SMITHSONIAN

HISTORY

OF NORTH AMERICA

MAP BY MAP

S M I T H S O N I A N
HISTORY
OF NORTH AMERICA
MAP BY MAP

10

INDIGENOUS NORTH AMERICA c. 30,000 YA–c. 1500

42

COLONIZATION AND CONFLICT 1500–1750

CONTENTS

Penguin Random House

DK LONDON

Senior Editor Hugo Wilkinson
Editors Abigail Ellis, Stephanie Farrow, Ian Fitzgerald, Clara Heathcock, Emily Kho, Alice Nightingale, Jo Stimfield
Senior US Editor Megan Douglass
Managing Editor Angeles Gavira Guerrero
Cartographers Lovell Johns, Ed Merritt
Senior Production Controller Meskerem Berhane

Senior Art Editor Duncan Turner
Jacket Development Manager Sophia MTT
Managing Art Editor Michael Duffy
Art Director Maxine Pedliham
Associate Publishing Director Liz Wheeler
Design Director Phil Ormerod
Managing Director Liz Gough

LOVELL JOHNS

Cartography and research Clare Varney
Research and editorial Sian Jenkins
Project management Louisa Keyworth

80

FROM EMPIRES TO INDEPENDENCE 1750–1820

116

EXPANDING NATIONS 1820–1850

DK DELHI

Senior Editor Anita Kakar
Editors Saumya Agarwal, Aashirwad Jain
Picture Research Manager Taiyaba Khatoon
Senior Jackets Coordinator Priyanka Sharma Saddi
Managing Editor Rohan Sinha
Pre-production Manager Balwant Singh
Senior Cartographer Mohammad Hassan
Cartographer Animesh Kumar Pathak
Cartography Manager Suresh Kumar
Production Editor Anita Yadav

Senior Art Editor Anjali Sachar
Project Art Editor Sonakshi Singh
Art Editors Arshti Narang, Mitravinda V K
Assistant Picture Researcher Nunhoih Guite
Senior Jacket Designer Suhita Dharamjit
Managing Art Editor Sudakshina Basu
Senior DTP Designer Harish Aggarwal
DTP Coordinator Vishal Bhatia
DTP Designers Nand Kishor Acharya, Bimlesh Tiwary
Production Manager Pankaj Sharma
Creative Head Malavika Talukder

CONTRIBUTORS

Katy Doll, Carrie Gibson, Mark Collins Jenkins,
Andrew Kerr-Jarrett, Joshua Newton, Shannon Reed,
Donald Sommerville, Marie Kesten Zahn

CONSULTANTS

Max Edelson (main consultant)
Professor of History, University of Virginia

Scott Hancock Associate Professor of History
and Africana Studies, Gettysburg College

Ashley Riley Sousa Associate Professor
of History, Middle Tennessee State University

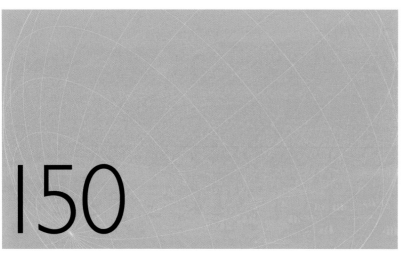

150

DISRUPTION AND EXPANSION 1850–1880

188

ACROSS NORTH AMERICA 1880–1914

First American Edition, 2024
Published in the United States by DK Publishing,
a division of Penguin Random House LLC
1745 Broadway, 20th Floor, New York, NY 10019

Copyright © 2024 Dorling Kindersley Limited
24 25 26 27 28 10 9 8 7 6 5 4 3 2 1
001–336950–Sep/2024

A catalog record for this book
is available from the Library of Congress.
ISBN 978-0-7440-9202-8

DK books are available at special discounts when purchased
in bulk for sales promotions, premiums, fund-raising, or
educational use. For details, contact: DK Publishing Special Markets,
1745 Broadway, 20th Floor, New York, NY 10019
SpecialSales@dk.com

Printed and bound in Malaysia

www.dk.com

Smithsonian

EXPERTS

For National Museum of American History: Bethanee Bemis, Museum Specialist; Frank Blazich, Curator,
Military History Division of Military and Society; Dan Cole, GIS Coordinator & Chief Cartographer;
Claire Jerry, Curator, Political History; Jennifer Jones, Chair and Curator, Armed Forces History Division;
Modupe Labode, Curator; Peter Liebhold, Curator Emeritus, Division of Work and Industry; Sara
Murphy, Collections Specialist, Collections Management; Manuel Rodriguez, Museum Curator, Division
of Political and Military History, National Museum of American History; Chris Wilson, African
American History Program Director; Cedric Yeh, Project Director, NYC Latino 9-11 Collecting
Initiative. For National Museum of the American Indian: Chris Turner, Cultural Information Specialist.

SMITHSONIAN

Established in 1846, the Smithsonian is the world's
largest museum and research complex, dedicated to
public education, national service, and scholarship in the
arts, sciences, and history. It includes 21 museums and
galleries and the National Zoological Park. The total
number of artifacts, works of art, and specimens in the
Smithsonian's collection is estimated at 155.5 million.

FOR SMITHSONIAN ENTERPRISES

Licensing Coordinator Avery Naughton
Editorial Lead Paige Towler
Senior Director, Licensed Publishing Jill Corcoran
**Vice President of
New Business and Licensing** Brigid Ferraro
President Carol LeBlanc

A WORLD AT WAR 1914–1945

POSTWAR NORTH AMERICA 1945–1980

GLOBAL NORTH AMERICA 1980–PRESENT

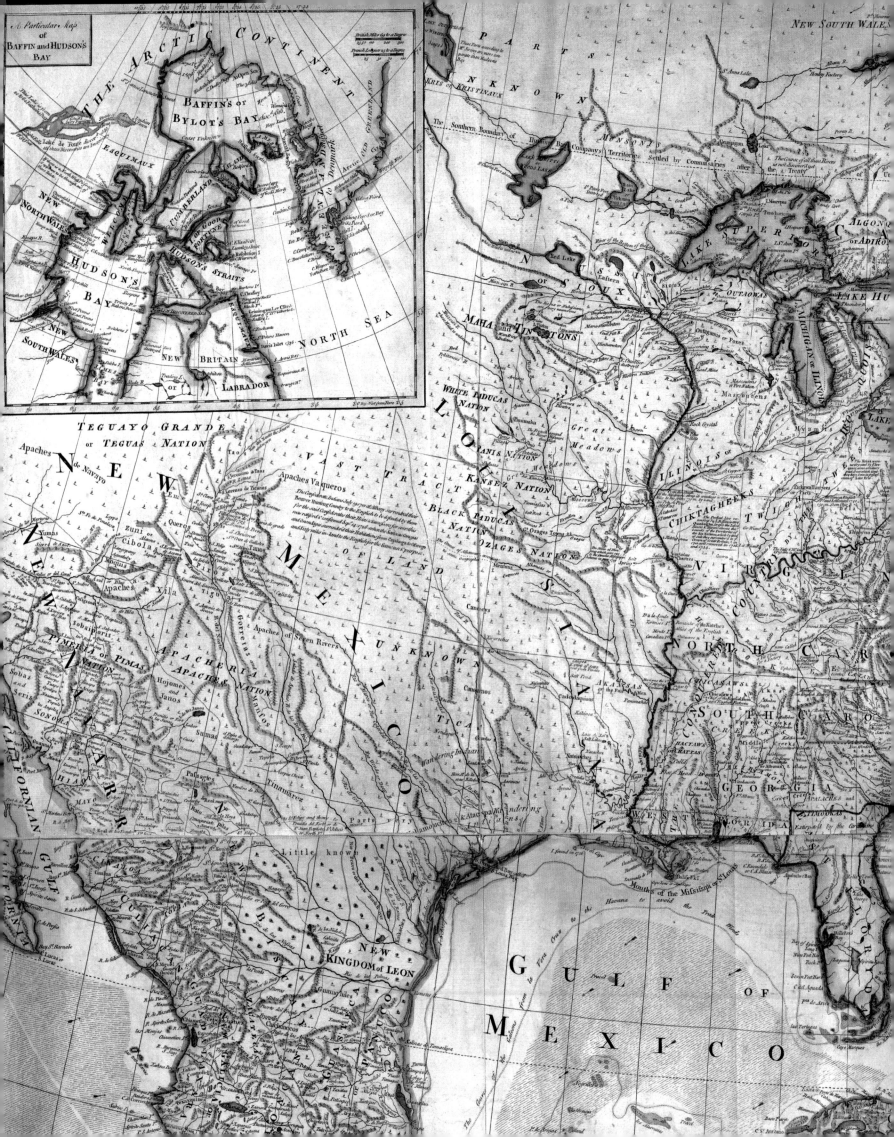

AN Accurate MAP OF NORTH AMERICA Describing and distinguishing the BRITISH and SPANISH Dominions on this great Continent; According to the Definitive Treaty Concluded at Paris 10 Feby 1763. Also all the WEST INDIA ISLANDS Belonging to, and possessed by the Several European Princes and States. The whole laid down according to the latest and Most authentick Improvements. By Eman Bowen Geogr to His MAJESTY And John Gibson Engraver

TERRA de LABRADOR NEW BRITAIN

GULF OF ST LAWRENCE RIVER

NEW FOUND LAND

THE GREAT FISHING BANK OF NEW FOUND LAND

Nova Scotia Fishing Banks

WESTERN OR

ATLANTIC OCEAN

BAHAMA or LUCAYOS ISLANDS

Tropic of

BERMUDAS or SUMMER'S Is.

North America, 1763
This map by Emanuel Bowen shows the new dimensions of British America after the Seven Years' War, as agreed in the Treaty of Paris (see pp. 94–95). Britain's efforts to reform its North American empire led to the American Revolution.

INDIGENOUS NORTH AMERICA

THE FIRST HUMANS TO ARRIVE IN NORTH AMERICA FROM SIBERIA FOUND A VARIED LANDSCAPE RICH IN NATURAL RESOURCES. AS THEY SPREAD ACROSS THE CONTINENT AND SOUTH TO MESOAMERICA AND BEYOND, SOPHISTICATED CIVILIZATIONS EMERGED AND FLOURISHED.

EARLY NORTH AMERICA

The first humans who migrated to North America, and their descendants, utilized its resources and altered its landscape over thousands of years. From ancestral populations of hunter-gatherers, they established trade, developed agriculture, and created civilizations.

△ **The first explorers**
Pathfinders of America, the millions of bison that once roamed the continent created a network of trails, called "traces," that later became Indigenous footpaths, settlers' byways, and railroad beds.

From the Arctic in the north to the southern tropics, the North American continent covers millions of square miles and contains an enormous variety of terrains. It separated millions of years ago from the massive continent known as Pangaea, which joined North America, South America, Europe, and Africa. Over time, new landscapes emerged—new worlds of lakes and forests and plains—which were actively shaped by the significant Pleistocene megafauna that survived environmental change, the American bison. The bison herds were the continent's wayfinders, finding the easiest routes across rivers and mountain ranges. The earliest human settlers,

▷ **Paleolithic tools**
In 1927, the discovery of Folsom spear points helped establish the presence of Indigenous people in North America 10,500–8,000 years ago, at the end of the Late Upper Paleolithic era—earlier than previously believed. These spear points had concave bases and central fluting, which helped fit them on to shafts.

who migrated from what is now Siberia, employed fire to further shape the landscape and create a great bison belt—a grassland biome stretching from Canada across most of the present-day US.

Archaeological horizons
The earliest Indigenous Americans left few traces. Archaeologists describe the majority of them based on spear point design—"Clovis" or "Folsom," although there are a now few uncovered spear points from 15,500 years ago that predate Clovis and Folsom. After several thousand more years, North America was crisscrossed by a growing network of trading paths, as people from different regions began bartering objects; for example, exchanging seashells from coastal areas for copper from the interior. Regional cultures emerged, and dialects evolved into discrete languages. Indigenous Americans used the continent's environment to good advantage. Whether living in the Pacific Northwest or the Southern Appalachians, the Great Lakes country or the expansive grasslands of the continental interior, these Indigenous cultures were well adapted to their world.

The rise of civilizations
For centuries, Indigenous Americans had collected and disseminated edible plants to secure their subsistence from the environment. However, full-fledged plant domestication occurred in the highlands of today's

ANCIENT WORLDS

Scholars have little knowledge of the early societies of North America, and ancient civilizations are often now named after important excavation sites. Other areas of uncertainty remain; for example, scholars still debate who built Teotihuacán, which dominated Mesoamerica for half a millennium, because so many ethnic groups proliferated there. New discoveries, however, are made every year.

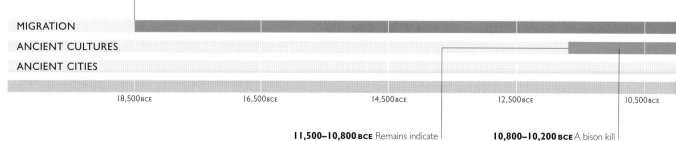

c.18,500–14,000 BCE The vast majority of Indigenous ancestors, who would migrate to both North and South America, arrive from Beringia, the Ice Age–era land bridge stretching from Siberia to Alaska

| MIGRATION |
| ANCIENT CULTURES |
| ANCIENT CITIES |

18,500 BCE   16,500 BCE   14,500 BCE   12,500 BCE   10,500 BCE

11,500–10,800 BCE Remains indicate a mammoth was killed around this time near Clovis, New Mexico, leading to the name of the Clovis culture

10,800–10,200 BCE A bison kill site near Folsom, New Mexico, is dated to this period, for which the Folsom culture is named

◁ **Zapotec Bowl with hummingbird rattle**
This ceramic bowl was cast c. 1300–1500, toward the end of
the Zapotec civilization. Hummingbirds were considered symbols
of resurrection—they wake up after periodic metabolic inactivity, as if
coming to life after death—and were venerated all over Mesoamerica.

*"Of all the quadrupeds … probably no other species has ever
marshaled such innumerable hosts as those of the American bison."*

WILLIAM TEMPLE HORNADAY, *THE EXTERMINATION OF THE AMERICAN BISON*, 1889

southwestern Mexico. Vine-grown squashes, being
easy to propagate, were grown first. However, it was
a grass that would nourish the Americas. Teosinte—a
grass with a tiny seed head—was selectively bred
over thousands of years, transforming into corn.

Fields of corn gave rise to settled village life.
Villages became towns, and towns became cities.
Mesoamerica's first civilization, the Olmecs,
arose in the tropical lowlands fronting the Gulf
of Mexico. Considered the "mother culture,"
the influence of the Olmecs was long-lasting
and far-spreading. Its impact transformed the
fertile highland valleys of Mexico and Oaxaca
into seats of successive empires, adorned with
monumental buildings and skyward reaching
pyramids. Mayan society was even more
advanced, with sophisticated architecture,
calendar and writing systems, and arts and
literature. At its peak, the densely populated
Maya territory was 96,000 square miles
(250,000 sq km) in size. An 800-square-mile
(2,070-sq-km) archaeological survey revealed
the remains of 60,000 structures, ranging from
palaces and temples to elevated highways and
agricultural terraces.

Mesoamerica's influence reached far north
into today's US, where the Chaco Canyon's
astronomical alignments and the massive

earthworks left by "mound builders" across the Southeast
testify to its impact. After thousands of years of settlement
within North America, the continent's Indigenous peoples,
living in isolation from the rest of the planet, lost the
acquired immunities their ancestors had to infectious
diseases endemic to Europe, Asia, and Africa.

▽ **Ancestral homeland**
The forested Southern Appalachians,
which include the Great Smoky Mountains,
were once the traditional homelands of
Iroquoian and Siouan speaking peoples.
Among the former, the Cherokee and
their ancestors have lived near the Great
Smokies for perhaps a thousand years.

c.9000 BCE Corn is
domesticated at the
Xihuatoxtla Shelter site
in the Balsas River Valley
in southwest Mexico

c.6800 BCE A wave of
Arctic Siberians gives rise to the
Athabaskan (Na-Dene) peoples
of northwestern North America

c.1200–400 BCE The
Olmecs, the "mother
culture" of Mesoamerica,
thrive in southern Mexico

c.250–900 CE The "classic
period" of Mesoamerican
civilization, as seen in the many
flourishing Maya cities

c.1000–1500 CE The Mississippian,
or "mound builder," culture dominates
the Ohio-Mississippi River valleys and
Southeast woodlands

c.1250 CE The migration of
Na-Dene people to Southwest
US includes present-day Navajo
and Apache peoples

8,500 BCE	6,500 BCE	4,500 BCE	2,500 BCE	500 BCE	1500 CE

c.1150–900 BCE San
Lorenzo, the earliest of
the Olmec capitals,
flourishes before being
destroyed by invaders

c.600 BCE–c.100 CE
El Mirador, an early Maya city of
200,000 people, is the capital of a
group of cities and settlements
containing around 1 million people

c.100 BCE–c.650 CE
Teotihuacán is the first
major city to arise in the
Valley of Mexico

c.500 BCE–c.850 CE
Monte Albán is the
formative city in
the Valley of Oaxaca

c.200–900 CE The city
of Tikal dominates the
Petén Basin (in present-day
Guatemala) of the Classic
Maya Civilization

c.850–1250 CE
Chaco Canyon is the
first urban complex
north of the Rio
Grande River

c.900–1350 CE Cahokia,
the largest Mississippian
culture site, boasts the
largest pyramid north
of Mexico

NORTH AMERICAN CONTINENT

Most of North America lies on a single tectonic plate, the North American Plate, with small parts of California on the adjoining Pacific Plate. The ancient rock underlying most of North America was once part of the supercontinent Pangaea, but about 200 million years ago it separated to form the modern continent.

The North American continent lies in the temperate Northern Hemisphere. Its geographical features include the Appalachian Mountains, one of the oldest mountain ranges on Earth, and the Sierra Nevada, which is among the youngest. Coal, oil, gas, and precious metals are abundant in both mountain ranges. Tectonic activity, including earthquakes and volcanic eruptions, occurs in the west along the boundary between the North American and Pacific Plates. The rich soils of the continent's Interior Plains are derived from sediments deposited by a network of rivers.

Glaciers sculpted the geologically young St. Lawrence River and Great Lakes. However, some eastern rivers, such as the Susquehanna, the Delaware, the Potomac, and the New River, might be even older than the Appalachians, as they appear to have cut water gaps transversely across the mountains. The Colorado River may have been slowly carving the Grand Canyon for 6 to 60 million years. Even the Mississippi, which means "Father of Waters," lives up to its name and may be four times as old as previously thought, flowing through its delta, for upward of 80 million years.

> *"Mountains, hills, plateaus, plains, and valleys, are here found, as elsewhere throughout the earth …"*
>
> JOHN WESLEY POWELL, "PHYSICAL FEATURES OF THE COLORADO VALLEY," *POPULAR SCIENCE MONTHLY*, AUGUST 1875

3 NORTH AMERICAN CORDILLERA
Stretching from Alaska to Central America, the comparatively young North American Cordillera arose when the North American Plate overrode the Pacific Plate approximately 80 million years ago. This mountain belt includes the Alaska Range, Brooks Range, Canadian and American Rockies, Coast Ranges, Sierra Nevada, Cascades, and the Sierra Madres.

▨ North American Cordillera

PACIFIC PLATE

PACIFIC OCEAN

△ **A geological phenomenon**
The mile-high (2 km) walls of the Grand Canyon display a banded sequence of geological layers dating back billions of years—a unique display of geological history.

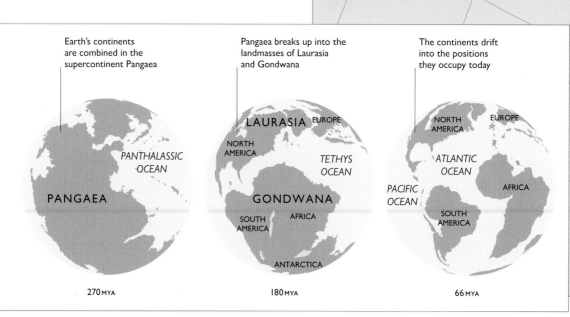

CONTINENTAL DRIFT
Earth's rocky continents are slowly carried around the planet's surface on gigantic subsurface tectonic plates. Collisions between the plates formed supercontinents that eventually broke up, leading to new configurations of land masses and water bodies. Such ruptures and collisions raise mountain ranges, fuel volcanoes, and cause earthquakes, shaping the world over a long span of geological time.

Earth's continents are combined in the supercontinent Pangaea

PANTHALASSIC OCEAN

PANGAEA

270 MYA

Pangaea breaks up into the landmasses of Laurasia and Gondwana

LAURASIA EUROPE

NORTH AMERICA

TETHYS OCEAN

GONDWANA

SOUTH AMERICA   AFRICA

ANTARCTICA

180 MYA

The continents drift into the positions they occupy today

NORTH AMERICA   EUROPE

ATLANTIC OCEAN

PACIFIC OCEAN   AFRICA

SOUTH AMERICA

66 MYA

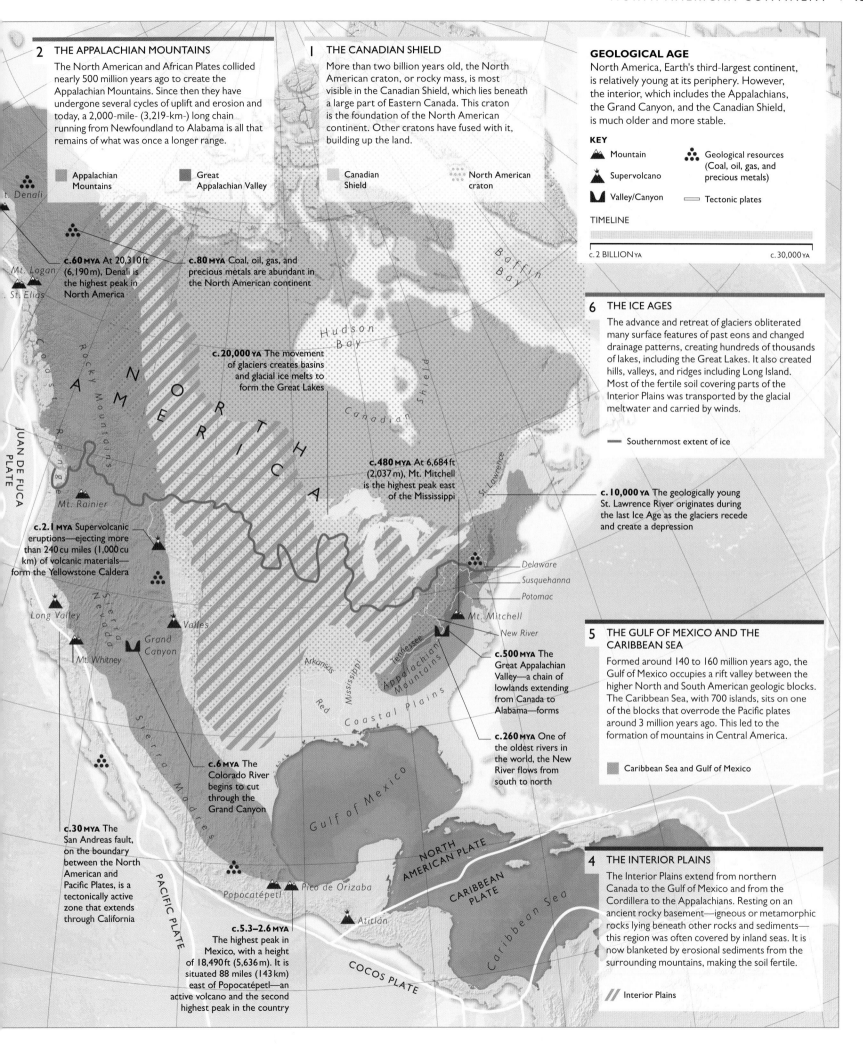

2 THE APPALACHIAN MOUNTAINS

The North American and African Plates collided nearly 500 million years ago to create the Appalachian Mountains. Since then they have undergone several cycles of uplift and erosion and today, a 2,000-mile- (3,219-km-) long chain running from Newfoundland to Alabama is all that remains of what was once a longer range.

Appalachian Mountains

Great Appalachian Valley

1 THE CANADIAN SHIELD

More than two billion years old, the North American craton, or rocky mass, is most visible in the Canadian Shield, which lies beneath a large part of Eastern Canada. This craton is the foundation of the North American continent. Other cratons have fused with it, building up the land.

Canadian Shield

North American craton

GEOLOGICAL AGE

North America, Earth's third-largest continent, is relatively young at its periphery. However, the interior, which includes the Appalachians, the Grand Canyon, and the Canadian Shield, is much older and more stable.

KEY

Mountain

Supervolcano

Valley/Canyon

Geological resources (Coal, oil, gas, and precious metals)

Tectonic plates

TIMELINE

c. 2 BILLION YA   c. 30,000 YA

6 THE ICE AGES

The advance and retreat of glaciers obliterated many surface features of past eons and changed drainage patterns, creating hundreds of thousands of lakes, including the Great Lakes. It also created hills, valleys, and ridges including Long Island. Most of the fertile soil covering parts of the Interior Plains was transported by the glacial meltwater and carried by winds.

Southernmost extent of ice

c.60 MYA At 20,310 ft (6,190 m), Denali is the highest peak in North America

c.80 MYA Coal, oil, gas, and precious metals are abundant in the North American continent

c.20,000 YA The movement of glaciers creates basins and glacial ice melts to form the Great Lakes

c.480 MYA At 6,684 ft (2,037 m), Mt. Mitchell is the highest peak east of the Mississippi

c.10,000 YA The geologically young St. Lawrence River originates during the last Ice Age as the glaciers recede and create a depression

c.2.1 MYA Supervolcanic eruptions—ejecting more than 240 cu miles (1,000 cu km) of volcanic materials—form the Yellowstone Caldera

c.500 MYA The Great Appalachian Valley—a chain of lowlands extending from Canada to Alabama—forms

5 THE GULF OF MEXICO AND THE CARIBBEAN SEA

Formed around 140 to 160 million years ago, the Gulf of Mexico occupies a rift valley between the higher North and South American geologic blocks. The Caribbean Sea, with 700 islands, sits on one of the blocks that overrode the Pacific plates around 3 million years ago. This led to the formation of mountains in Central America.

Caribbean Sea and Gulf of Mexico

c.6 MYA The Colorado River begins to cut through the Grand Canyon

c.260 MYA One of the oldest rivers in the world, the New River flows from south to north

c.30 MYA The San Andreas fault, on the boundary between the North American and Pacific Plates, is a tectonically active zone that extends through California

4 THE INTERIOR PLAINS

The Interior Plains extend from northern Canada to the Gulf of Mexico and from the Cordillera to the Appalachians. Resting on an ancient rocky basement—igneous or metamorphic rocks lying beneath other rocks and sediments—this region was often covered by inland seas. It is now blanketed by erosional sediments from the surrounding mountains, making the soil fertile.

Interior Plains

c.5.3–2.6 MYA The highest peak in Mexico, with a height of 18,490 ft (5,636 m). It is situated 88 miles (143 km) east of Popocatépetl—an active volcano and the second highest peak in the country

Delaware
Susquehanna
Potomac

Mt. Mitchell
New River

Denali
Mt. Logan
St. Elias
Mt. Rainier
Long Valley
Mt. Whitney
Valles
Grand Canyon
Pico de Orizaba
Popocatépetl
Atitlán

NORTH AMERICA
Rocky Mountains
Coast Ranges
Sierra Nevada
Sierra Madres
JUAN DE FUCA PLATE
PACIFIC PLATE
COCOS PLATE
NORTH AMERICAN PLATE
CARIBBEAN PLATE
Baffin Bay
Hudson Bay
Canadian Shield
St. Lawrence
Arkansas
Red
Mississippi
Tennessee
Appalachian Mountains
Coastal Plains
Gulf of Mexico
Caribbean Sea

NORTH AMERICAN LANDSCAPE

The vast North American landmass stretches from tropical regions near the equator to the frozen expanses of the Arctic, and it contains a wide variety of landscapes in between. This patchwork of different biomes was further diversified by the arrival of the first human inhabitants.

The North American continent—and its associated islands—is made up of almost every kind of biome, including grasslands, forest, desert, wetlands, arctic tundra, and more. Its climate covers a correspondingly wide range of temperatures and weather conditions.

These landscapes are the habitats for fauna largely unique to North America. This abundance of animal life played a key role in the initial settlement of the continent (see pp.18–19), because it provided valuable food sources for hunter-gathering peoples—from large animals such as bison and deer to smaller creatures such as rabbits and fish. The Indigenous peoples of North America used fire as a tool to alter the landscape—they lit fires to clear underbrush from vast deciduous forests in the east to create habitats for prey animals. In the Great Plains and the Appalachian valley, large, contained fires were burned to drive the resident herds of wildlife, especially bison, in desired directions. Such frequent fires turned this area into a grassy savanna. From Mexico to Mississippi, fires were used to clear land for farming and construction. The Caribbean islands were covered in dense, tropical vegetation, while taiga, tundra, and ice characterized the sparsely populated north.

> *"I had a most delightfull view of ... herds of Buffaloe, Elk, deer; & Antelopes feeding in one ... boundless pasture."*
>
> MERIWETHER LEWIS, *THE JOURNALS OF LEWIS AND CLARK*, 1805

△ Sunrise in Yosemite Park, California
Runoff from Ice Age glaciers carved and shaped much of the terrain of North America. The effects of past glacial activity are evident in the U-shaped valleys and jagged mountains of Yosemite National Park.

2 EASTERN DECIDUOUS FOREST

Covering nearly a third of the continent, forests range from boreal in the far north to subtropical and tropical around the Gulf of Mexico. At the heart of this vegetational complex are the eastern deciduous forests—temperate broadleaf forests that are especially rich in the southern Appalachians, where the Great Smoky Mountains are home to a diverse range of flora.

◼ Temperate broadleaf forest

3 TEMPERATE RAINFOREST

Towering conifers such as coast redwood, Douglas fir, and Sitka spruce populate the temperate rainforests that extend from northern California through Oregon, Washington, Vancouver Island, and British Columbia to Kodiak Island in southern Alaska. Perhaps the largest stretch of intact temperate rainforest in the world. This biome is also found in Florida and the east coast.

◼ Temperate coniferous forest

4 GRASSLAND BIOME

Ranging from south of the Rio Grande to far north-central Canada, the Great Plains include tall-grass prairie 6–8 feet (1.8–2.4m) high as well as usual short-grass prairie edging into steppe. Grasslands invaded the neighboring deciduous forest and Appalachian valley as Indigenous peoples including the Cherokee and Choctaw set fire to forests to create pastures and clear hunting grounds.

◼ Temperate grassland

5 STARKNESS AND ABUNDANCE

The deserts of the Great Basin and adjoining portions of Canyon Country are dry, harsh environments, so when the first humans to settle the continent arrived, they inhabited this area sparsely. West of the Sierra Nevada, however, was California's Central Valley, a mosaic of forest and meadow. The Yokut people here were hunter-gatherers who lived off the region's abundant fauna and flora.

◻ Desert and dry shrubland
◼ California's Central Valley

6 TROPICAL BIOMES

The rugged hills and low-lying plains of Southern Mexico, Central America, the Greater Antilles, and the Caribbean islands were covered in tropical vegetation. They comprised rainforests, high cloud forests, pine groves, seasonally dry woodlands, and savanna, depending on height, direction faced, and rainfall patterns. Mangrove thickets and coral reefs surrounded the islands.

◼ Tropical dry broadleaf
◻ Tropical broadleaf
◼ Tropical coniferous
◼ Tropical grassland

1896 The long Yukon River becomes the principal route to the gold strikes in its upper watershed

Novarupta

Jun 6, 1912 Novarupta volcanic eruption lasts 60 hours and results in the formation of Katmai caldera—now a lake covering an area of 4.7 square miles (12 sq km)

PACIFIC OCEAN

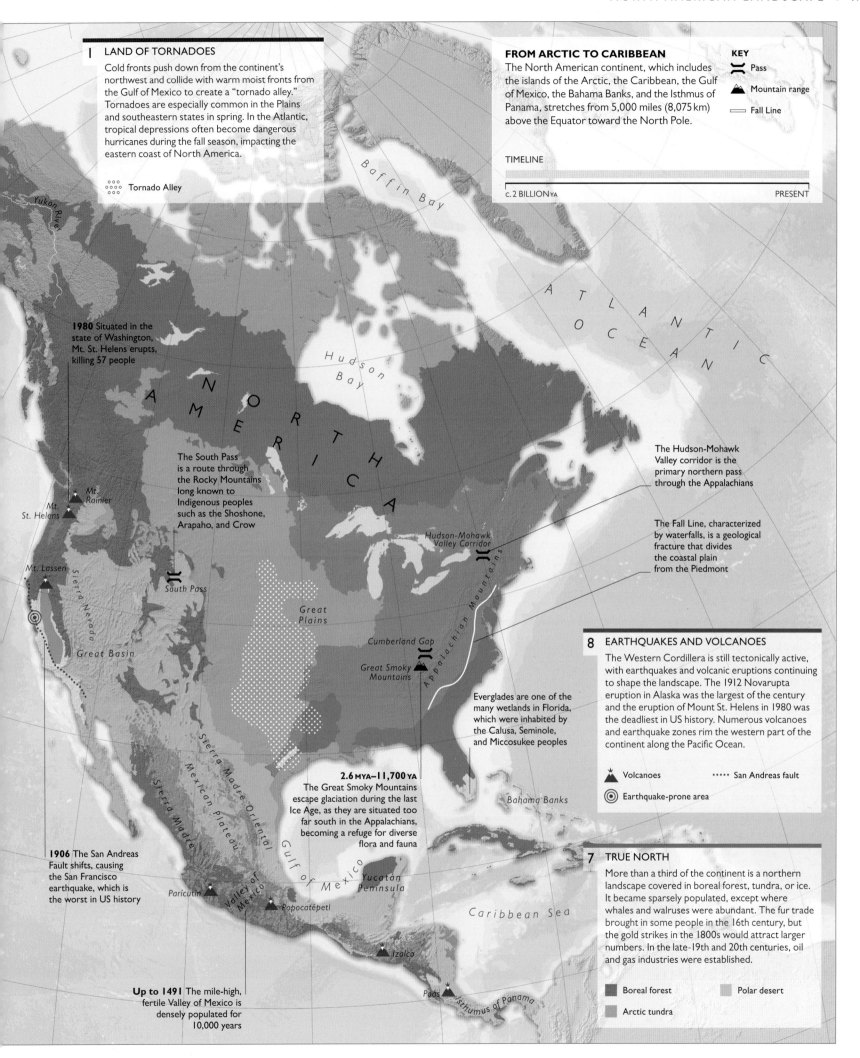

1 LAND OF TORNADOES

Cold fronts push down from the continent's northwest and collide with warm moist fronts from the Gulf of Mexico to create a "tornado alley." Tornadoes are especially common in the Plains and southeastern states in spring. In the Atlantic, tropical depressions often become dangerous hurricanes during the fall season, impacting the eastern coast of North America.

⠿ Tornado Alley

FROM ARCTIC TO CARIBBEAN

The North American continent, which includes the islands of the Arctic, the Caribbean, the Gulf of Mexico, the Bahama Banks, and the Isthmus of Panama, stretches from 5,000 miles (8,075 km) above the Equator toward the North Pole.

KEY

〰 Pass

⏶ Mountain range

▭ Fall Line

TIMELINE

c. 2 BILLION YA ———————————————— PRESENT

1980 Situated in the state of Washington, Mt. St. Helens erupts, killing 57 people

The South Pass is a route through the Rocky Mountains long known to Indigenous peoples such as the Shoshone, Arapaho, and Crow

The Hudson-Mohawk Valley corridor is the primary northern pass through the Appalachians

The Fall Line, characterized by waterfalls, is a geological fracture that divides the coastal plain from the Piedmont

8 EARTHQUAKES AND VOLCANOES

The Western Cordillera is still tectonically active, with earthquakes and volcanic eruptions continuing to shape the landscape. The 1912 Novarupta eruption in Alaska was the largest of the century and the eruption of Mount St. Helens in 1980 was the deadliest in US history. Numerous volcanoes and earthquake zones rim the western part of the continent along the Pacific Ocean.

▲ Volcanoes   ⋯⋯ San Andreas fault

◎ Earthquake-prone area

Everglades are one of the many wetlands in Florida, which were inhabited by the Calusa, Seminole, and Miccosukee peoples

2.6 MYA–11,700 YA The Great Smoky Mountains escape glaciation during the last Ice Age, as they are situated too far south in the Appalachians, becoming a refuge for diverse flora and fauna

1906 The San Andreas Fault shifts, causing the San Francisco earthquake, which is the worst in US history

7 TRUE NORTH

More than a third of the continent is a northern landscape covered in boreal forest, tundra, or ice. It became sparsely populated, except where whales and walruses were abundant. The fur trade brought in some people in the 16th century, but the gold strikes in the 1800s would attract larger numbers. In the late-19th and 20th centuries, oil and gas industries were established.

▮ Boreal forest   ▮ Polar desert

▮ Arctic tundra

Up to 1491 The mile-high, fertile Valley of Mexico is densely populated for 10,000 years

Map labels: Yukon River, Baffin Bay, ATLANTIC OCEAN, Hudson Bay, NORTH AMERICA, Mt. Rainier, Mt. St. Helens, Mt. Lassen, Sierra Nevada, South Pass, Great Basin, Great Plains, Hudson-Mohawk Valley Corridor, Appalachian Mountains, Cumberland Gap, Great Smoky Mountains, Sierra Madre, Mexican Plateau, Sierra Madre Oriental, Paricutín, Valley of Mexico, Popocatépetl, Gulf of Mexico, Yucatán Peninsula, Bahama Banks, Caribbean Sea, Izalco, Poás, Isthmus of Panama

THE FIRST MIGRATIONS

More than 15,000 years ago, the first settlers in North America traveled along the Bering Land Bridge between Siberia and Alaska and followed an ice-free corridor inland. Other theories exist but run counter to a broad scholarly consensus, backed by DNA and material evidence, for the Asian origins of the first Americans.

The people who traversed the ice-free corridor were once described as the "Clovis" culture, named for the site in New Mexico where their distinctive fluted spear points were first found. However, in the late 20th century, archaeological finds raised the possibility that an earlier population had preceded them. Excavations at Cactus Hill in Virginia unearthed compelling evidence that people were living on the East Coast long before a presumed ice-free corridor had opened in northwest Canada. Similar "pre-Clovis" traces have been found at Monte Verde in southern Chile. It has been argued that these settlements were established by Siberian, European, or even African seafarers exploring the coasts of both continents—or that these sites have been misdated and are not as old as is claimed. The rock art and artifacts of the Pedra Furada caves in Brazil are a particularly contentious example of this.

In the late 1980s, a breakthrough was made when the genome of the oldest human remains found in the Americas, the 13,000-year-old Anzick-1 skeleton, affirmed the Siberian ancestry of ancient Americans. Since then, all DNA collected from ancient remains and modern-day Indigenous Americans show that they originated in Siberia.

> *"We must believe they could come thither ... by land."*
>
> JOSÉ DE ACOSTA, SPANISH NATURALIST, ON HOW THE FIRST SETTLERS MAY HAVE COME TO THE AMERICAS, 1590

CACTUS HILL

Excavated primarily between 1993–2002, Cactus Hill in southeastern Virginia is one of North America's most intriguing archaeological sites. Artifacts discovered there indicate that humans inhabited the area at least 18,000 years ago. If ongoing scientific analysis confirms this, it may move back the commonly accepted arrival date of the continent's first settlers by at least 5,000 years.

Finds on display at Cactus Hill

2 DISCREDITED ATLANTIC THEORIES
c. 21,000 YA

Because "Solutrean"-style spear points like those used in France US have been found in southeastern US, a controversial theory suggested Europeans reached the continent via transatlantic pack ice. Alternatively, ancient but unverified artifacts from Brazil suggest settlers may have arrived by boat from Africa. Most scholars dismiss these theories.

■ ■ ➤ Theoretical movement of people

◆ Archaeological site

BERINGIA

SIBERIA

Anangula Village

c. 9,000 YA Pre-Inuit people leave Anangula Village to migrate north and east

1 A PACIFIC COAST MIGRATION
c. 30,000–c. 15,000 YA

It has been theorized that early sailors, traveling down the coasts of Siberia and North America, could have reached South America, setting up beachheads from which they moved inland. Based on this idea, some historians have dated sites such as Monte Verde in Chile to the pre-Clovis period.

■ ■ ➤ Theoretical movement of people

◆ Archaeological site

THEORIES OF THE FIRST AMERICANS

The majority of current scholarship favors the idea that settlers came across the land bridge from Siberia into what is now Alaska. Other theories have suggested coastal or transatlantic migration routes.

KEY

Extent of the ice sheet 24,000 YA

Extent of the ice sheet 15,000–12,500 YA

Land exposed by lower sea level at height of the Ice Age

TIMELINE

| 2 | 3 | 4 | 5 |

30,000 YA   25,000   20,000   15,000   10,000   5,000   0

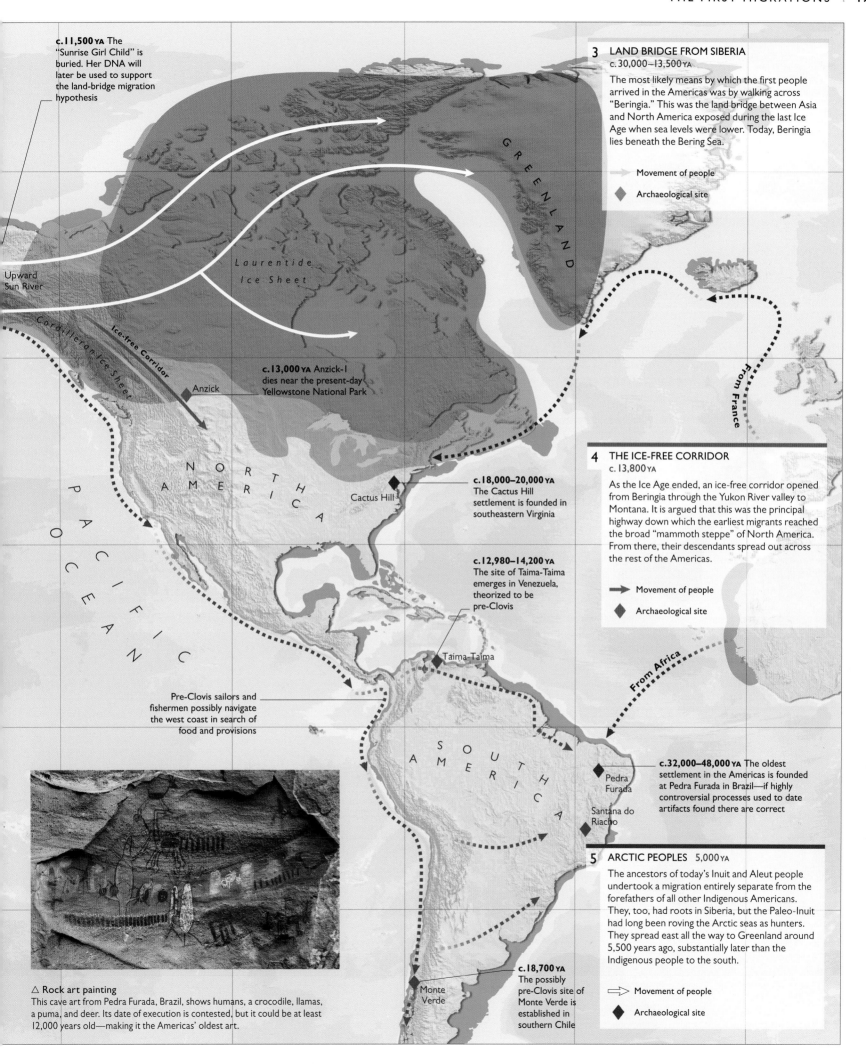

c.11,500 YA The "Sunrise Girl Child" is buried. Her DNA will later be used to support the land-bridge migration hypothesis

Upward Sun River

Cordilleran Ice Sheet

Ice-free Corridor

Laurentide Ice Sheet

GREENLAND

c.13,000 YA Anzick-1 dies near the present-day Yellowstone National Park

Anzick

NORTH AMERICA

PACIFIC OCEAN

Cactus Hill

c.18,000–20,000 YA The Cactus Hill settlement is founded in southeastern Virginia

c.12,980–14,200 YA The site of Taima-Taima emerges in Venezuela, theorized to be pre-Clovis

Taima-Taima

Pre-Clovis sailors and fishermen possibly navigate the west coast in search of food and provisions

SOUTH AMERICA

From France

From Africa

Pedra Furada

Santana do Riacho

Monte Verde

c.18,700 YA The possibly pre-Clovis site of Monte Verde is established in southern Chile

3 LAND BRIDGE FROM SIBERIA
c.30,000–13,500 YA

The most likely means by which the first people arrived in the Americas was by walking across "Beringia." This was the land bridge between Asia and North America exposed during the last Ice Age when sea levels were lower. Today, Beringia lies beneath the Bering Sea.

→ Movement of people

◆ Archaeological site

4 THE ICE-FREE CORRIDOR
c.13,800 YA

As the Ice Age ended, an ice-free corridor opened from Beringia through the Yukon River valley to Montana. It is argued that this was the principal highway down which the earliest migrants reached the broad "mammoth steppe" of North America. From there, their descendants spread out across the rest of the Americas.

→ Movement of people

◆ Archaeological site

c.32,000–48,000 YA The oldest settlement in the Americas is founded at Pedra Furada in Brazil—if highly controversial processes used to date artifacts found there are correct

5 ARCTIC PEOPLES 5,000 YA

The ancestors of today's Inuit and Aleut people undertook a migration entirely separate from the forefathers of all other Indigenous Americans. They, too, had roots in Siberia, but the Paleo-Inuit had long been roving the Arctic seas as hunters. They spread east all the way to Greenland around 5,500 years ago, substantially later than the Indigenous people to the south.

⇨ Movement of people

◆ Archaeological site

△ Rock art painting
This cave art from Pedra Furada, Brazil, shows humans, a crocodile, llamas, a puma, and deer. Its date of execution is contested, but it could be at least 12,000 years old—making it the Americas' oldest art.

Painting a picture
Rock art provides visual evidence of the beliefs and practices of ancient cultures. The large-eyed humanoids in this 1,500- to 4,000-year-old pictograph—painted by Ute peoples near present-day Thompson Springs, Utah— possibly depict spirit figures.

ANCIENT AMERICANS

North America's first human inhabitants, who arrived from Asia 30,000 years ago, were hunter-gatherers migrating with their prey. By 10,000 BCE, a common culture, now known as Clovis, had spread and by 1000 BCE, diversified to develop varied languages, religions, and societies.

Approximately 13,000 years ago, a common Clovis culture spread across North America. Ancient hunters used distinctive stone spear points to hunt bison, mammoth, and other megafauna. As the great glaciers of the ice age receded, distinctive ecosystems formed. Expanding forests and grasslands supported a wide range of smaller animals and wild plants. Ancient Americans utilized these regions, forming a variety of Indigenous societies during the Archaic period.

△ **Making a point**
Fluted and notched, the lance-shaped Clovis points were made of brittle materials such as chert.

Archaic peoples hunted deer and caribou, fished, and harvested oysters; and by 3000 BCE, they cultivated sunflower, maize, beans, and squash. They wove native grasses into baskets, mined copper, crafted earthenware vessels, improved farming output, and developed new hunting weapons and tactics.

Archaic sites in North America reveal a network of exchange that spanned the continent. Archaeologists have found widely dispersed trade goods, including useful minerals and valuable metals, in places far from where they were quarried or mined. South of the Rio Grande River, maize cultivation supported the growth of civilizations, including the empire of the Olmecs, which rose along Mesoamerica's tropical lowlands some 3,500 years ago (see pp. 22–23).

◁ **Enlightening excavations**
In 1936, excavations near Clovis, New Mexico, led to the discovery of the first lot of finely wrought stone projectile points. Similar points were found across the continent providing greater insight into a 13,000-year-old North American culture referred to as Clovis.

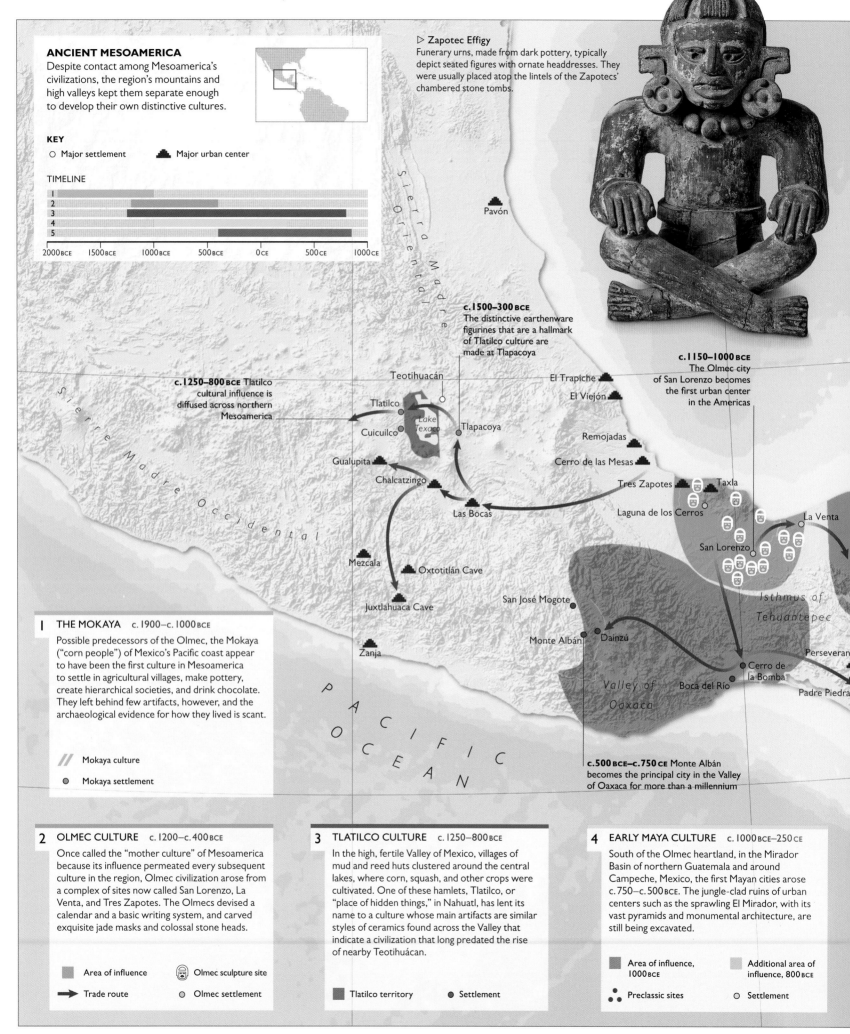

ANCIENT MESOAMERICA

Despite contact among Mesoamerica's civilizations, the region's mountains and high valleys kept them separate enough to develop their own distinctive cultures.

KEY

○ Major settlement ⛰ Major urban center

TIMELINE

	2000 BCE	1500 BCE	1000 BCE	500 BCE	0 CE	500 CE	1000 CE
1							
2							
3							
4							
5							

▷ **Zapotec Effigy**
Funerary urns, made from dark pottery, typically depict seated figures with ornate headdresses. They were usually placed atop the lintels of the Zapotecs' chambered stone tombs.

c.1500–300 BCE
The distinctive earthenware figurines that are a hallmark of Tlatilco culture are made at Tlapacoya

c.1150–1000 BCE
The Olmec city of San Lorenzo becomes the first urban center in the Americas

c.1250–800 BCE Tlatilco cultural influence is diffused across northern Mesoamerica

c.500 BCE–c.750 CE Monte Albán becomes the principal city in the Valley of Oaxaca for more than a millennium

1 THE MOKAYA c.1900–c.1000 BCE

Possible predecessors of the Olmec, the Mokaya ("corn people") of Mexico's Pacific coast appear to have been the first culture in Mesoamerica to settle in agricultural villages, make pottery, create hierarchical societies, and drink chocolate. They left behind few artifacts, however, and the archaeological evidence for how they lived is scant.

/// Mokaya culture

● Mokaya settlement

2 OLMEC CULTURE c.1200–c.400 BCE

Once called the "mother culture" of Mesoamerica because its influence permeated every subsequent culture in the region, Olmec civilization arose from a complex of sites now called San Lorenzo, La Venta, and Tres Zapotes. The Olmecs devised a calendar and a basic writing system, and carved exquisite jade masks and colossal stone heads.

▨ Area of influence ⬚ Olmec sculpture site

➡ Trade route ● Olmec settlement

3 TLATILCO CULTURE c.1250–800 BCE

In the high, fertile Valley of Mexico, villages of mud and reed huts clustered around the central lakes, where corn, squash, and other crops were cultivated. One of these hamlets, Tlatilco, or "place of hidden things," in Nahuatl, has lent its name to a culture whose main artifacts are similar styles of ceramics found across the Valley that indicate a civilization that long predated the rise of nearby Teotihuácan.

▨ Tlatilco territory ● Settlement

4 EARLY MAYA CULTURE c.1000 BCE–250 CE

South of the Olmec heartland, in the Mirador Basin of northern Guatemala and around Campeche, Mexico, the first Mayan cities arose c.750–c.500 BCE. The jungle-clad ruins of urban centers such as the sprawling El Mirador, with its vast pyramids and monumental architecture, are still being excavated.

▨ Area of influence, 1000 BCE ▨ Additional area of influence, 800 BCE

⋱ Preclassic sites ○ Settlement

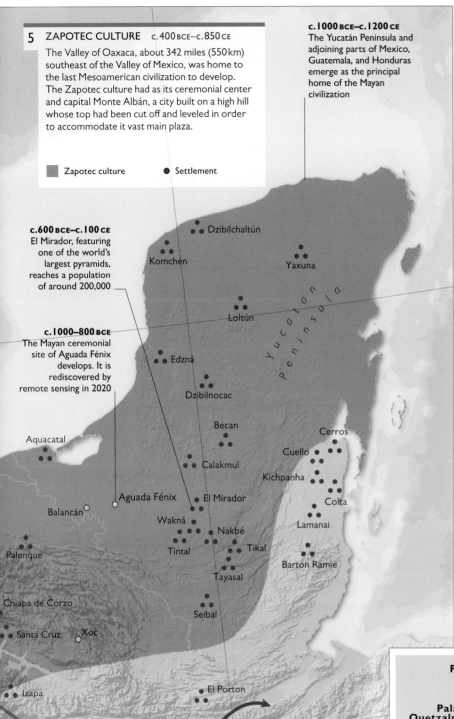

5 ZAPOTEC CULTURE c. 400 BCE–c. 850 CE

The Valley of Oaxaca, about 342 miles (550 km) southeast of the Valley of Mexico, was home to the last Mesoamerican civilization to develop. The Zapotec culture had as its ceremonial center and capital Monte Albán, a city built on a high hill whose top had been cut off and leveled in order to accommodate it vast main plaza.

■ Zapotec culture   ● Settlement

c. 1000 BCE–c. 1200 CE
The Yucatán Peninsula and adjoining parts of Mexico, Guatemala, and Honduras emerge as the principal home of the Mayan civilization

c. 600 BCE–c. 100 CE
El Mirador, featuring one of the world's largest pyramids, reaches a population of around 200,000

c. 1000–800 BCE
The Mayan ceremonial site of Aguada Fénix develops. It is rediscovered by remote sensing in 2020

c. 1400 BCE The earliest known ball court in Mesoamerica is constructed at Paso de la Amada, a possible Mokaya site

Dzibilchaltún
Komchén
Yaxuna
Loltún
Edzná
Dzibilnocac
Becan
Cerros
Cuello
Calakmul
Kichpanha
Aguada Fénix
El Mirador
Colta
Balancán
Wakná
Lamanai
Nakbé
Tintal
Tikal
Tayasal
Barton Ramie
Aquacatal
Palenque
Seibal
Chiapa de Corzo
Santa Cruz
Xoc
El Porton
Izapa
Copán
El Baúl
Kaminaljuyu
uiles
dán
Altamira Izapa Paso de la Amada
San Isidro Piedra Parada
La Victoria La Blanca
Abaj Takalik
Las Victorias
Chalchuapa

Yucatan Peninsula

MESOAMERICA'S FIRST CULTURES

Between about 1200 BCE and 200 BCE, Central America underwent a metamorphosis that saw its largely village-based culture transformed by the growth of large, sophisticated metropolitan centers dominated by hierarchical societies.

The domestication of corn, peppers, beans, and squash allowed Mesoamerican civilization to develop from initially small settlements into towns and then cities. The regular supply of crops provided by organized agriculture in this "Preclassic Era," or "Formative Period," offered nourishment and food security, and, later, surpluses that could be bartered and traded among different groups. As material abundance grew, the most successful of these emerging societies built gigantic pyramids, palaces, plazas, and other ceremonial structures. Calendrical systems and writing also developed.

The Olmec are thought to have emerged first, and their social structure, art, culture, and religious practices influenced many of the peoples that followed, such as the Maya, Zapotec, and Tlatilco. Successive regional cultures proliferated, from the swampy jungle lowlands to the high, fertile Valleys of Mexico and Oaxaca, where ceremonial cities such as Teotihuácan and Monte Albán arose, eventually becoming centers of warlike city-states. The rise of corn supported the origins of North American civilization.

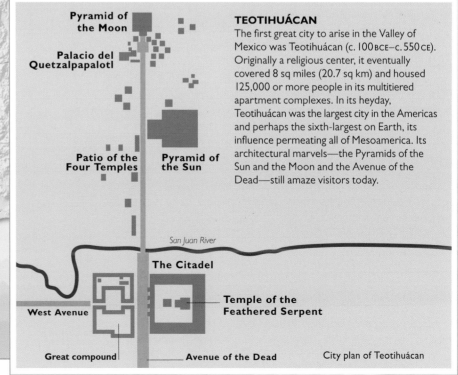

Pyramid of the Moon
Palacio del Quetzalpapalotl
Patio of the Four Temples
Pyramid of the Sun
San Juan River
The Citadel
West Avenue
Great compound
Temple of the Feathered Serpent
Avenue of the Dead

TEOTIHUÁCAN
The first great city to arise in the Valley of Mexico was Teotihuácan (c. 100 BCE–c. 550 CE). Originally a religious center, it eventually covered 8 sq miles (20.7 sq km) and housed 125,000 or more people in its multitiered apartment complexes. In its heyday, Teotihuácan was the largest city in the Americas and perhaps the sixth-largest on Earth, its influence permeating all of Mesoamerica. Its architectural marvels—the Pyramids of the Sun and the Moon and the Avenue of the Dead—still amaze visitors today.

City plan of Teotihuácan

Mississippian burial mound
This painting from around 1850 depicts a rounded burial mound in the Mississippi valley, possibly made between around 100 BCE and 200 CE. As well as the bodies of the deceased, various items were also interred.

MOUND BUILDERS

Mississippian culture flourished in eastern North America from 800 to 1600 CE, featuring tributary empires that built large earthen mounds in their most important towns. By the time the Spanish encountered Mississippian chiefdoms in the 1540s, this culture was already in decline.

The building of earthen burial and ceremonial mounds was carried out by various cultures. The Adena culture, centered around modern Ohio, flourished from 500 BCE to 100 CE and left behind elaborate earthworks. From 100 BCE to 500 CE, the Hopewell culture practiced metalwork and long-distance trade; they also built geometric earthen structures that tracked the paths of the sun and moon.

△ **Hopewell falcon**
This copper bird from c. 200 BCE is from a burial mound near Chillicothe, Ohio. Falcons were revered by the area's Hopewell people.

When farmers in the Mississippi River Valley began to produce an agricultural surplus of maize, squash, and beans, around 800 CE, it led to the growth of cities and craft industries, and the construction of large platform mounds, sites that became centers of power. As this civilization spread into modern Ohio, Oklahoma, Missouri, and the Carolinas, the largest chiefdoms ruled over smaller chiefdoms and villages. Archaeologists have excavated houses, temples, mounds, and luxury metal goods, indicating a wealthy ruling elite. Among the largest of the chiefdoms was Cahokia, a regional empire that used military might to grow. At its height in 1100 CE, more than 50,000 people lived within sight of Cahokia's central mound.

It is not known why this society declined, but diseases introduced by Europeans in the 16th century possibly hastened their downfall. Spanish explorer Hernando De Soto notably encountered the chiefdom of Cofitachequi in modern-day South Carolina in 1540.

GREAT SERPENT MOUND

Winding more than 1,300 ft (396 m) across an Ohio clifftop east of Cincinnati, the Great Serpent Mound is the best-known example of an effigy mound—human-made earthworks resembling a bird or an animal—which are common in the Great Lakes region and the upper Midwest. With gaping jaws and a spiral tail, the 3 ft- (91 cm-) high artifact was built between 900 and 2,300 years ago and is the largest serpent effigy in the world.

Serpent Mound, Ohio

CHACO CANYON CULTURE

The spectacular ruins lining Chaco Canyon in northwestern New Mexico are believed to have been built by the ancestral Pueblo people. The structures consist of public and ceremonial buildings, and were a hub for the people of the region. Six arrow-roads spread out upward of 50 miles (80 km), perhaps connecting another 30 gigantic buildings in a web of around 65,000 sq miles (168,300 sq km).

Pueblo Bonito—"Beautiful House"—is the most famous ruin in Chaco Canyon

CRADLE OF CULTURES

KEY
◆ Archaeological site

Mesoamerican peoples inhabited desert, mountain, plateau, and lowlands, while the Peruvian complex featured forests and mountains. Cultures of the American Southwest lived in harsh desert environments.

TIMELINE

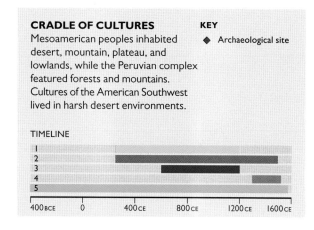

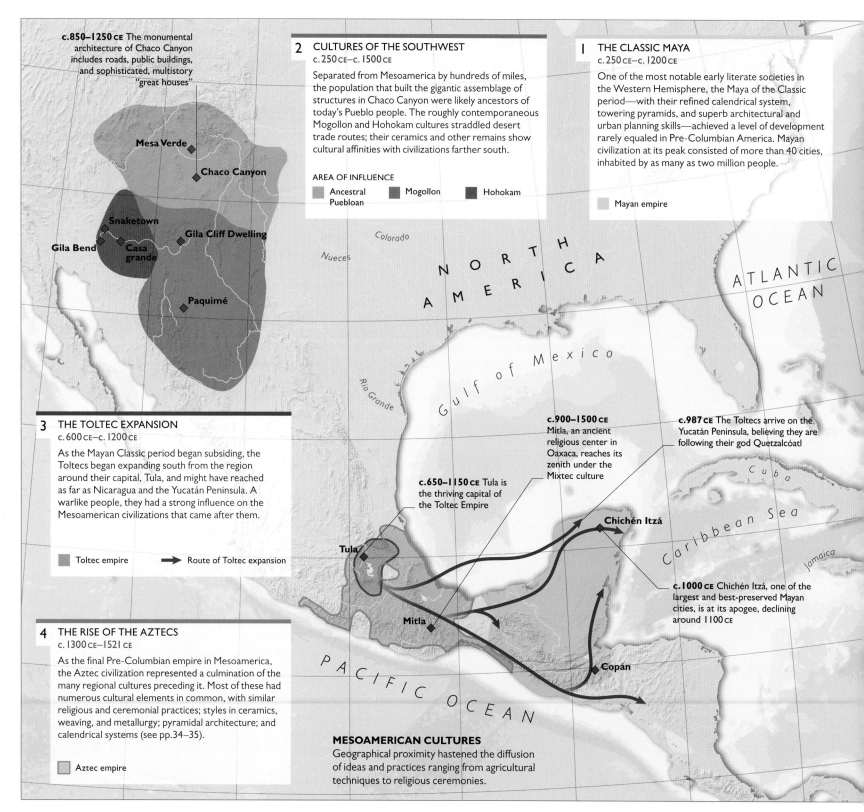

c.850–1250 CE The monumental architecture of Chaco Canyon includes roads, public buildings, and sophisticated, multistory "great houses"

2 CULTURES OF THE SOUTHWEST
c. 250 CE–c. 1500 CE

Separated from Mesoamerica by hundreds of miles, the population that built the gigantic assemblage of structures in Chaco Canyon were likely ancestors of today's Pueblo people. The roughly contemporaneous Mogollon and Hohokam cultures straddled desert trade routes; their ceramics and other remains show cultural affinities with civilizations farther south.

AREA OF INFLUENCE
Ancestral Puebloan / Mogollon / Hohokam

1 THE CLASSIC MAYA
c. 250 CE–c. 1200 CE

One of the most notable early literate societies in the Western Hemisphere, the Maya of the Classic period—with their refined calendrical system, towering pyramids, and superb architectural and urban planning skills—achieved a level of development rarely equaled in Pre-Columbian America. Mayan civilization at its peak consisted of more than 40 cities, inhabited by as many as two million people.

Mayan empire

3 THE TOLTEC EXPANSION
c. 600 CE–c. 1200 CE

As the Mayan Classic period began subsiding, the Toltecs began expanding south from the region around their capital, Tula, and might have reached as far as Nicaragua and the Yucatán Peninsula. A warlike people, they had a strong influence on the Mesoamerican civilizations that came after them.

Toltec empire / Route of Toltec expansion

c.900–1500 CE Mitla, an ancient religious center in Oaxaca, reaches its zenith under the Mixtec culture

c.650–1150 CE Tula is the thriving capital of the Toltec Empire

c.987 CE The Toltecs arrive on the Yucatán Peninsula, believing they are following their god Quetzalcóatl

c.1000 CE Chichén Itzá, one of the largest and best-preserved Mayan cities, is at its apogee, declining around 1100 CE

4 THE RISE OF THE AZTECS
c. 1300 CE–1521 CE

As the final Pre-Columbian empire in Mesoamerica, the Aztec civilization represented a culmination of the many regional cultures preceding it. Most of these had numerous cultural elements in common, with similar religious and ceremonial practices; styles in ceramics, weaving, and metallurgy; pyramidal architecture; and calendrical systems (see pp.34–35).

Aztec empire

MESOAMERICAN CULTURES
Geographical proximity hastened the diffusion of ideas and practices ranging from agricultural techniques to religious ceremonies.

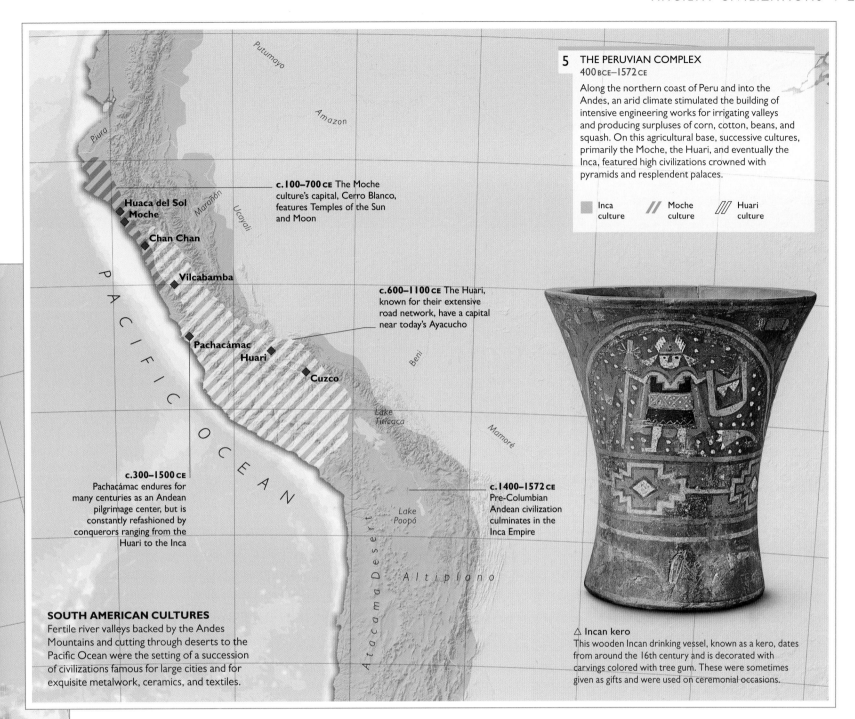

c.100–700 CE The Moche culture's capital, Cerro Blanco, features Temples of the Sun and Moon

Huaca del Sol
Moche

Chan Chan

Vilcabamba

c.600–1100 CE The Huari, known for their extensive road network, have a capital near today's Ayacucho

Pachacámac
Huari

Cuzco

c.300–1500 CE Pachacámac endures for many centuries as an Andean pilgrimage center, but is constantly refashioned by conquerors ranging from the Huari to the Inca

c.1400–1572 CE Pre-Columbian Andean civilization culminates in the Inca Empire

5 THE PERUVIAN COMPLEX
400 BCE–1572 CE

Along the northern coast of Peru and into the Andes, an arid climate stimulated the building of intensive engineering works for irrigating valleys and producing surpluses of corn, cotton, beans, and squash. On this agricultural base, successive cultures, primarily the Moche, the Huari, and eventually the Inca, featured high civilizations crowned with pyramids and resplendent palaces.

■ Inca culture   // Moche culture   /// Huari culture

SOUTH AMERICAN CULTURES
Fertile river valleys backed by the Andes Mountains and cutting through deserts to the Pacific Ocean were the setting of a succession of civilizations famous for large cities and for exquisite metalwork, ceramics, and textiles.

△ **Incan kero**
This wooden Incan drinking vessel, known as a kero, dates from around the 16th century and is decorated with carvings colored with tree gum. These were sometimes given as gifts and were used on ceremonial occasions.

ANCIENT CIVILIZATIONS

From around the middle of the first millennium BCE, many of the major civilizations of the Americas were characterized by a succession of overlapping empires, each of which dominated the cultural, religious, economic, and military life of their respective regions.

In Mesoamerica, the Mayan civilization (see pp.22–23) entered its key phase, the Classic Maya period, which featured grand cities, ornate metalwork, astronomy, and a hieroglyphic writing system. Influence began shifting from the Mayan lowlands to the plateaus of inland Mexico as the militaristic Toltecs expanded their influence. The Toltecs in turn were followed by the growth of the Aztecs—one of the last great Mesoamerican civilizations (see pp.34–35). There were broad overlaps among periods of hegemony, which were also periods of cultural and religious interchange when

cities arose, centered on ceremonial complexes topped with pyramids. Farther north, in what is now the Southwestern US and part of northern Mexico, previously nomadic peoples settled and built increasingly complex dwellings. Meanwhile, in the Andean region of South America, a succession of cultures, beginning with the Moche, grew and thrived through highly effective irrigation techniques. The Huari culture that followed them built a major network of roads, and the Inca build vast stone structures that can still be seen today.

EMPIRES AND INVADERS

While Indigenous American civilizations flourished in isolation from the rest of the world, newly-emerging European nation-states, blocked from the age-old trade routes to the East by the Muslim Ottoman Empire, began looking west, searching for sea passages to new lands, trade, and riches.

The first Europeans to reach North America came from the northwestern fringes of Eurasia, sailing across the North Atlantic and settling in Iceland and Greenland. These Norse seafarers did not set foot on the mainland itself but landed on Newfoundland, an island off the north coast that is geologically an extension of North America's Appalachian Mountains. However, the Norse settlement on Newfoundland's northern tip was abandoned after a few decades. The Norse presence in Greenland was also abandoned, leaving the Indigenous people of the Dorset Culture in full possession of the continent's ice-rimmed Arctic fringes. Interchange between the two groups appears to have been minimal, although Norse ships may have ranged as far south as the New England coast. Scandinavian explorer

◁ **Pectoral ornament**
This pendant, featuring a conch shell-section carved in jade and framed in ornamented gold, was probably worn on the chest of a priest impersonating the deity Quetzalcoatl—the "Feathered Serpent"—widely worshiped in the Aztec Empire.

Leif Erikson was later celebrated by his people as the first European to set foot in North America, although some historians have questioned this.

Conquest of the West Indies

Italian explorer Christopher Columbus also first set foot on an island of the Americas and not the mainland, but his first landing in the Bahamas paved the way for other European nations to later explore and colonize the entire continent. Although his expeditions were largely confined to the Caribbean islands, his successors gradually encroached on the continent itself. Another Italian explorer Amerigo Vespucci was the first to recognize the scale of those continents, and his Latinized name—"America"—

▽ **Europeans approach**
This late-19th century painting is a stylized depiction of Scandinavian explorer Leif Erikson's supposed voyage to North America around 1000. The US officially observes Leif Erikson Day each October 9.

"Columbus sought the golden shores of India ... He gave the world another world, and ruin
Brought upon blameless ... nations ... "

GEORGE SANTAYANA, *ODE #3*, 1922

TRADITION AND IMPERIALISM

The isolation of the Americas from the rest of the globe ensured the long preservation of its cultures, whose civilizations and artifacts—such as tools, ornaments, weapons, and pottery—changed and developed slowly over time. While the arrival of the Norse in Arctic America didn't affect the underlying patterns of Indigenous cultures, the coming of the Spanish to the Caribbean caused cataclysmic upheavals for the people of the regions.

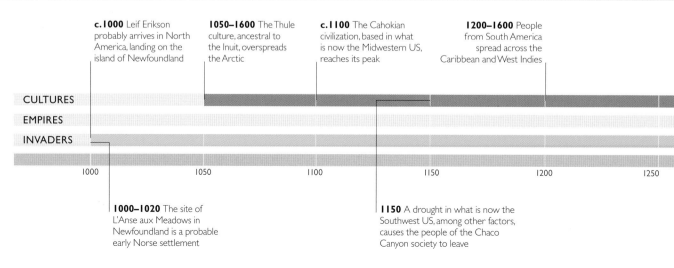

c.1000 Leif Erikson probably arrives in North America, landing on the island of Newfoundland

1050–1600 The Thule culture, ancestral to the Inuit, overspreads the Arctic

c.1100 The Cahokian civilization, based in what is now the Midwestern US, reaches its peak

1200–1600 People from South America spread across the Caribbean and West Indies

CULTURES

EMPIRES

INVADERS

1000   1050   1100   1150   1200   1250

1000–1020 The site of L'Anse aux Meadows in Newfoundland is a probable early Norse settlement

1150 A drought in what is now the Southwest US, among other factors, causes the people of the Chaco Canyon society to leave

▷ **Harpoon**
This ivory harpoon with an iron point was used by the Iñupiaq people of Alaska. It was primarily a tool for hunting and fishing, but could also be used in warfare.

was given to them. By 1500, Mesoamerican civilization in Central America, already thousands of years old, was reaching a new apex in the form of the Aztec Empire, which had replaced the Maya, Toltec, and Zapotec hegemonies preceding it. The Aztecs had traveled from a northern homeland to the Valley of Mexico, and built a new capital, Tenochtitlan. Far to the south, on the Pacific coast of South America, was the even larger Incan Empire, which remained largely isolated from the cultures of Mesoamerica. The Aztec and Incan empires were rich in gold, and both fell swiftly to the guns, diseases, and horses of the plundering Spanish conquistadors, who arrived in the early 1500s.

Across the continent

Interior North America was little affected by these developments, although Spanish incursions into the Great Plains and across the Southeast left death, disease, and destruction in their wake. Elsewhere, Indigenous peoples had been adapting their lifestyles to the continent's ever-changing ecosystems for millennia. Regional cultures had developed, especially where conditions were favorable for cultivating corn, although the great era of large towns built around huge mounds, like Cahokia, was on the wane during this period. In the deserts and sparse intermontane basins, hunting and gathering remained the norm, as it did along the coasts of the Pacific Northwest, where villagers lived off the sea. Families of nations, related through common linguistic stocks, expanded. Speakers of the Siouan languages mostly populated the Great Plains, but

offshoots had established themselves in the Southeastern hills. Algonquin and Iroquoian peoples spread out from a common homeland around the Great Lakes to the regions around Chesapeake Bay and along the Atlantic coastal plain and Piedmont, areas that would soon be encroached on by another group of invaders—the English.

◁ **Algonquin village**
This c. 1590 engraving of the "Town of Pomeiooc" in coastal North Carolina shows a typical Algonquin village with its bark-sheathed longhouses. Palisades were erected as a defense measure.

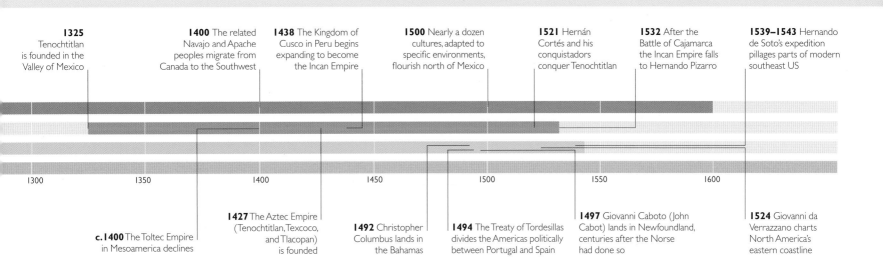

1325 Tenochtitlan is founded in the Valley of Mexico

1400 The related Navajo and Apache peoples migrate from Canada to the Southwest

1438 The Kingdom of Cusco in Peru begins expanding to become the Incan Empire

1500 Nearly a dozen cultures, adapted to specific environments, flourish north of Mexico

1521 Hernán Cortés and his conquistadors conquer Tenochtitlan

1532 After the Battle of Cajamarca the Incan Empire falls to Hernando Pizarro

1539–1543 Hernando de Soto's expedition pillages parts of modern southeast US

c.1400 The Toltec Empire in Mesoamerica declines

1427 The Aztec Empire (Tenochtitlan, Texcoco, and Tlacopan) is founded

1492 Christopher Columbus lands in the Bahamas

1494 The Treaty of Tordesillas divides the Americas politically between Portugal and Spain

1497 Giovanni Caboto (John Cabot) lands in Newfoundland, centuries after the Norse had done so

1524 Giovanni da Verrazzano charts North America's eastern coastline

NORSE VOYAGES

A Scandinavian people from the 8th–11th centuries, the Norse were accomplished seafarers, driven by their homeland's scarce pasture and arable land for farming but abundant timber for ships. They are thought to have been the first Europeans to reach North America.

The Norse sailed from what is now Denmark, Sweden, and Norway in their knarrs: long, wide, shallow-drafted ships with huge, square sails and long oars. They sailed south and west, often forcibly settling and ruling long-inhabited portions of the British Isles and Western Europe. The sparsely populated Orkney, Shetland, and Faroe Islands provided grazing for their herds. About a week's sailing west of the Faroes lay the island of Iceland. The Norse arrived there, according to tradition, around 870 CE, and began to settle. Soon they were looking even farther west.

The story of their settlement of Greenland—and perhaps North America—is told in the *Icelandic Sagas*, especially *The Saga of Erik the Red* and *The Saga of the Greenlanders*. Erik the Red chanced upon Greenland and planted Norse colonies there. In the latter saga, Bjarni Herjólfsson sighted new lands to the west of Greenland that could only be North America. In both accounts it was Erik's son, Leif Erikson, who became the first European to set foot on North American shores—nearly 500 years before Christopher Columbus.

> *"[Leif Erikson] … lighted upon lands of which before he had no expectation."*
>
> THE SAGA OF ERIK THE RED, 13TH CENTURY

ERIK THE RED
c.951–c.1000

Shown here in a 17th-century woodcut, the 10th-century Norseman Erik Thorvaldsson—more famous as "Erik the Red"—is known mainly through the 13th-century *Saga of Erik the Red*, composed and preserved in Iceland. Widely regarded as the first European to land on Greenland, he was credited with establishing the eastern and western settlements on the island's southwest corner. These colonies went on to be inhabited for around 500 years, and were a stepping stone in the Norse voyages to North America.

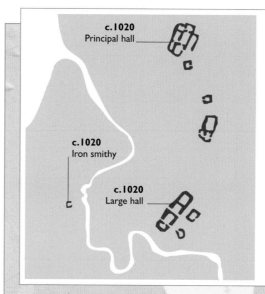

c.1020 Principal hall

c.1020 Iron smithy

c.1020 Large hall

L'ANSE AUX MEADOWS SETTLEMENT

A Norse presence in North America was purely conjectural until 1960, when Norwegian archaeologist Helge Ingstad began excavating the foundations of a Norse settlement, dated between the years 1000–1020, on the northeastern tip of Newfoundland. The scattered remnants might indicate a seasonal settlement, but the geographical description of Vinland in the sagas fits that of Newfoundland—if the wild grapes mentioned in the saga are understood to be berries instead.

5 PRESUMED VOYAGES TO NORTH AMERICA
1000–1400 CE

During the nearly five centuries the Norse inhabited Greenland, it is considered likely that they explored other parts of the North American littoral, perhaps coasting as far south as New England. Physical evidence is scant, but an 11th-century Norse silver coin found in Maine indicates trade, if not exploration.

→ Presumed voyages to North America

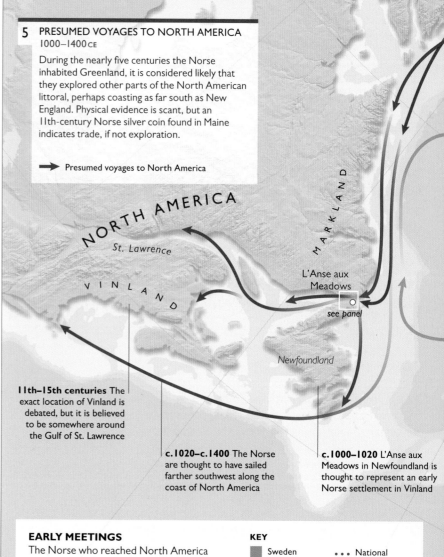

NORTH AMERICA

St. Lawrence

VINLAND

MARKLAND

L'Anse aux Meadows

see panel

Newfoundland

11th–15th centuries The exact location of Vinland is debated, but it is believed to be somewhere around the Gulf of St. Lawrence

c.1020–c.1400 The Norse are thought to have sailed farther southwest along the coast of North America

c.1000–1020 L'Anse aux Meadows in Newfoundland is thought to represent an early Norse settlement in Vinland

EARLY MEETINGS

The Norse who reached North America are thought to have encountered Indigenous peoples of the Americas. Little is known about their interactions but arrowheads have been found at Norse burial sites, suggesting conflict, while a silver coin (see above) suggests trade.

KEY

■ Sweden	⋯ National borders
■ Norway	
■ Denmark	— Holy Roman Empire border
■ Norse settlements	

TIMELINE

	740	850	960	1070	1180	1290	1400
1							
2							
3							
4							
5							

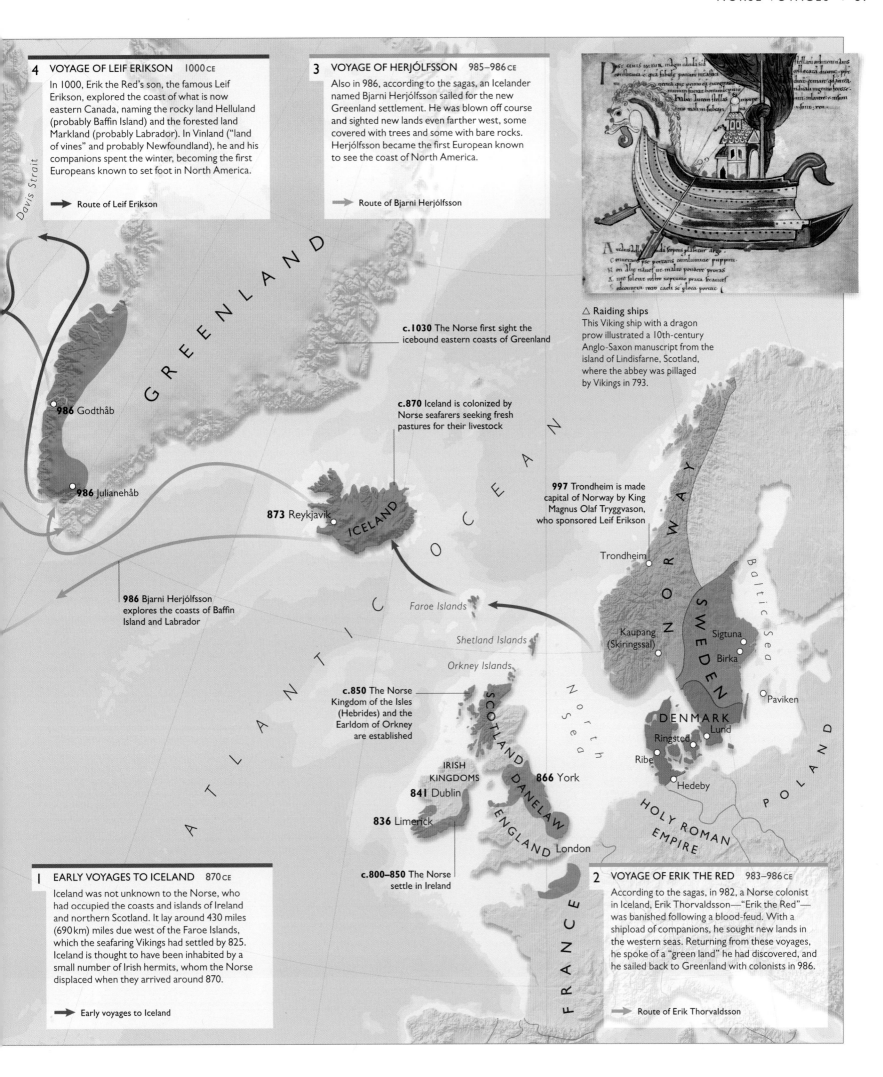

4 VOYAGE OF LEIF ERIKSON 1000 CE

In 1000, Erik the Red's son, the famous Leif Erikson, explored the coast of what is now eastern Canada, naming the rocky land Helluland (probably Baffin Island) and the forested land Markland (probably Labrador). In Vinland ("land of vines" and probably Newfoundland), he and his companions spent the winter, becoming the first Europeans known to set foot in North America.

→ Route of Leif Erikson

3 VOYAGE OF HERJÓLFSSON 985–986 CE

Also in 986, according to the sagas, an Icelander named Bjarni Herjólfsson sailed for the new Greenland settlement. He was blown off course and sighted new lands even farther west, some covered with trees and some with bare rocks. Herjólfsson became the first European known to see the coast of North America.

→ Route of Bjarni Herjólfsson

△ Raiding ships
This Viking ship with a dragon prow illustrated a 10th-century Anglo-Saxon manuscript from the island of Lindisfarne, Scotland, where the abbey was pillaged by Vikings in 793.

Davis Strait

G R E E N L A N D

c.1030 The Norse first sight the icebound eastern coasts of Greenland

986 Godthåb

c.870 Iceland is colonized by Norse seafarers seeking fresh pastures for their livestock

986 Julianehåb

997 Trondheim is made capital of Norway by King Magnus Olaf Tryggvason, who sponsored Leif Erikson

873 Reykjavik

ICELAND

A T L A N T I C   O C E A N

Trondheim

N O R W A Y

Baltic Sea

986 Bjarni Herjólfsson explores the coasts of Baffin Island and Labrador

Faroe Islands

Shetland Islands

North Sea

Orkney Islands

Kaupang (Skiringssal)

S W E D E N

Sigtuna

Birka

Paviken

c.850 The Norse Kingdom of the Isles (Hebrides) and the Earldom of Orkney are established

SCOTLAND

DENMARK

Lund

Ringsted

Ribe

IRISH KINGDOMS

DANELAW

866 York

Hedeby

841 Dublin

ENGLAND

London

P O L A N D

836 Limerick

HOLY ROMAN EMPIRE

c.800–850 The Norse settle in Ireland

F R A N C E

1 EARLY VOYAGES TO ICELAND 870 CE

Iceland was not unknown to the Norse, who had occupied the coasts and islands of Ireland and northern Scotland. It lay around 430 miles (690 km) miles due west of the Faroe Islands, which the seafaring Vikings had settled by 825. Iceland is thought to have been inhabited by a small number of Irish hermits, whom the Norse displaced when they arrived around 870.

→ Early voyages to Iceland

2 VOYAGE OF ERIK THE RED 983–986 CE

According to the sagas, in 982, a Norse colonist in Iceland, Erik Thorvaldsson—"Erik the Red"—was banished following a blood-feud. With a shipload of companions, he sought new lands in the western seas. Returning from these voyages, he spoke of a "green land" he had discovered, and he sailed back to Greenland with colonists in 986.

→ Route of Erik Thorvaldsson

32

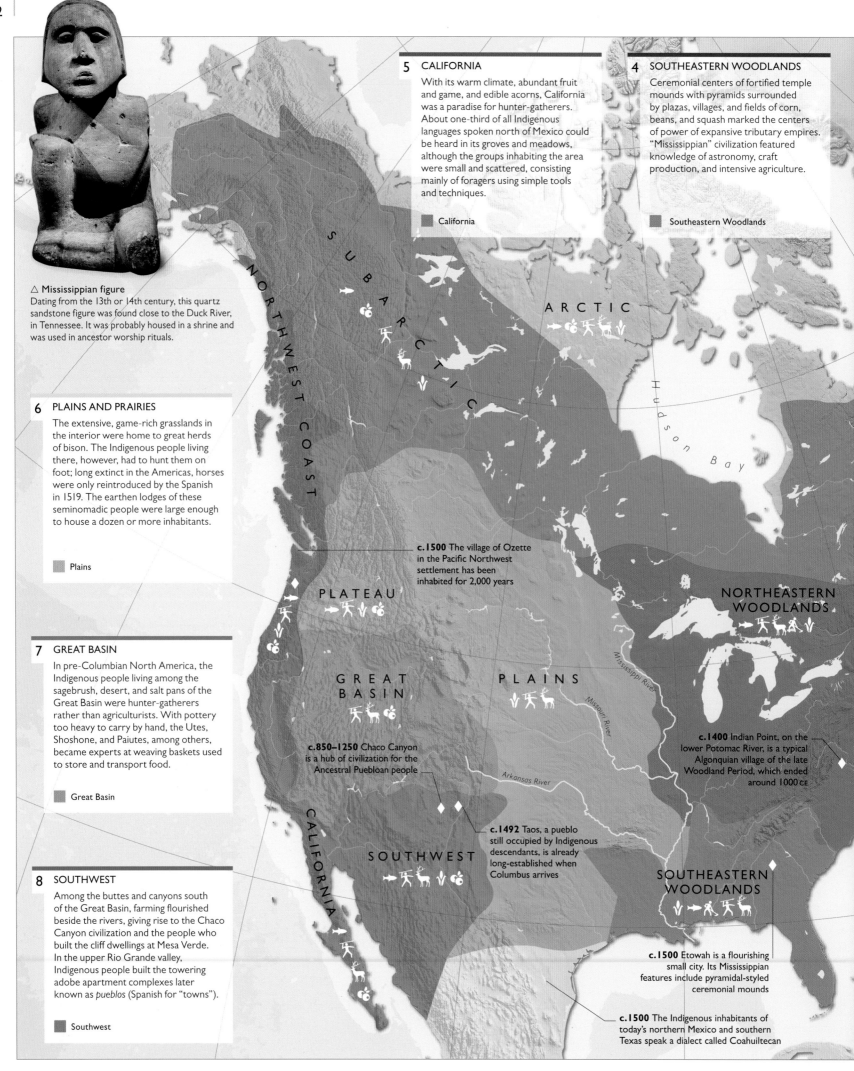

△ **Mississippian figure**
Dating from the 13th or 14th century, this quartz sandstone figure was found close to the Duck River, in Tennessee. It was probably housed in a shrine and was used in ancestor worship rituals.

5 CALIFORNIA

With its warm climate, abundant fruit and game, and edible acorns, California was a paradise for hunter-gatherers. About one-third of all Indigenous languages spoken north of Mexico could be heard in its groves and meadows, although the groups inhabiting the area were small and scattered, consisting mainly of foragers using simple tools and techniques.

◻ California

4 SOUTHEASTERN WOODLANDS

Ceremonial centers of fortified temple mounds with pyramids surrounded by plazas, villages, and fields of corn, beans, and squash marked the centers of power of expansive tributary empires. "Mississippian" civilization featured knowledge of astronomy, craft production, and intensive agriculture.

◻ Southeastern Woodlands

6 PLAINS AND PRAIRIES

The extensive, game-rich grasslands in the interior were home to great herds of bison. The Indigenous people living there, however, had to hunt them on foot; long extinct in the Americas, horses were only reintroduced by the Spanish in 1519. The earthen lodges of these seminomadic people were large enough to house a dozen or more inhabitants.

◻ Plains

7 GREAT BASIN

In pre-Columbian North America, the Indigenous people living among the sagebrush, desert, and salt pans of the Great Basin were hunter-gatherers rather than agriculturists. With pottery too heavy to carry by hand, the Utes, Shoshone, and Paiutes, among others, became experts at weaving baskets used to store and transport food.

◻ Great Basin

8 SOUTHWEST

Among the buttes and canyons south of the Great Basin, farming flourished beside the rivers, giving rise to the Chaco Canyon civilization and the people who built the cliff dwellings at Mesa Verde. In the upper Rio Grande valley, Indigenous people built the towering adobe apartment complexes later known as *pueblos* (Spanish for "towns").

◻ Southwest

c.1500 The village of Ozette in the Pacific Northwest settlement has been inhabited for 2,000 years

c.850–1250 Chaco Canyon is a hub of civilization for the Ancestral Puebloan people

c.1492 Taos, a pueblo still occupied by Indigenous descendants, is already long-established when Columbus arrives

c.1400 Indian Point, on the lower Potomac River, is a typical Algonquian village of the late Woodland Period, which ended around 1000 CE

c.1500 Etowah is a flourishing small city. Its Mississippian features include pyramidal-styled ceremonial mounds

c.1500 The Indigenous inhabitants of today's northern Mexico and southern Texas speak a dialect called Coahuiltecan

ARCTIC

SUBARCTIC

NORTHWEST COAST

PLATEAU

GREAT BASIN

PLAINS

NORTHEASTERN WOODLANDS

SOUTHWEST

CALIFORNIA

SOUTHEASTERN WOODLANDS

Hudson Bay

Mississippi River

Missouri River

Arkansas River

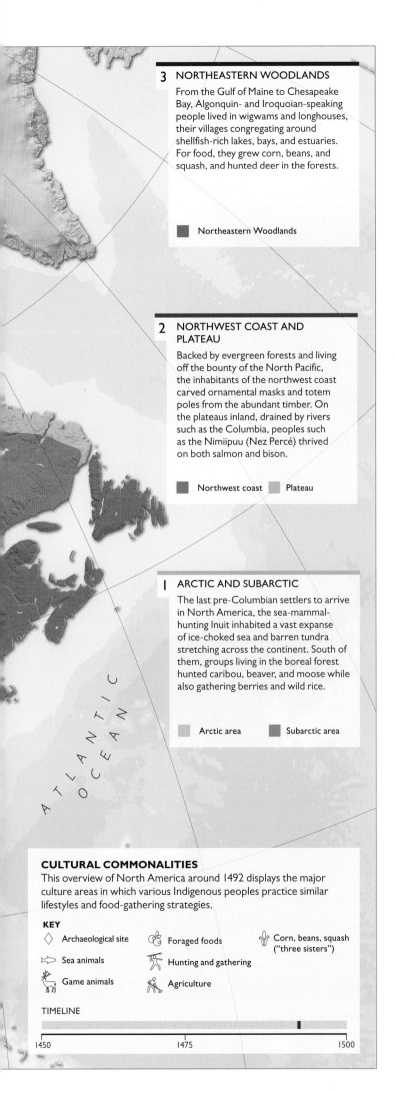

3 NORTHEASTERN WOODLANDS

From the Gulf of Maine to Chesapeake Bay, Algonquin- and Iroquoian-speaking people lived in wigwams and longhouses, their villages congregating around shellfish-rich lakes, bays, and estuaries. For food, they grew corn, beans, and squash, and hunted deer in the forests.

■ Northeastern Woodlands

2 NORTHWEST COAST AND PLATEAU

Backed by evergreen forests and living off the bounty of the North Pacific, the inhabitants of the northwest coast carved ornamental masks and totem poles from the abundant timber. On the plateaus inland, drained by rivers such as the Columbia, peoples such as the Nimiipuu (Nez Percé) thrived on both salmon and bison.

■ Northwest coast   ■ Plateau

1 ARCTIC AND SUBARCTIC

The last pre-Columbian settlers to arrive in North America, the sea-mammal-hunting Inuit inhabited a vast expanse of ice-choked sea and barren tundra stretching across the continent. South of them, groups living in the boreal forest hunted caribou, beaver, and moose while also gathering berries and wild rice.

■ Arctic area   ■ Subarctic area

CULTURAL COMMONALITIES

This overview of North America around 1492 displays the major culture areas in which various Indigenous peoples practice similar lifestyles and food-gathering strategies.

KEY

◇ Archaeological site   Foraged foods   Corn, beans, squash ("three sisters")

⊳ Sea animals   Hunting and gathering

Game animals   Agriculture

TIMELINE

1450   1475   1500

INDIGENOUS NORTH AMERICA

By the late 15th century, the Indigenous peoples of North America had been living there for at least 25,000 years. When they first arrived, the ancestors of the first human inhabitants of the continent brought with them a developed culture and sophisticated tools that enabled them to adapt to the ecosystems they encountered.

Millions of Indigenous people were living in North America at the time of Christopher Columbus's landfall. Over thousands of years and hundreds of generations, Indigenous societies had been established in every biome on the continent, where they followed the seasonal migration of animals; foraged for nuts, berries, and wild plants as hunter-gatherers; and created large cities and subordinate tributary empires.

Whether dwelling around agriculturally rich temple complexes in Mesoamerica and the Mississippi Valley, or foraging for scarce resources in the arid Great Basin between the Sierra Nevada and the Rocky Mountains, these societies adapted to life in diverse environments.

Even those living in areas too cold or too dry for agriculture benefited from vast networks of trade and exchange. From Mesoamerica, corn agriculture spread productive farming practices throughout the Americas. Native farmers prepared land for farming and animal grazing, using controlled burnings to replenish the soil and attract deer herds.

This Indigenous world was extensive but also very insular. In the whole of the Americas, it is likely that the only people from the other side of the world the Indigenous population ever encountered were the few Norse mariners who sailed to Greenland and Labrador, in modern Canada, from the late 10th century.

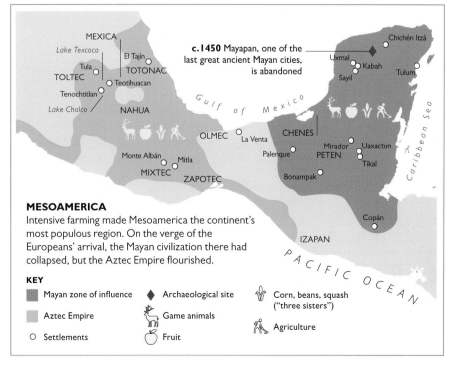

MESOAMERICA

Intensive farming made Mesoamerica the continent's most populous region. On the verge of the Europeans' arrival, the Mayan civilization there had collapsed, but the Aztec Empire flourished.

KEY

■ Mayan zone of influence   ◆ Archaeological site   Corn, beans, squash ("three sisters")

■ Aztec Empire   Game animals   Agriculture

○ Settlements   Fruit

THE AZTEC EMPIRE

The Aztec civilization was one of the last great Pre-Columbian Mesoamerican societies, existing around the 14th–16th centuries in central Mexico. Highly militaristic and religious, the civilization was rich in arts and culture.

The Aztecs produced finely crafted artifacts, including feathered headdresses and ceremonial masks adorned with feathers or turquoise, as well as epic narratives illustrated with detailed pictographs. Other disciplines included poetry, philosophy, music, and astronomy. They devised three calendar systems: a 365-day one; another 260-day version for charting annual religious ceremonies; and a long-count calendar tracking 52-year cycles for correlating movements of the heavens with the course of human affairs. The Aztec empire's capital, Tenochtitlan, rose above Lake Texcoco and consisted of around 80 palaces and ceremonial

△ **Double-headed serpent**
Made from cedro wood, turquoise, red thorny oyster shell, and conch, this Aztec serpent breastplate dates from around 1400–1521.

tepella

hom.camixpollo quetepellacuauhtla
rexcallcocon-canit-nenecamexica

quimamaintes

cuauhtla

rexcallco

Mountain scene at Chicomoztoc
Showing humans, animals, landscape, and pictograms, this ceremonial scene is from the Codex Azcatitlan, a 16th-century history of the Aztecs and their migration from the semi-mythical Aztlán to the Valley of Mexico.

buildings. On the Huēy Teōcalli, their sacred pyramid in the city, stood two shrines. One was dedicated to Huitzilopochtli, sun and war god who had led the Aztec's ancestors from Aztlán far to the north to the Valley of Mexico, while the other served Tlaloc, the fertility deity. Both gods demanded human sacrifices, which were supplied by an elite caste of warriors, who had established the empire (see p.26). The invasion of the Spanish in 1519 (see pp.48–49) heralded the end of the Aztec civilization.

"I have seen nothing that has so rejoiced my heart as these things."

ARTIST ALBRECHT DÜRER ON AZTEC ARTIFACTS, 1521

AZTEC AGRICULTURE

The Aztecs' highly productive system of agriculture was key in the formation of their empire. They grew corn, beans, and squash, supplemented by peppers and tomatoes, in fenced garden plots around the shores of Lake Texcoco. The plots were irrigated by complex waterworks featuring gates and aqueducts. Fish, waterfowl, turkeys, grasshoppers, and algae were also eaten, and cacao was used to make a bitter chocolate drink. Corn cultivation was especially associated with rites and ceremonies.

Illustration showing corn harvesting, 16th century

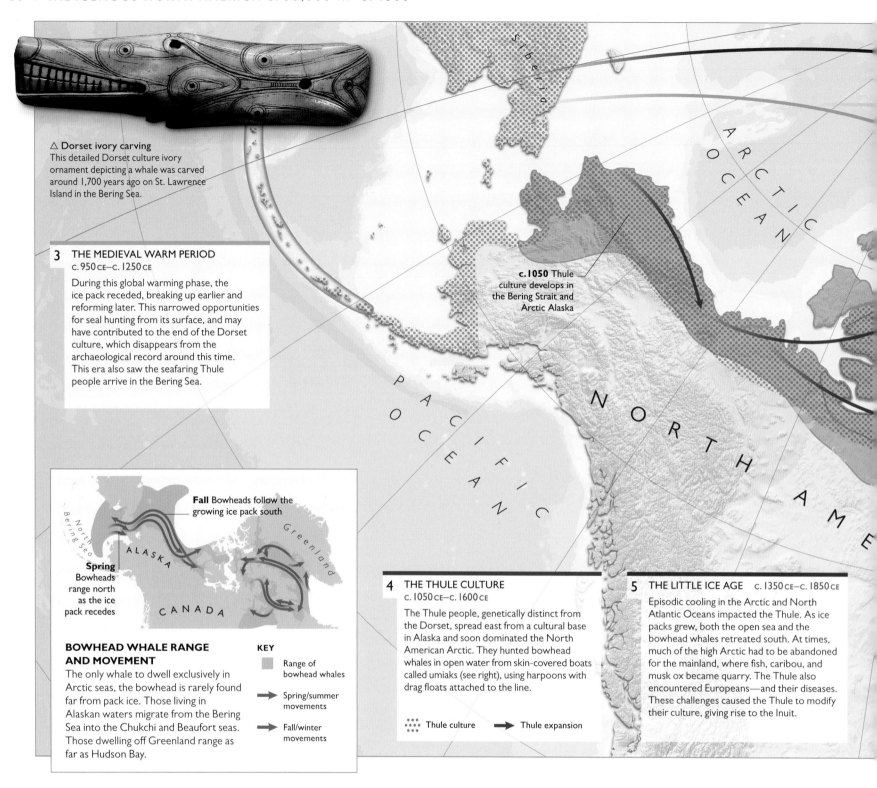

△ **Dorset ivory carving**
This detailed Dorset culture ivory ornament depicting a whale was carved around 1,700 years ago on St. Lawrence Island in the Bering Sea.

3 THE MEDIEVAL WARM PERIOD
c. 950 CE–c. 1250 CE

During this global warming phase, the ice pack receded, breaking up earlier and reforming later. This narrowed opportunities for seal hunting from its surface, and may have contributed to the end of the Dorset culture, which disappears from the archaeological record around this time. This era also saw the seafaring Thule people arrive in the Bering Sea.

c.1050 Thule culture develops in the Bering Strait and Arctic Alaska

Fall Bowheads follow the growing ice pack south

Spring Bowheads range north as the ice pack recedes

BOWHEAD WHALE RANGE AND MOVEMENT
The only whale to dwell exclusively in Arctic seas, the bowhead is rarely found far from pack ice. Those living in Alaskan waters migrate from the Bering Sea into the Chukchi and Beaufort seas. Those dwelling off Greenland range as far as Hudson Bay.

KEY

Range of bowhead whales

→ Spring/summer movements

→ Fall/winter movements

4 THE THULE CULTURE
c. 1050 CE–c. 1600 CE

The Thule people, genetically distinct from the Dorset, spread east from a cultural base in Alaska and soon dominated the North American Arctic. They hunted bowhead whales in open water from skin-covered boats called umiaks (see right), using harpoons with drag floats attached to the line.

::: Thule culture   → Thule expansion

5 THE LITTLE ICE AGE c. 1350 CE–c. 1850 CE

Episodic cooling in the Arctic and North Atlantic Oceans impacted the Thule. As ice packs grew, both the open sea and the bowhead whales retreated south. At times, much of the high Arctic had to be abandoned for the mainland, where fish, caribou, and musk ox became quarry. The Thule also encountered Europeans—and their diseases. These challenges caused the Thule to modify their culture, giving rise to the Inuit.

THE NORTH ATLANTIC WORLD

Today's Inuit are descendants of the first Arctic peoples, who lived on the shorelines and the ice pack of the Arctic seas—the Bering, Beaufort, and Chukchi. The first inhabitants of this region were distinct from the Indigenous peoples who first colonized the rest of North America; both originated in Siberia, but the Arctic peoples arrived thousands of years later.

Surrounded by shoreline and tundra, for thousands of years these peoples lived by hunting and gathering, killing mainly marine mammals such as whales, seals, and walruses, as well as caribou and polar bears. The massive bowhead whales in particular were an important resource (see above right). They slept on the ocean surface and so could be stealthily approached, but it was nevertheless a tremendous feat to kill one and wrestle it to shore. Nothing from the whale was wasted: meat, blubber, blood, skin, and organs were harvested for food, while tools, harpoons, needles, and other items were made from ivory and bone. Craftspeople also carved an early form of scrimshaw onto walrus tusks and sperm whale teeth, and whale ribs were used to build frames for dwellings.

The inhabitants of the North American Arctic were among the first Indigenous cultures to interact with Europeans. They are believed to have encountered medieval Norse explorers (see pp.30–31), but after

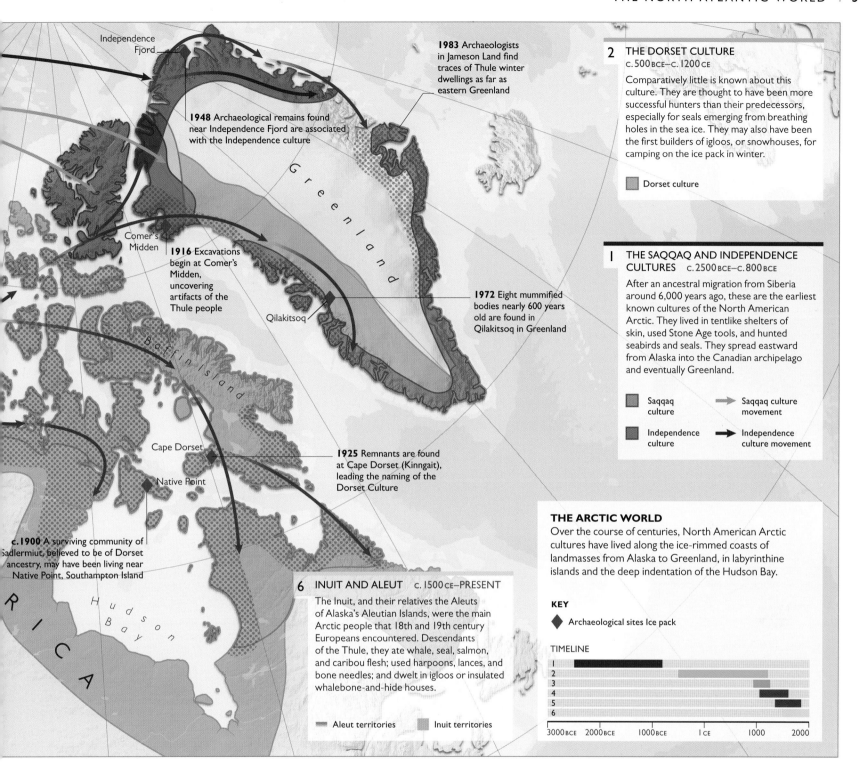

1983 Archaeologists in Jameson Land find traces of Thule winter dwellings as far as eastern Greenland

Independence Fjord

1948 Archaeological remains found near Independence Fjord are associated with the Independence culture

Comer's Midden

1916 Excavations begin at Comer's Midden, uncovering artifacts of the Thule people

Qilakitsoq

1972 Eight mummified bodies nearly 600 years old are found in Qilakitsoq in Greenland

Cape Dorset

Native Point

1925 Remnants are found at Cape Dorset (Kinngait), leading the naming of the Dorset Culture

c.1900 A surviving community of Sadlermiut, believed to be of Dorset ancestry, may have been living near Native Point, Southampton Island

2 THE DORSET CULTURE
c. 500 BCE–c. 1200 CE

Comparatively little is known about this culture. They are thought to have been more successful hunters than their predecessors, especially for seals emerging from breathing holes in the sea ice. They may also have been the first builders of igloos, or snowhouses, for camping on the ice pack in winter.

■ Dorset culture

1 THE SAQQAQ AND INDEPENDENCE CULTURES c. 2500 BCE–c. 800 BCE

After an ancestral migration from Siberia around 6,000 years ago, these are the earliest known cultures of the North American Arctic. They lived in tentlike shelters of skin, used Stone Age tools, and hunted seabirds and seals. They spread eastward from Alaska into the Canadian archipelago and eventually Greenland.

■ Saqqaq culture → Saqqaq culture movement
■ Independence culture → Independence culture movement

THE ARCTIC WORLD
Over the course of centuries, North American Arctic cultures have lived along the ice-rimmed coasts of landmasses from Alaska to Greenland, in labyrinthine islands and the deep indentation of the Hudson Bay.

KEY
◆ Archaeological sites Ice pack

6 INUIT AND ALEUT c. 1500 CE–PRESENT
The Inuit, and their relatives the Aleuts of Alaska's Aleutian Islands, were the main Arctic people that 18th and 19th century Europeans encountered. Descendants of the Thule, they ate whale, seal, salmon, and caribou flesh; used harpoons, lances, and bone needles; and dwelt in igloos or insulated whalebone-and-hide houses.

— Aleut territories ■ Inuit territories

TIMELINE
3000 BCE 2000 BCE 1000 BCE 1 CE 1000 2000

this they remained largely isolated from Europeans until the 19th century. The successive cultures of this region have now been traced back thousands of years by archaeologists, although artifacts from archaeological sites have revealed comparatively little. Like many ancient peoples, they are identified primarily by the regions they inhabited. The Thule culture is a notable exception to this, because it is named not only for a Greenland town but also for the ancient Greek name for a mythical northern land.

"The caribou feeds the wolf, but it is the wolf who keeps the caribou strong."

INUIT PROVERB

UMIAKS

First constructed by Thule people, the umiak is an open-water whaling boat made by stretching bearded seal hides over a whalebone or driftwood frame. Often powered by sails made of skins, each one can carry two dozen hunters. Captains of single boats or small fleets are still revered today.

Umiak illustration, 1892

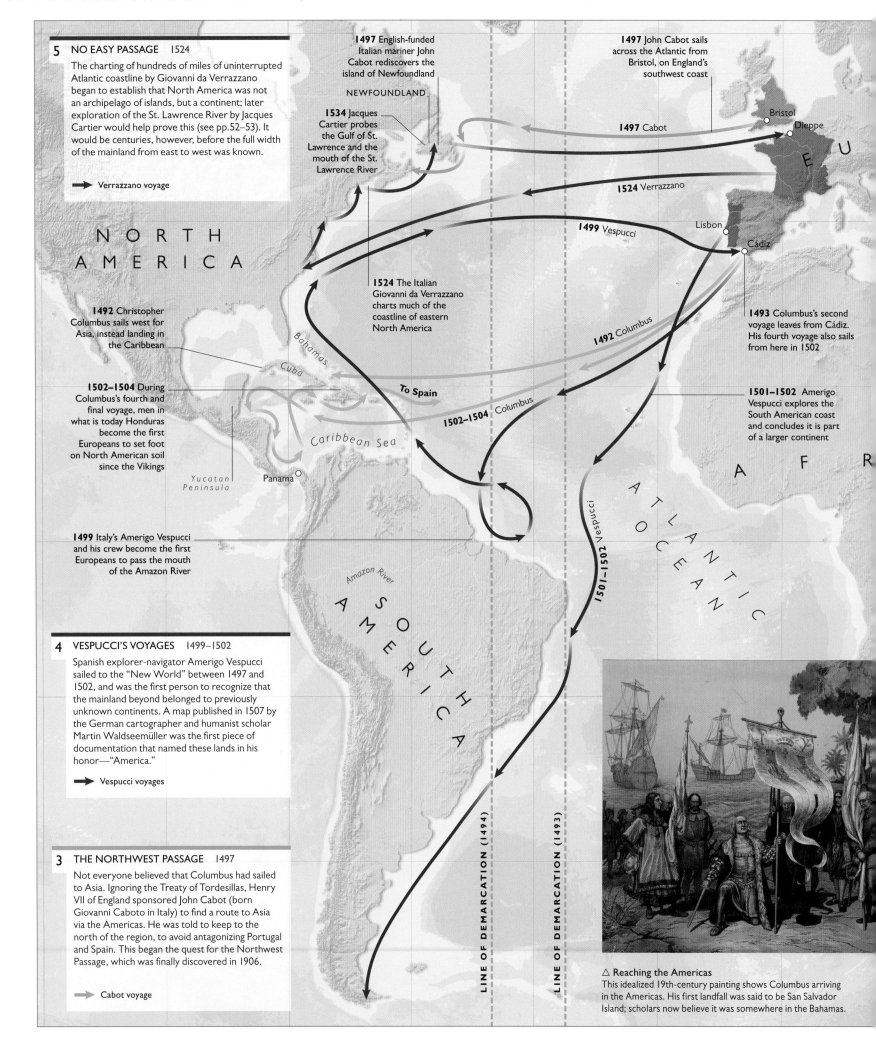

5 NO EASY PASSAGE 1524

The charting of hundreds of miles of uninterrupted Atlantic coastline by Giovanni da Verrazzano began to establish that North America was not an archipelago of islands, but a continent; later exploration of the St. Lawrence River by Jacques Cartier would help prove this (see pp.52–53). It would be centuries, however, before the full width of the mainland from east to west was known.

→ Verrazzano voyage

1497 English-funded Italian mariner John Cabot rediscovers the island of Newfoundland

NEWFOUNDLAND

1534 Jacques Cartier probes the Gulf of St. Lawrence and the mouth of the St. Lawrence River

1497 John Cabot sails across the Atlantic from Bristol, on England's southwest coast

Bristol
Dieppe
E U

1497 Cabot

1524 Verrazzano

1499 Vespucci

Lisbon
Cádiz

NORTH AMERICA

1492 Christopher Columbus sails west for Asia, instead landing in the Caribbean

1524 The Italian Giovanni da Verrazzano charts much of the coastline of eastern North America

1493 Columbus's second voyage leaves from Cádiz. His fourth voyage also sails from here in 1502

Bahamas
Cuba

1502–1504 During Columbus's fourth and final voyage, men in what is today Honduras become the first Europeans to set foot on North American soil since the Vikings

1492 Columbus

To Spain

1502–1504 Columbus

1501–1502 Amerigo Vespucci explores the South American coast and concludes it is part of a larger continent

Caribbean Sea

A F R

Yucatan Peninsula
Panama

1499 Italy's Amerigo Vespucci and his crew become the first Europeans to pass the mouth of the Amazon River

A T L A N T I C   O C E A N

1501–1502 Vespucci

Amazon River

S O U T H   A M E R I C A

4 VESPUCCI'S VOYAGES 1499–1502

Spanish explorer-navigator Amerigo Vespucci sailed to the "New World" between 1497 and 1502, and was the first person to recognize that the mainland beyond belonged to previously unknown continents. A map published in 1507 by the German cartographer and humanist scholar Martin Waldseemüller was the first piece of documentation that named these lands in his honor—"America."

→ Vespucci voyages

3 THE NORTHWEST PASSAGE 1497

Not everyone believed that Columbus had sailed to Asia. Ignoring the Treaty of Tordesillas, Henry VII of England sponsored John Cabot (born Giovanni Caboto in Italy) to find a route to Asia via the Americas. He was told to keep to the north of the region, to avoid antagonizing Portugal and Spain. This began the quest for the Northwest Passage, which was finally discovered in 1906.

→ Cabot voyage

LINE OF DEMARCATION (1494)

LINE OF DEMARCATION (1493)

△ **Reaching the Americas**
This idealized 19th-century painting shows Columbus arriving in the Americas. His first landfall was said to be San Salvador Island; scholars now believe it was somewhere in the Bahamas.

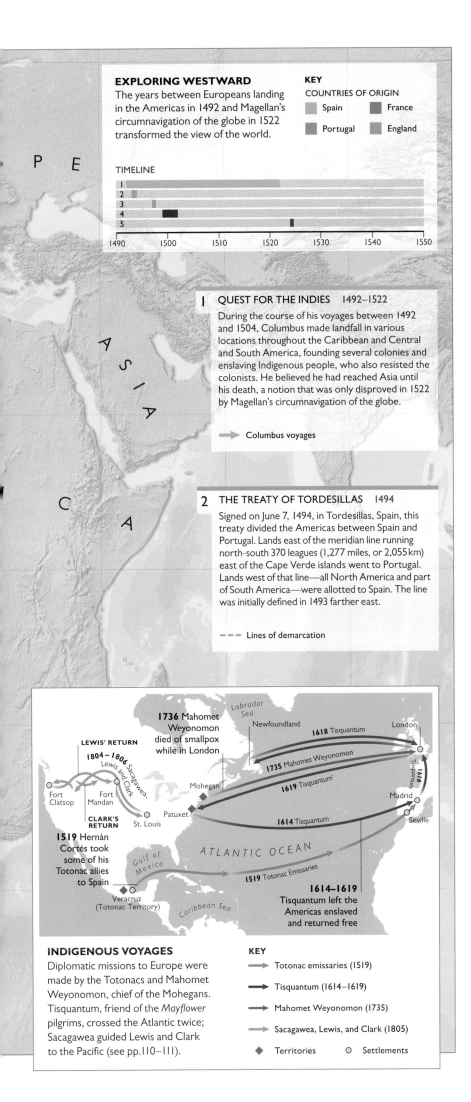

EXPLORING WESTWARD

The years between Europeans landing in the Americas in 1492 and Magellan's circumnavigation of the globe in 1522 transformed the view of the world.

KEY
COUNTRIES OF ORIGIN

Spain
Portugal
France
England

TIMELINE

1
2
3
4
5

1490   1500   1510   1520   1530   1540   1550

1 QUEST FOR THE INDIES   1492–1522

During the course of his voyages between 1492 and 1504, Columbus made landfall in various locations throughout the Caribbean and Central and South America, founding several colonies and enslaving Indigenous people, who also resisted the colonists. He believed he had reached Asia until his death, a notion that was only disproved in 1522 by Magellan's circumnavigation of the globe.

➝ Columbus voyages

2 THE TREATY OF TORDESILLAS   1494

Signed on June 7, 1494, in Tordesillas, Spain, this treaty divided the Americas between Spain and Portugal. Lands east of the meridian line running north-south 370 leagues (1,277 miles, or 2,055 km) east of the Cape Verde islands went to Portugal. Lands west of that line—all North America and part of South America—were allotted to Spain. The line was initially defined in 1493 farther east.

- - - Lines of demarcation

1736 Mahomet Weyonomon died of smallpox while in London

LEWIS' RETURN

1804–1806 Lewis and Clark

Fort Clatsop
Fort Mandan

CLARK'S RETURN
St. Louis

1519 Hernán Cortés took some of his Totonac allies to Spain

Veracruz (Totonac Territory)

Labrador Sea
Newfoundland
London
Mohegan
Patuxet
Madrid
Seville

1618 Tisquantum
1735 Mahomet Weyonomon
1619 Tisquantum
1618 Tisquantum
1614 Tisquantum

Gulf of Mexico
ATLANTIC OCEAN
Caribbean Sea

1519 Totonac Emissaries

1614–1619 Tisquantum left the Americas enslaved and returned free

INDIGENOUS VOYAGES

Diplomatic missions to Europe were made by the Totonacs and Mahomet Weyonomon, chief of the Mohegans. Tisquantum, friend of the *Mayflower* pilgrims, crossed the Atlantic twice; Sacagawea guided Lewis and Clark to the Pacific (see pp.110–111).

KEY

➝ Totonac emissaries (1519)
➝ Tisquantum (1614–1619)
➝ Mahomet Weyonomon (1735)
➝ Sacagawea, Lewis, and Clark (1805)
◆ Territories   ○ Settlements

EARLY VOYAGES

The fall of Constantinople to the Islamic Ottoman Empire in 1453 closed Asia's Silk Roads to Christian Europe, and European traders turned their attentions to the west. Improvements in navigation also spurred seafarers to voyage ever farther into the Atlantic.

Portugal led the way, its ships reaching the Madeira and Azores islands off western Africa. In 1492, however, Genoese navigator Christopher Columbus, serving the Spanish Court, landed in the Bahamas while searching for a western route to Asia. When news spread of his landfall, mariners from the Iberian peninsula set sail for the Americas in a race to claim its land, resources, and riches.

By 1494, Spain and Portugal had agreed to spheres of influence in the Americas and set about establishing empires there. However, they had not reckoned with other Atlantic-facing kingdoms such as France and England, who, while ostensibly still looking for a westward passage to Asia, were soon launching their own explorations of these lands, mostly to the north.

When the survivors of Ferdinand Magellan's circumnavigation of the world returned to Spain in 1522, European geographers could finally confirm that the western sea route to Asia was blocked by a vast new landmass—one on which the Europeans' impact would prove to be utterly transformational (see pp.46–47).

> *"More densely peopled and abounding in animals than our Europe or Asia or Africa ..."*
>
> AMERIGO VESPUCCI ON THE AMERICAS, 1504

MARTIN BEHAIM'S *ERDAPFEL*

The earliest surviving terrestrial globe, the *Erdapfel* (German for "earth apple") depicts an Atlantic Ocean stretching between western Europe and eastern Asia, a sea spangled with islands but no continents. Made between 1490–1492, it shows how Columbus's ideas about the shape of the world were widely accepted, especially by geographers like Martin Behaim (1459–1507). Behaim shared in particular Columbus's insistence that the "Western Ocean" was narrower than it proved to be.

Behaim's globe is a laminated linen ball.

VIEWS OF THE WORLD

Around the time Europeans first made contact with the Americas, human perceptions of the world and the universe varied greatly across cultures. However, these different cosmologies were similar in that they often consisted of a combination of geography, theory, and spiritual belief.

Few maps, charts, or artworks depicting the belief systems or mythological cosmos of Indigenous peoples of the Americas survive today. However, the worldview of people such as the Aztecs has been pieced together from various artifacts. It is known, for example, that their spiritual beliefs were highly syncretistic, meaning that they incorporated influences from other civilizations, especially the Maya. The Aztec belief in the Thirteen Heavens where the gods, stars, and planets reside, for example, incorporated the Mayan concept of time itself as a divinity manifesting itself through an unending series of cycles, each one lasting 900 or 1,200 years, that controlled human destiny.

The Catholicism that Spanish and Portuguese colonizers brought with them shared similarities with Indigenous beliefs—in the idea of death and rebirth, for example, or in a spiritual hierarchy from Earth to heaven—but differed because it was monotheistic, as opposed to polytheistic like the beliefs of the Maya and Aztec. While many Indigenous beliefs were fixed and based on observing set rituals in order to placate the gods, Christian beliefs changed during the era of European expansion; the Reformation began just 25 years after Columbus arrived in the Caribbean. Furthermore, the European vision of time was not cyclical but forward moving and unpredictable. It was something to be mastered, which gave rise to ideas such as a march toward progress, destiny, missionary

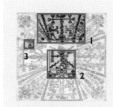

LOCATOR

KEY

1 The top of the cross represents east, the most important of the four cardinal directions. The tree is flanked by two "night lords."

2 The figure in the center is Xiuhtecuhtli, the god of fire, light, volcanoes, and more. The deity was rejuvenated by Aztec priests every 52 years in a ritual called the New Fire Ceremony.

3 The crocodile was the first of the *trecenas*, or 13-day periods of the calendar.

zeal, and imperial ambition. The encroachment of Europeans in the Americas led to centuries of conflict, possibly worsened by a mutual lack of understanding of each other's view of the world. Although Europeans destroyed Indigenous peoples in vast numbers, their descendants have survived and their holistic and spiritual outlook endures.

▷ **Cosmological map from the** *Fejérváry-Mayer Codex*
The god Xiuhtecuhtli dwells at the center of this c. 15th-century depiction of the spiritual cosmos. It was designed to be read counterclockwise from the bottom up. Birds, trees, and other sacred symbols each represent different aspects of the 260-day Aztec calendar.

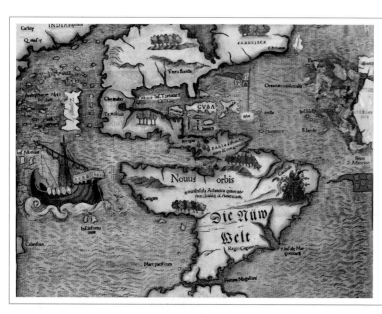

EUROPEAN VIEW
Europeans arriving in the Americas imposed a system of conquest and conversion formalized both by papal sanction and the 1494 Treaty of Tordesillas that divided the region into Spanish and Portuguese spheres of influence (see pp.38–39). Sebastian Münster, a German cartographer, priest, and theologian, epitomized this view in his 1540 depiction of the Americas, seen here in a 1561 copy. Ferdinand Magellan's ship *Victoria*, the first vessel to circumnavigate the world, represents the questing spirit of Christian Europe, while the Spanish flag above the West Indies and the Portuguese banner flying off Brazil symbolize the colonizers' supposed military and spiritual triumph over Indigenous populations.

COLONIZATION AND CONFLICT

AFTER INITIAL VOYAGES ACROSS THE ATLANTIC, EUROPEAN POWERS
SCRAMBLED TO EXPLORE AND COLONIZE THE VAST LANDS OF
THE AMERICAS, OFTEN BRINGING HARDSHIP, DISEASE, AND
DEATH TO THE INDIGENOUS PEOPLE THEY ENCOUNTERED.

EUROPEANS ARRIVE

In 1492, a party of Europeans mistakenly landed in the Americas. This ushered in an era that radically changed the course of history, with the subsequent rise of European colonialism, the destruction of Indigenous populations, and the introduction of enslaved Africans.

△ **Explorer and enslaver**
In his lifetime, English explorer Francis Drake was celebrated for his navigational prowess, now he is remembered for profiting from the slave trade.

Although the Genoese explorer Christopher Columbus believed he was sailing west to reach Asia in 1492, he did not realize there was an entirely different continent in his path. It was a navigational miscalculation that had far-reaching consequences for large swathes of the world.

The lands Columbus encountered across the Atlantic were populated by millions of culturally and linguistically diverse people. The first to meet Columbus's party were the Lucayan people of the Bahamas when he landed there in October 1492. On that same voyage Columbus tried to set up a colony on the island of Hispaniola among the Taíno people, who were part of the larger Arawak community of the Caribbean. They resisted fiercely.

New realities

There was much unfamiliarity on both sides. Europeans had never seen many of the plants and animals of these lands, tasted the food, or heard the languages of the people. Indigenous people were also exposed to new goods—including unfamiliar weaponry such as guns—and new foods, languages, animals, and customs abounded. Both groups were exposed to dangerous and unfamiliar diseases, with Indigenous people dying in vast numbers after exposure to European microbes.

"The city [Churultecal / Cholula] itself is more beautiful to look at than any in Spain."

HERNÁN CORTÉS, IN A LETTER TO EMPEROR CHARLES V, 1520

Europeans also brought with them their religions, and Columbus and later conquistadors in the Caribbean enslaved many of the Indigenous people, which they justified because they were not Christians. This practice would later end, though Indigenous labor continued to be exploited.

Spanish colonizers brought enslaved Africans to the Americas in 1502. This began the transatlantic slave trade, a destructive process that defined the colonial period. Europeans displaced Indigenous inhabitants and forced Africans to take their place as enslaved laborers.

△ **The Florentine Codex**
Spanish Franciscan monk Bernardino de Sahagún (1499–1590) complied this twelve-book ethnography covering many aspects of Mexican life after his arrival in 1529. Written in Nahuatl and lavishly illustrated by Nahua artists, this work is a crucial surviving source for post-conquest Mexico.

NEW WORLDS AND NEW CHALLENGES

The arrival of Europeans in the Americas quickly became a scramble for enrichment via exploitation and force. Piracy in the Caribbean eventually gave way to plantations, and settlement spread to the North and South American mainland. Such drastic changes came at a heavy price, as many Indigenous communities were destroyed, though not without decades of fierce resistance. The forced migration of enslaved Africans further transformed the region.

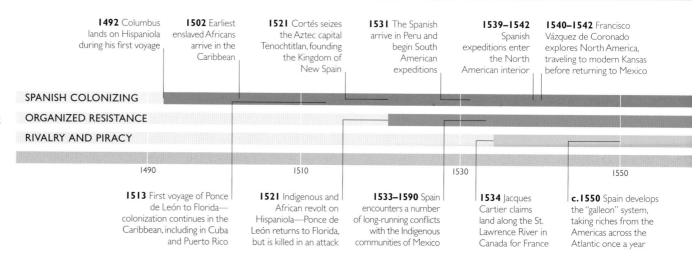

1492 Columbus lands on Hispaniola during his first voyage

1502 Earliest enslaved Africans arrive in the Caribbean

1521 Cortés seizes the Aztec capital Tenochtitlan, founding the Kingdom of New Spain

1531 The Spanish arrive in Peru and begin South American expeditions

1539–1542 Spanish expeditions enter the North American interior

1540–1542 Francisco Vázquez de Coronado explores North America, traveling to modern Kansas before returning to Mexico

SPANISH COLONIZING
ORGANIZED RESISTANCE
RIVALRY AND PIRACY

1490 — 1510 — 1530 — 1550

1513 First voyage of Ponce de León to Florida—colonization continues in the Caribbean, including in Cuba and Puerto Rico

1521 Indigenous and African revolt on Hispaniola—Ponce de León returns to Florida, but is killed in an attack

1533–1590 Spain encounters a number of long-running conflicts with the Indigenous communities of Mexico

1534 Jacques Cartier claims land along the St. Lawrence River in Canada for France

c.1550 Spain develops the "galleon" system, taking riches from the Americas across the Atlantic once a year

◁ **Hopi Bowl**
This Pueblo pottery shows a religious figure holding a scarlet macaw, which was associated with the sun and agricultural abundance.

Rivalry and growth

The colonization of North America did not happen in an instant, and it took more than century to take hold. It also required willing soldiers and sailors; money and ships; local cooperation, concessions, and compromise; and, most of the time, guns and conflict. The Spanish faced resistance throughout from Indigenous groups fighting to retain their homelands. Soon, there was external pressure, too, as other Europeans arrived in the 1500s. At first this took the form of pirates and privateers looking for ships to plunder, especially those in the Spanish Flota de Indias. Later, it involved state-sanctioned colonizing fleets from England, Denmark, France, and Holland.

Spanish efforts to colonize Mexica Tenochtitlan and Inca Peru had paid off in precious metals, as both places were rich in gold and silver. In addition, by the end of the 1560s Spain had set up a colony in Manila in the Philippines, and in St. Augustine in Florida. Before long, the Pacific and Atlantic worlds were linked, taking goods like silk from the east to the Pacific coast of Mexico, and from there onward to Spain.

Other European nations were eager to get their share of the riches, but as the age of piracy waned, some former pirates—and plenty of investors—realized other sorts of wealth could be found in the soil. Sugar plantations took root throughout the Caribbean—where growing conditions were ideal—with tobacco, cotton, and other crops also grown there. The French, English, Dutch, and Danish were among the powers competing for territory. They fought for land among themselves, against Spain, and constantly in the face of Indigenous opposition. Farther north, the

△ **Battles in the north**
This depiction, possibly from the 1590s, shows a group of Inuit people armed with bows and arrows fighting off European colonists armed with firearms in 1590.

English planted their Jamestown colony in 1607, and mainland South America saw the arrival of the Dutch and French along its north coast. Some of these colonies initially used indentured European servitude, but this soon gave way to the widespread use of African enslaved labor.

In little more than a century, the colonizing process that began in 1492 had changed the Americas forever. It began a genocidal assault on Indigenous peoples and repopulated their lands with European colonists and enslaved Africans.

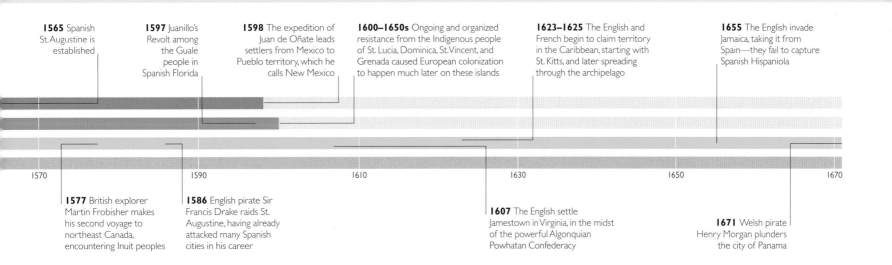

1565 Spanish St. Augustine is established

1597 Juanillo's Revolt among the Guale people in Spanish Florida

1598 The expedition of Juan de Oñate leads settlers from Mexico to Pueblo territory, which he calls New Mexico

1600–1650s Ongoing and organized resistance from the Indigenous people of St. Lucia, Dominica, St. Vincent, and Grenada caused European colonization to happen much later on these islands

1623–1625 The English and French begin to claim territory in the Caribbean, starting with St. Kitts, and later spreading through the archipelago

1655 The English invade Jamaica, taking it from Spain—they fail to capture Spanish Hispaniola

| 1570 | | 1590 | | 1610 | | 1630 | | 1650 | | 1670 |

1577 British explorer Martin Frobisher makes his second voyage to northeast Canada, encountering Inuit peoples

1586 English pirate Sir Francis Drake raids St. Augustine, having already attacked many Spanish cities in his career

1607 The English settle Jamestown in Virginia, in the midst of the powerful Algonquian Powhatan Confederacy

1671 Welsh pirate Henry Morgan plunders the city of Panama

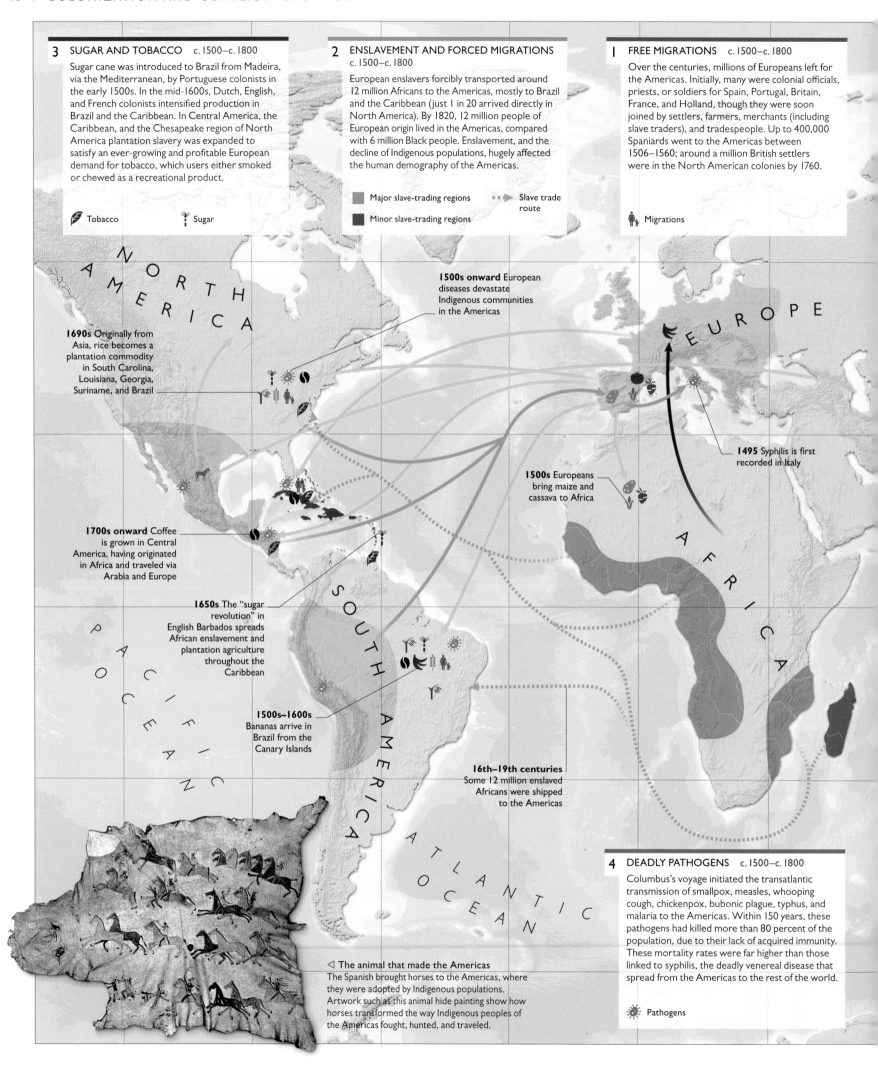

3 SUGAR AND TOBACCO c.1500–c.1800

Sugar cane was introduced to Brazil from Madeira, via the Mediterranean, by Portuguese colonists in the early 1500s. In the mid-1600s, Dutch, English, and French colonists intensified production in Brazil and the Caribbean. In Central America, the Caribbean, and the Chesapeake region of North America plantation slavery was expanded to satisfy an ever-growing and profitable European demand for tobacco, which users either smoked or chewed as a recreational product.

🌿 Tobacco   🌾 Sugar

2 ENSLAVEMENT AND FORCED MIGRATIONS c.1500–c.1800

European enslavers forcibly transported around 12 million Africans to the Americas, mostly to Brazil and the Caribbean (just 1 in 20 arrived directly in North America). By 1820, 12 million people of European origin lived in the Americas, compared with 6 million Black people. Enslavement, and the decline of Indigenous populations, hugely affected the human demography of the Americas.

■ Major slave-trading regions   ▪▪▶ Slave trade route
■ Minor slave-trading regions

1 FREE MIGRATIONS c.1500–c.1800

Over the centuries, millions of Europeans left for the Americas. Initially, many were colonial officials, priests, or soldiers for Spain, Portugal, Britain, France, and Holland, though they were soon joined by settlers, farmers, merchants (including slave traders), and tradespeople. Up to 400,000 Spaniards went to the Americas between 1506–1560; around a million British settlers were in the North American colonies by 1760.

👪 Migrations

1500s onward European diseases devastate Indigenous communities in the Americas

1690s Originally from Asia, rice becomes a plantation commodity in South Carolina, Louisiana, Georgia, Suriname, and Brazil

1700s onward Coffee is grown in Central America, having originated in Africa and traveled via Arabia and Europe

1650s The "sugar revolution" in English Barbados spreads African enslavement and plantation agriculture throughout the Caribbean

1500s–1600s Bananas arrive in Brazil from the Canary Islands

1495 Syphilis is first recorded in Italy

1500s Europeans bring maize and cassava to Africa

16th–19th centuries Some 12 million enslaved Africans were shipped to the Americas

◁ **The animal that made the Americas**
The Spanish brought horses to the Americas, where they were adopted by Indigenous populations. Artwork such as this animal hide painting show how horses transformed the way Indigenous peoples of the Americas fought, hunted, and traveled.

4 DEADLY PATHOGENS c.1500–c.1800

Columbus's voyage initiated the transatlantic transmission of smallpox, measles, whooping cough, chickenpox, bubonic plague, typhus, and malaria to the Americas. Within 150 years, these pathogens had killed more than 80 percent of the population, due to their lack of acquired immunity. These mortality rates were far higher than those linked to syphilis, the deadly venereal disease that spread from the Americas to the rest of the world.

✹ Pathogens

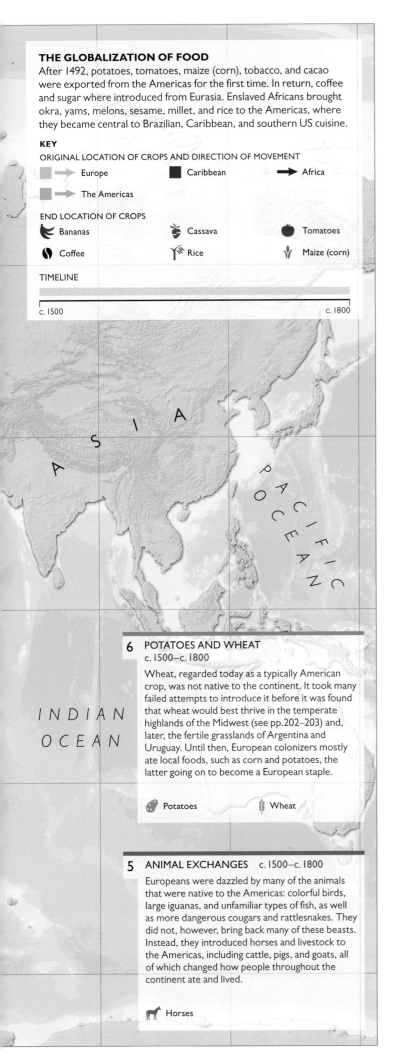

THE GLOBALIZATION OF FOOD

After 1492, potatoes, tomatoes, maize (corn), tobacco, and cacao were exported from the Americas for the first time. In return, coffee and sugar where introduced from Eurasia. Enslaved Africans brought okra, yams, melons, sesame, millet, and rice to the Americas, where they became central to Brazilian, Caribbean, and southern US cuisine.

KEY

ORIGINAL LOCATION OF CROPS AND DIRECTION OF MOVEMENT

Europe
The Americas
Caribbean
Africa

END LOCATION OF CROPS

Bananas
Cassava
Tomatoes
Coffee
Rice
Maize (corn)

TIMELINE

c. 1500 — c. 1800

6 POTATOES AND WHEAT
c. 1500–c. 1800

Wheat, regarded today as a typically American crop, was not native to the continent. It took many failed attempts to introduce it before it was found that wheat would best thrive in the temperate highlands of the Midwest (see pp.202–203) and, later, the fertile grasslands of Argentina and Uruguay. Until then, European colonizers mostly ate local foods, such as corn and potatoes, the latter going on to become a European staple.

Potatoes   Wheat

5 ANIMAL EXCHANGES   c. 1500–c. 1800

Europeans were dazzled by many of the animals that were native to the Americas: colorful birds, large iguanas, and unfamiliar types of fish, as well as more dangerous cougars and rattlesnakes. They did not, however, bring back many of these beasts. Instead, they introduced horses and livestock to the Americas, including cattle, pigs, and goats, all of which changed how people throughout the continent ate and lived.

Horses

THE COLUMBIAN EXCHANGE

The arrival of Europeans in the Americas from 1492 brought with it unexpected encounters with new cultures, foods, and animals—and deadly diseases. The biological and social interchanges that took place in the following centuries—the so-called "Columbian Exchange"—had a profound impact on the entire world.

Commissioned by the king and queen of Spain to find a direct maritime route to Asia, Christopher Columbus sailed west across the Atlantic Ocean and south into the tropical "Indies." When he landed in the Bahamas in 1492, Columbus believed he had reached a group of islands at the edges of Cathay (modern China). His discovery completed a circuit of exchange that connected Africa, Europe, and Asia to the Americas. Along these new routes came people, technology, plants, animals—and microorganisms: the impact of European diseases on Indigenous populations was severe, as was the reciprocal effect of the new pathogens exported from the Americas to the rest of the world.

New crops from the Americas—including potatoes, sweet potatoes, cassava, tomatoes, peanuts, and maize—redefined foodways across the Eastern Hemisphere. American chocolate, chiles, vanilla, and tobacco became profitable transatlantic commodities, and European colonizers came to depend on American quinine to fight malaria as they extended their empires into tropical territories. As labor, enslaved Africans were forcibly transported, first to clear lands once inhabited by Indigenous peoples and then plant them with both native and imported crops such as coffee, sugar, rubber, cotton, the indigo-dye-producing indigofera shrub, wheat, rice, and citrus fruits.

"Should I meet with gold or spices in great quantity, I shall remain till I collect as much as possible."

CHRISTOPHER COLUMBUS, JOURNAL ENTRY, 15TH CENTURY

CHOCOLATE

Of all the plants native to the Americas, the seeds of the *Theobroma cacao* remain the most popular, five centuries later. The Olmecs of Central America are believed to have domesticated the cacao tree more than 3,000 years ago. By the time of Columbus, chocolate was used as a drink, as food, and even as currency. Chocolate became hugely popular in Europe, especially as a drink—and particularly after sugar was added to it as a sweetener.

Maya god tending a cacao tree
Among cacao's many uses, it appears to have played a role in Maya religious rites and ceremonies.

SPANISH EXPLORATION

As conquistadors invaded Indigenous civilizations in Mexico and South America, some Spanish explorers looked to the mainland in the 1500s, traveling into Florida and the Southwest. Spanish invaders ultimately claimed much of the mainland despite Indigenous resistance efforts.

Spanish colonists in the early 1500s explored the waters around the Atlantic and the Gulf of Mexico, and some believed there was a larger landmass full of riches north of the Bahamas. Its existence was confirmed with the arrival of Juan Ponce de León in 1513, who landed around modern Cape Canaveral and named it La Florida. He did not stay long because the Ais people quickly drove him away. He eventually returned in 1521, this time to the southwest of Florida, where his attempts at colonization were again forcibly resisted, this time by the Calusa people. He later died from his injuries.

By this point word of the North American landmass had spread, and many went to Florida on their own hunt for wealth and land. In 1527, the expedition of Pánfilo de Narváez landed around modern Tampa and traveled west, encountering Apalachee and other Mississippian people along the Gulf coast. All but four of his men died, and survivors including Álvar Núñez Cabeza de Vaca and an enslaved African named Esteban de Dorantes covered some 2,000 miles (3,200 km) over land to return to New Spain.

Hernando de Soto's expedition traveled farther, starting in 1539 in western Florida, and from there crossing the Appalachian Mountains, and then west, making him the first documented European to cross the Mississippi River. Meanwhile Francisco Vázquez de Coronado traveled northeast from New Spain in 1540 on his two-year expedition, reaching as far as modern Kansas.

The extensive geographical knowledge of North America that Spanish explorers gained in this era fueled Spain's colonial ambitions for the continent.

KEY

1 Spain claimed the east coast as part of its territory, but English colonists challenged this, establishing Virginia in 1607.

2 In 1598 the Spanish gained a foothold in the southwest, among the Pueblo people.

3 Apalachee people along the Gulf Coast encountered the Narváez and de Soto expeditions.

LOCATOR

▷ **North America, from Johann Homann's atlas**
This 1720 map shows the later extent of Spain's claims in North America (yellow), also showing an expansive French Louisiana colony (red) that included Spanish Florida.

SPANISH EXPANSION IN EUROPE AND THE AMERICAS

By 1700, the Spanish had laid claim to European territories including Italy and Belgium, and notably, much of the landmass of the Americas. Their influence in South and Central America was undeniable, yet they had only outposts north of Mexico, where the number of Spanish settlements remained small as a result of Indigenous resistance.

1561 King Philip II moves his court to Madrid, and the city becomes the hub of Spain's empire

1545 Potosí, a mining town in the Andes mountains, becomes the main source of silver for Spain

KEY

▢ Area claimed by Spain in Europe and the Americas by 1700

MALINTZIN
c.1501–c.1529

Born around 1501 in Painalla, central Mesoamerica, Malintzin was an enslaved Nahua woman who served the Spanish conquistador Hernando Cortés. It is thought that she was stolen or enslaved as a child, ending up among the Chontal Maya people, who later gave her to Cortés. The Spanish used her baptismal name of doña Marina, or La Malinche, a misheard version of her actual name. Malintzin's fluency in the widely spoken Yucatec Mayan and Nahuatl languages led to her being appointed as a translator and guide by Cortés, whom she helped communicate with the Mexica emperor Montezuma II and other Indigenous leaders. She soon learned Spanish and became Cortés's only interpreter.

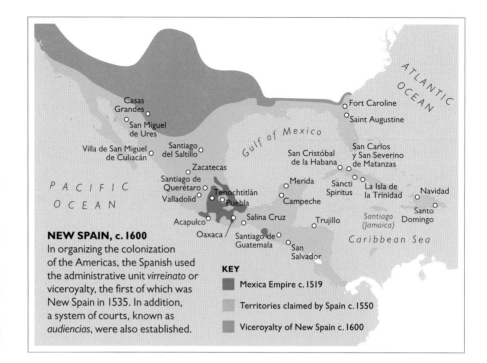

NEW SPAIN, c.1600
In organizing the colonization of the Americas, the Spanish used the administrative unit *virreinato* or viceroyalty, the first of which was New Spain in 1535. In addition, a system of courts, known as *audiencias*, were also established.

KEY
- Mexica Empire c.1519
- Territories claimed by Spain c.1550
- Viceroyalty of New Spain c.1600

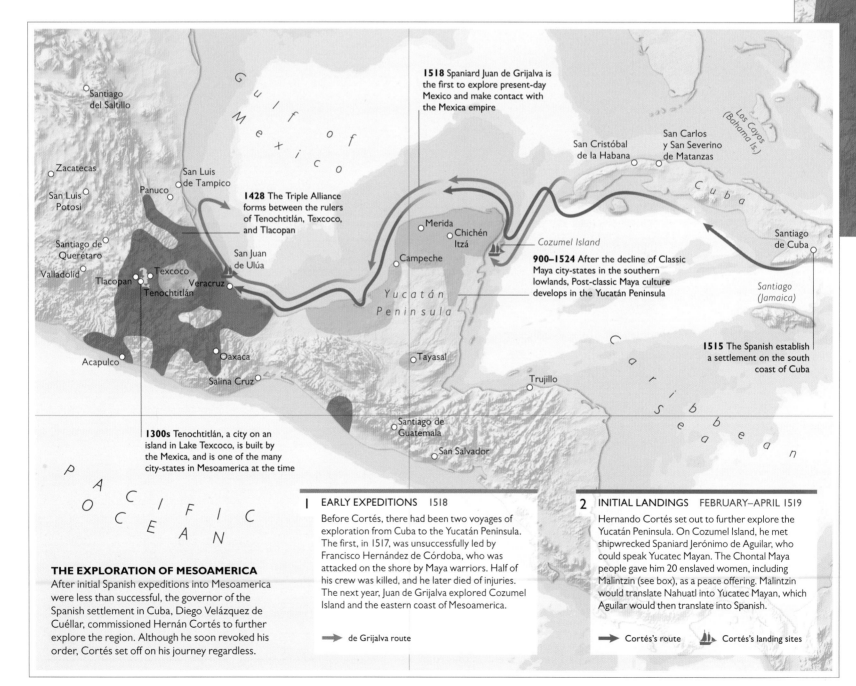

1518 Spaniard Juan de Grijalva is the first to explore present-day Mexico and make contact with the Mexica empire

1428 The Triple Alliance forms between the rulers of Tenochtitlán, Texcoco, and Tlacopan

900–1524 After the decline of Classic Maya city-states in the southern lowlands, Post-classic Maya culture develops in the Yucatán Peninsula

1515 The Spanish establish a settlement on the south coast of Cuba

1300s Tenochtitlán, a city on an island in Lake Texcoco, is built by the Mexica, and is one of the many city-states in Mesoamerica at the time

THE EXPLORATION OF MESOAMERICA
After initial Spanish expeditions into Mesoamerica were less than successful, the governor of the Spanish settlement in Cuba, Diego Velázquez de Cuéllar, commissioned Hernán Cortés to further explore the region. Although he soon revoked his order, Cortés set off on his journey regardless.

1 EARLY EXPEDITIONS 1518
Before Cortés, there had been two voyages of exploration from Cuba to the Yucatán Peninsula. The first, in 1517, was unsuccessfully led by Francisco Hernández de Córdoba, who was attacked on the shore by Maya warriors. Half of his crew was killed, and he later died of injuries. The next year, Juan de Grijalva explored Cozumel Island and the eastern coast of Mesoamerica.

→ de Grijalva route

2 INITIAL LANDINGS FEBRUARY–APRIL 1519
Hernando Cortés set out to further explore the Yucatán Peninsula. On Cozumel Island, he met shipwrecked Spaniard Jerónimo de Aguilar, who could speak Yucatec Mayan. The Chontal Maya people gave him 20 enslaved women, including Malintzin (see box), as a peace offering. Malintzin would translate Nahuatl into Yucatec Mayan, which Aguilar would then translate into Spanish.

→ Cortés's route   ⛵ Cortés's landing sites

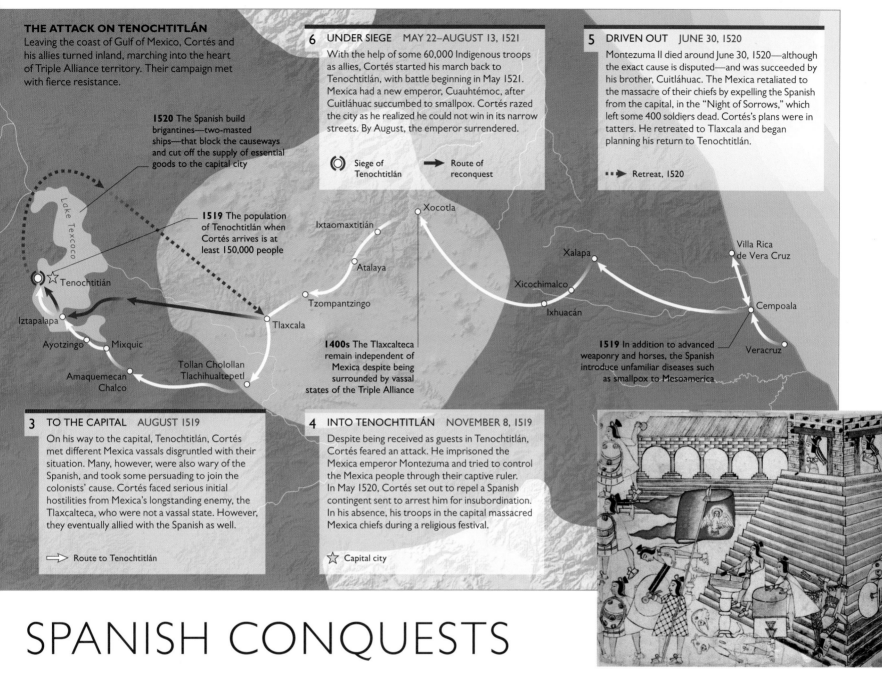

THE ATTACK ON TENOCHTITLÁN
Leaving the coast of Gulf of Mexico, Cortés and his allies turned inland, marching into the heart of Triple Alliance territory. Their campaign met with fierce resistance.

1520 The Spanish build brigantines—two-masted ships—that block the causeways and cut off the supply of essential goods to the capital city

1519 The population of Tenochtitlán when Cortés arrives is at least 150,000 people

6 UNDER SIEGE MAY 22–AUGUST 13, 1521
With the help of some 60,000 Indigenous troops as allies, Cortés started his march back to Tenochtitlán, with battle beginning in May 1521. Mexica had a new emperor, Cuauhtémoc, after Cuitláhuac succumbed to smallpox. Cortés razed the city as he realized he could not win in its narrow streets. By August, the emperor surrendered.

◎ Siege of Tenochtitlán

→ Route of reconquest

5 DRIVEN OUT JUNE 30, 1520
Montezuma II died around June 30, 1520—although the exact cause is disputed—and was succeeded by his brother, Cuitláhuac. The Mexica retaliated to the massacre of their chiefs by expelling the Spanish from the capital, in the "Night of Sorrows," which left some 400 soldiers dead. Cortés's plans were in tatters. He retreated to Tlaxcala and began planning his return to Tenochtitlán.

■■▶ Retreat, 1520

1400s The Tlaxcalteca remain independent of Mexica despite being surrounded by vassal states of the Triple Alliance

1519 In addition to advanced weaponry and horses, the Spanish introduce unfamiliar diseases such as smallpox to Mesoamerica

3 TO THE CAPITAL AUGUST 1519
On his way to the capital, Tenochtitlán, Cortés met different Mexica vassals disgruntled with their situation. Many, however, were also wary of the Spanish, and took some persuading to join the colonists' cause. Cortés faced serious initial hostilities from Mexica's longstanding enemy, the Tlaxcalteca, who were not a vassal state. However, they eventually allied with the Spanish as well.

⇨ Route to Tenochtitlán

4 INTO TENOCHTITLÁN NOVEMBER 8, 1519
Despite being received as guests in Tenochtitlán, Cortés feared an attack. He imprisoned the Mexica emperor Montezuma and tried to control the Mexica people through their captive ruler. In May 1520, Cortés set out to repel a Spanish contingent sent to arrest him for insubordination. In his absence, his troops in the capital massacred Mexica chiefs during a religious festival.

☆ Capital city

△ **Defending the temple**
This 16th-century codex depicts Mexica warriors defending Templo Mayor, the main temple of Tenochtitlán, against the Spanish conquistadors and their allies. The Spanish conquest resulted in the destruction of the temple.

SPANISH CONQUESTS

The Mexica empire fell in the 16th century, largely caused by the arrival of the Spanish conquistadors. However, an alliance of diverse Mesoamerican allies also aided the Spanish in their conquest.

In 1519, Spanish conquistador Hernando Cortés arrived on mainland Mexico, around present-day Veracruz, to find an incredibly diverse and politically complex world. The Triple Alliance—the Mexica (Aztecs) and their allies, the Texcoco and Tlacopan—dominated the area inland from the coast, known as the Valley of Mexico. The empire spread across the region, and its capital, Tenochtitlán, reflected the wealth the alliance received from their vassal states. The city, home to a population of at least 150,000 people at the time of the Spanish contact, sat on an island in the middle of Lake Texcoco.

Cortés wrote to the Spanish king Charles V praising the grandeur of the capital city. His admiration, however, did not deter him from destroying the city in his quest to conquer the Mexica empire. Over the course of two years, Cortés attacked the empire with the support of alliances he built with the Mexica's enemies and disgruntled subjects, amassing an army of tens of thousands. Cortés and his allies emerged victorious in 1521. However, for the Indigenous peoples, this victory was a double-edged sword—the rule of the Triple Alliance had ended only to make way for further incursions by the Spanish.

CONQUEST OF THE MEXICA
From 1519 to 1521, Cortés and his troops made their way up the Yucatán Peninsula, accumulating resources and garnering allies to topple the dominant Triple Alliance and pave the way for future Spanish conquests.

KEY

◼ Mexica Empire ◼ Tlaxcalteca ◼ Post-classic Maya states

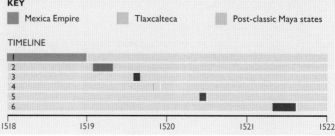

TIMELINE

◁ **Cartier's voyage**
This map by French cartographer Pierre Desceliers was made c. 1536–1542 using the information collected during Jacques Cartier's voyages to Canada, an area previously unfamiliar to Europeans.

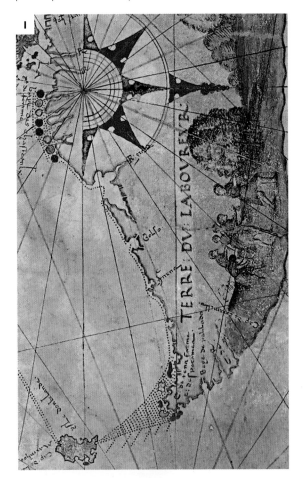

△ **Early arrivals**
Basque and Portuguese fishermen used the waters around Newfoundland and Labrador for at least two decades before Cartier's voyage.

▽ **Mid-Atlantic**
This area may represent the Chesapeake, making this one of the earliest nautical charts to connect the northern reaches of Canada to the US East Coast and the Caribbean.

△ **Indigenous land**
On his second voyage, Cartier traveled to a palisaded village of Iroquois-speaking people called Hochelaga, which was near today's Port of Montreal. He saw about 50 wooden houses there.

FRENCH AND ENGLISH EXPLORATION

Spain's conquests in the Americas spurred France and England to explore western waters as they searched for a more direct route to Asia. What they encountered instead was the rich natural world of northern Canada, New England, and the St. Lawrence River Valley.

French sailors had participated in some of the earliest Atlantic voyages (see pp.38–39), and by the 1500s the French king Francis I was taking an interest in sponsoring expeditions. Breton mariner Jacques Cartier won a commission from the crown, and in 1534 he left France with Asia as his intended destination, believing he knew the western route. Instead, he reached what is now Newfoundland.

He continued west, exploring the Gulf of St. Lawrence and claiming it for the king, despite the fact that it was inhabited by Indigenous peoples—some of whom he kidnapped and forcibly transported to France. He returned with a larger expedition the following year and sailed up the St. Lawrence River, establishing a base among Iroquois-speaking people and reaching the rapids near modern Montreal. After a brutal winter, he returned to France, then made a trip in 1541–1542 to establish a colony on the St. Lawrence River.

English mariners also began to explore North America in earnest during this period, and they were eager to find sites for possible settlement. The explorer Walter Raleigh

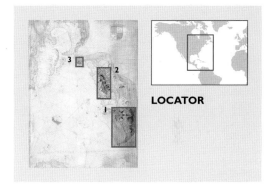

LOCATOR

oversaw two attempts to establish a colony on Roanoke Island, on the coast of modern North Carolina, between 1585 and 1587; his failure in these endeavors has been attributed to tensions with local Indigenous people.

Fellow English navigator Francis Drake became well known for his attacks on Spanish ships in the Atlantic and Caribbean before he circumnavigated the world in 1577–1580, during which time he is believed to have landed on the northern Pacific coast, somewhere north of San Francisco, in 1579.

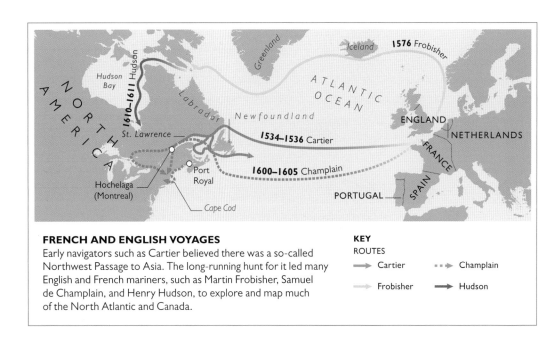

FRENCH AND ENGLISH VOYAGES
Early navigators such as Cartier believed there was a so-called Northwest Passage to Asia. The long-running hunt for it led many English and French mariners, such as Martin Frobisher, Samuel de Champlain, and Henry Hudson, to explore and map much of the North Atlantic and Canada.

KEY
ROUTES
⟶ Cartier
⟶ Frobisher
⇢ Champlain
⟶ Hudson

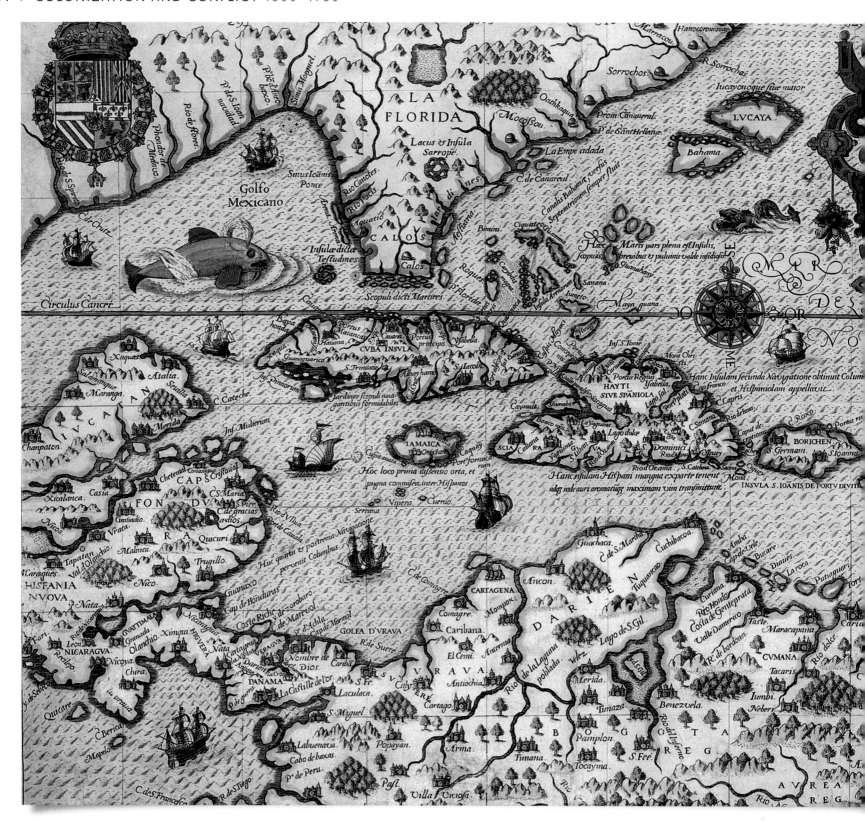

△ **Imagined islands**
Italian navigator Girolamo Benzoni explored the Americas in the 1540s and 1550s. His charts supplied the geographic information on this 1594 map, engraved by Flemish mapmaker Theodore De Bry.

▷ **Hispaniola**
The island of Quisqueya (also Ayiti), which the Spanish called Hispaniola, was the place of the first colony established by Christopher Columbus on his 1492 voyage.

△ **Nombre de Dios**
This port on the Isthmus of Panama was one of the earliest European colonies and would become a key shipping hub, as Peruvian silver and Mexican gold were brought from the Pacific and sent onward across the Atlantic to Spain.

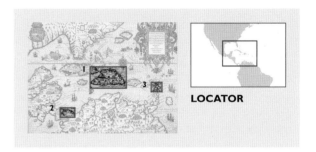

EUROPEANS IN THE CARIBBEAN

Spain initially claimed all the known islands of the West Indies, but other colonial powers were quick to move in, searching for gold and expanding their own growing empires.

Reports of Christopher Columbus's landfall in the Americas circulated rapidly around Europe, and mapmakers quickly tried to piece together the new geographical information. Demand was growing for up-to-date cartographical knowledge, and it was not long before other colonial powers—especially England, France, and Holland—began turning their attention to the potential for exploiting the land, resources, and riches in this territory.

With the help of these new maps, Europeans were soon finding their way across the Atlantic. They started as explorers, merchants, and even smugglers, but many would end up as colonizers. Spain tried to keep rival powers out, claiming the hemisphere as its own, but it could not effectively patrol the vast area. Nor was there a significant Spanish population across the islands to assist—gold in Mexico and silver in Peru had lured them away.

At first, much of the European activity was seaborne: exploration, trade, and piracy. However, by the 1600s, colonizers from western Europe were arriving and settling, with the English, French, Dutch, and later Danish claiming islands in rapid succession, often with fierce fighting as Indigenous people battled to keep their homelands. While the Spanish had found a substantial amount of precious metals, these newer arrivals were hoping to unearth a different kind of wealth from the ground. Many began experimenting with crops—at first tobacco, though eventually sugar would dominate the region. The Europeans forcibly brought enslaved Africans to work in the plantations that took root across nearly all the islands.

While this era brought thriving trade to the Caribbean, it relied on the suffering of vast numbers of Africans to stay profitable. Plantations continued to cause Indigenous deaths through overwork, violent land dispossession, and disease.

LOCATOR

△ Dominica
The island labeled as "Saint Dominica" would be one of the last to be colonized by Europeans, owing to the resistance of the Kalinago people.

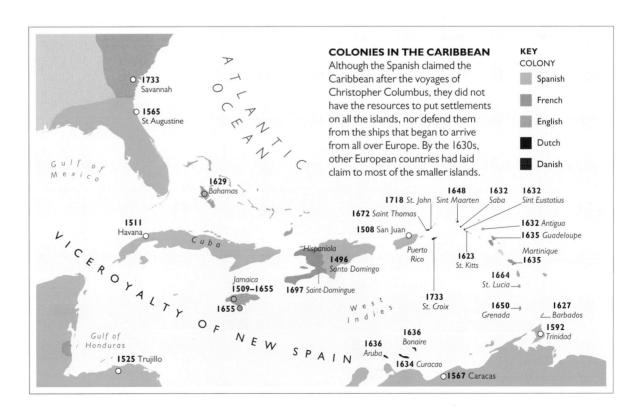

COLONIES IN THE CARIBBEAN
Although the Spanish claimed the Caribbean after the voyages of Christopher Columbus, they did not have the resources to put settlements on all the islands, nor defend them from the ships that began to arrive from all over Europe. By the 1630s, other European countries had laid claim to most of the smaller islands.

KEY
COLONY
- Spanish
- French
- English
- Dutch
- Danish

1733 Savannah
1565 St Augustine
ATLANTIC OCEAN
1629 Bahamas
1511 Havana
Cuba
Gulf of Mexico
VICEROYALTY
1509–1655 Jamaica
1655
Gulf of Honduras
1525 Trujillo
OF NEW SPAIN
Hispaniola
1496 Santo Domingo
1697 Saint-Domingue
West Indies
1508 San Juan
Puerto Rico
1672 Saint Thomas
1718 St. John
1648 Sint Maarten
1623 St. Kitts
1733 St. Croix
1632 Saba
1632 Sint Eustatius
1632 Antigua
1635 Guadeloupe
Martinique 1635
1664 St. Lucia
1650 Grenada
1636 Bonaire
1636 Aruba
1634 Curacao
1567 Caracas
1627 Barbados
1592 Trinidad

PIRACY AND PRIVATEERING

Depicted as treasure-hunting swashbucklers in popular culture, 17th-century pirates often undertook violent, political missions. They provided strategic naval support to the nations that commissioned them by plundering trading ships and colonies of their rivals.

Pirates, also known as buccaneers, have roamed non-territorial waters, or high seas, throughout history. When monarchs granted "letters of marque," they sailed legally during times of war as privateers. The 1650s–1730s is considered the golden age of piracy, when it yielded material rewards and geopolitical gains.

The Caribbean became a hotbed of piracy in the 17th century. The islands were rich in gold, silver, and gems, with enslaved people being brought in to harness these natural resources and more. Ships laden with riches en route to European destinations became a lucrative target for pirates. Some pirates even intercepted ships carrying enslaved people.

Some countries would commission private individuals, referred to as privateers, to undertake maritime attacks on vessels of enemy nations. When the Papacy allocated most of the Americas to Spain under the Treaty of Tordesillas (see pp.38–39), countries such as Britain and France funded privateers to undermine the Spanish navy and plunder their ships. In the Caribbean, Spanish assets were also attacked by buccaneers—French, English, or Dutch raiders who lived on the islands of Hispaniola, Tortuga, and Jamaica. They did not always hold valid commissions for their attacks.

Spanish fleets were subject to attack on grounds of religious differences as well. The period after the Protestant Reformation saw religious wars break out in Europe between Catholics and Protestants. Since Spain was a Catholic country, its ships were regularly raided by protestant pirates.

"The Pyrates at Sea, have the same sagacity with Robbers at Land"

A GENERAL HISTORY OF THE PYRATES, 1726

THE FEMALE PIRATES

Women also took to the high seas but often in a masculine disguise, because they were not allowed on European pirate ships. This engraved print from 1724 shows two female pirates, Irish-American Anne Bonny and Englishwoman Mary Read. Both dressed as men, and upon being captured in 1720, they had to reveal their sex—and that they were pregnant. They were spared execution and instead sent to prison for piracy.

Anne Bonny (left) and Mary Read

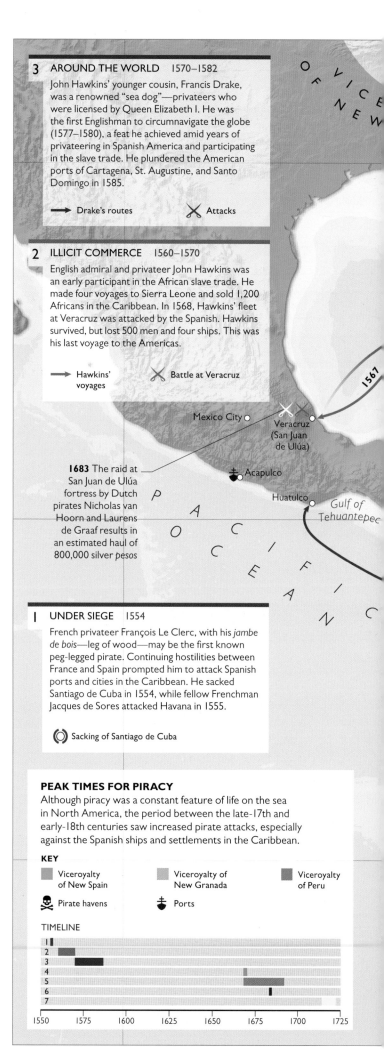

3 AROUND THE WORLD 1570–1582
John Hawkins' younger cousin, Francis Drake, was a renowned "sea dog"—privateers who were licensed by Queen Elizabeth I. He was the first Englishman to circumnavigate the globe (1577–1580), a feat he achieved amid years of privateering in Spanish America and participating in the slave trade. He plundered the American ports of Cartagena, St. Augustine, and Santo Domingo in 1585.

→ Drake's routes ✕ Attacks

2 ILLICIT COMMERCE 1560–1570
English admiral and privateer John Hawkins was an early participant in the African slave trade. He made four voyages to Sierra Leone and sold 1,200 Africans in the Caribbean. In 1568, Hawkins' fleet at Veracruz was attacked by the Spanish. Hawkins survived, but lost 500 men and four ships. This was his last voyage to the Americas.

→ Hawkins' voyages   ✕ Battle at Veracruz

Mexico City

Veracruz (San Juan de Ulúa)

1683 The raid at San Juan de Ulúa fortress by Dutch pirates Nicholas van Hoorn and Laurens de Graaf results in an estimated haul of 800,000 silver *pesos*

Acapulco

Huatulco

Gulf of Tehuantepec

1 UNDER SIEGE 1554
French privateer François Le Clerc, with his *jambe de bois*—leg of wood—may be the first known peg-legged pirate. Continuing hostilities between France and Spain prompted him to attack Spanish ports and cities in the Caribbean. He sacked Santiago de Cuba in 1554, while fellow Frenchman Jacques de Sores attacked Havana in 1555.

◉ Sacking of Santiago de Cuba

PEAK TIMES FOR PIRACY
Although piracy was a constant feature of life on the sea in North America, the period between the late-17th and early-18th centuries saw increased pirate attacks, especially against the Spanish ships and settlements in the Caribbean.

KEY

Viceroyalty of New Spain   Viceroyalty of New Granada   Viceroyalty of Peru

☠ Pirate havens   ⚓ Ports

TIMELINE

1550 1575 1600 1625 1650 1675 1700 1725

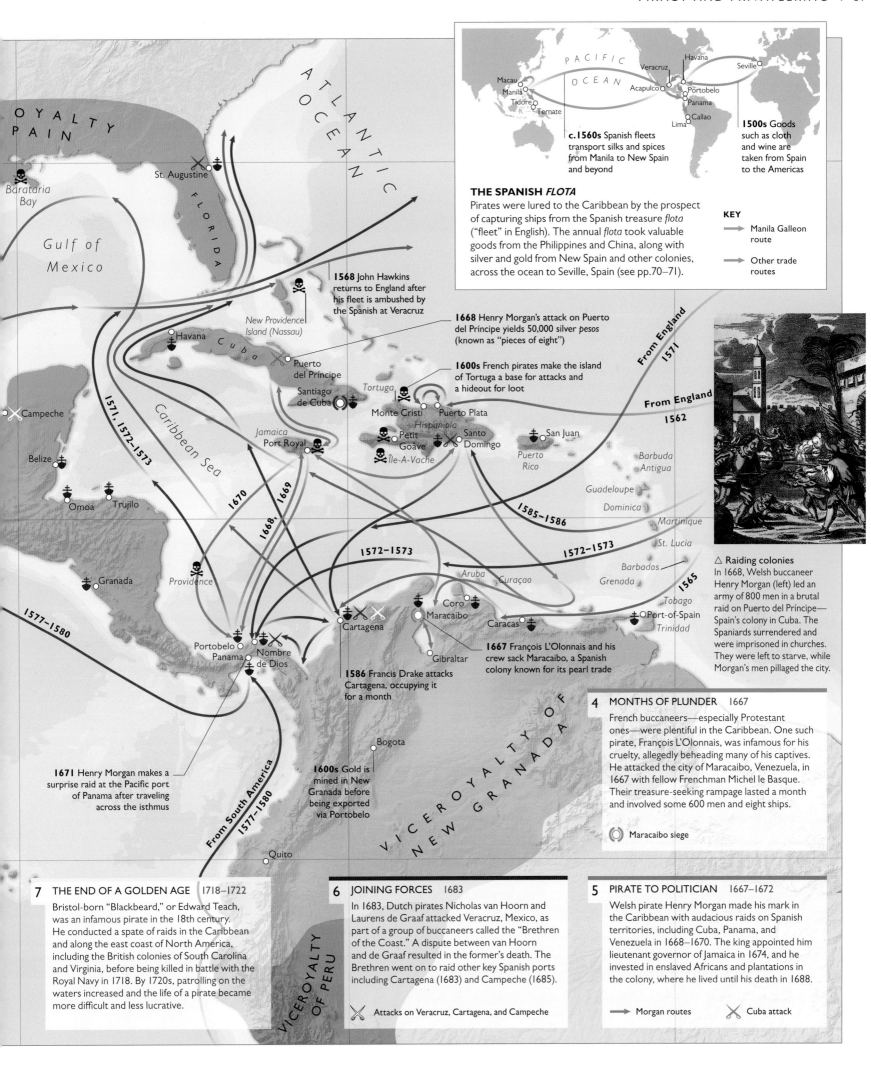

THE SPANISH *FLOTA*

c.1560s Spanish fleets transport silks and spices from Manila to New Spain and beyond

1500s Goods such as cloth and wine are taken from Spain to the Americas

Pirates were lured to the Caribbean by the prospect of capturing ships from the Spanish treasure *flota* ("fleet" in English). The annual *flota* took valuable goods from the Philippines and China, along with silver and gold from New Spain and other colonies, across the ocean to Seville, Spain (see pp.70–71).

KEY

→ Manila Galleon route

→ Other trade routes

1568 John Hawkins returns to England after his fleet is ambushed by the Spanish at Veracruz

1668 Henry Morgan's attack on Puerto del Príncipe yields 50,000 silver *pesos* (known as "pieces of eight")

1600s French pirates make the island of Tortuga a base for attacks and a hideout for loot

1586 Francis Drake attacks Cartagena, occupying it for a month

1667 François L'Olonnais and his crew sack Maracaibo, a Spanish colony known for its pearl trade

1671 Henry Morgan makes a surprise raid at the Pacific port of Panama after traveling across the isthmus

1600s Gold is mined in New Granada before being exported via Portobelo

△ Raiding colonies

In 1668, Welsh buccaneer Henry Morgan (left) led an army of 800 men in a brutal raid on Puerto del Príncipe—Spain's colony in Cuba. The Spaniards surrendered and were imprisoned in churches. They were left to starve, while Morgan's men pillaged the city.

⊚ Maracaibo siege

4 MONTHS OF PLUNDER 1667

French buccaneers—especially Protestant ones—were plentiful in the Caribbean. One such pirate, François L'Olonnais, was infamous for his cruelty, allegedly beheading many of his captives. He attacked the city of Maracaibo, Venezuela, in 1667 with fellow Frenchman Michel le Basque. Their treasure-seeking rampage lasted a month and involved some 600 men and eight ships.

7 THE END OF A GOLDEN AGE 1718–1722

Bristol-born "Blackbeard," or Edward Teach, was an infamous pirate in the 18th century. He conducted a spate of raids in the Caribbean and along the east coast of North America, including the British colonies of South Carolina and Virginia, before being killed in battle with the Royal Navy in 1718. By 1720s, patrolling on the waters increased and the life of a pirate became more difficult and less lucrative.

6 JOINING FORCES 1683

In 1683, Dutch pirates Nicholas van Hoorn and Laurens de Graaf attacked Veracruz, Mexico, as part of a group of buccaneers called the "Brethren of the Coast." A dispute between van Hoorn and de Graaf resulted in the former's death. The Brethren went on to raid other key Spanish ports including Cartagena (1683) and Campeche (1685).

✕ Attacks on Veracruz, Cartagena, and Campeche

5 PIRATE TO POLITICIAN 1667–1672

Welsh pirate Henry Morgan made his mark in the Caribbean with audacious raids on Spanish territories, including Cuba, Panama, and Venezuela in 1668–1670. The king appointed him lieutenant governor of Jamaica in 1674, and he invested in enslaved Africans and plantations in the colony, where he lived until his death in 1688.

→ Morgan routes   ✕ Cuba attack

COLONIZATION, WAR, AND TRADE

During the 17th century, Europeans increasingly established permanent colonies in North America, amid violent conflicts with Indigenous communities over land and resources. Meanwhile, the number of enslaved Africans brought over by the colonizers continued to rise.

Colonists from other parts of Europe followed the Spanish into North America by the early 1600s, spreading out along the east coast. French traders and priests lived among the Indigenous communities of the St. Lawrence River valley, while English arrivals established colonies among Algonquian peoples in Virginia and New England. The Dutch set up New Netherland in Algonquin territory, and farther south, Europeans were laying claim to Caribbean islands that Spain was unable to defend, starting with the British in St. Christopher in 1623.

Conflict and cooperation

A growing number of Europeans wanted to go to North America to engage in the cultivation and trade of lucrative goods, such as sugar and tobacco. Their arrival posed many threats, problems, and even some opportunities for Indigenous groups. Initially involved in trade with the settlers, the local peoples were soon engaged in long-running and violent disputes over land. Such factors led to a constantly shifting landscape of alliances among

> *"It was my misfortune to learn about the uprising … the night before it happened."*
>
> NEW MEXICO GOVERNOR ANTONIO DE OTERMÍN ON THE PUEBLO REVOLT, 1680

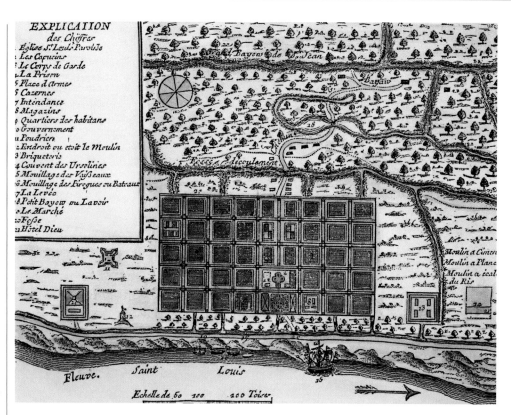

△ **Planning a city**
An engraving from 1753 shows the initial plan for the city of New Orleans, Louisiana, founded by the French in 1718 along the banks of the Mississippi River.

RESISTANCE AND FREEDOM-SEEKING

The arrival of the English, French, and Dutch in North America affected huge transformations across the parts of the continent that the Spanish had not explored or colonized as much. Relations with Indigenous communities were fragile to begin with, often escalating into violent conflict. Some among the growing number of enslaved Africans, especially in the Caribbean, resisted their enslavement through day-to-day resistance, escape, and armed conflict.

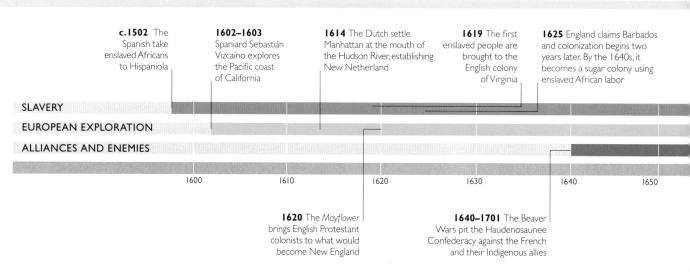

c.1502 The Spanish take enslaved Africans to Hispaniola

1602–1603 Spaniard Sebastián Vizcaíno explores the Pacific coast of California

1614 The Dutch settle Manhattan at the mouth of the Hudson River, establishing New Netherland

1619 The first enslaved people are brought to the English colony of Virginia

1625 England claims Barbados and colonization begins two years later. By the 1640s, it becomes a sugar colony using enslaved African labor

SLAVERY

EUROPEAN EXPLORATION

ALLIANCES AND ENEMIES

1600   1610   1620   1630   1640   1650

1620 The *Mayflower* brings English Protestant colonists to what would become New England

1640–1701 The Beaver Wars pit the Haudenosaunee Confederacy against the French and their Indigenous allies

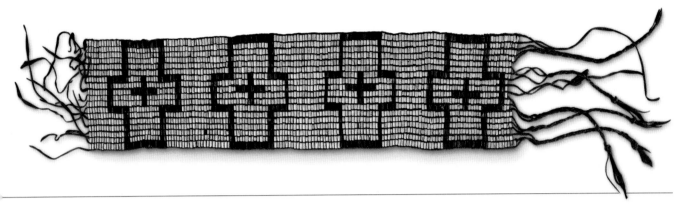

⊲ **Wampum belt**
This intricate belt from around 1680 is made with tiny beads called wampum. For some Indigenous peoples such as the Lenape and Haudenosaunee (see pp.74–75), these belts had great cultural importance.

⊲ **Maroon war**
Maroons were Africans who fled enslavement and set up independent communities near colonial settlements. Maroons in Jamaica fought the British in the First Maroon War (1728–1739).

the brutal system of slavery. Communities consisting of formerly enslaved people seeking freedom, known as maroons, began to appear throughout North America. In Jamaica, the maroons took on the British in a war, and managed to secure their freedom and autonomy by treaty in 1739, after more than a decade of fighting. Other enslaved people escaped to freedom with the help of Indigenous allies.

The first century of European colonization in North America was a disruptive, complicated, and often violent time. Indigenous people experienced permanent and damaging changes to their communities, ways of life, and ancestral land. At the same time, the arrival and growing influx of Europeans and Africans continued to transform the continent.

Indigenous peoples. Resistance and conflict became common in this era, as rival factions fought over everything from land to control over trade. The Beaver Wars (1640–1701) in the Great Lakes region pitted the Haudenosaunee people against the French and their allies, each vying for control of the trade in beaver pelts. To the South, the Yamasee, Creek, and other Indigenous peoples in the southeast joined together to devastate British Carolina during the Yamasee War (1715–1717). In 1680, the Pueblo people defeated the Spanish in a revolt in New Mexico.

Fighting for freedom
Large numbers of enslaved Africans were forced into this volatile situation, brought in to work the land and serve as laborers in expanding European colonies. They, too, engaged in rebellions and uprisings that challenged

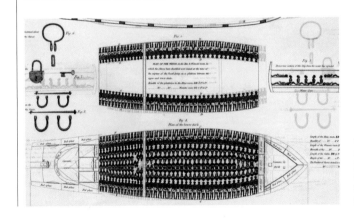

⊲ **Appalling ship conditions**
As more vessels carrying enslaved people crossed the Atlantic, diagrams such as this one, from around 1823, helped raise public awareness of the appalling conditions on board.

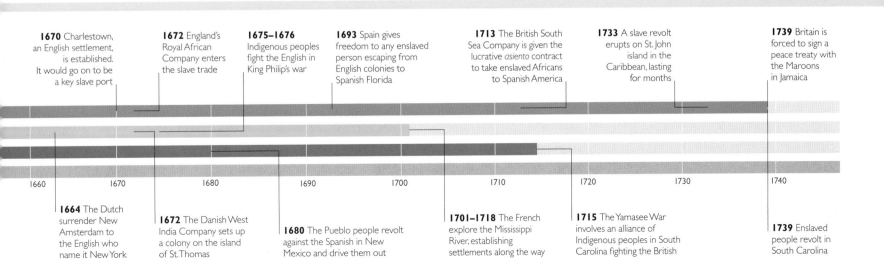

1670 Charlestown, an English settlement, is established. It would go on to be a key slave port

1672 England's Royal African Company enters the slave trade

1675–1676 Indigenous peoples fight the English in King Philip's war

1693 Spain gives freedom to any enslaved person escaping from English colonies to Spanish Florida

1713 The British South Sea Company is given the lucrative *asiento* contract to take enslaved Africans to Spanish America

1733 A slave revolt erupts on St. John island in the Caribbean, lasting for months

1739 Britain is forced to sign a peace treaty with the Maroons in Jamaica

1660   1670   1680   1690   1700   1710   1720   1730   1740

1664 The Dutch surrender New Amsterdam to the English who name it New York

1672 The Danish West India Company sets up a colony on the island of St. Thomas

1680 The Pueblo people revolt against the Spanish in New Mexico and drive them out

1701–1718 The French explore the Mississippi River, establishing settlements along the way

1715 The Yamasee War involves an alliance of Indigenous peoples in South Carolina fighting the British

1739 Enslaved people revolt in South Carolina

ANGLO-DUTCH COLONIZATION

The Dutch and English began to establish settlements along the Atlantic coast in the 1620s. Though they initiated the fur trade and established the mercantilist character of New York, Dutch colonies were short-lived. Their land was later ceded to the English.

In 1609, the Dutch East India Company contracted English explorer Henry Hudson to find a northeast passage from Europe to Asia. Unable to do so, Hudson tried charting a northwest route via North America, reaching the mouth of the river that would later bear his name, known as Mahicanituk by the local Canarsie people. The Dutch claimed this region, which was rich in natural resources, and established the New Netherland colony in 1614. In 1625, they founded New Amsterdam, the colony that would become modern Manhattan.

In 1620, a group of English colonists established Plymouth, the first colony of New England, to the northeast. The Pilgrims, a Puritan separatist group, were seeking religious freedom and economic opportunity. Initially beset with disease and hardship, the colonists depended on the cooperation of the area's Wampanoag people to survive.

Britain and the Netherlands vied for resources in the American colonies, with the English seizing the colony of New Amsterdam in

LOCATOR

KEY

1 Many Iroquois-speaking people lived west of Lake Champlain in present-day New York.

2 The Pilgrim settlers first landed at Plymouth Rock in 1620.

3 The Dutch established settlements on the western part of Long Island (Lange Eylandt).

1664. These hostilities led to the second Anglo-Dutch war (1665–1667) in which the Dutch captured England's South American colony of Suriname. The war ended with the Treaty of Breda (1667), allowing the Dutch to retain Suriname in exchange for New Netherland.

▷ **New beginnings**
This 1673 map shows the location of the former Dutch colony of New Netherland within the larger Indigenous world of Iroquoians, Abenakis, and Algonquians.

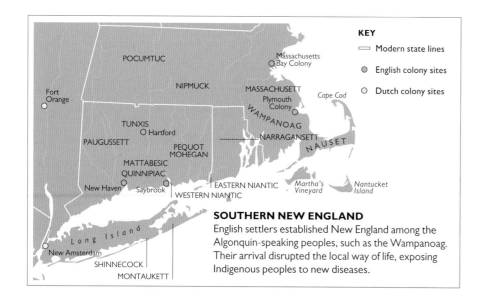

KEY

═══ Modern state lines

● English colony sites

○ Dutch colony sites

SOUTHERN NEW ENGLAND
English settlers established New England among the Algonquin-speaking peoples, such as the Wampanoag. Their arrival disrupted the local way of life, exposing Indigenous peoples to new diseases.

Nieuw-Amsterdam onlangs Nieuw jorck genaemt.
en nu hernomen by de Nederlanders op den 24 Aug 1673.

FRENCH COLONIZATION

The French founded their first settlements in North America in the early 1600s, starting along the St. Lawrence River valley and moving west and south along the Mississippi River, where they established the Gulf Coast port of New Orleans.

French explorers had begun to ply the waters of the Atlantic in the early 1500s, notably the Breton navigator Jacques Cartier, who first investigated the waterways around the St. Lawrence River valley in 1534 (see pp.52–53). He made two further voyages, establishing a link between the territory and France—although colonists would not arrive for many decades.

Farther south, in 1562 Protestant French Huguenots set up a short-lived settlement near today's Parris Island, South Carolina, followed by one in north Florida, from which they were ejected by Spain in 1565.

In 1603, French explorer Samuel de Champlain arrived in Canada, and in 1608 he established the trading post in the mouth of the St. Lawrence River that would become Quebec City. From that point on, commercial activity and further settlement followed, as did the arrival of Catholic religious orders. The territory became known as New France (*Nouvelle-France*). French explorers traveled into the Great Lakes region and along the Mississippi River,

founding the city of New Orleans in 1718 at its mouth. By this point, France had laid claim to the territory north and west of the Mississippi and all of Eastern Canada, as well as many Caribbean islands and the South American colony of Guiana (*Guyane*).

▷ New France in 1719
This map shows the extent of French North American claims in 1719, reaching from the mouth of the Mississippi River, north to the Great Lakes, and east to the Maritimes.

KEY

1 Quebec City and Montreal were established in 1608 and 1642 respectively.

2 New Orleans was founded at the mouth of the Mississippi in 1718.

3 Heading west toward the Great Lakes, the French encountered and allied with the Algonquian people.

LOCATOR

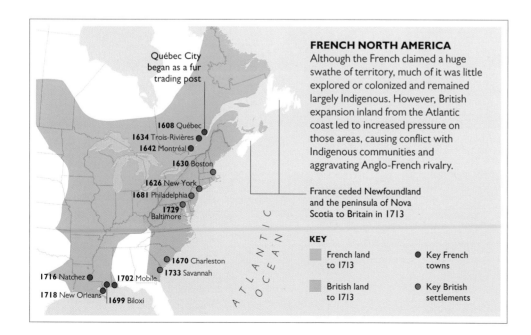

Québec City began as a fur trading post

1608 Québec
1634 Trois-Rivières
1642 Montréal
1630 Boston
1626 New York
1681 Philadelphia
1729 Baltimore
1670 Charleston
1733 Savannah
1716 Natchez
1702 Mobile
1718 New Orleans
1699 Biloxi

ATLANTIC OCEAN

FRENCH NORTH AMERICA
Although the French claimed a huge swathe of territory, much of it was little explored or colonized and remained largely Indigenous. However, British expansion inland from the Atlantic coast led to increased pressure on those areas, causing conflict with Indigenous communities and aggravating Anglo-French rivalry.

France ceded Newfoundland and the peninsula of Nova Scotia to Britain in 1713

KEY

French land to 1713	● Key French towns
British land to 1713	● Key British settlements

COLONIZING VIRGINIA

In 1607, the English established their first permanent colony in Virginia, North America. Its first few years were plagued by food shortages and hostile relations with the Indigenous communities whose land they had encroached on. While most of its inhabitants succumbed to starvation and disease, the survivors and new arrivals built what became an important mainland British colony.

After a number of failed attempts and casualties, 104 members of the Virginia Company—a group of English colonists—finally managed to get a foothold in North America. In May 1607, they established a colony, named Jamestown for King James I, on the shores of the Powhatan River (later known as James River) that flowed into Chesapeake Bay.

The land they occupied was that of the Paspahegh people, ruled by chief Wowinchopunk. His people were part of the dominant Algonquian-speaking Tsenacomoco confederation, under the paramount chief Wahunsenacawh (or Powhatan).

Drought, famine, disease, and attacks by Indigenous groups took a toll on the first colonists. Initially, Wahunsenacawh had extended help to the settlers, but soon their relations soured as English demand for food increased and they resorted to stealing. By the winter of 1609–1610, only one-sixth of the settlers survived—the rest died of starvation and illness.

New colonists and supplies arrived after being delayed by summer hurricanes, and the strengthened colony fought with the Indigenous people. They also experimented with the planting of a new crop, tobacco.

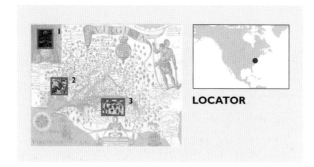

LOCATOR

One settler, John Rolfe, did so with great success. He married Wahunsenacawh's daughter Mataoka (or Pocahontas) in 1614, possibly by force after the English abducted her, and a temporary truce was agreed between the English and the people of Tsenacomoco.

Tobacco, which James I had denounced as a "filthie noveltie," became a mainstay of the colony's economy. The profit was used to bring in indentured labor and enslaved Africans. In 1619, the first documented group of Africans—abducted by English privateer *White Lion* from a Portuguese ship bound for Veracruz, New Spain—arrived in Virginia.

EUROPEAN COLONIES IN CHESAPEAKE AND THE LOWER SOUTH

Although Spain claimed the Atlantic coast as part of its Florida territory, it could not defend the area from European rivals. The British began to set up colonies, first in Jamestown then in New England, while France explored the Great Lakes region. Britain profited from tobacco planting, and, like France, found a viable trade option in the export of fish and fur. Rice and indigo were also grown.

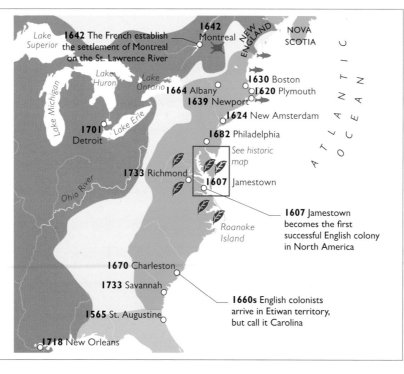

1642 The French establish the settlement of Montreal on the St. Lawrence River

Lake Superior

Lake Huron

Lake Michigan

Lake Ontario

Lake Erie

1642 Montreal

NOVA SCOTIA

NEW ENGLAND

1630 Boston
1620 Plymouth
1664 Albany
1639 Newport
1624 New Amsterdam

1701 Detroit

1682 Philadelphia

Ohio River

1733 Richmond

See historic map

1607 Jamestown

1607 Jamestown becomes the first successful English colony in North America

Roanoke Island

ATLANTIC OCEAN

1670 Charleston

1733 Savannah

1565 St. Augustine

1718 New Orleans

1660s English colonists arrive in Etiwan territory, but call it Carolina

KEY

- Territory claimed by the British/Scottish
- Territory claimed by the Spanish
- Territory claimed by the French
- 🌿 Tobacco planting
- ✴ Fur trading post
- ➤ Fisheries

POWHATAN
Held this state & fashion when Capt. Smith was delivered to him prisoner 1607

MAR-GOAGS
CHI-WONS
THE
VIRGINIA

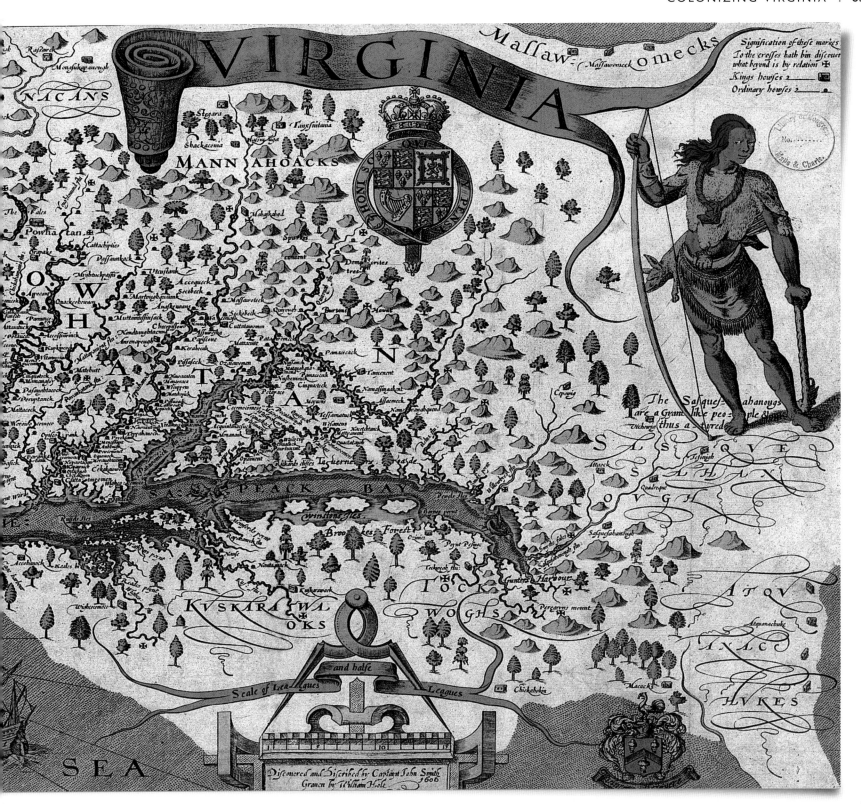

◁ **Wahunsenacawh**
The paramount chief presided over a political alliance of at least 30 Algonquian-speaking Indigenous groups, collectively called Tsenacomoco, or the Powhatan paramount chiefdom.

▷ **Jamestown settlement**
The English established their colony 60 miles (97km) upriver from Chesapeake Bay, at a point where they could safely anchor their ships. The colony was far enough from the river itself so as not to be an easy target for Spanish ships.

△ **Map of Virginia**
This rendering of Virginia was published in 1624 in Captain John Smith's account *The Generall Historie of Virginia, New-England, and the Summer Isles.*

◁ **Tobacco planting**
Colonists, indentured laborers, and enslaved Africans occupied abandoned Indigenous people's fields and cleared rich bottomlands along Chesapeake Bay to plant tobacco. It became an article of mass consumption in Europe after the Spanish introduced it from the Americas.

THE PUEBLO REVOLT

Angered by the oppressive practices of the Spanish colonial regime in the Southwest, the religious leader Po'pay organized an uprising, causing the settlers to leave for more than a decade and resulting in one of the most successful revolts of its time.

△ **Pueblo canteen**
Pueblo communities have long produced functional, decorative ceramics, like this 1870 canteen.

When Spanish explorers encountered the diverse peoples living along the northern Rio Grande Valley (in today's New Mexico), they called them *Pueblo*, the Castilian word for village, because they lived in settled communities. When colonists began to arrive, starting in 1598, they took land and food from the Indigenous population, and also tried to force them to convert to Christianity. This led to decades of oppression of the Pueblo by the Spanish. After several years of drought and famine in the 1670s, Spanish officials deepened resentments by accusing 47 Pueblo religious leaders of witchcraft, and executing three of

Rebellion reimagined
This 1936 mural by US artist Loren Mozley depicts the Pueblo Revolt. It is located in the US Federal Building and Courthouse in Albuquerque, New Mexico. It was funded as part of the New Deal (see pp.254–255).

them. The incident compelled one Tewa leader, Po'pay, to bring the Pueblo communities together in order to drive out the Spanish. They used messengers carrying knotted cords to plan the attack, which began on August 10, 1680. After ten days of fighting, the Spanish governor, Antonio de Otermín, was forced to retreat south, taking the settlers with him to El Paso. The Spanish did not return until 1692, making this one of the most successful Indigenous uprisings in the Americas.

> "I determined ... to fight with the enemy until dying or conquering."
>
> SPANISH GOVERNOR ANTONIO DE OTERMÍN, 1680

KIVAS

The great Kiva of Pueblo Bonito, in Chaco Canyon, northern New Mexico, is believed to be one of the oldest surviving examples of this type of structure. Kivas were large, circular, underground meeting areas and were important spiritual and ceremonial spaces. The Spanish destroyed many of them during the colonial era.

THE SOUTHEASTERN BORDERLANDS

Europeans wanted to colonize the southern Atlantic coast of North America, but Indigenous groups fought back fiercely and the process took several decades. The colonists also had to navigate complex Indigenous political and social networks in the region.

Spanish explorer Juan Ponce de León first landed on the southeastern coast of North America in 1513 and named it *La Florida*. His visit prompted other Spanish explorers to set out in this direction (see pp.48–49). Soon, Spanish Florida extended from the Atlantic coast to the Chesapeake Bay, its area dwindling as more Europeans arrived to stake their claims. Some Indigenous groups formed alliances with Spanish and English colonists, but other communities resisted. Europeans established vulnerable outposts that depended on trade and alliance with neighboring Indigenous peoples. French Protestants challenged Spanish claims with coastal

settlements in the 1560s. However, they failed to establish a lasting colony, because Spanish forces destroyed their settlements. The English landed in 1607 and founded Jamestown (see pp.64–65).

The incursion of Europeans had profound and long-lasting repercussions for southeastern Indigenous communities. Disease and conflict cost thousands of lives, but the region's political ecosystem was also altered. Indigenous people were pulled into wider European geopolitics as it was playing out among the settlements in the Americas. Similarly, the Europeans became caught up in larger Indigenous conflicts and realignments.

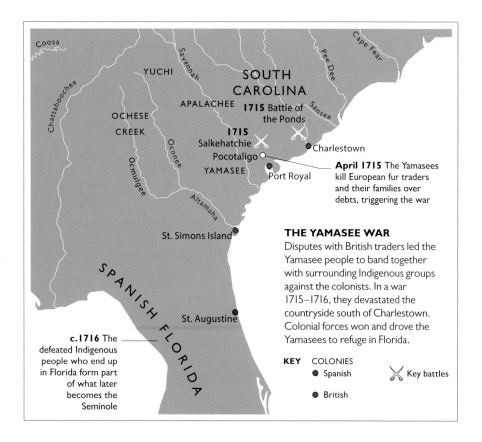

April 1715 The Yamasees kill European fur traders and their families over debts, triggering the war

c.1716 The defeated Indigenous people who end up in Florida form part of what later becomes the Seminole

THE YAMASEE WAR

Disputes with British traders led the Yamasee people to band together with surrounding Indigenous groups against the colonists. In a war 1715–1716, they devastated the countryside south of Charlestown. Colonial forces won and drove the Yamasees to refuge in Florida.

KEY   COLONIES
- ● Spanish
- ● British
- ✕ Key battles

3 INDIGENOUS CONFLICTS 1597–1715

This period saw several wars with Indigenous people fighting colonists. The Guale people revolted against Franciscan Catholics in 1597, while in Virginia, wars with the Powhatan, including devastating attacks in 1622 and 1644, destabilized the colony. Later, the Tuscarora War against British colonists in North Carolina took place in 1711–1715; the Yamasee War also began (see below left).

✊ Uprisings and conflicts

2 FRENCH COLONIZATION 1562–1565

In 1562, French Protestants, called Huguenots, traveled to North America to escape religious unrest in France. After a brief halt at the mouth of St. Johns River (near present-day Jacksonville), they sailed north, where they tried to settle. Plagued by Indigenous resistance and lack of resources, they returned to their landing point to set up Fort Caroline.

➡ Huguenot route

1 THE SPANISH ARRIVE 1513

In 1513, Spanish explorer Juan Ponce de León led an expedition to find the island of Bimini (Bahamas). He was looking for Lucayan people to enslave. However, he landed on the northeast coast of Florida, and the Ais (Ays) people drove him away. A later mission in 1521 also ended in failure, but these early travels opened the door to later Spanish colonization.

➡ Ponce de León route

INDIGENOUS LANDSCAPE

In the 16th century, southeastern North America comprised diverse Indigenous groups, customs, and languages. Indigenous alliances proved crucial to European success.

KEY

SELECTED INDIGENOUS
LANGUAGE GROUPS (APPROXIMATE)

- Iroquoian
- Timucua
- Siouan-Catawban
- Muskogean
- /// Algonquian

COLONIES AND FORTS

- ⊞ ● Spanish
- ⊞ ● French
- ⊞ ● English/Scottish

TIMELINE

	1500	1550	1600	1650	1700	1750

4 ENGLISH COLONIZATION 1607–1670

After the English colony at Jamestown, Virginia, took root in 1607, others began to appear in what Spain claimed was its Florida territory, including one at Charlestown (present-day South Carolina) in 1670. The two powers continued to contest each other's claims. Carolinians allied with the Muskogean Creeks to attack Indigenous mission communities allied with Spain and enslave Indigenous captives.

➡ English route

1622–1644 Powhatan War
Jamestown

1711–1715 Tuscarora War

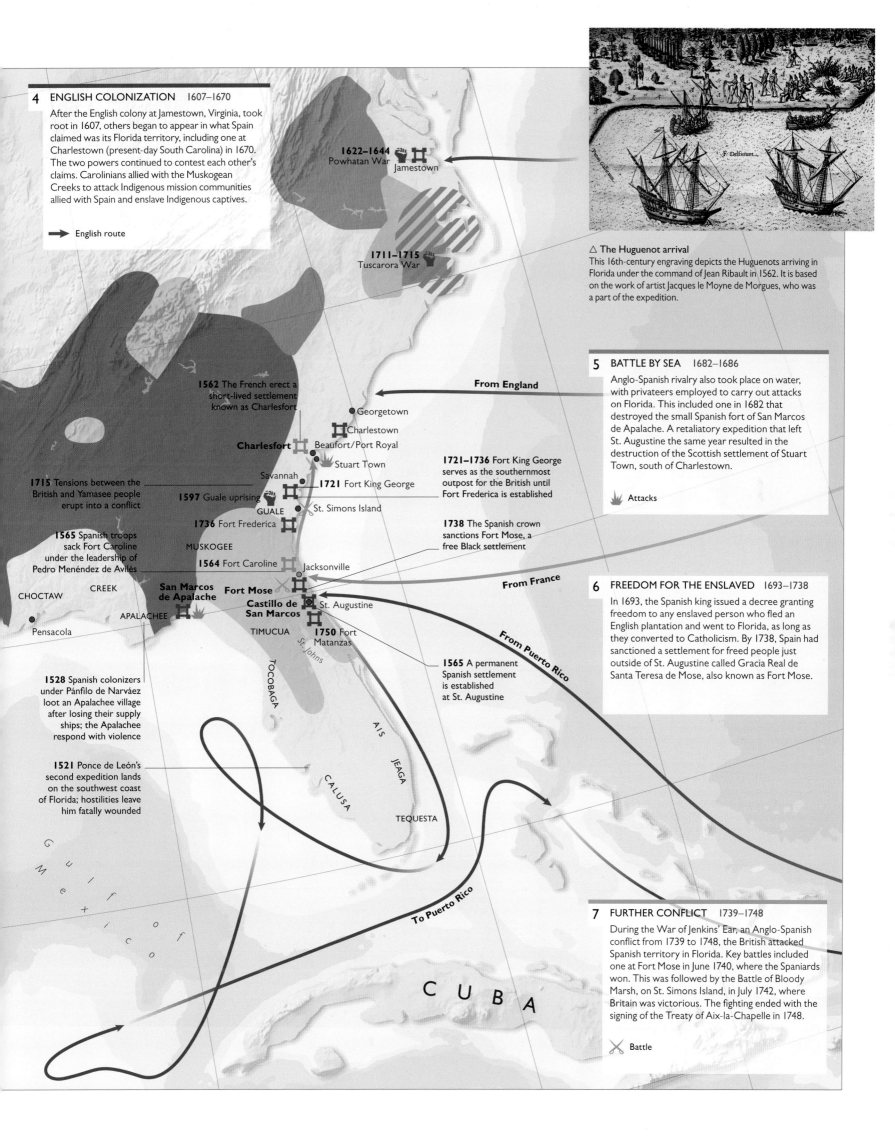

△ **The Huguenot arrival**
This 16th-century engraving depicts the Huguenots arriving in Florida under the command of Jean Ribault in 1562. It is based on the work of artist Jacques le Moyne de Morgues, who was a part of the expedition.

From England

1562 The French erect a short-lived settlement known as Charlesfort

Georgetown
Charlestown
Charlesfort Beaufort/Port Royal
Stuart Town
Savannah
1715 Tensions between the British and Yamasee people erupt into a conflict
1721 Fort King George
1597 Guale uprising
GUALE
1736 Fort Frederica
St. Simons Island
1565 Spanish troops sack Fort Caroline under the leadership of Pedro Menéndez de Avilés
MUSKOGEE
1564 Fort Caroline
Jacksonville
CREEK
San Marcos de Apalache **Fort Mose**
CHOCTAW **Castillo de San Marcos** St. Augustine
APALACHEE
Pensacola
TIMUCUA
1528 Spanish colonizers under Pánfilo de Narváez loot an Apalachee village after losing their supply ships; the Apalachee respond with violence
1750 Fort Matanzas
St. Johns
1565 A permanent Spanish settlement is established at St. Augustine
TOCOBAGA
1521 Ponce de León's second expedition lands on the southwest coast of Florida; hostilities leave him fatally wounded
AIS
JEAGA
CALUSA
TEQUESTA
From France
From Puerto Rico
To Puerto Rico
Gulf of Mexico
C U B A

1721–1736 Fort King George serves as the southernmost outpost for the British until Fort Frederica is established

1738 The Spanish crown sanctions Fort Mose, a free Black settlement

5 BATTLE BY SEA 1682–1686

Anglo-Spanish rivalry also took place on water, with privateers employed to carry out attacks on Florida. This included one in 1682 that destroyed the small Spanish fort of San Marcos de Apalache. A retaliatory expedition that left St. Augustine the same year resulted in the destruction of the Scottish settlement of Stuart Town, south of Charlestown.

🌿 Attacks

6 FREEDOM FOR THE ENSLAVED 1693–1738

In 1693, the Spanish king issued a decree granting freedom to any enslaved person who fled an English plantation and went to Florida, as long as they converted to Catholicism. By 1738, Spain had sanctioned a settlement for freed people just outside of St. Augustine called Gracia Real de Santa Teresa de Mose, also known as Fort Mose.

7 FURTHER CONFLICT 1739–1748

During the War of Jenkins' Ear, an Anglo-Spanish conflict from 1739 to 1748, the British attacked Spanish territory in Florida. Key battles included one at Fort Mose in June 1740, where the Spaniards won. This was followed by the Battle of Bloody Marsh, on St. Simons Island, in July 1742, where Britain was victorious. The fighting ended with the signing of the Treaty of Aix-la-Chapelle in 1748.

✗ Battle

LA CALI
TEATRO
LA COM

DON FERN

GRAN TEGUAIO

GRAN QUIVIRA   MOQUI

NUEVO

MARDE LAS CALIFORNAS Ò CAROLINAS Ò CARO

CALIFORNAS Ò CAROLINAS

MAR DEL SUR

Tropique de Cancer.

Tronco de Leguas Castellanas

10   20   30   40   50   60   70   80   90   100

NEW SPAIN IN THE WEST

The North American West was Spain's final imperial enterprise on the continent. By the late 1500s, it explored the Pacific coast, and by the late 1600s religious orders were pushing north from New Spain into Baja California and southern Arizona.

In 1598, the conquistador Juan de Oñate led an expedition into what is now New Mexico, establishing a colony in the north of the region. Later, Catholic missionaries started to move northwest into Baja California, placing missions there, and in the territory of the Pima nation (now Arizona), which the Spanish called *Pimería Alta*. Europeans knew little about Alta California, the territory to the northwest of New Spain and New Mexico. Although claimed by the Spanish, was inhabited by hundreds of thousands of Indigenous people. Spanish exploration into the Pacific focused on the Philippines in Asia, which Spain claimed in 1565. The Spanish established a centuries-long trading system that utilized New Spain's western ports, including Acapulco. Prior to later Spanish colonization (see pp.104–105),

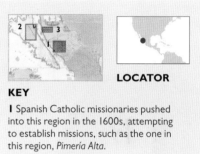

LOCATOR

KEY

1 Spanish Catholic missionaries pushed into this region in the 1600s, attempting to establish missions, such as the one in this region, *Pimería Alta*.

2 California was mistakenly depicted as an island on early maps.

3 The Spanish mistakenly believed the land of Quivira contained gold.

this area was populated by a variety of Indigenous peoples speaking a huge number of languages—including the Pueblos (see pp.66–67), the Chumash, the Pomo in the north, and the Miwok people in mountainous areas. Some communities were based in villages; others migrated according to the season. These populations would be transformed by the arrival of the Spanish.

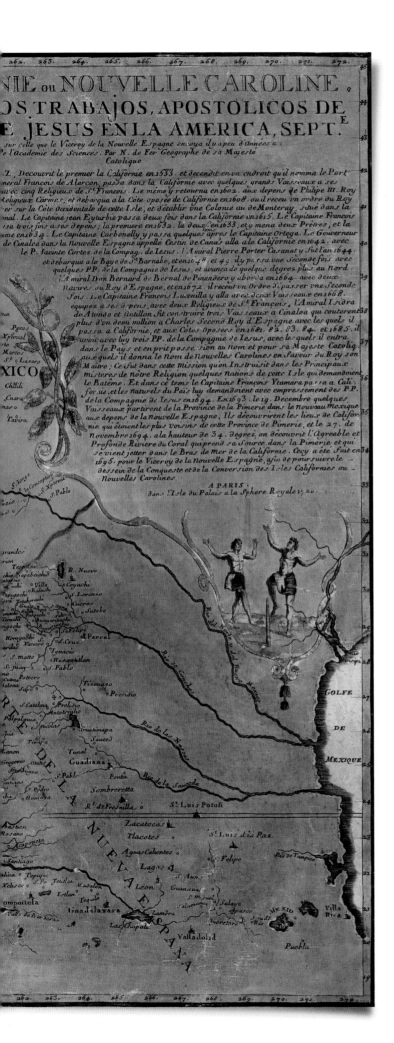

◁ **New Spain and California, 1720**
This map based on accounts of Spanish missionaries shows New Spain in dark green, New Mexico in pink, and California as an island.

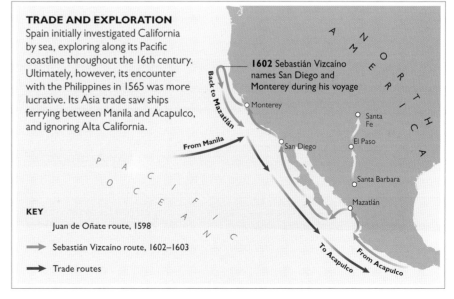

TRADE AND EXPLORATION
Spain initially investigated California by sea, exploring along its Pacific coastline throughout the 16th century. Ultimately, however, its encounter with the Philippines in 1565 was more lucrative. Its Asia trade saw ships ferrying between Manila and Acapulco, and ignoring Alta California.

1602 Sebastián Vizcaíno names San Diego and Monterey during his voyage

Back to Mazatlán

From Manila

Monterey

Santa Fe

San Diego

El Paso

Santa Barbara

Mazatlán

To Acapulco

From Acapulco

KEY

→ Juan de Oñate route, 1598

→ Sebastián Vizcaíno route, 1602–1603

→ Trade routes

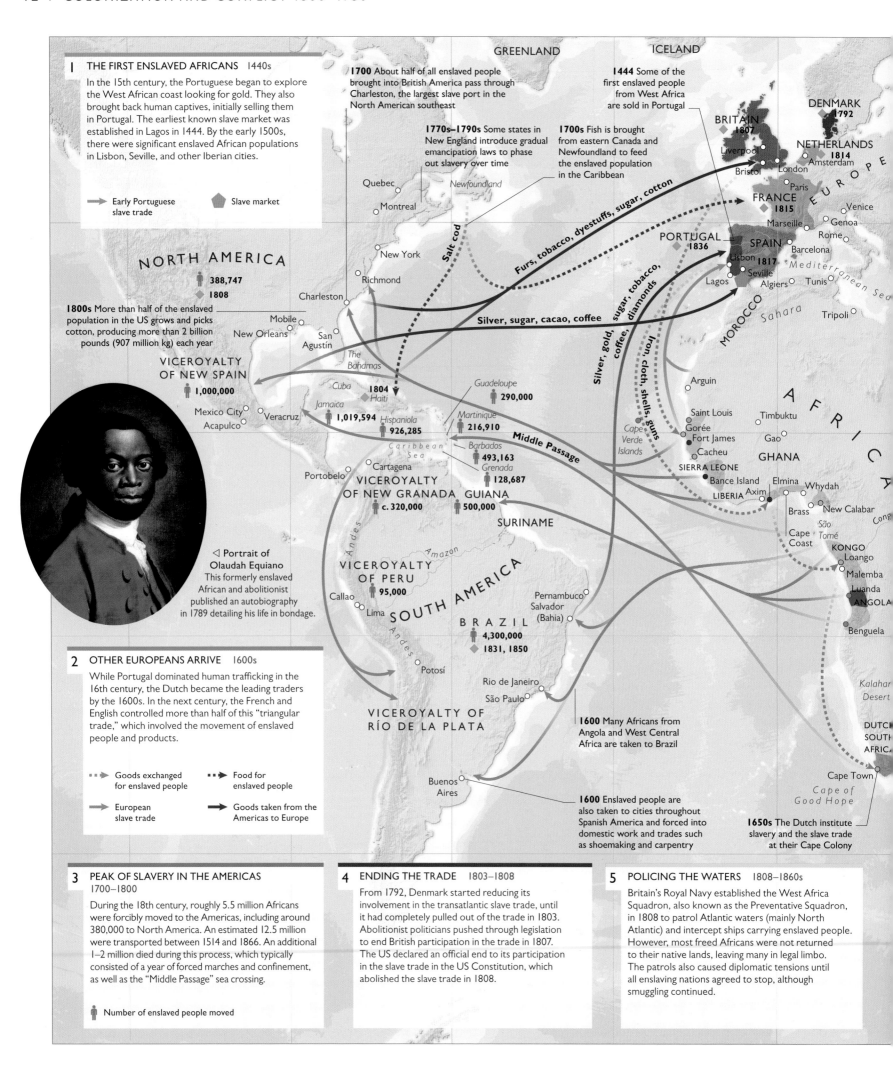

1 THE FIRST ENSLAVED AFRICANS 1440s

In the 15th century, the Portuguese began to explore the West African coast looking for gold. They also brought back human captives, initially selling them in Portugal. The earliest known slave market was established in Lagos in 1444. By the early 1500s, there were significant enslaved African populations in Lisbon, Seville, and other Iberian cities.

→ Early Portuguese slave trade

⬠ Slave market

1700 About half of all enslaved people brought into British America pass through Charleston, the largest slave port in the North American southeast

1770s–1790s Some states in New England introduce gradual emancipation laws to phase out slavery over time

1444 Some of the first enslaved people from West Africa are sold in Portugal

1700s Fish is brought from eastern Canada and Newfoundland to feed the enslaved population in the Caribbean

GREENLAND

ICELAND

DENMARK 1792

BRITAIN 1807

Liverpool

Bristol

London

NETHERLANDS 1814

Amsterdam

Paris

EUROPE

FRANCE 1815

Venice

Marseille

Genoa

Rome

Quebec

Newfoundland

Montreal

Salt cod

Furs, tobacco, dyestuffs, sugar, cotton

PORTUGAL 1836

SPAIN

Lisbon 1817

Seville

Barcelona

Mediterranean Sea

New York

Richmond

Silver, sugar, cacao, coffee

Silver, gold, sugar, tobacco, coffee, diamonds

Lagos

Algiers

Tunis

Tripoli

MOROCCO

Sahara

Charleston

Mobile

New Orleans

San Agustín

The Bahamas

1800s More than half of the enslaved population in the US grows and picks cotton, producing more than 2 billion pounds (907 million kg) each year

NORTH AMERICA

👤 388,747
◆ 1808

VICEROYALTY OF NEW SPAIN
👤 1,000,000

Mexico City

Acapulco

Veracruz

Cuba

Jamaica

1804 ◆ Haiti

1,019,594 Hispaniola

👤 926,285

Guadeloupe 290,000

Martinique 👤 216,910

Iron, cloth, shells, guns

Arguin

Saint Louis

Gorée

Fort James

Cacheu

Timbuktu

Gao

Cape Verde Islands

GHANA

SIERRA LEONE

Bance Island

Elmina

LIBERIA

Axim

Whydah

Brass

New Calabar

São Tomé

Cape Coast

KONGO

Loango

Malemba

Luanda

ANGOLA

Benguela

Portrait of Olaudah Equiano
This formerly enslaved African and abolitionist published an autobiography in 1789 detailing his life in bondage.

Caribbean Sea

Barbados

👤 493,163

Grenada

👤 128,687

Middle Passage

Cartagena

Portobelo

VICEROYALTY OF NEW GRANADA
👤 c. 320,000

GUIANA
👤 500,000

SURINAME

Andes

Amazon

VICEROYALTY OF PERU
👤 95,000

Callao

Lima

SOUTH AMERICA

Pernambuco

Salvador (Bahia)

BRAZIL
👤 4,300,000
◆ 1831, 1850

Andes

Potosí

Rio de Janeiro

São Paulo

VICEROYALTY OF RÍO DE LA PLATA

Buenos Aires

Kalahari Desert

DUTCH SOUTH AFRICA

Cape Town

Cape of Good Hope

2 OTHER EUROPEANS ARRIVE 1600s

While Portugal dominated human trafficking in the 16th century, the Dutch became the leading traders by the 1600s. In the next century, the French and English controlled more than half of this "triangular trade," which involved the movement of enslaved people and products.

- - -▶ Goods exchanged for enslaved people

▪ ▪▶ Food for enslaved people

→ European slave trade

➡ Goods taken from the Americas to Europe

1600 Many Africans from Angola and West Central Africa are taken to Brazil

1600 Enslaved people are also taken to cities throughout Spanish America and forced into domestic work and trades such as shoemaking and carpentry

1650s The Dutch institute slavery and the slave trade at their Cape Colony

👤 Number of enslaved people moved

3 PEAK OF SLAVERY IN THE AMERICAS 1700–1800

During the 18th century, roughly 5.5 million Africans were forcibly moved to the Americas, including around 380,000 to North America. An estimated 12.5 million were transported between 1514 and 1866. An additional 1–2 million died during this process, which typically consisted of a year of forced marches and confinement, as well as the "Middle Passage" sea crossing.

4 ENDING THE TRADE 1803–1808

From 1792, Denmark started reducing its involvement in the transatlantic slave trade, until it had completely pulled out of the trade in 1803. Abolitionist politicians pushed through legislation to end British participation in the trade in 1807. The US declared an official end to its participation in the slave trade in the US Constitution, which abolished the slave trade in 1808.

5 POLICING THE WATERS 1808–1860s

Britain's Royal Navy established the West Africa Squadron, also known as the Preventative Squadron, in 1808 to patrol Atlantic waters (mainly North Atlantic) and intercept ships carrying enslaved people. However, most freed Africans were not returned to their native lands, leaving many in legal limbo. The patrols also caused diplomatic tensions until all enslaving nations agreed to stop, although smuggling continued.

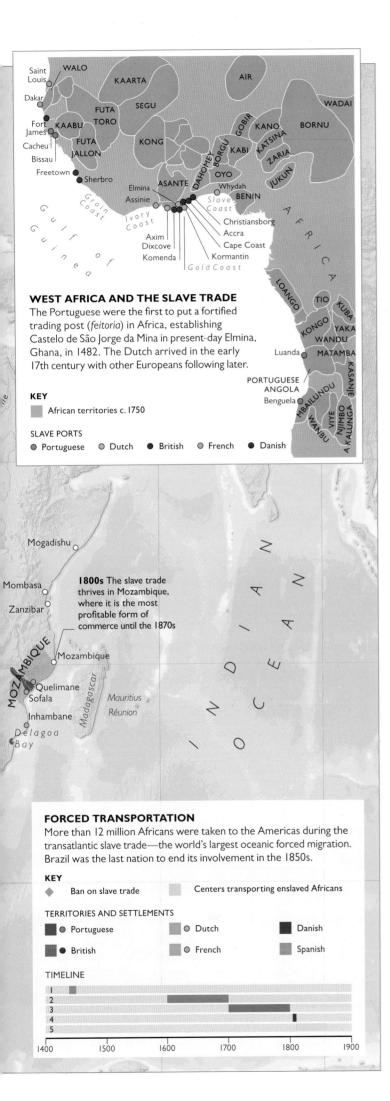

WEST AFRICA AND THE SLAVE TRADE
The Portuguese were the first to put a fortified trading post (*feitoria*) in Africa, establishing Castelo de São Jorge da Mina in present-day Elmina, Ghana, in 1482. The Dutch arrived in the early 17th century with other Europeans following later.

KEY

African territories c. 1750

SLAVE PORTS
● Portuguese ○ Dutch ● British ● French ● Danish

1800s The slave trade thrives in Mozambique, where it is the most profitable form of commerce until the 1870s

FORCED TRANSPORTATION
More than 12 million Africans were taken to the Americas during the transatlantic slave trade—the world's largest oceanic forced migration. Brazil was the last nation to end its involvement in the 1850s.

KEY

◆ Ban on slave trade   Centers transporting enslaved Africans

TERRITORIES AND SETTLEMENTS
■ ● Portuguese   ■ ○ Dutch   ■ Danish
■ ● British   ■ ○ French   ■ Spanish

TIMELINE

THE ATLANTIC SLAVE TRADE

The arrival of Portuguese explorers along the coast of West Africa in the 1440s set in motion a new era of trade, which soon focused on the transportation of human captives. Over the next four centuries, millions of enslaved people were forcibly taken to the Americas.

What began with Portuguese explorers taking West African captives back to Portugal expanded into the transatlantic slave trade, carried out by European nations and their colonies. The Spanish took enslaved Africans to the Caribbean island colony of Hispaniola as early as 1502. England participated in this trade starting in the 1560s, later founding the Royal African Company (RAC) in 1672, which became one of largest transporters of enslaved people to the Americas.

Europeans traded goods such as iron and textiles for humans in Africa. Enslaved Africans were taken to the Americas to work on plantations and produce crops such as sugar and cotton that were then sent to Europe. This came to be known as the "triangular trade."

By the late 18th century, public awareness and resistance by enslaved people led to a push for abolition. In 1792, Denmark became the first to agree to end its participation in the slave trade. A revolution in Haiti (see pp.106–107) led to the abolition of slavery on the island in 1804. The British pulled out of the slave trade in 1807, the US in 1808, with others following suit later. However, this was only the first stage of abolition; except for Haiti, the use of enslaved labor continued.

> *"But the whole business of slavery is … a most horrible iniquity to traffic with slaves and souls of men."*
>
> FORMERLY ENSLAVED MAN, QUOBNA OTTOBAH CUGOANO, *THOUGHTS AND SENTIMENTS ON THE EVIL OF SLAVERY*, 1787

THE *AMISTAD* MUTINY

In 1839, 53 African captives aboard the Spanish schooner *La Amistad*—sailing from Havana to Puerto Príncipe, Cuba—rose up in rebellion. They killed two crew members and told the surviving crew to take them back to Africa. Their ship ended up in US waters instead, where the freedom-seekers were charged with piracy and murder. Abolitionists in the US raised money and public awareness for their trial. Their case eventually went to the Supreme Court, which ruled that they were free.

PEOPLE OF THE LONGHOUSE

The Haudenosaunee formed a powerful confederation of Indigenous peoples in eastern North America. From the 1600s, they disrupted the French trade in beaver skins and exploited their strategic location between empires to expand their territories and influence.

△ War club
This carved and polished wooden stick with a ball attached to one end was a Haudenosaunee battle weapon, although similar types of clubs were also used in hunting.

As the French began exploring the Saint Lawrence River valley west toward the Great Lakes, they encountered the Haudenosaunee Confederacy, who they called "Iroquois." Haudenosaunee means "people of the longhouse," a communal, multifamily dwelling that was also a symbol of unity. Originally, the Haudenosaunee included the Mohawk, Oneida, Onondaga, Cayuga, and Seneca peoples, however in the 18th century the Tuscarora joined the union, after which they were collectively known as the Six Nations Confederacy.

A key figure in the creation of the confederacy in the 16th century was Hiawatha, who became the leader of the Iroquois. Following an encounter with a man known as "the Peacemaker," the initial Five Nations put their earlier cycles of animosity and conflict behind them and united under an oral constitution. This set of principles was known as the "Great Law of Peace," and set out the rules for a united society with democratic practices—the matrilineal clans that made up these Indigenous nations now had a say when selecting their leaders, including the powerful clan mothers.

Hiawatha's work lived on after his death and he was memorialized throughout the centuries, both in oral histories as well as in the 1855 epic poem by Henry Wadsworth Longfellow, *The Song of Hiawatha*.

THE BEAVER WARS c.1630–1701

The Beaver Wars arose from tensions between the Haudenosaunee and French colonists, who, in response to dwindling beaver pelts for trade, meddled in Indigenous affairs. Haudenosaunee conquests in the 1600s disrupted Indigenous life in the Northeast. From 1660, French and allied Indigenous forces counterattacked, devastating the Iroquoian homeland. Peace led to the Great Peace of Montreal in 1701, involving 39 Indigenous nations.

Front page of the Great Peace of Montreal

Warring factions
This engraving depicts French explorer Samuel de Champlain and his Indigenous allies in 1609, going into battle against the Haudenosaunee at Ticonderoga, in modern-day New York State.

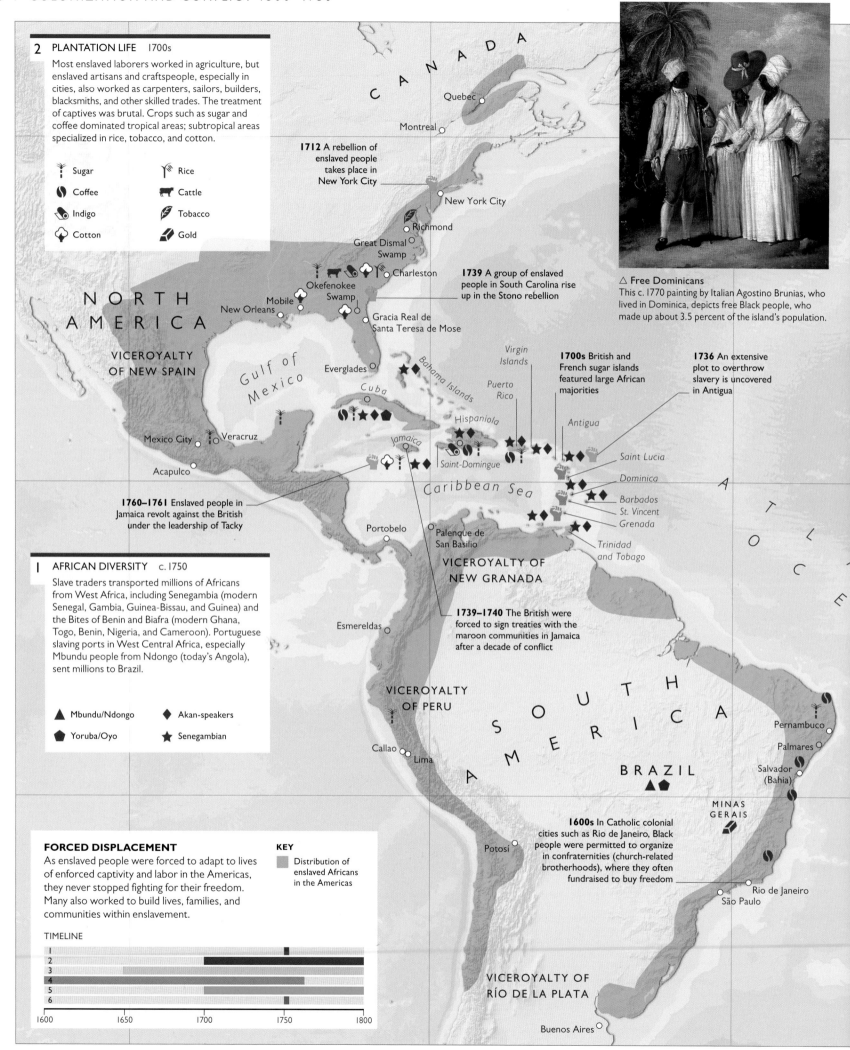

2 PLANTATION LIFE 1700s

Most enslaved laborers worked in agriculture, but enslaved artisans and craftspeople, especially in cities, also worked as carpenters, sailors, builders, blacksmiths, and other skilled trades. The treatment of captives was brutal. Crops such as sugar and coffee dominated tropical areas; subtropical areas specialized in rice, tobacco, and cotton.

- Sugar
- Coffee
- Indigo
- Cotton
- Rice
- Cattle
- Tobacco
- Gold

1712 A rebellion of enslaved people takes place in New York City

1739 A group of enslaved people in South Carolina rise up in the Stono rebellion

1700s British and French sugar islands featured large African majorities

1736 An extensive plot to overthrow slavery is uncovered in Antigua

△ **Free Dominicans**
This c. 1770 painting by Italian Agostino Brunias, who lived in Dominica, depicts free Black people, who made up about 3.5 percent of the island's population.

1760–1761 Enslaved people in Jamaica revolt against the British under the leadership of Tacky

1739–1740 The British were forced to sign treaties with the maroon communities in Jamaica after a decade of conflict

1 AFRICAN DIVERSITY c. 1750

Slave traders transported millions of Africans from West Africa, including Senegambia (modern Senegal, Gambia, Guinea-Bissau, and Guinea) and the Bites of Benin and Biafra (modern Ghana, Togo, Benin, Nigeria, and Cameroon). Portuguese slaving ports in West Central Africa, especially Mbundu people from Ndongo (today's Angola), sent millions to Brazil.

- ▲ Mbundu/Ndongo
- ⬟ Yoruba/Oyo
- ◆ Akan-speakers
- ★ Senegambian

1600s In Catholic colonial cities such as Rio de Janeiro, Black people were permitted to organize in confraternities (church-related brotherhoods), where they often fundraised to buy freedom

FORCED DISPLACEMENT

As enslaved people were forced to adapt to lives of enforced captivity and labor in the Americas, they never stopped fighting for their freedom. Many also worked to build lives, families, and communities within enslavement.

KEY

Distribution of enslaved Africans in the Americas

TIMELINE

	1600	1650	1700	1750	1800
1					
2					
3					
4					
5					
6					

Map labels:
CANADA, Quebec, Montreal, New York City, Richmond, Great Dismal Swamp, Charleston, Okefenokee Swamp, New Orleans, Mobile, NORTH AMERICA, VICEROYALTY OF NEW SPAIN, Gulf of Mexico, Everglades, Gracia Real de Santa Teresa de Mose, Cuba, Bahama Islands, Virgin Islands, Puerto Rico, Mexico City, Veracruz, Hispaniola, Antigua, Acapulco, Jamaica, Saint-Domingue, Caribbean Sea, Saint Lucia, Dominica, Barbados, St. Vincent, Grenada, Trinidad and Tobago, Portobelo, Palenque de San Basilio, VICEROYALTY OF NEW GRANADA, Esmereldas, VICEROYALTY OF PERU, SOUTH AMERICA, BRAZIL, Pernambuco, Palmares, Salvador (Bahia), MINAS GERAIS, Callao, Lima, Potosí, Rio de Janeiro, São Paulo, VICEROYALTY OF RÍO DE LA PLATA, Buenos Aires, ATLANTIC OCEAN

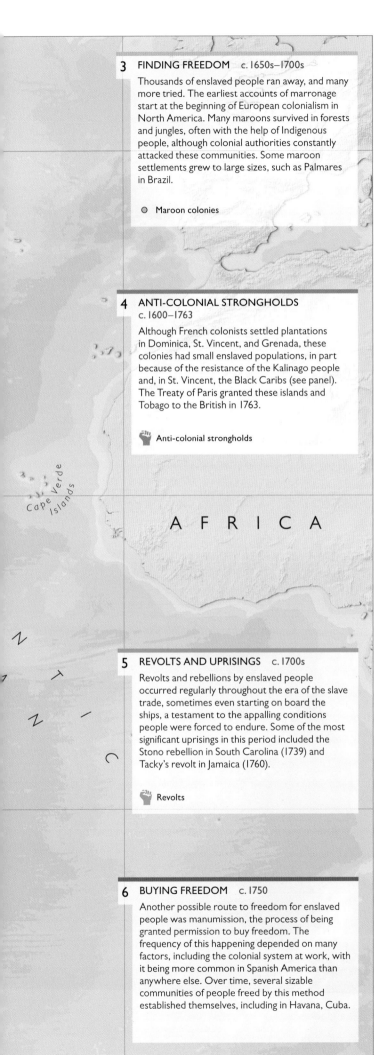

3 FINDING FREEDOM c. 1650s–1700s

Thousands of enslaved people ran away, and many more tried. The earliest accounts of marronage start at the beginning of European colonialism in North America. Many maroons survived in forests and jungles, often with the help of Indigenous people, although colonial authorities constantly attacked these communities. Some maroon settlements grew to large sizes, such as Palmares in Brazil.

● Maroon colonies

4 ANTI-COLONIAL STRONGHOLDS c. 1600–1763

Although French colonists settled plantations in Dominica, St. Vincent, and Grenada, these colonies had small enslaved populations, in part because of the resistance of the Kalinago people and, in St. Vincent, the Black Caribs (see panel). The Treaty of Paris granted these islands and Tobago to the British in 1763.

✊ Anti-colonial strongholds

Cape Verde Islands

A F R I C A

5 REVOLTS AND UPRISINGS c. 1700s

Revolts and rebellions by enslaved people occurred regularly throughout the era of the slave trade, sometimes even starting on board the ships, a testament to the appalling conditions people were forced to endure. Some of the most significant uprisings in this period included the Stono rebellion in South Carolina (1739) and Tacky's revolt in Jamaica (1760).

✊ Revolts

6 BUYING FREEDOM c. 1750

Another possible route to freedom for enslaved people was manumission, the process of being granted permission to buy freedom. The frequency of this happening depended on many factors, including the colonial system at work, with it being more common in Spanish America than anywhere else. Over time, several sizable communities of people freed by this method established themselves, including in Havana, Cuba.

AFRICANS IN THE AMERICAS

The transatlantic slave trade resulted in the forcible dispersion across the Americas of enslaved Africans from diverse cultures. Their struggle to be free never wavered. Some found a way to purchase their freedom, while others engaged in rebellions or joined freedom-seeking maroon communities.

The enslaved people forced across the Atlantic (see pp.72–73) were from diverse areas of Africa, ranging from the Senegambian region south of the Sahara Desert, to the kingdoms of Kongo and Angola in West Central Africa, and even at times from parts of East Africa such as Madagascar. They brought with them regional cultural traditions—including art, language, music, and food—which would ultimately become integral parts of North American culture.

During the more than four centuries of the slave trade, enslaved people's quest for freedom never faltered. Sometimes revolts even started on the ships, before those captured ever reached the Americas. Although millions lived and died in bondage, others managed to escape the system. Some did this by running away to join freedom-seeking communities known as maroons, often living in remote places like mountains or swamps. Maroons fought with colonial authorities, occasionally winning their freedom. More often, however, their rebellions ended in their deaths.

Some paid enslavers to be freed. However, many more gained agency amid oppression by forming their own organizations, languages, and cultural traditions within captivity.

"Plucking up courage, I told him I was free, and he could not by law serve me so."

THE INTERESTING NARRATIVE OF THE LIFE OF OLAUDAH EQUIANO, 1789

THE "BLACK CARIBS"

The so-called "Black Caribs"—today known as the Garifuna—inhabited St. Vincent and the Grenadines and were descended from Africans and the Kalinago people. When the British Empire attempted to push them out of their homelands on the eastern (windward) side of St. Vincent, the "Black Caribs" fought back in the First Carib War (1769–1773). After the end of the Second Carib War (1795–1797), the British deported the Garifuna to Roatán, Honduras, and later to Belize.

Engraving depicting "Black Caribs"

Explanation.

The Provinces belonging to England before the War, lye on the Eastern S... of the dotted Line, & the Cessions m... by France & Spain to England, by... Peace, lye between that and the Riv... Mississipi.

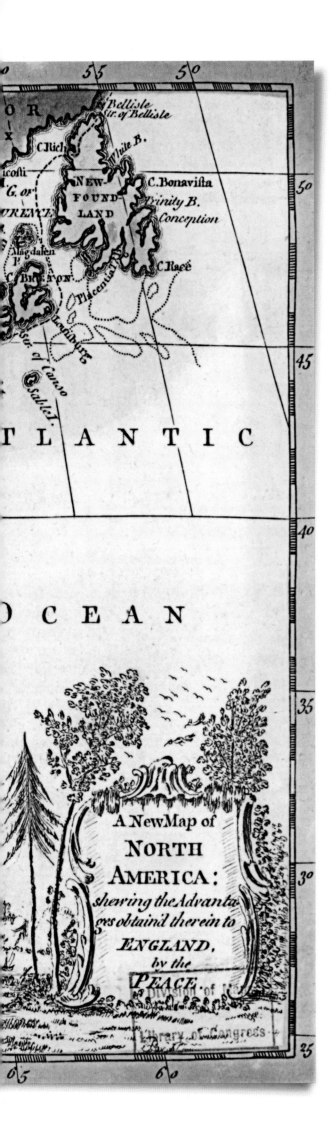

COLONIES AND INDIGENOUS LANDS

From the 1500s to the 1700s, Europeans arrived in a diverse Indigenous world in eastern North America, encountering cultures and people they often misunderstood but also relied on for survival. As European colonization grew, so, too, did Indigenous resistance.

There was wariness between European colonists and Indigenous peoples of the Americas. Despite instances of cooperation and even friendliness, as colonization intensified, relations between the groups became increasingly violent, especially over the issue of land. Dispossession, warfare and European diseases caused millions of deaths, with the Indigenous population falling from an estimated 8 million to 2 million people.

As Spanish, French, and English colonies emerged in Florida, Virginia, the Great Lakes, New England, and New Mexico, Indigenous peoples often used European rivalries to their advantage. They frequently took sides in armed disputes, such as the French and Indian War of 1754–1763 (see pp.84–85).

◁ Encroaching empire, 1763
This map shows British, Spanish, and French territory after the Seven Years' War (see pp.84–85). It also attempts to show the Proclamation Line (see p.88). Indigenous leaders were not consulted on how the land would be demarcated.

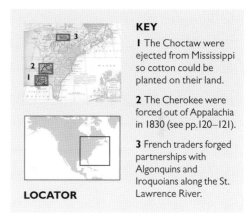

KEY

1 The Choctaw were ejected from Mississippi so cotton could be planted on their land.

2 The Cherokee were forced out of Appalachia in 1830 (see pp.120–121).

3 French traders forged partnerships with Algonquins and Iroquoians along the St. Lawrence River.

LOCATOR

However, there was also economic and cultural interaction. Trade networks were important, and a range of goods were exchanged including beaver, deer, and other animal pelts for textiles and guns from Europe. Linguistic and cultural lines were also crossed, with friendships, partnerships, and even families formed amid the battles over colonization and land.

COLONIES AND CULTURES
By 1750, much of the Indigenous world of North America had been threatened by European colonial claims. Each of the main Indigenous culture areas shown here contained a large variety of linguistic and cultural groupings.

KEY
INDIGENOUS CULTURE AREAS

Arctic	California
Subarctic	Great Basin
Northwest	Southwest
Plateau	Southeast
Plains	Mesoamerica
Northeast	Caribbean

COLONIAL TERRITORIAL CLAIMS BY 1750

French   British   Spanish

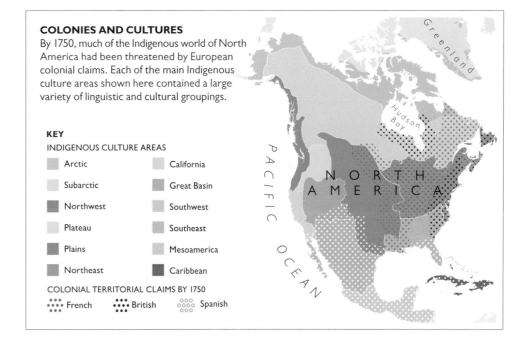

FROM EMPIRES TO INDEPENDENCE

WIDE-RANGING WARS AND POWER STRUGGLES CHANGED THE MAP OF NORTH AMERICA IN THIS ERA, INCLUDING THE REVOLUTION THAT SAW THE BIRTH OF THE US. TO THE SOUTH, MEXICO ALSO SUCCESSFULLY FOUGHT FOR ITS INDEPENDENCE.

CLASH OF THE COLONIES

Through a series of military victories, British North America evolved from a collection of struggling small settlements into a powerful colonial bloc. However, its most dramatic battle was still to come, as some of Britain's own subjects decided to fight for their independence.

△ **Victory commemorated**
This 1759 medal celebrates the British capture of French Quebec during the Seven Years' War, after which France ceded its Canadian territory.

As large populations of British colonists and enslaved Africans expanded into new territories, victories in a series of global conflicts gave Britain more land and power in North America—at least temporarily. The consequences of the Seven Years' War (which included the French and Indian War in North America, 1756–1763) were particularly important. In the war's aftermath, Britain received France's Canadian territory and some of its Caribbean possessions. Spain ceded Florida to Britain in exchange for the return of conquered Havana, which Britain had occupied since 1762. These gains left Britain the dominant European power in North America, but it was not on secure footing.

Rumblings of discontent

Keeping control of North American territories and their people was not straightforward. During the war, the British military expelled some 10,000 French Acadian settlers from the Maritime provinces because of fears about their loyalty in the contested province of Nova Scotia. Farther south, previously loyal subjects were becoming angered by a series of repressive taxes such as the Stamp Act of 1765, which was levied in part to pay for the expense of the Seven Years' War.

British subjects in the 13 colonies began to complain openly about taxation without representation. This disquiet soon turned into serious talk of freeing themselves from imperial

◁ **Leading a revolution**
This 1851 painting by Emanuel Leutze shows General George Washington guiding the Continental Army across the Delaware River in December 1776, a key turning point.

FROM COLONY TO NEW NATION

Britain became the dominant European power in North America after the Seven Years' War, but it was a position that was short-lived as the anger of British subjects in the 13 colonies began to rise. By 1775 they were in full revolt, and in 1783 they secured their freedom and established the United States. A new chapter in the political development of the entire hemisphere had begun, and it would bring profound changes in the decades to come.

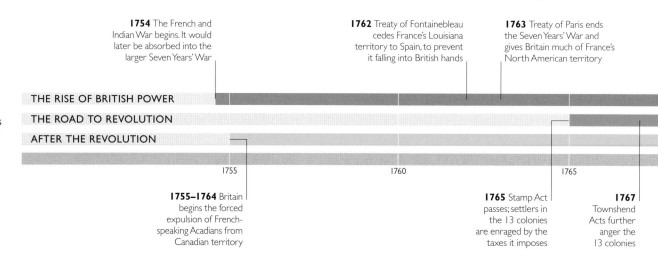

1754 The French and Indian War begins. It would later be absorbed into the larger Seven Years' War

1762 Treaty of Fontainebleau cedes France's Louisiana territory to Spain, to prevent it falling into British hands

1763 Treaty of Paris ends the Seven Years' War and gives Britain much of France's North American territory

THE RISE OF BRITISH POWER

THE ROAD TO REVOLUTION

AFTER THE REVOLUTION

1755   1760   1765

1755–1764 Britain begins the forced expulsion of French-speaking Acadians from Canadian territory

1765 Stamp Act passes; settlers in the 13 colonies are enraged by the taxes it imposes

1767 Townshend Acts further anger the 13 colonies

rule. The public mood darkened further when British troops fired on an angry crowd in 1770, killing five in what became known as the Boston Massacre. Then, in 1773, activists dumped British tea chests in Boston Harbor, creating a "tea party" to protest the East India Company's tea monopoly and to voice their frustration with the colonial government.

On April 19, 1775, the first shots of the independence struggle were fired in Lexington, a town outside of Boston. The war would go on to last eight years. While the battles raged, the Continental Congress made a case for autonomy in the Declaration of Independence (1776), based on the rights to "Life, Liberty, and the pursuit of Happiness." At the same time, Americans wrestled with the status of enslaved Africans. Virginia's royal governor, John Murray (Lord Dunmore) offered enslaved people freedom if they would fight for the British; these troops became known as the Black Loyalists. However, thousands of other enslaved and free Black people sided with the "Patriots," including Crispus Attucks, the first person killed in the Boston Massacre. Victory for the Patriots was never assured, and they received a huge boost when France entered the war.

Spain also sent aid. Bernardo de Gálvez, then the governor of Spanish Louisiana, led his troops to a key victory at the Battle of Pensacola in 1781. In 1783, Britain capitulated, and US independence was secured by the Treaty of Paris, which recognized the 13 colonies as a sovereign nation and forced Britain to return Florida to Spain.

Uncertain futures

Many of the people who had fought for or supported Britain began to leave, including the Black Loyalists. Some of Britain's Indigenous allies abandoned their lands and headed to Canada, which remained under British control. In the end, around 100,000 Loyalists departed. Approximately half of these headed north, and the others moved to Britain or other parts of British North America, such as Jamaica and the Bahamas.

For those who remained, serious questions and challenges lay ahead over the building of this new nation and the establishment of its place in the world.

△ **Decisive battle**
Two lines of ships fire broadside in an image from a French logbook of the Battle of Yorktown in 1781. This critical engagement lasted 21 days, and Britain's defeat in the battle led to its defeat in the American Revolution.

▽ **Loyalist departure**
Many thousands of Loyalists had to be resettled when the war ended. Britain provided them with land in its colonies and spread pro-Loyalist propaganda to ensure they would be welcomed.

"On these shores freedom has planted her standard dipped in the purple tide that flowed from the veins of her martyred heroes."

MERCY WARREN OTIS, QUOTED IN *WORDS OF THE FOUNDING FATHERS*

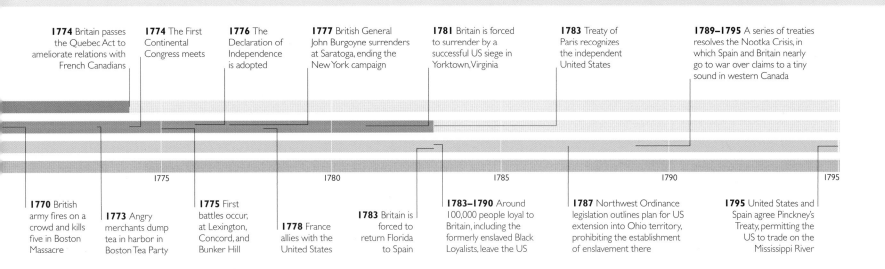

1774 Britain passes the Quebec Act to ameliorate relations with French Canadians

1774 The First Continental Congress meets

1776 The Declaration of Independence is adopted

1777 British General John Burgoyne surrenders at Saratoga, ending the New York campaign

1781 Britain is forced to surrender by a successful US siege in Yorktown, Virginia

1783 Treaty of Paris recognizes the independent United States

1789–1795 A series of treaties resolves the Nootka Crisis, in which Spain and Britain nearly go to war over claims to a tiny sound in western Canada

1775   1780   1785   1790   1795

1770 British army fires on a crowd and kills five in Boston Massacre

1773 Angry merchants dump tea in harbor in Boston Tea Party

1775 First battles occur, at Lexington, Concord, and Bunker Hill

1778 France allies with the United States

1783 Britain is forced to return Florida to Spain

1783–1790 Around 100,000 people loyal to Britain, including the formerly enslaved Black Loyalists, leave the US

1787 Northwest Ordinance legislation outlines plan for US extension into Ohio territory, prohibiting the establishment of enslavement there

1795 United States and Spain agree Pinckney's Treaty, permitting the US to trade on the Mississippi River

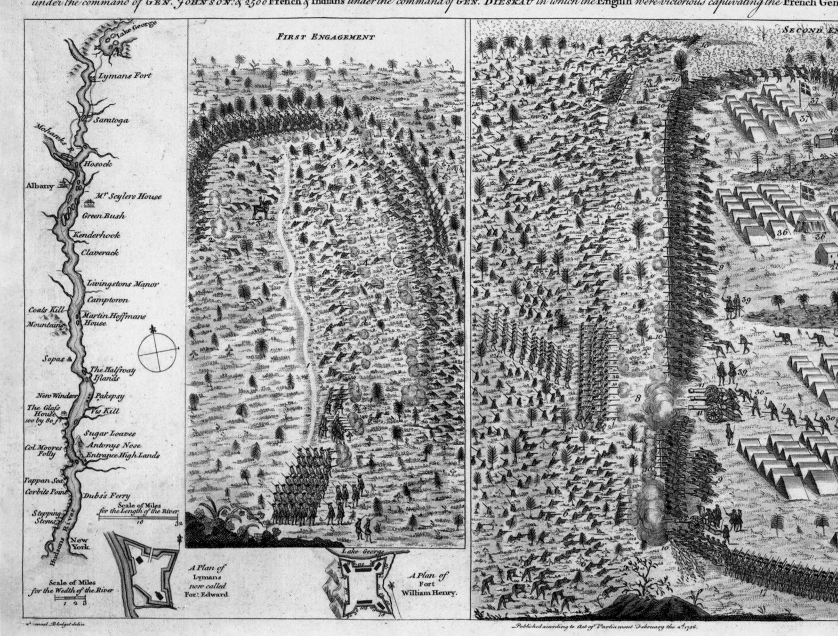

A Prospective View of the BATTLE fought near Lake George, on the 8.th of Sep.r 1755, between ... under the command of Gen.r JOHNSON & 2500 French & Indians under the command of Gen.r DIESKAU in which the English were victorious captivating the French Gen ...

FIRST ENGAGEMENT

SECOND EN...

A Plan of Lymans now called Fort Edward.

A Plan of Fort William Henry.

Published according to Act of Parliament February the 2.d 1756.

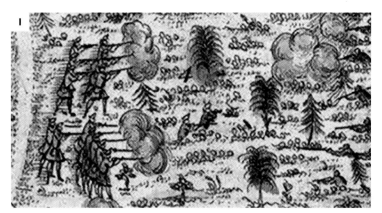

△ First engagement
The French and their Indigenous allies ambushed British and Mohawk troops on the road between Fort Edward and Lake George. The British and their allies initially took heavy casualties.

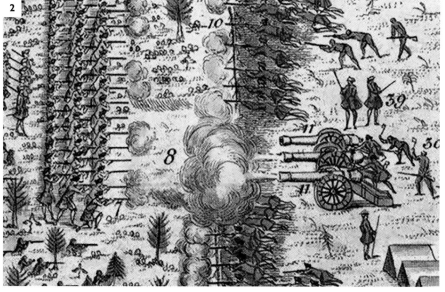

▷ Second engagement
The British successfully retaliated in the next two rounds of fighting, and when reinforcements arrived they were able to defeat the French, although both sides suffered significant losses.

English, with 250 Mohawks,
...mber of his Men killing 700 & putting the rest to flight.

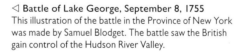

BATTLE FOR NORTH AMERICA

The struggle between Britain and France for dominance in North America became part of a much larger global conflict that was known as the Seven Years' War, the outcome of which changed the course of world politics for centuries to come.

The conflict known as the French and Indian War (1754–1763) began over the question of which European power would control the land around the Ohio River Valley, an area being eyed by colonists and speculators from the British empire. This was of great concern to Indigenous peoples, who did not want their territory to fall under British control and be taken by colonists. France, too, was hostile to its longtime rival encroaching on its colonies. When this tension spilled over into a conflict, it took the form of an ongoing series of battles that soon became subsumed into a larger global confrontation known as the Seven Years' War (1756–1763). In this conflict, which is often considered to be the first "world war," Britain and its Prussian allies fought

LOCATOR

European rivals including France and Spain, with battles taking place in South America, India, West Africa, and elsewhere around the world.

In the North American theater, France and its Indigenous allies fought against Britain and the Haudenosaunee and Cherokee, with key battles taking place around the Ohio and St. Lawrence rivers. The conflict was brought to an end by the 1763 Treaty of Paris (see pp.88–89), which ceded large amounts of territory to Britain and ultimately led to the redrawing of the colonial and Indigenous maps of North America.

◁ **Battle of Lake George, September 8, 1755**
This illustration of the battle in the Province of New York was made by Samuel Blodget. The battle saw the British gain control of the Hudson River Valley.

3

△ **Indigenous allies**
Relationships with Indigenous communities were critical for British and French military efforts in North America. The French had the support of a number of allies across Indigenous groups in the northeast, while the British had connections to the Haudenosaunee and Cherokees.

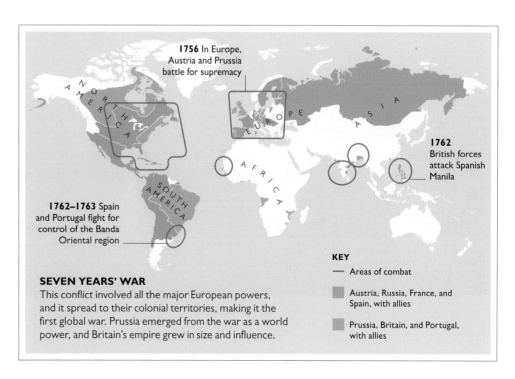

1756 In Europe, Austria and Prussia battle for supremacy

1762 British forces attack Spanish Manila

1762–1763 Spain and Portugal fight for control of the Banda Oriental region

SEVEN YEARS' WAR
This conflict involved all the major European powers, and it spread to their colonial territories, making it the first global war. Prussia emerged from the war as a world power, and Britain's empire grew in size and influence.

KEY
— Areas of combat

Austria, Russia, France, and Spain, with allies

Prussia, Britain, and Portugal, with allies

THE ACADIAN EXPULSION

In 1755, colonists of French descent in northeastern Canada were violently forced from their homes by the British. They were driven into exile across the continent in what became known as the "great upheaval."

△ **A fight for dominance**
The French-controlled fortress and port of Louisbourg in Nova Scotia succumbed to two British sieges, in 1745 and 1758, which helped to cement Britain's control of the region.

The Acadians were mostly French Catholic settlers who, from 1604, established farms and communities in what are now Canada's Maritime provinces: the island of Nova Scotia, southern New Brunswick, parts of northern Maine, and some of southern Quebec. French Acadians settled among the Mi'kmaq in the Dawnland, the territories of the Wabanaki Confederacy.

By 1680, around 1,000 Acadians were living in the region, but their occupancy came under threat in 1713, when the island of Nova Scotia was ceded to the British by France under the terms of the Treaty of Utrecht, an agreement signed during the long-running War of the Spanish Succession (1701–1714). At first, the British allowed the Acadians to remain in place, and their population grew to around 15,000. But by 1755 imperial officials had become distrustful of the community's loyalty to France—especially after they refused to take an oath of allegiance to Britain—and they began a campaign of expulsion.

Ultimately, at least 10,000 Acadians were compelled to leave, their crops destroyed and homes burned down. Most were displaced across North America, while some were deported to England and France. Others died of disease, starvation, and in shipwrecks. A number headed for Louisiana. Formerly a French territory, from 1762 it passed under Spanish control—the two Catholic nations were allies and the Acadian settlers were welcomed into the region, where in time they formed the basis of Louisiana's Cajun community.

BRITANNIA

This flag with the image of Britannia was carried on a British expedition against France to capture the fort at Louisbourg in 1745. The figure of Britannia was commonly used to represent British imperial power. She was usually shown—as here—holding a trident and shield, and wearing a Roman-style helmet.

Eviction on an epic scale
This 19th-century engraving shows the violent and dramatic events of 1755, as the French Acadian community in northern Canada were driven out of their homes by British troops and forced southward into exile.

COLONIAL BRITISH NORTH AMERICA

Britain emerged from the Seven Years' War with territorial gains, including all of French Canada and Spanish Florida. The Treaty of Paris (1763) also profoundly reconfigured the power balance between Europeans and their Indigenous allies.

The Treaty of Paris 1763 that ended the Seven Years' War (see pp.84–85) significantly changed the colonial map of North America, making Britain the dominant European power. Britain gained control of France's colonies in Canada, and of the contested Caribbean islands of Grenada, St. Vincent and the Grenadines, Dominica, and Tobago. Britain also received Spanish Florida in exchange for ending its occupation of Havana, Cuba. Spain had received the vast French Louisiana territory in 1762, in a secret treaty designed to keep it out of British hands, and the deal meant French America now consisted of a handful of Caribbean islands including Saint-Domingue, Martinique, and Guadeloupe.

The peace deal was greeted by a great deal of anger. France's Indigenous allies were enraged by the prospect of British control in the St. Lawrence River and Great Lakes area. In 1763 Ottawa chief Pontiac organized a confederacy with the Potawatomi and Ojibwe people to attack the British, starting around the Great Lakes region. The fighting spread east to the edges of New York and Virginia, and a peace was not brokered until 1766. In the years that followed, there was a significant ongoing effort by the French to retake its Caribbean islands, as well as fierce resistance from the Indigenous communities there.

LOCATOR

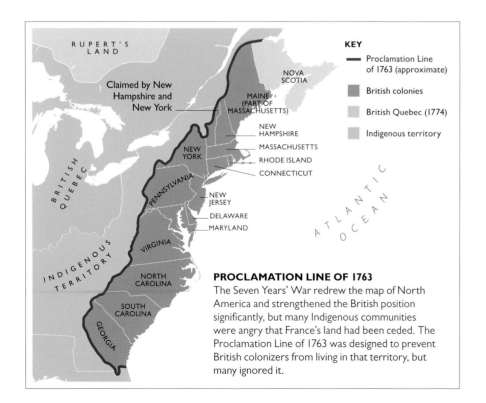

PROCLAMATION LINE OF 1763
The Seven Years' War redrew the map of North America and strengthened the British position significantly, but many Indigenous communities were angry that France's land had been ceded. The Proclamation Line of 1763 was designed to prevent British colonizers from living in that territory, but many ignored it.

△ **North America by Carington Bowles, c. 1774**
This map reflects the new arrangement after the controversial Treaty of Paris (1763), and includes some of the articles of the treaty, which granted new territories to Great Britain, including all of French Canada; the Caribbean islands of Grenada, St. Vincent and the Grenadines, Dominica, and Tobago; and Spanish Florida.

△ **Pontiac's War (1763–1765)**
Angered by the cessation of French land to the British, Indigenous communities in the Great Lakes region launched a rebellion in 1763, under the leadership of Ottawa chief Pontiac.

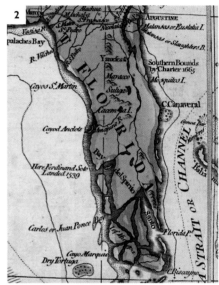

△ **Florida**
Spain ceded Florida in exchange for Havana, Cuba, which the British occupied in 1762. Britain split it into East Florida and West Florida, then retroceded it to Spain in 1783; Spain ceded Florida to the US in 1819.

△ **The Lesser Antilles**
Britain took control of the islands of Grenada, St. Vincent and the Grenadines, Dominica, and Tobago. A mixture of French and British sugar planters, enslaved Africans, and the Kalinago people inhabited them after 1763.

REVOLUTIONARY WAR IN THE NORTH

The first phase of the American Revolution began near Boston and took place mostly in the northeast, with the conflict reaching into Canada. In 1778, French forces joined the strengthening Continental Army against Britain. The war was far from over, but the tide was turning in favor of the rebellious "Patriots."

Britain was left with empty coffers at the end of the Seven Years' War in 1763, and it levied unpopular taxes on its colonies through measures such as the Stamp Act of 1765 and the Townshend Acts of 1767–1768 (see pp.88–89).

Colonists in North America reacted with boycotts and riots. In Boston, on March 5, 1770, soldiers fired on civilians harassing a soldier, killing five protesters. Known as the "Boston Massacre," this precipitated further resistance; five years later, the colonists and Britain were at war.

The first three years of the conflict were largely fought in the northern colonies and Canada. Most of the political organization also took place in the north; it was from Philadelphia, for example, that the Continental Congress issued the Declaration of Independence.

Early military campaigns by the Patriots involved invading Canadian positions, partly in the hope of bringing on board disaffected French-Canadians. In the end, their support failed to materialize; there was little enthusiasm from British Canadians, too.

Indigenous communities had divided loyalties during the conflict. The Cherokee supported the British, as did most of the Haudenosaunee Confederacy, of which only the Oneida and the Tuscarora backed the Patriots.

> *"If particular care and attention is not paid to the ladies, we are determined to foment a rebellion."*
>
> ABIGAIL ADAMS, FUTURE FIRST LADY (1797–1801), IN A 1776 LETTER TO HER HUSBAND, JOHN ADAMS

THE DECLARATION OF INDEPENDENCE

With their opening salvo of "We hold these truths to be self-evident, that all men are created equal," the Patriots of the 13 Colonies made the case for separating the future US from Britain in one of the most influential political statements ever written. The Declaration of Independence was ratified on July 4, 1776, and its main author was Thomas Jefferson, a Virginia landowner and enslaver who served as president from 1801–1809. Many of the other 56 men who signed the document would hold important government posts in the first decades of the new nation's history.

Signing the Declaration of Independence

4 PHILADELPHIA CAMPAIGN
1777–1778

The Patriots' defeat at the Battle of Brandywine Creek in September 1777 left the British under General William Howe free to seize Philadelphia. Farther north, however, the Continental Army's fortunes were looking up. Its victory in October 1777 over the British at Saratoga in the Hudson Valley was a key turning point in the conflict.

▬ Campaign area

5 FRANCE ENTERS THE CONFLICT
1778

Having recently lost out to Britain in the Seven Years' War, France funneled arms and money to the Continental Army in the early years of the rebellion. When it became clear after Saratoga that the Patriots might win, France joined the war. Its first military involvement was at the inconclusive Battle of Rhode Island on August 29, 1778.

✗ Key battle

Lake Ontario

Fort Niagara

Lake Erie

UPPER OHIO FRONTIER

1778 Patriot forces under George Rogers Clark head west and seize British-held Cahokia and Kaskaskia

Fort Pitt (or Pittsburg)

Redstone Fort

VIRGINIA

To Cahokia

1775 In November, Virginia's governor, Lord Dunmore, offers freedom to Patriot-held enslaved people willing to fight for Britain

KENTUCKY FRONTIER

WINS AND LOSSES

The fortunes of both sides varied in the first three years of the conflict, with the Continental Army facing serious setbacks early on.

KEY

○ Settlements	···· State lines	▬ ▬ The 13 Colonies, 1775
▨ Northern colonies	✠ Forts	✗ Other battles

MOVEMENTS, WITH DATE AND LEADER NAME

➡ British   ➡ Patriots   ➡ French

TIMELINE

1   2   3   4   5

1775   1776   1777   1778   1779

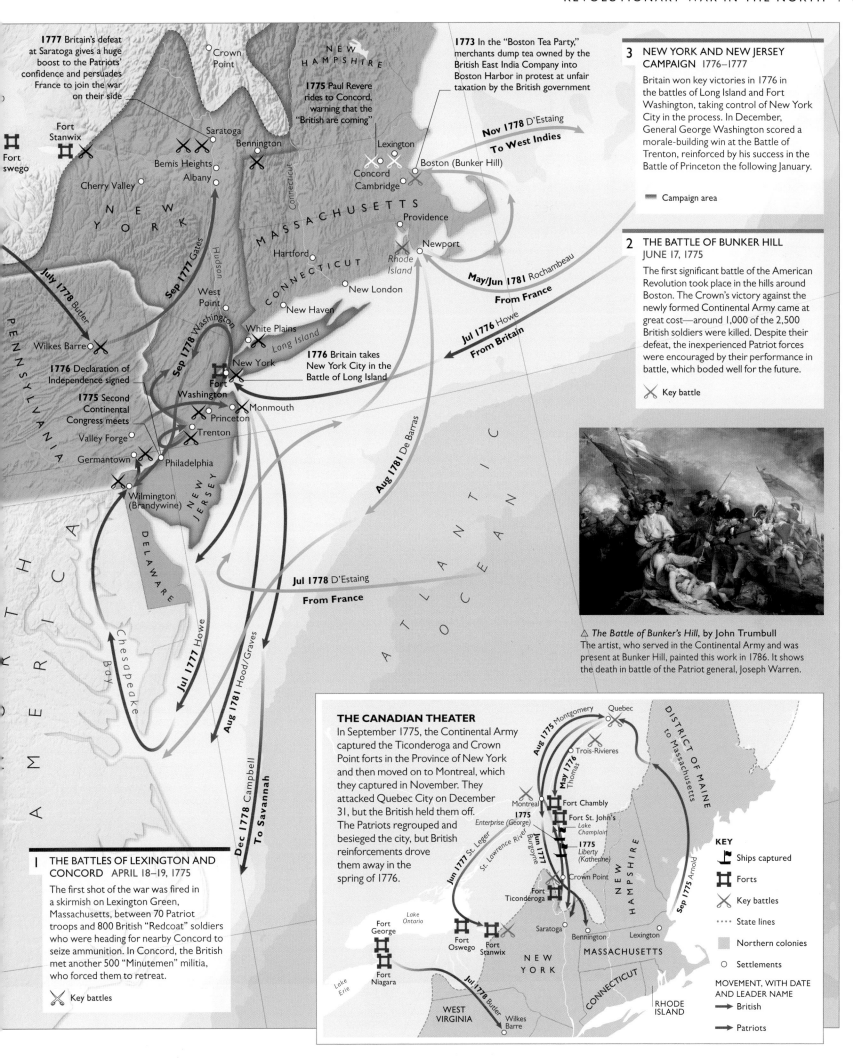

1777 Britain's defeat at Saratoga gives a huge boost to the Patriots' confidence and persuades France to join the war on their side

1775 Paul Revere rides to Concord, warning that the "British are coming"

1773 In the "Boston Tea Party," merchants dump tea owned by the British East India Company into Boston Harbor in protest at unfair taxation by the British government

1776 Britain takes New York City in the Battle of Long Island

1776 Declaration of Independence signed

1775 Second Continental Congress meets

3 NEW YORK AND NEW JERSEY CAMPAIGN 1776–1777

Britain won key victories in 1776 in the battles of Long Island and Fort Washington, taking control of New York City in the process. In December, General George Washington scored a morale-building win at the Battle of Trenton, reinforced by his success in the Battle of Princeton the following January.

▬ Campaign area

2 THE BATTLE OF BUNKER HILL JUNE 17, 1775

The first significant battle of the American Revolution took place in the hills around Boston. The Crown's victory against the newly formed Continental Army came at great cost—around 1,000 of the 2,500 British soldiers were killed. Despite their defeat, the inexperienced Patriot forces were encouraged by their performance in battle, which boded well for the future.

✕ Key battle

△ *The Battle of Bunker's Hill*, by John Trumbull
The artist, who served in the Continental Army and was present at Bunker Hill, painted this work in 1786. It shows the death in battle of the Patriot general, Joseph Warren.

1 THE BATTLES OF LEXINGTON AND CONCORD APRIL 18–19, 1775

The first shot of the war was fired in a skirmish on Lexington Green, Massachusetts, between 70 Patriot troops and 800 British "Redcoat" soldiers who were heading for nearby Concord to seize ammunition. In Concord, the British met another 500 "Minutemen" militia, who forced them to retreat.

✕ Key battles

THE CANADIAN THEATER

In September 1775, the Continental Army captured the Ticonderoga and Crown Point forts in the Province of New York and then moved on to Montreal, which they captured in November. They attacked Quebec City on December 31, but the British held them off. The Patriots regrouped and besieged the city, but British reinforcements drove them away in the spring of 1776.

KEY

⚑ Ships captured

Ħ Forts

✕ Key battles

┈ State lines

▢ Northern colonies

○ Settlements

MOVEMENT, WITH DATE AND LEADER NAME

→ British

→ Patriots

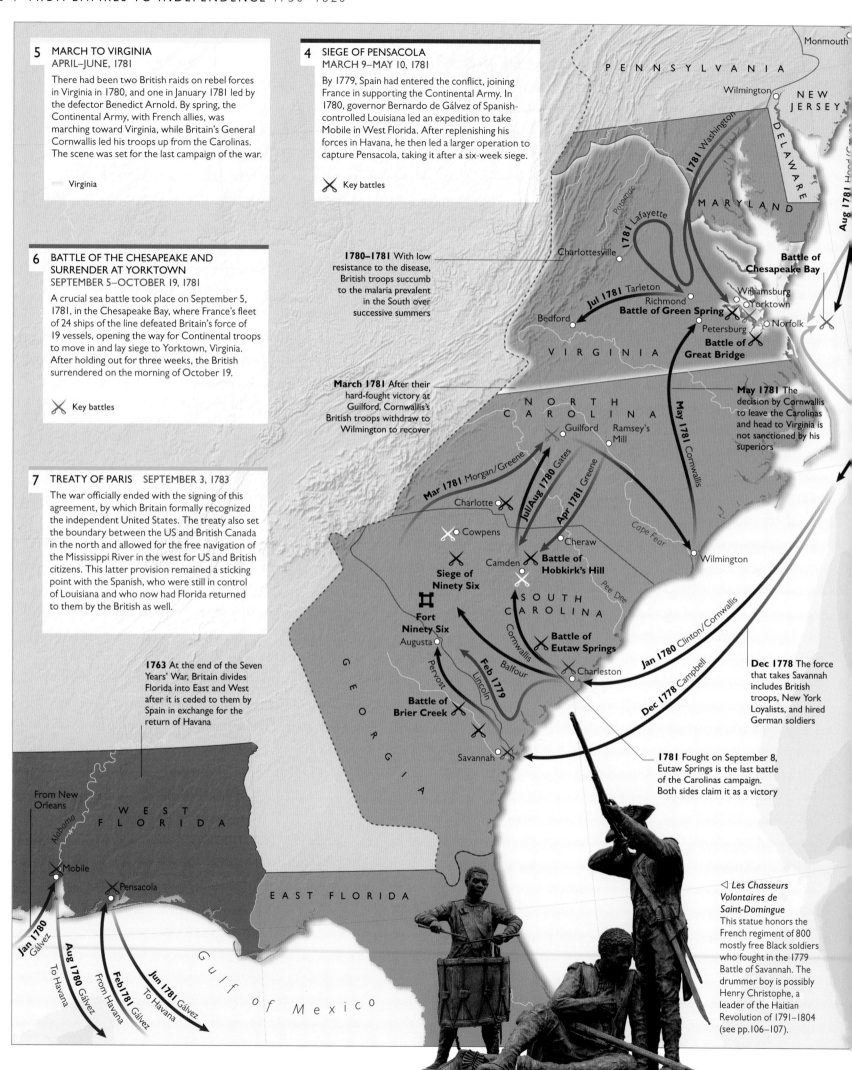

5 MARCH TO VIRGINIA
APRIL–JUNE, 1781

There had been two British raids on rebel forces in Virginia in 1780, and one in January 1781 led by the defector Benedict Arnold. By spring, the Continental Army, with French allies, was marching toward Virginia, while Britain's General Cornwallis led his troops up from the Carolinas. The scene was set for the last campaign of the war.

Virginia

4 SIEGE OF PENSACOLA
MARCH 9–MAY 10, 1781

By 1779, Spain had entered the conflict, joining France in supporting the Continental Army. In 1780, governor Bernardo de Gálvez of Spanish-controlled Louisiana led an expedition to take Mobile in West Florida. After replenishing his forces in Havana, he then led a larger operation to capture Pensacola, taking it after a six-week siege.

✕ Key battles

6 BATTLE OF THE CHESAPEAKE AND SURRENDER AT YORKTOWN
SEPTEMBER 5–OCTOBER 19, 1781

A crucial sea battle took place on September 5, 1781, in the Chesapeake Bay, where France's fleet of 24 ships of the line defeated Britain's force of 19 vessels, opening the way for Continental troops to move in and lay siege to Yorktown, Virginia. After holding out for three weeks, the British surrendered on the morning of October 19.

✕ Key battles

7 TREATY OF PARIS   SEPTEMBER 3, 1783

The war officially ended with the signing of this agreement, by which Britain formally recognized the independent United States. The treaty also set the boundary between the US and British Canada in the north and allowed for the free navigation of the Mississippi River in the west for US and British citizens. This latter provision remained a sticking point with the Spanish, who were still in control of Louisiana and who now had Florida returned to them by the British as well.

1763 At the end of the Seven Years' War, Britain divides Florida into East and West after it is ceded to them by Spain in exchange for the return of Havana

1780–1781 With low resistance to the disease, British troops succumb to the malaria prevalent in the South over successive summers

March 1781 After their hard-fought victory at Guilford, Cornwallis's British troops withdraw to Wilmington to recover

May 1781 The decision by Cornwallis to leave the Carolinas and head to Virginia is not sanctioned by his superiors

Dec 1778 The force that takes Savannah includes British troops, New York Loyalists, and hired German soldiers

1781 Fought on September 8, Eutaw Springs is the last battle of the Carolinas campaign. Both sides claim it as a victory

◁ *Les Chasseurs Volontaires de Saint-Domingue*
This statue honors the French regiment of 800 mostly free Black soldiers who fought in the 1779 Battle of Savannah. The drummer boy is possibly Henry Christophe, a leader of the Haitian Revolution of 1791–1804 (see pp.106–107).

Map labels

PENNSYLVANIA
NEW JERSEY
DELAWARE
MARYLAND
VIRGINIA
NORTH CAROLINA
SOUTH CAROLINA
GEORGIA
WEST FLORIDA
EAST FLORIDA
Gulf of Mexico

Monmouth
Wilmington
Aug 1781 Hood/Grave
1781 Washington
Potomac
Lafayette
Charlottesville
1781
Jul 1781 Tarleton
Richmond
Bedford
Battle of Green Spring
Williamsburg
Yorktown
Norfolk
Petersburg
Battle of Chesapeake Bay
Battle of Great Bridge
May 1781 Cornwallis
Guilford
Ramsey's Mill
Mar 1781 Morgan/Greene
Jul/Aug 1780 Gates
Apr 1781 Greene
Charlotte
Cowpens
Cheraw
Camden
Battle of Hobkirk's Hill
Cape Fear
Wilmington
Siege of Ninety Six
Fort Ninety Six
Augusta
Cornwallis
Battle of Eutaw Springs
Pee Dee
Jan 1780 Clinton/Cornwallis
Feb 1779
Balfour
Lincoln
Perysor
Charleston
Dec 1778 Campbell
Battle of Brier Creek
Savannah
From New Orleans
Alabama
Mobile
Pensacola
Jan 1780 Gálvez
To Havana
Aug 1780 Gálvez
From Havana
Feb 1781 Gálvez
Jun 1781 Gálvez
To Havana

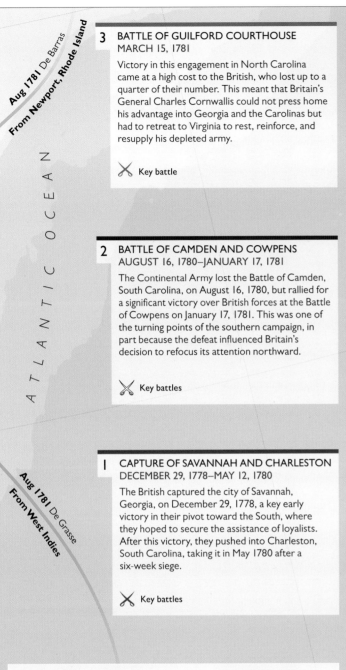

Aug 1781 De Barras
From Newport, Rhode Island

ATLANTIC OCEAN

3 BATTLE OF GUILFORD COURTHOUSE
MARCH 15, 1781

Victory in this engagement in North Carolina came at a high cost to the British, who lost up to a quarter of their number. This meant that Britain's General Charles Cornwallis could not press home his advantage into Georgia and the Carolinas but had to retreat to Virginia to rest, reinforce, and resupply his depleted army.

✕ Key battle

2 BATTLE OF CAMDEN AND COWPENS
AUGUST 16, 1780–JANUARY 17, 1781

The Continental Army lost the Battle of Camden, South Carolina, on August 16, 1780, but rallied for a significant victory over British forces at the Battle of Cowpens on January 17, 1781. This was one of the turning points of the southern campaign, in part because the defeat influenced Britain's decision to refocus its attention northward.

✕ Key battles

1 CAPTURE OF SAVANNAH AND CHARLESTON
DECEMBER 29, 1778–MAY 12, 1780

The British captured the city of Savannah, Georgia, on December 29, 1778, a key early victory in their pivot toward the South, where they hoped to secure the assistance of loyalists. After this victory, they pushed into Charleston, South Carolina, taking it in May 1780 after a six-week siege.

✕ Key battles

Aug 1781 De Grasse
From West Indies

SOUTHERN STRATEGIES
Britain's commanders turned south in late 1778, believing they could shore up loyalist support in the region. This strategic error resulted in British Army forces becoming trapped in Virginia in 1781.

KEY

▮ Southern colonies	╫ Fort	╌ Thirteen Colonies, 1775
▮ East Florida	— State lines	✕ Other battles
▮ West Florida	○ Settlements	

MOVEMENT, WITH DATE AND LEADER NAME
➡ British ➡ French ➡ Patriots ➡ Spanish

TIMELINE
1 2 3 4 5 6 7
1778 1779 1780 1781 1782 1783 1784

REVOLUTIONARY WAR IN THE SOUTH

The second phase of the American Revolution began with the British capture of Savannah. British southern strategy soon unraveled, as the Continental Army—along with French and Spanish allies—won victories that ultimately led to Britain's surrender.

After their defeat at Saratoga in 1777 (see pp.90–91), the British looked toward the South for their next campaign, believing supporters there could help them secure the region. It was a costly miscalculation. While British troops scored initial victories in Savannah and Charleston, it was soon evident that there was plenty of support for independence in the South.

Spain entered the conflict in 1779 on the side of the Continental Army and France, providing further challenges for the British. The Spanish had been quietly supplying arms and goods since the start of the war, but in 1780–1781 Louisiana governor Bernardo de Gálvez launched attacks in West Florida, taking Mobile and Pensacola from the British.

In early 1781, the British suffered a costly defeat at the battle of Cowpens and a narrow, Pyrrhic victory at Guilford Courthouse that led their forces to turn back toward Virginia. By September, George Washington was moving his forces south, with plans to lay siege to the British garrison at Yorktown. There, on October 19, 1781, the Continental Army joined the French navy to secure final victory over the British.

"We are at the end of our tether, and now or never, our deliverance must come."

GEORGE WASHINGTON TO COL. JOHN LAURENS, APRIL 9, 1781

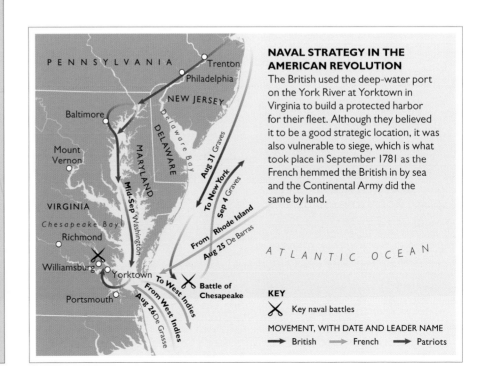

NAVAL STRATEGY IN THE AMERICAN REVOLUTION

The British used the deep-water port on the York River at Yorktown in Virginia to build a protected harbor for their fleet. Although they believed it to be a good strategic location, it was also vulnerable to siege, which is what took place in September 1781 as the French hemmed the British in by sea and the Continental Army did the same by land.

KEY

✕ Key naval battles

MOVEMENT, WITH DATE AND LEADER NAME
➡ British ➡ French ➡ Patriots

THE BIRTH OF THE UNITED STATES

The peace conference in Paris, France, that ended the American Revolution established the borders of the new nation. However, there were ongoing boundary disputes with rival colonial powers as well as with Indigenous communities, who had not been represented at the treaty negotiations.

After the US won its independence from Britain, it almost doubled in size under the terms of the 1783 Treaty of Paris. This accord set the boundary of the US along the entire length of the Mississippi River, from its source in present-day Minnesota to its mouth in the Gulf of Mexico. However, this vast area was Indigenous land, which was home to, among others, the Chickasaw and the Choctaw in the south and the Anishinaabe (know in the period of the map as "Chipawas") around the Great Lakes in the north. Many Indigenous communities had supported the British during the war and felt betrayed by the terms agreed in the treaty.

The US also found itself bordered by Britain and its Canadian territory, and by Spain, which regained Florida and retained the rest of its vast holdings beyond the Mississippi River. The newly-formed country soon faced problems in all directions. To the north, there was a disagreement with Britain over the border of Maine. To the west, in the territory between the 13 colonies and the new boundary, Indigenous residents resisted the arrival of US colonists looking for land. Spain, too, would be a source of tensions, including a diplomatic fight over the location of the US–Florida border and heated negotiations over access rights for US shipping on the Spanish-controlled Mississippi River (See below).

While the Treaty of Paris ended one major conflict, it left the US with several smaller—but nonetheless troublesome—disputes that ran for decades to come.

KEY

1 Indigenous people clashed with settlers arriving west of the Appalachian Mountains.

2 Florida was ceded back to Spain after being under British rule from 1763–1783.

3 Spain continued to control the vast Louisiana territory until 1801.

4 The boundary between Maine and British Canada (in modern New Brunswick) was disputed until 1842, in part due to imprecise wording in the Treaty of Paris.

LOCATOR

◁ **The US after the 1783 Treaty of Paris**
The agreements reached in 1783 in the French capital defined the borders of the newly formed US, extending its western frontier from the eastern seaboard across to the banks of the Mississippi River.

TREATY OF PARIS AND PINCKNEY'S TREATY
The Treaty of Paris in 1783 dramatically redrew the map of North America, so the new United State stretched from the Atlantic coast to the Mississippi River. Twelve years later, the Treaty of San Lorenzo (also known as Pinckney's Treaty) set the southern boundary and gave the US a commercial boost by allowing its merchant and trading ships access to the Mississippi River, which was then still under Spanish control.

KEY

- Spanish possessions
- British North America
- United States
- Area disputed with Spain before 1795
- Line of Pinckney's Treaty, 1795

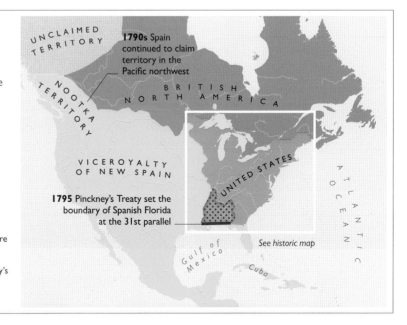

UNCLAIMED TERRITORY

1790s Spain continued to claim territory in the Pacific northwest

NOOTKA TERRITORY

BRITISH NORTH AMERICA

VICEROYALTY OF NEW SPAIN

1795 Pinckney's Treaty set the boundary of Spanish Florida at the 31st parallel

UNITED STATES

ATLANTIC OCEAN

See historic map

Gulf of Mexico

Cuba

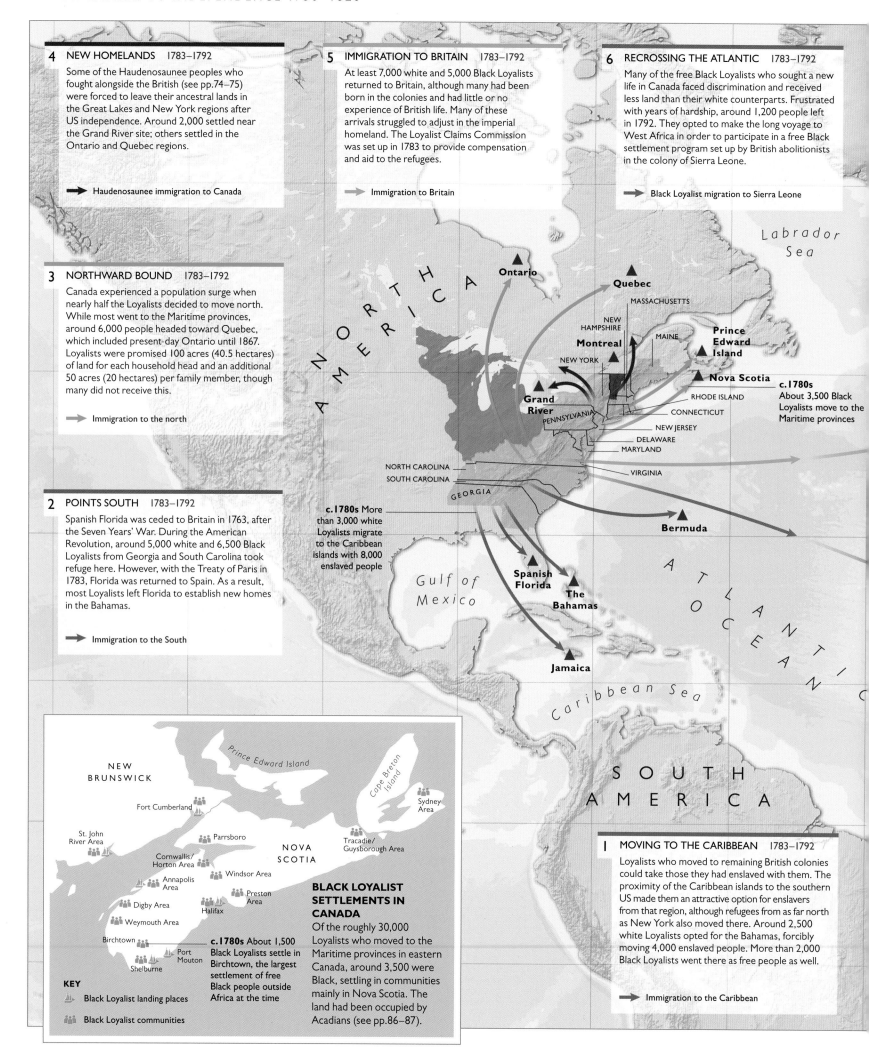

4 NEW HOMELANDS 1783–1792

Some of the Haudenosaunee peoples who fought alongside the British (see pp.74–75) were forced to leave their ancestral lands in the Great Lakes and New York regions after US independence. Around 2,000 settled near the Grand River site; others settled in the Ontario and Quebec regions.

➤ Haudenosaunee immigration to Canada

5 IMMIGRATION TO BRITAIN 1783–1792

At least 7,000 white and 5,000 Black Loyalists returned to Britain, although many had been born in the colonies and had little or no experience of British life. Many of these arrivals struggled to adjust in the imperial homeland. The Loyalist Claims Commission was set up in 1783 to provide compensation and aid to the refugees.

➤ Immigration to Britain

6 RECROSSING THE ATLANTIC 1783–1792

Many of the free Black Loyalists who sought a new life in Canada faced discrimination and received less land than their white counterparts. Frustrated with years of hardship, around 1,200 people left in 1792. They opted to make the long voyage to West Africa in order to participate in a free Black settlement program set up by British abolitionists in the colony of Sierra Leone.

➤ Black Loyalist migration to Sierra Leone

3 NORTHWARD BOUND 1783–1792

Canada experienced a population surge when nearly half the Loyalists decided to move north. While most went to the Maritime provinces, around 6,000 people headed toward Quebec, which included present-day Ontario until 1867. Loyalists were promised 100 acres (40.5 hectares) of land for each household head and an additional 50 acres (20 hectares) per family member, though many did not receive this.

➤ Immigration to the north

2 POINTS SOUTH 1783–1792

Spanish Florida was ceded to Britain in 1763, after the Seven Years' War. During the American Revolution, around 5,000 white and 6,500 Black Loyalists from Georgia and South Carolina took refuge here. However, with the Treaty of Paris in 1783, Florida was returned to Spain. As a result, most Loyalists left Florida to establish new homes in the Bahamas.

➤ Immigration to the South

c.1780s More than 3,000 white Loyalists migrate to the Caribbean islands with 8,000 enslaved people

c.1780s About 3,500 Black Loyalists move to the Maritime provinces

Map labels

NORTH AMERICA

Labrador Sea

Ontario
Quebec
MASSACHUSETTS
NEW HAMPSHIRE
MAINE
Prince Edward Island
Montreal
NEW YORK
Nova Scotia
Grand River
RHODE ISLAND
PENNSYLVANIA
CONNECTICUT
NEW JERSEY
DELAWARE
MARYLAND
VIRGINIA
NORTH CAROLINA
SOUTH CAROLINA
GEORGIA
Bermuda

Gulf of Mexico

Spanish Florida
The Bahamas
Jamaica

ATLANTIC OCEAN

Caribbean Sea

SOUTH AMERICA

BLACK LOYALIST SETTLEMENTS IN CANADA

Of the roughly 30,000 Loyalists who moved to the Maritime provinces in eastern Canada, around 3,500 were Black, settling in communities mainly in Nova Scotia. The land had been occupied by Acadians (see pp.86–87).

Inset map labels

NEW BRUNSWICK
Prince Edward Island
Cape Breton Island
Sydney Area
Fort Cumberland
St. John River Area
Parrsboro
NOVA SCOTIA
Tracadie/ Guysborough Area
Cornwallis/ Horton Area
Windsor Area
Annapolis Area
Digby Area
Preston Area
Halifax
Weymouth Area
Birchtown
Port Mouton
Shelburne

c.1780s About 1,500 Black Loyalists settle in Birchtown, the largest settlement of free Black people outside Africa at the time

KEY

⚓ Black Loyalist landing places

👪 Black Loyalist communities

1 MOVING TO THE CARIBBEAN 1783–1792

Loyalists who moved to remaining British colonies could take those they had enslaved with them. The proximity of the Caribbean islands to the southern US made them an attractive option for enslavers from that region, although refugees from as far north as New York also moved there. Around 2,500 white Loyalists opted for the Bahamas, forcibly moving 4,000 enslaved people. More than 2,000 Black Loyalists went there as free people as well.

➤ Immigration to the Caribbean

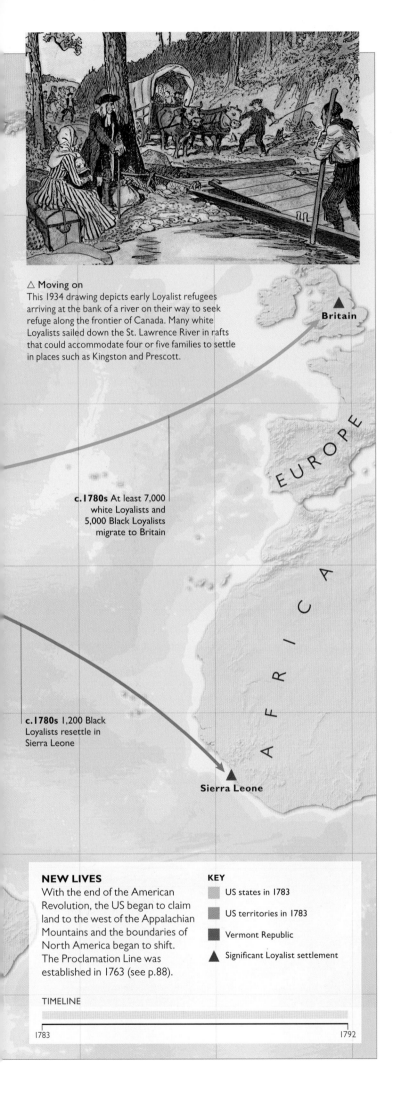

△ **Moving on**
This 1934 drawing depicts early Loyalist refugees arriving at the bank of a river on their way to seek refuge along the frontier of Canada. Many white Loyalists sailed down the St. Lawrence River in rafts that could accommodate four or five families to settle in places such as Kingston and Prescott.

Britain

EUROPE

c.1780s At least 7,000 white Loyalists and 5,000 Black Loyalists migrate to Britain

AFRICA

c.1780s 1,200 Black Loyalists resettle in Sierra Leone

Sierra Leone

NEW LIVES
With the end of the American Revolution, the US began to claim land to the west of the Appalachian Mountains and the boundaries of North America began to shift. The Proclamation Line was established in 1763 (see p.88).

KEY
- US states in 1783
- US territories in 1783
- Vermont Republic
- ▲ Significant Loyalist settlement

TIMELINE

1783   1792

LOYALIST MIGRATIONS

The American Revolution heralded the birth of a new nation, but it also gave rise to an uncertain future for the people in North America who had sided with Britain. Up to 100,000 of them, including thousands of Black Loyalists, left the US to rebuild their lives elsewhere.

The American Revolution left the victors with a new nation to organize (see pp.100–101). However, the newly formed United States was inhabited in part by many thousands of defeated combatants, as well as civilians who remained loyal to the British cause. In the end, around 80,000 to 100,000 Loyalists decided to leave.

A large contingent of Black Loyalists, many of whom had served in the army, left for Nova Scotia (see opposite), while thousands of other Black Loyalists went elsewhere, including the Bahamas and Britain. Around 2,000 Indigenous allies also settled in Canada. At the same time, white Loyalists could take those

they had enslaved with them, and so thousands more Black people were forcibly moved. Another estimated 20,000 enslaved people used the chaos of the conflict to seek freedom.

Historians have not been able to agree on final numbers, partly because the exodus and arrival of Loyalists were not systematically recorded across all the places they sought refuge, but estimates illustrate profound shifts. Loyalist arrivals altered the fortunes of many places, including the Maritime provinces of Canada, which saw their populations boom, and the Bahamas, where southern enslavers pushed the islands toward a plantation economy.

> "The place is beyond description wretched ... I think I never saw such wretchedness and poverty."
>
> VISITOR TO BIRCHTOWN, NOVA SCOTIA, 1788

UPPER AND LOWER CANADA

After the American Revolution, there was an influx of Loyalists into Canada, which already had a large French population. In an attempt to better organize this diverse population, the British government passed the Constitutional Act of 1791. This divided Canada into the predominantly French and Catholic Lower Canada (Quebec) and the mostly British and Protestant Upper Canada (present-day Ontario), each with its own provincial legislature. The Maritime provinces of New Brunswick, Nova Scotia, and Prince Edward Island joined them to form a confederated Dominion of Canada in 1867.

A 20th-century painting depicting the Legislative Assembly of Lower Canada, 1793

BRITISH CANADA

Canada experienced profound social transformations in the decades after the American Revolution, with Loyalists flocking to the colony rapidly altering the population. British colonial authorities used political means to exert control over French and Indigenous populations.

During the Seven Years' War (see pp.84–85), British forces expelled thousands of French Acadians from Nova Scotia between 1755 and 1764 because of their suspected disloyalty. With the ceding of France's Canadian territory to Britain in 1763, authorities and new French subjects of the British king struggled to define the new colony. With the Quebec Act of 1774, Britain attempted to win the loyalty of the French-speaking majority by protecting Catholic worship and reinstituting French property claims under British law.

British attitudes to Canada's Indigenous populations were never so conciliatory, and would lead to repression of their cultural, linguistic, religious, and geographical freedoms (see p.209). Large areas remained untouched by colonists, with few venturing to northern and western Canada in this era.

Britain's defeat in the American Revolution and the arrival of tens of thousands of Loyalists in Canada presented another challenge. In the Constitution Act of 1791, Britain divided the province of Quebec into Upper Canada (roughly today's southern Ontario), where many Loyalists settled, and Lower Canada (St. Lawrence River Valley), which was heavily French,

giving each group its own legislature (see p.97). The Act also strengthened the role of governor, thus tightening colonial ties to London.

At the same time Britain was in an ongoing bitter dispute with Spain over control of the valuable fur trade near Nootka Sound (see p.104). It took multiple rounds of treaty negotiations to avoid war.

KEY

1 Nootka Sound was where Captain James Cook encountered the Nuu-chah-nulth people in 1778, and where the British interfered in trade, angering Spain and almost leading to war in 1789.

2 Upper Canada was already home to many Indigenous communities when British Loyalists arrived.

3 Lower Canada remained populated by a sizable French-speaking community.

LOCATOR

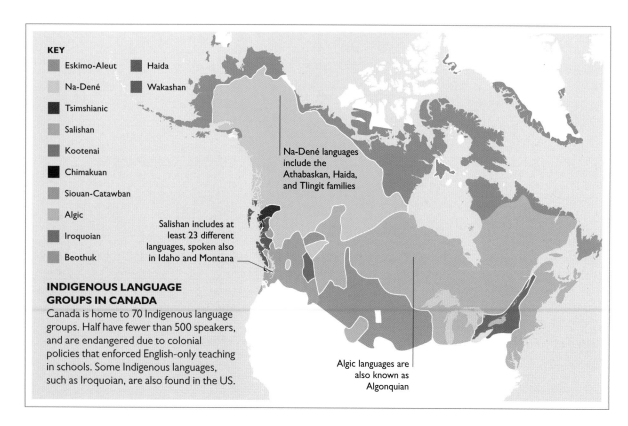

KEY
- Eskimo-Aleut
- Na-Dené
- Tsimshianic
- Salishan
- Kootenai
- Chimakuan
- Siouan-Catawban
- Algic
- Iroquoian
- Beothuk
- Haida
- Wakashan

Na-Dené languages include the Athabaskan, Haida, and Tlingit families

Salishan includes at least 23 different languages, spoken also in Idaho and Montana

Algic languages are also known as Algonquian

INDIGENOUS LANGUAGE GROUPS IN CANADA
Canada is home to 70 Indigenous language groups. Half have fewer than 500 speakers, and are endangered due to colonial policies that enforced English-only teaching in schools. Some Indigenous languages, such as Iroquoian, are also found in the US.

△ **Map of British North America**
This 1855 map shows the territorial extent of British Canada, reaching from the border of the US into the Arctic. Colonists from Europe and the US were mostly concentrated in the south, though the fur and lumber trade took them to all parts. Indigenous peoples continued to live throughout the region.

"A great many settlers come daily from the United States, some even from
the Carolinas, about 2,000 miles."

ELIZABETH SIMCOE, *THE DIARY OF MRS. SIMCOE*, 1911 (WRITTEN IN 1792–1796)

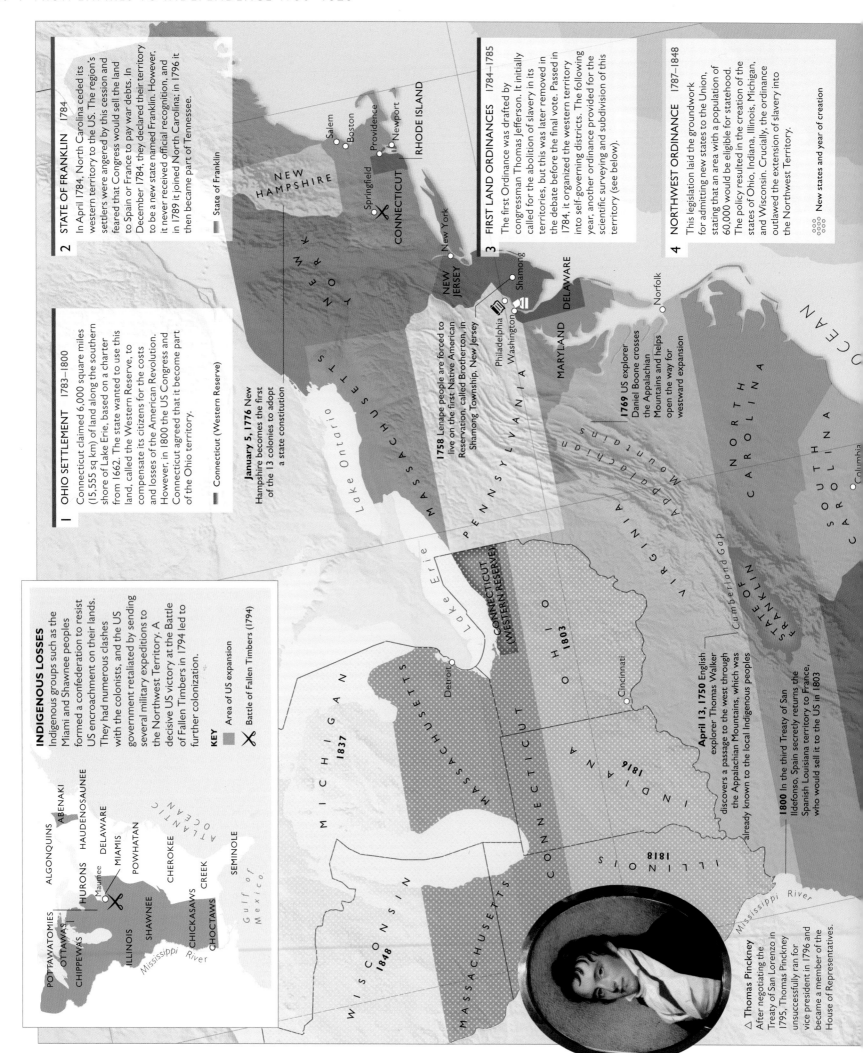

1 OHIO SETTLEMENT 1783–1800

Connecticut claimed 6,000 square miles (15,555 sq km) of land along the southern shore of Lake Erie, based on a charter from 1662. The state wanted to use this land, called the Western Reserve, to compensate its citizens for the costs and losses of the American Revolution. However, in 1800 the US Congress and Connecticut agreed that it become part of the Ohio territory.

 Connecticut (Western Reserve)

January 5, 1776 New Hampshire becomes the first of the 13 colonies to adopt a state constitution

2 STATE OF FRANKLIN 1784

In April 1784, North Carolina ceded its western territory to the US. The region's settlers were angered by this cession and feared that Congress would sell the land to Spain or France to pay war debts. In December 1784, they declared their territory to be a new state named Franklin. However, it never received official recognition, and in 1789 it joined North Carolina; in 1796 it then became part of Tennessee.

 State of Franklin

3 FIRST LAND ORDINANCES 1784–1785

The first Ordinance was drafted by congressman Thomas Jefferson. It initially called for the abolition of slavery in its territories, but this was later removed in the debate before the final vote. Passed in 1784, it organized the western territory into self-governing districts. The following year, another ordinance provided for the scientific surveying and subdivision of this territory (see below).

1758 Lenape people are forced to live on the first Native American Reservation, called Brotherton, in Shamong Township, New Jersey

1769 US explorer Daniel Boone crosses the Appalachian Mountains and helps open the way for westward expansion

4 NORTHWEST ORDINANCE 1787–1848

This legislation laid the groundwork for admitting new states to the Union, stating that an area with a population of 60,000 would be eligible for statehood. The policy resulted in the creation of the states of Ohio, Indiana, Illinois, Michigan, and Wisconsin. Crucially, the ordinance outlawed the extension of slavery into the Northwest Territory.

 New states and year of creation

INDIGENOUS LOSSES

Indigenous groups such as the Miami and Shawnee peoples formed a confederation to resist US encroachment on their lands. They had numerous clashes with the colonists, and the US government retaliated by sending several military expeditions to the Northwest Territory. A decisive US victory at the Battle of Fallen Timbers in 1794 led to further colonization.

KEY

 Area of US expansion

✂ Battle of Fallen Timbers (1794)

POTTAWATOMIES
OTTAWAS
CHIPPEWAS
ALGONQUINS
ABENAKI
HAUDENOSAUNEE
HURONS
DELAWARE
MIAMIS
POWHATAN
Maumee
ILLINOIS
SHAWNEE
CHEROKEE
CHICKASAWS
CREEK
CHOCTAWS
SEMINOLE

Gulf of Mexico
Mississippi River
ATLANTIC OCEAN

April 13, 1750 English explorer Thomas Walker discovers a passage to the west through the Appalachian Mountains, which was already known to the local Indigenous peoples

1800 In the third Treaty of San Ildefonso, Spain secretly returns the Spanish Louisiana territory to France, who would sell it to the US in 1803

△ **Thomas Pinckney**
After negotiating the Treaty of San Lorenzo in 1795, Thomas Pinckney unsuccessfully ran for vice president in 1796 and became a member of the House of Representatives.

Lake Ontario

Lake Erie

CONNECTICUT RESERVE (WESTERN RESERVE)

NEW HAMPSHIRE
NEW YORK
MASSACHUSETTS
CONNECTICUT
RHODE ISLAND
Salem
Boston
Providence
Newport
Springfield
New York
NEW JERSEY
Shamong
PENNSYLVANIA
Philadelphia
Washington
DELAWARE
MARYLAND
Norfolk
VIRGINIA
NORTH CAROLINA
SOUTH CAROLINA
Columbia
Appalachian Mountains
Cumberland Gap
FRANKLIN

MICHIGAN 1837
WISCONSIN 1848
MASSACHUSETTS
CONNECTICUT
Detroit
OHIO 1803
Cincinnati
INDIANA 1816
ILLINOIS 1818
Mississippi River

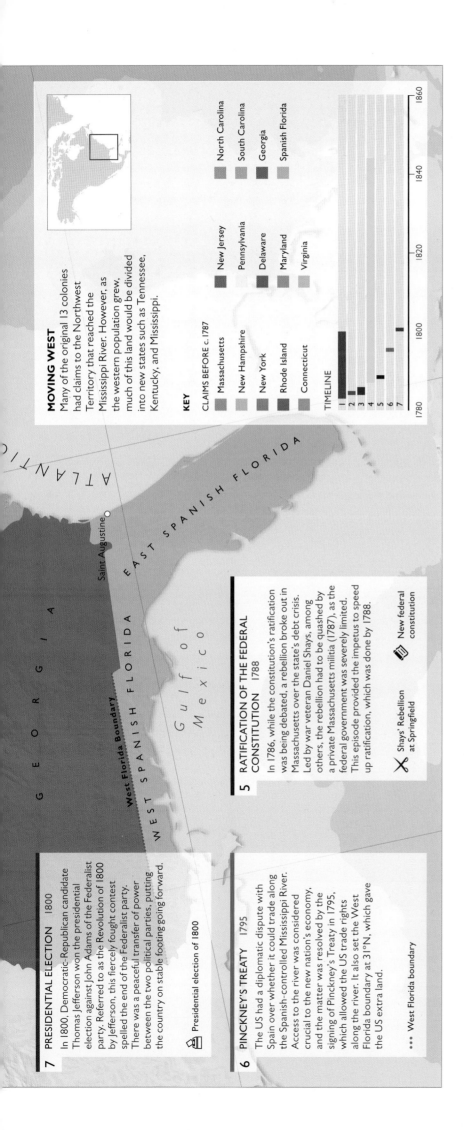

MOVING WEST

Many of the original 13 colonies had claims to the Northwest Territory that reached the Mississippi River. However, as the western population grew, much of this land would be divided into new states such as Tennessee, Kentucky, and Mississippi.

KEY

CLAIMS BEFORE c.1787

Massachusetts	New Jersey
New Hampshire	Pennsylvania
New York	Delaware
Rhode Island	Maryland
Connecticut	Virginia

North Carolina
South Carolina
Georgia
Spanish Florida

TIMELINE

1
2
3
4
5
6
7

1780   1800   1820   1840   1860

---

7 PRESIDENTIAL ELECTION 1800

In 1800, Democratic-Republican candidate Thomas Jefferson won the presidential election against John Adams of the Federalist party. Referred to as the Revolution of 1800 by Jefferson, this fiercely fought contest spelled the end of the Federalist party. There was a peaceful transfer of power between the two political parties, putting the country on stable footing going forward.

🏛 Presidential election of 1800

6 PINCKNEY'S TREATY 1795

The US had a diplomatic dispute with Spain over whether it could trade along the Spanish-controlled Mississippi River. Access to the river was considered crucial to the new nation's economy, and the matter was resolved by the signing of Pinckney's Treaty in 1795, which allowed the US trade rights along the river. It also set the West Florida boundary at 31°N, which gave the US extra land.

··· West Florida boundary

5 RATIFICATION OF THE FEDERAL CONSTITUTION 1788

In 1786, while the constitution's ratification was being debated, a rebellion broke out in Massachusetts over the state's debt crisis. Led by war veteran Daniel Shays, among others, the rebellion had to be quashed by a private Massachusetts militia (1787), as the federal government was severely limited. This episode provided the impetus to speed up ratification, which was done by 1788.

✂ Shays' Rebellion at Springfield

📖 New federal constitution

LAND CLAIMS AND GOVERNANCE

From the 1780s, the new nation of the United States faced the logistical challenge of organizing its new lands and its own government, both of which were fraught with disputes and setbacks.

The Treaty of Paris (see pp.94–95) had granted the US a large territory to the west, most of which had already been claimed by some of the original 13 colonies. Settlers began to push into the new areas, especially the Northwest Territory—north and west of the Ohio River. Ordinances were drawn up to organize this process, such as the Northwest Ordinance (1787) prohibiting slavery in the area. In 1787, delegates met in Philadelphia and drafted a new constitution. The process of ratification dragged out, with some anti-Federalist states opposing it, but was concluded in 1789. This allowed a more powerful federal government to form, with George Washington as its first

president, and promoted western settlement. The expansion of territory created as many problems as it did opportunities. Settlers were involved in constant conflict with Indigenous peoples who rejected US claims on the lands reserved for them (see pp.88–89). After a number of battles and raids, the Treaty of Greenville in 1795 brokered a short-lived peace that crumbled as the US continued its expansion.

The presidential election of 1800 saw the victorious Thomas Jefferson selected by the House of Representatives following a tie in votes. It marked a turning point in US politics and ushered in an era of Democratic–Republican rule that favored territorial expansion.

PUBLIC LAND SURVEY SYSTEM

This map shows three counties in Ohio surveyed under the Land Ordinance of 1785, which laid the basis for all land surveying in the US. The resulting maps were used to divide land that was going up for sale, initially in the Northwest Territory. The grid system used on this map was common, as land was divided into townships and then subdivided into lots for sale.

ATLANTIC

EAST SPANISH FLORIDA

Saint Augustine

GEORGIA

West Florida Boundary

WEST SPANISH FLORIDA

Gulf of Mexico

EXPANSION AND REVOLUTION

The creation of the US was followed by other revolutions, ushering in a turbulent period throughout North America. With the US purchase of French Louisiana and Spanish efforts to colonize California, frontiers were being redefined in the west.

The era of upheaval in the Americas that followed the creation of the US is often known as the "Age of Revolution." The next significant independence struggle took place in Saint-Domingue (present-day Haiti), France's prized sugar colony in the Caribbean. This conflict, which became known as the Haitian Revolution, erupted in 1791 (see pp.106–107). It followed the French Revolution, which had begun in 1789 and whose motto *liberté, égalité, fraternité* (liberty, equality, and fraternity) had a particular resonance on an island with 500,000 enslaved people. The struggle for Haitian independence lasted 13 years, led by two formerly enslaved men—Toussaint L'Ouverture and, after his death, Jean-Jacques Dessalines. The creation of an independent Haiti had one very crucial difference to the foundation of the US—full emancipation for the enslaved population. This was made clear in the constitution adopted in 1805 with the words "slavery is forever abolished." It would be decades before any of Haiti's neighbors followed suit.

◁ **Fighting for freedom**
This 19th-century painting depicts Haitian leader Jean-Jacques Dessalines leading his troops to victory against the French in 1803, securing independence for Haiti.

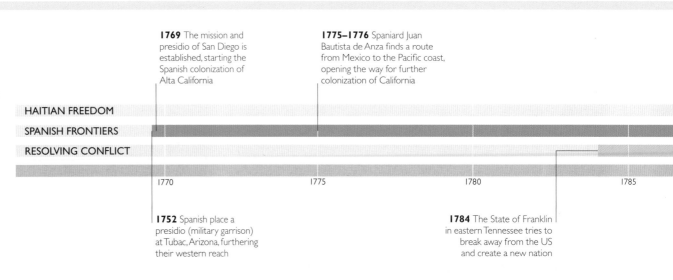

△ **Indigenous artifact**
This basket was made by Pomo artisans, one of the many Indigenous groups in California during Spanish colonization in the late 18th century.

Spanish losses

Spain had claimed the lands along the Pacific coast of North America through the Treaty of Tordesillas (1494) but did not explore the region much. In the 1770s, threatened by the southward expansion of the Russian and British fur trade in Alaska, Spain began to establish settlements in Alta California (see pp.104–105), trading and warring with the Indigenous communities along the way.

In 1808, when French emperor Napoleon Bonaparte placed his brother, Joseph, on the Spanish throne, it wreaked havoc in Spain and throughout Spanish America, as Spain's colonies began debating their futures. Mexico was the first to break away under the leadership of Miguel Hidalgo y Costilla. His *Grito de Dolores* (Cry of Dolores)—a rallying call for independence made in 1810 from Dolores, a small town in Mexico—became the first salvo to be fired in what became a battle for independence throughout Spain's colonies. By the 1820s, most of Spanish America had gained independence, with the exception of Cuba

NEW FRONTIERS AND POLITICAL CLASHES

Spain started establishing settlements in California by the late-18th century, but by the start of the 19th century, its empire had begun to disintegrate. Many Spanish-American colonies became independent, joining new countries such as the US (1776) and Haiti (1804). However, there were continued threats and interference from European powers for some time, often resulting in conflicts, such as the War of 1812 between the US and Britain.

1769 The mission and presidio of San Diego is established, starting the Spanish colonization of Alta California

1775–1776 Spaniard Juan Bautista de Anza finds a route from Mexico to the Pacific coast, opening the way for further colonization of California

HAITIAN FREEDOM

SPANISH FRONTIERS

RESOLVING CONFLICT

1770   1775   1780   1785

1752 Spanish place a presidio (military garrison) at Tubac, Arizona, furthering their western reach

1784 The State of Franklin in eastern Tennessee tries to break away from the US and create a new nation

◁ **Igniting a revolution**
This 1937 work by Mexican muralist José Clemente Orozco depicts national hero Padre Miguel Hidalgo y Costilla waving his fiery torch of revolution at the colonial enslavers and oppressors.

and Puerto Rico. Santo Domingo, Spain's oldest colony, was under Haitian rule from 1822 to 1844, after which it became the independent Dominican Republic.

Growing pains
The newly created US had to weather its own challenges during this time. Barbary pirates were holding American ships to ransom in the Mediterranean, demanding large tributes for their safe passage. In the early 19th century, the US fought a series of battles at sea against the Barbary states to end this extortion (see pp.108–109). The US also went to war with Britain in 1812 over naval matters. Britain was impressing, or forcefully recruiting, US vessels—and sometimes sailors—to aid its navy in the Napoleonic Wars (1799–1815). Moreover, Britain tried to restrict the US from trading with France. These provocations turned into a full-scale war between the two nations, which ended in a bloody stalemate. The US

territory greatly expanded during this period, nearly doubling in size, with Napoleon Bonaparte selling the vast French Louisiana territory to the US in 1803 to manage the cost of battling the revolution in Haiti and funding the impending war against Britain.

▷ **War uniform**
This uniform was worn by US general Andrew Jackson during the Battle of New Orleans (1815)—the final battle in the War of 1812. Later, he entered public life, and became the US president in 1829.

"Yes, I have saved my country—I have avenged America. The avowal I made of it in the face of earth and heaven, constitutes my pride and my glory."

JEAN-JACQUES DESSALINES, HAITIAN DECLARATION OF INDEPENDENCE, JUNE 12, 1804

1789 The French Revolution begins in France, and news of it spreads to its colonies

1791 Enslaved people rise up in France's Caribbean colony of Saint-Domingue

1794 The French governor abolishes slavery in Saint-Domingue

1795 A number of revolts—mostly concerning slavery—take place across the Caribbean, including in Jamaica, St.Vincent, Venezuela, and Curaçao

1802 Napoleon sends an expeditionary force to Saint-Domingue to reassert control

1804 The independent nation of Haiti is established, and slavery is entirely abolished—becoming the first country in the Americas to do so

1812 Britain wages another war with the US on land and at sea

1794 Haitian general Toussaint L'Ouverture quits fighting for Spain

1799 L'Ouverture consolidates his control of Saint-Domingue after suppressing internal strife

1800 Spain returns the Louisiana territory to France in a secret deal with Napoleon Bonaparte, who sells it to the US for $15 million, in part to pay for the war in Haiti

1801 L'Ouverture declares himself governor of Hispaniola for life and issues a constitution

1803 L'Ouverture dies in a prison in France. Jean-Jacques Dessalines assumes command, driving off the French

1810 Mexican priest Miguel Hidalgo y Costilla starts the Mexican fight for independence from Spain

1815 The end of the second Barbary war stops long-running North African piracy attacks on the US vessels in the Mediterranean

1790 1795 1800 1805 1810 1815

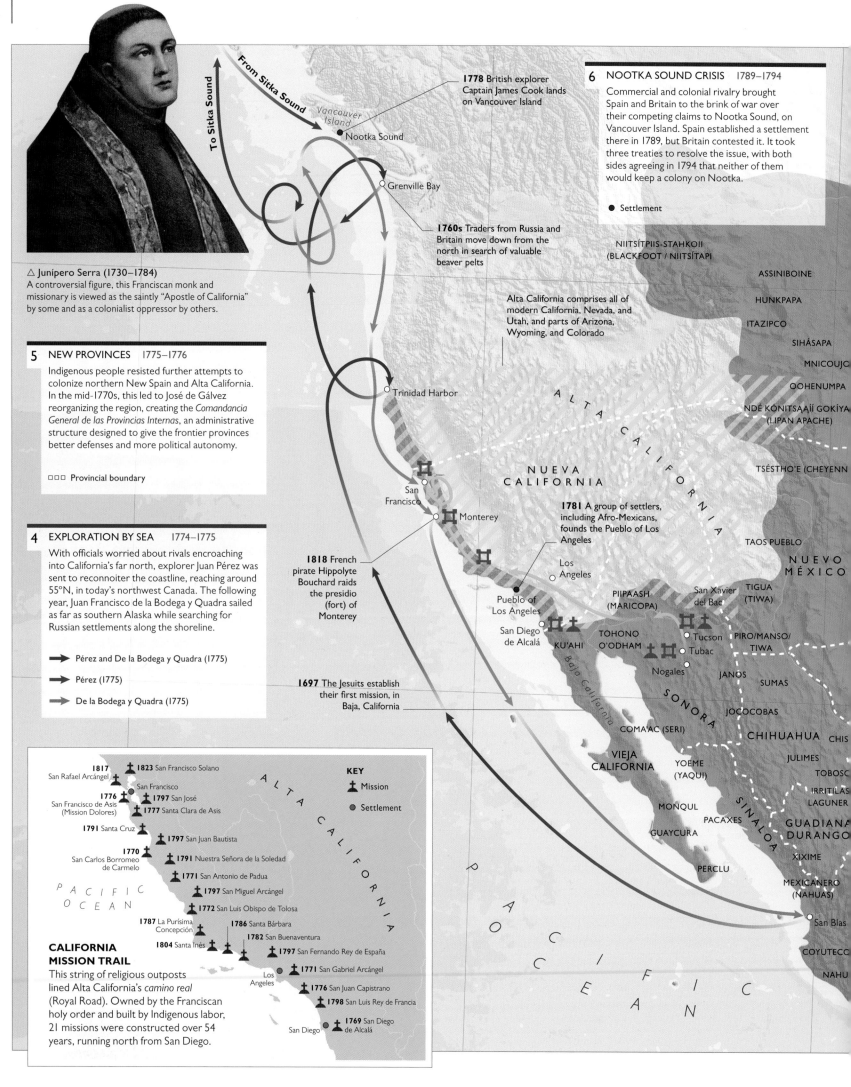

104

1778 British explorer Captain James Cook lands on Vancouver Island

Vancouver Island

Nootka Sound

From Sitka Sound

To Sitka Sound

Grenville Bay

1760s Traders from Russia and Britain move down from the north in search of valuable beaver pelts

6 NOOTKA SOUND CRISIS 1789–1794

Commercial and colonial rivalry brought Spain and Britain to the brink of war over their competing claims to Nootka Sound, on Vancouver Island. Spain established a settlement there in 1789, but Britain contested it. It took three treaties to resolve the issue, with both sides agreeing in 1794 that neither of them would keep a colony on Nootka.

● Settlement

NIITSÍTPIIS-STAHKOII
(BLACKFOOT / NIITSÍTAPI)

ASSINIBOINE

HUNKPAPA

ITAZIPCO

SIHÁSAPA

MNICOUJO

OOHENUMPA

NDÉ KÓNITSAAÍÍ GOKÍYA
(LIPAN APACHE)

TSÉSTHO'E (CHEYENN

△ **Junípero Serra (1730–1784)**
A controversial figure, this Franciscan monk and missionary is viewed as the saintly "Apostle of California" by some and as a colonialist oppressor by others.

Alta California comprises all of modern California, Nevada, and Utah, and parts of Arizona, Wyoming, and Colorado

5 NEW PROVINCES 1775–1776

Indigenous people resisted further attempts to colonize northern New Spain and Alta California. In the mid-1770s, this led to José de Gálvez reorganizing the region, creating the *Comandancia General de las Provincias Internas*, an administrative structure designed to give the frontier provinces better defenses and more political autonomy.

□□□ Provincial boundary

Trinidad Harbor

A L T A   C A L I F O R N I A

N U E V A
C A L I F O R N I A

San Francisco

Monterey

1818 French pirate Hippolyte Bouchard raids the presidio (fort) of Monterey

4 EXPLORATION BY SEA 1774–1775

With officials worried about rivals encroaching into California's far north, explorer Juan Pérez was sent to reconnoiter the coastline, reaching around 55°N, in today's northwest Canada. The following year, Juan Francisco de la Bodega y Quadra sailed as far as southern Alaska while searching for Russian settlements along the shoreline.

➤ Pérez and De la Bodega y Quadra (1775)

➤ Pérez (1775)

➤ De la Bodega y Quadra (1775)

1781 A group of settlers, including Afro-Mexicans, founds the Pueblo of Los Angeles

Los Angeles

Pueblo of Los Angeles

San Diego de Alcalá

KU'AHI

PIIPAASH
(MARICOPA)

TOHONO
O'ODHAM

Nogales

San Xavier del Bac

Tucson

Tubac

TIGUA
(TIWA)

PIRO/MANSO/
TIWA

JANOS

SUMAS

N U E V O
M É X I C O

TAOS PUEBLO

1697 The Jesuits establish their first mission, in Baja, California

Baja California

COMA'AC (SERI)

VIEJA
CALIFORNIA

YOEME
(YAQUI)

MONQUI

PACAXES

GUAYCURA

PERCLU

S O N O R A

JOCOCOBAS

CHIHUAHUA   CHIS

JULIMES

TOBOSO

IRRITILAS
LAGUNER

S I N A L O A

GUADIANA
DURANGO

XIXIME

MEXICANERO
(NAHUAS)

San Blas

COYUTEC

NAHU

CALIFORNIA MISSION TRAIL

A L T A   C A L I F O R N I A

KEY

✝ Mission

● Settlement

1817 San Rafael Arcángel

✝ **1823** San Francisco Solano

San Francisco

1776 San Francisco de Asis (Mission Dolores)

✝ **1797** San José

✝ **1777** Santa Clara de Asis

1791 Santa Cruz

1770 San Carlos Borromeo de Carmelo

✝ **1797** San Juan Bautista

✝ **1791** Nuestra Señora de la Soledad

✝ **1771** San Antonio de Padua

✝ **1797** San Miguel Arcángel

✝ **1772** San Luis Obispo de Tolosa

1787 La Purísima Concepción

1786 Santa Bárbara

1804 Santa Inés

1782 San Buenaventura

✝ **1797** San Fernando Rey de España

Los Angeles

✝ **1771** San Gabriel Arcángel

✝ **1776** San Juan Capistrano

✝ **1798** San Luis Rey de Francia

San Diego

✝ **1769** San Diego de Alcalá

P A C I F I C   O C E A N

This string of religious outposts lined Alta California's *camino real* (Royal Road). Owned by the Franciscan holy order and built by Indigenous labor, 21 missions were constructed over 54 years, running north from San Diego.

P A C I F I C   O C E A N

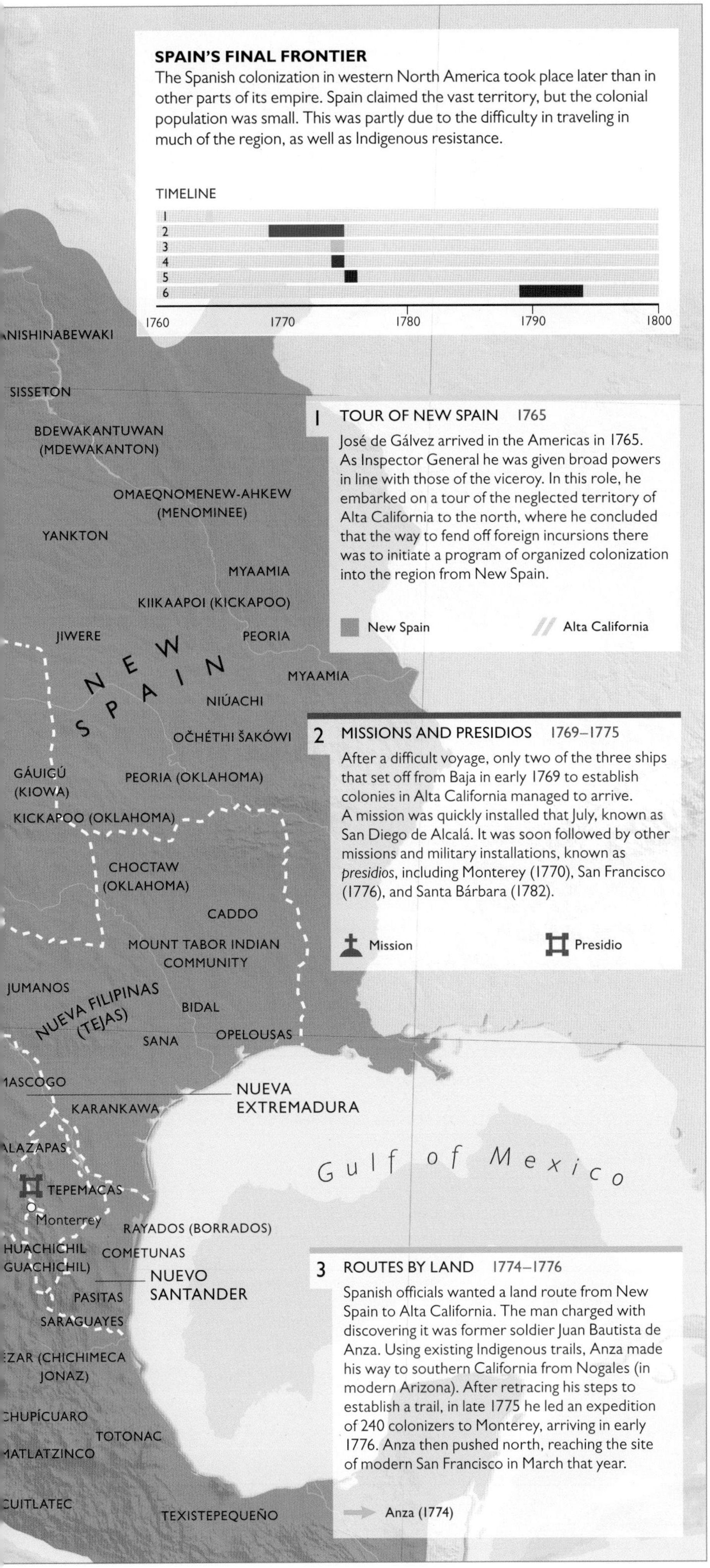

SPAIN'S FINAL FRONTIER

The Spanish colonization in western North America took place later than in other parts of its empire. Spain claimed the vast territory, but the colonial population was small. This was partly due to the difficulty in traveling in much of the region, as well as Indigenous resistance.

TIMELINE

1					
2					
3					
4					
5					
6					

1760   1770   1780   1790   1800

1   TOUR OF NEW SPAIN   1765

José de Gálvez arrived in the Americas in 1765. As Inspector General he was given broad powers in line with those of the viceroy. In this role, he embarked on a tour of the neglected territory of Alta California to the north, where he concluded that the way to fend off foreign incursions there was to initiate a program of organized colonization into the region from New Spain.

▪ New Spain   ⁄⁄ Alta California

2   MISSIONS AND PRESIDIOS   1769–1775

After a difficult voyage, only two of the three ships that set off from Baja in early 1769 to establish colonies in Alta California managed to arrive. A mission was quickly installed that July, known as San Diego de Alcalá. It was soon followed by other missions and military installations, known as *presidios*, including Monterey (1770), San Francisco (1776), and Santa Bárbara (1782).

✝ Mission   ⌂ Presidio

3   ROUTES BY LAND   1774–1776

Spanish officials wanted a land route from New Spain to Alta California. The man charged with discovering it was former soldier Juan Bautista de Anza. Using existing Indigenous trails, Anza made his way to southern California from Nogales (in modern Arizona). After retracing his steps to establish a trail, in late 1775 he led an expedition of 240 colonizers to Monterey, arriving in early 1776. Anza then pushed north, reaching the site of modern San Francisco in March that year.

→ Anza (1774)

Map labels: ANISHINABEWAKI, SISSETON, BDEWAKANTUWAN (MDEWAKANTON), OMAEQNOMENEW-AHKEW (MENOMINEE), YANKTON, MYAAMIA, KIIKAAPOI (KICKAPOO), JIWERE, PEORIA, NEW SPAIN, MYAAMIA, NIÚACHI, OČHÉTHI ŠAKÓWIŊ, GÁUIGÚ (KIOWA), PEORIA (OKLAHOMA), KICKAPOO (OKLAHOMA), CHOCTAW (OKLAHOMA), CADDO, MOUNT TABOR INDIAN COMMUNITY, JUMANOS, NUEVA FILIPINAS (TEJAS), BIDAL, SANA, OPELOUSAS, MASCOGO, KARANKAWA, NUEVA EXTREMADURA, Gulf of Mexico, ALAZAPAS, TEPEMACAS, Monterrey, RAYADOS (BORRADOS), HUACHICHIL (GUACHICHIL), COMETUNAS, NUEVO SANTANDER, PASITAS, SARAGUAYES, EZAR (CHICHIMECA JONAZ), CHUPÍCUARO, TOTONAC, MATLATZINCO, CUITLATEC, TEXISTEPEQUEÑO

LATER SPANISH EXPLORATION

Concerned by fears that European, Russian, and US rivals would encroach on Alta California, a territory they had claimed for centuries but barely investigated, the Spanish from the mid-1700s began to colonize the region, initially through the building of missions.

Although Spain long considered the entire Pacific coast of North America part of its empire (see pp.70–71), it established few settlements north of the Baja peninsula or New Mexico. By the 1760s, however, fur traders from Russia and British North America (and later from the US) began to explore the northern parts of this region, forcing officials in New Spain to act. After traveling extensively around the region, José de Gálvez, New Spain's Inspector General, reported back that what Alta California needed most of all was more Spanish colonizers and closer links with New Spain.

One of the first people to follow the advice of Gálvez was the Franciscan friar Junípero Serra, who established the first church in San Diego, in 1769. From there, the Spanish made their way along the coast, building churches and engaging in forcible conversions, forced labor, and massacres of the Indigenous communities, including the Chumash and Ohlone. There were about 310,000 Indigenous people in Alta California before the Spanish arrived, but conflict and disease would cause that number drop dramatically.

"Thanks be to God, I arrived here … at this port of San Diego. It is beautiful to behold".

JUNÍPERO SERRA, 1769

NDÉ (APACHE) RESISTANCE

The Ndé (Apache) are a diverse, nomadic people who were living across much of the southwestern borderlands when Europeans first arrived in the Americas. With the Spanish reintroduction of horses on the continent (see pp.46–47), the Ndé became expert riders and used the animal in warfare against Spanish as well as other Indigenous groups, such as the Pueblo. Ndé defenses against colonization continued well into the 19th century inhibiting future European settlement.

A painted Ndé leather shield

THE HAITIAN REVOLUTION

The fight for freedom conducted by the enslaved people in the French colony of Saint-Domingue, present-day Haiti, was among the most successful revolutions in the Americas. It led to the establishment of the only independent nation with a commitment to full emancipation from its founding.

By the late-18th century, French Saint-Domingue on the island of Hispaniola was the most profitable colony in the world. It was the leading producer of sugar, an industry that was built on and exacted a heavy toll on enslaved labor. On August 22, 1791, a group of enslaved people set the sugarcane fields of northern Saint-Domingue ablaze, triggering a 13-year revolt. The Haitian Revolution was inspired by the French Revolution, which started in 1789 and pitted republicans against monarchists. Other conflicts unfolding during the Haitian Revolution stemmed from colonial rivalry, as Spain and Britain made forays into Saint-Domingue. Divisions among the enslaved and free people of color also led to strife.

In an effort to quell the revolt and bolster their numbers against British and Spanish attacks, the French Revolutionary government officially freed the enslaved majority on the island in 1794. General Toussaint L'Ouverture, a formerly enslaved man and rebel leader allied with this government to take over Spanish Santo Domingo in 1801. The following year, he proclaimed himself governor of the island for life.

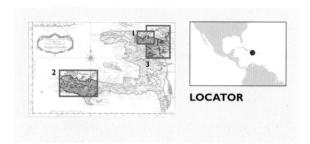

LOCATOR

Napoleon Bonaparte assumed power in France in 1799 and planned to reinstitute slavery in the colony. He imprisoned L'Ouverture, who died in captivity in 1803. Jean-Jacques Dessalines, L'Ouverture's successor, led the next, bloody phase of the struggle in which some 30,000 French soldiers were killed. Bonaparte capitulated, and on January 1, 1804, independent Haiti was established, returning to its Indigenous name. It was the second free nation in the Americas, after the US. Given its ambivalent stance on slavery at the time (see pp.130–131), the US did not recognize Haitian independence for another six decades.

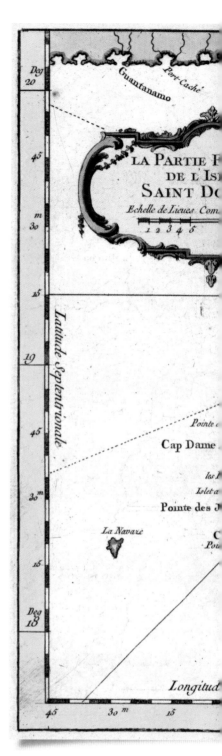

△ **French Saint-Domingue**
This 1764 map shows the western third of Hispaniola, which formally became a French colony with the 1697 Treaty of Rijswijk.

▽ **The revolution begins**
The rebellion began around Le Cap, possibly preceded by a voudon (voodoo) ceremony organized by enslaved leader Dutty Boukman.

A REGION IN REVOLT

There were a number of rebellions led by enslaved people across the Caribbean in 1795, during the height of the Haitian Revolution. Similarly, the American (see pp.90–94) and French revolutions spread the idea of breaking free from oppression. There were also renewed phases of long-running conflicts that involved enslaved or formerly enslaved people, including the Second Carib War in St. Vincent. Fought between the Carib people and the British, this war led to the Caribs being exiled to Honduras.

KEY

▢ Region of revolt

UNITED STATES

Pointe Coupée Parish

Louisiana

Gulf of Mexico

Apr 1795 Pointe Coupée conspiracy is uncovered in Spanish Louisiana leading to several enslaved people being arrested

ATLANTIC OCEAN

Santo Domingo (Dominican Republic)

Cuba

1795–1796 Britain hoped to take advantage of the strife in Saint-Domingue to claim the colony as its own

Jamaica

Puerto Rico

Saint-Domingue (Haiti)

May 1795 Venezuela is rocked by the Coro slave revolt

Caribbean Sea

Curaçao

Dominica
St. Lucia
St. Vincent
Grenada

1795–1797 Africans living independently in the mountains of Jamaica, known as Maroons, revolt against the violation of the terms set after the first Maroon War (1738)

VENEZUELA

Demerara

COLOMBIA

GUYANA

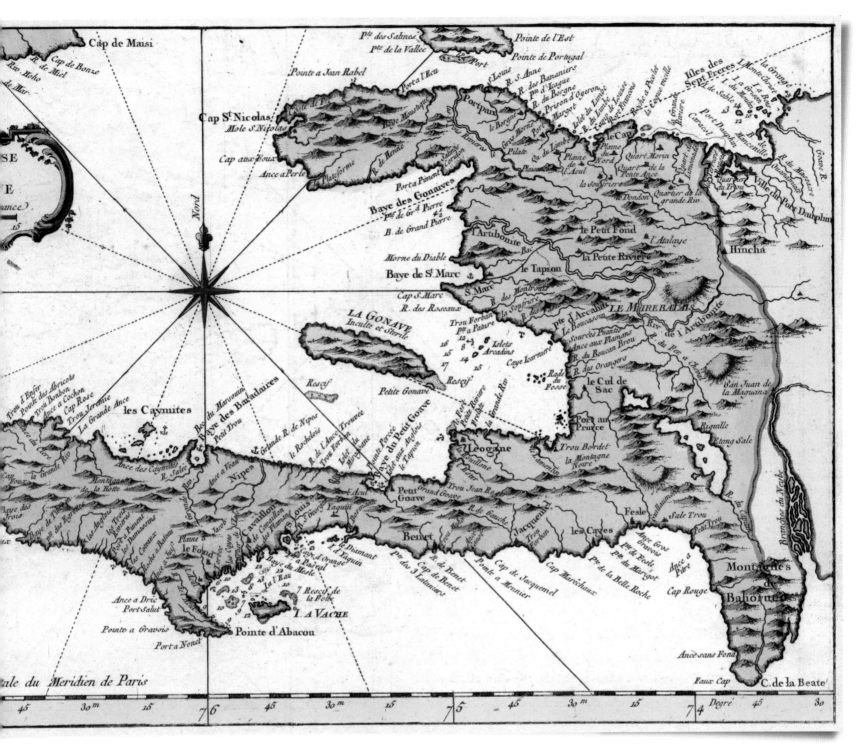

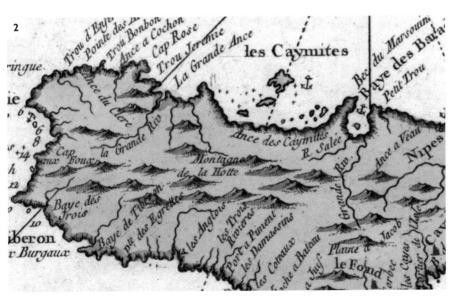

◁ The British arrive

Britain hoped to take advantage of the existing strife in Saint-Domingue to claim the colony for their own. In 1793, they sent 600 troops from Jamaica and occupied the port of Jérémie (shown here as Trou Jeremie, upper left). In a war that lasted five years, the British lost to the French.

▷ Across the border

Spanish Santo Domingo lay to the east of Hispaniola. The Spanish covertly aided the Haitian rebels, with a view to ousting the French from the island. Border regions such as Fort Dauphin (shown here as Port Dauphin) were key areas for rebels to trade resources with the Spanish.

THE BARBARY WARS

One of the first overseas conflicts for the new United States involved a series of battles against the North African Barbary states, after mounting anger that US ships were being captured and ransomed while trading in the Mediterranean.

Within a few decades of independence, the young US found itself in a war in the Mediterranean, fighting what were known as the Barbary states of Morocco, Algiers, Tunis, and Tripoli in Islamic North Africa—often under Ottoman or other colonial control. For centuries, state-affiliated pirates from this region had targeted European ships, taking their goods, kidnapping Christian crews, and attacking coastal villages.

Captives were put to work on Barbary vessels or ransomed for a high payout. To avoid this, most European nations paid money, known as "tribute," but this did not always protect them. The US wanted to trade with Europe, but it no longer had the protection of Britain's Royal Navy.

At first, the US paid tribute but still suffered attacks, also forcing it to pay money for ransoms. However, by the time of Thomas Jefferson's presidency (1801–1809) the US Navy had grown strong enough to go to war. The First Barbary War (1801–1805) was mostly fought with Tripoli and, although it demonstrated the growing naval power of the US and ended with a peace treaty, it failed to end US ransom payments. The short-lived Second Barbary War (1815) was mostly fought with Algiers, and it ended with a treaty that permitted the US tribute-free shipping rights in the Mediterranean.

> "As peace is better than war, war is better than tribute."
>
> US PRESIDENT JAMES MADISON, 1816

STEPHEN DECATUR 1779–1820

Stephen Decatur was a navy captain who led the US to victory in the Barbary Wars. His exploits in the First Barbary War, including the 1804 raid to set the US frigate *Philadelphia* on fire after it was captured in Tripoli, made him a national hero. This became a defining exploit in the US Navy's early history. He was also known for his involvement in the War of 1812 (see pp.112–113). Decatur died five years after his return from the Second Barbary War, in a pistol duel with a fellow naval officer.

Attack on Tripoli
On August 3, 1804, US Commodore Edward Preble launched a series of attacks in Tripoli's harbor. The bombardment lasted for more than a month but did not bring the conflict to a close. Fighting continued until the spring of 1805.

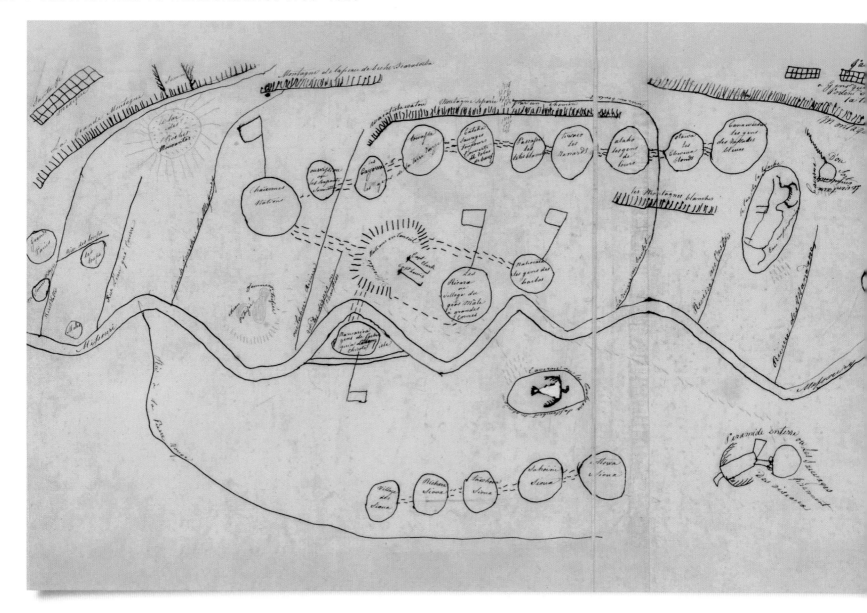

THE LEWIS AND CLARK EXPEDITION

△ Along the Missouri River
Drawn by Arikara leader Too Né around 1805, this map depicts the Missouri River running through more than 30 different Indigenous communities and sacred sites, providing a spiritual geography of the region. Too Né accompanied Lewis and Clark for part of their expedition.

After the US acquired the vast Louisiana territory from France in 1803, a group of US surveyors journeyed into parts of the land where no Europeans had ventured before. Along the way, they met diverse Indigenous communities, whom they relied on heavily for guidance, and mapped the way for colonization in western North America.

With the acquisition of the Louisiana territory in 1803, the US almost doubled its area. However, the government knew little about this region beyond the Mississippi River. Despite having been under Spanish and then French control, it remained virtually unexplored by Europeans. In a bid to find a route to the Pacific Ocean and trade with the Indigenous people who lived in western North America, President Thomas Jefferson commissioned a survey of these lands.

Led by explorers Meriwether Lewis and William Clark, the expedition company was referred to as the Corps of Discovery. The Corps initially comprised 30 people—soldiers, interpreters, oarsmen, and an enslaved man named York. In late 1804, they were joined by a Shoshone woman, Sacagawea, who helped the party as an interpreter, mediator, guide, and forager. By the end, a total of about 45 people, including members of Indigenous communities such as the Arikara, had participated in various parts of the journey, which took place between May 1804 and September 1806. The surveyors met people from around 50 different communities and kept detailed notes regarding the flora, fauna, and lands they observed along the way.

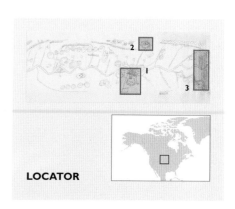

LOCATOR

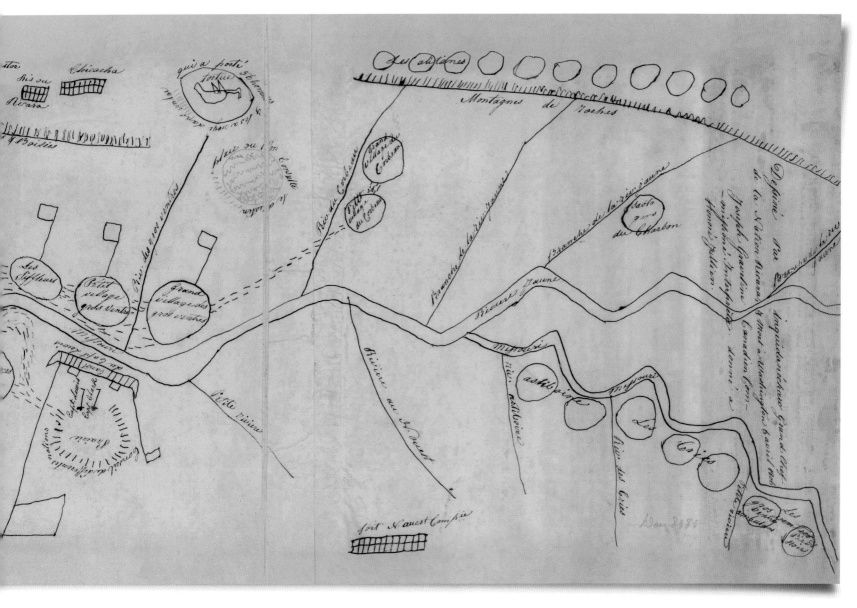

▷ **Lewis's boat**
The expedition relied on a variety of boats to traverse the waterways. In addition to dugout canoes, they used a keelboat. This shallow riverboat could be maneuvered in strong currents using oars, poles, sails, and towlines.

1

▷ **The Turtle that carried 56 men**
The map marks the location of an Arikara legend about a group of men that came across a snapping turtle. All climbed its back but one, who walked beside it. Staying stuck to the turtle as it walked into a lake, the men drowned and were thought to watch over the Arikara people.

2

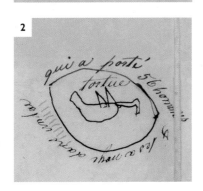

3

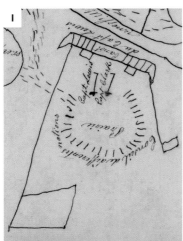

△ **Chief's signature**
The writing indicates that this is the map of *Inquidanécharo,* an Arikara word meaning "band chief" or "chiefly village." It was also used to refer to their leader Too Né.

THE FULL ROUTE OF LEWIS AND CLARK
The Lewis and Clark expedition set out along the Missouri River in May 1804. The party traversed a total of some 8,000 miles (12,875 km), passing through the lands of diverse Indigenous groups including the Sioux, Shoshone, Nimiipuu (Nez Percé), and Mandan. Their journey spanned 16 present-day states, from Missouri to Oregon, and they reached the Pacific Ocean, via the Columbia River, in November 1805.

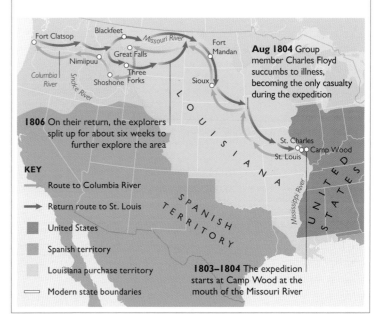

Aug 1804 Group member Charles Floyd succumbs to illness, becoming the only casualty during the expedition

1806 On their return, the explorers split up for about six weeks to further explore the area

1803–1804 The expedition starts at Camp Wood at the mouth of the Missouri River

KEY

— Route to Columbia River

→ Return route to St. Louis

▮ United States

▮ Spanish territory

▮ Louisiana purchase territory

▭ Modern state boundaries

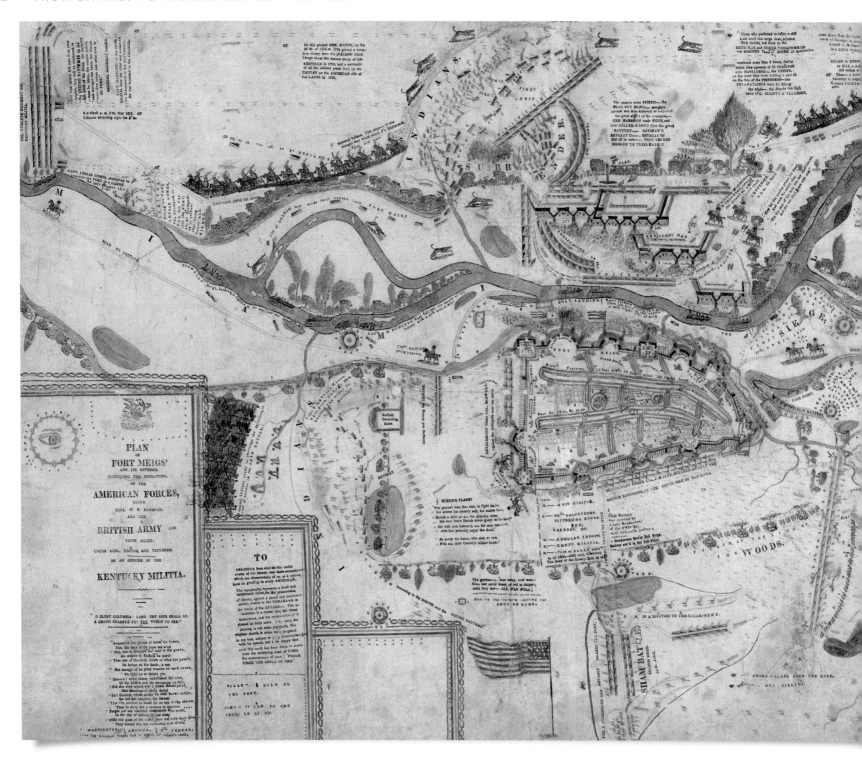

△ Siege of Fort Meigs
Fort Meigs was built on the Maumee River in Ohio in February 1813, in anticipation of British attacks, which came in both April and July. This plan of the fort was painted by a Kentucky militia officer, William Sebree, who fought in the siege.

▷ North side defenses
In April, most of the British forces were deployed to the north of the fort, and their artillery fire was largely ineffective against the heavy earthwork defenses.

△ British naval force
The War of 1812 began on water, although it later progressed to land. The British land forces attacking Fort Meigs were supported by two gunboats on the river.

▷ Indigenous support
The Shawnee leader Tecumseh organized a confederacy opposed to further colonizing encroachment, and joined the war as an ally of the British.

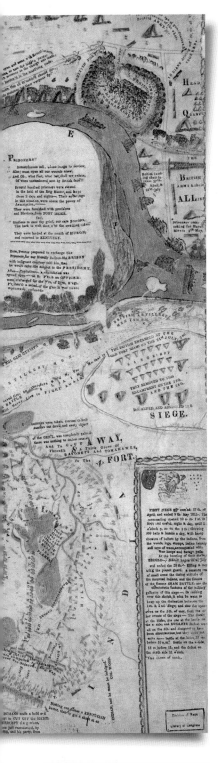

THE WAR OF 1812

A conflict between the US and Britain over maritime rights led to numerous battles on water and on land, and involved Britain's Indigenous allies. It eventually ended in a draw, with no clear victor and no changes to any of the existing map boundaries.

The War of 1812 was initially fought over the question of US trade neutrality with Britain and France, who were fighting the Napoleonic Wars (c. 1799–1815). The conflict started when the British attacked neutral US merchant ships, sometimes press-ganging their sailors. It quickly moved on land as the British convinced Indigenous allies, under their Shawnee leader Tecumseh, to attack US positions along the northwest frontier with Canada, pushing Congress to declare war on Britain.

The conflict started with US losses in Montreal and Detroit, and two sieges by the British on Fort Meigs. Detroit was recaptured by 1813 in the Battle of the Thames, where Tecumseh was killed. Frustration about increasing US encroachment on their territory among the Creek people, who were British allies, then led to the eruption of the Creek War in Alabama in the summer of 1813. Fighting also continued on the water, with key US victories on Lake Erie in 1813 and on Lake Champlain in 1814. However, the British

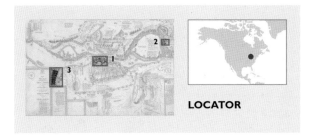

LOCATOR

managed to blockade the east coast and used their position in the Chesapeake Bay to attack Washington, D.C., burning the US Capitol and the White House before being driven out in the Battle of Baltimore.

The final front was in New Orleans, where future president Andrew Jackson won in January 1815. However, unknown to the combatants, the Treaty of Ghent had officially ended the war two weeks earlier. With no clear victory, it restored Anglo-American relations to what they had been before the war.

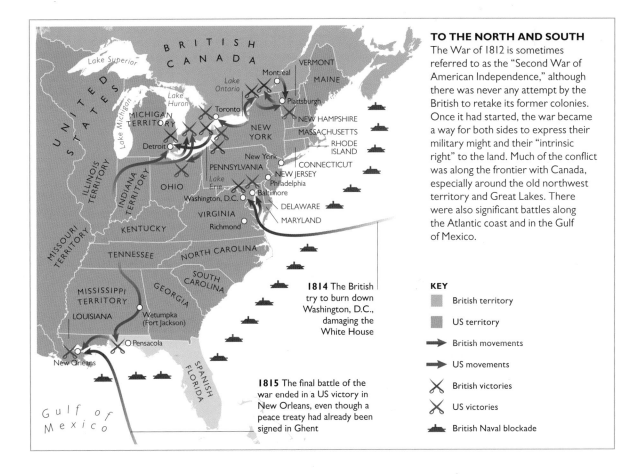

TO THE NORTH AND SOUTH
The War of 1812 is sometimes referred to as the "Second War of American Independence," although there was never any attempt by the British to retake its former colonies. Once it had started, the war became a way for both sides to express their military might and their "intrinsic right" to the land. Much of the conflict was along the frontier with Canada, especially around the old northwest territory and Great Lakes. There were also significant battles along the Atlantic coast and in the Gulf of Mexico.

1814 The British try to burn down Washington, D.C., damaging the White House

1815 The final battle of the war ended in a US victory in New Orleans, even though a peace treaty had already been signed in Ghent

KEY

- British territory
- US territory
- British movements
- US movements
- British victories
- US victories
- British Naval blockade

The Cry of Dolores
This mural by Juan O'Gorman, painted in 1960, depicts the moment Father Miguel Hidalgo y Costilla rang the parish bell and delivered the *Grito de Dolores* ("Cry of Dolores") a cry for freedom and call to revolt.

MEXICAN INDEPENDENCE

Mexico's bid for independence from Spain started with an insurgency organized by a priest in 1810. The struggle lasted for more than a decade, after which the new nation faced further internal unrest over the question of governance.

△ **Flag of the empire**
The First Mexican Empire's motto of "independence, religion, and union" is emblazoned on this tricolor military banner from 1821.

In 1808, French emperor Napoleon Bonaparte invaded Spain and put his brother, Joseph, on the Spanish throne, forcing the previous king Charles IV to abdicate. This change of rule triggered a larger imperial crisis as Spain's colonies debated the question of sovereignty and their futures. In Mexico's case, long-simmering resentments between criollos (see below) and Spanish-born officials also contributed to the growing calls for independence.

On the morning of September 16, 1810, a priest and revolutionary named Miguel Hidalgo y Costilla issued a cry for independence in the town of Dolores, Mexico. Thousands joined his cause, and it began the long-running and inconclusive Mexican War of Independence between insurgents and royalists. In 1820, Agustín de Iturbide, a criollo former royalist commander, reached out to Vicente Guerrero, a prominent insurgent leader, to find a way forward. The result was the 1820 Plan of Iguala, which promised "independence, religion, and union" in the form of a constitutional monarchy. It also protected existing privileges for the church and military, thereby securing their crucial support. The First Mexican Empire was established by treaty with Spain in 1821, and by 1822 Iturbide was emperor. However, other political problems quickly emerged. By 1823, the first empire was over, to be replaced by a republic.

CRIOLLOS AND PENINSULARES

One of the underlying tensions that led to calls for Mexican independence was the animosity between people of Spanish heritage born in New Spain, called criollos (right), and those who came from mainland Spain, peninsulares, who were often in positions of power, such as viceroys or judges. By the mid-17th century, the number of criollos far outnumbered peninsulares. Criollos claimed that peninsulares discriminated against them, especially in the awarding of political positions.

EXPANDING NATIONS

AS THE YOUNG US PUSHED WESTWARD INTO NEW TERRITORIES, INDIGENOUS PEOPLE WERE INCREASINGLY FORCED FROM THEIR LANDS. THE US ALSO BEGAN GROWING ITS INFLUENCE OVERSEAS, WHILE THE MEXICAN-AMERICAN WAR RESHAPED THE TWO NATIONS' BORDERS.

THE GROWTH OF NORTH AMERICA

The first half of the 19th century saw the rapid expansion of the US. This was driven by the economic opportunities of farming, the fur trade, and mining—but also by the wider ideal of "manifest destiny," the popular notion that the people of the US were fated to control the continent.

△ **The Monroe Doctrine**
Proclaimed by President James Monroe in his seventh annual message to Congress on December 2, 1823, the doctrine that bears his name declared that the Western Hemisphere lay within the US sphere of interest and was off-limits to European powers.

This era unfolded against a backdrop of conflicts between the US, other colonizing powers, and Indigenous and First Nations peoples. Disputes over land, resources, and cultural differences were a large part of the problem. Some of these were resolved by settlements made between the different parties, but they were not always honored—particularly those agreed with Indigenous peoples whose lands were increasingly being taken from them by the colonizing nations.

The Convention of 1818, delineated the border between the US and British North America along the 49th parallel. It specified clear spheres of influence between the US and Britain in the north of the continent. It was followed a year later by the Adams-Onís Treaty between the US and Spain. By its terms, Spain ceded its claims on Texas and accepted US control over Florida, allowing the US to devote its attention to colonizing the south and west of its new territory. Meanwhile, Britain focused on consolidating its control over British North America, where it built settlements, constructed roads and canals, and established trading posts in the far

north. This laid the groundwork for the eventual confederation of the British North American colonies into the Dominion of Canada in 1867.

Away from the mainland, having lost possession of the Thirteen Colonies in 1783, Britain invested in the defense and development of its valuable colonies, such as Jamaica, Barbados, and other islands in the Caribbean. Technological advances transformed lives and accelerated economic

△ **Sutter's Mill and the California Gold Rush**
While building this sawmill for businessman John Sutter in January 1848, workers discovered gold. Within weeks, tens of thousands of prospectors had headed West, hoping to make their fortunes.

> *"The American claim is by the right of our manifest destiny ... to possess the whole ... continent which [God] has given us ..."*
>
> US COLUMNIST JOHN L. O'SULLIVAN, 1845

EXPANSION AND ENGAGEMENT

The newly independent US established its borders through agreements and treaties with European powers as it acquired land to the south and west. At the same time, the US developed trade links with Asia and Europe, becoming a global commercial power. Territorial growth and economic opportunity expanded with the acquisition of new territories—but such gains came at the cost of the violent dispossession of the continent's Indigenous people.

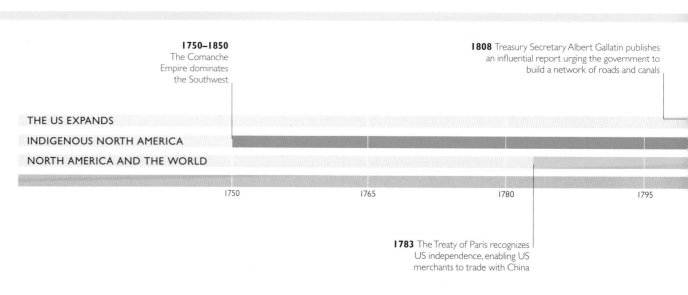

1750–1850 The Comanche Empire dominates the Southwest

1808 Treasury Secretary Albert Gallatin publishes an influential report urging the government to build a network of roads and canals

THE US EXPANDS

INDIGENOUS NORTH AMERICA

NORTH AMERICA AND THE WORLD

1750   1765   1780   1795

1783 The Treaty of Paris recognizes US independence, enabling US merchants to trade with China

◁ **Leather and wood Comanche whip**
The Comanche dominated much of the
Southwest and Mexico before European
settlers arrived. Their empire was based on
conquest and trade, especially in horses.

growth in this period. Factories emerged, especially in
the Northeast, leading to urbanization as people moved
from rural areas in search of employment. The invention
of the telegraph changed how people communicated,
allowing for the rapid transmission of information over long
distances. The development of steam-powered locomotives
and riverboats revolutionized travel and trade. Railroads,
canals, and paved roads vastly improved the speed and
efficiency with which people and goods crossed the country.
Local economies became regional, national, and finally
international as the continent became ever-more connected.

Industrialization and immigration

The growing industrial and commercial economy, and
expanding transportation networks, attracted immigrants
from around the world seeking better lives and employment
opportunities in the US. While European arrivals were
significant during this period, there was also a sizable
influx of Asian immigrants, particularly from China, who
were attracted by the promise of work in industries such
as mining, railroad construction, and agriculture. While
these immigrants played a crucial role in the labor force,
contributing to the growth and diversification of the
economy, they remained subjected to harsh discrimination
and racial prejudice throughout the 19th century.

The period 1820–1850 was a time of profound change
and transformation in North America. It saw the US assume
control over North American territory from the Atlantic to the

Pacific, however it was only through the brutality of
Indigenous dispossession and expanding enslavement of
Black people that made this growth possible. This left the
US with a painful legacy of violence and discrimination that
would eventually continue to impact the nation's social and
political landscape through to the Civil War.

▽ **Settler revolution in Texas**
At the Battle of San Jacinto in 1836,
imagined in this 1901 painting, General
Sam Houston and his forces secured
Texan independence from Mexico in an
engagement that lasted just 18 minutes.

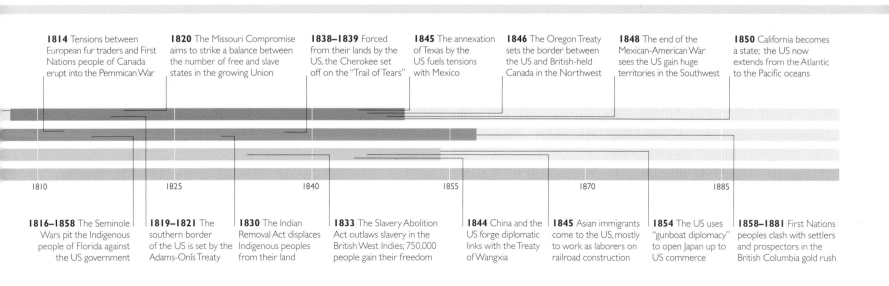

1814 Tensions between European fur traders and First Nations people of Canada erupt into the Pemmican War

1820 The Missouri Compromise aims to strike a balance between the number of free and slave states in the growing Union

1838–1839 Forced from their lands by the US, the Cherokee set off on the "Trail of Tears"

1845 The annexation of Texas by the US fuels tensions with Mexico

1846 The Oregon Treaty sets the border between the US and British-held Canada in the Northwest

1848 The end of the Mexican-American War sees the US gain huge territories in the Southwest

1850 California becomes a state; the US now extends from the Atlantic to the Pacific oceans

1810   1825   1840   1855   1870   1885

1816–1858 The Seminole Wars pit the Indigenous people of Florida against the US government

1819–1821 The southern border of the US is set by the Adams-Onís Treaty

1830 The Indian Removal Act displaces Indigenous peoples from their land

1833 The Slavery Abolition Act outlaws slavery in the British West Indies; 750,000 people gain their freedom

1844 China and the US forge diplomatic links with the Treaty of Wangxia

1845 Asian immigrants come to the US, mostly to work as laborers on railroad construction

1854 The US uses "gunboat diplomacy" to open Japan up to US commerce

1858–1881 First Nations peoples clash with settlers and prospectors in the British Columbia gold rush

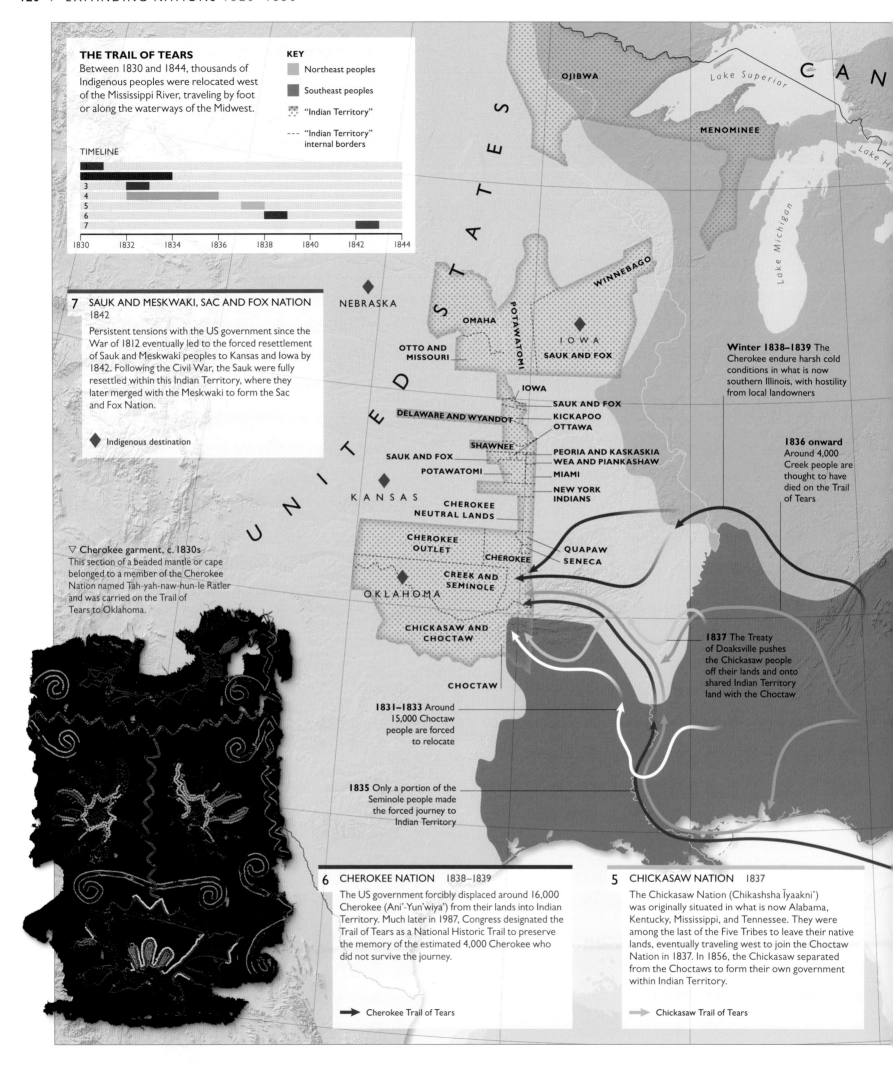

THE TRAIL OF TEARS

Between 1830 and 1844, thousands of Indigenous peoples were relocated west of the Mississippi River, traveling by foot or along the waterways of the Midwest.

KEY

- Northeast peoples
- Southeast peoples
- "Indian Territory"
- --- "Indian Territory" internal borders

TIMELINE

1830 1832 1834 1836 1838 1840 1842 1844

7 SAUK AND MESKWAKI, SAC AND FOX NATION 1842

Persistent tensions with the US government since the War of 1812 eventually led to the forced resettlement of Sauk and Meskwaki peoples to Kansas and Iowa by 1842. Following the Civil War, the Sauk were fully resettled within this Indian Territory, where they later merged with the Meskwaki to form the Sac and Fox Nation.

◆ Indigenous destination

▽ Cherokee garment, c. 1830s
This section of a beaded mantle or cape belonged to a member of the Cherokee Nation named Tah-yah-naw-hun-le Ratler and was carried on the Trail of Tears to Oklahoma.

Winter 1838–1839 The Cherokee endure harsh cold conditions in what is now southern Illinois, with hostility from local landowners

1836 onward Around 4,000 Creek people are thought to have died on the Trail of Tears

1837 The Treaty of Doaksville pushes the Chickasaw people off their lands and onto shared Indian Territory land with the Choctaw

1831–1833 Around 15,000 Choctaw people are forced to relocate

1835 Only a portion of the Seminole people made the forced journey to Indian Territory

6 CHEROKEE NATION 1838–1839

The US government forcibly displaced around 16,000 Cherokee (Ani'-Yun'wiya') from their lands into Indian Territory. Much later in 1987, Congress designated the Trail of Tears as a National Historic Trail to preserve the memory of the estimated 4,000 Cherokee who did not survive the journey.

➡ Cherokee Trail of Tears

5 CHICKASAW NATION 1837

The Chickasaw Nation (Chikashsha Ĭyaakni') was originally situated in what is now Alabama, Kentucky, Mississippi, and Tennessee. They were among the last of the Five Tribes to leave their native lands, eventually traveling west to join the Choctaw Nation in 1837. In 1856, the Chickasaw separated from the Choctaws to form their own government within Indian Territory.

➡ Chickasaw Trail of Tears

Map labels: OJIBWA, MENOMINEE, Lake Superior, Lake Michigan, CAN[ADA], WINNEBAGO, NEBRASKA, OMAHA, POTAWATOMI, IOWA, OTTO AND MISSOURI, SAUK AND FOX, IOWA, UNITED STATES, SAUK AND FOX, KICKAPOO, OTTAWA, DELAWARE AND WYANDOT, SHAWNEE, PEORIA AND KASKASKIA, WEA AND PIANKASHAW, MIAMI, SAUK AND FOX, POTAWATOMI, NEW YORK INDIANS, KANSAS, CHEROKEE NEUTRAL LANDS, CHEROKEE OUTLET, CHEROKEE, QUAPAW, SENECA, CREEK AND SEMINOLE, OKLAHOMA, CHICKASAW AND CHOCTAW, CHOCTAW

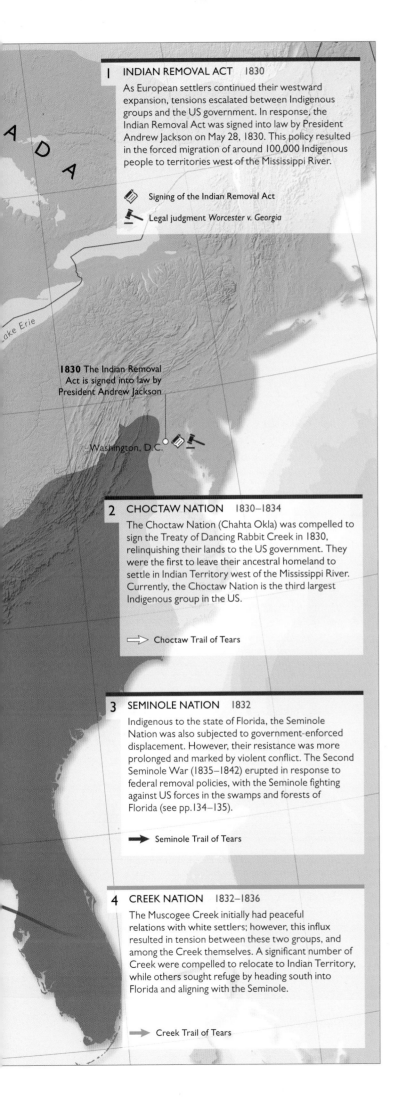

1 INDIAN REMOVAL ACT 1830

As European settlers continued their westward expansion, tensions escalated between Indigenous groups and the US government. In response, the Indian Removal Act was signed into law by President Andrew Jackson on May 28, 1830. This policy resulted in the forced migration of around 100,000 Indigenous people to territories west of the Mississippi River.

🖋 Signing of the Indian Removal Act

⚖ Legal judgment *Worcester v. Georgia*

1830 The Indian Removal Act is signed into law by President Andrew Jackson

Washington, D.C.

2 CHOCTAW NATION 1830–1834

The Choctaw Nation (Chahta Okla) was compelled to sign the Treaty of Dancing Rabbit Creek in 1830, relinquishing their lands to the US government. They were the first to leave their ancestral homeland to settle in Indian Territory west of the Mississippi River. Currently, the Choctaw Nation is the third largest Indigenous group in the US.

⇨ Choctaw Trail of Tears

3 SEMINOLE NATION 1832

Indigenous to the state of Florida, the Seminole Nation was also subjected to government-enforced displacement. However, their resistance was more prolonged and marked by violent conflict. The Second Seminole War (1835–1842) erupted in response to federal removal policies, with the Seminole fighting against US forces in the swamps and forests of Florida (see pp.134–135).

➡ Seminole Trail of Tears

4 CREEK NATION 1832–1836

The Muscogee Creek initially had peaceful relations with white settlers; however, this influx resulted in tension between these two groups, and among the Creek themselves. A significant number of Creek were compelled to relocate to Indian Territory, while others sought refuge by heading south into Florida and aligning with the Seminole.

➡ Creek Trail of Tears

THE TRAIL OF TEARS

From 1830 to 1850, thousands of Indigenous peoples were forcibly relocated from their ancestral homelands by coercive treaties and US military intervention. This "Trail of Tears" was characterized by extreme temperatures, unsanitary conditions, and inadequate supplies that led to widespread suffering and death.

Throughout the presidencies of George Washington, John Adams, Thomas Jefferson, and James Madison, the US government lived up to its treaty obligations to Indigenous nations when faced with the growing demands by European settlers for land. The Louisiana Purchase of 1803 (see p.111) greatly expanded federal territory west of the Mississippi River, but this provoked conflict with the Indigenous communities already inhabiting these areas.

Tensions escalated when President Jefferson proposed a relocation plan for eastern Indigenous peoples into these western territories. This policy was eventually enacted into law in 1824 and saw the resettlement of large groups of people. These early stages of "Indian Removal" gained momentum under Andrew Jackson, who first announced his intention to relocate Indigenous populations in his 1829 inaugural address. Under his administration, hundreds of thousands of Indigenous groups were forcibly removed to newly designated "Indian Territories." These communities, collectively known as the "Five Civilized Tribes," experienced the threat of erasure of established social structures, languages, and traditional ways of life due to their forced displacement. Although Indian Territory initially spanned from Texas to Canada, this land gradually reduced to an area that would later form the state of Oklahoma.

"Many days pass, and people die very much. We bury close by trail."

UNKNOWN TRAIL OF TEARS SURVIVOR, 19TH CENTURY

JOHN ROSS 1790–1866

John Ross, or Guwisguwi, of mixed Cherokee and Scottish ancestry, was the Principal Chief of the Cherokee Nation from 1828 to 1866. In the War of 1812, he led a Cherokee regiment under Andrew Jackson. Ross later advocated for Cherokee land rights, promoting peaceful coexistence between Indigenous peoples and their white neighbors. He, along with thousands of Cherokee followers, opposed the deceptive treaties the US government used to justify the forced removal of Indigenous communities from their native lands.

An 1848 oil painting of Ross by John Neagle

BRITISH AMERICA

First Nations, British, and French cultures; political dynamics; and economic expansion combined to form the character of British Canada by the mid 1800s. Montreal emerged as a vibrant commercial hub, facilitating trade along the St. Lawrence River and serving as a meeting point for diverse cultural influences.

Colonial British Canada in the St. Lawrence River Valley was characterized by a blend of British governance and French Canadian culture. The river served as a vital transportation artery, facilitating trade and communication between settlements in the region and with other parts of British North America. Nova Scotia, New Brunswick, Prince Edward Island, Newfoundland, Labrador, British Columbia, and Vancouver Island were also under British rule, as was Rupert's Land—a territory owned by the Hudson's Bay Company comprising parts of present-day Manitoba, Saskatchewan, Ontario, Quebec, and Alberta, as well as many Indigenous lands of the Arctic Archipelago and Northwest Territories. Elsewhere in the Americas, Britain's Caribbean colonies played a prominent role in trade during the 19th century. The British West Indies, including Jamaica, were

▽ Map of the Province of Canada, 1861
The Province of Canada was established in 1840 by the British North America Act, replacing Upper Canada (present-day Ontario), settled during the American Revolution, and Lower Canada (present-day Quebec), established in 1791.

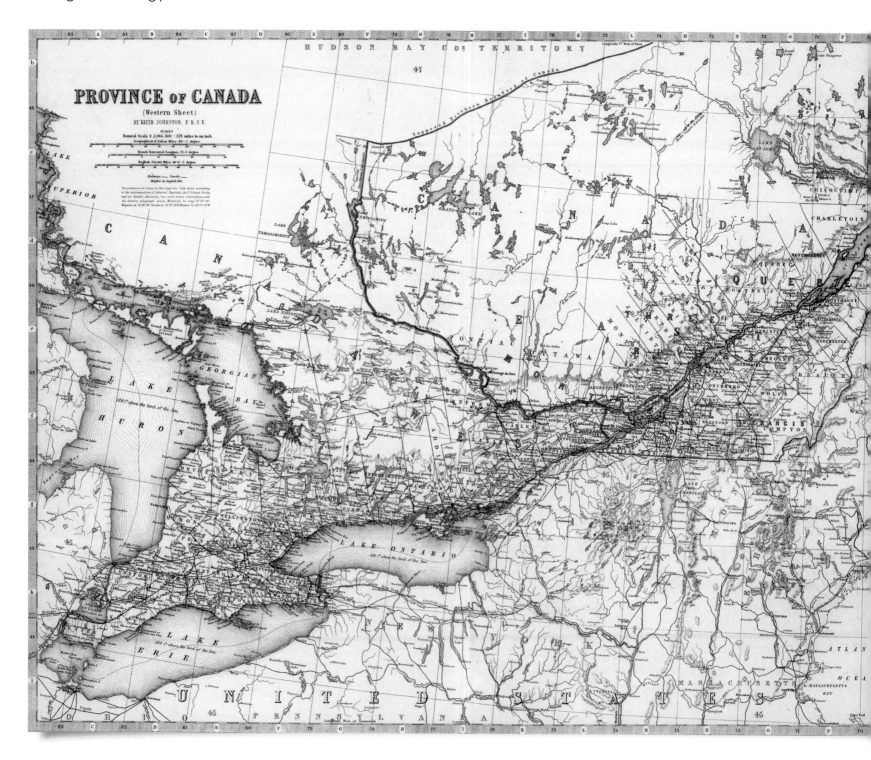

known for sugar plantations that relied heavily on enslaved labor from Africa. Additional territories included the Bahamas, Barbados, and Trinidad and Tobago. From the late 19th century, proposals urged British Caribbean colonies such as Jamaica and the Bahamas to join the Canadian Confederation, but nothing came of this.

LOCATOR

KEY

1 The St. Lawrence River was an important water route into Canada.

2 The Gulf of St. Lawrence was a thriving area of maritime trade.

3 The vast Hudson's Bay Company territory known as Rupert's Land comprised the drainage basin of Hudson Bay.

HUDSON'S BAY COMPANY

Incorporated in England in May 1670, the Hudson's Bay Company traded furs throughout Rupert's Land via Hudson Bay. In 1821, the British Parliament merged the company with its rival, the North West Company, and granted it sole trading rights in the Northwest Territories, creating a continent-spanning commercial enterprise. Governed from Britain until 1931 but now headquartered in Toronto, the Hudson's Bay Company remains active in merchandising, natural resources, and real estate, and is known as Canada's oldest corporation.

Fort Garry, in present-day Winnipeg, was a trading post for the company from 1822 to 1878.

PROVINCE of CANADA
(Eastern Sheet)
NEW BRUNSWICK, NOVA SCOTIA,
PRINCE EDWARD I? CAPE BRETON I? AND
NEWFOUNDLAND.
BY KEITH JOHNSTON, F.R.S.E

NEWFOUNDLAND
ON SAME SCALE

THE US AND THE HEMISPHERE

Emboldened by its territorial expansion and growing influence, the US used the 1823 Monroe Doctrine to tell Europeans they could no longer colonize territory in its hemisphere—and to signal to its neighbors that it was now the dominant power in North, South, and Central America.

In his annual message to Congress on December 2, 1823, President James Monroe made clear his frustration with the European powers. He was irritated by Russia and Britain encroaching on the northwest coast of North America, as well as Spain's ongoing efforts at resisting the independence movements across its crumbling empire farther south.

△ **James Monroe**
Hailing from Virginia, James Monroe (1758–1831) served as the fifth president of the US from 1817 until 1825.

He told the assembled congressmen that "the American continents, by the free and independent condition which they have assumed and maintain, are henceforth not to be considered as subjects for future colonization by any European powers."

It was not thought of as a "doctrine" at the time—nor was it exclusively Monroe's, having been drafted by his cabinet—but was labeled as such later. This moment represented the arrival of a confident young nation standing up to European rivals wherever and whenever they might meddle in the Americas. The Monroe Doctrine also made it clear to the emerging republics of Latin America that the US claimed the right to speak for all of North, South, and Central America. Couched within Monroe's statement was an assumption of US superiority over its neighbors that shaped what US policy in the Americas would look like in the decades to come (see pp.228–229).

△ **A nation extends its reach**
In *The Birth of the Monroe Doctrine*, painted by Clyde O. DeLand in 1912, President James Monroe's proprietorial hand rests on the hemisphere as he discusses the details of the policy bearing his name with his cabinet—whose members include future president John Quincy Adams (far left) and future vice-president John C. Calhoun (third from right).

WESTWARD MIGRATION

In the first half of the 19th century, colonists navigated the vast Great Plains and rugged Rocky Mountains in the North American West, driven by the promise of land and economic opportunities in this largely unexplored region of the continent.

Colonists migrated to newly acquired western territories (see pp.94–95) in the US, transforming once-frontier districts into organized territories with elected legislatures and governors appointed by the president. These territories were eligible for statehood once their populations surpassed 100,000 people. St. Louis, strategically positioned along the Mississippi River, emerged as a major frontier town. It served as a crucial gateway for westward travel and a vital trading center for Mississippi River traffic and inland commerce. The arrival of settlers via the Oregon Trail in the early 1840s solidified US control of the region.

The end of Spanish missions in Alta California saw the first group of US settlers arriving in the region in 1841. The terms that concluded the Mexican-American War (see pp.138–139) defined the boundary between the US and Mexico and granted full US citizenship to those in the annexed areas of Upper California.

The belief that Indigenous peoples (see pp.128–129) were not utilizing the land to its full potential, particularly in terms of agriculture, became a pretext for the assertion of Manifest Destiny (see below). European-Americans believed that it was their duty to develop the land they regarded as wilderness through settlement and agricultural and industrial development.

KEY

1 The US acquired the Oregon Territory through a treaty with Britain in 1846.

2 By August 1846, the US had wrested control of New Mexico and Upper California from Mexico.

3 A transcontinental railroad was proposed, connecting the West from Oregon to New York City through Indigenous territory.

▷ **Mapping the West, 1846**
This map was issued during the Mexican-American War. It shows US control over the ceded Mexican territories of Upper California and New Mexico in the West (both pink). Mexico with its new border is shown in yellow.

MANIFEST DESTINY

The westward expansion of the US was driven by the concept of "manifest destiny," a term coined in 1845, and asserted the nation's inherent right to expand its territory. Manifest destiny provided a moral rationale for seizing the western territories, and opening them to land speculators and settlers. This painting shows a female figure—representing the US—leading settlers westward, while Indigenous peoples and herds of bison run away in fear.

American Progress (1872) by John Gast

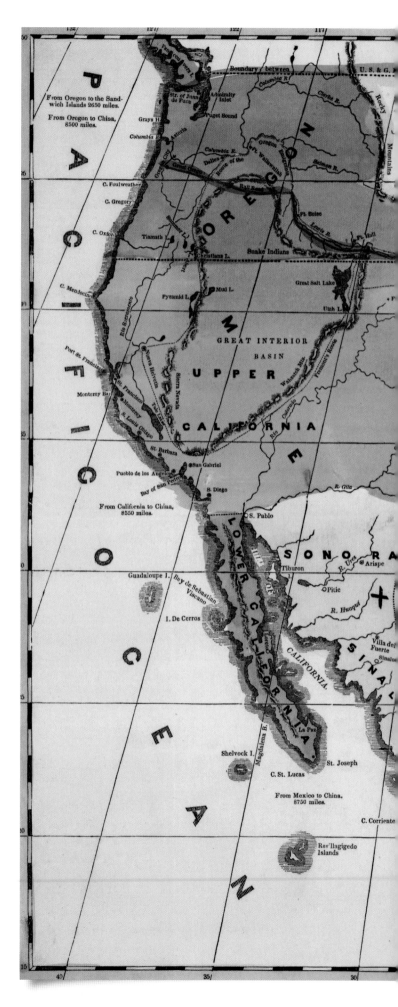

PHELPS'
ORNAMENTAL
MAP
OF THE
UNITED STATES
AND
MEXICO.

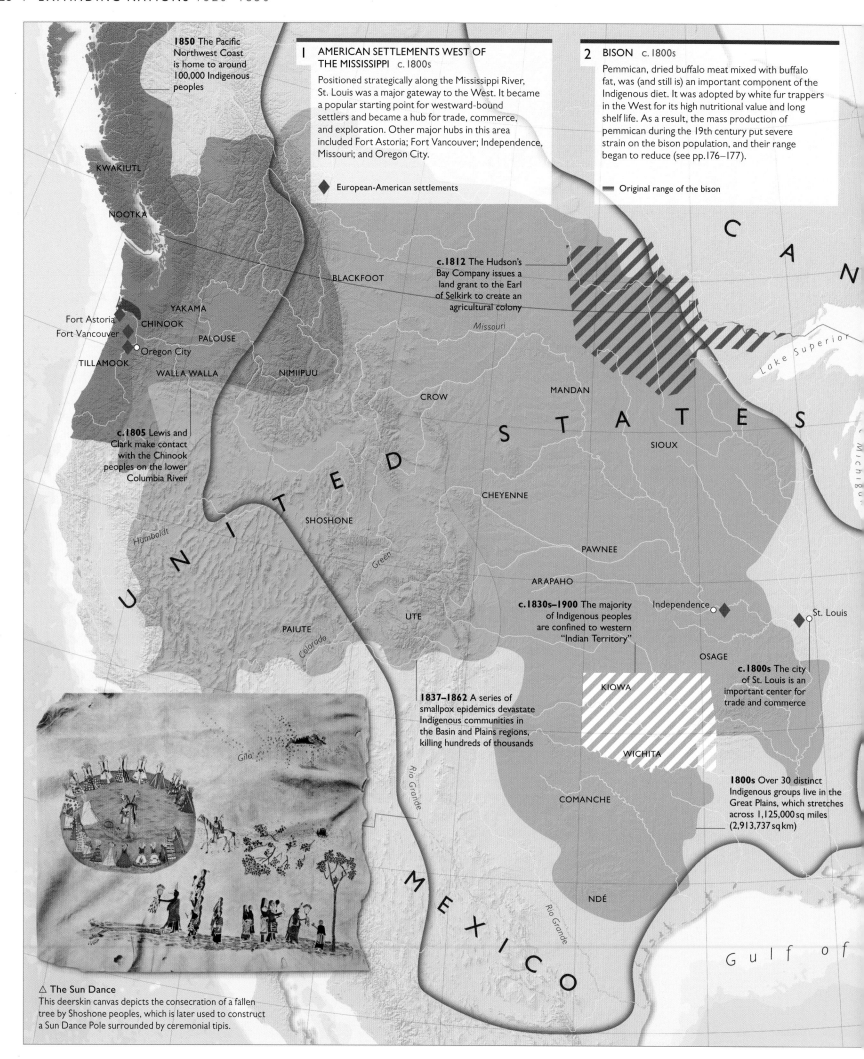

1850 The Pacific Northwest Coast is home to around 100,000 Indigenous peoples

1 AMERICAN SETTLEMENTS WEST OF THE MISSISSIPPI c.1800s

Positioned strategically along the Mississippi River, St. Louis was a major gateway to the West. It became a popular starting point for westward-bound settlers and became a hub for trade, commerce, and exploration. Other major hubs in this area included Fort Astoria; Fort Vancouver; Independence, Missouri; and Oregon City.

◆ European-American settlements

2 BISON c.1800s

Pemmican, dried buffalo meat mixed with buffalo fat, was (and still is) an important component of the Indigenous diet. It was adopted by white fur trappers in the West for its high nutritional value and long shelf life. As a result, the mass production of pemmican during the 19th century put severe strain on the bison population, and their range began to reduce (see pp.176–177).

▬ Original range of the bison

KWAKIUTL

NOOTKA

BLACKFOOT

c.1812 The Hudson's Bay Company issues a land grant to the Earl of Selkirk to create an agricultural colony

YAKAMA

Fort Astoria
Fort Vancouver
CHINOOK
Oregon City
PALOUSE
TILLAMOOK
WALLA WALLA
NIMIIPUU

c.1805 Lewis and Clark make contact with the Chinook peoples on the lower Columbia River

CROW
MANDAN

SIOUX

SHOSHONE
CHEYENNE

PAWNEE

ARAPAHO

c.1830s–1900 The majority of Indigenous peoples are confined to western "Indian Territory"

Independence
St. Louis

UTE

OSAGE

PAIUTE

c.1800s The city of St. Louis is an important center for trade and commerce

1837–1862 A series of smallpox epidemics devastate Indigenous communities in the Basin and Plains regions, killing hundreds of thousands

KIOWA

WICHITA

1800s Over 30 distinct Indigenous groups live in the Great Plains, which stretches across 1,125,000 sq miles (2,913,737 sq km)

COMANCHE

NDÉ

C A N
Lake Superior
Michigan
U N I T E D   S T A T E S
Missouri
Humboldt
Green
Colorado
Gila
Rio Grande
M E X I C O
Rio Grande
Gulf of

△ **The Sun Dance**
This deerskin canvas depicts the consecration of a fallen tree by Shoshone peoples, which is later used to construct a Sun Dance Pole surrounded by ceremonial tipis.

KEY

/// Western "Indian Territory"

CULTURE AREAS

■ Northwest Coast

■ Plateau

■ Great Basin

■ Great Plains

TIMELINE

1800 1820 1840 1860 1880 1900

3 PEOPLES OF THE GREAT BASIN c.1800s

Smallpox, measles, and other illnesses took a heavy toll on the Indigenous populations of the Great Basin, an area spanning portions of California, Nevada, Utah, Idaho, Oregon, and Wyoming. Affected peoples included the Ute, Washoe, and Shoshone, all of whom suffered from the introduced diseases brought by Euro-American traders.

c.1889 American bison are reduced to only 541 animals from nearly 60 million at the end of the 18th century

4 EARLY CONTACT WITH THE CHINOOK c.1805

The Chinook are a major group of the Northwest region, noted for their trading links with other peoples. Lewis and Clark's was the first US expedition to gather information on them, estimating their population at 16,000, around one third of the total Indigenous population of Oregon Country. Contact with Europeans led to a decline in their numbers.

■ Chinook territory

5 THE SELKIRK CONCESSION 1812

An agreement between Lord Selkirk and the Hudson's Bay Company (HBC) granted Selkirk a large tract in the Red River Valley to establish a fur-trading colony for displaced Scottish farmers in what is now part of Manitoba, Canada. An attempt to monopolize fur trading by HBC led to the Pemmican War (1812–1816) between white traders and the Métis peoples.

/// Selkirk Concession

WESTERN LANDS AND PEOPLES

The prospect of new land and economic opportunity generated a relentless westward expansion by white colonists that stretched the boundaries of the US from coast to coast. New forts and colonies in the West played a crucial role in shaping the new political structure of the continent.

The Indigenous peoples of the Great Plains and Canadian Prairies were known for their mobility, endurance, and horsemanship. These Indigenous populations practiced nomadic lifestyles and largely became the basis for the white colonists' archetypal view of "American Indians," alongside the non-nomadic communities of the Northwest Coast and Plateau regions.

While early European explorers had made contact with these Indigenous communities in the West, it was not until the early 1800s that the first US and Canadian expeditions extensively explored the region. In 1804, the Lewis and Clark expedition (see pp.110–111) marked the first instance of white Americans living among the Indigenous peoples of Oregon, observing and reporting back on their unique dress, diet, and cultural practices.

Although initial relations between Indigenous groups and white settlers were cordial, the eventual influx of European and US migrants into the southern Plateau region—comprising modern-day Montana, Idaho, Oregon, and Washington—in the 1840s initiated open conflict as Indigenous peoples resisted the growing demands of the fur trade that developed extensively in the area. Formidable warriors, the Great Plains and Prairie peoples often triumphed in battle against the US army. However, they faced limitations in undertaking lengthy campaigns because warriors also needed to hunt for their families. Eventually, treaties were brokered between the Indigenous inhabitants of these regions and the US government, yielding concessions such as safe passage for traders on the Santa Fe and Oregon trails that crossed Indigenous lands.

This increased interaction between white colonists and Indigenous populations across the Northwest Coast, Plateau, Basin, and Plains led to a growing number of coercive treaties that forcibly confined many Plateau peoples into smaller reservations (see pp.176–177), disrupting their traditional nomadic lifestyle.

WASHAKIE c.1804–1900

Chief Washakie was a prominent leader of the Eastern Shoshone during the mid-19th century. At the urging of white fur traders, he represented a contingent of Shoshone at the council meetings of the Treaty of Fort Laramie, which secured safe passage for westward-bound white settlers on the Oregon Trail. At the 1868 Fort Bridger negotiations, Washakie surrendered the Green River Valley of eastern Utah and southern Wyoming to the construction of the new Union Pacific Railroad.

Photograph of Chief Washakie, c.1900

THE EXPANSION OF SLAVERY

As the US continued to grow in size, the issue of human trafficking grew in scale alongside it. The original legislation and compromises of the past were no longer holding firm, and the nation's expansion was pushing it toward a crisis over which new states would prohibit slavery and which would allow it.

Slavery was a political and social issue that stalked the US from its inception. During the American Revolution a number of northern colonies, beginning with Vermont (1777), enacted gradual abolition measures. In 1787, Congress passed the Northwest Ordinance, prohibiting slavery in the territory that would become Ohio, Indiana, Illinois, Michigan, and Wisconsin. However, new states south of the Ohio River protected the rights of enslavers to traffic in human beings. Demand for American cotton drove the expansion of plantation slavery from the 1790s to 1820 into the modern-day states of South Carolina, Georgia, Alabama, Mississippi, and Louisiana. This fueled a lucrative internal trade that trafficked enslaved Black people from the Atlantic seaboard to the cotton belt.

Applications for statehood from Maine and Missouri triggered a political crisis between states that allowed slavery and states that prohibited it, leading to the 1820 Missouri Compromise. Maine would enter

prohibiting slavery, and Missouri allowing it. Some Black people sought freedom from the slaveholding South. Joined by allies, including free Black and white abolitionists, they walked along trails, roads, and rivers. This has been called the "Underground Railroad."

▷ Reynolds's political map of the US, c. 1856
This map shows states that prohibited slavery (red) and allowed it (gray), and the territory open to slavery or freedom per the Missouri Compromise (yellow/blue).

LOCATOR

KEY

1 The Missouri Compromise line of 1820 divided states that prohibited or allowed slavery.

2 States that formed north of the Ohio River did not allow slavery due to the 1787 Northwest Ordinance.

3 The labor of enslaved Black people generated riches in the Mississippi Delta.

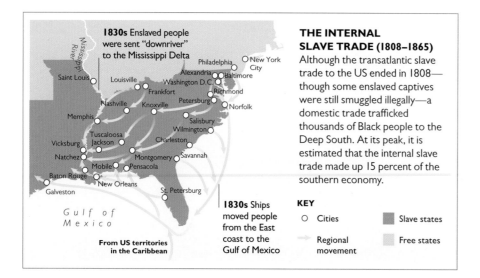

1830s Enslaved people were sent "downriver" to the Mississippi Delta

Cities shown: Saint Louis, Louisville, Frankfort, Nashville, Knoxville, Petersburg, Memphis, Tuscaloosa, Jackson, Vicksburg, Natchez, Mobile, Pensacola, Baton Rouge, New Orleans, Galveston, St. Petersburg, Savannah, Montgomery, Charleston, Wilmington, Salisbury, Norfolk, Richmond, Washington D.C., Alexandria, Baltimore, Philadelphia, New York City

Gulf of Mexico

1830s Ships moved people from the East coast to the Gulf of Mexico

From US territories in the Caribbean

THE INTERNAL SLAVE TRADE (1808–1865)
Although the transatlantic slave trade to the US ended in 1808— though some enslaved captives were still smuggled illegally—a domestic trade trafficked thousands of Black people to the Deep South. At its peak, it is estimated that the internal slave trade made up 15 percent of the southern economy.

KEY
- ○ Cities
- → Regional movement
- Slave states
- Free states

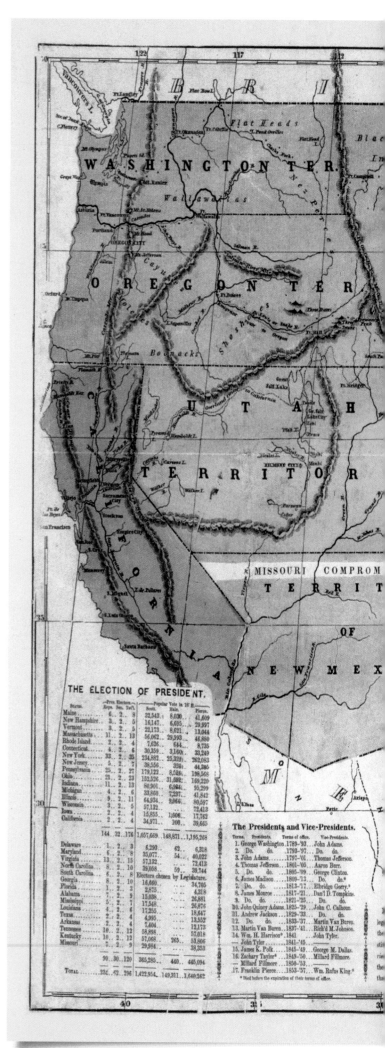

SLAVEHOLDERS.—Of the 6,222,418 white inhabitants of the South, only 347,525 are owners of slaves. And yet this faction controls every branch of the Federal Government, and wields its influence for the increase and perpetuation of Slavery. Classification of the Slaveholders in 1850:

Holders of 1 slave	68,820
Holders of 1 and under 5	105,683
Holders of 5 and under 10	80,765
Holders of 10 and under 20	54,595
Holders of 20 and under 50	29,733
Holders of 50 and under 100	6,196
Holders of 100 and under 200	1,479
Holders of 200 and under 300	187
Holders of 300 and under 500	56
Holders of 500 and under 1,000	9
Holders of 1,000 and over	2
Total number of Slaveholders	347,525

CONGRESSIONAL REPRESENTATION.

HOUSE OF REPRESENTATIVES.

The Free States have a total of 144 members.

The Slave States have a total of 90 members.

One Free State Representative represents 91,935 white men and women.

One Slave State Representative represents 68,725 white men and women.

Slave Representation gives to Slavery an advantage over Freedom of 30 votes in the House of Representatives.

UNITED STATES SENATE.

16 Free States, with a white population of 13,238,670 have 32 Senators.

15 Slave States, with a white population of 6,186,477, have 30 Senators.

So that 413,708 Free Men of the North enjoy but the same political privileges in the U.S. Senate as is given to 206,215 Slave Propagandists.

POST-OFFICE STATISTICS FOR A SINGLE YEAR.

Chief Items of the Accounts.	Free States.	Slave States.
Amount received for Postages	$4,391,360 80	$1,486,984 08
Paid for Transportation of Mails	2,381,607 16	2,087,266 05
	$2,010,253 64	$600,281 99

Showing that there is received yearly in the Free States, Two Millions of Dollars ($2,000,000) MORE THAN IS EXPENDED, while in the Slave States the EXPENDITURES EXCEED THE RECEIPTS over Six Hundred Thousand Dollars ($600,000).

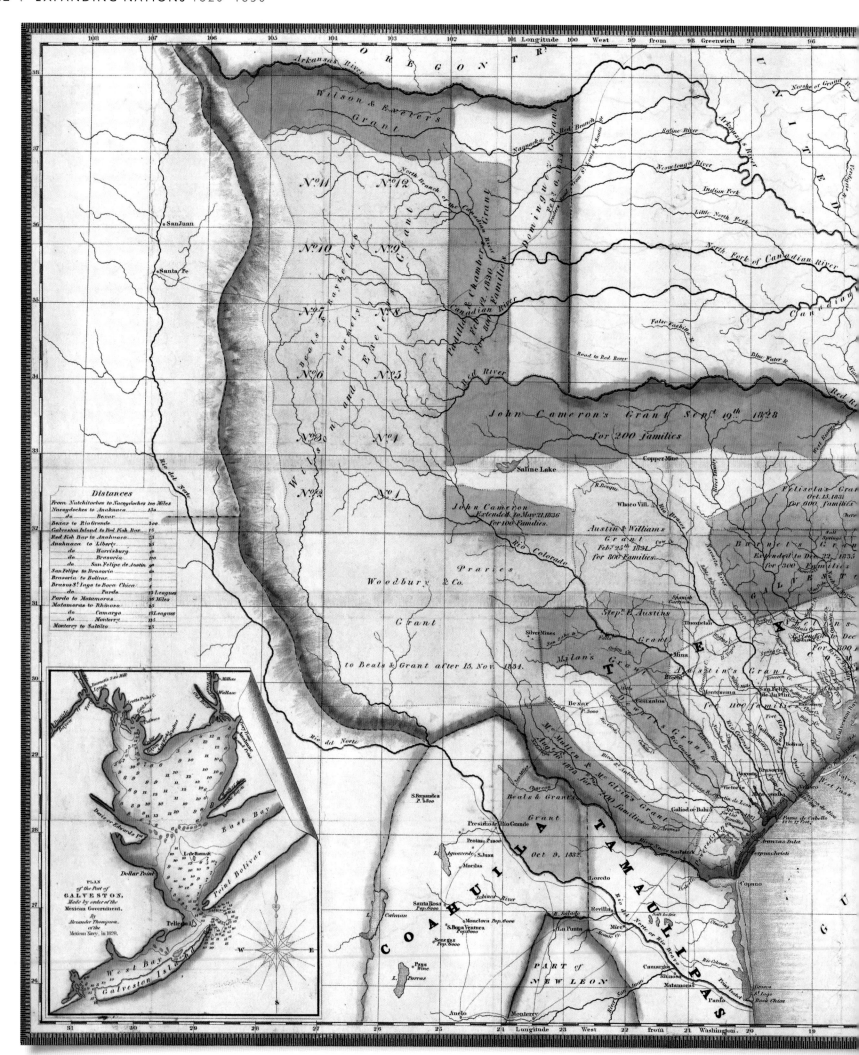

Distances

From Natchitoches to Nacogdoches	100 Miles
Nacogdoches to Anahuaca	150
do do Bexar	
Bexar to Rio Grande	300
Galveston Island to Red Fish Bar	15
Red Fish Bar to Anahuaca	25
Anahuaca to Liberty	20
do do Harrisburg	60
do do Brasoria	120
do do San Felipe de Austin	90
San Felipe to Brasoria	60
Brasoria to Bolivar	8
Brasos St. Iago to Boca Chica	
do do Pardo	15 Leagues
Pardo to Matamoras	36 Miles
Matamoras to Rhinoso	25
do do Camargo	18 Leagues
do do Monterry	115
Monterry to Saltilto	25

PLAN
of the Port of
GALVESTON,
Made by order of the
Mexican Government,
By
Alexander Thompson,
of the
Mexican Navy, in 1829.

TEXAS JOINS THE UNION

Settlers from the US arrived in the remote Mexican state of Coahuila y Tejas, bringing enslaved Africans with them. When Mexico banned slavery, it prompted the state to break away as an independent republic before joining the US as Texas in 1845.

Dominated by Indigenous peoples, the state of Texas was among the most remote in the newly formed republic of Mexico. In a bid to mitigate Indigenous resistance and exert greater control over the region, the Mexican government picked up where their Spanish predecessors had left off. In 1821, they renegotiated a deal with Stephen Austin—brokered the year before by his businessman father Moses Austin and the outgoing Spanish authorities—to settle 300 American families in Texas. By the early 1820s there were some 3,000 US settlers, or "Texians," and 2,500 Mexican Tejanos in the region.

Texians brought enslaved workers to build new cotton plantations. In 1829, Mexico abolished enslavement and tried to limit US immigration, because the Texian population had grown to around 30,000. However, the Mexican authorities did not have the resources to enforce either order.

◁ **Settling Texas**
This 1835 map shows Texian settlements, many of which were ideally positioned along waterways, such as the Brazos, Colorado, and Sabine Rivers. Shaded sections indicate land grants allocated within Texas.

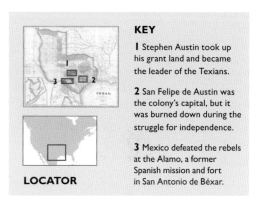

LOCATOR

KEY

1 Stephen Austin took up his grant land and became the leader of the Texians.

2 San Felipe de Austin was the colony's capital, but it was burned down during the struggle for independence.

3 Mexico defeated the rebels at the Alamo, a former Spanish mission and fort in San Antonio de Béxar.

Texians resisted and armed skirmishes followed, growing in intensity through 1835. By March 2, 1836, a declaration of independence for Texas had been adopted, secured in the battle of San Jacinto (see below).

Independent Texians wanted to join the US, a country that stood divided on the issue of enslavement. By early 1845—despite a heated debate about its implications—the US annexed Texas. On December 29, it became the 28th US state. US president James K. Polk welcomed this move with a view to procuring even more Mexico territory (see pp.138–139).

THE TEXAS REVOLUTION

Tensions between the Texians and the Mexican government came to a head in October 1835 and a revolution broke out. After suffering an early defeat in December, Mexico sent troops to Texas, resulting in a in a series of battles, including the key Battle of the Alamo. The defeat there fueled Texian retaliation and they prevailed upon Mexican forces at the decisive battle of San Jacinto in April 1836.

KEY

→ Texian troops

→ Mexican troops

✕ Major battles

▢ Republic of Texas

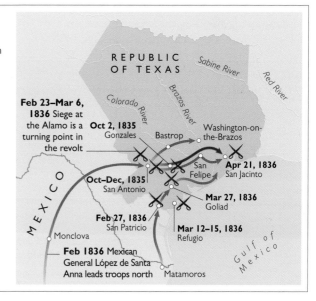

Battle of Withlacoochee
Significant US losses in 1835 during the Dade Battle and the Battle of Withlacoochee, which was fought at the ford of the Withlacoochee River, incited Congress to designate $600,000 in funding for the Second Seminole War.

SEMINOLE WARS

The Seminole Wars marked a turbulent chapter in the expansion of the US into Indigenous territory, with US forces seizing Indigenous lands on the Florida peninsula and forcing many Seminoles to move west.

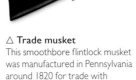

△ **Trade musket**
This smoothbore flintlock musket was manufactured in Pennsylvania around 1820 for trade with Indigenous peoples.

The Seminoles are an Indigenous nation of Creek origin who migrated to Florida. Their resistance to European settlers under British rule and their role in providing sanctuary for enslaved people set the stage for the conflicts that escalated into the First Seminole War. Led by the future President Andrew Jackson, this war spanned Florida and southern Georgia, pushing the Seminoles farther south.

Spain's cession of Florida to the US in 1821 initiated a policy of relocating the region's Indigenous populations. While some Seminole leaders signed a treaty in 1832 and relocated in the west (see pp.120–121), others resisted, utilizing guerrilla tactics that outmatched the numerically superior US forces, giving rise to the Second Seminole War. Rather than continuing direct skirmishes, US troops began destroying Seminole settlements and supplies. The US considered the Second Seminole War to have ended in 1842, without a formal peace treaty.

Persistent US military presence across Florida escalated into the Third Seminole War in 1855. Though there were no large-scale battles, these years were marked by raids and minor skirmishes. Suffering from starvation and a loss of morale, many Seminole, including the leader Holata Micco (also known as Billy Bowlegs), surrendered and were relocated to Indian Territory. In 1858, the United States declared an end to the conflicts, having relocated more than 3,000 Seminole west of the Mississippi River.

OSCEOLA c.1804–1838

Osceola led a group of warriors during the Second Seminole War, as an adviser to Micanopy, the principal chief of the Seminole. Osceola and Micanopy were captured under a flag of truce and imprisoned by the US Army, causing an uproar on both sides of the conflict. Osceola died while in custody in 1838, and he became a symbol of inspiration for Indigenous resistance.

EXPANSION OF TRANSPORTATION

The 19th century saw the construction of an expanding network of roads, canals, and railroads in the US that integrated the vast spaces of North America, dramatically reducing travel and freight times. The nation's economy reaped the benefits, with a boost in commercial agriculture and industry.

In 1794, the nation's first toll road opened between Philadelphia and Lancaster, Pennsylvania. Initiated in 1811 by the Army Corps of Engineers, the Cumberland Road, or "National Road," allowed travel across the Appalachian Mountains, extending overland travel between the Potomac and Ohio rivers by 1818.

River transportation experienced a revolutionary advancement with the application of steam power. US engineer Robert Fulton and his paddle wheel ship, *Clermont*, marked a significant breakthrough in 1807 by achieving a speed of 5 mph (8 kph) on its maiden voyage up the Hudson River. Steamboats became integral to river traffic, facilitating two-way transportation and the movement of freight cargo. The development of canals extended the reach of maritime transportation, as these enabled farmers in the Midwest and Southwest to efficiently transport goods to market. Steamboats could travel 50–100 miles (80–160 km) a day, compared to the 7–12 miles (11–19 km) possible via stagecoach or wagon. In the early 1800s, journeys between New York City and Chicago required approximately six weeks. By the 1830s, the travel time for a passenger to reach Chicago from New York City was down to two to three weeks.

The development of railroads in the US began with horse-drawn train cars, evolving rapidly with the introduction of steam technology made possible by fuels such as coal. After construction was complete, railroads lowered the cost of transporting many kinds

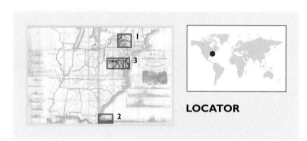

LOCATOR

of goods, causing a growth in other industries such as iron and steel production. By 1830, more than 200 railroads were proposed or under construction, with about 1,000 miles (1,600 km) in operation. By 1840, the US had nearly 3,000 miles (4,800 km) of track, tripling to over 9,000 miles (14,480 km) in 1850 and stretching from the East Coast to the Midwest. In 1857, the travel time from New York City to Chicago was reduced to a two-day journey. A trip from New York to California could now be completed in one month. The completion of the first transcontinental railroad, the "Overland Route," in 1869 joined the lines of the Central Pacific and Union Pacific Railroad Companies (see pp.194–195).

▷ **Railroad and canal map of the US, 1834**
The integration of waterways and railroads facilitated the expansion of the American frontier and the development of a national industrial economy. By 1840, the US had dug more than 3,000 miles (4,800 km) of canals.

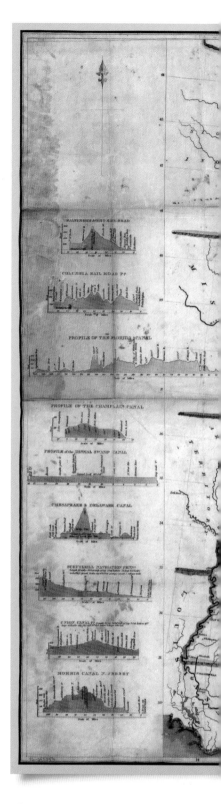

STEAMBOATS

Various types of steamboats served different functions, from carrying passengers and cargo to clearing river obstacles. Showboats emerged as floating entertainment venues, with theaters, ballrooms, and saloons, contributing to the tourism of river towns. Despite their benefits, steamboats posed safety risks due to boiler explosions, limiting their lifespans and cost-effectiveness. Steamboat captains would often race each other and attempt speed records along their routes.

Steamboats race on the Mississippi River

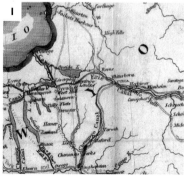

△ **Erie Canal**
Built 1817–1825 to connect the cities of Buffalo and Albany, the Erie Canal reduced travel times and shipping costs, making New York City a commercial and financial hub.

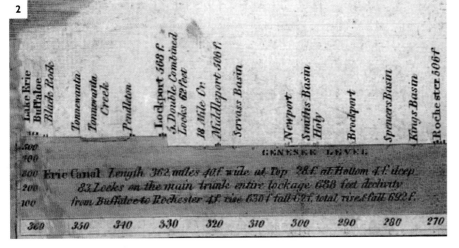

◁ Erie Canal elevation profile
The Eerie Canal cut through forests, swamps, fields, and cliffs on its 363-mile (584-km) route, and used 83 locks to overcome hills.

△ Baltimore and Ohio Railroad
Established in 1827, this first public-use railroad carried the first telegraph message, and spanned 10,000 miles (16,100 km) in track lines.

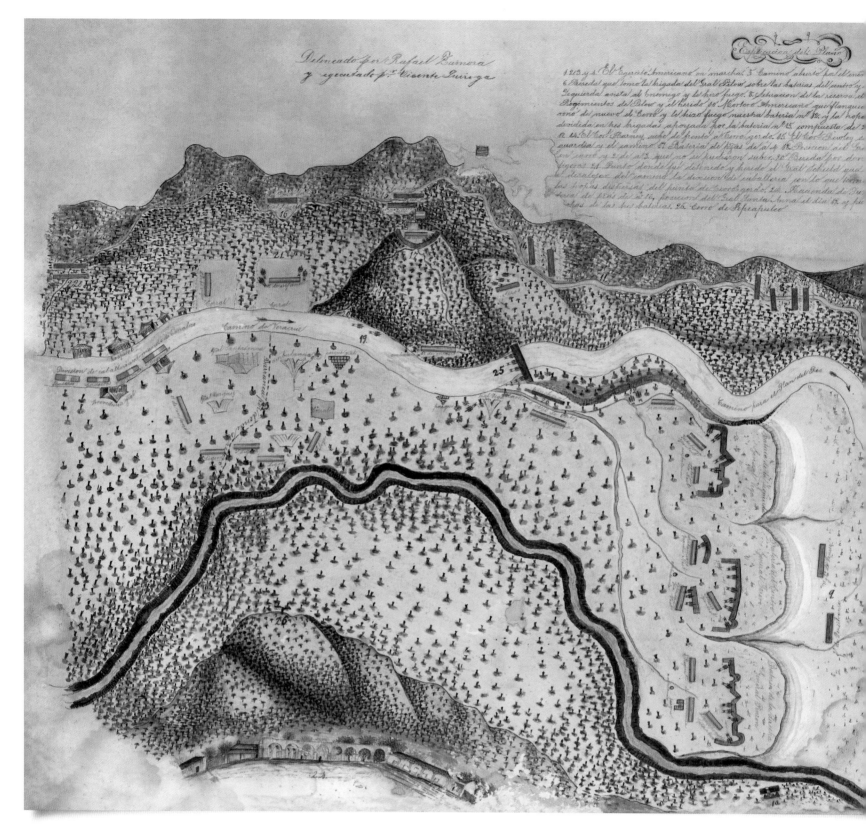

Delineado por Rafael Zamora
y ejecutado p.r Vicente Guiroga

Esplicacion del Plano

△ **Battle of Cerro Gordo**
This watercolor sketch by Mexican soldiers shows the positions of US and Mexican troops during the confrontation at the mountain pass north of the port of Veracruz.

▷ **Santa Anna's tent**
Antonio López de Santa Anna, the politician and general who had presided over the loss of Texas, returned to the battlefield with 12,000 soldiers in tow.

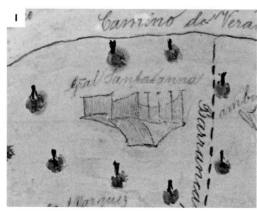

◁ **Blocked roads**
Mexican troops closed off the roads and took up positions in the hills, but US soldiers found paths to go around, above, and behind them to launch surprise attacks.

▷ **The US camp**
General Winfield Scott's force of 8,500 troops spent five days in camp while US Army scouts reconnoitered the Mexican positions at Cerro Gordo.

MEXICAN-AMERICAN WAR

The animosity between US and Mexico worsened after the latter's loss of Texas in 1836, turning into a full war a decade later. US military forces quickly took the upper hand, and the war concluded with a huge expansion of territory for the US.

The issue of Texas heightened growing tensions between the US and Mexico, with the Mexican government refusing to accept Texas's annexation in 1845 (see pp.132–133). Relations were further strained by an ongoing dispute about where the boundary between the two countries lay. The US claimed it was at the Rio Grande; Mexico said it was farther north, at the Nueces River.

US president James K. Polk (1845–1849) had run for office on an expansionist platform, and he was determined to obtain territory. He began by offering to buy parts of northern Mexico, including California, but was refused. In spring 1845, he dispatched troops to the Nueces River area. Some of these troops later moved to the Rio Grande area, which Mexico considered an act of provocation.

In April 1846, Mexican troops attacked a US scouting party, and the war began. The US initially sent one force south to invade Mexico, while another occupied California and New Mexico. A turning point

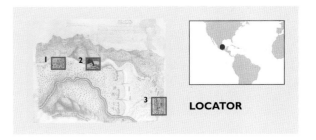

LOCATOR

came in 1847, when General Winfield Scott sailed to the port city of Veracruz and began marching inland toward the capital, Mexico City. The US army also won a crucial victory at the battle of Cerro Gordo (shown left) on April 18, 1847, during its approach.

Negotiations to end the conflict broke down when Mexico disputed the terms on offer. Fighting carried on until the US captured Mexico City in September 1847 and the Mexican government capitulated. The subsequent Treaty of Guadalupe Hidalgo (see below) ceded 51 percent of Mexican land to the US.

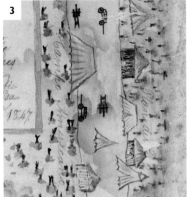

AFTERMATH OF THE WAR
Mexico suffered great losses under the 1848 Treaty of Guadalupe Hidalgo, ceding just over half of its remaining territory to the US. The area of land totaled 525,000 square miles (1.36 million square km) and included much of what is now Nevada, Utah, California, New Mexico, Texas, and western Colorado. The US also added around 150,000 new residents, as some Mexicans decided to stay in their homes, even though they were now governed by new country.

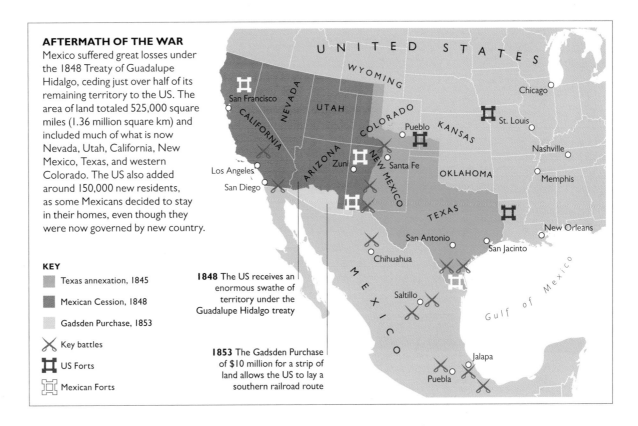

1848 The US receives an enormous swathe of territory under the Guadalupe Hidalgo treaty

1853 The Gadsden Purchase of $10 million for a strip of land allows the US to lay a southern railroad route

KEY

- Texas annexation, 1845
- Mexican Cession, 1848
- Gadsden Purchase, 1853
- ✗ Key battles
- ⊞ US Forts
- ⊞ Mexican Forts

POPULATION BOOM

Once the news of the discovery of gold in northern California began to circulate, the region experienced waves of migration. Prospective miners from the eastern US and places as far away as China and Australia came to seek their fortunes.

TIMELINE

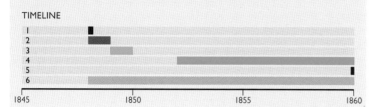

ENVIRONMENTAL IMPACT

Gold mining increasingly involved going deeper into the ground. Such excavations led to erosion and deforestation. Hydraulic mining used jets of water to clear rock and sediment, the runoff from which contaminated nearby water bodies.

Hydraulic mining at Old Hilltop Mine, Michigan Bar, 1849

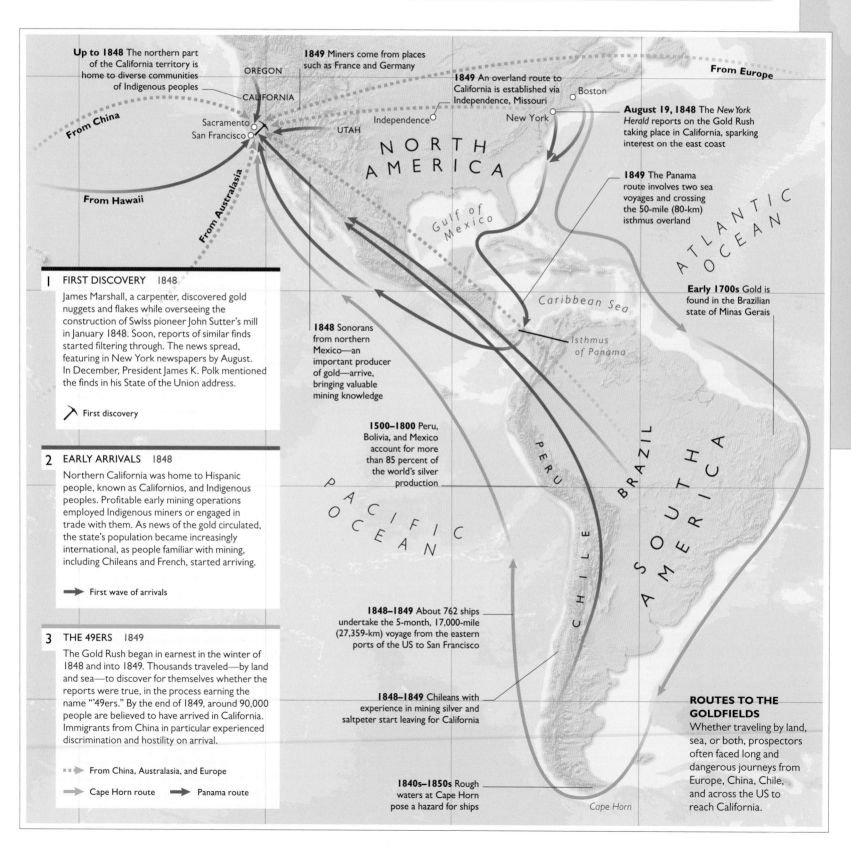

Up to 1848 The northern part of the California territory is home to diverse communities of Indigenous peoples

1849 Miners come from places such as France and Germany

From Europe

1849 An overland route to California is established via Independence, Missouri

August 19, 1848 The *New York Herald* reports on the Gold Rush taking place in California, sparking interest on the east coast

OREGON
CALIFORNIA
From China
Sacramento
San Francisco
From Hawaii
From Australasia

Boston
Independence
New York

1849 The Panama route involves two sea voyages and crossing the 50-mile (80-km) isthmus overland

NORTH AMERICA

Gulf of Mexico

ATLANTIC OCEAN

Caribbean Sea

Early 1700s Gold is found in the Brazilian state of Minas Gerais

Isthmus of Panama

1 FIRST DISCOVERY 1848

James Marshall, a carpenter, discovered gold nuggets and flakes while overseeing the construction of Swiss pioneer John Sutter's mill in January 1848. Soon, reports of similar finds started filtering through. The news spread, featuring in New York newspapers by August. In December, President James K. Polk mentioned the finds in his State of the Union address.

⚒ First discovery

2 EARLY ARRIVALS 1848

Northern California was home to Hispanic people, known as Californios, and Indigenous peoples. Profitable early mining operations employed Indigenous miners or engaged in trade with them. As news of the gold circulated, the state's population became increasingly international, as people familiar with mining, including Chileans and French, started arriving.

➡ First wave of arrivals

3 THE 49ERS 1849

The Gold Rush began in earnest in the winter of 1848 and into 1849. Thousands traveled—by land and sea—to discover for themselves whether the reports were true, in the process earning the name "'49ers." By the end of 1849, around 90,000 people are believed to have arrived in California. Immigrants from China in particular experienced discrimination and hostility on arrival.

▪▪▶ From China, Australasia, and Europe
➡ Cape Horn route   ➡ Panama route

1848 Sonorans from northern Mexico—an important producer of gold—arrive, bringing valuable mining knowledge

1500–1800 Peru, Bolivia, and Mexico account for more than 85 percent of the world's silver production

PACIFIC OCEAN

PERU
BRAZIL
CHILE
SOUTH AMERICA

1848–1849 About 762 ships undertake the 5-month, 17,000-mile (27,359-km) voyage from the eastern ports of the US to San Francisco

1848–1849 Chileans with experience in mining silver and saltpeter start leaving for California

1840s–1850s Rough waters at Cape Horn pose a hazard for ships

Cape Horn

ROUTES TO THE GOLDFIELDS

Whether traveling by land, sea, or both, prospectors often faced long and dangerous journeys from Europe, China, Chile, and across the US to reach California.

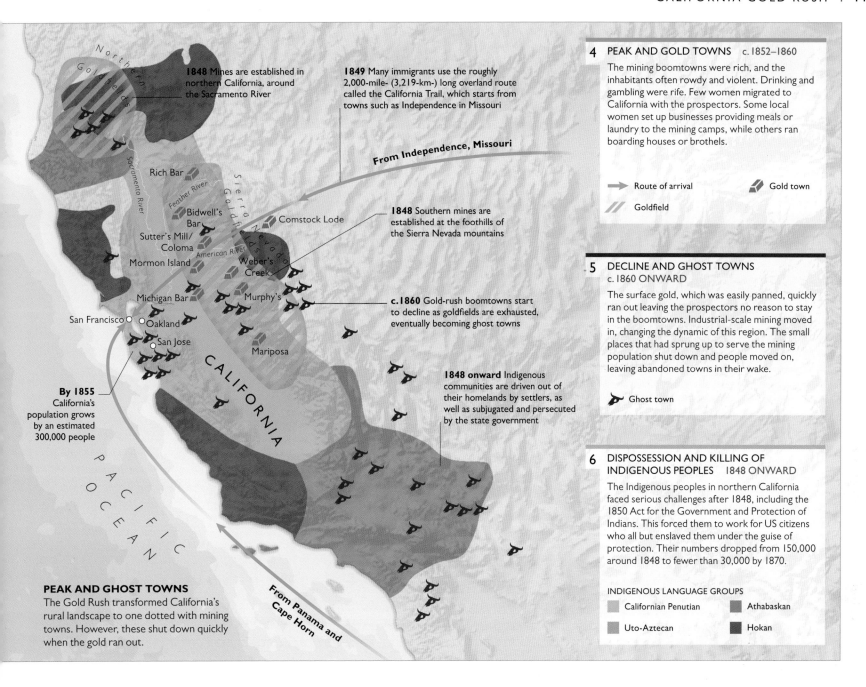

1848 Mines are established in northern California, around the Sacramento River

1849 Many immigrants use the roughly 2,000-mile- (3,219-km-) long overland route called the California Trail, which starts from towns such as Independence in Missouri

From Independence, Missouri

Rich Bar

Bidwell's Bar

Sutter's Mill/ Coloma

Mormon Island

Comstock Lode

Weber's Creek

1848 Southern mines are established at the foothills of the Sierra Nevada mountains

Michigan Bar

Murphy's

San Francisco

Oakland

San Jose

Mariposa

c.1860 Gold-rush boomtowns start to decline as goldfields are exhausted, eventually becoming ghost towns

By 1855 California's population grows by an estimated 300,000 people

CALIFORNIA

1848 onward Indigenous communities are driven out of their homelands by settlers, as well as subjugated and persecuted by the state government

PACIFIC OCEAN

From Panama and Cape Horn

PEAK AND GHOST TOWNS
The Gold Rush transformed California's rural landscape to one dotted with mining towns. However, these shut down quickly when the gold ran out.

4 PEAK AND GOLD TOWNS c.1852–1860
The mining boomtowns were rich, and the inhabitants often rowdy and violent. Drinking and gambling were rife. Few women migrated to California with the prospectors. Some local women set up businesses providing meals or laundry to the mining camps, while others ran boarding houses or brothels.

→ Route of arrival   Gold town

Goldfield

5 DECLINE AND GHOST TOWNS c.1860 ONWARD
The surface gold, which was easily panned, quickly ran out leaving the prospectors no reason to stay in the boomtowns. Industrial-scale mining moved in, changing the dynamic of this region. The small places that had sprung up to serve the mining population shut down and people moved on, leaving abandoned towns in their wake.

Ghost town

6 DISPOSSESSION AND KILLING OF INDIGENOUS PEOPLES 1848 ONWARD
The Indigenous peoples in northern California faced serious challenges after 1848, including the 1850 Act for the Government and Protection of Indians. This forced them to work for US citizens who all but enslaved them under the guise of protection. Their numbers dropped from 150,000 around 1848 to fewer than 30,000 by 1870.

INDIGENOUS LANGUAGE GROUPS

Californian Penutian	Athabaskan
Uto-Aztecan	Hokan

CALIFORNIA GOLD RUSH

News of the discovery of gold in the Sierra Nevada mountains drew thousands of migrants to California, transforming its economy. However, its Indigenous communities did not fare as well, suffering terrible violence and land dispossession during the Gold Rush.

The search for gold is tied to the history of colonialism in the Americas, and by the 19th century there were profitable mines across Latin America. However, the discovery of gold in 1848 at Sutter's Mill—on the American River, west of Sacramento, California— was accidental. Once it became clear that there were substantial gold deposits in the area, nearly 100,000 miners from around the world poured in, including enslaved Black people brought against their will.

The timing was ideal—what had been the state of Alta California in Mexico was now part of the United States, ceded in 1848 under the Treaty of

Guadalupe Hidalgo (see p.138) and granted statehood in 1850. By 1854, gold valued at around $345 million (at the time) had been mined. Soon, many of the overseas arrivals were being pushed out. A foreign miners' tax was instituted in 1850, which required non-US citizens to pay a monthly fee to continue mining in the state. Local ordinances targeting Hispanic people and Indigenous peoples were also put in place. Indigenous communities were subjugated, murdered, and massacred with little to no recourse to federal protection. California was forever transformed by this tumultuous time.

△ **Panning for gold**
A miner uses a shallow pan to sift for gold in California's American River in 1850. Panning was difficult, manual work, with no guarantee of actually finding gold.

North America's first Chinatown
The San Francisco Chinatown is the oldest such enclave in North America. This photograph shows Chinese immigrants at the entrance to a temple, many of which were established in Chinese communities.

IMMIGRATION FROM EAST ASIA

People from East Asia began migrating to North America in large numbers from the middle of the 19th century. Despite facing hardship and discrimination as immigrants, they made a vital and lasting contribution to the long-term development of the US and Canada.

While Asians had long been present in the US, it was the 1848 gold rush (see pp.140–141) that brought large numbers from China in search of better economic opportunities. The 1858 gold rush in British Columbia then drew Chinese prospectors from San Francisco, leading to the first Chinese community in Canada in Barkerville. Thousands of laborers from China worked on railroads, but they also set up businesses and found employment in a range of industries. "Chinatowns" sprung up in cities across the continent, most famously in San Francisco. Although governments were initially welcoming, these new arrivals were met with fear, suspicion, and often violence.

Laws restricting Asian immigration

US laws increasingly targeted Chinese people, culminating in the Chinese Exclusion Act of 1882, which banned Chinese immigration for more than 60 years. In 1885, Canada set a restrictive tax for incoming Chinese immigrants. However, North America remained attractive for migrants from countries not affected by these laws, especially Japan from the 1880s onward. More than 400,000 Japanese people migrated to the US before 1911, especially to Hawaii and the west coast. They, too, faced hostility and restrictive legislation. In 1924, the US banned immigration from East Asia, including Japan, Korea, and the Philippines, and Canada banned Chinese immigration.

JAPANESE IMMIGRATION TO HAWAII

From 1885, Japanese workers were employed on sugar-cane plantations in Hawaii. Their work was physical and exhausting, and their lives were strictly controlled by the companies that employed them. Despite this, the Japanese community prospered, bringing with them their cultural traditions, cuisine, language, and religious beliefs. By the 1920s, more than 40 percent of the population of Hawaii was of Japanese descent.

This 1885 painting shows Japanese laborers at Spreckelsville Plantation, on Maui.

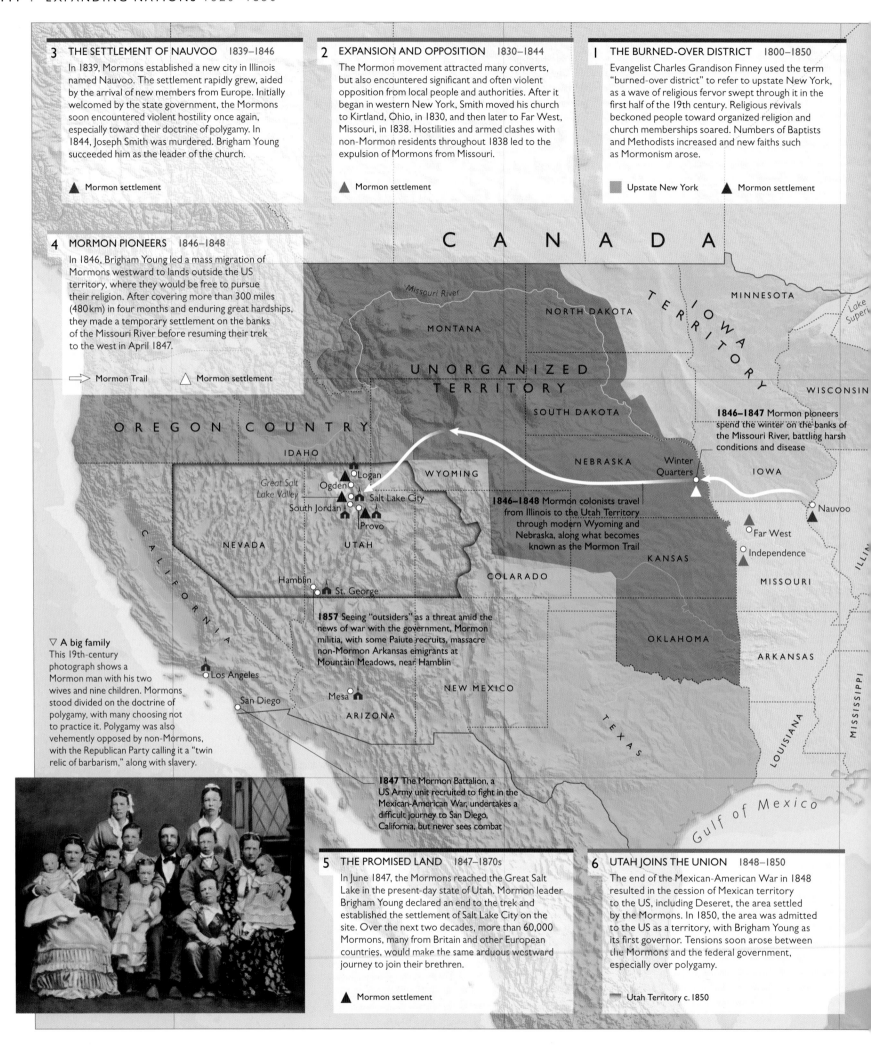

3 THE SETTLEMENT OF NAUVOO 1839–1846

In 1839, Mormons established a new city in Illinois named Nauvoo. The settlement rapidly grew, aided by the arrival of new members from Europe. Initially welcomed by the state government, the Mormons soon encountered violent hostility once again, especially toward their doctrine of polygamy. In 1844, Joseph Smith was murdered. Brigham Young succeeded him as the leader of the church.

▲ Mormon settlement

2 EXPANSION AND OPPOSITION 1830–1844

The Mormon movement attracted many converts, but also encountered significant and often violent opposition from local people and authorities. After it began in western New York, Smith moved his church to Kirtland, Ohio, in 1830, and then later to Far West, Missouri, in 1838. Hostilities and armed clashes with non-Mormon residents throughout 1838 led to the expulsion of Mormons from Missouri.

▲ Mormon settlement

1 THE BURNED-OVER DISTRICT 1800–1850

Evangelist Charles Grandison Finney used the term "burned-over district" to refer to upstate New York, as a wave of religious fervor swept through it in the first half of the 19th century. Religious revivals beckoned people toward organized religion and church memberships soared. Numbers of Baptists and Methodists increased and new faiths such as Mormonism arose.

■ Upstate New York ▲ Mormon settlement

4 MORMON PIONEERS 1846–1848

In 1846, Brigham Young led a mass migration of Mormons westward to lands outside the US territory, where they would be free to pursue their religion. After covering more than 300 miles (480km) in four months and enduring great hardships, they made a temporary settlement on the banks of the Missouri River before resuming their trek to the west in April 1847.

⟹ Mormon Trail △ Mormon settlement

1846–1847 Mormon pioneers spend the winter on the banks of the Missouri River, battling harsh conditions and disease

1846–1848 Mormon colonists travel from Illinois to the Utah Territory through modern Wyoming and Nebraska, along what becomes known as the Mormon Trail

1857 Seeing "outsiders" as a threat amid the news of war with the government, Mormon militia, with some Paiute recruits, massacre non-Mormon Arkansas emigrants at Mountain Meadows, near Hamblin

1847 The Mormon Battalion, a US Army unit recruited to fight in the Mexican-American War, undertakes a difficult journey to San Diego, California, but never sees combat

▽ A big family
This 19th-century photograph shows a Mormon man with his two wives and nine children. Mormons stood divided on the doctrine of polygamy, with many choosing not to practice it. Polygamy was also vehemently opposed by non-Mormons, with the Republican Party calling it a "twin relic of barbarism," along with slavery.

5 THE PROMISED LAND 1847–1870s

In June 1847, the Mormons reached the Great Salt Lake in the present-day state of Utah. Mormon leader Brigham Young declared an end to the trek and established the settlement of Salt Lake City on the site. Over the next two decades, more than 60,000 Mormons, many from Britain and other European countries, would make the same arduous westward journey to join their brethren.

▲ Mormon settlement

6 UTAH JOINS THE UNION 1848–1850

The end of the Mexican-American War in 1848 resulted in the cession of Mexican territory to the US, including Deseret, the area settled by the Mormons. In 1850, the area was admitted to the US as a territory, with Brigham Young as its first governor. Tensions soon arose between the Mormons and the federal government, especially over polygamy.

— Utah Territory c. 1850

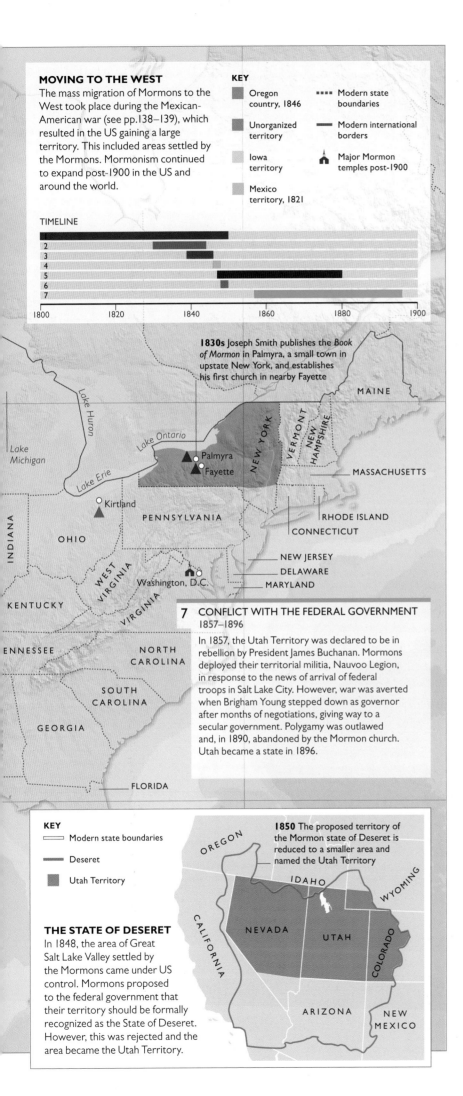

MOVING TO THE WEST

The mass migration of Mormons to the West took place during the Mexican-American war (see pp.138–139), which resulted in the US gaining a large territory. This included areas settled by the Mormons. Mormonism continued to expand post-1900 in the US and around the world.

KEY

- Oregon country, 1846
- Unorganized territory
- Iowa territory
- Mexico territory, 1821
- ▪▪▪▪ Modern state boundaries
- ▬ Modern international borders
- ⛪ Major Mormon temples post-1900

TIMELINE

1 2 3 4 5 6 7

1800 1820 1840 1860 1880 1900

1830s Joseph Smith publishes the *Book of Mormon* in Palmyra, a small town in upstate New York, and establishes his first church in nearby Fayette

MAINE

Lake Huron

Lake Michigan

Lake Ontario

Lake Erie

Palmyra

Fayette

VERMONT

NEW HAMPSHIRE

NEW YORK

MASSACHUSETTS

Kirtland

PENNSYLVANIA

RHODE ISLAND

CONNECTICUT

INDIANA

OHIO

NEW JERSEY

DELAWARE

MARYLAND

Washington, D.C.

WEST VIRGINIA

VIRGINIA

KENTUCKY

TENNESSEE

NORTH CAROLINA

SOUTH CAROLINA

GEORGIA

FLORIDA

7 CONFLICT WITH THE FEDERAL GOVERNMENT 1857–1896

In 1857, the Utah Territory was declared to be in rebellion by President James Buchanan. Mormons deployed their territorial militia, Nauvoo Legion, in response to the news of arrival of federal troops in Salt Lake City. However, war was averted when Brigham Young stepped down as governor after months of negotiations, giving way to a secular government. Polygamy was outlawed and, in 1890, abandoned by the Mormon church. Utah became a state in 1896.

KEY

- ▭ Modern state boundaries
- ▬ Deseret
- ▪ Utah Territory

THE STATE OF DESERET

In 1848, the area of Great Salt Lake Valley settled by the Mormons came under US control. Mormons proposed to the federal government that their territory should be formally recognized as the State of Deseret. However, this was rejected and the area became the Utah Territory.

1850 The proposed territory of the Mormon state of Deseret is reduced to a smaller area and named the Utah Territory

OREGON

IDAHO

WYOMING

CALIFORNIA

NEVADA

UTAH

COLORADO

ARIZONA

NEW MEXICO

THE RISE OF MORMONISM

In the mid-19th century, the Latter Day Saint movement was founded in the US. Its adherents, known as Mormons, played an important role in the settling of the US West.

In the early 19th century, upstate New York was in the throes of the "Second Great Awakening," a period of intense religious revival and experimentation that saw the creation of many new faiths and movements within the protestant Christian tradition. The most successful of these was Mormonism—also known as the Church of Jesus Christ of Latter-Day Saints—founded by US prophet Joseph Smith in 1830. Smith claimed to have received an angelic revelation of a new scripture written on plates of gold. He drew many new followers to his cause, but the new church also attracted hostility from the wider public, especially over the doctrine of plural marriage, or polygamy. Mormons were hounded across the Midwest, and Smith was murdered in 1844. After his death, the leadership of the Mormons fell to his disciple Brigham Young.

In 1846, Mormons undertook one of the most significant mass migrations in US history to escape religious persecution—an arduous, 1,300-mile (2,090-km) westward trek to the Great Salt Lake. They settled in this region, which in 1850 was incorporated into the US as the Utah Territory. The federal government disagreed with many Mormon practices, resulting in the occupation of Utah by federal troops. After this, relations remained peaceful, if tense, culminating in full statehood for Utah in 1896. A strong Mormon presence remains in Utah today.

SPREADING THE FAITH

Missionary activity—both in the US and abroad—was a significant feature of the Mormon church from its earliest days. After Joseph Smith established a missionary branch in Britain in 1837, the country became a major source of new recruits, reaching 80,000 members by 1890. The Pacific was another area of missionary efforts in the mid-19th century, with new branches established in Australia (1844), Hawaii (1850), and New Zealand (1855). The Laie Hawaii Temple on O'ahu Island (below) was established in 1850, and is the oldest continually operating Mormon temple outside of Utah.

COMANCHE EMPIRE

The Comanche Nation, known as "Numunuu" or "The People" in their own language, migrated across what is now the US Southwest and northern Mexico seeking opportunities to trade and raid. This land became Comanche country, or Comanchería, and by 1750, their population had grown to 15,000.

By the early 1700s, the Comanche acquired horses from the Spanish and widened the range of bison hunting across the Great Plains. By expanding their territory the Comanche gained access to trade goods and weaponry. Skilled traders, they controlled much of the commerce of the Southern Plains, bartering buffalo products and horses with colonists for manufactured items and foodstuffs. Horses became a symbol of Comanche wealth and the most valuable trade commodity. As the Comanche extended south, they fought with nations such as the Ndé (Apache) and communities in northern Mexico. With the decline of Spanish influence in the early 1800s, Comanche raids on Spanish settlements became more frequent, strategically disrupting the region's resources and forcing the Spanish to depend on Comanche trade. By raiding settlements for goods to trade with white traders entering Texas, the Comanche gained greater access to arms and ammunition, and a market for their horses.

In the 1830s, displaced Indigenous nations settling in "Indian Territory" turned to Comanchería for horses for trade, travel, hunting, and war. In their new surroundings, the nations forged alliances with the Comanche via intermarriage and assimilation. The Indian Removal Act of 1830 (see pp.120–121) saw the forced relocation of thousands of Indigenous peoples, and the territories controlled by the Comanche shrank. The culmination of this was the signing of the Treaty of Medicine Lodge Creek in 1867, designating a reservation for the Comanche, Kiowa, and Ndé in southwest "Indian Territory" between the Washita and Red rivers.

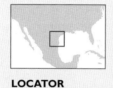

LOCATOR

KEY

1 Santa Fe, New Mexico, was a center of colonial trade and was also sometimes the target of Comanche raids.

2 Northern and Middle Comanche territory included the Red River, an important source of trade with the Kiowa people also nearby.

3 Southern Comanche territory extended down to Mexico.

▷ **Colton's map of Texas, 1855**
Parts of Texas were inhabited by the Comanche. On this 1855 map, "Indian Territory" (now Oklahoma) can be seen top right, with coloring indicating different counties.

CYNTHIA ANN PARKER
c.1817–1871

In May 1836, Comanches and their allies raided Fort Parker, a colonial settlement near the Navasota River in central Texas, resulting in the deaths of several colonists and the abduction of five hostages, among them a child named Cynthia Ann Parker. While the other captives were later released, Parker remained with the Comanche for 24 years. She became the wife of Chief Peta Nocona and bore three children, one of whom, Quanah Parker, would become the last chief of the Comanche. Various traders and soldiers encountered Parker on several occasions, but she refused to leave her Comanche family until she was forcibly recaptured in 1860.

TEXAS

PUBLISHED BY J.H. COLTON & Co. No. 172 WILLIAM ST NEW YORK.

SCALE OF MILES.

The Perry Expedition, 1852–1853
Ordered by President Millard Fillmore, the Perry Expedition sought to open trade with Japan through "gunboat diplomacy," the use of military force to achieve foreign policy goals. This print by Toshu Shogetsu depicts the arrival of Perry's "Black Ships" into Edo Bay in 1853.

THE PACIFIC WORLD

In February 1784, the *Empress of China* became the first ship to successfully complete a historic voyage from the US to China, opening up trade between the two nations. Commodities such as tea, silk, porcelain, sugar, spices, and opium characterized this new commerce across the Pacific world.

△ **A new import**
This Chinese *gaiwan* was traditionally used for drinking tea, which accounted for 36 percent of US imports from China in 1822.

The westward expansion of the US during the 19th century extended far beyond the confines of North America, as this period witnessed a sustained effort to establish a more robust US presence across the vast expanse of the Pacific Ocean. The allure of potential profits earned from trade with China motivated US officials, and later citizens, to venture into the Pacific region, with a growing stream of merchants embarking on journeys to China and its surrounding territories.

The 1844 Treaty of Wangxia, the first of the unequal treaties imposed on the Qing dynasty by the US, established consulates and residences for US ministers in the capital Beijing (then Peking) and key port cities, strengthening diplomatic ties and solidifying US engagement in the Pacific region. In 1854, the Convention of Kanagawa reestablished trade and communication with Japan, and US embassies were established in Fiji (1844), Samoa (1856), and the Marshall Islands (1881) as merchants sought new supplies and trade goods. The island Kingdom of Hawai'i was identified as a strategic and substantial Pacific base to support western interests in China, and saw a rising US presence in the area. This eventually led to the annexation of the islands by the US in 1898 (see pp.196–197).

MATTHEW C. PERRY 1794–1858

US naval officer Commodore Matthew C. Perry served in the War of 1812 (see pp.112–113) and the Mexican-American War (see pp.138–139). He made two expeditions to Japan in 1852–1854 and played a pivotal role in the signing of the Convention of Kanagawa in 1854, marking the end of Japan's 220-year-old policy of national seclusion. He was an early advocate of the use of steam power in the US Navy, and is known as "the father of the steam navy."

DISRUPTION AND EXPANSION

THE ISSUE OF SLAVERY IN THE US REACHED A BREAKING POINT, SPARKING A CIVIL WAR THAT REDEFINED THE NATION. IN THE NORTH, COLONIAL TERRITORIES UNITED AS THE DOMINION OF CANADA, AND THE VAST LANDS OF ALASKA WERE ADDED TO THE US.

A NATION DIVIDED

In the mid-19th century, civil war erupted in the US between the abolitionist North and the pro-slavery South. The North prevailed, but the abolition of slavery further widened the rift between the two camps.

◁ **Battle at Fort Sumter**
Federal troops occupied Fort Sumter in South Carolina after the state's secession. On April 12, 1861, Confederate forces bombarded the fort to reclaim it, sparking a civil war. This engraving shows Union forces returning Confederate fire.

By 1850, sectional strife in the US was reaching a breaking point. Longstanding differences between the North and the South were exacerbated by disputes over the future of slavery. The US Constitution permitted Congress to abolish the slave trade after 1808, but it did not determine the legality of enslavement in newly acquired western lands (see pp.154–155). Legislative compromises between the North and South foundered on this dilemma, and led to the ending of the Whig Party in 1854, shattering the two-party system and making any national agreement over enslavement even more difficult. No fewer than four candidates ran for the presidency in the 1860 election. The winner, Republican candidate Abraham Lincoln, swept the North, but could not claim a popular majority or a single Electoral College vote from the South.

△ **Antislavery token**
This copper coin was made in 1838 for the American Anti-Slavery Society. The engraving depicts an enslaved woman and the words "Am I not a woman & a sister."

Secession and Civil War

Following the Republican victory, seven southern states seceded from the Union to form the Confederate States of America. After the Confederacy attacked the Union-held

YEARS OF STRIFE

From 1850 to 1877, the US faced a national crisis over the question of slavery and its aftermath. Rising tensions between the free North and the slaveholding South culminated in a civil war that claimed more than 750,000 lives. Divisions persisted after the war, with white Southerners resisting federal Reconstruction policies. The Compromise of 1877 eventually promoted white political reconciliation, but at the sacrifice of Black civil rights.

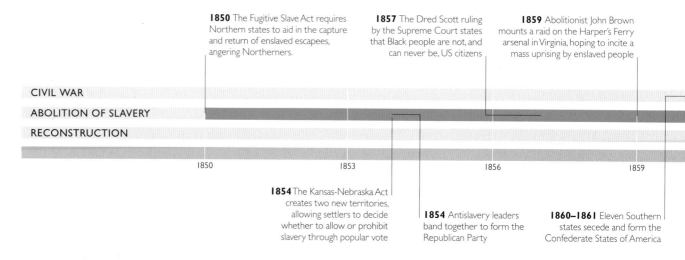

1850 The Fugitive Slave Act requires Northern states to aid in the capture and return of enslaved escapees, angering Northerners.

1857 The Dred Scott ruling by the Supreme Court states that Black people are not, and can never be, US citizens

1859 Abolitionist John Brown mounts a raid on the Harper's Ferry arsenal in Virginia, hoping to incite a mass uprising by enslaved people

CIVIL WAR

ABOLITION OF SLAVERY

RECONSTRUCTION

1850   1853   1856   1859

1854 The Kansas-Nebraska Act creates two new territories, allowing settlers to decide whether to allow or prohibit slavery through popular vote

1854 Antislavery leaders band together to form the Republican Party

1860–1861 Eleven Southern states secede and form the Confederate States of America

◁ **Emancipation Day**
This photograph is of an "Emancipation Day" celebration in Texas in 1900. Also known as "Juneteenth," this national holiday commemorates the day when the enslaved people in Texas learned of their emancipation—two years after it had been declared—on June 19, 1865.

Fort Sumter, four additional states joined the rebellion. The country descended into war, with Northerners fighting to protect the Union and white Southerners fighting to preserve slavery. As armies clashed on numerous battlefields, Black people joined the fight against the Confederacy by the thousands. Union officers and political leaders responded by granting refugees their freedom as a war aim. In 1863, Lincoln issued the Emancipation Proclamation, declaring enslaved people in Confederate-held territory to be free. On April 9, 1865, Confederate General Robert E. Lee surrendered at Appomattox.

Failure of Reconstruction

The US government passed three amendments to the Constitution, designed to grant full citizenship to Black Americans in the reconstituted Union. This included the Thirteenth Amendment, which abolished slavery. After the Union victory, early Reconstruction policies (see pp.170–171) allowed Southerners to form state governments if they fulfilled certain conditions, including paying war debts, swearing loyalty to the Union, and upholding the Thirteenth Amendment. However, these Southern governments elected former Confederate leaders as new officials who instituted "black codes"—laws to keep new

"freedmen" in check. This provoked a furious response from Republicans in Congress, who passed a series of Reconstruction Acts designed to overturn the old order in the South and place Black Americans, newly empowered by Constitutional Amendments (see pp.164–165), in state capitols. White supremacist groups such as the Ku Klux Klan (KKK) fought these attempts with violent campaigns of terror and intimidation, and by the late 1860s thousands of Black people had been killed. In the Compromise of 1877, Democrats agreed to back a Republican candidate for president during an election standoff in return for the removal of federal troops from former Confederate states, eventually giving white Southerners free reign to run their own state governments. They denied Black Americans basic civil rights, enforced racial segregation, and used the police to subjugate the Black population. The end of Reconstruction betrayed the promise of freedom for Black Americans in the South.

▷ **Ku Klux Klan**
This illustration appears in the 1924 book *Authentic History Ku Klux Klan, 1865–1877*. The Ku Klux Klan was the first, and most infamous, of the ex-Confederate paramilitaries that terrorized Black Americans and their supporters.

> *"With malice toward none; with charity for all ... let us strive to finish the work we are in; to bind up the nation's wounds ..."*
>
> ABRAHAM LINCOLN, SECOND INAUGURAL ADDRESS, 1865

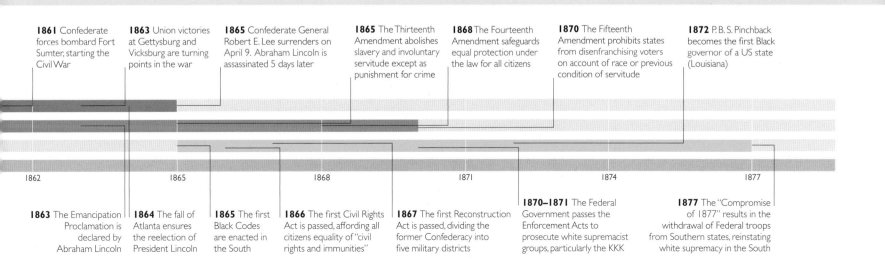

1861 Confederate forces bombard Fort Sumter, starting the Civil War

1863 Union victories at Gettysburg and Vicksburg are turning points in the war

1865 Confederate General Robert E. Lee surrenders on April 9. Abraham Lincoln is assassinated 5 days later

1865 The Thirteenth Amendment abolishes slavery and involuntary servitude except as punishment for crime

1868 The Fourteenth Amendment safeguards equal protection under the law for all citizens

1870 The Fifteenth Amendment prohibits states from disenfranchising voters on account of race or previous condition of servitude

1872 P. B. S. Pinchback becomes the first Black governor of a US state (Louisiana)

1862   1865   1868   1871   1874   1877

1863 The Emancipation Proclamation is declared by Abraham Lincoln

1864 The fall of Atlanta ensures the reelection of President Lincoln

1865 The first Black Codes are enacted in the South

1866 The first Civil Rights Act is passed, affording all citizens equality of "civil rights and immunities"

1867 The first Reconstruction Act is passed, dividing the former Confederacy into five military districts

1870–1871 The Federal Government passes the Enforcement Acts to prosecute white supremacist groups, particularly the KKK

1877 The "Compromise of 1877" results in the withdrawal of Federal troops from Southern states, reinstating white supremacy in the South

DRED SCOTT V. SANDFORD

Enslaved couple Dred and Harriet Scott sued the state of Missouri for their freedom, arguing that they had lived in the free Wisconsin territory and the free state of Illinois. In its 1857 *Dred Scott v. Sandford* ruling, the Supreme Court declared that Black people were not US citizens and had no rights in law. The court also ruled that Congress had no power to ban slavery, which helped sow the seeds of the Civil War.

Statue of Dred and Harriet Scott at the Old Courthouse, St. Louis, Missouri

A HOUSE DIVIDED

The deepening North-South rift over slavery worsened with every expansion of national territory. The fierce debates and partisan violence this led to would escalate into full-blown civil war.

KEY

Slavery prohibited	– – State boundaries, 1820
Slavery permitted	
Decision left to territory	—— State boundaries, 1854
★ Clashes and other key events	

TIMELINE

1
2
3
4
5

1810   1830   1850   1870   1890

1803 The US acquires the Louisiana Purchase (see pp.110–111) from France

1820 The border is established in the West between free states (to the north) and slave states (to the south)

36°30'N

Nat Turner Revolt ★

1831 A four-day uprising by enslaved and free Black people results in scores of deaths

A COUNTRY IN TRANSITION

The territories the expanding US came into contact with, and eventually subsumed, altered the political, cultural, and economic face of the nation.

1 AFTERMATH OF THE MISSOURI COMPROMISE FROM 1820

This 1820 Act of Congress outlawed slavery in the lands comprising the Louisiana Purchase north of the 36°30' line of latitude. The one exception to this—the special case that gave the act its name—was Missouri. Because the free state of Maine was admitted to the US in 1820, it was agreed in the interests of parity to allow Missouri to join as a slave state at the same time.

—— Latitude 36°30'N   ▓ Louisiana Purchase

2 MEXICAN CESSION AND FREE TERRITORIES 1821

In 1821, Spain accepted Mexican independence and ceded its North American territories stretching from Texas to California to the new nation. North of this lay the "Free Territories," lands as yet not part of the US, the Mexican Empire, or Britain's imperial holdings. If, as seemed likely, they would one day join the US, the question remained as to whether they would be free or slave states.

▓ Free territories   ▓ Mexican cession

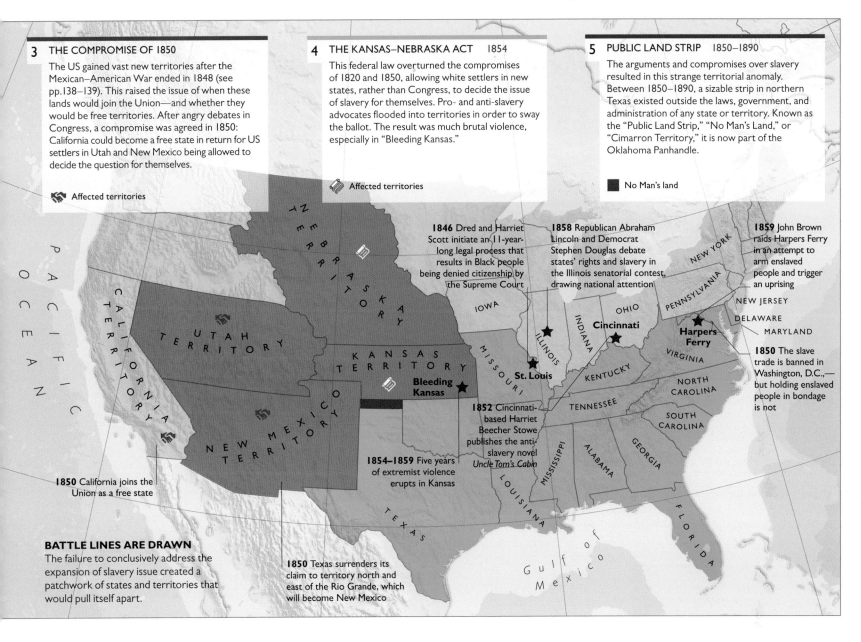

3 THE COMPROMISE OF 1850

The US gained vast new territories after the Mexican–American War ended in 1848 (see pp.138–139). This raised the issue of when these lands would join the Union—and whether they would be free territories. After angry debates in Congress, a compromise was agreed in 1850: California could become a free state in return for US settlers in Utah and New Mexico being allowed to decide the question for themselves.

Affected territories

4 THE KANSAS–NEBRASKA ACT 1854

This federal law overturned the compromises of 1820 and 1850, allowing white settlers in new states, rather than Congress, to decide the issue of slavery for themselves. Pro- and anti-slavery advocates flooded into territories in order to sway the ballot. The result was much brutal violence, especially in "Bleeding Kansas."

Affected territories

5 PUBLIC LAND STRIP 1850–1890

The arguments and compromises over slavery resulted in this strange territorial anomaly. Between 1850–1890, a sizable strip in northern Texas existed outside the laws, government, and administration of any state or territory. Known as the "Public Land Strip," "No Man's Land," or "Cimarron Territory," it is now part of the Oklahoma Panhandle.

No Man's land

1846 Dred and Harriet Scott initiate an 11-year-long legal process that results in Black people being denied citizenship by the Supreme Court

1858 Republican Abraham Lincoln and Democrat Stephen Douglas debate states' rights and slavery in the Illinois senatorial contest, drawing national attention

1859 John Brown raids Harpers Ferry in an attempt to arm enslaved people and trigger an uprising

1850 The slave trade is banned in Washington, D.C.,—but holding enslaved people in bondage is not

1852 Cincinnati-based Harriet Beecher Stowe publishes the anti-slavery novel *Uncle Tom's Cabin*

1854–1859 Five years of extremist violence erupts in Kansas

1850 California joins the Union as a free state

BATTLE LINES ARE DRAWN
The failure to conclusively address the expansion of slavery issue created a patchwork of states and territories that would pull itself apart.

1850 Texas surrenders its claim to territory north and east of the Rio Grande, which will become New Mexico

SLAVERY AND WESTWARD EXPANSION

As the US expanded westward throughout the first half of the 19th century, it carried the issue of slavery into each new territory that was settled. In time, slavery divided the nation into irreconcilable factions that fought a bloody civil war.

Congress became increasingly divided between pro-slavery and anti-slavery politicians as abolitionist sentiment grew. In 1820, even though a demarcation line was legally established across the Louisiana Purchase territory, north of which slavery would not be permitted, Missouri, north of the line, was allowed to join the Union as a slave state through a concept known as paired admissions. Maine, a non-slave state, joined the Union at the same time, thus creating four new seats in the Senate, two from a new slave state and two from a new free state. This plan was introduced by Kentucky senator Henry Clay and came

to be known as the Missouri Compromise, the first of several failed compromises. In addition, provocative federal regulations such as the 1850 Fugitive Slave Law—which demanded that free states return escaped Black people to slavery—inflamed tensions further. The Kansas-Nebraska Act of 1854 undid the Missouri Compromise by allowing the inhabitants of new territories north of the line to vote on slavery's legal status under the doctrine of "popular sovereignty." In 1859, a failed anti-slavery attack in Virginia demonstrated the potential for violence that lurked beneath these uneasy agreements.

△ **Fugitive Slave Act**
This law required citizens and governments of free states to assist enslavers attempting to recapture freedom seekers within their borders.

SOUTHERN SECESSION

Decades of conflict over the legal status of enslavement in the US fractured the Union after Abraham Lincoln's election in 1860. Eleven states seceded to form the Confederate States of America, triggering the US Civil War.

When Abraham Lincoln won the US presidential election in November 1860, many Southerners felt that his Republican Party would force the abolition of enslavement upon their states (see pp.154–155). One such state, South Carolina, officially severed its ties with the federal Union on December 20, 1860, in a Secession Convention in Charleston. Over the next few weeks, the "Cotton States" of the Deep South—Mississippi, Alabama, Florida, Louisiana, Georgia, and Texas—followed suit. On February 4, 1861, these seven states combined to form the unrecognized republic known as the Confederate States of America.

That same month, prominent national figures attended a peace conference in Washington to forge a compromise and keep the remaining eight slave states from seceding. The convention might have succeeded but for the events that transpired soon after. Lincoln, inaugurated in March, ignored secessionist South Carolina's calls for US troops to evacuate Fort Sumter situated in its city of Charleston. Instead, he chose to resupply the fort's garrison. Confederate batteries shelled the fort on April 12–13, and Lincoln called on union states to supply 75,000 militiamen to quell an "insurrection." At this threat of military coercion, the slave states of Virginia, North Carolina, Arkansas,

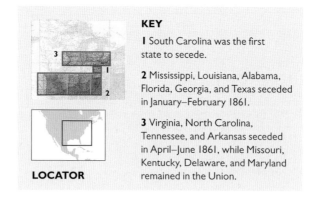

KEY

1 South Carolina was the first state to secede.

2 Mississippi, Louisiana, Alabama, Florida, Georgia, and Texas seceded in January–February 1861.

3 Virginia, North Carolina, Tennessee, and Arkansas seceded in April–June 1861, while Missouri, Kentucky, Delaware, and Maryland remained in the Union.

LOCATOR

and Tennessee joined the Confederacy. Kentucky declared its neutrality, while Missouri and Delaware remained in the Union. On the border of the US capital of Washington, D.C., the strategically important state of Maryland was quickly occupied by Union troops. The Civil War had begun.

▷ **Choosing sides**
The shaded portions in this 1861 map of the US represent the 15 slave states, 11 of which seceded to form the Confederate States of America. Clashes between the Union and the Confederacy at Charleston (inset) triggered the Civil War.

"*I felt a nervous dread and horror of this break with so great a power as the United States, but I was ready and willing …*"

MARY BOYKIN CHESNUT, CONFEDERATE DIARIST, *A DIARY FROM DIXIE*, 1905

A DIVIDED UNITED STATES
At the outbreak of Civil War in 1861, the nation's population lay mostly east of the Mississippi River. California and Oregon were outliers to the conflict. The territories of the Louisiana Purchase had yet to be settled. With no formal government, the unorganized "Indian Territory" had divided loyalties in the war.

KEY

■ Union states

■ States seceding from the Union in 1861

♦ Enslavement legal

US Territories

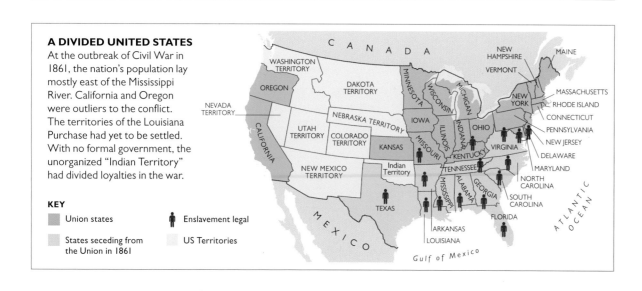

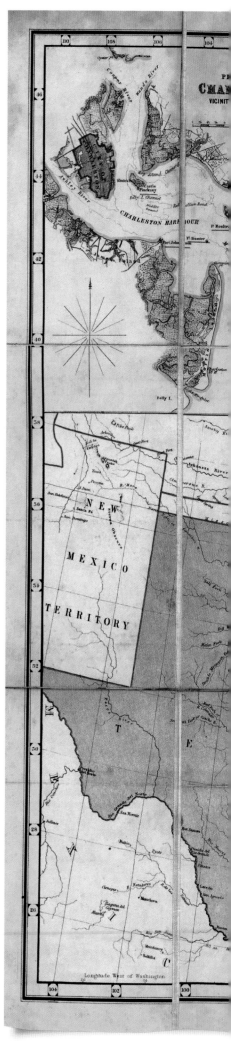

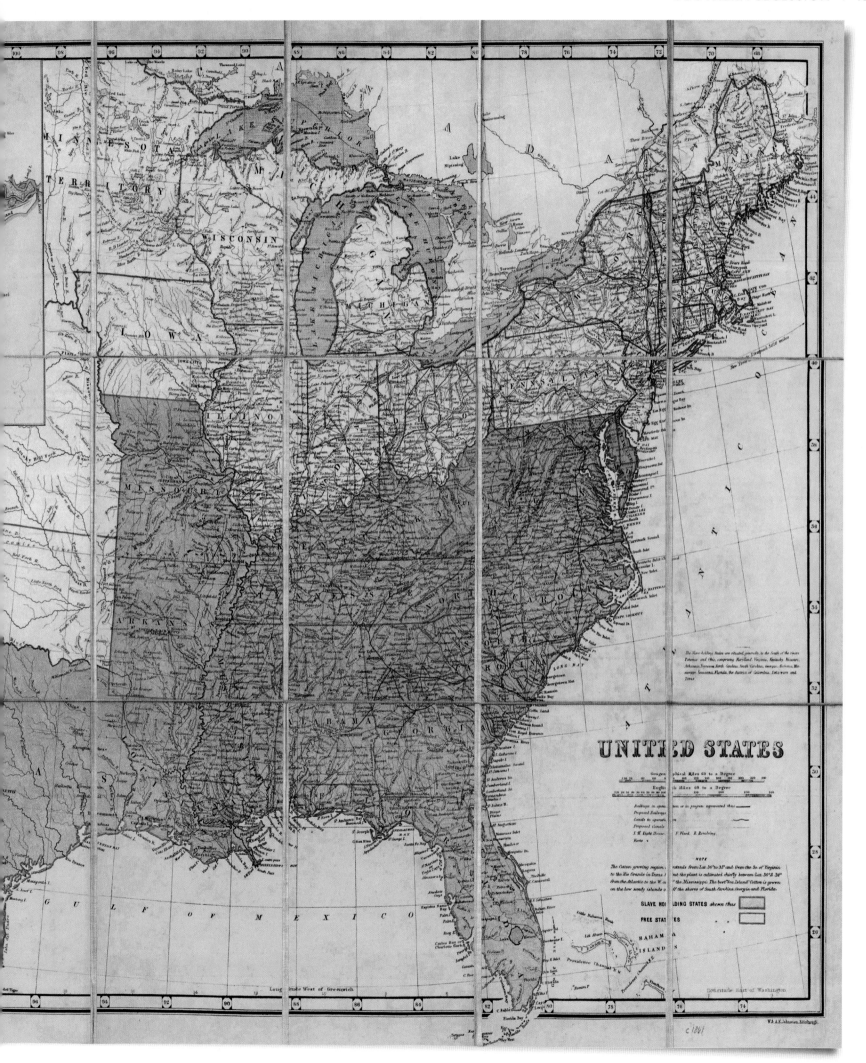

UNITED STATES

NOTE

The Cotton-growing region extends from Lat. 30° to 35° and from the So. of Virginia to the Rio Grande in Texas. But the plant is cultivated chiefly between Lat. 30° & 34° from the Atlantic to the W. of the Mississippi. The best Sea Island Cotton is grown on the low sandy islands of the shores of South Carolina, Georgia and Florida.

SLAVE HOLDING STATES shown thus

FREE STATES

CIVIL WAR IN THE EAST

The first two years of fighting in the Eastern theater were dominated by Confederate victories, thanks to Robert E. Lee, who became the South's most senior commander. His two invasions of the North, however, were failures, with Gettysburg marking the war's turning point.

After the attack on Fort Sumter finally ignited war between the North and South, the Union's strategy was to deny the Confederacy foreign recognition, blockade its ports by naval force, and divide it by seizing control of the Mississippi River system. Richmond, Virginia became the Confederate capital on May 8, 1861, turning the 100 miles (160 km) of forest and farmland separating it from Washington, D.C., into a battleground.

This region became the scene of at least a dozen major battles and countless minor engagements during the four years of war. Initially, most of the victories were won by the Confederate Army of Northern Virginia, led from June 1862 by General Robert E. Lee, and assisted by his lieutenant, Thomas J. "Stonewall" Jackson. However, Jackson was mortally wounded in battle at the Confederates' biggest victory, Chancellorsville, and Lee's subsequent invasion of Pennsylvania was defeated at the Battle of Gettysburg by the Army of the Potomac and its commander, General George Gordon Meade.

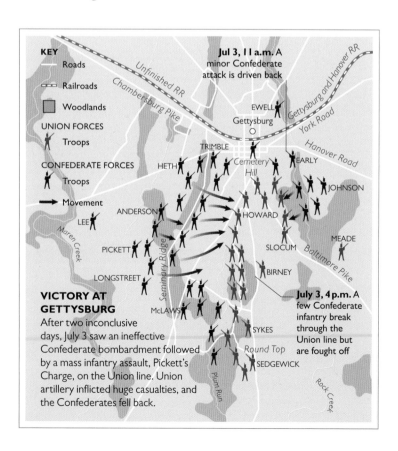

VICTORY AT GETTYSBURG

After two inconclusive days, July 3 saw an ineffective Confederate bombardment followed by a mass infantry assault, Pickett's Charge, on the Union line. Union artillery inflicted huge casualties, and the Confederates fell back.

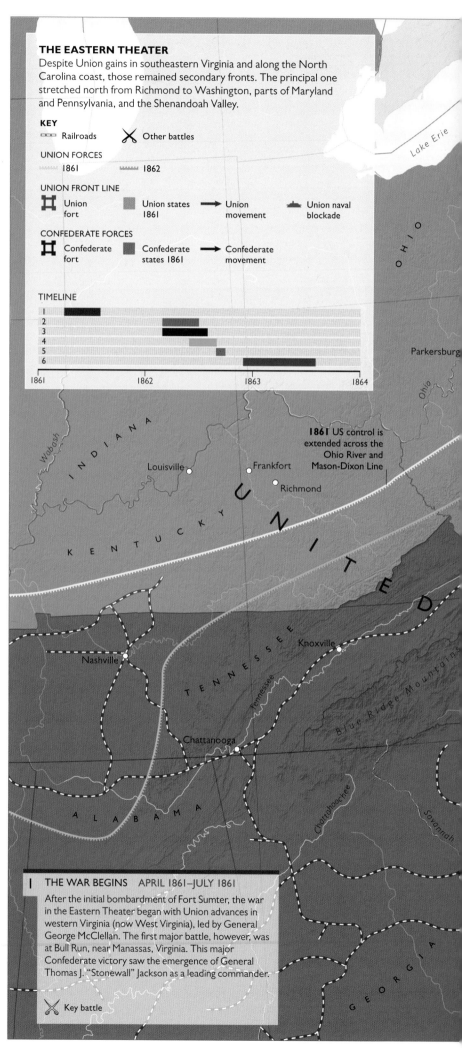

THE EASTERN THEATER

Despite Union gains in southeastern Virginia and along the North Carolina coast, those remained secondary fronts. The principal one stretched north from Richmond to Washington, parts of Maryland and Pennsylvania, and the Shenandoah Valley.

1861 US control is extended across the Ohio River and Mason-Dixon Line

THE WAR BEGINS   APRIL 1861–JULY 1861

After the initial bombardment of Fort Sumter, the war in the Eastern Theater began with Union advances in western Virginia (now West Virginia), led by General George McClellan. The first major battle, however, was at Bull Run, near Manassas, Virginia. This major Confederate victory saw the emergence of General Thomas J. "Stonewall" Jackson as a leading commander.

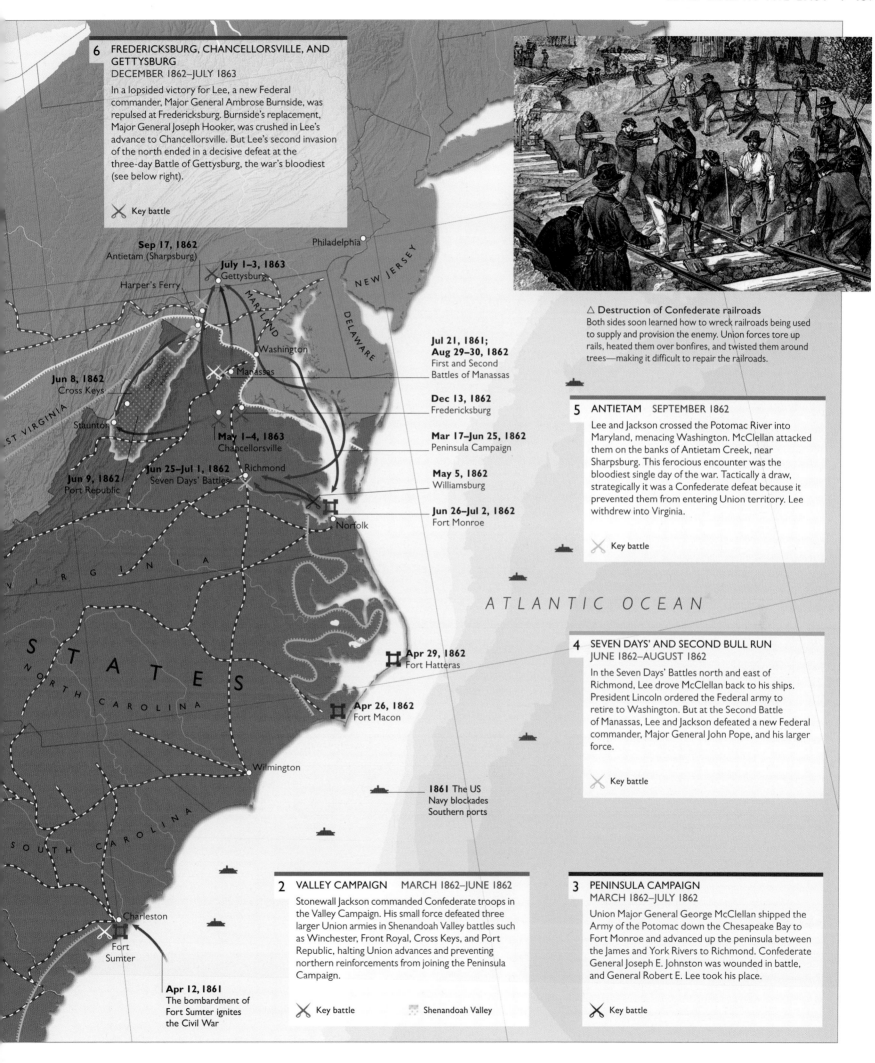

6 FREDERICKSBURG, CHANCELLORSVILLE, AND GETTYSBURG
DECEMBER 1862–JULY 1863

In a lopsided victory for Lee, a new Federal commander, Major General Ambrose Burnside, was repulsed at Fredericksburg. Burnside's replacement, Major General Joseph Hooker, was crushed in Lee's advance to Chancellorsville. But Lee's second invasion of the north ended in a decisive defeat at the three-day Battle of Gettysburg, the war's bloodiest (see below right).

✕ Key battle

Sep 17, 1862
Antietam (Sharpsburg)

Philadelphia

July 1–3, 1863
Gettysburg

Harper's Ferry

NEW JERSEY

MARYLAND

DELAWARE

Washington

Jun 8, 1862
Cross Keys

Manassas

**Jul 21, 1861;
Aug 29–30, 1862**
First and Second
Battles of Manassas

ST VIRGINIA

Staunton

Dec 13, 1862
Fredericksburg

May 1–4, 1863
Chancellorsville

Mar 17–Jun 25, 1862
Peninsula Campaign

Jun 25–Jul 1, 1862
Seven Days' Battles

Richmond

May 5, 1862
Williamsburg

Jun 9, 1862
Port Republic

Jun 26–Jul 2, 1862
Fort Monroe

Norfolk

V I R G I N I A

△ **Destruction of Confederate railroads**
Both sides soon learned how to wreck railroads being used to supply and provision the enemy. Union forces tore up rails, heated them over bonfires, and twisted them around trees—making it difficult to repair the railroads.

5 ANTIETAM   SEPTEMBER 1862

Lee and Jackson crossed the Potomac River into Maryland, menacing Washington. McClellan attacked them on the banks of Antietam Creek, near Sharpsburg. This ferocious encounter was the bloodiest single day of the war. Tactically a draw, strategically it was a Confederate defeat because it prevented them from entering Union territory. Lee withdrew into Virginia.

✕ Key battle

A T L A N T I C   O C E A N

S T A T E S

N O R T H   C A R O L I N A

Apr 29, 1862
Fort Hatteras

Apr 26, 1862
Fort Macon

4 SEVEN DAYS' AND SECOND BULL RUN
JUNE 1862–AUGUST 1862

In the Seven Days' Battles north and east of Richmond, Lee drove McClellan back to his ships. President Lincoln ordered the Federal army to retire to Washington. But at the Second Battle of Manassas, Lee and Jackson defeated a new Federal commander, Major General John Pope, and his larger force.

✕ Key battle

Wilmington

1861 The US
Navy blockades
Southern ports

S O U T H   C A R O L I N A

Charleston

Fort
Sumter

Apr 12, 1861
The bombardment of
Fort Sumter ignites
the Civil War

2 VALLEY CAMPAIGN   MARCH 1862–JUNE 1862

Stonewall Jackson commanded Confederate troops in the Valley Campaign. His small force defeated three larger Union armies in Shenandoah Valley battles such as Winchester, Front Royal, Cross Keys, and Port Republic, halting Union advances and preventing northern reinforcements from joining the Peninsula Campaign.

✕ Key battle   ▨ Shenandoah Valley

3 PENINSULA CAMPAIGN
MARCH 1862–JULY 1862

Union Major General George McClellan shipped the Army of the Potomac down the Chesapeake Bay to Fort Monroe and advanced up the peninsula between the James and York Rivers to Richmond. Confederate General Joseph E. Johnston was wounded in battle, and General Robert E. Lee took his place.

✕ Key battle

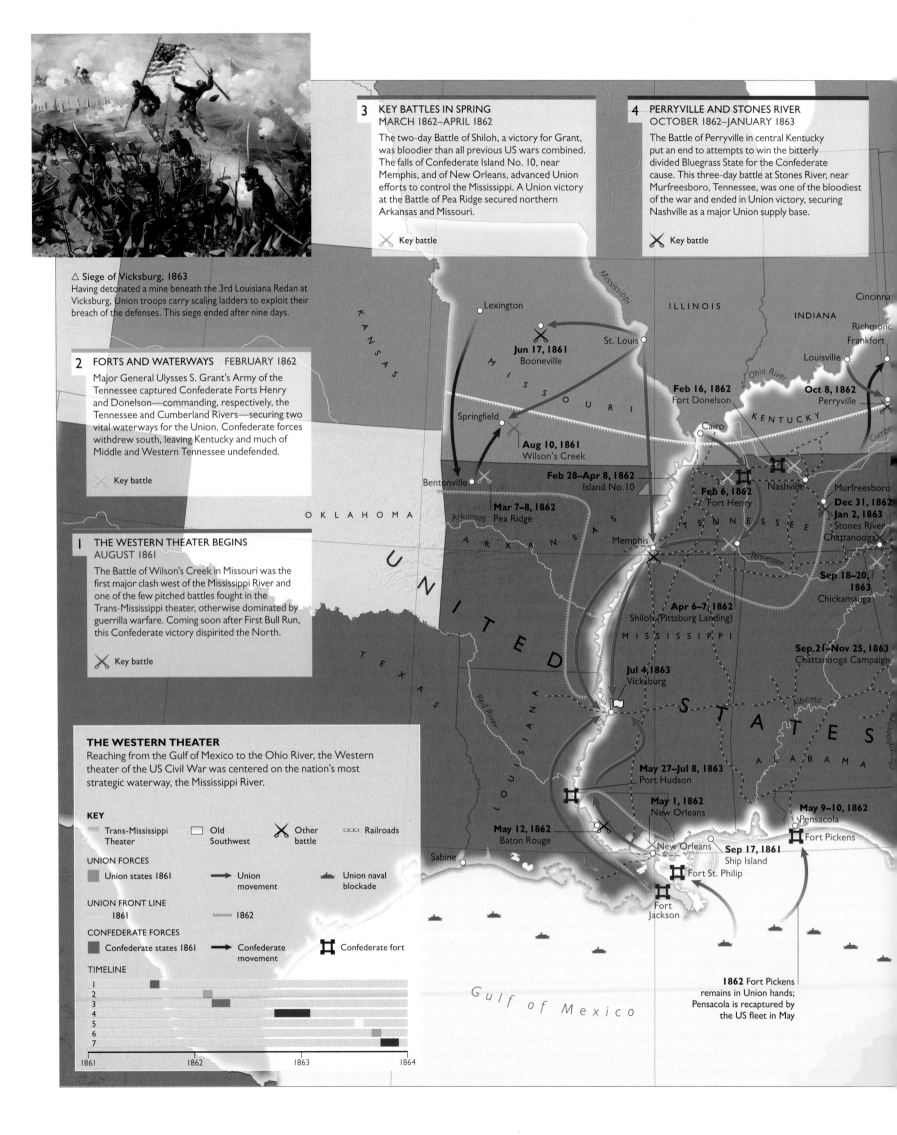

3 KEY BATTLES IN SPRING
MARCH 1862–APRIL 1862

The two-day Battle of Shiloh, a victory for Grant, was bloodier than all previous US wars combined. The falls of Confederate Island No. 10, near Memphis, and of New Orleans, advanced Union efforts to control the Mississippi. A Union victory at the Battle of Pea Ridge secured northern Arkansas and Missouri.

✕ Key battle

4 PERRYVILLE AND STONES RIVER
OCTOBER 1862–JANUARY 1863

The Battle of Perryville in central Kentucky put an end to attempts to win the bitterly divided Bluegrass State for the Confederate cause. This three-day battle at Stones River, near Murfreesboro, Tennessee, was one of the bloodiest of the war and ended in Union victory, securing Nashville as a major Union supply base.

✕ Key battle

△ Siege of Vicksburg, 1863
Having detonated a mine beneath the 3rd Louisiana Redan at Vicksburg, Union troops carry scaling ladders to exploit their breach of the defenses. This siege ended after nine days.

2 FORTS AND WATERWAYS   FEBRUARY 1862

Major General Ulysses S. Grant's Army of the Tennessee captured Confederate Forts Henry and Donelson—commanding, respectively, the Tennessee and Cumberland Rivers—securing two vital waterways for the Union. Confederate forces withdrew south, leaving Kentucky and much of Middle and Western Tennessee undefended.

✕ Key battle

1 THE WESTERN THEATER BEGINS
AUGUST 1861

The Battle of Wilson's Creek in Missouri was the first major clash west of the Mississippi River and one of the few pitched battles fought in the Trans-Mississippi theater, otherwise dominated by guerrilla warfare. Coming soon after First Bull Run, this Confederate victory dispirited the North.

✕ Key battle

THE WESTERN THEATER
Reaching from the Gulf of Mexico to the Ohio River, the Western theater of the US Civil War was centered on the nation's most strategic waterway, the Mississippi River.

KEY

▢ Trans-Mississippi Theater	▢ Old Southwest	✕ Other battle	▭▭▭ Railroads

UNION FORCES
▢ Union states 1861   → Union movement   ⚓ Union naval blockade

UNION FRONT LINE
—— 1861   ⋯⋯ 1862

CONFEDERATE FORCES
▢ Confederate states 1861   → Confederate movement   ▥ Confederate fort

TIMELINE
1
2
3
4
5
6
7

1861   1862   1863   1864

Map labels:

Lexington
St. Louis
ILLINOIS
INDIANA
Cincinna
Richmon
Frankfort
Jun 17, 1861 Booneville
Louisville
Ohio River
Feb 16, 1862 Fort Donelson
Oct 8, 1862 Perryville
KENTUCKY
KANSAS
MISSOURI
Springfield
Cairo
Aug 10, 1861 Wilson's Creek
Feb 28–Apr 8, 1862 Island No. 10
Feb 6, 1862 Fort Henry
Nashville
Murfreesboro
Bentonville
Mar 7–8, 1862 Pea Ridge
Dec 31, 1862 Jan 2, 1863 Stones River
Chattanooga
OKLAHOMA
Arkansas
Memphis
Tennessee
ARKANSAS
Sep 18–20, 1863 Chickamauga
UNITED
Apr 6–7, 1862 Shiloh (Pittsburg Landing)
MISSISSIPPI
Sep 21–Nov 25, 1863 Chattanooga Campaign
TEXAS
Jul 4, 1863 Vicksburg
STATES
Alabama
Red River
ALABAMA
LOUISIANA
May 27–Jul 8, 1863 Port Hudson
May 1, 1862 New Orleans
May 9–10, 1862 Pensacola
May 12, 1862 Baton Rouge
Fort Pickens
Sabine
New Orleans
Sep 17, 1861 Ship Island
Fort St. Philip
Fort Jackson
Gulf of Mexico

1862 Fort Pickens remains in Union hands; Pensacola is recaptured by the US fleet in May

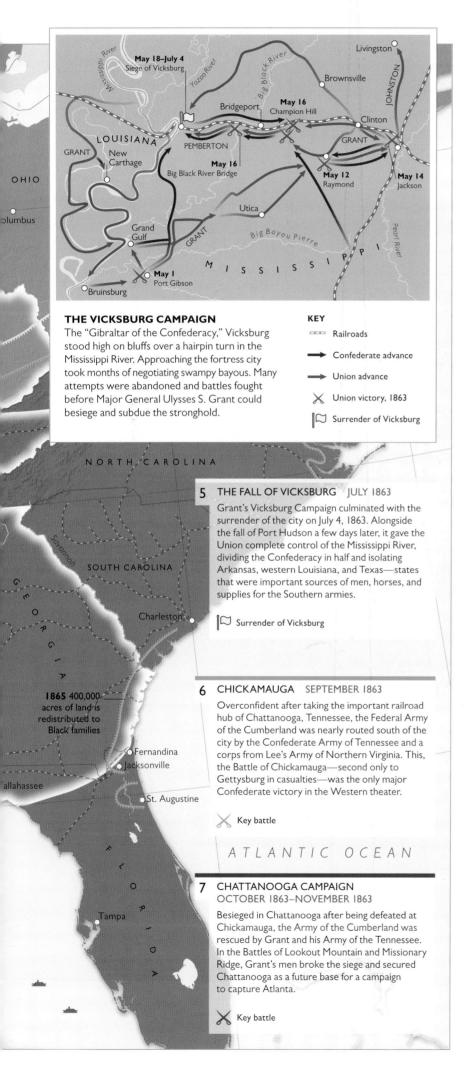

May 18–July 4
Siege of Vicksburg

Livingston

Brownsville

Bridgeport

May 16
Champion Hill

Clinton

JOHNSTON

GRANT

LOUISIANA

PEMBERTON

GRANT

New
Carthage

OHIO

May 16
Big Black River Bridge

May 12
Raymond

May 14
Jackson

Utica

Big Bayou Pierre

Pearl River

Grand
Gulf

olumbus

M I S S I S S I P P I

May 1
Port Gibson

Bruinsburg

GRANT

THE VICKSBURG CAMPAIGN

The "Gibraltar of the Confederacy," Vicksburg stood high on bluffs over a hairpin turn in the Mississippi River. Approaching the fortress city took months of negotiating swampy bayous. Many attempts were abandoned and battles fought before Major General Ulysses S. Grant could besiege and subdue the stronghold.

KEY

- 🔲🔲🔲 Railroads
- ➡ Confederate advance
- ➡ Union advance
- ✕ Union victory, 1863
- 🏳 Surrender of Vicksburg

NORTH CAROLINA

SOUTH CAROLINA

Savannah

G E O R G I A

Charleston

1865 400,000 acres of land is redistributed to Black families

Fernandina

Jacksonville

St. Augustine

allahassee

F L O R I D A

Tampa

5 THE FALL OF VICKSBURG   JULY 1863

Grant's Vicksburg Campaign culminated with the surrender of the city on July 4, 1863. Alongside the fall of Port Hudson a few days later, it gave the Union complete control of the Mississippi River, dividing the Confederacy in half and isolating Arkansas, western Louisiana, and Texas—states that were important sources of men, horses, and supplies for the Southern armies.

🏳 Surrender of Vicksburg

6 CHICKAMAUGA   SEPTEMBER 1863

Overconfident after taking the important railroad hub of Chattanooga, Tennessee, the Federal Army of the Cumberland was nearly routed south of the city by the Confederate Army of Tennessee and a corps from Lee's Army of Northern Virginia. This, the Battle of Chickamauga—second only to Gettysburg in casualties—was the only major Confederate victory in the Western theater.

✕ Key battle

ATLANTIC OCEAN

7 CHATTANOOGA CAMPAIGN
OCTOBER 1863–NOVEMBER 1863

Besieged in Chattanooga after being defeated at Chickamauga, the Army of the Cumberland was rescued by Grant and his Army of the Tennessee. In the Battles of Lookout Mountain and Missionary Ridge, Grant's men broke the siege and secured Chattanooga as a future base for a campaign to capture Atlanta.

✕ Key battle

CIVIL WAR IN THE WEST

The Western theater occupied the vast expanse between the Appalachians and the Mississippi, as well as states bordering the plains and prairies. Both sides studied maps of this sprawling area and planned similar strategies.

Early fighting in the Western theater was dominated by the struggle to win and control the border states, especially Kentucky and Tennessee. The former was officially neutral, the latter officially Confederate, but both states had divided loyalties. Even army names reflected the fight for these territories. The chief Confederate force in the West was the Army of Tennessee, and the principal Union forces were named after rivers: the Army of the Tennessee, the Army of the Cumberland, and the Army of the Ohio.

Securing the major Gulf of Mexico ports (especially New Orleans, Mobile, and Pensacola—all of which except Mobile were under Federal control by 1862) was also strategically important. However, the key to the Western Theater as a whole was control of the Mississippi River. Despite the presence of US Navy gunboats on the river, it took the North two years to capture the 110-mile section between the fortified cities of Port Hudson in Louisiana and Vicksburg in Mississippi. That happened in July 1863, finally severing the Confederacy in two.

> *"The Father of Waters again goes unvexed to the sea."*
>
> ABRAHAM LINCOLN ON THE MISSISSIPPI RIVER, 1863

THE 1862 US–DAKOTA WAR

When Minnesota's Santee— the band of Dakota that was led by Chief Little Crow— killed neighboring settlers in response to longstanding grievances, a new war erupted within the wider one. Several hundred more settlers were slain before the Army intervened, killing an estimated 75–100 Dakota soldiers. Some 303 Dakota were sentenced to die in a mass hanging; President Lincoln commuted the death sentences of all but 38 of them.

Dakota chief during the war, 1862

GENERAL SHERMAN'S ADVANCE

While the two factions spent most of 1864 locked in a titanic duel around Richmond and Petersburg in Virginia, Union general William T. Sherman led a dramatically successful campaign in Georgia that helped hasten the end of the Civil War.

△ **Railroad route**
The Western and Atlantic Railroad, running between Chattanooga to the northwest and Atlanta in the south, became the axis of Sherman's advance once he started on May 5, 1864. It was also his supply lifeline.

△ **First major battle**
The Battle of Resaca (May 13–15) was typical of the campaign's fighting: Johnston fought from entrenchments, hoping to bleed Sherman dry, but the latter always outflanked the Southern forces.

General William T. Sherman drove a Union force south from Chattanooga to battle the defensive-minded General Joseph Johnston for Atlanta, the Confederacy's railroad and supply hub. Enduring two months of skirmishing and inconclusive battles, Sherman eventually outflanked Johnston's defenses, and by mid-July was approaching Atlanta.

Confederate president Jefferson Davis, feeling that Johnston was too cautious, replaced him with General John Bell Hood, who launched futile attacks all around the beleaguered city. However, one by one its vital railroads were cut. Hood withdrew, and on September 2, Sherman's troops captured Atlanta. Hoping to wage "total war" on the Confederacy, Sherman took most of his force on an epic march to Savannah two months later. Meeting minimal resistance, they plundered and destroyed plantations on their way. Savannah surrendered on December 21.

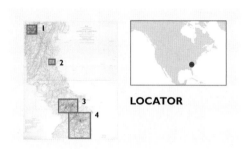

LOCATOR

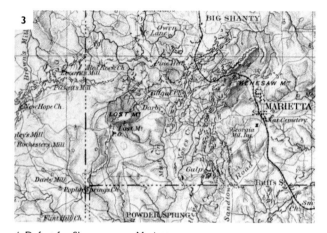

△ **Defeat for Sherman near Marietta**
The cluster of clashes around Marietta, including the battles of New Hope Church and Pickett's Mill, culminated in Sherman's only serious defeat, the Battle of Kennesaw Mountain on June 27, just west of Marietta.

"I beg to present you, as a Christmas gift, the City of Savannah."

GENERAL WILLIAM T. SHERMAN TO
PRESIDENT ABRAHAM LINCOLN, DECEMBER 22, 1864

THE MARCH TO THE SEA
In November 1864, Sherman took 62,000 troops on a "scorched earth" march to Savannah that aimed to destroy the Confederacy's economy in the Southeast. Seizing food and burning farms and plantations, Sherman sought to demoralize white Southerners and weaken their support for the war.

KEY
➡ Union 14th Corps
➡ Union 15th Corps
➡ Union 17th Corps
➡ Union 20th Corps
┅➤ Cavalry

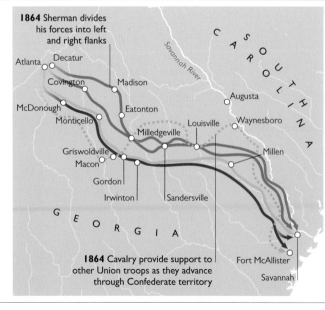

1864 Sherman divides his forces into left and right flanks

1864 Cavalry provide support to other Union troops as they advance through Confederate territory

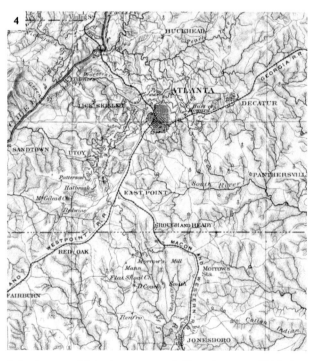

△ **Battles around Atlanta**
Sherman's troops clashed with Hood's in a series of battles around Atlanta (including the battles of Peachtree Creek, Atlanta, Ezra Church, and Jonesborough), as the Union forces attempted to capture the strategically important city.

▷ **Campaign map, c. 1864**
Drawn by Sherman's chief engineer, Colonel Orlando Poe, this is a topographical map of the campaign, published in the *Official Records of the War of the Rebellion.* Battle lines are sketched in blue (Union) and red (Confederate).

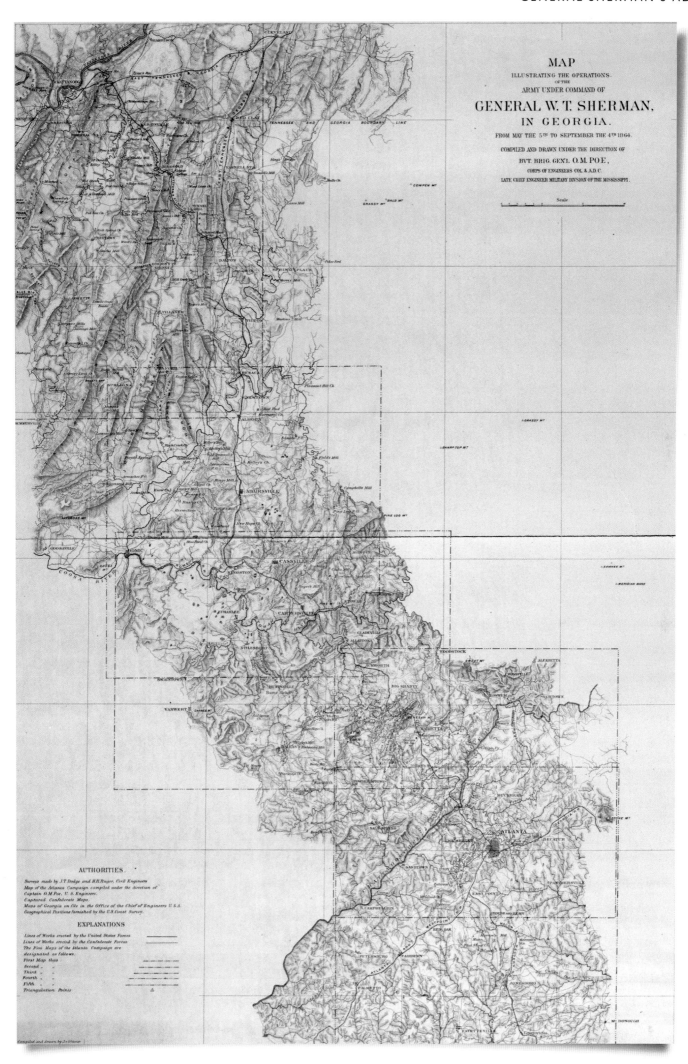

MAP
ILLUSTRATING THE OPERATIONS.
OF THE
ARMY UNDER COMMAND OF
GENERAL W. T. SHERMAN,
IN GEORGIA.
FROM MAY THE 5TH TO SEPTEMBER THE 4TH 1864.
COMPILED AND DRAWN UNDER THE DIRECTION OF
BVT. BRIG. GEN'L. O. M. POE,
CORPS OF ENGINEERS COL. & A.D.C.
LATE CHIEF ENGINEER MILITARY DIVISION OF THE MISSISSIPPI.

Scale

AUTHORITIES.
Surveys made by J.T. Dodge and R.H. Ruger, Civil Engineers
Map of the Atlanta Campaign compiled under the direction of
Captain O.M. Poe, U. S. Engineers.
Captured Confederate Maps.
Maps of Georgia on file in the Office of the Chief of Engineers U.S.A.
Geographical Positions furnished by the U.S Coast Survey.

EXPLANATIONS
Lines of Works erected by the United States Forces
Lines of Works erected by the Confederate Forces
The Five Maps of the Atlanta Campaign are
designated as follows.
First Map this
Second
Third
Fourth
Fifth
Triangulation Points

THE END OF CIVIL WAR

The final year of war in the Eastern Theater was dominated by a struggle between Robert E. Lee and Ulysses S. Grant, while Union victories in the western theater helped secure Abraham Lincoln's reelection.

In March 1864, General Ulysses S. Grant was promoted to commander-in-chief of all US armies. He decided to accompany the Army of the Potomac in Virginia, clashing with Robert E. Lee, a wily commander he had once idolized. The Union's final strategy now pivoted to trapping and destroying Lee's Army of Northern Virginia, then taking Richmond, the Confederate capital. This was one part of a double-headed attack, with General William T. Sherman's successful advance on Atlanta (see pp.162–163) comprising the other. The Southern strategy, meanwhile, was to play for time in the hopes that the "Peace Party" in the North would offer a negotiated peace if President Lincoln were unseated in that year's election.

The latter outcome seemed increasingly likely in the summer of 1864, when Confederate forces advanced close to the Union capital, Washington, D.C., while Grant and Lee's forces had become deadlocked at Petersburg. However, following Union victories at Atlanta, Mobile Bay, and the Shenandoah Valley, Abraham Lincoln was reelected president. The Confederate surrender followed in spring 1865.

> *"Hold on with a bulldog grip, and chew and choke as much as possible."*
>
> ABRAHAM LINCOLN TO ULYSSES S. GRANT, 1864

AFRICAN AMERICAN TROOPS

Of the nearly 180,000 Black people who served as members of the Union Army's "US Colored Troops," around 10,000 were killed, while 16 soldiers won Congressional Medals of Honor. African American regiments fought bravely at Fort Wagner, near Charleston, South Carolina; at Port Hudson, Louisiana; at Nashville, Tennessee; and at the Battle of the Crater outside Petersburg, Virginia.

Private William Wright of the "US Colored Troops"

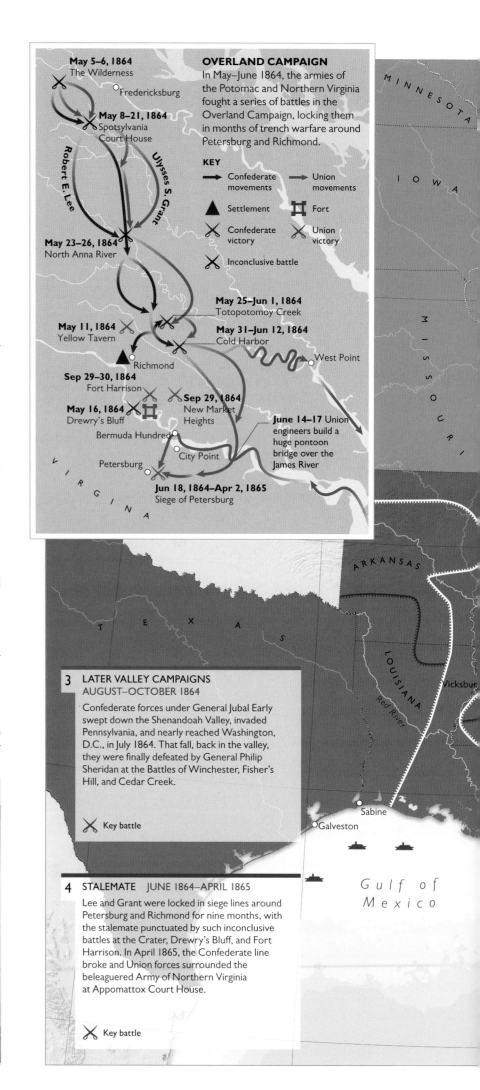

OVERLAND CAMPAIGN

In May–June 1864, the armies of the Potomac and Northern Virginia fought a series of battles in the Overland Campaign, locking them in months of trench warfare around Petersburg and Richmond.

KEY

→ Confederate movements
→ Union movements
▲ Settlement
⊞ Fort
⚔ Confederate victory
⚔ Union victory
⚔ Inconclusive battle

May 5–6, 1864
The Wilderness

Fredericksburg

May 8–21, 1864
Spotsylvania Court House

Robert E. Lee

Ulysses S. Grant

May 23–26, 1864
North Anna River

May 11, 1864
Yellow Tavern

May 25–Jun 1, 1864
Totopotomoy Creek

May 31–Jun 12, 1864
Cold Harbor

West Point

Richmond

Sep 29–30, 1864
Fort Harrison

May 16, 1864
Drewry's Bluff

Sep 29, 1864
New Market Heights

June 14–17 Union engineers build a huge pontoon bridge over the James River

Bermuda Hundred

City Point

Petersburg

Jun 18, 1864–Apr 2, 1865
Siege of Petersburg

VIRGINIA

MINNESOTA
IOWA
MISSOURI
ARKANSAS
TEXAS
LOUISIANA
Vicksburg
Red River

3 LATER VALLEY CAMPAIGNS
AUGUST–OCTOBER 1864

Confederate forces under General Jubal Early swept down the Shenandoah Valley, invaded Pennsylvania, and nearly reached Washington, D.C., in July 1864. That fall, back in the valley, they were finally defeated by General Philip Sheridan at the Battles of Winchester, Fisher's Hill, and Cedar Creek.

⚔ Key battle

Sabine
Galveston

4 STALEMATE JUNE 1864–APRIL 1865

Lee and Grant were locked in siege lines around Petersburg and Richmond for nine months, with the stalemate punctuated by such inconclusive battles at the Crater, Drewry's Bluff, and Fort Harrison. In April 1865, the Confederate line broke and Union forces surrounded the beleaguered Army of Northern Virginia at Appomattox Court House.

⚔ Key battle

Gulf of Mexico

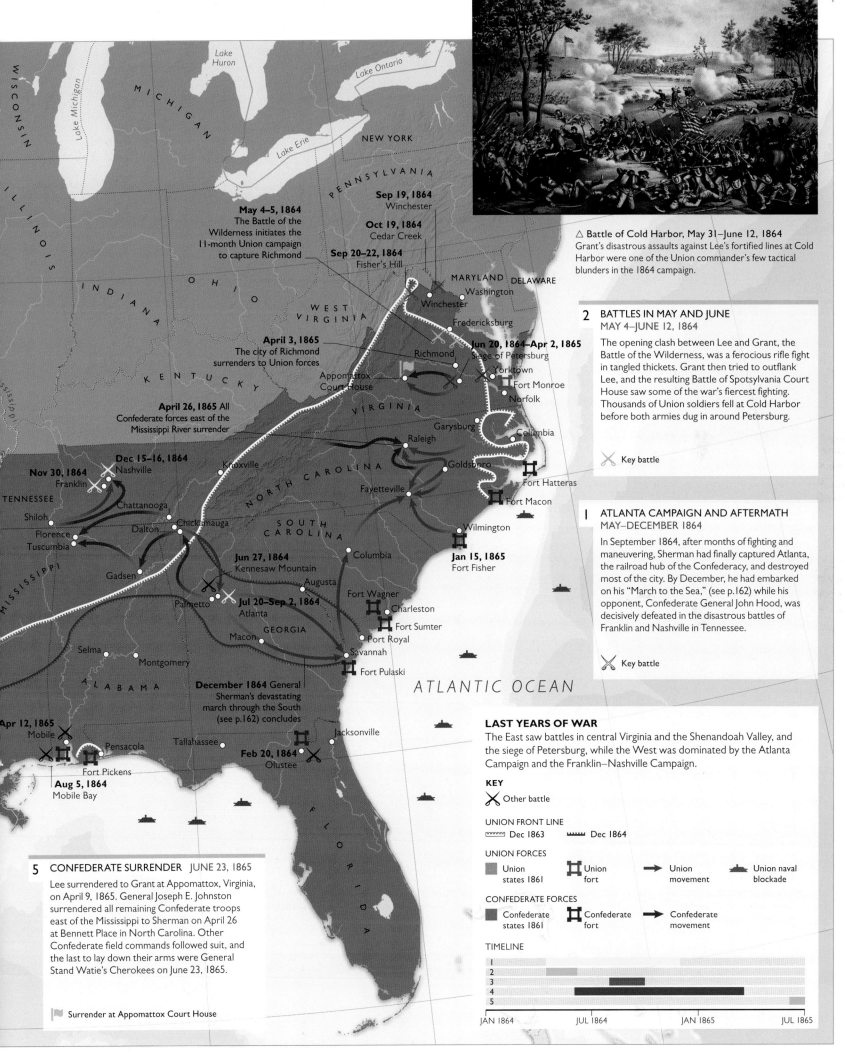

May 4–5, 1864
The Battle of the
Wilderness initiates the
11-month Union campaign
to capture Richmond

Sep 19, 1864
Winchester

Oct 19, 1864
Cedar Creek

Sep 20–22, 1864
Fisher's Hill

April 3, 1865
The city of Richmond
surrenders to Union forces

April 26, 1865 All
Confederate forces east of the
Mississippi River surrender

Dec 15–16, 1864
Nashville

Nov 30, 1864
Franklin

Jun 27, 1864
Kennesaw Mountain

Jul 20–Sep 2, 1864
Atlanta

December 1864 General
Sherman's devastating
march through the South
(see p.162) concludes

Apr 12, 1865
Mobile

Aug 5, 1864
Mobile Bay

Feb 20, 1864
Olustee

Jun 20, 1864–Apr 2, 1865
siege of Petersburg

Jan 15, 1865
Fort Fisher

△ **Battle of Cold Harbor, May 31–June 12, 1864**
Grant's disastrous assaults against Lee's fortified lines at Cold
Harbor were one of the Union commander's few tactical
blunders in the 1864 campaign.

2 BATTLES IN MAY AND JUNE
MAY 4–JUNE 12, 1864

The opening clash between Lee and Grant, the
Battle of the Wilderness, was a ferocious rifle fight
in tangled thickets. Grant then tried to outflank
Lee, and the resulting Battle of Spotsylvania Court
House saw some of the war's fiercest fighting.
Thousands of Union soldiers fell at Cold Harbor
before both armies dug in around Petersburg.

✗ Key battle

1 ATLANTA CAMPAIGN AND AFTERMATH
MAY–DECEMBER 1864

In September 1864, after months of fighting and
maneuvering, Sherman had finally captured Atlanta,
the railroad hub of the Confederacy, and destroyed
most of the city. By December, he had embarked
on his "March to the Sea," (see p.162) while his
opponent, Confederate General John Hood, was
decisively defeated in the disastrous battles of
Franklin and Nashville in Tennessee.

✗ Key battle

LAST YEARS OF WAR
The East saw battles in central Virginia and the Shenandoah Valley, and
the siege of Petersburg, while the West was dominated by the Atlanta
Campaign and the Franklin–Nashville Campaign.

KEY

✗ Other battle

UNION FRONT LINE
〰 Dec 1863   ▬ Dec 1864

UNION FORCES

| Union states 1861 | Union fort | → Union movement | Union naval blockade |

CONFEDERATE FORCES

| Confederate states 1861 | Confederate fort | → Confederate movement |

TIMELINE

5 CONFEDERATE SURRENDER JUNE 23, 1865

Lee surrendered to Grant at Appomattox, Virginia,
on April 9, 1865. General Joseph E. Johnston
surrendered all remaining Confederate troops
east of the Mississippi to Sherman on April 26
at Bennett Place in North Carolina. Other
Confederate field commands followed suit, and
the last to lay down their arms were General
Stand Watie's Cherokees on June 23, 1865.

⚑ Surrender at Appomattox Court House

JAN 1864   JUL 1864   JAN 1865   JUL 1865

WARTIME EMANCIPATION

The Emancipation Proclamation of 1863 legally freed enslaved people in areas under rebellion against the US. The 13th Amendment two years later formally ended slavery—in most, but not all, of its forms. A long struggle for equality lay ahead for Black Americans.

△ **Ending slavery**
A colored engraving of the 1863 proclamation. It began the legal process that ultimately abolished most forms of slavery in the US.

When Lincoln issued the Emancipation Proclamation on January 1, 1863, it freed enslaved people in the rebellious Southern states, declaring that, "all persons held as slaves within any State ... in rebellion against the United States, shall be then, thenceforward, and forever free."

The Proclamation did not free enslaved people in the loyal border states of West Virginia, Tennessee, Maryland, and Missouri. It did not end slavery in practice in rebel-held territory either, as Lincoln's government could not enforce the law in land it did not control. What it did do, though, was ratify the efforts undertaken by enslaved people to free themselves during the Civil War. From the beginning of the conflict, thousands of Black people sought freedom from their enslavers, seeking protection behind US lines. Sympathetic Union generals declared them "contraband of war" and Congress passed two "Confiscation Acts" that acknowledged the freedom of those who escaped.

The willingness of liberated Black people to fight for the US encouraged Congress to pass the Militia Act, which led some 200,000 to enlist and lay their lives on the line to defend the US and end enslavement. They were rewarded on December 6, 1865, by the ratification of the 13th Amendment that ended the practice. The amendment did—and still does—allow enslavement to remain in use as a punishment for some crimes.

THE PORT ROYAL EXPERIMENT

After US forces took South Carolina's Port Royal and the surrounding Sea Islands in 1861, some 10,000 formerly enslaved people stayed on the plantations, working and sometimes buying the land for themselves. Many Sea Islanders and their descendants owned and farmed the land there well into the 20th century.

Sweet potato planting in Port Royal after its liberation.

Fighting for freedom
Black soldiers in United States Army uniforms pose for a photograph during the Civil War. Hundreds of thousands of free and enslaved Black people volunteered to join the military; around 40,000 of them died in the war, 30,000 of the deaths were from infection or disease.

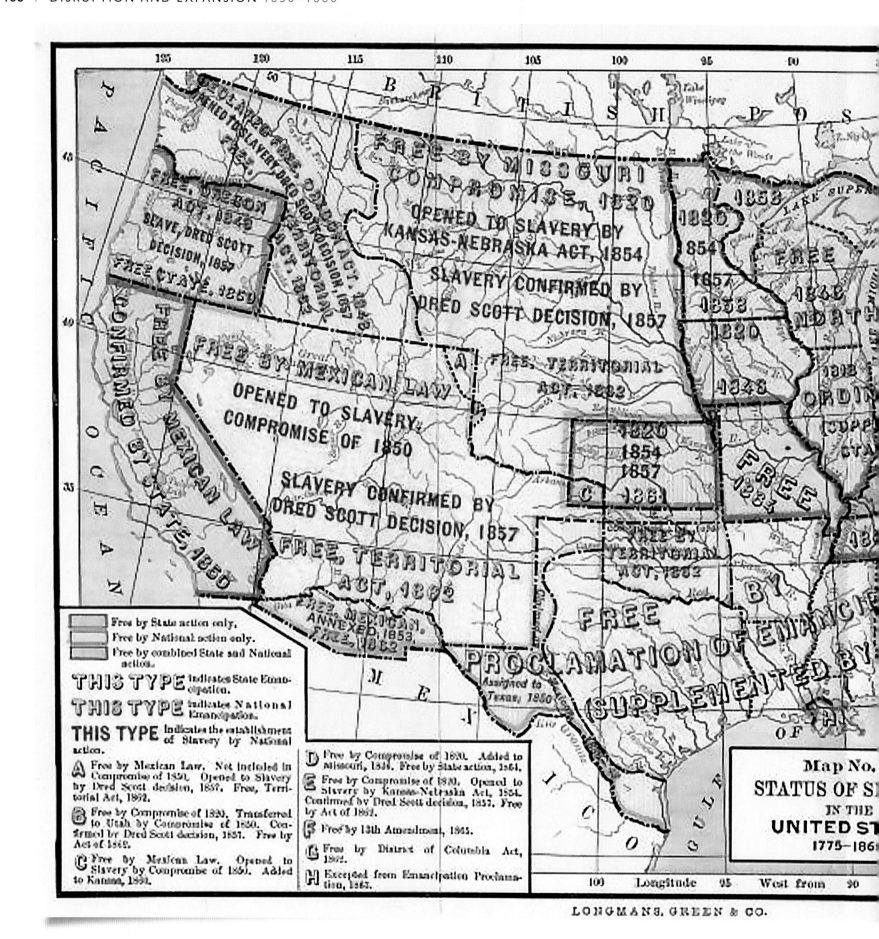

"I do order and declare that all persons held as slaves … are, and henceforward shall be free."

ABRAHAM LINCOLN, IN THE EMANCIPATION PROCLAMATION, JANUARY 1, 1863

THE ABOLITION OF SLAVERY

Legal enslavement in the US ended with the Civil War in 1865. However it continued for decades longer in Puerto Rico, Cuba, and Brazil. Complete emancipation across the hemisphere did not come into effect until 1888.

Northern states abolished enslavement and passed gradual manumission laws from the 1770s, but enslavement was not formally abolished in the US until the 13th Amendment in 1865. Other nations took the lead in formal abolition, including Haiti (1804), Britain (1833), France (1848), and Holland (1863), with republics in former Spanish America abolishing it from the early 19th century. Puerto Rico, Cuba, and Brazil remained as slave societies after the Civil War; their abolitions took effect in 1873, 1886, and 1888 respectively.

In the US, by the end of the Civil War, not all enslaved people had been told they were free, most notoriously in Texas. News of the 1863 Emancipation Proclamation was not made public until June 19, 1865. That day, known as Juneteenth, is now a federal holiday.

After the Civil War, the US entered the Reconstruction period (1865–1877), in which the government attempted to

bring equality and representation to formerly enslaved people (see pp.170–171). One such effort was the 14th Amendment (1868), which made Black people citizens and overturned the Dred Scott decision of 1857 (see p.154). However, reconstruction largely failed and was followed by increased segregation and inequality.

LOCATOR

KEY

1 West Virginia broke away from Virginia in 1863 to avoid joining the confederacy.

2 Texas became the last state to enforce the 1863 Emancipation Proclamation in 1865.

3 In 2013, Mississippi was the last state to ratify the amendment abolishing enslavement.

△ **Legal landscape of enslavement in the US**
Established by European colonists, enslavement persisted in the US when it was founded in 1776. This 1893 map shows the laws used to implement, and eventually abolish, enslavement. Purple areas indicate abolishment through state laws; pink shows national laws; and the green denotes a combination of the two.

ABOLITION IN THE AMERICAS
The US was one of the last countries in the Americas to end the practice of enslavement, with the first being Haiti in 1804 (see p.106), and the last being Brazil in 1888. Enslavement did not always cease immediately and in some places—for instance Pennsylvania, New Hampshire, and Connecticut—abolition came through gradual measures that could last for years, such as forced apprenticeships.

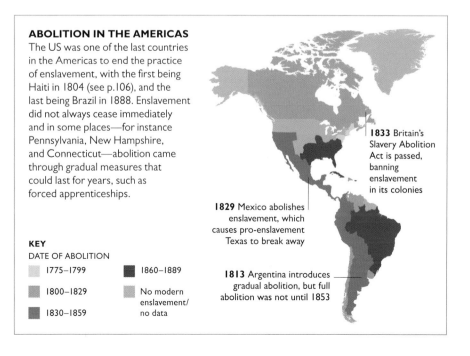

1833 Britain's Slavery Abolition Act is passed, banning enslavement in its colonies

1829 Mexico abolishes enslavement, which causes pro-enslavement Texas to break away

1813 Argentina introduces gradual abolition, but full abolition was not until 1853

KEY
DATE OF ABOLITION

1775–1799	1860–1889
1800–1829	No modern enslavement/ no data
1830–1859	

RECONSTRUCTION AND THE SOUTH

The Reconstruction Era (1865–1877) saw the US attempt to address the injustice of slavery and readmit the rebel states into the Union. The moderate approach proposed by Abraham Lincoln was overtaken by a more punitive attitude toward the South; violent resistance ensued, and racial inequality continued.

Barely two weeks after Lincoln's death, his successor Andrew Johnson offered to pardon ex-Confederates and return confiscated lands to any Southerners who swore an oath of loyalty to the US. His moderate attitude emboldened Southern leaders, who were already enacting repressive "Black Codes," laws to control formerly enslaved populations. Many in the North argued for confiscated land to be allocated to freed people to help them establish economic independence. Johnson's leniency toward the Southern white population lost him support in Congress and led to his impeachment in 1868.

Meanwhile, the Radical Republicans, a faction committed to racial justice, took control of the Reconstruction process. In 1867, they enacted bills to disenfranchise ex-Confederates, enfranchise freedmen, and end the South's most egregious racial practices. This met fierce resistance, and ex-Confederate paramilitaries launched a campaign of terror in the South.

The financial panic of 1873 drove the South into a depression. In 1877, as part of an agreement to elect Republican Rutherford B. Hayes president, Federal troops withdrew from the South, where white Democrats gained power to enforce white supremacy. When Johnson pardoned ex-rebels in December 1868, former enslavers were still the South's main landowners, with Black Americans the primary labor force once more, having exchanged enslavement for the peonage of sharecropping.

> "The slave went free; stood for a brief moment in the sun; then moved back again toward slavery."
>
> W. E. B. DU BOIS, *BLACK RECONSTRUCTION*, 1935

"40 ACRES AND A MULE"

In January 1865, General William T. Sherman issued Special Field Order No. 15, reserving 40,000 acres of confiscated or abandoned lands on the southeast coast for freed people. Each person was allocated up to 40 acres. When the US Army offered to provide mules, the order became known colloquially as the "forty acres and a mule" policy. After President Johnson restored all property and land to its ex-Confederate owners, the "Sherman Reserve" was lost.

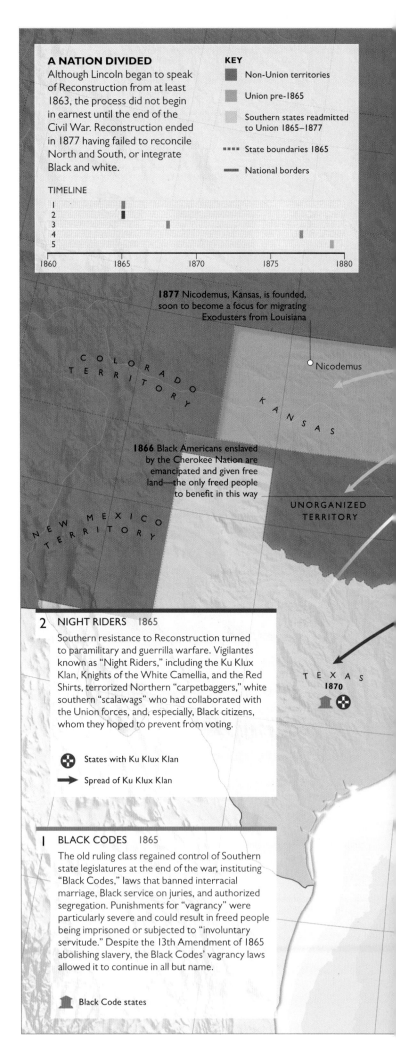

A NATION DIVIDED

Although Lincoln began to speak of Reconstruction from at least 1863, the process did not begin in earnest until the end of the Civil War. Reconstruction ended in 1877 having failed to reconcile North and South, or integrate Black and white.

KEY
- Non-Union territories
- Union pre-1865
- Southern states readmitted to Union 1865–1877
- ···· State boundaries 1865
- — National borders

TIMELINE

1877 Nicodemus, Kansas, is founded, soon to become a focus for migrating Exodusters from Louisiana

1866 Black Americans enslaved by the Cherokee Nation are emancipated and given free land—the only freed people to benefit in this way

2 NIGHT RIDERS 1865

Southern resistance to Reconstruction turned to paramilitary and guerrilla warfare. Vigilantes known as "Night Riders," including the Ku Klux Klan, Knights of the White Camellia, and the Red Shirts, terrorized Northern "carpetbaggers," white southern "scalawags" who had collaborated with the Union forces, and, especially, Black citizens, whom they hoped to prevent from voting.

- ✪ States with Ku Klux Klan
- → Spread of Ku Klux Klan

1 BLACK CODES 1865

The old ruling class regained control of Southern state legislatures at the end of the war, instituting "Black Codes," laws that banned interracial marriage, Black service on juries, and authorized segregation. Punishments for "vagrancy" were particularly severe and could result in freed people being imprisoned or subjected to "involuntary servitude." Despite the 13th Amendment of 1865 abolishing slavery, the Black Codes' vagrancy laws allowed it to continue in all but name.

- 🏛 Black Code states

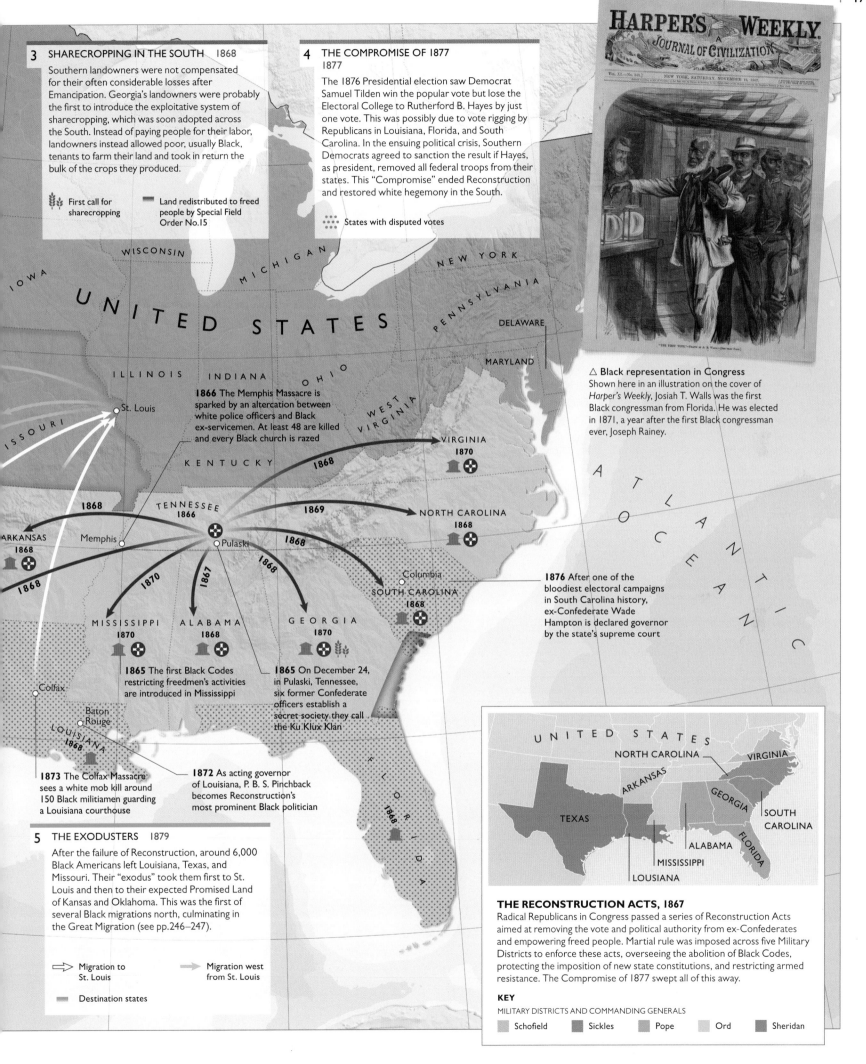

3 SHARECROPPING IN THE SOUTH 1868

Southern landowners were not compensated for their often considerable losses after Emancipation. Georgia's landowners were probably the first to introduce the exploitative system of sharecropping, which was soon adopted across the South. Instead of paying people for their labor, landowners instead allowed poor, usually Black, tenants to farm their land and took in return the bulk of the crops they produced.

🌾 First call for sharecropping

▬ Land redistributed to freed people by Special Field Order No.15

4 THE COMPROMISE OF 1877 1877

The 1876 Presidential election saw Democrat Samuel Tilden win the popular vote but lose the Electoral College to Rutherford B. Hayes by just one vote. This was possibly due to vote rigging by Republicans in Louisiana, Florida, and South Carolina. In the ensuing political crisis, Southern Democrats agreed to sanction the result if Hayes, as president, removed all federal troops from their states. This "Compromise" ended Reconstruction and restored white hegemony in the South.

⣿ States with disputed votes

△ **Black representation in Congress**
Shown here in an illustration on the cover of *Harper's Weekly*, Josiah T. Walls was the first Black congressman from Florida. He was elected in 1871, a year after the first Black congressman ever, Joseph Rainey.

1866 The Memphis Massacre is sparked by an altercation between white police officers and Black ex-servicemen. At least 48 are killed and every Black church is razed

1876 After one of the bloodiest electoral campaigns in South Carolina history, ex-Confederate Wade Hampton is declared governor by the state's supreme court

1865 The first Black Codes restricting freedmen's activities are introduced in Mississippi

1865 On December 24, in Pulaski, Tennessee, six former Confederate officers establish a secret society they call the Ku Klux Klan

1873 The Colfax Massacre sees a white mob kill around 150 Black militiamen guarding a Louisiana courthouse

1872 As acting governor of Louisiana, P. B. S. Pinchback becomes Reconstruction's most prominent Black politician

5 THE EXODUSTERS 1879

After the failure of Reconstruction, around 6,000 Black Americans left Louisiana, Texas, and Missouri. Their "exodus" took them first to St. Louis and then to their expected Promised Land of Kansas and Oklahoma. This was the first of several Black migrations north, culminating in the Great Migration (see pp.246–247).

⇨ Migration to St. Louis

➜ Migration west from St. Louis

▬ Destination states

THE RECONSTRUCTION ACTS, 1867

Radical Republicans in Congress passed a series of Reconstruction Acts aimed at removing the vote and political authority from ex-Confederates and empowering freed people. Martial rule was imposed across five Military Districts to enforce these acts, overseeing the abolition of Black Codes, protecting the imposition of new state constitutions, and restricting armed resistance. The Compromise of 1877 swept all of this away.

KEY

MILITARY DISTRICTS AND COMMANDING GENERALS

▢ Schofield ▢ Sickles ▢ Pope ▢ Ord ▢ Sheridan

ECONOMY, PEOPLE, AND TERRITORY

Industrialization and the growth of transportation hugely impacted the economies of North America in the 19th century. While colonizers and armies pushed Indigenous people out of their homelands, an influx of Europeans immigrated to the US.

The second half of the 19th century saw immense growth of the US economy, largely made possible by the rapid development of railroads. By 1869, when the first transcontinental rail line was built, coast-to-coast journeys that would take months to complete could now be accomplished in less than 84 hours. Expanding rail networks were revolutionizing the transportation of people, food, and machinery, while also establishing infrastructure for transcontinental trade. Cities, such as Chicago, sprang up at railroad junctions, which, in turn, attracted to their crowded streets goods and people from an immense hinterland. Outside the US, industrialization also resulted in a manufacturing boom in Canada, while mechanization boosted the sugar industry in the Caribbean. The Canadian economy grew on the back of increased exports of fish and fur, among other commodities.

People on the move

Immigrants poured into the US after 1865, many of them Scandinavians, attracted to the "Big Woods" and lumber mills of the Great Lakes country, or Czechs to the plains and prairies of the Midwest. Others began to arrive from eastern and southern Europe to escape crop failures and political turmoil at home. Italians began arriving in considerable numbers by the 1880s, as did Eastern European Jews fleeing anti-Semitic violence and lack

△ **Bow case and quiver**
Made from otter skin, wool cloth, and ermine, and adorned with glass beads and a silk ribbon, this bow case and quiver were fashioned by a Nimiipuu (Nez Percé) artist c. 1870.

△ **Indentured laborers in the West Indies, c. 1900**
This painting shows indentured laborers working at a sugar mill. After the abolition of slavery, the British brought indentured laborers from their colonies in South and East Asia to work the Caribbean sugar plantations.

of economic opportunities. While many of these newcomers found sanctuary in the big cities of the Northeast, such as Boston and New York, this rapid modernization of the US also provoked a rise in exploitative labor practices, especially against Chinese workers, who began to arrive in the US in high numbers during this era. Large swathes of canal and railroad were built by Chinese immigrant labor, along with many Irish, yet they still faced discrimination and hostility. In 1882, Congress passed the Chinese Exclusion Act, heavily restricting Chinese immigration. Many

GROWTH AND CONTRACTION

Railroads, lengthening and spreading every year, spurred growth in the economy and the acquisition of territory for both the US and Canada. Waves of new European emigrants started arriving from the 1820s, adding to the stream of settlers heading west. At the same time, Indigenous territories continued shrinking with each new legislative change that was introduced in reservation policy.

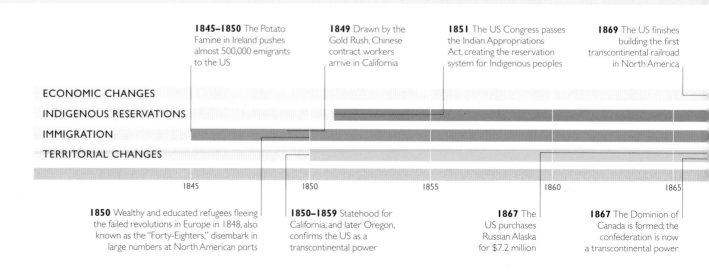

1845–1850 The Potato Famine in Ireland pushes almost 500,000 emigrants to the US

1849 Drawn by the Gold Rush, Chinese contract workers arrive in California

1851 The US Congress passes the Indian Appropriations Act, creating the reservation system for Indigenous peoples

1869 The US finishes building the first transcontinental railroad in North America

ECONOMIC CHANGES
INDIGENOUS RESERVATIONS
IMMIGRATION
TERRITORIAL CHANGES

1845   1850   1855   1860   1865

1850 Wealthy and educated refugees fleeing the failed revolutions in Europe in 1848, also known as the "Forty-Eighters," disembark in large numbers at North American ports

1850–1859 Statehood for California, and later Oregon, confirms the US as a transcontinental power

1867 The US purchases Russian Alaska for $7.2 million

1867 The Dominion of Canada is formed; the confederation is now a transcontinental power

▷ **Fur trappers in Alaska**
Fur seal hunters were among the first Europeans to settle in Alaska. This photograph from 1890 shows a group of trappers with their pack horses and dogs.

immigrants from southern Europe settled elsewhere in the Americas, including Mexico, Cuba, and Argentina. In the Caribbean, indentured laborers from India were shipped to British colonies to replace formerly enslaved persons who refused to return to the cane fields and sugar mills after the 1834 emancipation of slavery in the British West Indies.

Territorial aspirations

The British united Canada, Nova Scotia, and New Brunswick into the self-governing Dominion of Canada in 1867. Although this confederation was put together by an act of the British Parliament, it was given substance by the trans-Canada railroad. In the same year, the US purchased what was formerly Russian Alaska; however, it was only from the late 1870s, with the discovery of salmon and gold there, that the US began to explore and colonize it. Territorial expansion in the US meant encroachment on Indigenous lands, and Indigenous Alaskans fought back. The last of the

"Indian Wars" (see pp.176–177) demonstrated the power of Indigenous resistance, but ultimately failed to stem the tide of US settlement and exploitation. By the end of the 19th century, settlers occupied good agricultural lands in the West, and the US government forced Indigenous peoples to relocate. In 1887, the General Allotment Act, also known as the Dawes Act, was passed, designed to dissolve autonomous Indigenous communities and force the sale of their lands.

◁ **Residence card**
This Certificate of Residence was issued to a Chinese farmer in California. The Geary Act of 1892 required all Chinese immigrants in the US to carry this document to prove their legal presence in the country. An absence of this ID would result in deportation.

> "The Wheat is one force, the Railroad, another, and there is the law that governs them—supply and demand."
>
> FRANK NORRIS, THE OCTOPUS: A STORY OF CALIFORNIA, 1901

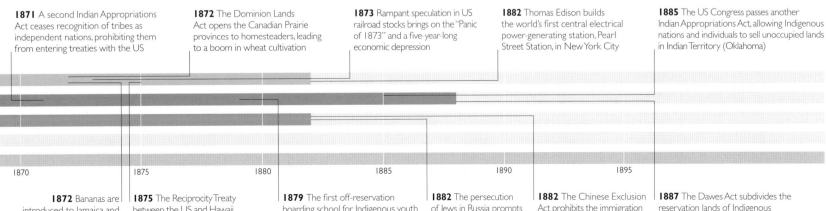

1871 A second Indian Appropriations Act ceases recognition of tribes as independent nations, prohibiting them from entering treaties with the US

1872 The Dominion Lands Act opens the Canadian Prairie provinces to homesteaders, leading to a boom in wheat cultivation

1873 Rampant speculation in US railroad stocks brings on the "Panic of 1873" and a five-year-long economic depression

1882 Thomas Edison builds the world's first central electrical power-generating station, Pearl Street Station, in New York City

1885 The US Congress passes another Indian Appropriations Act, allowing Indigenous nations and individuals to sell unoccupied lands in Indian Territory (Oklahoma)

1870   1875   1880   1885   1890   1895

1872 Bananas are introduced to Jamaica and replace sugar as the primary export crop by 1890

1875 The Reciprocity Treaty between the US and Hawaii grants special economic privileges to the US

1879 The first off-reservation boarding school for Indigenous youth opens in Pennsylvania, attempting to forcibly assimilate students

1882 The persecution of Jews in Russia prompts mass immigration to the US

1882 The Chinese Exclusion Act prohibits the immigration of Chinese laborers to the US for 10 years

1887 The Dawes Act subdivides the reservation lands of Indigenous nations by apportioning land to individuals and selling the surplus

A GROWING ECONOMY

In the 19th century, developments in transportation and industry transformed the largely agrarian and rural US economy into an industrial one, while the economies of neighboring British North America and the Caribbean also experienced growth.

Despite periodic stagnations and depressions, the US economy grew at a rapid rate in the second half of the 19th century. The expansion of land ownership played a key role in this growth, while the arrival of steamships, railroads, and the telegraph facilitated trade and communication across the country and beyond. Manufacturing grew, and factories were soon making a wide range of goods. Cotton, cultivated by enslaved people in the US South before the Civil War, remained a leading export. People flocked to urban centers to seek work and millions of immigrants poured in, hoping to find a better life. As a result, the US population increased from around 2.3 million in 1774 to about 92 million by 1909. Consumption became an important economic driver, as buying power improved.

During this period, the economy of Canada (then part of British North America) grew at a steady rate, relying on export of staples such as fish, fur, timber, and wheat. Its manufacturing industry would flourish by the end of the century. In the Caribbean, mechanization boosted the sugar industry further. Sugar planters imported indentured workers from India, China, Indonesia, and elsewhere to replace enslaved labor after Britain abolished enslavement in 1834.

> *"One can hardly believe there has been a revolution ... so rapid, so extensive, so complete."*
>
> JOHN DEWEY, *THE SCHOOL AND SOCIETY*, 1899

△ Canadian powerhouse
Canada enjoyed rising prosperity in the 19th century. Among its largest cities, Montreal was a hub of trade and industry, as seen in this 1892 illustration of its bustling harbor. Lumber, agriculture, and manufacturing were key.

Sorting cotton
Not everyone in the US equally benefited from the growing economy. Many people, such as these Black American cotton workers in Florida (c. 1905), had to endure poor working conditions and low pay.

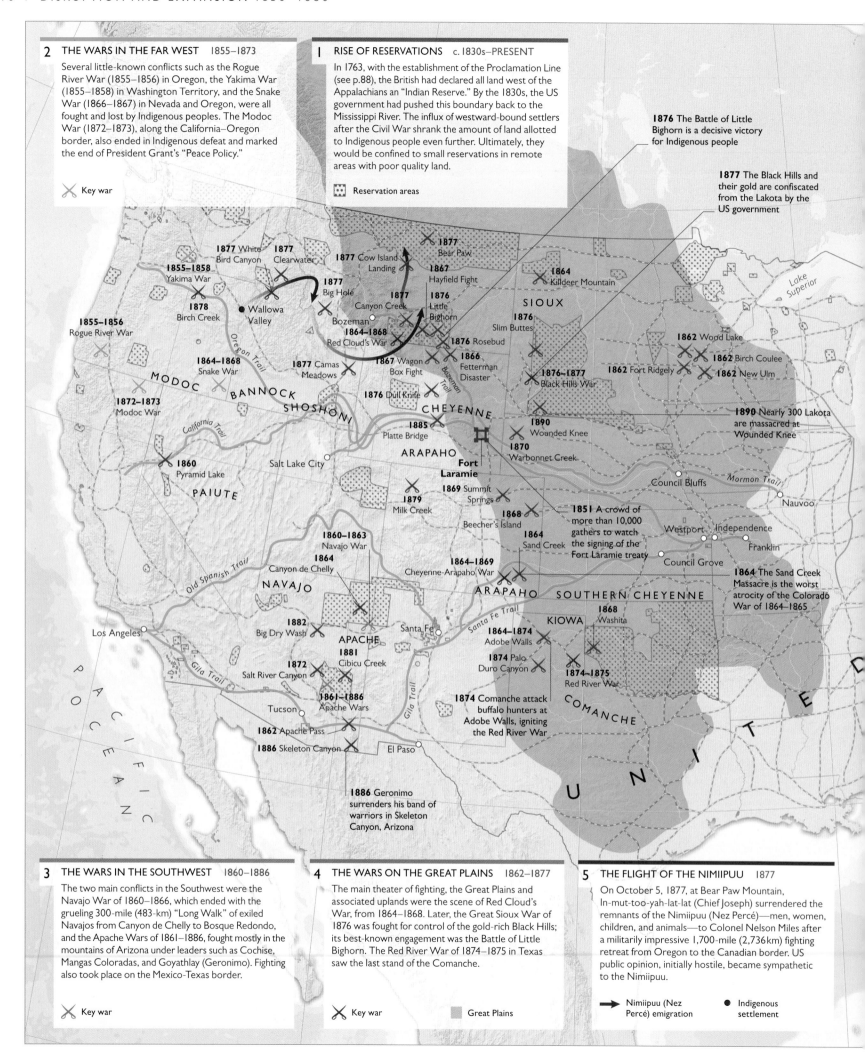

2 THE WARS IN THE FAR WEST 1855–1873

Several little-known conflicts such as the Rogue River War (1855–1856) in Oregon, the Yakima War (1855–1858) in Washington Territory, and the Snake War (1866–1867) in Nevada and Oregon, were all fought and lost by Indigenous peoples. The Modoc War (1872–1873), along the California–Oregon border, also ended in Indigenous defeat and marked the end of President Grant's "Peace Policy."

✕ Key war

1 RISE OF RESERVATIONS c.1830s–PRESENT

In 1763, with the establishment of the Proclamation Line (see p.88), the British had declared all land west of the Appalachians an "Indian Reserve." By the 1830s, the US government had pushed this boundary back to the Mississippi River. The influx of westward-bound settlers after the Civil War shrank the amount of land allotted to Indigenous people even further. Ultimately, they would be confined to small reservations in remote areas with poor quality land.

▦ Reservation areas

1876 The Battle of Little Bighorn is a decisive victory for Indigenous people

1877 The Black Hills and their gold are confiscated from the Lakota by the US government

1877 White Bird Canyon
1877 Clearwater
1855–1858 Yakima War
1877 Cow Island Landing
1877 Bear Paw
1867 Hayfield Fight
1864 Killdeer Mountain
1877 Big Hole
1855–1856 Rogue River War
1877 Canyon Creek
1877 Little Bighorn
1876 Little Bighorn
1876 Slim Buttes
1864–1868 Snake War
1864–1868 Red Cloud's War
1876 Rosebud
1862 Wood Lake
1878 Birch Creek
Wallowa Valley
Bozeman
1876 Dull Knife
1866 Fetterman Disaster
1862 Fort Ridgely
1862 Birch Coulee
1862 New Ulm
1877 Camas Meadows
1867 Wagon Box Fight
1876–1877 Black Hills War
SIOUX
1872–1873 Modoc War
MODOC
BANNOCK
SHOSHONI
CHEYENNE
1885 Platte Bridge
1890 Wounded Knee
1890 Nearly 300 Lakota are massacred at Wounded Knee
1860 Pyramid Lake
Salt Lake City
ARAPAHO
Fort Laramie
1870 Warbonnet Creek
PAIUTE
1879 Milk Creek
1869 Summit Springs
1868 Beecher's Island
1851 A crowd of more than 10,000 gathers to watch the signing of the Fort Laramie treaty
Council Bluffs
Westport Independence
Nauvoo
Franklin
1860–1863 Navajo War
1864 Canyon de Chelly
1864 Sand Creek
1864–1869 Cheyenne-Arapaho War
Council Grove
1864 The Sand Creek Massacre is the worst atrocity of the Colorado War of 1864–1865
NAVAJO
Los Angeles
ARAPAHO
SOUTHERN CHEYENNE
1882 Big Dry Wash
Santa Fe
KIOWA
1868 Washita
APACHE
1881 Cibicu Creek
1864–1874 Adobe Walls
1872 Salt River Canyon
1874 Palo Duro Canyon
1874–1875 Red River War
Tucson
1861–1886 Apache Wars
1874 Comanche attack buffalo hunters at Adobe Walls, igniting the Red River War
COMANCHE
1862 Apache Pass
1886 Skeleton Canyon
El Paso
UNITED
PACIFIC OCEAN
1886 Geronimo surrenders his band of warriors in Skeleton Canyon, Arizona
Lake Superior
Oregon Trail
California Trail
Old Spanish Trail
Gila Trail
Mormon Trail
Bozeman Trail
Santa Fe Trail

3 THE WARS IN THE SOUTHWEST 1860–1886

The two main conflicts in the Southwest were the Navajo War of 1860–1866, which ended with the grueling 300-mile (483-km) "Long Walk" of exiled Navajos from Canyon de Chelly to Bosque Redondo, and the Apache Wars of 1861–1886, fought mostly in the mountains of Arizona under leaders such as Cochise, Mangas Coloradas, and Goyathlay (Geronimo). Fighting also took place on the Mexico-Texas border.

✕ Key war

4 THE WARS ON THE GREAT PLAINS 1862–1877

The main theater of fighting, the Great Plains and associated uplands were the scene of Red Cloud's War, from 1864–1868. Later, the Great Sioux War of 1876 was fought for control of the gold-rich Black Hills; its best-known engagement was the Battle of Little Bighorn. The Red River War of 1874–1875 in Texas saw the last stand of the Comanche.

✕ Key war   ▨ Great Plains

5 THE FLIGHT OF THE NIMIIPUU 1877

On October 5, 1877, at Bear Paw Mountain, In-mut-too-yah-lat-lat (Chief Joseph) surrendered the remnants of the Nimiipuu (Nez Percé)—men, women, children, and animals—to Colonel Nelson Miles after a militarily impressive 1,700-mile (2,736km) fighting retreat from Oregon to the Canadian border. US public opinion, initially hostile, became sympathetic to the Nimiipuu.

→ Nimiipuu (Nez Percé) emigration   ● Indigenous settlement

As the US increased its efforts to displace Indigenous peoples from their lands in the West, it was inevitable that conflict would arise.

KEY

✕ Other wars

⊞ US fort

┄ Railroads, 1870–1890

▬ Overland trails

— State boundaries, 1880

TIMELINE

1 2 3 4 5

1800 1850 1900 1950 2000 2050

▽ The Battle of Little Bighorn, June 25, 1876
This hide painting depicts the Battle of Little Bighorn, a comprehensive victory for the Indigenous war leaders Tatanka Iyotake (Sitting Bull) and Ta-sunko-witko (Crazy Horse).

INDIGENOUS PEOPLE IN THE WEST

With the Treaty of Fort Laramie in 1851, the US government conceded that much of the Great Plains was Indigenous territory and denied any claim to it. Most European Americans, however, disagreed and thought that the land was in the public domain and open to settlement. Clashes were inevitable.

This uncertainty continued for more than a decade. Then, in 1862, President Abraham Lincoln initiated both the Homestead Act, which encouraged US citizens to colonize the West, and the construction of the transcontinental railroads. Two years later in 1864, he endorsed the public domain argument.

This led to Red Cloud's War, starting in 1864, in which an alliance of Indigenous people in Wyoming and Montana conducted raids against colonists and US Army forts along the Bozeman Trail. A short-lived "Peace Policy" introduced by President Ulysses S. Grant was derailed by political opposition, and violence continued across the US through the 1870s. Although much of the fighting was instigated by

colonists, in 1873 US Army forces at Fort Clark on the Rio Grande began a series of extralegal raids into Mexico to quell Ndé (Apache) attacks. Three years later, General George Custer was killed along with all his men at the Battle of Little Bighorn by Lakota, Cheyenne, and Arapaho warriors angered by settlers and prospectors encroaching on their land.

Although Indigenous peoples mobilized serious resistance to superior US forces, they were overwhelmed. A symbolic moment came with the capture of the Ndé resistance leader Goyathlay (Geronimo) in 1886, followed in 1890 by the Battle of Wounded Knee, where 300 people of the Pine Ridge Reservation were massacred by US Army troops.

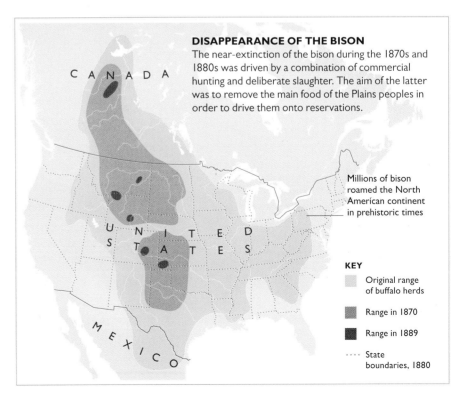

DISAPPEARANCE OF THE BISON
The near-extinction of the bison during the 1870s and 1880s was driven by a combination of commercial hunting and deliberate slaughter. The aim of the latter was to remove the main food of the Plains peoples in order to drive them onto reservations.

Millions of bison roamed the North American continent in prehistoric times

KEY

Original range of buffalo herds

Range in 1870

Range in 1889

State boundaries, 1880

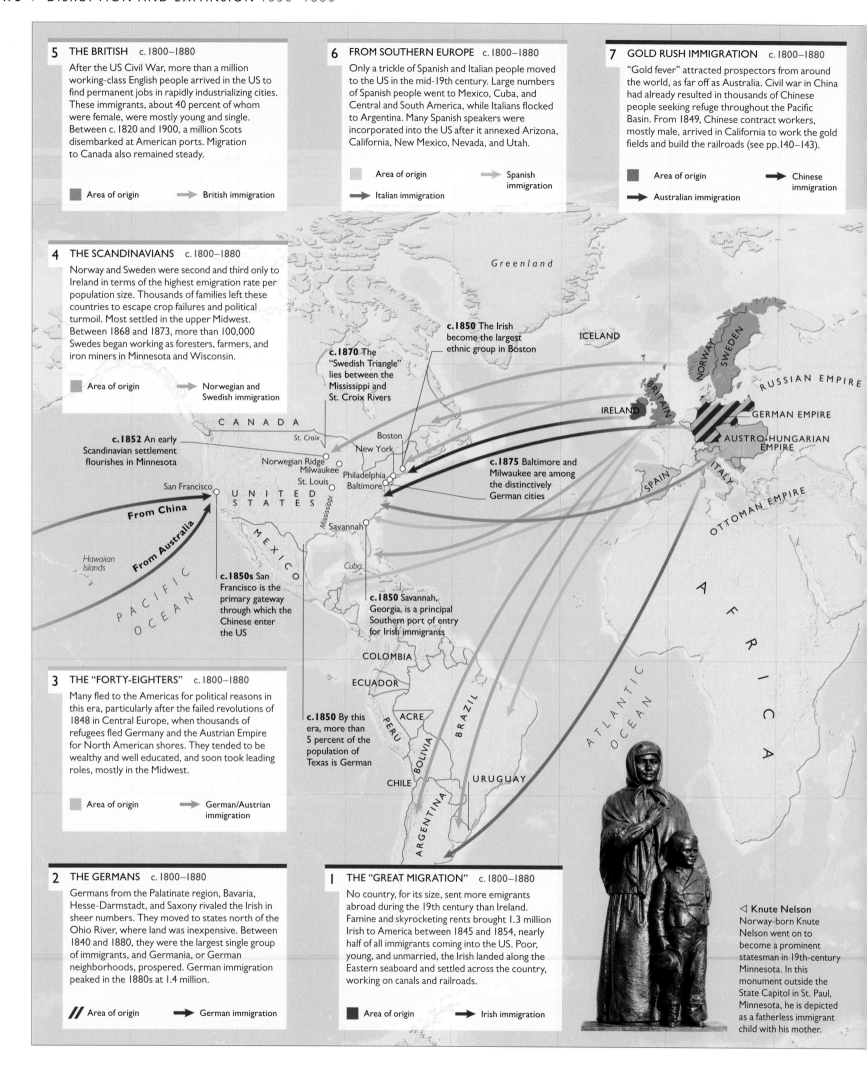

5 THE BRITISH c. 1800–1880

After the US Civil War, more than a million working-class English people arrived in the US to find permanent jobs in rapidly industrializing cities. These immigrants, about 40 percent of whom were female, were mostly young and single. Between c. 1820 and 1900, a million Scots disembarked at American ports. Migration to Canada also remained steady.

■ Area of origin → British immigration

6 FROM SOUTHERN EUROPE c. 1800–1880

Only a trickle of Spanish and Italian people moved to the US in the mid-19th century. Large numbers of Spanish people went to Mexico, Cuba, and Central and South America, while Italians flocked to Argentina. Many Spanish speakers were incorporated into the US after it annexed Arizona, California, New Mexico, Nevada, and Utah.

□ Area of origin → Spanish immigration
→ Italian immigration

7 GOLD RUSH IMMIGRATION c. 1800–1880

"Gold fever" attracted prospectors from around the world, as far off as Australia. Civil war in China had already resulted in thousands of Chinese people seeking refuge throughout the Pacific Basin. From 1849, Chinese contract workers, mostly male, arrived in California to work the gold fields and build the railroads (see pp.140–143).

■ Area of origin → Chinese immigration
→ Australian immigration

4 THE SCANDINAVIANS c. 1800–1880

Norway and Sweden were second and third only to Ireland in terms of the highest emigration rate per population size. Thousands of families left these countries to escape crop failures and political turmoil. Most settled in the upper Midwest. Between 1868 and 1873, more than 100,000 Swedes began working as foresters, farmers, and iron miners in Minnesota and Wisconsin.

□ Area of origin → Norwegian and Swedish immigration

c.1850 The Irish become the largest ethnic group in Boston

c.1870 The "Swedish Triangle" lies between the Mississippi and St. Croix Rivers

c.1852 An early Scandinavian settlement flourishes in Minnesota

c.1875 Baltimore and Milwaukee are among the distinctively German cities

c.1850s San Francisco is the primary gateway through which the Chinese enter the US

c.1850 Savannah, Georgia, is a principal Southern port of entry for Irish immigrants

c.1850 By this era, more than 5 percent of the population of Texas is German

From China
From Australia

3 THE "FORTY-EIGHTERS" c. 1800–1880

Many fled to the Americas for political reasons in this era, particularly after the failed revolutions of 1848 in Central Europe, when thousands of refugees fled Germany and the Austrian Empire for North American shores. They tended to be wealthy and well educated, and soon took leading roles, mostly in the Midwest.

□ Area of origin → German/Austrian immigration

2 THE GERMANS c. 1800–1880

Germans from the Palatinate region, Bavaria, Hesse-Darmstadt, and Saxony rivaled the Irish in sheer numbers. They moved to states north of the Ohio River, where land was inexpensive. Between 1840 and 1880, they were the largest single group of immigrants, and Germania, or German neighborhoods, prospered. German immigration peaked in the 1880s at 1.4 million.

// Area of origin → German immigration

1 THE "GREAT MIGRATION" c. 1800–1880

No country, for its size, sent more emigrants abroad during the 19th century than Ireland. Famine and skyrocketing rents brought 1.3 million Irish to America between 1845 and 1854, nearly half of all immigrants coming into the US. Poor, young, and unmarried, the Irish landed along the Eastern seaboard and settled across the country, working on canals and railroads.

■ Area of origin → Irish immigration

◁ **Knute Nelson**
Norway-born Knute Nelson went on to become a prominent statesman in 19th-century Minnesota. In this monument outside the State Capitol in St. Paul, Minnesota, he is depicted as a fatherless immigrant child with his mother.

IMMIGRATION IN THE 1800s

For nearly 30 years, the French Revolution, Napoleonic Wars, and War of 1812 curtailed shipping in the North Atlantic, limiting immigration to the US. After 1820, the first great influx began, originating mostly from northwestern Europe.

Large numbers of Irish people came to the US by the 1820s. Many were single young men in search of a better future. The Irish were stereotyped as boisterous Roman Catholics in a Protestant nation. However, they continued coming to the US in large numbers, including families during the Great Famine (1845–1852), and became a familiar part of US society. They were matched by an influx of Germans—well-educated families who were welcomed in growing Midwestern cities. In the 1840s–1850s, more than 70 percent of immigrants were Irish or German. By contrast, the slave trade (see pp.72–73) also caused forced immigration in this period.

The principal immigration ports were Baltimore, Philadelphia, Boston, and New York, with Savannah and New Orleans receiving immigrants in the South. After the US Civil War, when the Scandinavians arrived in considerable numbers, they migrated from northern ports to populate the forests and prairies of the upper Midwest, helping make the region even more diverse. In 1849, prospectors from around the globe, including Asia, began landing in California, where gold had been discovered (see pp.140–141). By 1875, when the first restrictions on immigration began, nearly 100,000 Chinese people were living in California (see pp.142–143).

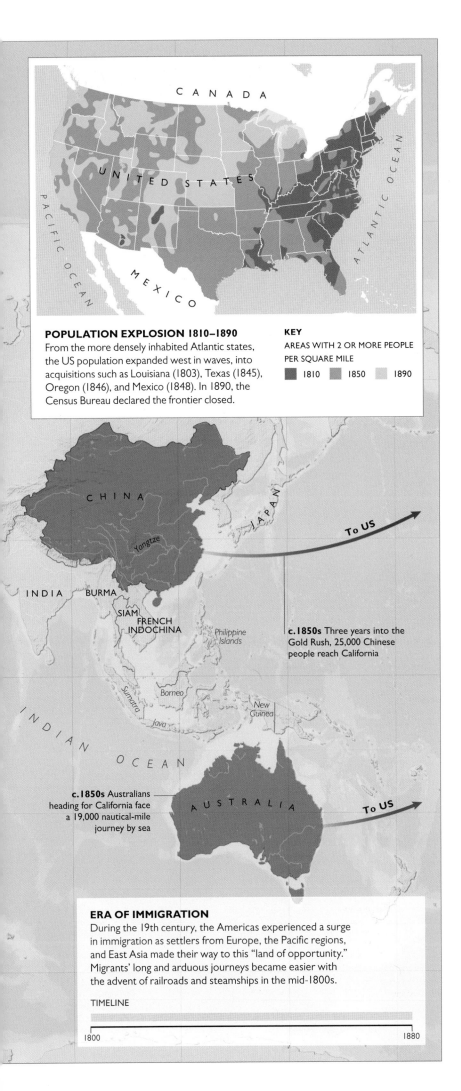

POPULATION EXPLOSION 1810–1890
From the more densely inhabited Atlantic states, the US population expanded west in waves, into acquisitions such as Louisiana (1803), Texas (1845), Oregon (1846), and Mexico (1848). In 1890, the Census Bureau declared the frontier closed.

KEY
AREAS WITH 2 OR MORE PEOPLE PER SQUARE MILE
█ 1810   █ 1850   ░ 1890

c.1850s Three years into the Gold Rush, 25,000 Chinese people reach California

c.1850s Australians heading for California face a 19,000 nautical-mile journey by sea

ERA OF IMMIGRATION
During the 19th century, the Americas experienced a surge in immigration as settlers from Europe, the Pacific regions, and East Asia made their way to this "land of opportunity." Migrants' long and arduous journeys became easier with the advent of railroads and steamships in the mid-1800s.

TIMELINE

1800   1880

CASTLE GARDEN EMIGRANT LANDING DEPOT

Located on the southwestern tip of Manhattan Island, Castle Garden was originally a fort. In 1855 it became the nation's first immigrant processing station. Long lines of prospective new citizens shuffled into its vast waiting rooms to be inspected, registered, and closely questioned as to their intentions and destinations. In its 35-year history, an estimated 8 million people passed through Castle Garden. It closed in 1890, amid allegations of overcrowding and corruption.

JEWISH IMMIGRATION

From 1820 to 1924, Jewish immigration into North America began slowly and grew into a major influx of refugees. Jewish communities thrived and became a notable part of the continent's cultural landscape.

△ **Prayer book**
Printed in Germany in 1842, this tiny prayer book was compiled for the use of Jewish emigrants bound for "the nation of America."

The first Jewish congregation in North America was formed in 1654 in Dutch New Amsterdam, later renamed New York City. Settlement remained sporadic for nearly two centuries before the first big wave of Jewish migration began. Between 1820 and 1880, an estimated 300,000 German-speaking Jews arrived from Central Europe in the US alone, most of them following the paths of German settlements in the northeast and Midwest.

From 1881 to 1924, in a second wave, upward of 2.5 million Eastern European Jews disembarked in North America, most of them in New York City, making it the largest Jewish urban population in the world by 1910. The vast majority had fled pogroms and persecutions in Czarist Russia, exchanging towns and villages in the Russian empire for teeming tenements in eastern North American cities. Soon, Jewish immigrants were making their mark in North American culture. One such immigrant from this era was music composer Irving Berlin, who went on to write many classic songs including "God Bless America" and "White Christmas."

This influx finally ebbed in 1924, when new US immigration quotas and restrictions stemmed the flow of people entering the country (see pp.244–245). In the 1930s, however, Jewish refugees from Nazi Germany—novelist Thomas Mann, physicist Albert Einstein, and director Billy Wilder among them—formed another wave of immigrants making their way across the Atlantic.

ARRIVING IN NEW YORK

From the end of the 19th century, Jewish immigrants arriving in New York Harbor after a long voyage across the Atlantic Ocean from Eastern Europe would pass the new Statue of Liberty. The words on the statue's base famously proclaim "Give me your tired, your poor, your huddled masses yearning to breathe free." Those lines had been written by the poet Emma Lazarus, herself a descendant of an early New York Jewish immigrant family.

Jewish refugees, 1892

A Jewish neighborhood
This photograph from 1900 shows a street market in Manhattan's Lower East Side thronging with newly arrived Jewish immigrants. Many immigrants sport the attire prevalent in their Eastern European homelands.

CANADIAN CONFEDERATION

In 1850, British North America consisted of four Maritime Colonies (New Brunswick, Nova Scotia, Prince Edward Island, and Newfoundland), the Province of Canada, and Vancouver Island. Unification would soon follow.

The desire to confederate, or unify politically, these fragmented territories had gained widespread support by the mid-19th century. Concerted efforts were underway by 1864; the civil war that was raging in the US was a reminder that any attempt at union would have to be carefully planned. These efforts were resolved in London, where Parliament passed the 1867 British North America Act establishing the new Dominion of Canada. This initial confederation comprised what had been Upper and Lower Canada (Ontario and Quebec respectively), New Brunswick, and Nova Scotia. The capital was to be Ottawa in Ontario, where a new Parliament of Canada was overseen by a royally-appointed Governor General.

The new Dominion grew quickly. By 1871 it incorporated all the land west and north of Ontario, much of it purchased from the North-West Company, inheritor of the Hudson's Bay

LOCATOR

KEY

1 The province of Quebec (yellow) was formerly known as Lower Canada.

2 Ontario (pink) was formerly Upper Canada.

3 The mass of light green territory was formerly controlled by Hudson's Bay Company (known as "Rupert's Land"). Originally the basin of Hudson Bay, it had been extended west to the Pacific in the decades before confederation.

Company domains known as "Rupert's Land" (see pp.122–123). Vancouver and the new British Columbia were absorbed that same year. In 1873, the last holdout, Prince Edward Island, joined. A united Canada now stretched from Atlantic to Pacific and far into the Arctic.

HISTORY OF THE FLAGS OF CANADA

After Confederation, the Canadian Red Ensign became the Dominion's unofficial flag, combining the Union Jack with the shield of Canada. Many different versions appeared, some sporting provincial coats of arms, royal crowns, and even beavers. Iconographic maple leaves, however, increasingly assumed symbolic importance. Today's official Canadian Flag, centered on a red maple leaf, was adopted in 1965.

An early Canadian Red Ensign combining the Union Jack with the shield of Canada

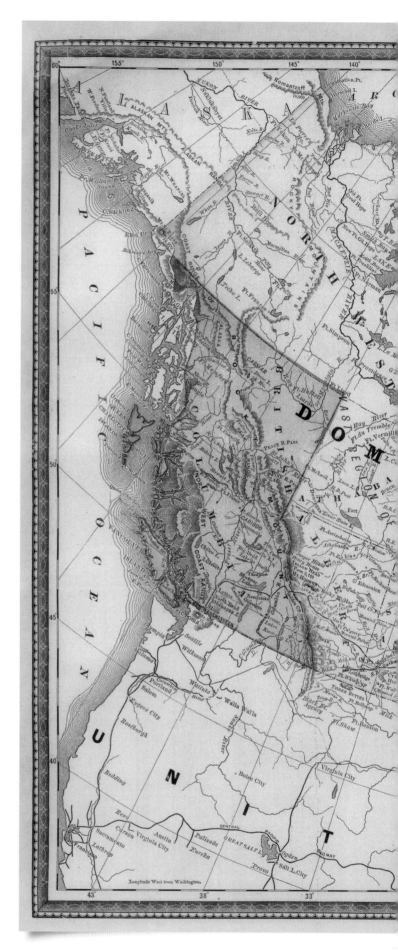

△ The Dominion of Canada in 1889
This 1889 map drafted by Rand McNally and Company depicts the Dominion of Canada shortly after Confederation. Manitoba has already become a province, but today's Alberta, Saskatchewan, Yukon, and Nunavut have yet to be established. Newfoundland, including Labrador, would not join until 1949.

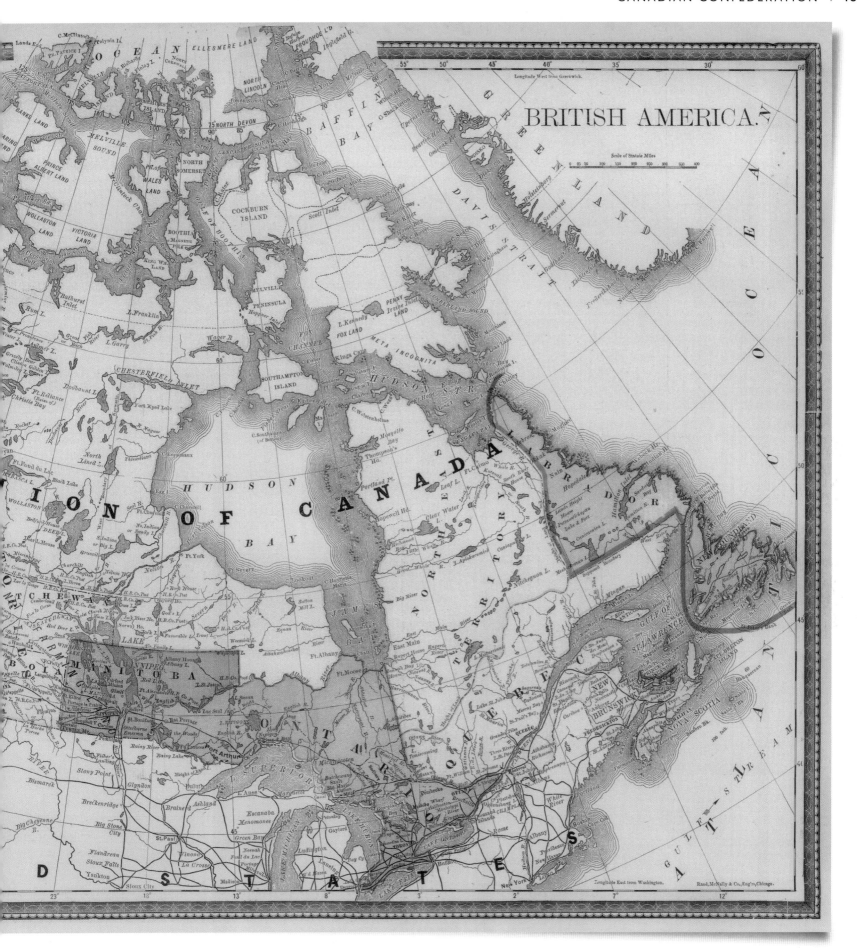

"*As to it I have no help … Whatever is good or ill in the
Constitution is mine*"

SIR JOHN A. MACDONALD, THE DOMINION'S FIRST PRIME MINISTER, 1867

CHICAGO AND THE GREAT WEST

The Chicago Portage, a six-mile stretch of marshy ground between the Great Lakes and the vast watershed of the Mississippi River, was a key geographical pivot for a continental empire. Sparsely inhabited before 1830, it soon became the fastest growing city in the US.

Chicago benefited from its position in the direct path of a stream of immigrants, arriving via the Erie Canal and a new federal road, who were heading west for the fertile prairies of Illinois, Iowa, Nebraska, and the Dakotas. Because of its proximity to a major lake, plain, and forest, Chicago could transfer timber for building prairie homesteads and towns from Michigan and Wisconsin via the new Illinois and Michigan Canal. Farmers in the West sent their wheat back to the booming city, where huge grain elevators lined the waterfronts. Twenty years later in 1840, a population of 40,000 had soared to 109,000.

Railroads soon supplanted the canal, and by the late 19th century Chicago was the nation's railroad hub, the "Gate City" to a vast hinterland from Canada to Texas. This was the "Great West" the metropolis had largely created. Millions of livestock were taken off trains at the sprawling Union Stock Yards, to be slaughtered and shipped as meat in refrigerated cars to East Coast cities. Chicago's financiers created the continent's largest futures

LOCATOR

market to guard against fluctuations in agricultural commodities. After a devastating fire in 1871, the city recovered so quickly that by 1885, it was home to the world's first skyscraper. The railroads also distributed catalogs of two Chicago-based retailers—Montgomery Ward and Sears, Roebuck—all over the country, offering consumer goods to remote locations via mail-order for the first time.

By 1893, when the city hosted the World's Columbian Exposition on its lakeshore front—a fair attended by over 27 million people—Chicago was competing with New York City as the foremost metropolis in North America.

△ **The city of Chicago, 1874**
This birds-eye view of Chicago published by New York printmakers Currier & Ives, with the Great West stretching far into the distance, depicts a city almost recovered from the 1871 fire that nearly destroyed it.

▽ **The Union Stock Yards**
Thousands of densely packed pens held tens of thousands of cattle, hogs, and sheep at the Union Stock Yards, the largest abattoir in the country.

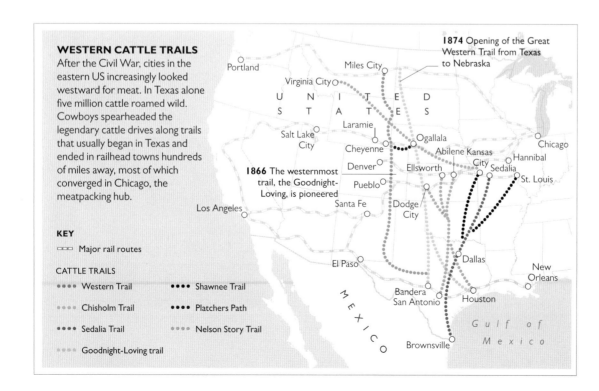

WESTERN CATTLE TRAILS
After the Civil War, cities in the eastern US increasingly looked westward for meat. In Texas alone five million cattle roamed wild. Cowboys spearheaded the legendary cattle drives along trails that usually began in Texas and ended in railhead towns hundreds of miles away, most of which converged in Chicago, the meatpacking hub.

1874 Opening of the Great Western Trail from Texas to Nebraska

1866 The westernmost trail, the Goodnight-Loving, is pioneered

Portland · Miles City · Virginia City · Salt Lake City · Laramie · Cheyenne · Ogallala · Chicago · Abilene · Kansas City · Hannibal · Denver · Ellsworth · Sedalia · St. Louis · Pueblo · Santa Fe · Dodge City · Los Angeles · El Paso · Dallas · New Orleans · Bandera · San Antonio · Houston · Brownsville

UNITED STATES · MEXICO · Gulf of Mexico

KEY

▭▭ Major rail routes

CATTLE TRAILS

•••• Western Trail   •••• Shawnee Trail

•••• Chisholm Trail   •••• Platchers Path

•••• Sedalia Trail   •••• Nelson Story Trail

•••• Goodnight-Loving trail

◁ Exposition building
The 1872 Chicago Interstate Exposition Building, with its 220,000 square feet of exhibition space, was the largest structure built in North America at the time.

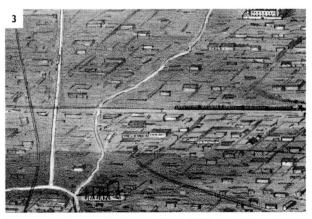

◁ Illinois and Michigan Canal
Ships thronged the South Branch of the Chicago River just downstream from its intersection with the Illinois and Michigan Canal, the first link in Chicago's transcontinental journey. Factories and railroads lined the banks.

EXPLORING ALASKA

For three decades after it purchased Alaska in 1867, the US practically ignored this distant region. According to the 1890 census, it was inhabited by 32,000 people, only 4,300 of whom were non-Indigenous. It remained a huge, underpopulated district under military rule until the discovery of gold in 1896.

"Russian America," as Alaska was referred to in the late 18th and early 19th centuries, was sold by Czar Alexander II's government to the US for $7.2 million. At the time the Russians first arrived in 1741, this region was home to tens of thousands of Indigenous peoples; major groups included the Inupiaq, Siberian and Central Yupiit, Sugpiaq, Aleut, Tlingit, Haida, Tsimshians, and Athabaskans.

The few European settlers who ventured there were whalers and hunters of fur seals and sea otters. An abundance of salmon in the waters led to canneries being set up by 1878. Starting from the late 1890s, a series of gold strikes brought thousands to the Klondike region in nearby Canada (see pp.222–223). As these prospectors began moving on to Alaska, the towns of Sitka and Skagway grew, and others, such as Circle City, Nome, Juneau, and Fairbanks sprang up. Only Anchorage was established as a railroad town.

In 1899, US financier and railroad magnate Edward Harriman undertook an expedition into Alaska. The first thorough survey of the region's geography, geology, botany, and zoology, it posited Alaska as the "Last Frontier," praised for its scenic grandeur and wealth of natural resources. Situated at the North Pacific rim, it allowed the US greater access to the Pacific world for further expansion. However, Alaska remained geographically isolated from the rest of the US, an outlier well into the 20th century.

KEY

1 The Alaskan gold rush started in 1896, with the discovery of gold along the Klondike River.

2 In 1897, Mt. Logan was considered the highest mountain in North America; Alaska's Denali had not yet been explored by Europeans.

3 The Alaskan panhandle's boundary was a subject of debate between the UK and the US, and would only be settled in 1903.

▷ **Map of the gold fields**
In J. J. Millroy's 1897 map, red dashed lines depict routes to get to the Klondike gold fields. Many prospectors traveled by sea to the US military post of St. Michael and up the Yukon River to the gold fields.

"But this [description] would require a volume, while here I have only space to add—Go to Alaska, go and see."

JOHN MUIR, "ALASKA," *THE AMERICAN GEOLOGIST*, VOLUME XI, NUMBER 5, MAY 1893

THE ALASKAN TELEGRAPH LINE

In the early 1860s, the Western Union Telegraph Company made plans to lay an overland telegraph line from the Pacific northwest across Siberia to Moscow with the aim of opening a path of communication and trade with Asia. It funded a Russian-American Telegraph Expedition, headed by US businessman Perry McDonough Collins, into the wilds of Alaska. From 1865 to 1867, members of the expedition strung cable through the vast and previously unmapped terrain of central Alaska. However, the success of an Atlantic telegraph in 1866 eventually put an end to this initiative.

Painting by John Clayton White (1835–1907) of work underway on the Alaskan telegraph line, also known as the Collins' overland telegraph line.

MILLROY'S MAP OF ALASKA AND THE KLONDYKE GOLD FIELDS.
J. J. MILLROY, MAP PUBLISHER, SALT LAKE CITY, UTAH.
COMPILED FROM GOVERNMENT AND PRIVATE SURVEYS.

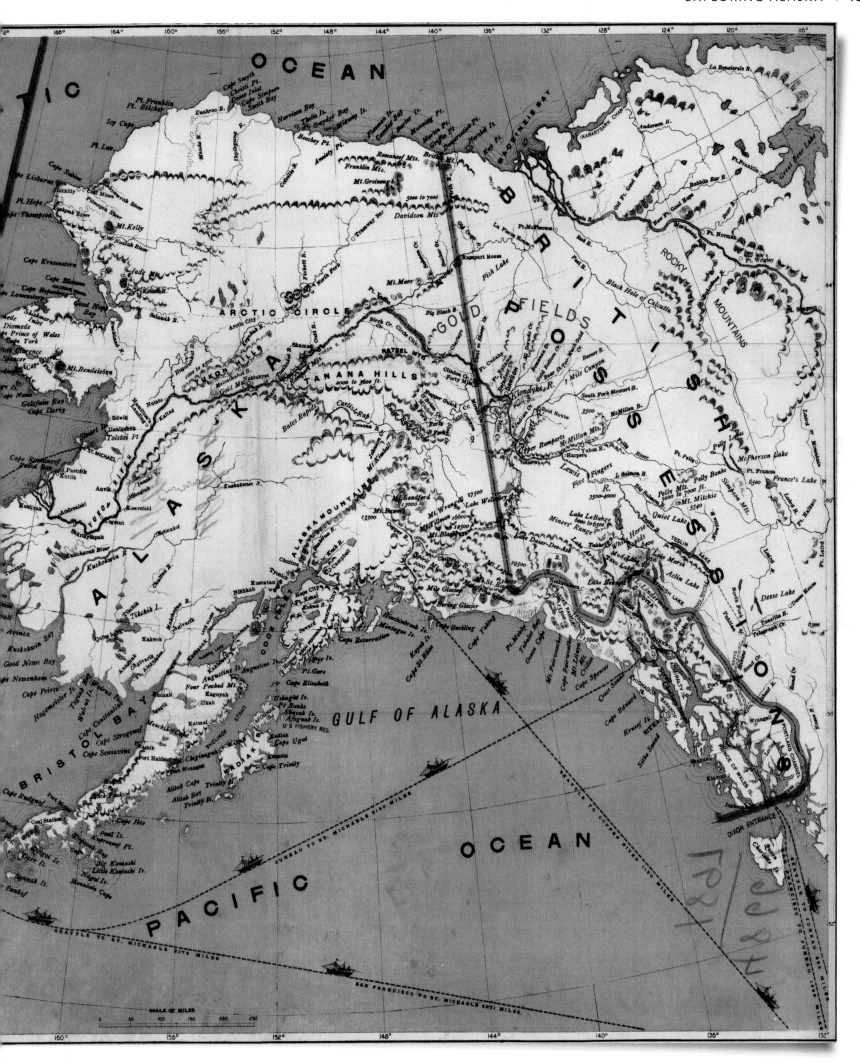

ACROSS
NORTH AMERICA

AS CITIES GREW AND TRANSPORTATION NETWORKS EXPANDED ACROSS NORTH AMERICA, THE US WAS ALSO EXTENDING ITS IMPERIAL REACH OVERSEAS. AT HOME, IMMIGRATION TO THE US GREW, WHILE INDIGENOUS PEOPLE WERE FURTHER MARGINALIZED.

SOCIETY, CITIES, AND EMPIRE

In the last decades of the 19th century, the growing transportation and communication network in the US led to the growth of its cities, powered by heavy industry and peopled by a new wave of immigrants. By 1900, the expansionist policies of the US secured it an overseas empire.

△ **Early trains**
This illustration depicts the *Jupiter* locomotive of the Central Pacific Railroad. It was one of the two locomotives present at the 1869 Golden Spike ceremony celebrating the first transcontinental railroad. By 1900, US railroad track had more than tripled, and five transcontinental railroads spanned the nation.

Despite periodic economic slumps, the North American economy grew at a rapid pace in the late 19th and early 20th centuries, with the railroads continuing to be a driving force behind this growth. In the US, the railroad network kept expanding until 1916, when it reached its peak. It moved people, freight, and livestock from farmlands to urban centers including Boston, Chicago, and New York City, among others. The locomotives of such lines as the Great Northern and Pennsylvania Railroads carried grain from the wheat belts and iron ore from the Great Lakes to the mills and steelworks in the Midwest (see pp.202–203). The railroads created a new landscape in the US, one of trestles, crossings, depots, sidings, and warehouses. The 1894 Pullman Strike (see pp.206–207), by virtually shutting down the major railroads, proved how indispensable they were to the nation. Meanwhile, local rail counterparts—electrified streetcar lines, elevated trains, and underground subway systems—enabled new mobility in increasingly populous industrial cities.

Labor strikes and immigration
By 1894, labor union strikes frequently halted industrial momentum, as organized labor rose to fight on behalf of exploited workers. Strikes impacted every major segment of industry, and corporations retaliated with lockouts, injunctions, and violence. Women, who made up nearly a fifth of the US labor force by 1900, joined men on the picket lines.

Other strikers were newcomers to the US, having just arrived with the great wave of immigration between the 1880s and 1920s (see pp.198–199). Many of these

△ **Men of steel**
In this 1909 image, Pittsburgh steelworkers pose beside a gigantic foundry ladle, used to transport and pour molten metal. The city was then the leading steel producer in the nation, with the US being the top producer in the world.

EXPLOSIVE GROWTH
Between 1880 and 1914, the US entered a new era of urban living for many of its citizens, thanks to the explosive growth of cities, industries, and immigration. Various new developments and improvements in technology and infrastructure were matched by the growth of huge corporations and trusts, which also gave rise to an organized labor movement. After defeating Spain in 1898, the US also acquired many of the former's Pacific territories.

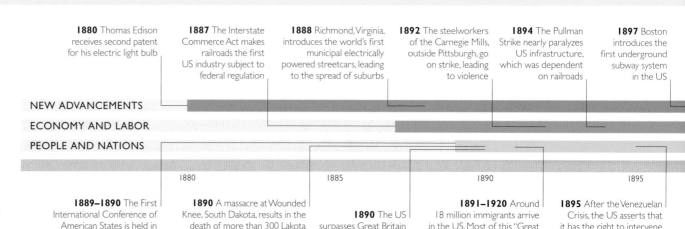

1880 Thomas Edison receives second patent for his electric light bulb

1887 The Interstate Commerce Act makes railroads the first US industry subject to federal regulation

1888 Richmond, Virginia, introduces the world's first municipal electrically powered streetcars, leading to the spread of suburbs

1892 The steelworkers of the Carnegie Mills, outside Pittsburgh, go on strike, leading to violence

1894 The Pullman Strike nearly paralyzes US infrastructure, which was dependent on railroads

1897 Boston introduces the first underground subway system in the US

NEW ADVANCEMENTS
ECONOMY AND LABOR
PEOPLE AND NATIONS

1880   1885   1890   1895

1889–1890 The First International Conference of American States is held in Washington, D.C., giving rise to the Pan-American Union

1890 A massacre at Wounded Knee, South Dakota, results in the death of more than 300 Lakota people. It is the last significant fighting in the "Indian Wars"

1890 The US surpasses Great Britain as the world's leading steel producer

1891–1920 Around 18 million immigrants arrive in the US. Most of this "Great Wave" comes from southern and eastern Europe

1895 After the Venezuelan Crisis, the US asserts that it has the right to intervene in the affairs of any Latin American nation

◁ **Women Strikers**
New York City's shirtwaist factory strike of 1909, sometimes called the "Uprising of the 20,000," was then the largest ever strike mounted by women workers in the US. The strikers were predominantly Jewish immigrants—many of them from Russia.

immigrants ended up in the tenements and sweatshops of the cities. As immigrant communities grew in New York City and beyond, so influences from a range of different countries became absorbed into cultural and intellectual life in the US.

US imperialism

Despite holding fast to the Monroe Doctrine (see pp.124–125), the US had largely refrained from military interference in the western hemisphere—except for Mexico and Cuba—until the 1880s, when it began embracing the Pan-Americanism then sweeping through Latin America. However, its version, the "Big Brother" policy, entailed intervention in the affairs of nations to its south (see pp.210–211). Across the Pacific, the US had long profited from trade with China, even keeping a naval force called the Yangtze Patrol to protect its interests in China's vast but turbulent empire. However, after the Spanish-American War of 1898 ended, most of the Spanish possessions in the Pacific, including the Philippines, came under US control. As Filipino freedom fighters resisted US occupation, the latter waged a bloody war. Back in the US, Indigenous peoples faced an "assimilation" campaign amounting to cultural extermination (see pp.208–209).

▷ **Indigenous reservation**
In this picture from 1885, white colonizers and members of the Ndé pose at a general store and post office in Ruidoso, on the Ndé Reservation in New Mexico. The reservation was established by President Ulysses S. Grant in 1873.

> "[T]he blackness below me was split by the fiery eye of a monster engine ... rattling a hundred claws of steel ..."

MARY ANTIN, *THE PROMISED LAND*, 1912

1902 Italian inventor Guglielmo Marconi transmits the first radio signal across the Atlantic from Glace Bay, Canada, to Poldhu, United Kingdom

1903 US inventors the Wright Brothers demonstrate the feasibility of "heavier-than-air" flight at Kitty Hawk, North Carolina

1909 A three-month nonviolent strike organized by the Ladies' Garment Workers' Union results in wage increases and a reduced 52-hour workweek

1911 The Standard Oil Company—a huge monopoly in the oil sector—is dissolved into 34 companies by the US Supreme Court

1915 Scottish-born US inventor Alexander Graham Bell makes the first official transcontinental telephone call from New York City to San Francisco

1900   1905   1910   1915   1920

1898 The US annexes the Republic of Hawaii, while Spain cedes the Philippines, Puerto Rico, and Guam to the US

1899–1902 The Philippine-American War leads to hundreds of thousands of Filipino civilian deaths

1902 US Steel, the nation's first billion-dollar conglomerate, is founded

1914 The Colorado National Guard, along with the Colorado Fuel and Iron Company guards, open fire on the tents of protesting miners, killing 25 people, including women and children

"Technology gives us the facilities that lessen the barriers of time and distance—the telegraph and cable, the telephone, radio, and the rest."

EMILY GREENE BALCH (1867–1961), US ECONOMIST AND SOCIOLOGIST

TRAVEL AND COMMUNICATION

Around the end of the 19th century, North America was moving into a new era of travel and information exchange, both locally and globally. Cities in particular were transformed by improved transportation networks such as streetcars and light rail lines.

By the late 19th century, an extensive network of railroads covered the US and parts of Mexico and Canada. This carried people, goods, and mail, and led to the use of standardized railroad time. Train stations provided transportation hubs in expanding cities, where commuters could take electricity-powered streetcars and local light rail lines to new suburbs. In this way "walking cities," in which people lived near where they worked and shopped, were surpassed by wider urban areas connected by local transportation systems. On an international scale, steamship lines prospered, making speedy global travel possible. Freight was also widely hauled in the US by water in this era, notably on the Mississippi and via canals.

First laid in the 1850s, undersea telegraph cables were well established by this time, providing a worldwide communications network. In the US, telephony continued expanding, and by the early 1900s, the Bell Telephone Company was wiring the Northeast and Midwest and a national network was planned.

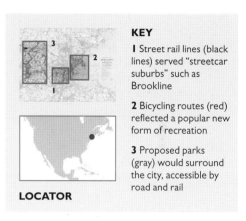

KEY

1 Street rail lines (black lines) served "streetcar suburbs" such as Brookline

2 Bicycling routes (red) reflected a popular new form of recreation

3 Proposed parks (gray) would surround the city, accessible by road and rail

LOCATOR

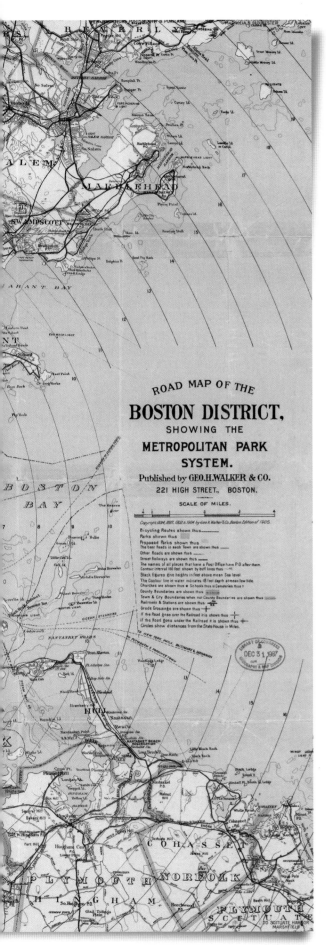

△ **The growth of Boston**
This 1905 edition of a Boston street map highlights the city's new Metropolitan Park System, an attempt to preserve green spaces in the fast-growing metropolis. The map also shows how the spread of road and rail networks made it easier for the city to expand outward into new suburbs from its original center around Boston Harbor.

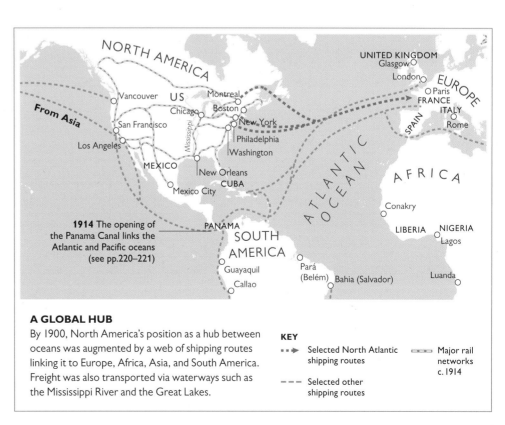

A GLOBAL HUB
By 1900, North America's position as a hub between oceans was augmented by a web of shipping routes linking it to Europe, Africa, Asia, and South America. Freight was also transported via waterways such as the Mississippi River and the Great Lakes.

KEY

‣ ‣ ▶ Selected North Atlantic shipping routes

– – – Selected other shipping routes

▭▭▭ Major rail networks c.1914

Connecting east and west
On May 10, 1869, railroad officials and employees were photographed by A. J. Russell at Promontory Summit, Utah Territory, to celebrate the completion of the first transcontinental railroad linkage. The Chinese laborers were not pictured.

BUILDING THE RAILROADS

In the early 19th century, a new form of transportation surpassed rivers, canals, turnpikes, and coastal schooners in North America. Trains were fast, could travel long distances, and were not dependent on weather.

The first steam locomotive to carry passengers debuted in England in 1825. Three years later, work started on the first US railroad, the Baltimore and Ohio. By 1870, a rail network spanned the country east of the Mississippi River and an extensive rail network was beginning to emerge in the South, built by enslaved and, after 1863, free laborers.

△ **Golden link**
A ceremonial golden spike was hammered in to join the tracks at the meeting of the Central Pacific and Union Pacific railroads. It was later replaced with an iron spike.

In 1862, Congress approved the extension of the rail network to the Pacific Coast in California. Two companies were given the job: Central Pacific Railroad and Union Pacific Railroad. After the Civil War ended in 1865 (see pp.164–165), Central Pacific extended its line east from California, crossing the Sierra Nevada mountain range. Eighty percent of its workforce comprised immigrant Chinese laborers who faced discrimination and reduced pay. Union Pacific drove west across the prairies, mostly employing Irish immigrants. The two lines met at Promontory Summit in Utah Territory.

By 1883, five railroad lines stretched from the Atlantic to the Pacific in the US, with one line in Canada by 1885. However, for the Indigenous communities displaced by the construction of the lines, it was yet another invasion and expropriation of their lands.

"… the one immediate vital need of the entire Republic, is the Pacific Railroad."

ROCKY MOUNTAIN NEWS, 1866

◁ **Changing landscape**
This 1875 wood engraving depicts railroad construction on the Great Plains. The US government granted railroad companies huge tracts of western land to facilitate the expansion of the nation's rail network. Many of these areas were Indigenous homelands rich in gold and other key minerals, which encouraged the immigration of white laborers to the region and led to the displacement of the Cheyenne peoples (among others) from their ancestral lands.

5 THE "OPEN DOOR" POLICIES 1899–1900

Manila was the gateway to China, the largest market in East Asia, which was so weakened by wars and rebellions that it was being carved into "concessions" by foreign powers. US diplomats espoused "open door" policies, opening China's trade equally to all countries, while joining their gunboats with others in shows of imperial force.

○ Chinese concessions　　⚓ US gunboats

4 CHAIN OF ISLANDS 1856–1900

Following the annexation of Hawaii, the US was able to establish sea routes to the Philippines. In the latter half of the 19th century, it gradually established a chain of Pacific islands with coaling-and-cable stations and naval bases linking the West Coast of the US to Manila via Hawaii, Midway Island, and Wake Island. The cession of Guam by Spain in 1899 was the final link.

▬ Area controlled by the US

3 THE ANNEXATION OF HAWAII 1898

While the US had been claiming Pacific islands since the mid-19th century, their acquisition of the Philippines necessitated the annexation of the Hawaiian Islands, the crossroads of the North Pacific. Some factions in the US had been calling for this for decades, but all efforts had been stalled in Congress. President William McKinley authorized the annexation in July 1898, and Honolulu became a key US base.

⚑ Annexation of Hawaii　　⚓ US naval base
▬ Area controlled by the US

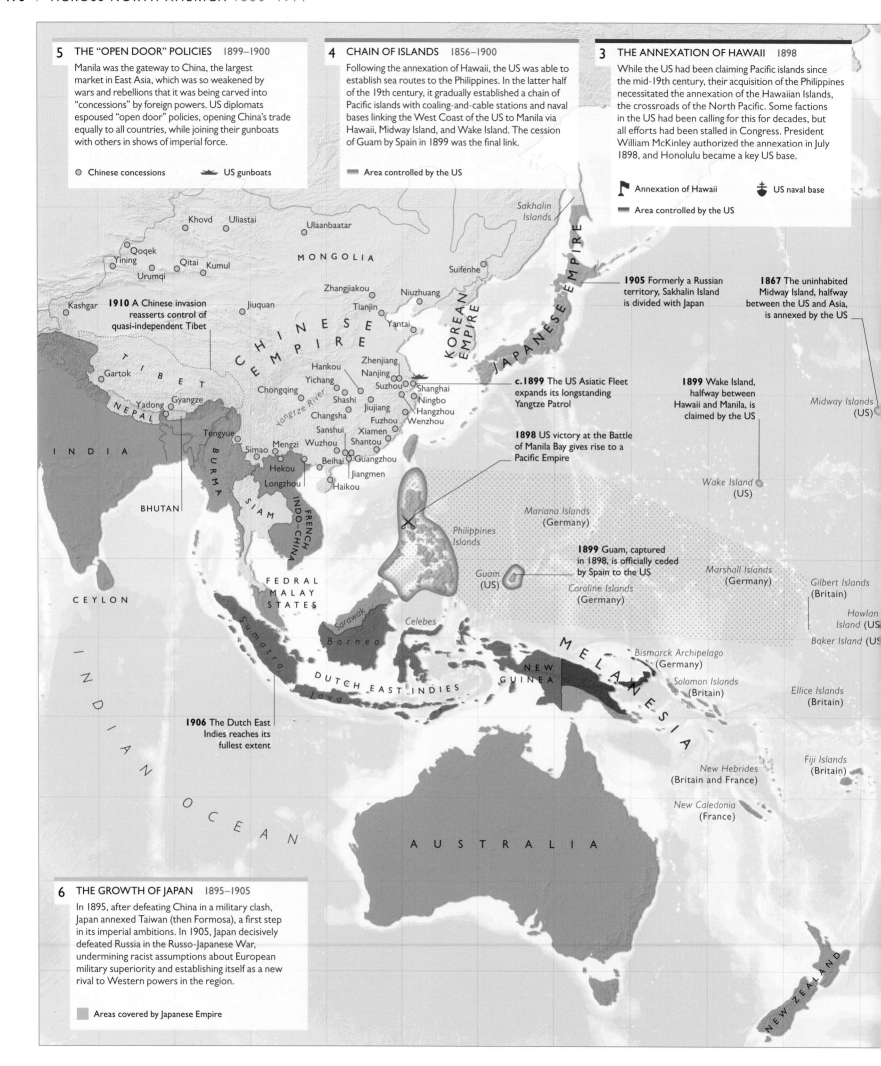

1905 Formerly a Russian territory, Sakhalin Island is divided with Japan

1867 The uninhabited Midway Island, halfway between the US and Asia, is annexed by the US

1910 A Chinese invasion reasserts control of quasi-independent Tibet

c.1899 The US Asiatic Fleet expands its longstanding Yangtze Patrol

1899 Wake Island, halfway between Hawaii and Manila, is claimed by the US

1898 US victory at the Battle of Manila Bay gives rise to a Pacific Empire

1899 Guam, captured in 1898, is officially ceded by Spain to the US

1906 The Dutch East Indies reaches its fullest extent

6 THE GROWTH OF JAPAN 1895–1905

In 1895, after defeating China in a military clash, Japan annexed Taiwan (then Formosa), a first step in its imperial ambitions. In 1905, Japan decisively defeated Russia in the Russo-Japanese War, undermining racist assumptions about European military superiority and establishing itself as a new rival to Western powers in the region.

▨ Areas covered by Japanese Empire

US IMPERIALISM IN THE PACIFIC

Having begun annexing territory in the mid-19th century, by around 1900 the US had a Pacific empire, maintained by a fleet based in Hawaii. It bordered both China and an increasingly militaristic Japan.

By the mid-19th century, sailing ships departing East Coast harbors for California or Oregon rounded Cape Horn and, due to currents and trade winds, usually called at Hawaii before reaching their final destinations in Asia. Failed attempts by the US to annex these islands lasted for decades, and it took the Spanish-American War (see pp.216–217) to persuade the US public that Hawaii was the key to the Pacific.

Hawaii became the stepping stone to a huge overseas US empire. So untested were the empire's administrators, however, that shortly after arriving in Manila in the Philippines, they stumbled into a war—the Philippine-American War of 1899–1902—which the US won after causing the deaths of around 200,000 Filipino civilians, as well as 20,000 combatants.

A weakened China was also close at hand, and the US quickly became involved in the scramble for territorial "concessions" such as Shanghai, which it defended with a fleet of naval gunboats. The US was building its principal naval base in Hawaii's Pearl Harbor, but the new empire's administrators were soon facing anti-imperialist sentiments at home, and the growing assertiveness of the nearby Japanese empire.

"From San Juan, Porto Rico, to Manila, in the Philippines, is almost halfway around the world"

DR. ISAIAH BOWMAN, *THE NEW WORLD*, 1921

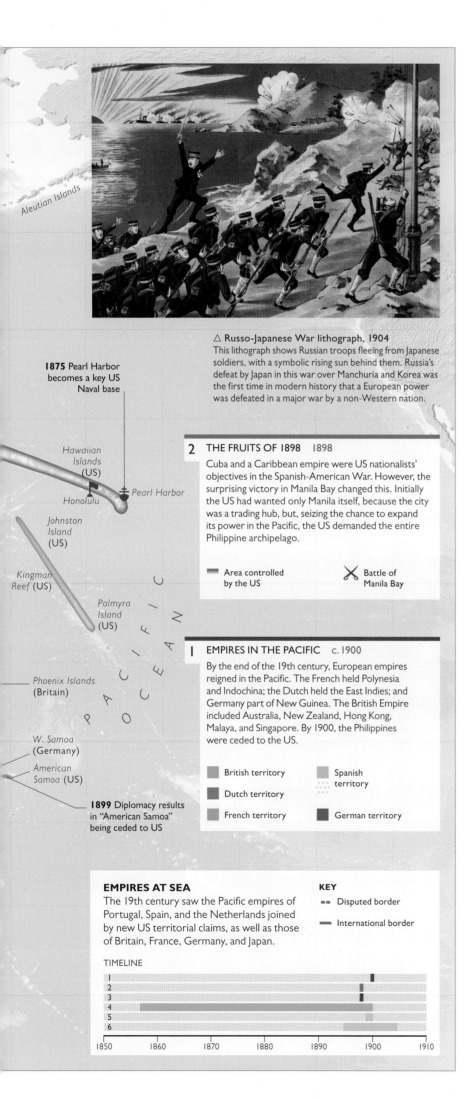

△ Russo-Japanese War lithograph, 1904
This lithograph shows Russian troops fleeing from Japanese soldiers, with a symbolic rising sun behind them. Russia's defeat by Japan in this war over Manchuria and Korea was the first time in modern history that a European power was defeated in a major war by a non-Western nation.

1875 Pearl Harbor becomes a key US Naval base

Hawaiian Islands (US)

Honolulu

Pearl Harbor

Johnston Island (US)

Kingman Reef (US)

Palmyra Island (US)

Phoenix Islands (Britain)

W. Samoa (Germany)

American Samoa (US)

1899 Diplomacy results in "American Samoa" being ceded to US

Aleutian Islands

PACIFIC OCEAN

2 THE FRUITS OF 1898 1898

Cuba and a Caribbean empire were US nationalists' objectives in the Spanish-American War. However, the surprising victory in Manila Bay changed this. Initially the US had wanted only Manila itself, because the city was a trading hub, but, seizing the chance to expand its power in the Pacific, the US demanded the entire Philippine archipelago.

Area controlled by the US

Battle of Manila Bay

1 EMPIRES IN THE PACIFIC c.1900

By the end of the 19th century, European empires reigned in the Pacific. The French held Polynesia and Indochina; the Dutch held the East Indies; and Germany part of New Guinea. The British Empire included Australia, New Zealand, Hong Kong, Malaya, and Singapore. By 1900, the Philippines were ceded to the US.

British territory
Dutch territory
French territory
Spanish territory
German territory

EMPIRES AT SEA

The 19th century saw the Pacific empires of Portugal, Spain, and the Netherlands joined by new US territorial claims, as well as those of Britain, France, Germany, and Japan.

KEY
Disputed border
International border

TIMELINE

1850 1860 1870 1880 1890 1900 1910

IMPERIALISTS AND ANTI-IMPERIALISTS IN THE US

The events of 1898 reignited a longstanding argument in the US, one that dated back to the Louisiana Purchase and Mexican Cessions. Expansionists were in favor of territorial acquisitions, and their opponents were not. The latter insisted there was no Constitutional warrant for land grabs, and that the Philippines were not essential to national security. However, the expansionists prevailed.

Puck magazine illustration, 1904

A NEW WAVE OF IMMIGRATION

The decades following the end of the US Civil War (1861–1865) and the establishment of the Confederation of Canada (1867) brought an unprecedented upsurge in immigration to North America. While many of the previous immigrants had origins in northwestern Europe, a large proportion of the 18 million people who arrived between 1891 and 1920 came from southern and eastern Europe.

By the late 19th century, railroads had reached the more isolated parts of the Austro-Hungarian, Russian, and Turkish Ottoman Empires, where overpopulation and political oppression were driving many to seek other shores. These railroads led to ports in the Black, Adriatic, and North Seas, where steamships offered inexpensive passage to a rapidly industrializing North America with seemingly abundant job opportunities.

Most numerous were the roughly four million Italians, who primarily came from southern Italy and Sicily (see pp.200–201). Another four million were Slavs from Austria-Hungary and Russia, nearly half of them Poles. Close to two million Eastern European Jews, largely from Russia but also from Austria-Hungary and Romania, left to escape persecution and pogroms. They arrived as families and settled in tightly knit communities, such as the half a million migrants who lived in an area of less than 2 square miles (5 square km) in New York City's Lower East Side.

▽ **Neighborhoods of New York**
This 1920 map of Manhattan and part of the Bronx shows the diverse ethnic populations settled in the area. These included Eastern European Jews (red), Irish (green), Chinese (yellow), and French (blue).

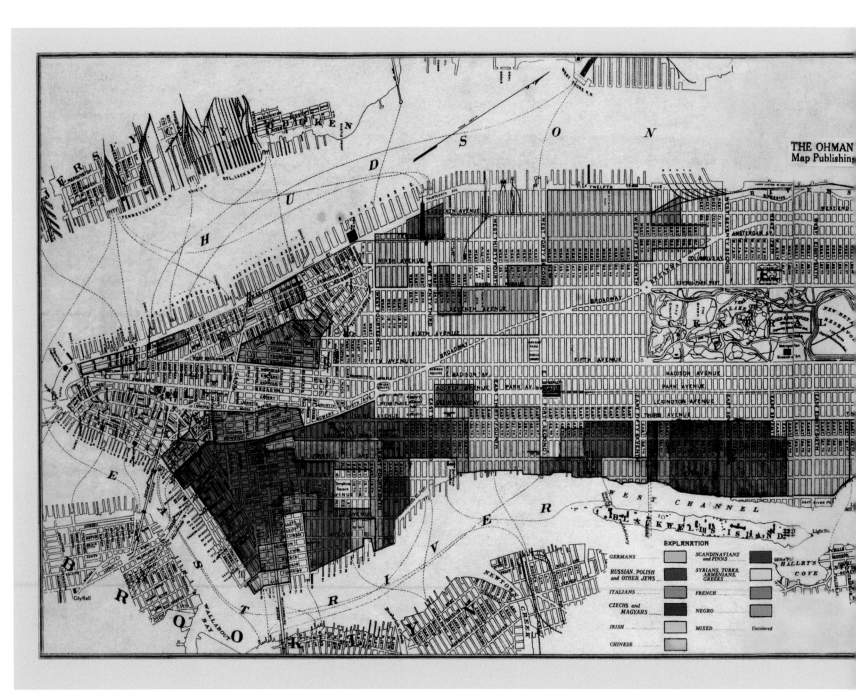

Hungarians, Lithuanians, and Romanians entered the country, as did nearly half a million Armenians and Christian Arabs from Lebanon and Syria. Almost as many Greeks followed, and around 185,000 Portuguese became commercial fishermen in New England and California. Most of these immigrants funneled through Ellis Island in New York Harbor and settled in industrial cities, such as Boston and Chicago. Many practiced "chain migration," sending for relatives and friends to join them.

FROM EAST AND WEST

Mexico and Canada also received large numbers of immigrants in this period, albeit fewer than the US. They came mainly from Europe, with a small but significant contingent from East Asia. Racial discrimination was a factor in immigration policies such as the Chinese Exclusion Act of 1882 in the US.

KEY

→ Long-distance immigration routes

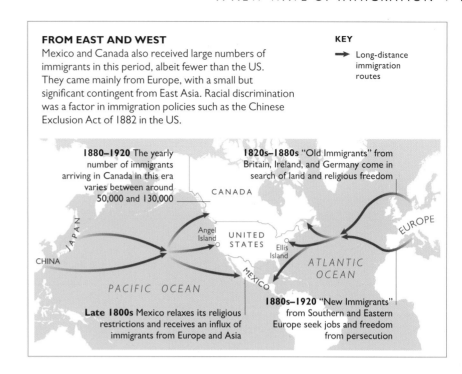

1880–1920 The yearly number of immigrants arriving in Canada in this era varies between around 50,000 and 130,000

1820s–1880s "Old Immigrants" from Britain, Ireland, and Germany come in search of land and religious freedom

Late 1800s Mexico relaxes its religious restrictions and receives an influx of immigrants from Europe and Asia

1880s–1920 "New Immigrants" from Southern and Eastern Europe seek jobs and freedom from persecution

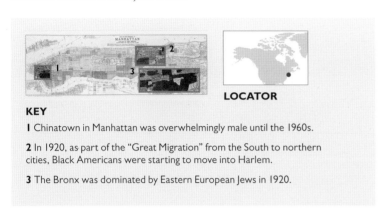

LOCATOR

KEY

1 Chinatown in Manhattan was overwhelmingly male until the 1960s.

2 In 1920, as part of the "Great Migration" from the South to northern cities, Black Americans were starting to move into Harlem.

3 The Bronx was dominated by Eastern European Jews in 1920.

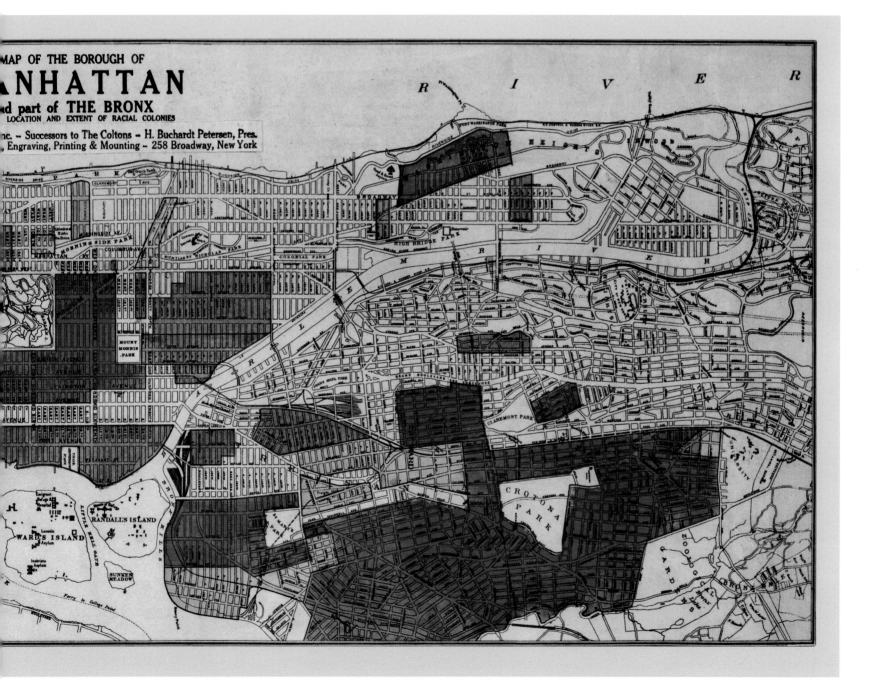

MAP OF THE BOROUGH OF **MANHATTAN** and part of **THE BRONX** LOCATION AND EXTENT OF RACIAL COLONIES

Home away from home
The bustling market on Mulberry Street in New York City, as it appeared around 1900, was the domestic, social, and commercial heart of the Lower East Side neighborhood, whose residents were mostly Italian.

ITALIAN IMMIGRANTS

Italians were the largest ethnic group out of southern Europe in the great wave of immigration between 1880 and 1920. They established settlements called "Little Italy" in cities across North America and left an indelible mark on the region's cultural landscape.

In the "push-pull" model of human migration, the factors that pushed millions of people out of southern Italy and Sicily in the late 19th and early 20th centuries included poverty, agricultural collapse, and the aftershocks of the wars for Italian unification. The "pull" for many immigrants was the economic potential of North America, especially the US, in terms of employment opportunities.

Initially, young Italian men referred to as "birds of passage" worked in the US for a few years and returned home. After 1900, families and occasionally entire villages made the move. They arrived *en masse* into the cities of Baltimore, Philadelphia, and New Orleans. A great majority of them passed through the immigrant inspection station on Ellis Island and into the environs of New York City.

△ **Blending cultures**
This 1910 advertisement is for an Italian drink, which bears the name and the emblem of the "land of liberty."

Making ends meet

More than 4 million Italians arrived in the US as part of this wave of immigration. While some eventually returned to Italy, many stayed on. In many cases illiterate and with little to no work experience, they undertook low-paid, unskilled jobs in poor working conditions. Child labor was common in farms, mines, and factories.

△ **Gateway to the New World**
Upon their arrival at Ellis Island, immigrants were subjected to medical checks, failing which they could be deported. In the 1900s, more than two million Italians passed through Ellis Island in making their way into the "land of opportunity."

US INDUSTRY AND AGRICULTURE

At the turn of the 20th century, the US Midwest and surrounding area was becoming an agricultural and industrial powerhouse. Home to some of the farming "belts," it had large milling and livestock-processing facilities, plus significant warehousing and steelwork industries.

In 1859, petroleum was discovered in Pennsylvania and within 15 years it ranked third in national exports. A network of pipelines and refineries spread from the Northeast across to the Midwest, which, fed by railroads, was becoming a vast manufacturing area. Enormous mills began mass-producing steel, and in 1890, the US surpassed Britain as the world's top steel producer. The cities of Gary, Indiana, and Cleveland, Ohio, boomed because of proximity to the Great Lakes, which were used to transport iron ore from the northern Mesabi Range to various steelworks. By 1904, Pittsburgh had 34 mills lining the city's three rivers.

In 1901, financier J. P. Morgan merged three steel companies to form the US Steel Corporation, the nation's first billion-dollar conglomerate, which eventually controlled many of the country's major producers and suppliers of steel. Deemed a monopoly alongside

John D. Rockefeller's Standard Oil, this merger forced other businesses to adopt new strategies to prevent ruinous, inflationary price battles. In 1911, the Supreme Court ruled that Standard Oil be broken up into smaller companies. However, US Steel remained intact.

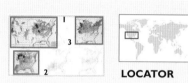

LOCATOR

KEY

1 Wheat production flourished in multiple locations due to improved varieties and mechanization.

2 Corn thrived in the eastern half of the country and supported hog farming.

3 Hay, composed primarily of grasses and clover, was a key animal fodder.

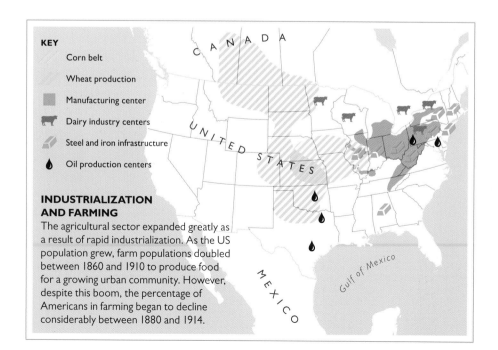

KEY

- Corn belt
- Wheat production
- Manufacturing center
- Dairy industry centers
- Steel and iron infrastructure
- Oil production centers

INDUSTRIALIZATION AND FARMING

The agricultural sector expanded greatly as a result of rapid industrialization. As the US population grew, farm populations doubled between 1860 and 1910 to produce food for a growing urban community. However, despite this boom, the percentage of Americans in farming began to decline considerably between 1880 and 1914.

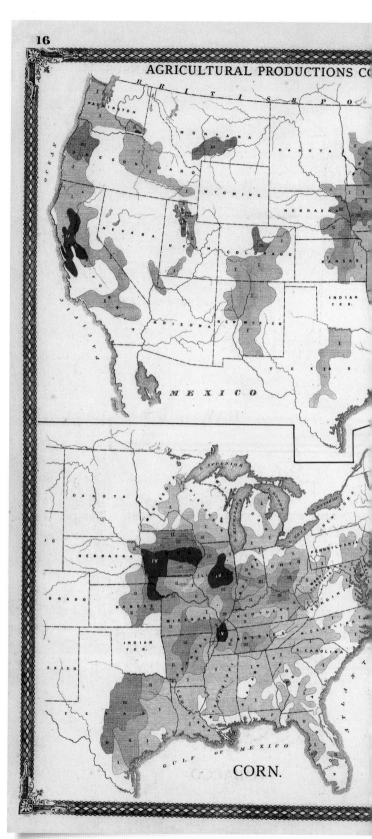

△ Agrarian spread, 1870
This 1876 map depicts the primary growing regions and quantities of five major crops: wheat, hay, corn, cotton, and tobacco. It uses data compiled from the 1870 US Census and shows the Midwest as an area of increasing agricultural development and production for three of the five crops during this period.

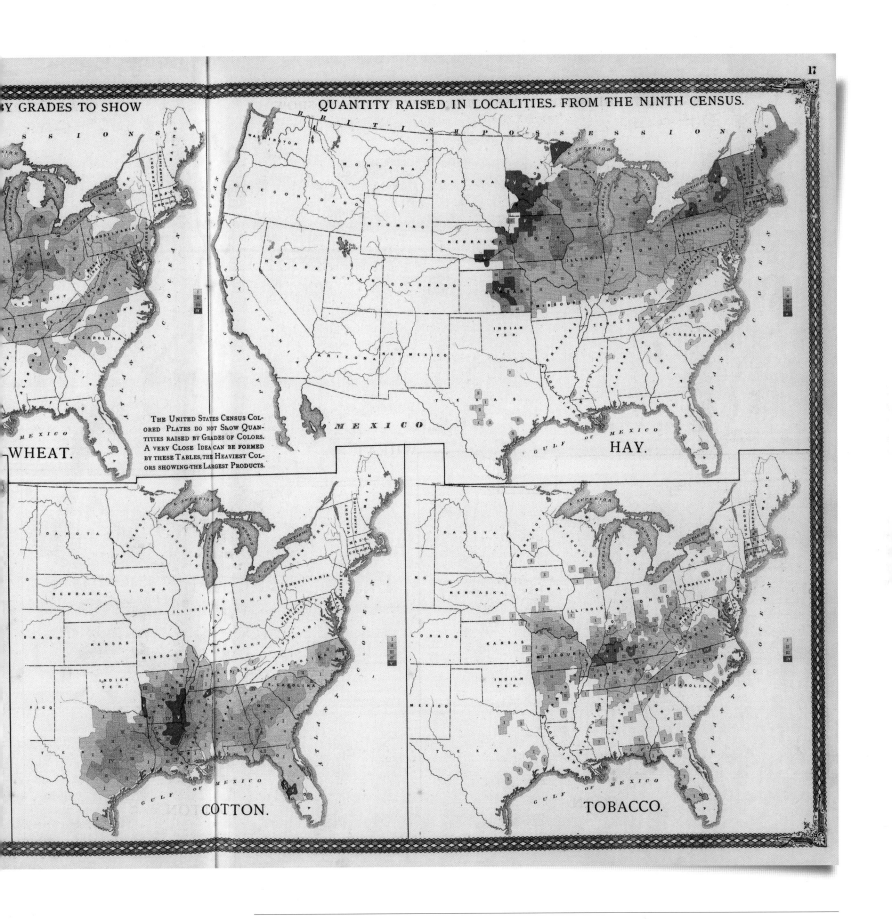

BY GRADES TO SHOW

QUANTITY RAISED IN LOCALITIES. FROM THE NINTH CENSUS.

THE UNITED STATES CENSUS COL-
ORED PLATES DO NOT SHOW QUAN-
TITIES RAISED BY GRADES OF COLORS.
A VERY CLOSE IDEA CAN BE FORMED
BY THESE TABLES, THE HEAVIEST COL-
ORS SHOWING THE LARGEST PRODUCTS.

WHEAT.

HAY.

COTTON.

TOBACCO.

"The assimilative power of … industrial forces is enormous, especially when this influence proceeds from … the American people."

URBANIZATION AND GROWING CITIES

At the birth of the US, just 10 percent of the population lived in urban areas. By 1920, that figure reached 50 percent for the first time, and continued to grow. This shift heralded a new era of growing cities.

By the early 1900s, the US was undergoing a period of prosperity, and this was reflected in growing cities that offered increasing numbers of jobs and higher wages. Many people moved to urban areas, including rural families and immigrants drawn by the prospect of jobs in the new industrial era (see pp.202–203).

The expansion of railroad networks by the end of the 19th century made travel and the movement of goods easier and more reliable (see pp.192–195). The introduction of electricity, indoor plumbing, and heating systems improved living and working conditions for many, making cities appear attractive.

By 1890, up to five million people were living in the highly urbanized Boston-to-Washington, D.C., corridor. The rapidly growing city of Chicago was close behind, followed by Buffalo, Cleveland, Cincinnati, Pittsburgh, St. Louis, Detroit, and Milwaukee in the Midwest. By 1920, these places were connected by rail, electricity cables, and telephone lines—and by roads built for the increasingly popular automobile. This, and the extension of bus and streetcar services, encouraged the development of suburban living. Los Angeles,

for example, tripled in size in 1910–1920. However, the era's prosperity and improved living standards did not include everyone. Thousands of those who moved to cities suffered poverty and lived in overcrowded and unsanitary conditions. Reform movements attempted to help those in need, but poverty, labor exploitation, and economic inequality continued to worsen.

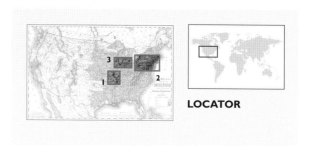

LOCATOR

▷ **Rand McNally's map of the US, 1890**
This map depicts the population density of the US in 1890. The expanding cities of the industrialized eastern regions become population hubs in this era.

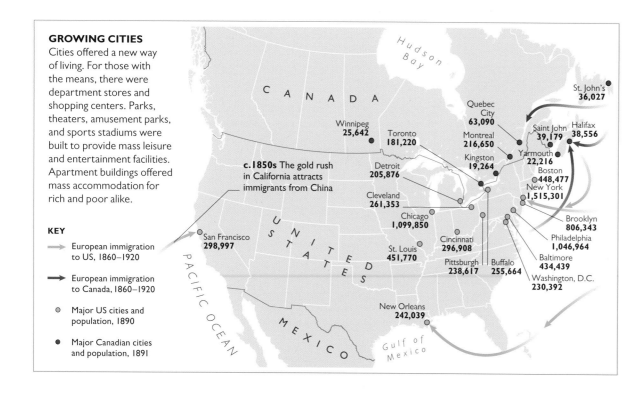

GROWING CITIES
Cities offered a new way of living. For those with the means, there were department stores and shopping centers. Parks, theaters, amusement parks, and sports stadiums were built to provide mass leisure and entertainment facilities. Apartment buildings offered mass accommodation for rich and poor alike.

KEY

→ European immigration to US, 1860–1920

➤ European immigration to Canada, 1860–1920

○ Major US cities and population, 1890

● Major Canadian cities and population, 1891

△ **Cities across the river**
Between 1870–1920, St. Louis, Missouri, was the fourth-largest city in the US. Its growth stimulated that of East St. Louis, Illinois, on the opposite side of the Mississippi River.

Rand, McNally & Co.'s
MAP OF THE
UNITED STATES
SHOWING, IN SIX DEGREES,
THE
Density of Population,
1890.
EXPLANATION:

Below 2 Inhabitants to a Square Mile
2 to 6 "
6 to 18 "
18 to 45 "
45 to 90 "
Above 90 "

Center of Population 1790 to 1890 ✦

Average Density of Population for the United States (not incl. Alaska), 1890: 20.77 inhabitants per sq. mile
Average Density of Population for the United States (not incl. Alaska), 1880: 16.58 inhabitants per sq. mile
An Increase in 10 years of 4.19 inhabitants per sq. mile

Division of Maps
Library of Congress

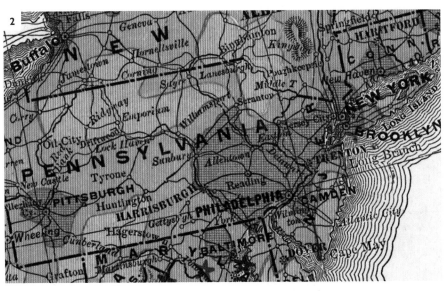

◁ East coast expansion
By 1890, the string of cities from Boston to Washington, D.C., were extending toward each other—today known as the "BosWash megalopolis."

△ Detroit and Chicago
Located at the southwestern side of the Great Lakes and northern termini of railroads, these two cities became industrial powerhouses.

LABOR UNREST

Organized labor came of age in the US from the late 19th to early 20th centuries. Between 1881–1894, there were 14,800 strikes involving four million workers. Large corporations fought back with lockouts, injunctions, and armed guards.

△ **Call to action**
This pamphlet from 1886 calls for a mass meeting at Chicago's Haymarket Square to protest against police's violent response to a workers' strike.

Rapid industrialization and immigration created problems such as low wages, long hours, and poor working conditions. As workers began to organize themselves, strikes became more frequent and were met with retaliation. In 1892, workers of the Carnegie Steel Company outside Pittsburgh protested against wage cuts. Several people were killed in the violent clash that followed. In 1914, around 20 people were massacred by the National Guard when workers at the Ludlow coal mine in Colorado went on strike for better pay and shorter hours.

In 1894, the American Railway Union protested against the Pullman Company for reducing already low wages further, bringing the railroad-dependent national infrastructure to a grinding halt. President Grover Cleveland called in the US Army to quell the strike, resulting in at least 30 people being killed and scores more wounded.

President Cleveland declared the first Monday of September as Labor Day—a holiday for workers. In 1902, President Theodore Roosevelt chose to arbitrate an end to the five-month Scranton coal mine strike in Pennsylvania rather than use force, setting a precedent for peaceful agreements. In a court case in 1905, however, the Supreme Court made it harder for governments to regulate labor, undoing laws that improved working conditions until 1937.

△ **Heavy-handed response**
Chicago policemen were called in to protect a train carrying perishable goods from a mob of rioting workers during the Pullman Strike. The strike resulted in millions of dollars being lost—for both the railroads and the striking workers.

Commotion in the city
Rioters assaulted a horse-drawn trolley car on Philadelphia's Kensington Avenue during a streetcar strike in 1910 for better wages and work hours. Violence brought the city to a standstill and sympathy strikes were staged along the East Coast.

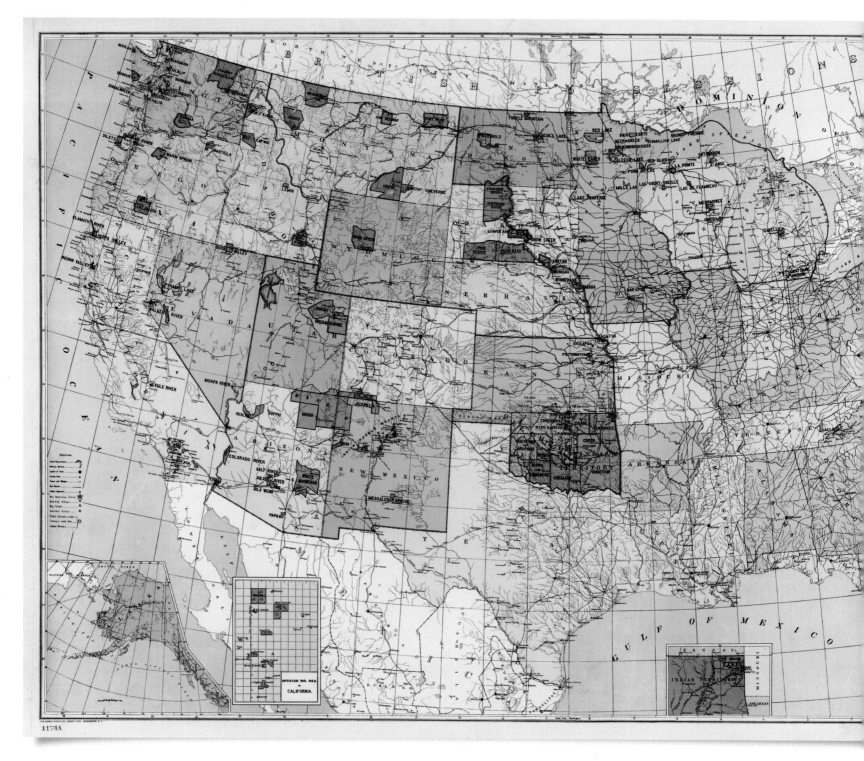

△ **Indigenous reservations**
This 1892 map displays the range of Indigenous Reservations across the US. Most were west of the Mississippi River, and almost all of them would shrink over the next half-century.

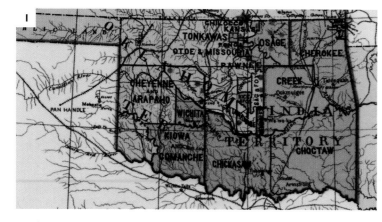

△ **The "Five Civilized Tribes"**
The so-called "Indian Territory" of the Cherokee, Choctaw, Chickasaw, Creek, and Seminole people was absorbed by the new state of Oklahoma in 1906.

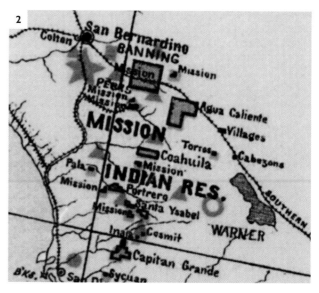

▷ **Reservations in California**
These small enclaves were created for "Mission Indians," the descendants of the peoples who worked the Franciscan missions under the Spanish Empire.

RESERVATIONS AND ASSIMILATION

As settlement spread across the country, US forces dispossessed Indigenous people of their homelands, pushing them onto what became known as reservations. The process of forced relocation and cultural indoctrination continued under successive laws and statutes until the 1930s.

Although reservations were established on lands communally owned by Indigenous populations, the 1887 General Allotment Act (or Dawes Act) further restricted them by allocating the head of each family a 160-acre (64-ha) parcel of land. Once each family had received its allotment, the remaining land was made available for anyone to buy. Within 50 years, the people living on reservations saw almost two-thirds of their reserved land sold off, mostly to white settlers.

Having been relocated onto reservations in order to separate them from the rest of the population, Indigenous people were also expected to relinquish their cultural identity in an enforced policy of assimilation. Until their role was abolished in 1908, federally-appointed "Indian Agents" administered and inspected reservations, ensuring—not always successfully—that Indigenous people replaced their customary hunting practices with European-style farming techniques, wore European clothing, learned English, and renounced their spiritual beliefs in favor of Christianity. They removed Indigenous children from their families and educated—or indoctrinated—

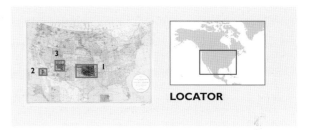

LOCATOR

them at residential schools in the US and Canada, where they were kept in unsanitary and disease-ridden conditions, and where many were subjected to physical and sexual abuse.

In 1928, the Institute for Government Research's Meriam Report declared these schools to be ineffective and revealed that most Indigenous people on reservations lived well below the poverty line and that their health care ranked among the worst in the nation. In 1934, the Dawes Act was replaced with the Indian Reorganization Act that aimed to reverse the failed policy of forced assimilation and return some lost land to Indigenous people.

△ **Navajo reservation**
Established in 1868, this territory covers parts of New Mexico, Utah, and Arizona. Due to land deals, it has grown over the years—from 3.3 million acres (1.36 million ha) to 17.5 million acres (7.1 million ha) today.

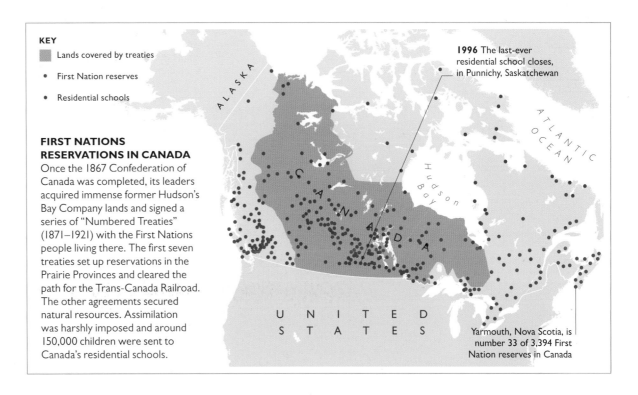

KEY
- Lands covered by treaties
- First Nation reserves
- Residential schools

FIRST NATIONS RESERVATIONS IN CANADA
Once the 1867 Confederation of Canada was completed, its leaders acquired immense former Hudson's Bay Company lands and signed a series of "Numbered Treaties" (1871–1921) with the First Nations people living there. The first seven treaties set up reservations in the Prairie Provinces and cleared the path for the Trans-Canada Railroad. The other agreements secured natural resources. Assimilation was harshly imposed and around 150,000 children were sent to Canada's residential schools.

1996 The last-ever residential school closes, in Punnichy, Saskatchewan

Yarmouth, Nova Scotia, is number 33 of 3,394 First Nation reserves in Canada

INDEPENDENT LATIN AMERICA

By the end of the 19th century, many formerly colonized nations within Latin America were independent. However, the young republics faced many challenges, both internally and from the US. The latter contributed to the economic growth of the region, but was not above using force to secure its interests there.

The 1800s were a period of profound transformation across Latin America, as colonized nations asserted their national sovereignty and new republican governments assumed power. Continual improvements in technology and infrastructure, including expanded railroad networks and ports, encouraged growing trade in commodities and manufactured goods. Social and political progression was reflected in the gradual abolition of slavery across the continent— Brazil became the last republic to outlaw slavery in 1888. However, many nations still suffered from dictatorship, civil war, and border disputes. They also had to manage their challenging relationship with the US. In 1904, President Roosevelt outlined the "Roosevelt Corollary," which built upon the existing Monroe Doctrine (see pp.124–125) by stating that the US would intervene in the affairs of Latin America if any of its interests or investments were threatened. "If a nation shows that it knows how to act with reasonable efficiency and decency in social and political matters … it need fear no interference from the United States," he promised. However, events would prove otherwise, and the US became deeply involved in Latin American affairs.

> "Once the United States is in Cuba, who will drive it out?"
>
> CUBAN INDEPENDENCE LEADER JOSÉ MARTÍ, 1895

RUBBER AND GUANO

Rubber and guano, two of the industrial world's most important commodities, were found abundantly in South America. The latex sap that was used to make rubber was discovered in a tree species native to the continent, whereas guano was the waste of seabirds and bats, and contained chemicals used in the manufacture of gunpowder and fertilizer. The mass-production and export of both items led to environmental degradation and regional conflict across South America.

A rubber plantation in Brazil

April 1914 US troops land in Veracruz during the Mexican Revolution and some 3,500 troops occupy the city for seven months

3 WAR OF THE PACIFIC   1879–1883

The Atacama desert in modern-day Chile was an area rich in valuable guano (see below left). This area saw a boundary and taxation dispute between Chile and the combined forces of Peru and Bolivia, which erupted into violent conflict in 1879. By the time the war ended in 1883, Chile had emerged the victor, with Bolivia suffering the disastrous loss of its Pacific coastline, leaving it landlocked and without a crucial port.

- Chile before 1874
- Gained from Bolivia
- Gained from Peru
- Conquered by Chile
- ✕ Battle

2 COMMODITIES BOOM   1870s–1920s

In the late 19th century, Latin America experienced a wave of expanding railroads and ports that facilitated a growing range of new exports, such as coffee from Brazil, tin from Bolivia, and beef from Argentina. However, many of the companies were foreign-owned, and local people received little of the proceeds.

- Ports
- Coffee
- Nitrates
- Rubber
- Beef
- Tin
- Bananas

1 PARAGUAYAN WAR   1864–70

One of the most significant disputes of the 19th century, this conflict pitted Paraguay against the "Triple Alliance" of Argentina, Brazil, and Uruguay. It was triggered by long-running, post-independence territorial disputes, and ended with Paraguay losing the war, its land claims, and approximately 60 percent of its population, especially young men.

- Area after war
- Lost area

A TIME OF TRANSITION

In the latter half of the 19th century, Latin America saw a boom in its exports and some prosperity, but this period was also marked by international conflict and US interference and occupation.

KEY

- Countries under European influence
- Railroad network

TIMELINE

July 3, 1898 The Battle of Santiago de Cuba is fought as part of the Spanish-American War

July 1, 1898 The Battle of San Juan Hill is fought as part of the Spanish-American War

July 25, 1898 The US invades Puerto Rico. By October it is ceded to the US after their victory in the Spanish-American War

1915–1934 US Marines occupy Haiti from 1915–1934 and the Dominican Republic from 1916–1924

1797 Britain seizes Trinidad from Spain

1815 The Dutch cede three territories that become British Guiana

1903 US supports Panama's independence with gunboats

1914 The Panama Canal opens, drastically cutting international shipping time. The "canal zone" is put under US control

1890–1920 Manaus flourishes as the center of the rubber boom in the Amazon region

1870 Control of the large Gran Chaco region remains contested after the Paraguayan War. Paraguay and Bolivia go to war over it again from 1932–1935

1914 Around 21,000 miles (34,000 km) of train track is laid in Argentina between the 1850s and 1914

1884 Work begins on enlarging the port of Buenos Aires, funded by the British Barings bank

△ **Battle of Santiago de Cuba**
This painting depicts the destruction of the Spanish fleet during the Spanish-American War. The US victory in 1898 marked the end of Spanish imperialism in the Americas.

4 US INTERVENTION 1898–1935

In the early 20th century, US troops embarked on military intervention and occupation across Latin America, such as in Cuba, Mexico, Panama, Nicaragua, Honduras, Haiti, and the Dominican Republic. The US government used justifications including debt collection and the "protection" of US interests to explain its use of armed force against these republics.

■ Countries under US influence

5 SPANISH-AMERICAN WAR 1898

Cuba had been fighting for independence from Spain since 1895. Tensions escalated in 1898 when the *USS Maine* exploded in Havana's harbor and the US army became involved (see pp.216–217). Although Spain was defeated and Cuba won its independence, the new island nation's autonomy was limited. Puerto Rico was also ceded to the US.

✕ Key battles

6 MEXICAN REVOLUTION 1910–1921

More than thirty years under the dictatorship of Porfirio Díaz had left Mexico with a more robust economy, but an increasingly widening wealth gap between rich and poor. Tensions reached breaking point during the Mexican Revolution, which began in 1910 and left the nation socially and politically transformed (see pp.238–239).

✊ Revolution

THE US WEST

The last half of the 19th century witnessed the birth of the legendary cattle drives and the closing of the frontier as large numbers of farmers, herders, and prospectors traveled west to the Great Plains and Great Basin regions. They were incentivized by the extension of railroads to these areas and federal grants of free land and housing.

After 1865, the open-range cattle herding of the antebellum South reached Texas, combining with roping and riding techniques from Mexico—and so the American cowboy was born. Huge cattle drives traveled along the northern reaches of known trails, encountering newly built railheads, and the rowdy saloon towns that surrounded them, along the way. Routes such as the Chisholm Trail to Wichita and Abilene, the Great Western to Dodge City, and the long Goodnight-Loving Trail to Cheyenne, Miles City, and Bozeman were discovered during this period. Each new trail and cattle town extended a little further west. This era also saw the continuation of the forcible displacement of Indigenous populations (see pp.176–177 and 208–209).

Silver lodes in Nevada and gold strikes in Colorado and South Dakota resulted in new boomtowns. Shepherds turned west after Congress passed the Desert Land Act extension in 1877, allotting 640 acres to settlers for a nominal fee and a promise to irrigate the land. The original Homestead Act of 1862 promised 160 acres of the public domain to be given freely to any American citizen who would reside there for five years and improve the acreage for agriculture. This was a turning point in the peopling and farming of the windy, arid Plains as colonists swarmed into the Dakotas as soon as railroads opened the region. The combination of rail transportation, mechanized agriculture, and the development of cold-tolerant cultivars of hard spring wheat extended the "Wheat Belt" of the Midwest (see pp.202–203) to the Great Plains, enabling the US to become a leading producer of the crop.

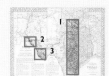

LOCATOR

KEY

1 Between 1861 and 1873, more than 1.5 million cattle were driven up the Chisholm Trail.

2 El Paso was an important railroad hub on the border with Mexico.

3 The discovery of a lode of silver created the boomtown of Shafter in Presidio County, Texas.

▷ **Westward bound**
This 1876 map by US geographer S. A. Mitchell shows cattle trail routes running through Texas and New Mexico, including the Shawnee, Chisholm, Great Western, Great Eastern, and Goodnight-Loving trails.

THE END OF THE OPEN RANGE

In 1874, the first commercially-successful barbed wire was introduced in the US by Joseph Glidden. Farmers and ranchers across the sparsely settled Plains and intermontane basins took advantage of this commodity to enclose their grazing lands and reservoirs, effectively denying rights of passage to other ranchers' herds. By the end of the 19th century, this single invention signaled the end of the open range.

An 1876 lithographic advertisement for Glidden steel barbed wire

1876
TEXAS
AND
INDIAN TERRITORY
MAP OF
SOUTHWESTERN
CATTLE TRAILS
SECOND EDITION

From the earliest days of the republic until almost the end of the 1800's, millions of cattle were driven to destinations that included the Midwestern states, New Orleans and western territories. By far the largest number were herded in a northerly direction aft Civil War to emerging railheads in Kansas and often even further north to Nebraska, Col Wyoming and Montana. These drives were the inspiration for many fictional western s including the epic Lonesome Dove novel.

The drives moved slowly to allow the cattle to fatten along the way. The routes, while ge ly following a beaten path, would vary according to the availability of forage and water

▪▪▪▪▪▪ Chisholm Trail
1867 to 1884. The Chisholm Trail was the major route out of Texas for livestock. Although there were many feeder trails in South Texas, the trunk of what cattlemen referred to as the Chisholm Trail began in San Antonio and followed the old Shawnee trial through Austin, Waco and Fort Worth. Most historians agree however that the trail established by Jesse Chisholm in 1867 began where the trail entered Indian Territory at Red River Crossing in Montague County (see map). The trail terminated at different times in different places in Kansas including Abilene, Ellsworth, Junction City, Newton, Wichita or Caldwell.

▪ ▪ ▪ Shawnee Trail
1840's to 1867. The earliest and easternmost trail used to move Texas long-horn cattle north before and just after the Civil War was the Shawnee Trail. Texas herds were taken up the Shawnee Trail as early as the 1840s and use of the route gradually increased, however by 1853 trouble had begun to plague some of the drovers as farmers tried to block their passage because the longhorns carried ticks that bore a serious disease that the farmers called Texas fever.

1874 to 1893. The the Fort Griffin Tra who herded 3,500 from South Texas Nebraska. Followin Lytle's route suppla 1879 the Western bound for northern

▪ ▪ ▪ ▪ P
1883 to 1889. One Potter-Blocker Trai crossed more barrer lar trail after 1885 range. During the la its herds to pastures to the Panhandle a north impractical af

Entered according to Act of Congress in the year 1876 by S. Augustus Mitchell in the Office of the Librarian of Congress at W

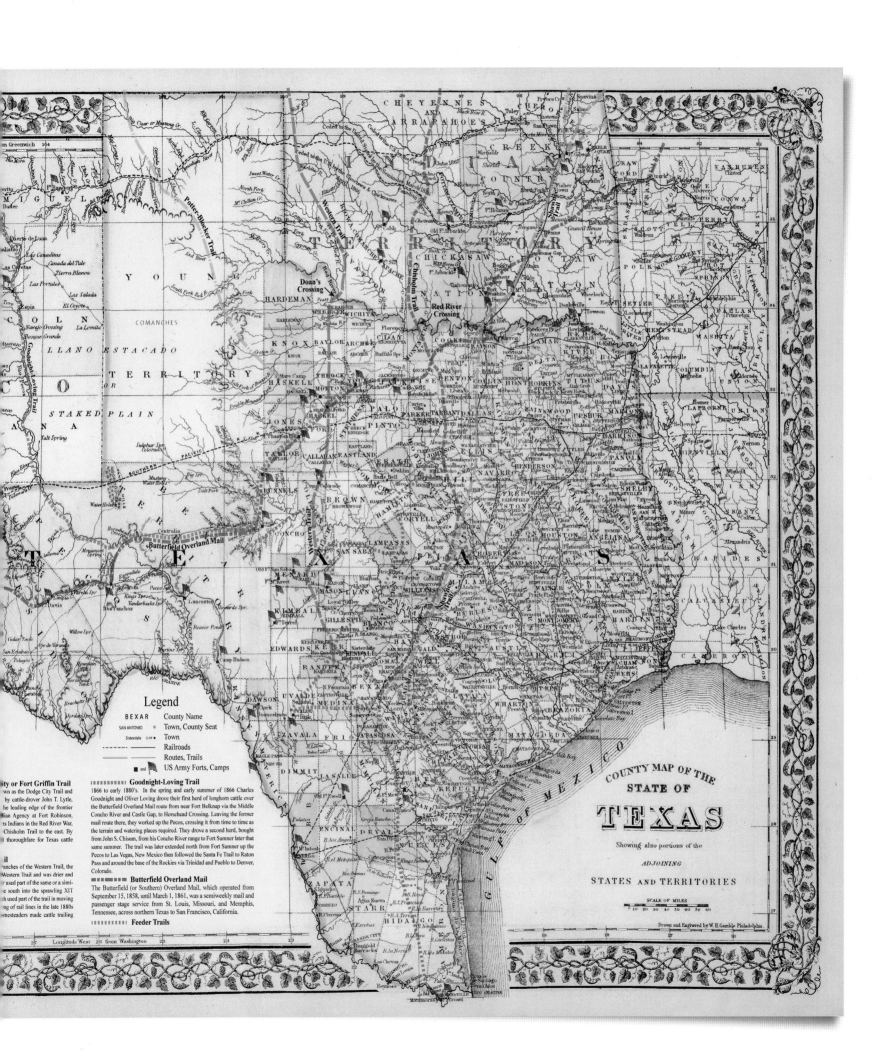

Legend

BEXAR — County Name
SAN ANTONIO ○ — Town, County Seat
Sisterdale ○ or ● — Town
━━━━━ — Railroads
┄┄┄┄┄ — Routes, Trails
▪ and ⚑ — US Army Forts, Camps

▪▪▪▪▪ ty or Fort Griffin Trail
wn as the Dodge City Trail and
by cattle-drover John T. Lytle,
he leading edge of the frontier
as Indians in the Red River War,
Chisholm Trail to the east. By
thoroughfare for Texas cattle

▪▪▪▪ il
anches of the Western Trail, the
Western Trail and was drier and
used part of the same or a simi-
south into the sprawling XIT
h used part of the trail in moving
ing of rail lines in the late 1880s
homesteaders made cattle trailing

▪▪▪▪▪▪ Goodnight-Loving Trail
1866 to early 1880's. In the spring and early summer of 1866 Charles
Goodnight and Oliver Loving drove their first herd of longhorn cattle over
the Butterfield Overland Mail route from near Fort Belknap via the Middle
Concho River and Castle Gap, to Horsehead Crossing. Leaving the former
mail route there, they worked up the Pecos, crossing it from time to time as
the terrain and watering places required. They drove a second herd, bought
from John S. Chisum, from his Concho River range to Fort Sumner later that
same summer. The trail was later extended north from Fort Sumner up the
Pecos to Las Vegas, New Mexico then followed the Santa Fe Trail to Raton
Pass and around the base of the Rockies via Trinidad and Pueblo to Denver,
Colorado.

▪▪▪▪▪▪ Butterfield Overland Mail
The Butterfield (or Southern) Overland Mail, which operated from
September 15, 1858, until March 1, 1861, was a semiweekly mail and
passenger stage service from St. Louis, Missouri, and Memphis,
Tennessee, across northern Texas to San Francisco, California.

▪▪▪▪▪▪ Feeder Trails

COUNTY MAP OF THE
STATE OF
TEXAS
Showing also portions of the
ADJOINING
STATES AND TERRITORIES

SCALE OF MILES
2 10 20 30 40 50 60 70 80

Drawn and Engraved by W.H.Gamble Philadelphia

GROWTH AND CHANGE

At the turn of the 20th century, the US made the transition from a transcontinental power to a global one. Already an economic colossus, after 1898 it became an imperial state as well. However, this era also saw continued inequality at home.

△ **The fight for Cuba**
This engraving depicts Cuban freedom fighters gathered around a command post in Santa Clara during the Cuban War of Independence (1895–1898). Their struggle against Spain escalated into the Spanish–American War.

North Americans began realizing the vast potential of their continent's northern reaches when gold was discovered in the Yukon River watershed in Alaska in 1896. Gold Rush towns like Whitehorse and Nome not only attracted hordes of prospectors but also railroads, then approaching their peak years as engines of the US economy. Railroads were also being built at a steady pace in Canada and Mexico. Telegraph poles, telephone wires, and undersea cables connected North American ports to the far ends of the globe. Soon after, the automobile and air-travel revolution changed the face of the transportation industry on the continent. With its economy growing rapidly, the US entered into its Gilded Age (see pp.218–219). However, this era was fraught with inequality.

Second-class citizens

The turn of the century was an ominous time for Black Americans. Across the South and in many other parts of the country, legally sanctioned racial segregation permeated every aspect of social life. Jim Crow laws (see pp.218–219) imposed poll taxes and literacy tests on potential Black-American voters, effectively disenfranchising most Black people. Even streetcars were strictly segregated. When an industrial boom spread textile plants across the Southern Piedmont region from southern Virginia to upland South Carolina, the mill owners hired only white employees, relegating Black people to sharecropping in the fields or processing tobacco in barns. Black people in this era were also under threat from frequent outbreaks of lynching by white supremacist terrorist groups, such as the Ku Klux Klan, which often went unpunished.

An imperial power

In 1895, the US intervened in Cuba's War of Independence against Spain, later prompting the Spanish–American War in 1898. The conflict resulted in a US victory, with the country gaining control of Guam, Puerto Rico, and the Philippines, among other territories, and emerging as a global colonial power (see pp.216–217). After its victory in the

◁ **Tlingit rattle**
Prospectors flocking to the Yukon River watershed during the Gold Rush might have bought carvings and metalwork crafted specifically for them by Indigenous Alaskans, such as this rattle made by a Tlingit artisan in the late 19th century.

A YOUNG GIANT

In the late 19th and early 20th centuries, the US became a world power, supported by a booming economy and strong military. War in Cuba and unrest throughout the Caribbean islands posed threats to US interests and resulted in increased US intervention in those regions. Domestically, the US grew more divided as racial segregation policies were legally condoned. In Canada, the economy expanded on the back of transcontinental railroads. Mexico witnessed growth, but in 1910, entered into a period of civil war.

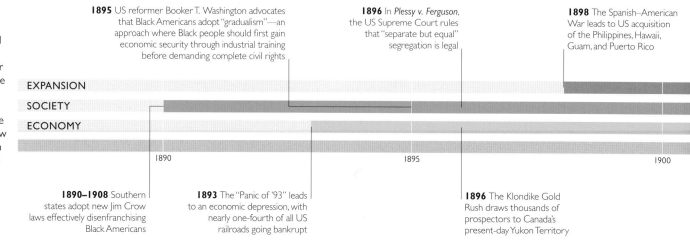

1895 US reformer Booker T. Washington advocates that Black Americans adopt "gradualism"—an approach where Black people should first gain economic security through industrial training before demanding complete civil rights

1896 In *Plessy v. Ferguson*, the US Supreme Court rules that "separate but equal" segregation is legal

1898 The Spanish–American War leads to US acquisition of the Philippines, Hawaii, Guam, and Puerto Rico

EXPANSION

SOCIETY

ECONOMY

1890

1895

1900

1890–1908 Southern states adopt new Jim Crow laws effectively disenfranchising Black Americans

1893 The "Panic of '93" leads to an economic depression, with nearly one-fourth of all US railroads going bankrupt

1896 The Klondike Gold Rush draws thousands of prospectors to Canada's present-day Yukon Territory

◁ **Porfirio Díaz**
In 1910, Porfirio Díaz secured himself a seventh term as Mexico's president by rigging the election. A year later, his 30-year dictatorship ended after an armed rebellion by revolutionary forces.

Spanish-American War, the US strove to protect its interests in the Caribbean and Latin America by using military force, guided by the principle of US hegemony in the hemisphere put forward by the Monroe Doctrine (see pp.210–211).

The US used its power to assure control over the security of the strategically vital Panama Canal Zone, wrested from Colombia in 1903 and soon the scene of one of the most complex engineering efforts the world had then seen. Four years later, when President Theodore Roosevelt dispatched the "Great White Fleet"—white for the color the 16 battleships' hulls were painted—around the world in a display of US naval might, one flotilla had to transit from the Atlantic to the Pacific via the Strait of Magellan near the tip of South America. After the completion of the Panama Canal in 1914, it was easier than ever to shuttle between oceans. The US was now an imperial power, stretching from the Philippines to Alaska and Puerto Rico.

In the early 20th century, US companies made huge profits by investing in the infrastructure and industry of Mexico, then under the rule of Porfirio Díaz. However, comparatively few of Mexico's citizens benefited from the US investment (see pp.228–229). Díaz was later overthrown.

"[T]he problem of the twentieth century is the problem of the color line—the relation of the darker to the lighter races of men …"

W. E. B. DU BOIS, *THE SOULS OF BLACK FOLK,* 1903

△ **Through the continent**
This late-19th-century engraving depicts the cutting of the Panama Canal through the continental divide at Culebra. This feat of engineering was achieved using dredges with giant buckets, rail-mounted steam shovels, rail-track shifters, cranes, and 60 million lb (27 million kg) of dynamite.

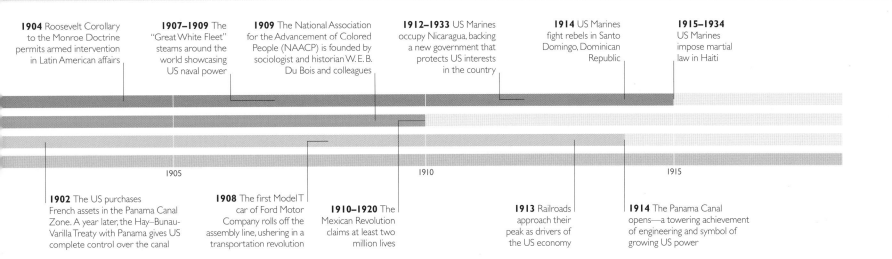

1904 Roosevelt Corollary to the Monroe Doctrine permits armed intervention in Latin American affairs

1907–1909 The "Great White Fleet" steams around the world showcasing US naval power

1909 The National Association for the Advancement of Colored People (NAACP) is founded by sociologist and historian W. E. B. Du Bois and colleagues

1912–1933 US Marines occupy Nicaragua, backing a new government that protects US interests in the country

1914 US Marines fight rebels in Santo Domingo, Dominican Republic

1915–1934 US Marines impose martial law in Haiti

1905   1910   1915

1902 The US purchases French assets in the Panama Canal Zone. A year later, the Hay–Bunau-Varilla Treaty with Panama gives US complete control over the canal

1908 The first Model T car of Ford Motor Company rolls off the assembly line, ushering in a transportation revolution

1910–1920 The Mexican Revolution claims at least two million lives

1913 Railroads approach their peak as drivers of the US economy

1914 The Panama Canal opens—a towering achievement of engineering and symbol of growing US power

THE SPANISH–AMERICAN WAR

An 1895 uprising by Cuban rebels against their Spanish colonizers sparked a US military intervention on humanitarian grounds that quickly led to the emergence of the US as a world power, with dominance in the Caribbean and a growing Pacific empire that included Hawaii and the Philippines.

Since 1895, Spain's troops had been failing to suppress a bloody insurrection in Cuba, the Spanish island on the southern doorstep of the US. Many people in the US favored military intervention in the conflict, sympathizing with the Cuban struggle for independence. The situation flared on February 15, 1898, when the US battleship *Maine*, having been dispatched to Havana Harbor to protect American interests, exploded and sank. Although the cause of the blast was unknown, by late April Spain and the US were at war.

Notable battles between US and Spanish forces took place in the Philippines' Manila Bay and in Santiago, in southeast Cuba (including the Battle of San Juan Hill, in which Teddy Roosevelt's Rough Riders advanced shoulder to shoulder with the African American 10th Cavalry). A month-long land offensive in Puerto Rico brought the conflict to an end in the US's favor, and on August 12, Spain sued for peace. After the Treaty of Paris

was ratified in 1899, Cuba became a US protectorate, Guam and Puerto Rico became US territories, and the Philippines was made a US colony. A global empire was born, with Hawaii also having been annexed in 1898. In response, Roosevelt, US president from 1901, expanded the navy and invested in the Panama Canal (see pp.220–221).

LOCATOR

KEY

1 Santiago de Cuba was the principal scene of combat, both military and naval.

2 Havana Harbor was the site of the unsolved sinking of the USS *Maine*.

3 San Juan was shelled by the US Navy during the 1898 Puerto Rican Campaign.

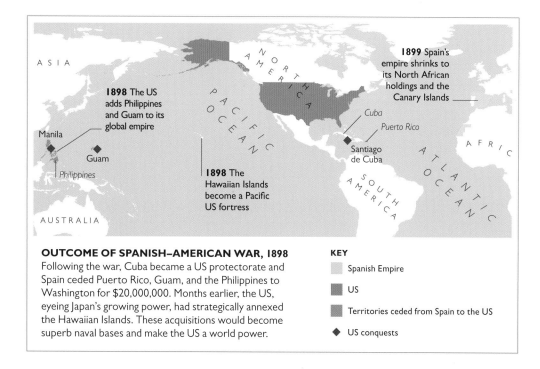

OUTCOME OF SPANISH–AMERICAN WAR, 1898
Following the war, Cuba became a US protectorate and Spain ceded Puerto Rico, Guam, and the Philippines to Washington for $20,000,000. Months earlier, the US, eyeing Japan's growing power, had strategically annexed the Hawaiian Islands. These acquisitions would become superb naval bases and make the US a world power.

1898 The US adds Philippines and Guam to its global empire

1898 The Hawaiian Islands become a Pacific US fortress

1899 Spain's empire shrinks to its North African holdings and the Canary Islands

KEY

Spanish Empire

US

Territories ceded from Spain to the US

◆ US conquests

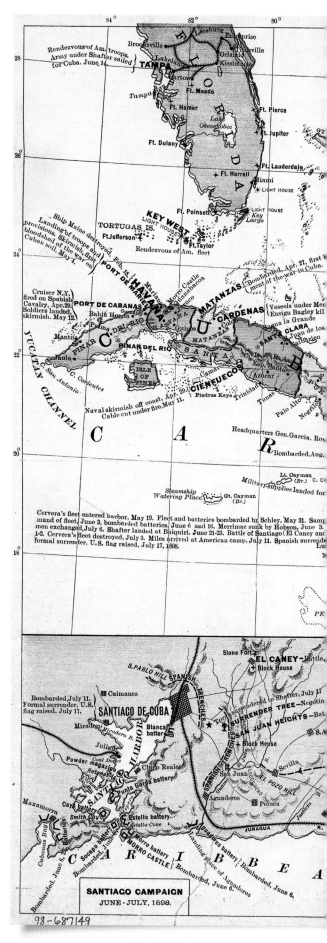

△ Caribbean battle sites
The insets on historian Eugenia Goff's 1898 "Historical Map" of the war depict all of its principal locales—Havana Harbor; the battles of El Caney and San Juan Hill; and the Puerto Rico Campaign—missing only the Battle of Manila Bay in the Philippines.

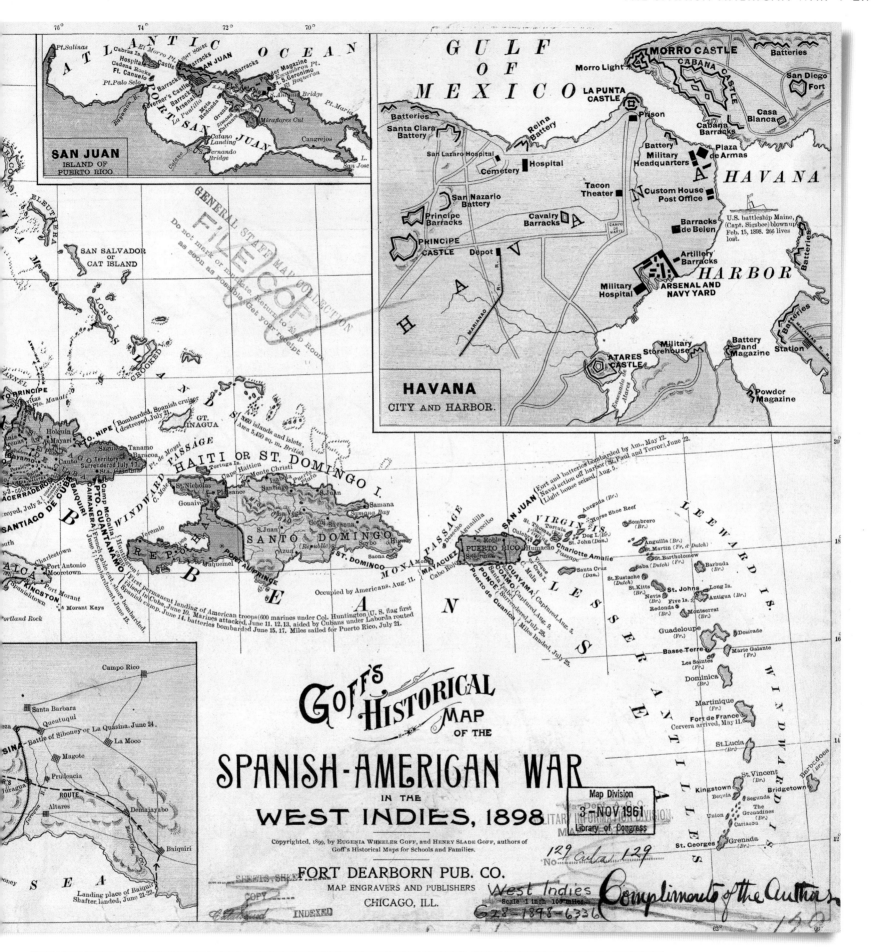

Goff's HISTORICAL MAP OF THE SPANISH-AMERICAN WAR IN THE WEST INDIES, 1898

Copyrighted, 1899, by Eugenia Wheeler Goff, and Henry Slade Goff, authors of Goff's Historical Maps for Schools and Families.

FORT DEARBORN PUB. CO.

MAP ENGRAVERS AND PUBLISHERS

CHICAGO, ILL.

"It has been a splendid little war, begun with the highest motives, carried on with magnificent intelligence and spirit, favored by that fortune that loves the brave."

JOHN HAY, US AMBASSADOR TO THE UK, TO THEODORE ROOSEVELT, 1898

INDUSTRY AND SEGREGATION

Rapid industrialization in the wake of the Civil War led to unprecedented growth in the US economy. At the same time, Black Americans in the South saw their fortunes decline as a system of segregation took hold, causing millions to leave for northern states.

Although the Civil War (see pp.164–165) disrupted its economy, by the beginning of the 20th century the US was rapidly becoming the wealthiest nation in North America and the world. The railroad, oil, and manufacturing sectors all played a critical role in boosting the economy. Agriculture was also vital to the country, with widely grown crops such as cotton and tobacco becoming valuable commodities. This era of rapid industrialization and economic growth came to be known as the Gilded Age. While it created many millionaires, it also widened the gulf between the rich and the poor.

For Black Americans in the Deep South, this was a time of great fear and uncertainty. The failure of postwar reconstruction initiatives (see pp.168–169) meant there was little to no federal protection of their hard-earned rights. Southern states began to institute legally mandated segregationist policies, demarcating separate facilities for the Black population—from schools and parks to public phone booths and water fountains. Millions of Black people left for the northern states in a relocation known as the Great Migration. In addition to looking for better job opportunities away from the low wages of domestic work and sharecropping, they sought to escape the racial violence endemic to the South.

> "I always tried to turn every disaster into an opportunity."
>
> JOHN D. ROCKEFELLER, FOUNDER OF STANDARD OIL

JIM CROW SOUTH

Laws enforcing racial segregation and disenfranchisement in the US South were known as Jim Crow laws, after a derogatory term for Black people. Marking the end of the Reconstruction period, such laws were upheld by a Supreme Court ruling in the case of *Plessy v Ferguson* (1896) that cited "separate but equal" treatment as being constitutional.

A segregated water fountain in Oklahoma, 1939

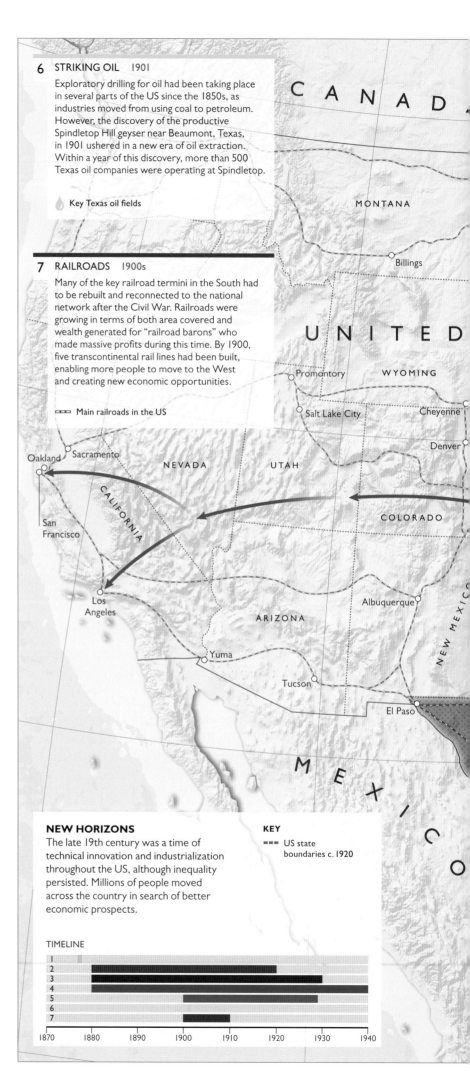

6 STRIKING OIL 1901

Exploratory drilling for oil had been taking place in several parts of the US since the 1850s, as industries moved from using coal to petroleum. However, the discovery of the productive Spindletop Hill geyser near Beaumont, Texas, in 1901 ushered in a new era of oil extraction. Within a year of this discovery, more than 500 Texas oil companies were operating at Spindletop.

⬥ Key Texas oil fields

7 RAILROADS 1900s

Many of the key railroad termini in the South had to be rebuilt and reconnected to the national network after the Civil War. Railroads were growing in terms of both area covered and wealth generated for "railroad barons" who made massive profits during this time. By 1900, five transcontinental rail lines had been built, enabling more people to move to the West and creating new economic opportunities.

▭▭▭ Main railroads in the US

NEW HORIZONS

The late 19th century was a time of technical innovation and industrialization throughout the US, although inequality persisted. Millions of people moved across the country in search of better economic prospects.

KEY

▬▬▬ US state boundaries c. 1920

TIMELINE

	1870	1880	1890	1900	1910	1920	1930	1940
1								
2								
3								
4								
5								
6								
7								

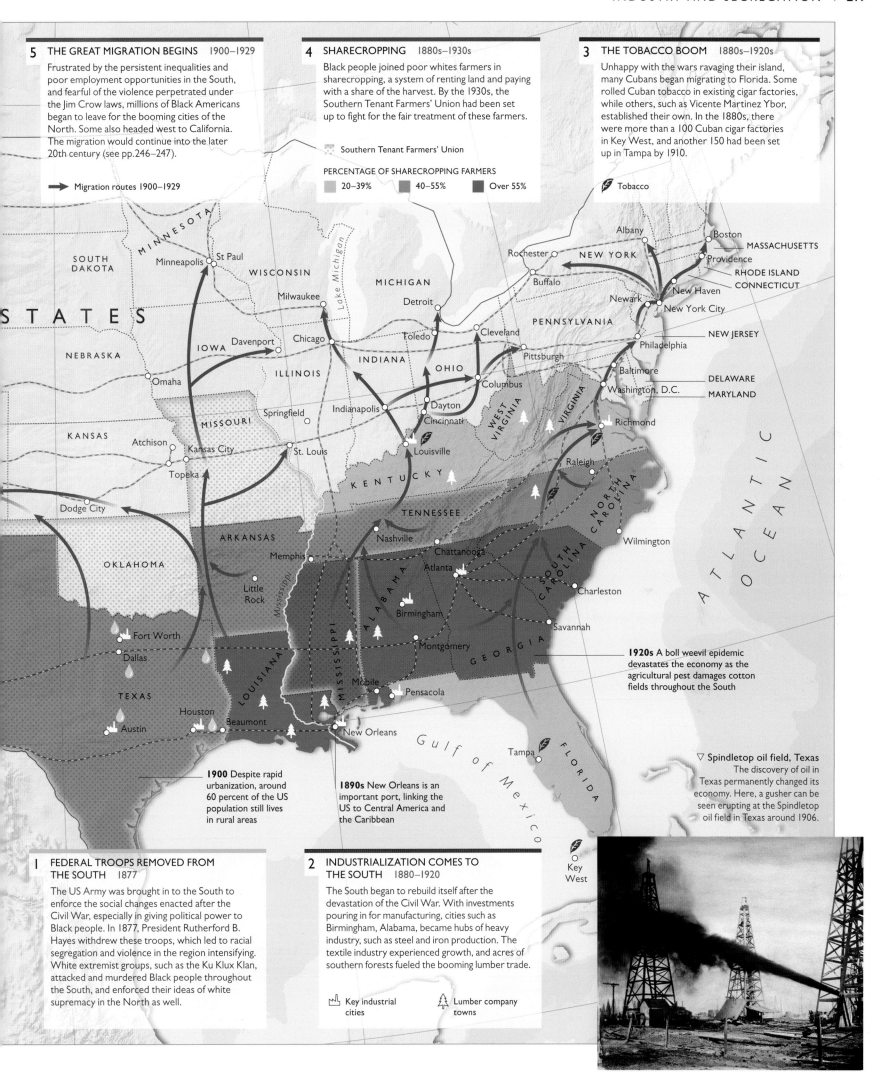

5 THE GREAT MIGRATION BEGINS 1900–1929

Frustrated by the persistent inequalities and poor employment opportunities in the South, and fearful of the violence perpetrated under the Jim Crow laws, millions of Black Americans began to leave for the booming cities of the North. Some also headed west to California. The migration would continue into the later 20th century (see pp.246–247).

➜ Migration routes 1900–1929

4 SHARECROPPING 1880s–1930s

Black people joined poor whites farmers in sharecropping, a system of renting land and paying with a share of the harvest. By the 1930s, the Southern Tenant Farmers' Union had been set up to fight for the fair treatment of these farmers.

▦ Southern Tenant Farmers' Union

PERCENTAGE OF SHARECROPPING FARMERS

◻ 20–39%   ◼ 40–55%   ◼ Over 55%

3 THE TOBACCO BOOM 1880s–1920s

Unhappy with the wars ravaging their island, many Cubans began migrating to Florida. Some rolled Cuban tobacco in existing cigar factories, while others, such as Vicente Martinez Ybor, established their own. In the 1880s, there were more than a 100 Cuban cigar factories in Key West, and another 150 had been set up in Tampa by 1910.

🌿 Tobacco

1920s A boll weevil epidemic devastates the economy as the agricultural pest damages cotton fields throughout the South

▽ **Spindletop oil field, Texas**
The discovery of oil in Texas permanently changed its economy. Here, a gusher can be seen erupting at the Spindletop oil field in Texas around 1906.

1900 Despite rapid urbanization, around 60 percent of the US population still lives in rural areas

1890s New Orleans is an important port, linking the US to Central America and the Caribbean

1 FEDERAL TROOPS REMOVED FROM THE SOUTH 1877

The US Army was brought in to the South to enforce the social changes enacted after the Civil War, especially in giving political power to Black people. In 1877, President Rutherford B. Hayes withdrew these troops, which led to racial segregation and violence in the region intensifying. White extremist groups, such as the Ku Klux Klan, attacked and murdered Black people throughout the South, and enforced their ideas of white supremacy in the North as well.

2 INDUSTRIALIZATION COMES TO THE SOUTH 1880–1920

The South began to rebuild itself after the devastation of the Civil War. With investments pouring in for manufacturing, cities such as Birmingham, Alabama, became hubs of heavy industry, such as steel and iron production. The textile industry experienced growth, and acres of southern forests fueled the booming lumber trade.

🏭 Key industrial cities   🌲 Lumber company towns

THE PANAMA CANAL

In 1914, the dream of carving a channel between the Atlantic and Pacific oceans came true—but its construction was a struggle that took more than three decades and cost millions of dollars.

In 1855, the Panama Canal Railway Company opened a railroad to transport passengers and freight from coast to coast. This engineering feat revived the old idea of cutting a passage through the narrow Isthmus of Panama for ships to make the same journey.

French diplomat Ferdinand de Lesseps, the man behind the building of the Suez Canal, began the first attempt in 1880, but impenetrable jungle and tropical diseases that killed thousands of his workers forced him to abandon the project in 1889.

In 1902, the US decided to restart work on the canal. The Spanish-American War of 1898 had seen a victorious US take over former Spanish territories in both the Caribbean and the Philippines—the control of which would be made much easier if US Navy ships could reach them by sailing through the Americas rather than around them. However, the land the US wanted to cut through lay in Colombia,

whose senate refused to lease it to the US. In response, the US aided independence fighters who, in 1903, seceded from Colombia and set up the Republic of Panama—whose new rulers gave the US the land it needed.

The 50-mile (80-km) canal opened in 1914, reducing the sea journey from ocean to ocean by around 9,200 miles (14,800 km). The canal zone remained under US control until 1999.

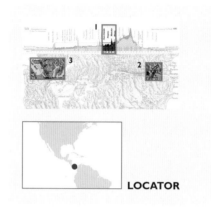

LOCATOR

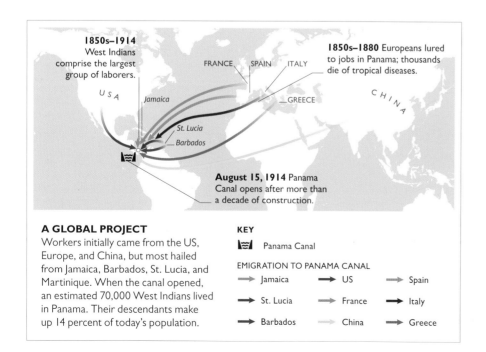

1850s–1914 West Indians comprise the largest group of laborers.

1850s–1880 Europeans lured to jobs in Panama; thousands die of tropical diseases.

August 15, 1914 Panama Canal opens after more than a decade of construction.

A GLOBAL PROJECT

Workers initially came from the US, Europe, and China, but most hailed from Jamaica, Barbados, St. Lucia, and Martinique. When the canal opened, an estimated 70,000 West Indians lived in Panama. Their descendants make up 14 percent of today's population.

KEY

🛶 Panama Canal

EMIGRATION TO PANAMA CANAL

→ Jamaica   → US   → Spain
→ St. Lucia   → France   → Italy
→ Barbados   → China   → Greece

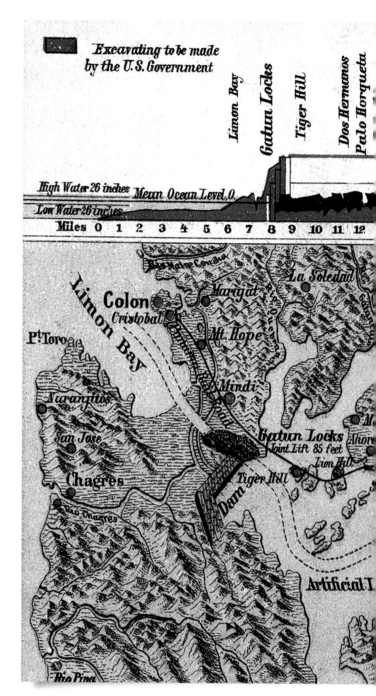

△ **Canal construction**
This 1914 postcard marks the opening of the canal, with a graphic representation of the excavations made by the French- and US-run stages of the project (top). The canal's cost on completion was an estimated $700 million; at least 25,000 people lost their lives helping to build it.

▷ **French excavations**
When France abandoned its attempt to build a canal through the Isthmus of Panama, it sold its construction rights and equipment to the US for $40 million. The canal's new builders also took over many of the dig sites the French had initiated.

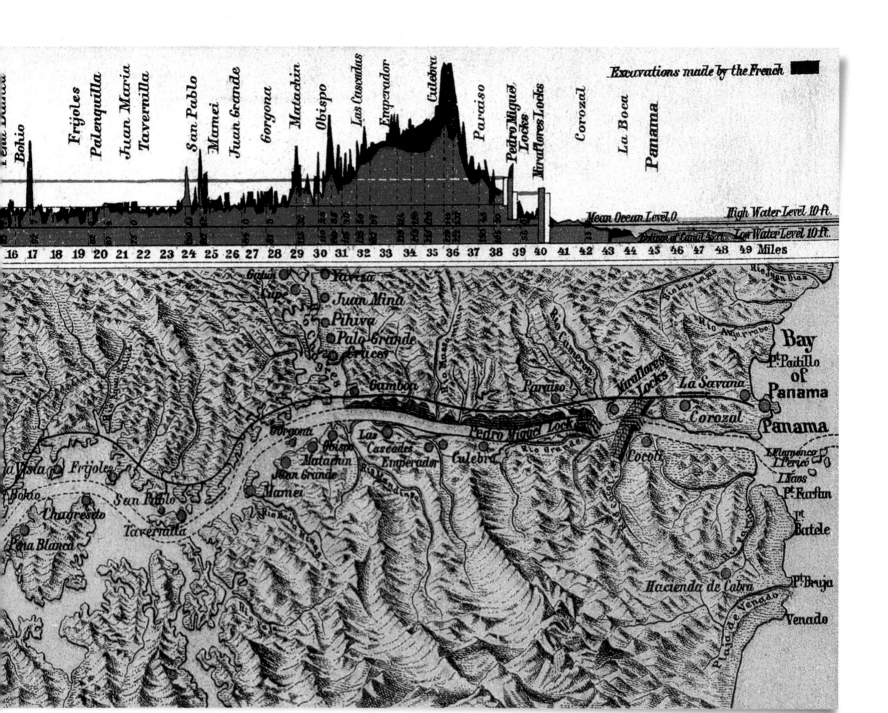

Excavations made by the French

Bohío Frijoles Palenquilla Juan Maria Tavernilla San Pablo Mamei Juan Grande Gorgona Matachin Obispo Las Cascadas Emperador Culebra Paraiso Pedro Miguel Locks Miraflores Locks Corozal La Boca Panama

Mean Ocean Level, 0.   High Water Level 10 ft.

Bottom of Canal 35 ft.   Low Water Level 10 ft.

16 17 18 19 20 21 22 23 24 25 26 27 28 29 30 31 32 33 34 35 36 37 38 39 40 41 42 43 44 45 46 47 48 49 Miles

2

3

◁ Indigenous displacement
Several thousand Indigenous people living along the route of the railroad and canal path were displaced by the construction, notably around Colón and Gatun. At least 21 small towns and settlements were submerged by the new waterway.

◁ Eastern lock
The US chose the site for the Miraflores locks in part because it was far enough inland to avoid naval attacks. The locks rise and fall 54 ft (16.5 m).

THE EXPANSION OF CANADA

The construction of the continent-spanning Canadian Pacific Railway unified the country for the first time and fostered the expansion of commerce, industry, and international trade. However, a divide remained between Canada's large Francophone minority and their English-speaking compatriots.

The transcontinental railroad opened up the nation's prairies for colonization and farming, which was aided by the development of cold-resistant wheat varieties. Indigenous groups such as the Cree and Kanienkehaka (Mohawk) had their ancestral lands taken from them, and resistance was suppressed. Eastern European immigrants, attracted by work on cattle ranches and wheat farms, joined other hopefuls heading west, helping the population of the prairies swell to more than one million and encouraging the growth of Saskatchewan and Alberta, which would formally become Canadian provinces in 1905.

Meanwhile, the country's northern expansion took in Hudson's Bay and the Klondike, the latter leading to a border dispute with Alaska between 1896 and 1903. In the east, industry spread along the St. Lawrence River, thanks to rail-shipped coal and a number of hydroelectric plants opened at Niagara Falls in the early 1900s.

LOCATOR

By 1911, Canada was home to 7.2 million people. A third of these were French speakers, mainly in Quebec, a province whose identity even today is quite distinct from the rest of Canada. Its cultural differences aside, by the end of the decade the unified nation boasted three transcontinental railroads, extending into the US and linking Canada's international ports, indicating the country's new-found global reach.

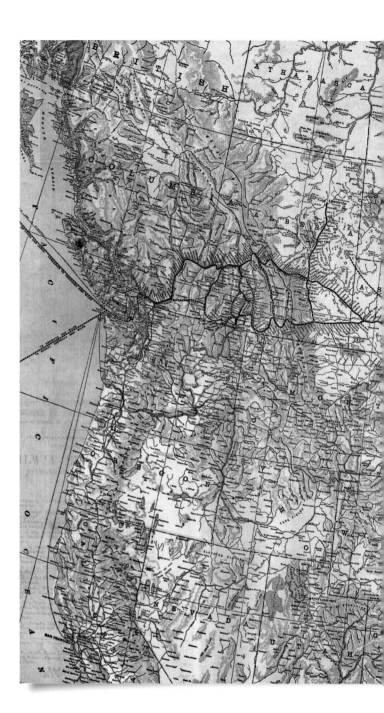

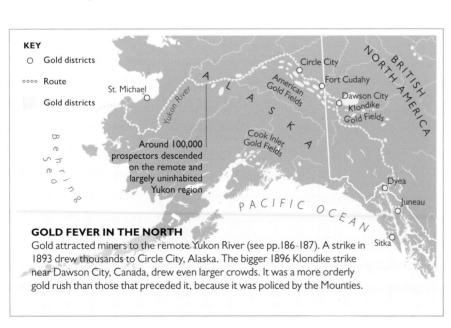

KEY

- ○ Gold districts
- ∘∘∘∘ Route
- Gold districts

Around 100,000 prospectors descended on the remote and largely uninhabited Yukon region

GOLD FEVER IN THE NORTH
Gold attracted miners to the remote Yukon River (see pp.186-187). A strike in 1893 drew thousands to Circle City, Alaska. The bigger 1896 Klondike strike near Dawson City, Canada, drew even larger crowds. It was a more orderly gold rush than those that preceded it, because it was policed by the Mounties.

△ **Last spike at Craigellachie**
An engineering marvel, the Canadian Pacific Railway was built in just four years, and its construction involved blasting through the soaring Rocky Mountains and erecting bridges across steep-sided valleys and passes. The last spike was driven at Craigellachie, British Columbia, on November 7, 1885—six years ahead of the scheduled completion date.

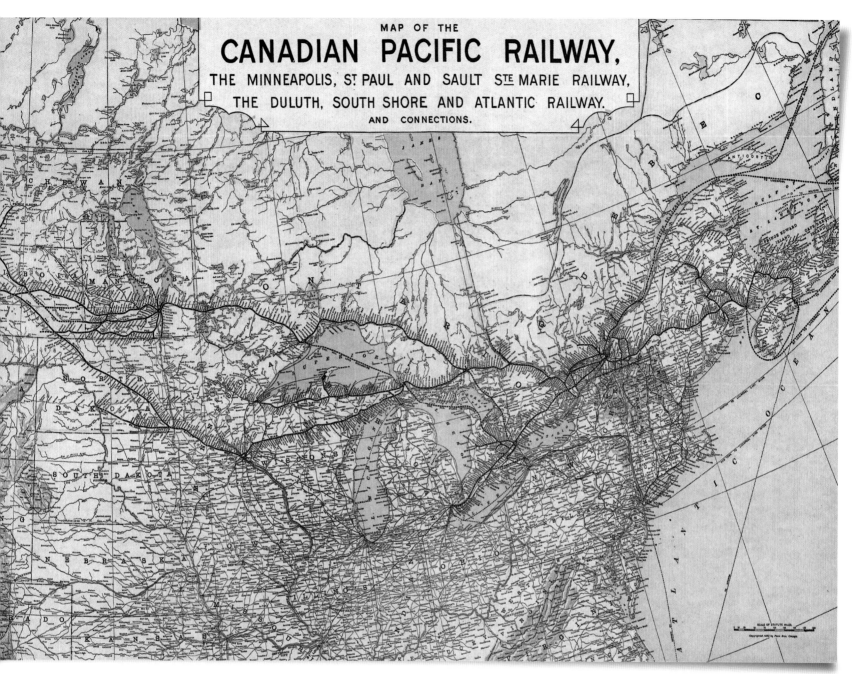

MAP OF THE
CANADIAN PACIFIC RAILWAY,
THE MINNEAPOLIS, ST. PAUL AND SAULT STE. MARIE RAILWAY,
THE DULUTH, SOUTH SHORE AND ATLANTIC RAILWAY.
AND CONNECTIONS.

2

◁ North-West Rebellion 1885
In Rupert's Land, comprising most of modern Saskatchewan and Manitoba, descendants of Indigenous peoples and French Canadians known as the Métis resisted assimilation. Almost 100 of them died during their struggle.

▷ Farms and townships
From 1871, the prairies were surveyed and divided into townships, with farmland offered free to settlers. In 1873, the famed North-West Mounted Police— the Mounties—was formed in order to keep the peace in the remote region.

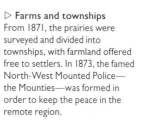

3

△ Canadian Pacific Railway
The symbolic joining of the port of Halifax on the Atlantic with that of Vancouver on the Pacific is commemorated on this 1893 map, published by the Poole Brothers of Chicago.

EXPANDING HORIZONS

By the early 20th century, at the beginning of "The American Century," North America was undergoing a period of rapid technological change that revolutionized transportation, communication, standards of living, and the global balance of power.

When Grand Central Station in New York City was completed in 1913, its architectural grandeur testified to the importance of railroads in uniting the US and Canada. Trains had enabled travel across vast distances and made cities out of inland settlements. They peaked in 1916, the same year US industrialist Henry Ford's Michigan assembly lines crossed the half-million mark for the production of Model T automobiles. By this time, the transcontinental Lincoln Highway had been constructed, the first transcontinental telephone call had been made, and the Panama Canal had officially opened (see pp.220–221).

Cities were increasingly being powered by electricity and illuminated by US inventor Thomas Edison's new electric light bulbs. Phonographs and motion pictures made in the US were also growing in popularity. Wireless communication technology, pioneered by Italian inventor Guglielmo Marconi, was in use across the US by the early 20th century, with the US subsidiary of the Marconi Company dominating the market. At the same time, this era of technological advances also saw the US strengthening its power on the world stage by growing its naval fleet to rival that of Britain.

WRIGHT BROTHERS

Brothers Orville (left) and Wilbur Wright owned a bicycle shop in Dayton, Ohio, when on December 17, 1903, they became the first people to fly heavier-than-air machines. They made four powered and sustained flights on their first day, aboard the *Wright Flyer*. Orville's famous first flight lasted 12 seconds and covered 120 ft (36 m), while Wilbur, on the final attempt, covered 852 ft (259 m) in 59 seconds. In 1909, the *Wright Military Flyer* became the world's first military aircraft.

2 THE GOLDEN AGE OF RAILROADS
1875–1930

The end of the 19th century marked the start of the golden age of railroads in North America, moving people, freight, and livestock quickly and efficiently across the continent. The network grew from 35,000 miles (56,327 km) of tracks to more than a quarter of a million miles (402,300 km) in 1916, before beginning a decline due to the growth of other modes of transportation.

▭▭▭ Main railroads

▬▬▬ Travel time from New York by railroad, 1930

1915 The Lincoln Highway from Manhattan's Times Square to San Francisco's Lincoln Park is the continent's first paved transcontinental automobile road

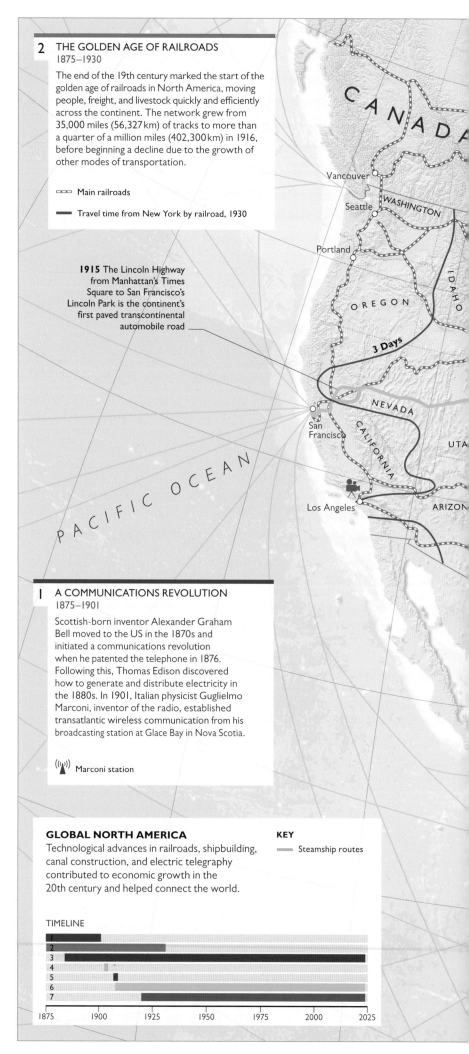

1 A COMMUNICATIONS REVOLUTION
1875–1901

Scottish-born inventor Alexander Graham Bell moved to the US in the 1870s and initiated a communications revolution when he patented the telephone in 1876. Following this, Thomas Edison discovered how to generate and distribute electricity in the 1880s. In 1901, Italian physicist Guglielmo Marconi, inventor of the radio, established transatlantic wireless communication from his broadcasting station at Glace Bay in Nova Scotia.

((ᵀ)) Marconi station

GLOBAL NORTH AMERICA

Technological advances in railroads, shipbuilding, canal construction, and electric telegraphy contributed to economic growth in the 20th century and helped connect the world.

KEY

▬▬ Steamship routes

TIMELINE

2					
3					
4					
5					
6					
7					

1875   1900   1925   1950   1975   2000   2025

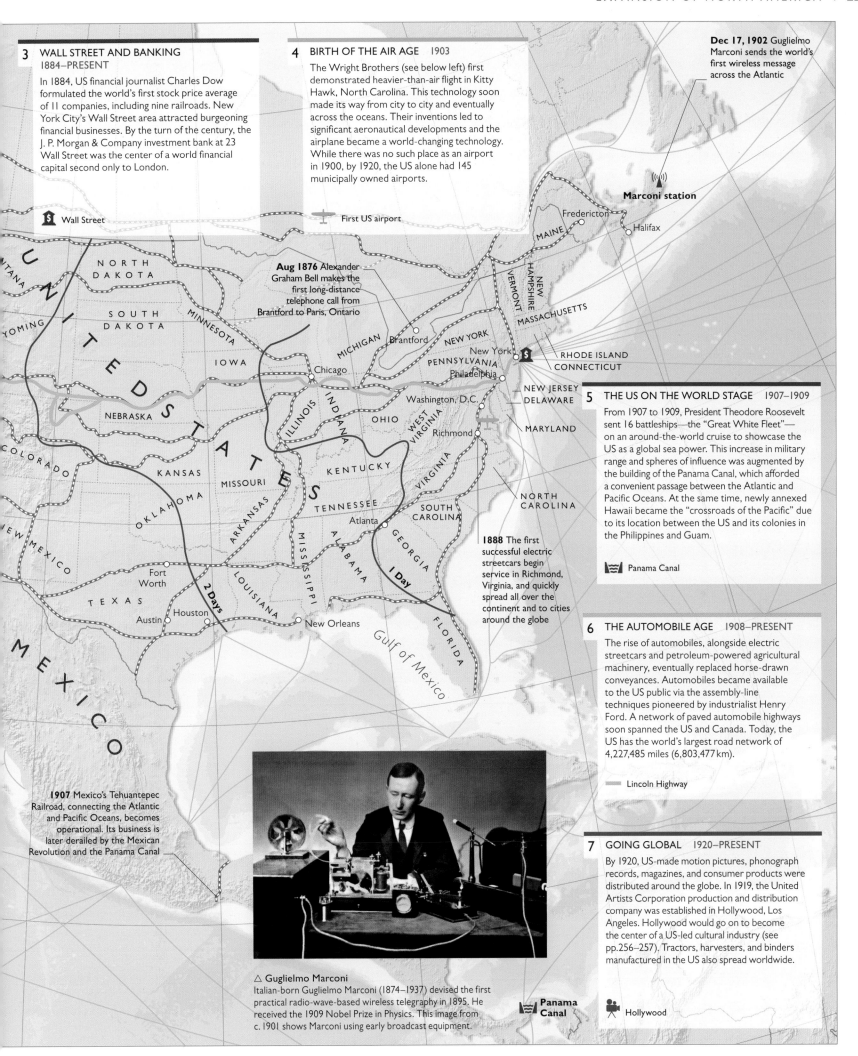

3 WALL STREET AND BANKING
1884–PRESENT

In 1884, US financial journalist Charles Dow formulated the world's first stock price average of 11 companies, including nine railroads. New York City's Wall Street area attracted burgeoning financial businesses. By the turn of the century, the J. P. Morgan & Company investment bank at 23 Wall Street was the center of a world financial capital second only to London.

💲 Wall Street

4 BIRTH OF THE AIR AGE 1903

The Wright Brothers (see below left) first demonstrated heavier-than-air flight in Kitty Hawk, North Carolina. This technology soon made its way from city to city and eventually across the oceans. Their inventions led to significant aeronautical developments and the airplane became a world-changing technology. While there was no such place as an airport in 1900, by 1920, the US alone had 145 municipally owned airports.

First US airport

Dec 17, 1902 Guglielmo Marconi sends the world's first wireless message across the Atlantic

Marconi station

Aug 1876 Alexander Graham Bell makes the first long-distance telephone call from Brantford to Paris, Ontario

1888 The first successful electric streetcars begin service in Richmond, Virginia, and quickly spread all over the continent and to cities around the globe

5 THE US ON THE WORLD STAGE 1907–1909

From 1907 to 1909, President Theodore Roosevelt sent 16 battleships—the "Great White Fleet"—on an around-the-world cruise to showcase the US as a global sea power. This increase in military range and spheres of influence was augmented by the building of the Panama Canal, which afforded a convenient passage between the Atlantic and Pacific Oceans. At the same time, newly annexed Hawaii became the "crossroads of the Pacific" due to its location between the US and its colonies in the Philippines and Guam.

Panama Canal

6 THE AUTOMOBILE AGE 1908–PRESENT

The rise of automobiles, alongside electric streetcars and petroleum-powered agricultural machinery, eventually replaced horse-drawn conveyances. Automobiles became available to the US public via the assembly-line techniques pioneered by industrialist Henry Ford. A network of paved automobile highways soon spanned the US and Canada. Today, the US has the world's largest road network of 4,227,485 miles (6,803,477 km).

Lincoln Highway

1907 Mexico's Tehuantepec Railroad, connecting the Atlantic and Pacific Oceans, becomes operational. Its business is later derailed by the Mexican Revolution and the Panama Canal

7 GOING GLOBAL 1920–PRESENT

By 1920, US-made motion pictures, phonograph records, magazines, and consumer products were distributed around the globe. In 1919, the United Artists Corporation production and distribution company was established in Hollywood, Los Angeles. Hollywood would go on to become the center of a US-led cultural industry (see pp.256–257). Tractors, harvesters, and binders manufactured in the US also spread worldwide.

△ **Guglielmo Marconi**
Italian-born Guglielmo Marconi (1874–1937) devised the first practical radio-wave-based wireless telegraphy in 1895. He received the 1909 Nobel Prize in Physics. This image from c. 1901 shows Marconi using early broadcast equipment.

Panama Canal

Hollywood

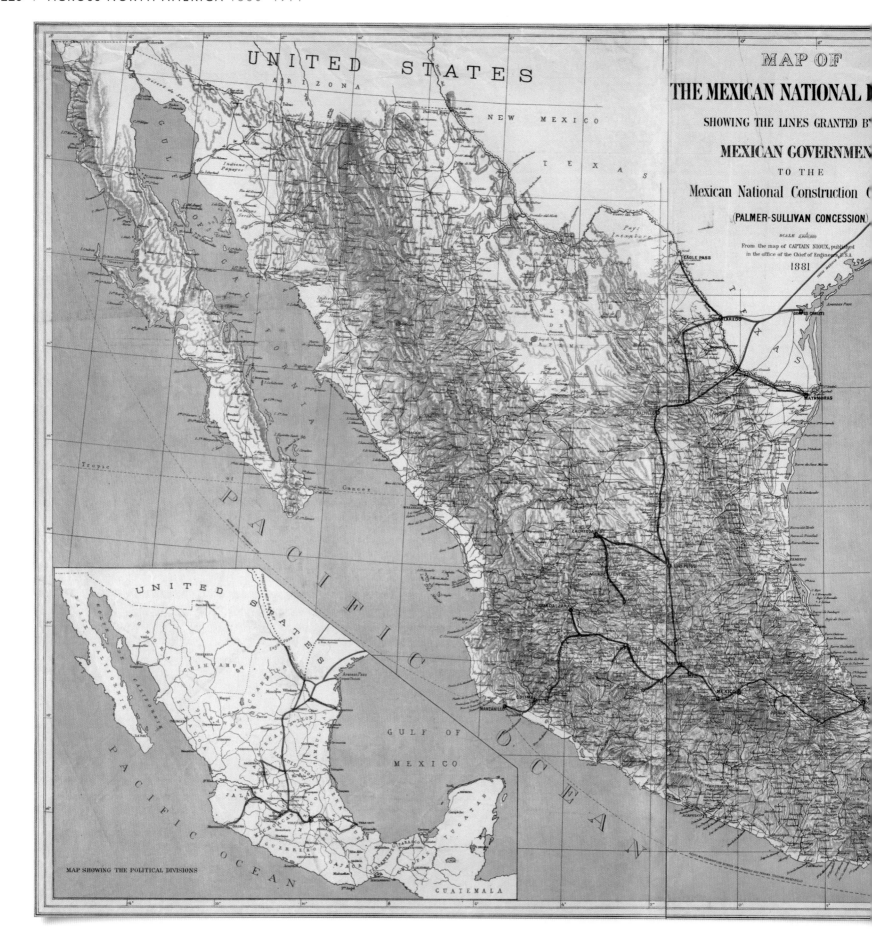

MAP OF

THE MEXICAN NATIONAL R

SHOWING THE LINES GRANTED BY

MEXICAN GOVERNMENT

TO THE

Mexican National Construction C

(PALMER-SULLIVAN CONCESSION)

SCALE

From the map of CAPTAIN SIOUX, published
in the office of the Chief of Engineers, U.S.A.

1881

MAP SHOWING THE POLITICAL DIVISIONS

"Pity poor Mexico, so far from God, so close to the United States."

PORFIRIO DÍAZ, PRESIDENT OF MEXICO
(1876–1880, 1884–1911)

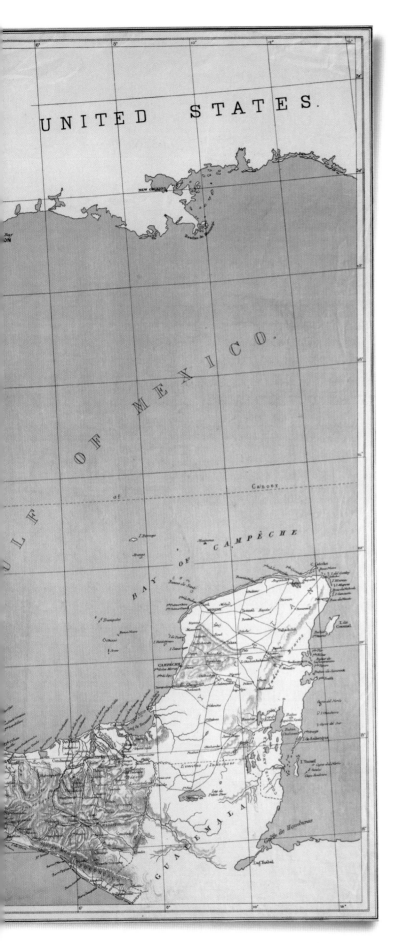

△ Mexican railroads
This 1881 map shows some of the Mexican National Railway lines between the US and Mexico. This rail network was crucial for trade and attracted substantial US investment. As a result, rail lines grew from 700 miles (1,127 km) in 1880 to more than 15,000 miles (24,140 km) by 1910.

THE MEXICAN BORDERLANDS

At the end of the 19th century, the US invested heavily in, and profited handsomely from, Mexico's infrastructure. However, many Mexicans were losing their lands and livelihoods.

The Mexican-American War (see pp.138–139) vastly reconfigured the map of North America. While the war damaged the relationship between the two nations, it became clear they needed each other to prosper. Mexico was rich in raw materials and agricultural goods, while the US had plenty of capital and eager markets. Mexico also had a ready supply of labor. From the end of the 19th century and into the 20th, people worked and lived straddling the border between the two countries. They inhabited border towns—fluid, multilingual, and multicultural places that also included workers from Europe and Asia.

This period coincided with the *Porfiriato* in Mexico—the decades-long presidency of Porfirio Díaz. He was eager to attract US investment to modernize Mexico, as well as enrich the oligarchy running the country. While most US capital went into the railroads, industries such as mining and ranching

LOCATOR

KEY

1 Mexico City's population grew as people who lost their lands in the rest of the country arrived in search of work.

2 Mining areas such as Zacatecas saw an influx of US capital, but not much of the profits.

3 The border town of Laredo benefited from the arrival of the railroads, with thousands of workers crossing the border every day.

4 The northern border states received US investment for ranching and industry.

benefited as well. Poorer Mexicans found themselves being pushed off their lands to make way for foreign interests. By the early 20th century, this combination of rich foreign interests and impoverished local communities was fraught with tension.

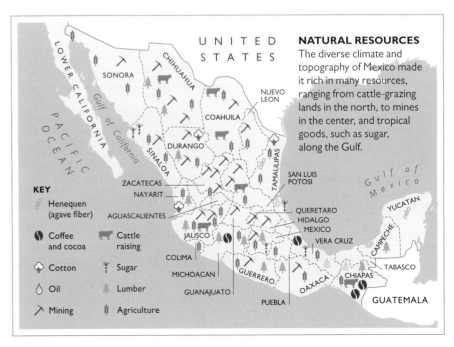

NATURAL RESOURCES
The diverse climate and topography of Mexico made it rich in many resources, ranging from cattle-grazing lands in the north, to mines in the center, and tropical goods, such as sugar, along the Gulf.

KEY
- Henequen (agave fiber)
- Coffee and cocoa
- Cotton
- Oil
- Mining
- Cattle raising
- Sugar
- Lumber
- Agriculture

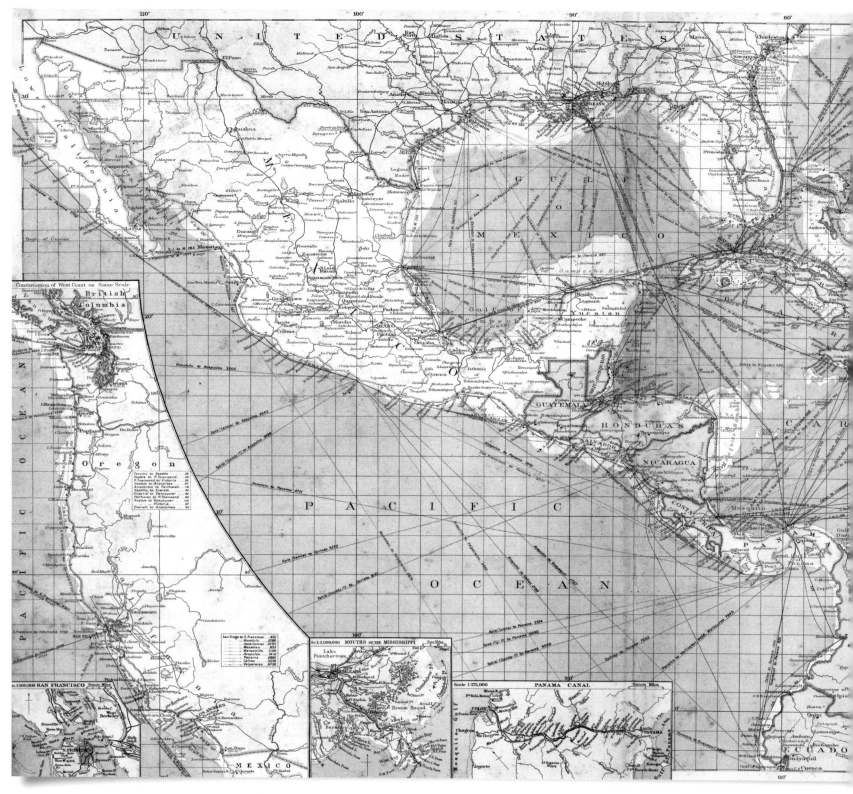

△ Havana
The Cuban capital's port was, in the early decades of the 20th century, the departure point for millions of tons of sugar exported to the US.

◁ New Orleans
This Gulf port played a critical role in supplying US markets with Central American and Caribbean produce, particularly coffee.

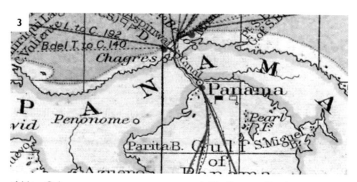

△ The Panama Canal
The opening of this waterway in 1914 provided the US with a strong military, economic, and strategic presence in Central America.

US INFLUENCE IN THE CARIBBEAN

The US entered the 20th century as a major hemispheric power, asserting itself in Central America and the Caribbean through the use of military bases, political leverage, and dominance over trade.

The end of the Spanish–American War (see pp.216–217) reinforced the ascendant position of the US in Central America and the Caribbean. Puerto Rico was ceded to the US by Spain in 1898, while the nominal autonomy of Cuba was undermined by a US-imposed clause in its constitution known as the Platt Amendment. Its provisions allowed the US to involve itself in Cuban affairs at will—and, in 1903, to establish the naval base at Guantánamo Bay still in use today.

In Central America, US gunboats supported Panama's successful fight for independence from Colombia in 1903. In return, the US was allowed to finish building the Panama Canal (see pp. 220–221) and set up its own zone of control several miles wide along the entire length of the waterway.

LOCATOR

In his 1904 State of the Union address, President Theodore Roosevelt laid out his "corollary" to the Monroe Doctrine of 1823 (see pp.124-125), stating that the US reserved the right to intervene in the affairs of other nations in the Americas. This allowed US forces to occupy Nicaragua, in 1912; Veracruz, Mexico, in 1914; and Santa Domingo, in the Dominican Republic, in 1916, when political instability in those places threatened the country's strategic and economic interests. The US occupation of Haiti in 1915 lasted until 1934.

△ **Central American and West Indian ports**
The US dominated trade in the Caribbean, and was a key market and destination for the region's agricultural cash crops, such as sugar, bananas, and tobacco.

◁ **Tampico and Veracruz**
These were Mexico's main ports for trading with the US and other Central and South American states. Veracruz was an important mercantile center; Tampico exported oil.

THE US AND THE CARIBBEAN
After taking control of Puerto Rico in 1898, the US widened its presence in the Caribbean by building military installations in the region over the next half century. The San Isidro Air Base in the Dominican Republic, for example, was set up as late as 1953.

1820–1860s The strategically vital Fort Jefferson and Fort Zachary Taylor are built on the Florida Keys

1903 US agrees a lease with Cuba to open a naval base at Guantánamo Bay

KEY
◼ Areas of US control c. 1900
⚓ US naval base

A WORLD AT WAR

WORLD WAR I MARKED A NEW ERA OF GLOBAL CONFLICT.
POPULATION SHIFTS AND A WORLDWIDE RECESSION
FOLLOWED, AND THE NEW GEOPOLITICAL LANDSCAPE
SOON LED THE US, CANADA, AND MEXICO INTO
ANOTHER, EVEN DEADLIER WORLD WAR.

WAR AND PROGRESS

North America and its relationship with the world underwent a transformation in the early 20th century. Industrialization, internal strife, and a global war would test the resilience of societies in the US, Canada, and Mexico.

△ **U-boats at war**
This 1916 illustration depicts a German U-boat attacking an English merchant ship. Such indiscriminate German attacks on merchant and passenger ships, called "unrestricted submarine warfare," pushed the US to abandon its policy of neutrality.

At the dawn of the 20th century, North America was a continent in transition. The US, which had overtaken Britain as the world's most industrialized nation, experienced a period of rapid economic growth that transformed a primarily rural, agrarian society into a country of large towns and cities connected by railroads, telegraph lines, and roads. It was also an era of new progressive politics that pushed back against what was seen as the corruption of the late 19th century.

In Mexico, there was widespread opposition to the nearly three decade-long rule of Porfirio Díaz, which was marked by corruption and the concentration of wealth among the elite few. This led to the outbreak of a revolution in 1910 that would consume the country for the next decade. A series of regional military uprisings, led most famously by figures such as Emiliano Zapata and Pancho Villa, challenged the authority of successive federal regimes. A landmark new constitution was drafted in 1917 that laid the basis for a new form of government and civil settlement. Beginning in 1929,

▷ **Centenary of the Mexican Revolution**
This 2010 coin features the Mexico coat of arms on one side and a "Soldadera" or female soldier of the Mexican revolution on the other.

the National Revolutionary Party, later renamed the Institutional Revolutionary Party (PRI), would govern Mexico for the next 70 years.

A global war

The outbreak of World War I in 1914 was as much a decisive turning point for the nations of North America as it was for the main European belligerents. Canada, along with Newfoundland (then a separate British Dominion), joined the war effort at once. More than 650,000 British North Americans fought in the war, many at the Somme, Passchendaele, and on Vimy Ridge. Back home, Canadian society was mobilized in support of the war effort.

The US initially attempted to stay out of the war, with its government declaring neutrality. The enormous demand of Allied nations for munitions and other supplies from the US provided an immediate stimulus to the American economy and created a strong demand for labor in Northern factories. For Black Americans, who still overwhelmingly lived in the rural South, this was an opportunity. In what became known as the Great Migration, millions of Black Americans fled Jim Crow segregation and moved to the cities in the Northern, Midwest, and Western states in search of better economic opportunities. The US commitment to neutrality collapsed in

NORTH AMERICA IN A GLOBAL CONTEXT

The early 20th century was an era of increased globalization. The nations of North America were bound to those of Europe, Asia, and South America by unprecedented economic, technological, and cultural links. Before 1914, many people believed that this interdependence meant a major war between industrialized countries was unlikely ever to happen again.

Sept 6, 1901 US President William McKinley is assassinated in Buffalo, New York

1910 The Great Migration starts, as millions of Black Americans leave the South to seek employment in the industrial North

May 25, 1911 Porfirio Díaz resigns as president of Mexico

Feb 5, 1917 The Constituent Congress approves the Mexican Constitution

POLITICS

SOCIETY

THE WIDER WORLD

1910

1913

1916

Aug 4, 1914 Britain declares war on Germany. As a British Dominion, Canada declares war the same day

May 7, 1915 A German submarine, sinks the *RMS Lusitania* killing 1,195 people, including 128 US citizens

Apr 6, 1917 The US declares war on Germany

◁ **The Great Migration**
En route to New Jersey in 1940, this group of migrants from Florida were among millions of Black workers who made their way to the industrial North after the onset of World War I in 1914. This migration continued until the 1970s.

1917 in part due to continued German submarine attacks on commercial ships. US forces intercepted a German telegram to Mexico, promising US territory as a reward for siding with Germany. The US declared war on Germany, and US troops arrived in Europe in June 1917. The intervention of the US, with its vast reserves of soldiers, weaponry, and industrial production, finally allowed the Allies to break the stalemate on the Western Front that had persisted since 1914. Faced with the collapse of its army, the German government surrendered on November 11, 1918.

Postwar progress

The vision of President Woodrow Wilson would have a major impact on shaping the postwar peace. His famous "Fourteen Points" laid the basis for new cooperation between independent nations built on self-determination, collective security, and disarmament.

The end of the war saw Canada and the US enter a decade of economic expansion, technological change, and cultural experimentation. This was also a period of social transition and the continued struggle for rights by Black, Indigenous, and immigrant North Americans, often in the face of violent repression. In the US, women gained the right to vote in 1920, a right Canadian women had exercised in federal elections since 1918. The US national prohibition against alcohol brought a surge in organized crime and smuggling, often across the US–Canada border. As the decade drew to a close, overproduction and overspeculation led the economy to falter and eventually crash, resulting in a global economic crisis.

THE LARGEST HOTEL *in the* BRITISH EMPIRE

The ROYAL YORK TORONTO CANADA
A CANADIAN PACIFIC HOTEL

▷ **Canadian economic boom**
Canada experienced an economic boom after World War I. Linked to the wider British empire but also possessed of a growing sense of nationhood, Canada in the 1920s was a prosperous society.

> *"The chief business of the American people is business."*
>
> PRESIDENT CALVIN COOLIDGE, 1925

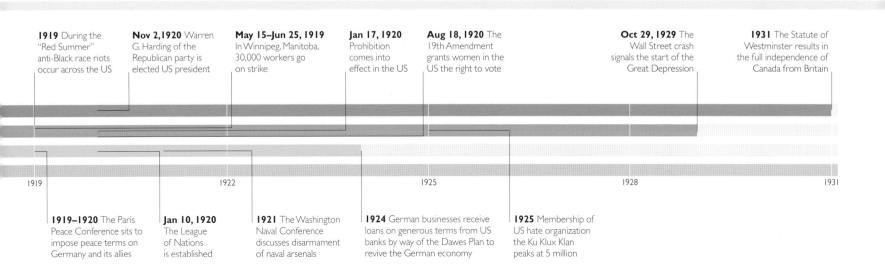

1919 During the "Red Summer" anti-Black race riots occur across the US

Nov 2, 1920 Warren G. Harding of the Republican party is elected US president

May 15–Jun 25, 1919 In Winnipeg, Manitoba, 30,000 workers go on strike

Jan 17, 1920 Prohibition comes into effect in the US

Aug 18, 1920 The 19th Amendment grants women in the US the right to vote

Oct 29, 1929 The Wall Street crash signals the start of the Great Depression

1931 The Statute of Westminster results in the full independence of Canada from Britain

1919   1922   1925   1928   1931

1919–1920 The Paris Peace Conference sits to impose peace terms on Germany and its allies

Jan 10, 1920 The League of Nations is established

1921 The Washington Naval Conference discusses disarmament of naval arsenals

1924 German businesses receive loans on generous terms from US banks by way of the Dawes Plan to revive the German economy

1925 Membership of US hate organization the Ku Klux Klan peaks at 5 million

URBANIZATION IN THE 20TH CENTURY

The population shift away from the countryside was one of the most important changes brought by the industrial revolution in the US. It transformed what had been an overwhelmingly rural and agrarian society—President Thomas Jefferson's "nation of farmers"—into one dominated by towns and cities.

As industrialization increased, the growth of jobs in factories, railroads, construction, and shipping from the middle of the 19th century led to the concentration of the workforce in new and expanding urban areas in the US. The arrival of European immigrants also contributed to the swelling population of cities in the North and Midwest.

This transformation of the American social order was rapid and dramatic. In 1830, only New York City had a population greater than 100,000 people. By 1920, there were 70 such cities in the US, three of which had more than one million inhabitants.

US cities of the 19th and early 20th centuries were contradictory places, with the prosperous upper classes enjoying high levels of urban comfort and luxury alongside the grinding poverty and daily struggle endured by the working masses.

Rapid technological growth during this period meant that the environment of US cities was in a state of constant flux. New infrastructure, construction techniques, and forms of transportation left their mark with every passing decade. By the 1960s, US cities and their growing suburbs had been transformed from the early industrial metropolises of the 19th century (see pp.278–279).

> *"The great city can teach something that no university by itself can altogether impart."*
>
> SETH LOW, MAYOR OF NEW YORK CITY, 1902–1903

WONDER AND SQUALOR

New building technologies allowed for the construction of monumental architecture that became symbolic of the age, such as the Empire State Building in New York City and San Francisco's Golden Gate Bridge. But the rapid expansion of cities also had less beneficial effects. Manhattan's Hell's Kitchen district, for example, first grew up as a shanty town for mainly Irish railroad and dock workers. The tenements that replaced these encampments were little better. Immigrant and Black American "ghettos" developed, where jobs were scarce and poorly paid, and where overcrowding, crime, and disease were endemic.

A tenement in one of New York City's crowded immigrant neighborhoods

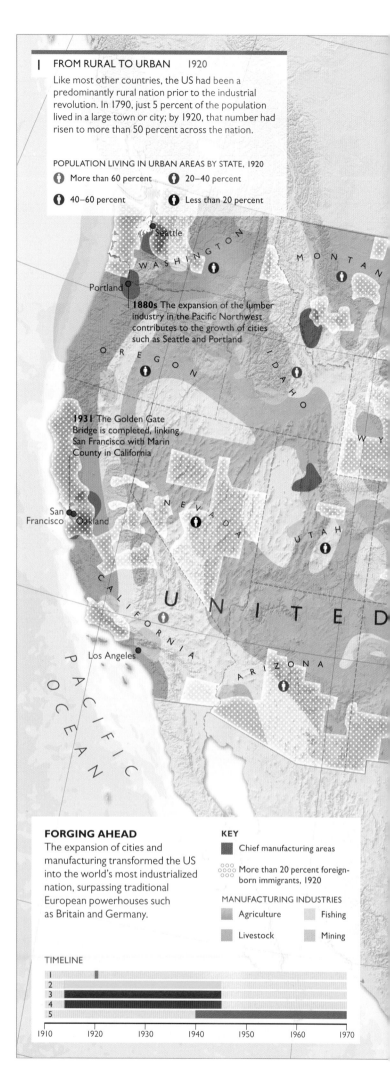

FROM RURAL TO URBAN   1920

Like most other countries, the US had been a predominantly rural nation prior to the industrial revolution. In 1790, just 5 percent of the population lived in a large town or city; by 1920, that number had risen to more than 50 percent across the nation.

POPULATION LIVING IN URBAN AREAS BY STATE, 1920

- More than 60 percent
- 20–40 percent
- 40–60 percent
- Less than 20 percent

1880s The expansion of the lumber industry in the Pacific Northwest contributes to the growth of cities such as Seattle and Portland

1931 The Golden Gate Bridge is completed, linking San Francisco with Marin County in California

FORGING AHEAD
The expansion of cities and manufacturing transformed the US into the world's most industrialized nation, surpassing traditional European powerhouses such as Britain and Germany.

KEY

- Chief manufacturing areas
- More than 20 percent foreign-born immigrants, 1920

MANUFACTURING INDUSTRIES

- Agriculture
- Fishing
- Livestock
- Mining

TIMELINE

1910 1920 1930 1940 1950 1960 1970

2 THE INDUSTRIAL NORTH 1914–1945

Early industrialization was concentrated in the North and Midwest. This created a new workforce in cities such as Chicago, Boston, New York, Baltimore, Philadelphia, and Pittsburgh. The growth of these cities was also fueled by the new railroads that facilitated the rapid transportation of raw materials and manufactured goods across the country.

◎ The North's largest cities

3 WESTERN CITIES 1914–1945

There had been large settlements in the western part of the US since the mid-19th century—for example, San Francisco, which expanded during the California Gold Rush. However, the completion of the transcontinental railroad in 1869 drove rapid urbanization in places such as Los Angeles, Oakland, Seattle, and Portland, especially after World War I.

● The West's largest cities

4 URBAN INFRASTRUCTURE 1914–1945

Modern modes of transportation, including railroads, ferries, subways, and, most importantly, highways and the automobile, transformed the infrastructure of towns and cities. They also allowed for the growth of suburbs after World War II, when new building technologies allowed for homes to be built inexpensively for the prosperous middle classes.

1925 New York City overtakes London, UK as the world's biggest city

1906 The publication of Upton Sinclair's novel *The Jungle* draws attention to the poor conditions of immigrant stockyard workers in Chicago

1910 Pittsburgh, Pennsylvania, produces 60 percent of US steel

1950 Houston surpasses New Orleans as the largest city in the South

▽ **Aerial view**
Many skyscrapers in the 1920s and 1930s were constructed in the Art Deco style. These included the Chrysler Building (below), the tallest building in the world when it was completed in 1930.

5 THE URBAN SOUTH 1940s–1960s

The South remained largely rural until after World War II, much longer than other parts of the US. The urbanization of the South was in part driven by federal government projects, including facilities for the space program in Florida, Texas, and Alabama. Cities such as Atlanta, Miami, New Orleans, and Houston experienced rapid growth during this period.

● The South's largest cities

WORLD WAR I IN NORTH AMERICA

Provoked by repeated attacks on its shipping, the US declared war on Germany in spring 1917. The country's military involvement came late in the war but provided a boost in strength and morale for the Allies, as well as hastening social change on the home front.

△ **Emotional impact**
The sinking of the British liner *Lusitania* on May 7, 1915, claimed 1,198 lives, including 128 US citizens. It helped to turn public opinion in the US against Germany.

When war broke out in Europe in 1914, most people in the US were happy to stay out of the conflict. This is partly why they reelected President Woodrow Wilson in 1916, when he ran on the slogan: "He kept us out of war." Canada, by contrast, as part of the British Empire, sent large forces to fight in France throughout the conflict.

Opinion changed when German submarines began to sink merchant ships in the Atlantic, killing US civilians. By spring 1917, Germany was operating a policy of unrestricted submarine warfare, attacking US and any other ships it suspected of aiding the Allies. This led in April that year to the US entering the war.

In time, some 2 million men of the American Expeditionary Force (AEF) crossed the Atlantic, most of them landing in France to be trained and equipped. The only major action that US troops saw was the Meuse–Argonne campaign in northeast France, from September 1918.

In the meantime, President Wilson had in January that year laid out his Fourteen Points plan for a peace settlement, only a few of which were included in the finished peace treaty, the Treaty of Versailles of 1919. One of these was the founding of what became the League of Nations—although Congress blocked the US from joining it after refusing to ratify the terms of the Treaty of Versailles.

US WOMEN'S RIGHTS IN WARTIME

Millions of women in the US participated in World War I as nurses, factory workers, and much else. Their active contribution to the war effort reinforced prewar calls for women's voting rights— which were partly gained by the 19th Amendment to the US Constitution, ratified in August 1920.

US suffragettes in 1915

The "Harlem Hellfighters"
Most Black Americans were given noncombat roles in the segregated US Army of World War I. The "Harlem Hellfighters" 369th Infantry Regiment was an exception—although it was sent to fight with a French, rather than US, division.

MEXICO

SCALES

Statute Miles, 98 = 1 Inch.

Kilometres, 157 = 1 Inch.

Copyright by Rand McNally & Co.
1913

STATE OF MEXICO
AND
SURROUNDING
COUNTRY
(Enlarged Scale)

Statute Miles, 23 = 1 Inch.

Kilometres, 53 = 1 Inch.

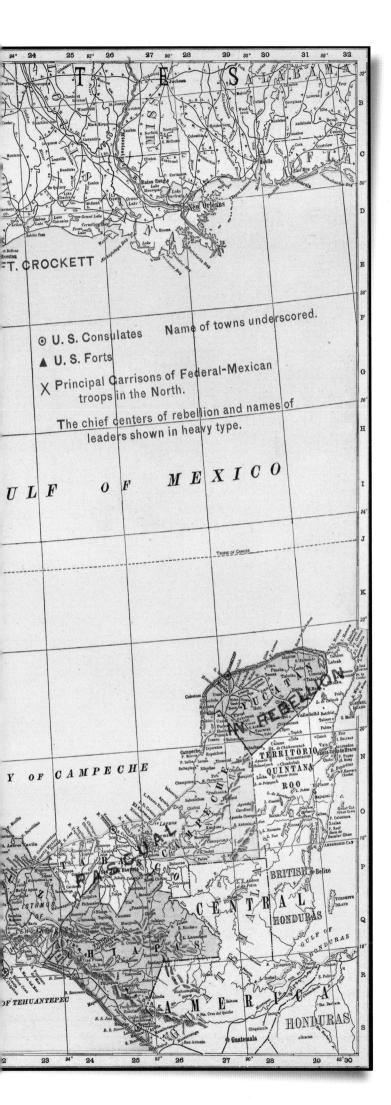

THE MEXICAN REVOLUTION

In 1910, an uprising against Mexican president Porfirio Diaz sparked a decade-long revolution, whose leaders included the guerrilla commanders Emiliano Zapata and Pancho Villa. Armed rebellions, civil war, and regime changes persisted until 1920, when ruling generals imposed order with state power.

In November 1910, Mexican opposition leader Francisco Madero called for an armed revolt against Porfirio Díaz—president of more than three decades—after he had rigged the 1910 election to "return" as president. Several revolutionary factions united in a revolt that led to Díaz resigning by the end of May 1911 and going into exile in Paris.

Madero won the elections later that year but proved to be an ineffective president. Forced to resign—and shot—in 1913, he was replaced by Victoriano Huerta, whose dictatorial rule met with fierce resistance. In 1914, a coalition of Constitutionalists under Venustiano Carranza and revolutionary forces led by Emiliano Zapata and Pancho Villa toppled Huerta. The coalition then fell apart over the question of who would assume the presidency, leading to a civil war. Constitutionalists dominated

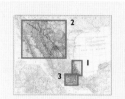

LOCATOR

KEY

1 The detention of nine US sailors in Tampico escalated US–Mexico tensions, resulting in the US occupation of Veracruz.

2 Carranza's Constitutionalists controlled a swathe of northern Mexico. Pancho Villa dominated in Chihuahua.

3 Zapata's Liberation Army of the South controlled Morelos, an important state due to its proximity to the capital.

following commander Álvaro Obregón's defeat of Villa at Celaya in 1915. Carranza assumed the presidency in 1917 and made provisions for radical reforms. When he failed to deliver on his promises, Carranza was overthrown by Obregón in 1920 and killed while trying to escape. In the 1920s and 1930s, Obregón and succeeding presidents implemented programs of economic and land reform.

◁ **The end of the Huerta regime**
This "war map" shows the rebel forces operating in Mexico in 1913. In Mexico City, Huerta was under pressure from both the north and south; with the US briefly drawn into the conflict on the Caribbean coast.

EMILIANO ZAPATA
1879–1919

An idealistic Mexican revolutionary leader, Zapata was born in 1879 in the sugarcane-growing state of Morelos, which remained his primary stronghold. In 1911, he drafted a document, the *Plan of Ayala*, in which he rejected the presidency of Francisco Madero and provided a blueprint for land reform in Mexico. A gifted guerrilla leader, Zapata found himself isolated after Villa's defeat in 1915. In 1919, he was assassinated by Carranza loyalists.

CHARLES A. LINDBERGH

Charles A. Lindbergh was the first person to fly nonstop and solo across the Atlantic—in his plane, *Spirit of St. Louis* (right), in 1927. Although this flight made him an international hero, he later became a leading voice for US isolationism. Initially a supporter of Nazi Germany and the isolationist America First Committee, he later joined the US fight against Japan in World War II. Lindbergh's story can be seen as one example of the conflicting views in the US over the country's place in the new world order.

THE BURDEN OF POWER

The US emerged as a global power in the wake of World War I. The debate between internationalist and isolationist factions continued, but it was clear that US power and influence had been decisive in the war's outcome and in the postwar settlement.

KEY

New countries created after the war

LAND LOST BY EUROPE
- Germany
- Austro-Hungary
- Russia

TIMELINE

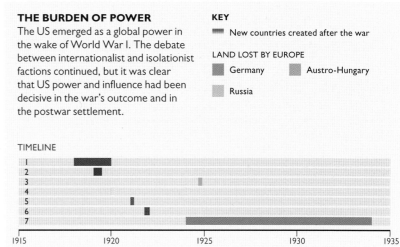

1915   1920   1925   1930   1935

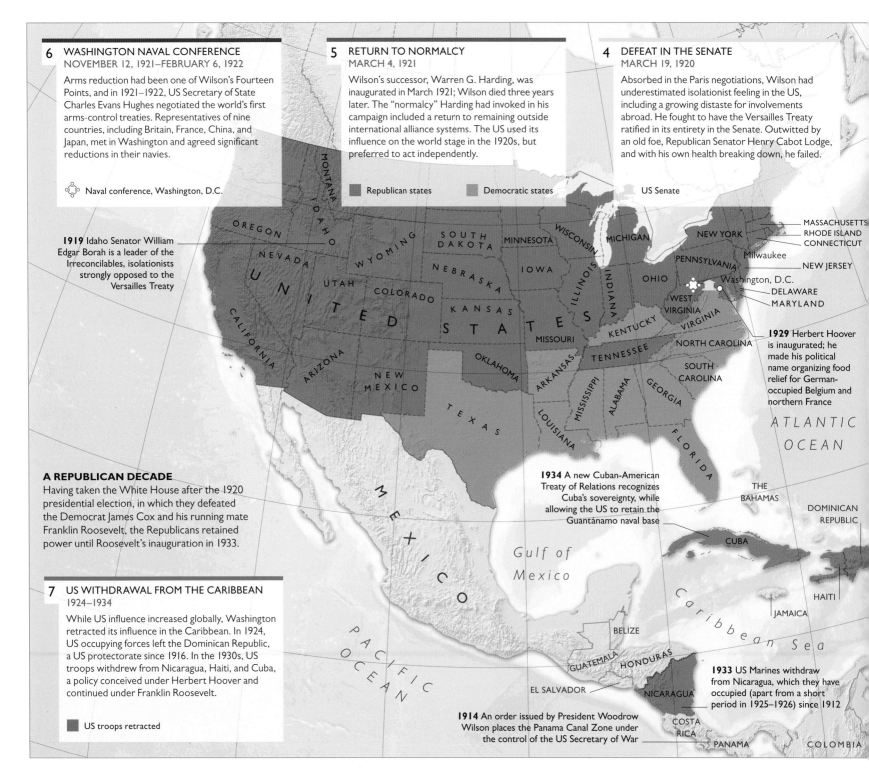

6 WASHINGTON NAVAL CONFERENCE
NOVEMBER 12, 1921–FEBRUARY 6, 1922

Arms reduction had been one of Wilson's Fourteen Points, and in 1921–1922, US Secretary of State Charles Evans Hughes negotiated the world's first arms-control treaties. Representatives of nine countries, including Britain, France, China, and Japan, met in Washington and agreed significant reductions in their navies.

Naval conference, Washington, D.C.

5 RETURN TO NORMALCY
MARCH 4, 1921

Wilson's successor, Warren G. Harding, was inaugurated in March 1921; Wilson died three years later. The "normalcy" Harding had invoked in his campaign included a return to remaining outside international alliance systems. The US used its influence on the world stage in the 1920s, but preferred to act independently.

Republican states   Democratic states

4 DEFEAT IN THE SENATE
MARCH 19, 1920

Absorbed in the Paris negotiations, Wilson had underestimated isolationist feeling in the US, including a growing distaste for involvements abroad. He fought to have the Versailles Treaty ratified in its entirety in the Senate. Outwitted by an old foe, Republican Senator Henry Cabot Lodge, and with his own health breaking down, he failed.

US Senate

1919 Idaho Senator William Edgar Borah is a leader of the Irreconcilables, isolationists strongly opposed to the Versailles Treaty

1929 Herbert Hoover is inaugurated; he made his political name organizing food relief for German-occupied Belgium and northern France

A REPUBLICAN DECADE
Having taken the White House after the 1920 presidential election, in which they defeated the Democrat James Cox and his running mate Franklin Roosevelt, the Republicans retained power until Roosevelt's inauguration in 1933.

1934 A new Cuban-American Treaty of Relations recognizes Cuba's sovereignty, while allowing the US to retain the Guantánamo naval base

7 US WITHDRAWAL FROM THE CARIBBEAN
1924–1934

While US influence increased globally, Washington retracted its influence in the Caribbean. In 1924, US occupying forces left the Dominican Republic, a US protectorate since 1916. In the 1930s, US troops withdrew from Nicaragua, Haiti, and Cuba, a policy conceived under Herbert Hoover and continued under Franklin Roosevelt.

US troops retracted

1933 US Marines withdraw from Nicaragua, which they have occupied (apart from a short period in 1925–1926) since 1912

1914 An order issued by President Woodrow Wilson places the Panama Canal Zone under the control of the US Secretary of War

3 DAWES PLAN AUGUST 16, 1924

With hyperinflation threatening Germany's ability to make its reparations payments, US banker and future vice president Charles G. Dawes chaired an international committee set up to resolve the crisis. The success of the resulting Dawes Plan earned Dawes the Nobel Peace Prize. US industrialist Owen D. Young headed the committee that created the follow-up Young Plan (1929).

🖈 Dawes Plan

2 PARIS PEACE CONFERENCE JANUARY–JUNE 1919

Thirty-two nationalities, although none of the defeated nations, took part in the Paris conference, with the "Big Four" of Britain, France, Italy, and the US dominating. The Treaty of Versailles with Germany, signed in the Hall of Mirrors, would be followed by treaties with Germany's former allies.

✹ Palace of Versailles

1 NATIONAL SELF-DETERMINATION 1918–1920

In Paris, Wilson tried unsuccessfully to reduce the harsh reparations imposed on Germany. He had more success with his principle of self-determination—the right of nations to sovereignty. A clutch of new states emerged in central and eastern Europe from the remains of the Austro-Hungarian and Ottoman empires, as well as the splintering of the former Russian czarist realms.

1922 The Permanent Court of International Justice meets for the first time in The Hague—without US participation

1928 The US and France negotiate the Kellogg–Briand Pact, supposedly a treaty for the "renunciation of war"

A NEW MAP OF EUROPE
Finland and the Baltics shook off Russian imperial rule. Poland reemerged as a sovereign nation with territory from the old Russian, German, and Austro-Hungarian empires. Czechoslovakia and Yugoslavia were newly created.

1917 The Jones–Shafroth Act creates a Senate and bill of rights for Puerto Rico and grants US citizenship to Puerto Ricans born since 1899

THE NEW WORLD ORDER

The post-World War I Paris Peace Conference created a new map of Europe and new international institutions. The US, led by President Woodrow Wilson, was a commanding presence at the conference; back home, however, Wilson fell foul of isolationist forces.

△ **League of Nations**
A graphic from a popular dictionary shows the member states of the League of Nations, which opened with 42 members in Geneva in November 1920. The US never joined.

Addressing Congress in January 1918, President Wilson laid out 14 principles for building a lasting peace. His "Fourteen Points" included free trade among nations, arms reduction, the right to national self-determination, and the creation of a "general association of nations" to guarantee states' independence and territorial integrity. In November, the Fourteen Points were the basis on which Germany agreed to the Armistice.

In December, Wilson sailed for Europe—the first incumbent president to do so—and stayed for six months at the Paris conference. Driven by a vision of a world order based on principles of international justice, Wilson fought for the creation of a League

of Nations, the "general association" from his Fourteen Points. The charter for the League was enshrined as Part 1 of the Treaty of Versailles signed on June 28, 1919.

In Washington, some Republicans were suspicious of foreign "entanglements" and hostile to membership of the League. The Versailles Treaty needed ratification in the Senate by a two-thirds majority. Refusing compromise, Wilson set off on a tour of the West to drum up support—until incapacitated by a stroke. In March 1920, the treaty was defeated in the Senate. Elections in November saw victory for the Republican Warren G. Harding. In 1921, a new bilateral treaty confirmed peace between Germany and the US.

INTERWAR CANADA

World War I had forged a new sense of nationhood for Canada. The post-war years brought industrial unrest and severe unemployment during the Depression, but Canadian national identity remained strong.

△ **Mobilized**
This World War II propaganda depicts a soldier, an industrial worker, and an agricultural worker—all equally vital.

War had changed Canada economically and socially, establishing new industries and bringing women into the workforce in greater numbers to meet wartime needs. Peacetime brought its own upheavals, including high inflation, militancy by unionized industrial workers, and tumbling produce prices. The crisis peaked in 1919 with a six-week general strike in Winnipeg, Manitoba, which was harshly suppressed by the federal government. A more progressive move was the 1918 Act that gave most Canadian women—though not Asian, Inuit, or First Nations women— the right to vote in federal elections.

The 1921 election swept the Liberal William Lyon Mackenzie King to power. Canada had a new sense of international importance, with its own seat at the League of Nations. The Statute of Westminster, passed by British Parliament in 1931, confirmed Canada's near-complete autonomy from Britain. However, reliance on exports made it vulnerable to the downturn in world trade during the Great Depression. By 1933, unemployment had engulfed 30 percent of the Canadian workforce. Full employment would return to the nation only with World War II.

> *"If some countries have too much history, we have too much geography."*
>
> WILLIAM LYON MACKENZIE KING, 1936

THE PERSONS CASE

Under the 1867 Constitution Act, only "qualified persons" were eligible for Canada's Senate—and "persons," it was understood, meant men. In 1927–1929, five women— Emily Murphy, Nellie McClung, Irene Parlby, Louise McKinney, and Henrietta Muir Edwards—successfully legally challenged this, and, in 1930, Cairine Mackay Wilson became Canada's first woman senator.

Nellie McClung

Right to relief
Young unemployed men, all unmarried, stage a sit-down protest in Ottawa in May 1939. The plight of single men without work could be desperate: government relief favored married men with families.

REPRESSION AND PROSPERITY

In 1919 and 1920, a postwar surge in industrial unrest provoked fears of communist political agitation in the US. In an attempt to curb this unrest, the government instituted several repressive policies. The 1920s also brought unprecedented prosperity for many, until the Wall Street Crash of 1929.

In 1919, a five-day general strike brought Seattle to a halt as nearly 65,000 workers took to the streets. In solidarity, workers throughout the city joined shipyard workers in protest for better wages. Seattle's mayor Ole Hanson, fearing a leftist uprising similar to events during Russia's Bolshevik revolution, responded with force, deploying soldiers, sailors, marines, and police to quell the strike.

The Seattle strike was the first major episode in a "red scare" that continued until 1920. In the economic slump that followed World War I, many people were drawn to left-wing groups, some of which used violent means to attack capitalism. Riots erupted in cities such as Chicago and Cleveland. Anarchist letter bombing campaigns targeted key public figures, including US Attorney-General Alexander Mitchell Palmer, who responded to the unrest with a series of raids. About 6,000 suspected socialist agitators were arrested, with many immigrants among them being deported.

In November 1920, Republican Warren Harding won the presidential election, promising a return to "normalcy." The "normal" US that emerged saw nationwide Prohibition and revival of the white supremacist vigilante group, the Ku Klux Klan. At the same time, women were finally guaranteed the right to vote (see below right), and a steady rise in wages went some way toward restoring economic well-being. However, no effort was made to regulate the stock market, resulting in the calamitous collapse of Wall Street in October 1929.

> "After all, the chief business of the American people is business."

CALVIN COOLIDGE, US PRESIDENT, 1925

THE ROARING TWENTIES

The 1920s were a time of new freedoms and trends. Automobile ownership shot up— four in five US families had a car by 1929. Young women who defied the norm by wearing short skirts and bobbed hair were known as "flappers." In 1925, F. Scott Fitzgerald published *The Great Gatsby*—a novel showing the hollowness this era of prosperity, also referred to as the Jazz Age after the music of the time. In 1927, Charles Lindbergh made the first solo transatlantic flight, from New York to Paris.

An early 20th century flapper

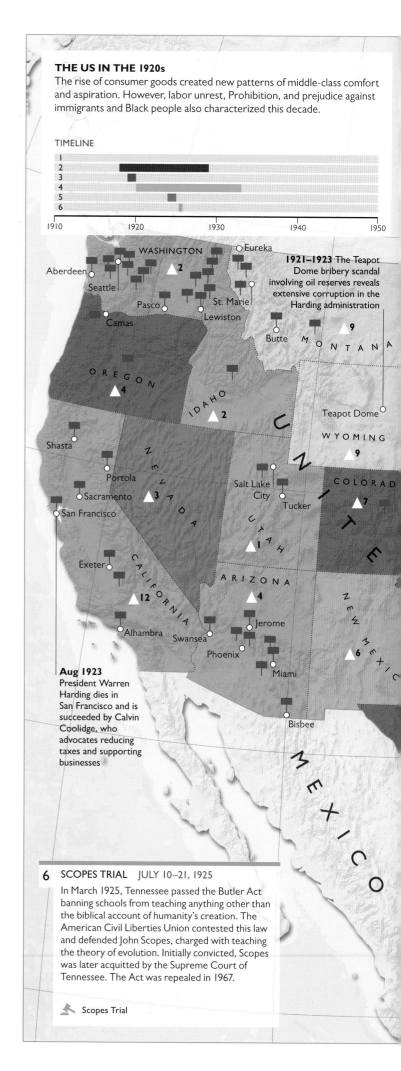

THE US IN THE 1920s
The rise of consumer goods created new patterns of middle-class comfort and aspiration. However, labor unrest, Prohibition, and prejudice against immigrants and Black people also characterized this decade.

1921–1923 The Teapot Dome bribery scandal involving oil reserves reveals extensive corruption in the Harding administration

Aug 1923 President Warren Harding dies in San Francisco and is succeeded by Calvin Coolidge, who advocates reducing taxes and supporting businesses

6 SCOPES TRIAL JULY 10–21, 1925
In March 1925, Tennessee passed the Butler Act banning schools from teaching anything other than the biblical account of humanity's creation. The American Civil Liberties Union contested this law and defended John Scopes, charged with teaching the theory of evolution. Initially convicted, Scopes was later acquitted by the Supreme Court of Tennessee. The Act was repealed in 1967.

Scopes Trial

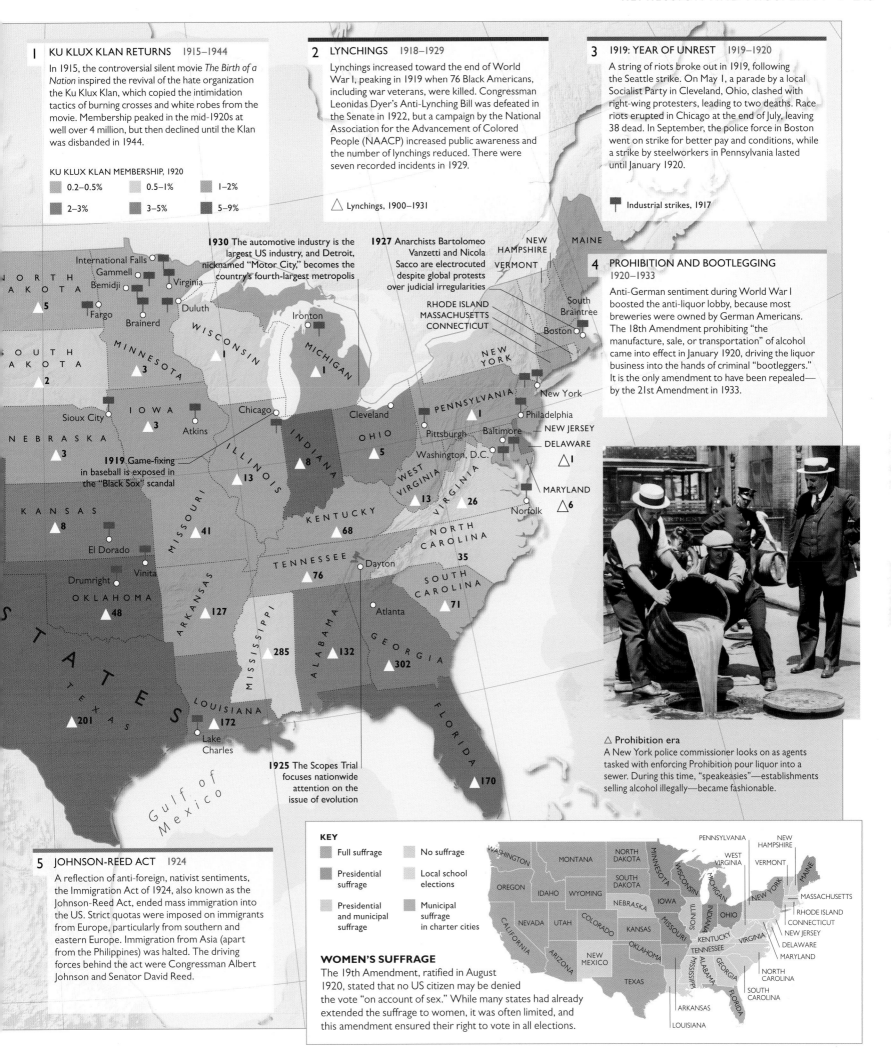

1 | KU KLUX KLAN RETURNS 1915–1944

In 1915, the controversial silent movie *The Birth of a Nation* inspired the revival of the hate organization the Ku Klux Klan, which copied the intimidation tactics of burning crosses and white robes from the movie. Membership peaked in the mid-1920s at well over 4 million, but then declined until the Klan was disbanded in 1944.

KU KLUX KLAN MEMBERSHIP, 1920

- 0.2–0.5%
- 0.5–1%
- 1–2%
- 2–3%
- 3–5%
- 5–9%

2 | LYNCHINGS 1918–1929

Lynchings increased toward the end of World War I, peaking in 1919 when 76 Black Americans, including war veterans, were killed. Congressman Leonidas Dyer's Anti-Lynching Bill was defeated in the Senate in 1922, but a campaign by the National Association for the Advancement of Colored People (NAACP) increased public awareness and the number of lynchings reduced. There were seven recorded incidents in 1929.

△ Lynchings, 1900–1931

3 | 1919: YEAR OF UNREST 1919–1920

A string of riots broke out in 1919, following the Seattle strike. On May 1, a parade by a local Socialist Party in Cleveland, Ohio, clashed with right-wing protesters, leading to two deaths. Race riots erupted in Chicago at the end of July, leaving 38 dead. In September, the police force in Boston went on strike for better pay and conditions, while a strike by steelworkers in Pennsylvania lasted until January 1920.

■ Industrial strikes, 1917

1930 The automotive industry is the largest US industry, and Detroit, nicknamed "Motor City," becomes the country's fourth-largest metropolis

1927 Anarchists Bartolomeo Vanzetti and Nicola Sacco are electrocuted despite global protests over judicial irregularities

4 | PROHIBITION AND BOOTLEGGING 1920–1933

Anti-German sentiment during World War I boosted the anti-liquor lobby, because most breweries were owned by German Americans. The 18th Amendment prohibiting "the manufacture, sale, or transportation" of alcohol came into effect in January 1920, driving the liquor business into the hands of criminal "bootleggers." It is the only amendment to have been repealed—by the 21st Amendment in 1933.

1919 Game-fixing in baseball is exposed in the "Black Sox" scandal

1925 The Scopes Trial focuses nationwide attention on the issue of evolution

△ **Prohibition era**
A New York police commissioner looks on as agents tasked with enforcing Prohibition pour liquor into a sewer. During this time, "speakeasies"—establishments selling alcohol illegally—became fashionable.

Map labels (states and cities)

NORTH DAKOTA — 5
International Falls, Gammell, Bemidji, Virginia, Fargo, Brainerd, Duluth
SOUTH DAKOTA — 2
MINNESOTA — 3
WISCONSIN — 1
MICHIGAN — 1
Ironton
NEW HAMPSHIRE, MAINE, VERMONT
RHODE ISLAND, MASSACHUSETTS, CONNECTICUT
South Braintree
Boston
NEW YORK
New York
IOWA — 3
Sioux City, Atkins
NEBRASKA — 3
Chicago
ILLINOIS — 13
INDIANA — 8
OHIO — 5
Cleveland
PENNSYLVANIA — 1
Philadelphia
Pittsburgh, Baltimore
NEW JERSEY
DELAWARE — 1
MARYLAND — 6
Washington, D.C.
WEST VIRGINIA — 13
VIRGINIA — 26
Norfolk
KANSAS — 8
El Dorado
MISSOURI — 41
KENTUCKY — 68
NORTH CAROLINA — 35
Drumright, Vinita
OKLAHOMA — 48
ARKANSAS — 127
TENNESSEE — 76
Dayton
SOUTH CAROLINA — 71
Atlanta
GEORGIA — 302
MISSISSIPPI — 285
ALABAMA — 132
TEXAS — 201
LOUISIANA — 172
Lake Charles
FLORIDA — 170
Gulf of Mexico

5 | JOHNSON-REED ACT 1924

A reflection of anti-foreign, nativist sentiments, the Immigration Act of 1924, also known as the Johnson-Reed Act, ended mass immigration into the US. Strict quotas were imposed on immigrants from Europe, particularly from southern and eastern Europe. Immigration from Asia (apart from the Philippines) was halted. The driving forces behind the act were Congressman Albert Johnson and Senator David Reed.

KEY

- Full suffrage
- Presidential suffrage
- Presidential and municipal suffrage
- No suffrage
- Local school elections
- Municipal suffrage in charter cities

WOMEN'S SUFFRAGE

The 19th Amendment, ratified in August 1920, stated that no US citizen may be denied the vote "on account of sex." While many states had already extended the suffrage to women, it was often limited, and this amendment ensured their right to vote in all elections.

Suffrage map state labels

WASHINGTON, OREGON, CALIFORNIA, NEVADA, IDAHO, UTAH, ARIZONA, MONTANA, WYOMING, COLORADO, NEW MEXICO, NORTH DAKOTA, SOUTH DAKOTA, NEBRASKA, KANSAS, OKLAHOMA, TEXAS, MINNESOTA, IOWA, MISSOURI, ARKANSAS, LOUISIANA, WISCONSIN, ILLINOIS, MICHIGAN, INDIANA, OHIO, KENTUCKY, TENNESSEE, MISSISSIPPI, ALABAMA, GEORGIA, FLORIDA, SOUTH CAROLINA, NORTH CAROLINA, VIRGINIA, WEST VIRGINIA, PENNSYLVANIA, NEW YORK, MAINE, NEW HAMPSHIRE, VERMONT, MASSACHUSETTS, RHODE ISLAND, CONNECTICUT, NEW JERSEY, DELAWARE, MARYLAND

THE GREAT MIGRATION

At the start of the 20th century, the overwhelming majority of Black Americans still lived in the southern states. Over the following decades until around 1970, more than 6 million would leave, escaping violence to seek better lives in the North and West.

While slavery had been abolished at the end of the Civil War in 1865, conditions for Black Americans in the South at the start of the 20th century remained grim. Jim Crow laws subjected Black people to severe discrimination and segregation, while the economic system of sharecropping was exploited to trap many in rural poverty. However, the outbreak of World War I and the entry of the US into the conflict in 1917 created new industrial job opportunities in the North and West for Black workers, and as a result millions left the South, migrating to cities such as New York City, Chicago, Pittsburgh, and Detroit. This "Great Migration," as it came to be called, had begun in its earliest form around 1890 (see pp.218–219). It was one of the most significant internal migrations in US history, reshaping both the demographic makeup of the US and the position of Black Americans within it.

After World War II, a second wave of migrants left the South, particularly for cities on the West Coast. Although Black migrants escaped the overt persecution of the South and managed to access new job opportunities, they still faced significant hardship in the North, including economic inequality with white workers; flagrant hostility and racism; and de facto discrimination in housing, education, and healthcare.

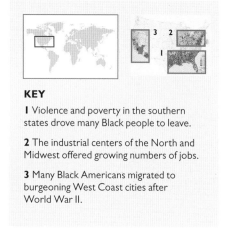

KEY

1 Violence and poverty in the southern states drove many Black people to leave.

2 The industrial centers of the North and Midwest offered growing numbers of jobs.

3 Many Black Americans migrated to burgeoning West Coast cities after World War II.

▷ **Black American population in 1950**
This map from a 1956 statistical atlas by Samuel Fitzsimmons shows the distribution of Black Americans by county in 1950, indicating counties with a population of 500 or more Black people (yellow and below in key).

THE HARLEM RENAISSANCE

The Harlem Renaissance was a blossoming of Black culture in the Manhattan neighborhood of Harlem during the 1920s. Music flourished, with jazz artists such as Louis Armstrong and Billie Holiday inspiring this cultural movement. Literature and scholarship also thrived, as seen in the poetry of Langston Hughes and the pioneering anthropological work of Zora Neale Hurston.

Jazz musician Cootie Williams at the Savoy Ballroom in Harlem c.1930s

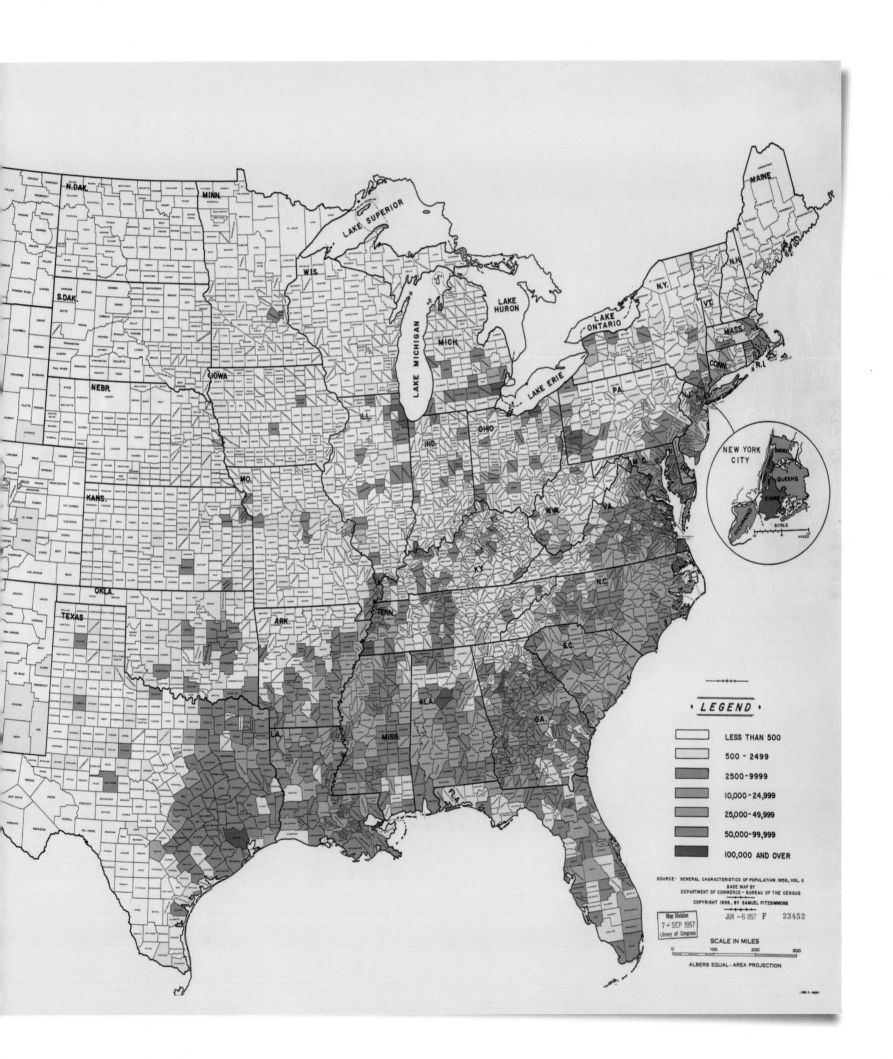

LEGEND

	LESS THAN 500
	500 - 2499
	2500 - 9999
	10,000 - 24,999
	25,000 - 49,999
	50,000 - 99,999
	100,000 AND OVER

SOURCE: GENERAL CHARACTERISTICS OF POPULATION 1950, VOL. II
BASE MAP BY
DEPARTMENT OF COMMERCE - BUREAU OF THE CENSUS
COPYRIGHT 1956, BY SAMUEL FITZSIMMONS

Map Division
7 - SEP 1957
Library of Congress

JUN -6 1957 F   23452

SCALE IN MILES

0   100   200   300

ALBERS EQUAL - AREA PROJECTION

NEW YORK CITY

GREAT DEPRESSION AND WORLD WAR II

North America experienced a period of crisis from 1929 to 1945. The Great Depression threatened to erode the foundations of society, while World War II brought the US, Canada, and Mexico into the global struggle against fascism.

△ **Great Depression**
There was little relief available for the unemployed in the early days of the Great Depression. This image shows people lining up outside a soup kitchen in Chicago in 1931.

The Wall Street crash of October 1929 was one of the turning points of the 20th century. It brought the decade of prosperity known as the Roaring Twenties to a halt and marked the start of the worst economic downturn of modern times, the Great Depression. The Depression began in the US but swiftly became a global economic crisis that saw the collapse of industrial production, the failure of banks and other financial institutions, and a sharp contraction in trade. In the US, this led to homelessness and mass unemployment, which peaked at 25 percent in 1933. Large numbers of people were forced to seek refuge in encampments or shanty towns nicknamed "Hoovervilles" after President Herbert Hoover, who was blamed for the crisis and the ineffective relief efforts of the federal government.

Adding to this misery was the onset in the 1930s of severe drought and dust storms that ravaged the southern plains of the US, earning the region the name "Dust Bowl" (see pp.252–253). The resulting erosion destroyed farms, ruined crops, and rendered vast areas of land unsuitable for agriculture. With their homes and livelihoods severely compromised, thousands of people from the region became refugees, who migrated west to California in search of jobs.

The New Deal

Against this backdrop of hardship, Franklin D. Roosevelt was elected president in 1932, promising to make a "New Deal" between the federal government and US citizens (see pp.254–255). Between 1933 and 1939, his administration enacted a series of programs to provide temporary relief to

△ **Supporting the arts**
As part of the New Deal initiative, the federal government commissioned works from artists, writers, and musicians to support them during the Depression. This painting depicts life on a farm during the 1930s.

> *"The United States of America was suddenly and deliberately attacked by naval and air forces of the Empire of Japan."*
>
> FRANKLIN D. ROOSEVELT, DECEMBER 8, 1941

FROM DEPRESSION TO A WORLD WAR

The economic suffering caused by the Great Depression was alleviated gradually during the 1930s thanks to economic initiatives such as the New Deal. However, it was the full-scale mobilization of industry, society, and the workforce required to fight World War II that finally brought an end to more than a decade of economic malaise.

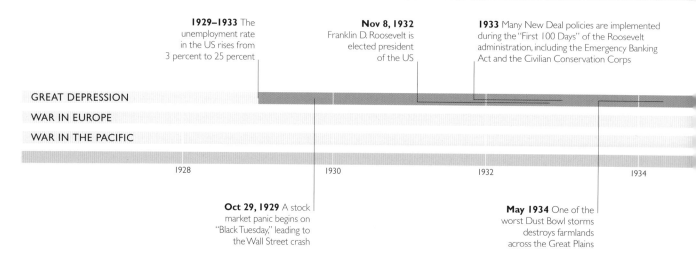

1929–1933 The unemployment rate in the US rises from 3 percent to 25 percent

Nov 8, 1932 Franklin D. Roosevelt is elected president of the US

1933 Many New Deal policies are implemented during the "First 100 Days" of the Roosevelt administration, including the Emergency Banking Act and the Civilian Conservation Corps

GREAT DEPRESSION

WAR IN EUROPE

WAR IN THE PACIFIC

1928   1930   1932   1934

Oct 29, 1929 A stock market panic begins on "Black Tuesday," leading to the Wall Street crash

May 1934 One of the worst Dust Bowl storms destroys farmlands across the Great Plains

▽ Attack on Pearl Harbor
Mitsubishi A6M Zero fighter planes played a key role in the Japanese attack on Pearl Harbor, a preemptive strike designed to prevent the US from intervening in the Pacific. Of the four US battleships sunk in the attack, three were eventually repaired and returned to active duty.

▽ The Manhattan Project
The Manhattan Project was the code name given to the US effort to develop an atomic bomb. This image shows the project team based at the Los Alamos National Laboratory in New Mexico.

the unemployed, bolster the US economy, and reform the financial system to prevent a similar crisis from happening again. With its signature public works programs which employed thousands of workers in construction and infrastructure projects, the New Deal represented a dramatically increased role for the federal government in the management of the economy and the daily lives of individuals. People sought refuge from their bleak circumstances in entertainment, particularly cinema. Hollywood productions progressed from the older silent films into the new "talkies," which became an affordable and enormously popular escape.

World War II

While Canada supported Britain by declaring war on Germany in September 1939, the US initially attempted to stay out of the conflict. This changed after the bombing of the Pearl Harbor naval base by Japan in December 1941, marking the entry of the US into the conflict, followed by Mexico in 1942. Nearly 18 million North Americans fought in World War II, both in Europe against Germany and its allies and in the Pacific against Japan. Millions more contributed to the war effort on the home front. Germany capitulated in May 1945, but Japan fought on for three more months until the atomic bombings of Hiroshima and Nagasaki forced their surrender. While North American cities and towns survived the war unscathed, the victory was hard-won, exacting a heavy toll in human life and struggle.

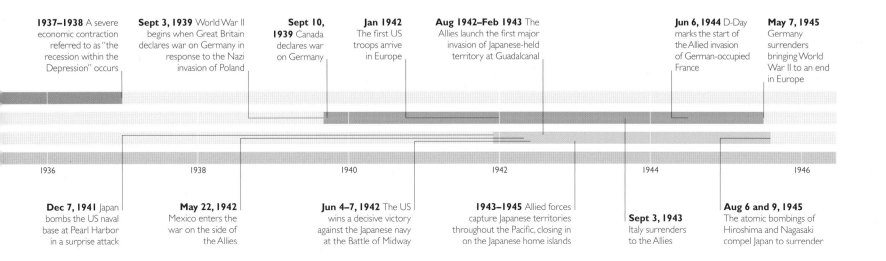

1937–1938 A severe economic contraction referred to as "the recession within the Depression" occurs

Sept 3, 1939 World War II begins when Great Britain declares war on Germany in response to the Nazi invasion of Poland

Sept 10, 1939 Canada declares war on Germany

Jan 1942 The first US troops arrive in Europe

Aug 1942–Feb 1943 The Allies launch the first major invasion of Japanese-held territory at Guadalcanal

Jun 6, 1944 D-Day marks the start of the Allied invasion of German-occupied France

May 7, 1945 Germany surrenders bringing World War II to an end in Europe

1936   1938   1940   1942   1944   1946

Dec 7, 1941 Japan bombs the US naval base at Pearl Harbor in a surprise attack

May 22, 1942 Mexico enters the war on the side of the Allies

Jun 4–7, 1942 The US wins a decisive victory against the Japanese navy at the Battle of Midway

1943–1945 Allied forces capture Japanese territories throughout the Pacific, closing in on the Japanese home islands

Sept 3, 1943 Italy surrenders to the Allies

Aug 6 and 9, 1945 The atomic bombings of Hiroshima and Nagasaki compel Japan to surrender

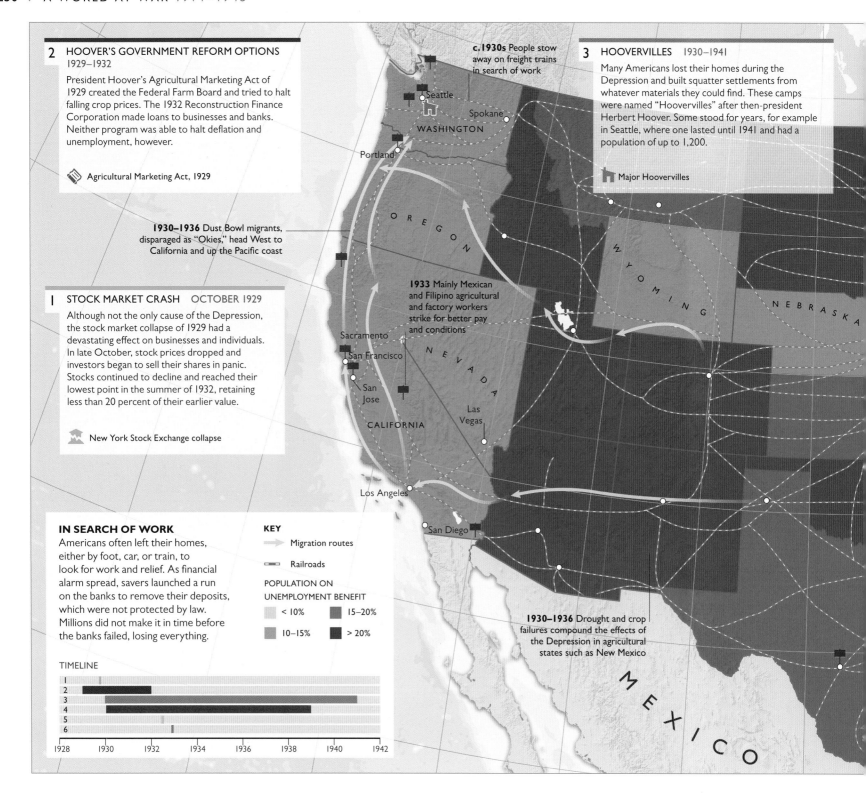

2 HOOVER'S GOVERNMENT REFORM OPTIONS 1929–1932

President Hoover's Agricultural Marketing Act of 1929 created the Federal Farm Board and tried to halt falling crop prices. The 1932 Reconstruction Finance Corporation made loans to businesses and banks. Neither program was able to halt deflation and unemployment, however.

Agricultural Marketing Act, 1929

c.1930s People stow away on freight trains in search of work

3 HOOVERVILLES 1930–1941

Many Americans lost their homes during the Depression and built squatter settlements from whatever materials they could find. These camps were named "Hoovervilles" after then-president Herbert Hoover. Some stood for years, for example in Seattle, where one lasted until 1941 and had a population of up to 1,200.

Major Hoovervilles

1930–1936 Dust Bowl migrants, disparaged as "Okies," head West to California and up the Pacific coast

1933 Mainly Mexican and Filipino agricultural and factory workers strike for better pay and conditions

1 STOCK MARKET CRASH OCTOBER 1929

Although not the only cause of the Depression, the stock market collapse of 1929 had a devastating effect on businesses and individuals. In late October, stock prices dropped and investors began to sell their shares in panic. Stocks continued to decline and reached their lowest point in the summer of 1932, retaining less than 20 percent of their earlier value.

New York Stock Exchange collapse

IN SEARCH OF WORK

Americans often left their homes, either by foot, car, or train, to look for work and relief. As financial alarm spread, savers launched a run on the banks to remove their deposits, which were not protected by law. Millions did not make it in time before the banks failed, losing everything.

KEY

→ Migration routes

Railroads

POPULATION ON UNEMPLOYMENT BENEFIT
< 10%
10–15%
15–20%
> 20%

TIMELINE

1930–1936 Drought and crop failures compound the effects of the Depression in agricultural states such as New Mexico

THE GREAT DEPRESSION

In the 1930s, the US sank into a financial, economic, and social crisis on an unprecedented scale. Millions lost their jobs and their homes. Banks and businesses went bust and the state was forced to intervene. People turned to reforming politicians, including Franklin Roosevelt, in the hope that they would bring relief to the struggling nation.

The 1920s was a decade of progress and prosperity in the US. However, that came to an end with the Wall Street Crash of October 1929, when the country's overstretched economy collapsed in spectacular fashion. Almost overnight, the US—followed by much of the developed world—was plunged into the Great Depression. Caught unawares, the federal government struggled to find solutions as joblessness soared and almost 90,000 businesses closed. More than 9,000 banks failed, taking their customers' savings with them.

Before the Depression, unemployment stood at just 3.1 percent; by 1933, it was at 25 percent. Localities, states, and some private charities provided assistance, but it was not enough. Writers such as Meridel LeSueur chronicled the experiences of women looking for jobs and assistance; musician Woody Guthrie sang of the plight of rural farmers and laborers; and photographers such as Dorothea Lange captured haunting images of human suffering.

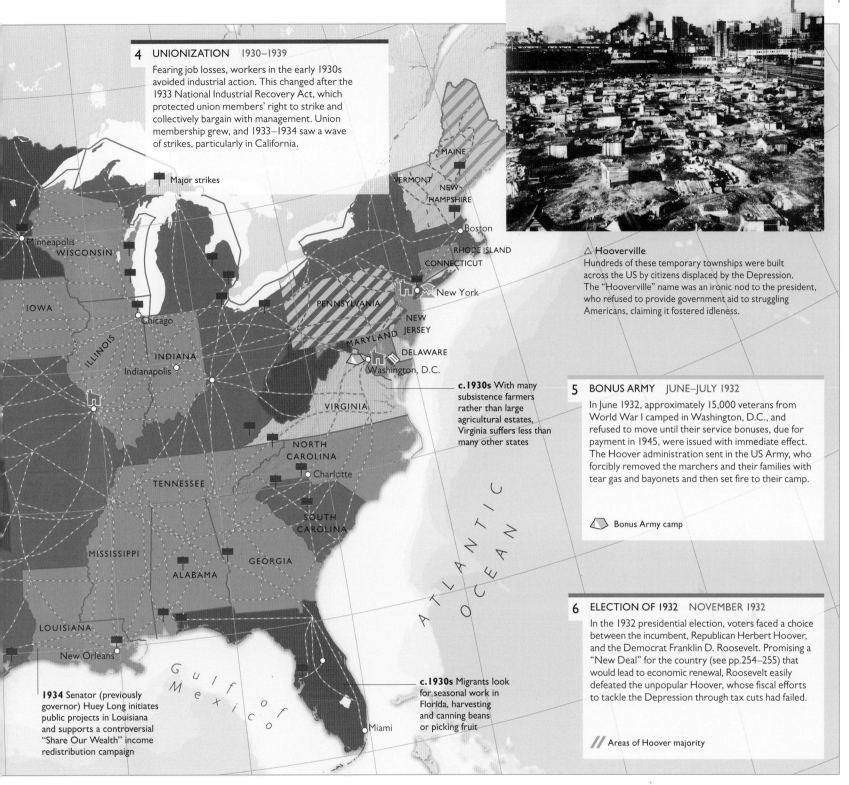

4 UNIONIZATION 1930–1939

Fearing job losses, workers in the early 1930s avoided industrial action. This changed after the 1933 National Industrial Recovery Act, which protected union members' right to strike and collectively bargain with management. Union membership grew, and 1933–1934 saw a wave of strikes, particularly in California.

■ Major strikes

MAINE

VERMONT

NEW HAMPSHIRE

Boston

RHODE ISLAND

CONNECTICUT

Minneapolis
WISCONSIN

New York

IOWA

PENNSYLVANIA

Chicago

NEW JERSEY

INDIANA

MARYLAND DELAWARE

Indianapolis

Washington, D.C.

ILLINOIS

VIRGINIA

c.1930s With many subsistence farmers rather than large agricultural estates, Virginia suffers less than many other states

NORTH CAROLINA

Charlotte

TENNESSEE

SOUTH CAROLINA

MISSISSIPPI

GEORGIA

ALABAMA

LOUISIANA

New Orleans

Gulf of Mexico

Miami

1934 Senator (previously governor) Huey Long initiates public projects in Louisiana and supports a controversial "Share Our Wealth" income redistribution campaign

c.1930s Migrants look for seasonal work in Florida, harvesting and canning beans or picking fruit

A T L A N T I C   O C E A N

△ **Hooverville**
Hundreds of these temporary townships were built across the US by citizens displaced by the Depression. The "Hooverville" name was an ironic nod to the president, who refused to provide government aid to struggling Americans, claiming it fostered idleness.

5 BONUS ARMY JUNE–JULY 1932

In June 1932, approximately 15,000 veterans from World War I camped in Washington, D.C., and refused to move until their service bonuses, due for payment in 1945, were issued with immediate effect. The Hoover administration sent in the US Army, who forcibly removed the marchers and their families with tear gas and bayonets and then set fire to their camp.

⬡ Bonus Army camp

6 ELECTION OF 1932 NOVEMBER 1932

In the 1932 presidential election, voters faced a choice between the incumbent, Republican Herbert Hoover, and the Democrat Franklin D. Roosevelt. Promising a "New Deal" for the country (see pp.254–255) that would lead to economic renewal, Roosevelt easily defeated the unpopular Hoover, whose fiscal efforts to tackle the Depression through tax cuts had failed.

// Areas of Hoover majority

During the Great Depression, farmers, ordinary workers, and—especially—Black Americans were hit hardest. In some places, Black unemployment rose to 50 percent, and there was a rise in racial violence, not just in the South, where the incidence of lynchings rose from 8 in 1932 to 28 in 1933, but in the North, too, some called for firing Black people to make jobs for unemployed white people. In the Midwest, meanwhile, economic hardship and several years of drought from 1930 drove people off the land as the country's fertile prairies were transformed into a "dust bowl" (see pp.252–253).

"Use it up, wear it out, make do or do without."

COMMON DEPRESSION-ERA SAYING

BONNIE PARKER AND CLYDE BARROW

Perhaps the Depression-era's most famous outlaws, Bonnie Parker and Clyde Barrow captured the public's attention with their gang's series of bank robberies, murders, kidnappings, and attempted jailbreaks from 1932 to 1934. The two were public enemies, but many were fascinated by their story, which, although shocking, combined an element of romance with a sense of the desperation that many felt during the depths of the Depression. Bonnie and Clyde were just 23 and 25 years old respectively when they were shot dead by law enforcement in 1934.

Bonnie and Clyde in 1932

DUST BOWL

During the Great Depression, farmers in the southern Great Plains suffered an environmental catastrophe. Drought and poor farming practices led to fertile topsoil being lost in devastating dust storms.

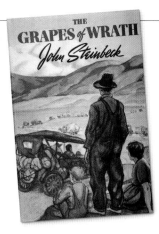

△ **Dust Bowl saga**
John Steinbeck's 1939 novel tells the story of a Dust Bowl family who travel to California in search of a better life, which eludes them at every turn.

Located in the region where Colorado, Kansas, Oklahoma, Texas, and New Mexico meet, the Dust Bowl—a term coined by Associated Press reporter Robert E. Geiger in 1935—saw millions of acres of farming land made barren through the loss of topsoil. In the early 20th century, farmers had plowed up the deep-rooted, moisture-retaining native grasses that kept the land stable and fertile to plant crops such as wheat. When drought struck in the 1930s, winds swept up the dry topsoil, creating a self-intensifying cycle that generated terrifying "black blizzards." Dust blotted out the sun, as the storms left behind a wasteland of dust drifts.

On the road

Their lands compromised, farming families lost their livelihoods. In one of the largest migrations in US history, 2.5 million people set out to search for work. Many ended up in California's Central Valley, where the "Okies"—nominally people from Oklahoma, but applied to Dust Bowl refugees in general—eked out livings in makeshift camps, picking fruit and vegetables for work. From 1933, relief for the Dust Bowl states came from New Deal initiatives (see pp.254–255), hiring displaced farmers to plant trees as windbreaks and resow native grasses. Farming started to pick up in the 1940s, with the return of the rains.

BLACK SUNDAY

One of the most intense black blizzards descended on the town of Beaver in northwestern Oklahoma at about 4 p.m. on Sunday, April 14, 1935. From there it spread south and east across Oklahoma and Texas. Wind speeds in the storm reached nearly 60 mph (100 kph). In places, the air was so thick with dust that people could not see their own hands.

Trekking east
The Dust Bowl uprooted entire families, driving them toward an uncertain future. Photographer Dorothea Lange captured this image in 1936 of a Texan family on the road to Arkansas, where they hoped to find work picking cotton.

THE NEW DEAL

Politicians in the US struggled to formulate a response to the Great Depression—with the exception of Franklin D. Roosevelt, whose wide-ranging program of reform created jobs, steadied the banks, and established a social safety net.

Roosevelt took office as president in March 1933, promising a "New Deal" to help people struggling through the economic disaster plaguing the country. His Relief, Recovery, and Reform program ("Three Rs") provided immediate assistance and the promise of future protection, stability, and growth.

The New Deal marked an important change in federal policy, with the government becoming directly involved in major economic decisions across all sectors, and a host of new organizations providing jobs and support. The Works Progress Administration employed more than 8.5 million people, including artists and writers. The Agricultural Adjustment Act helped farmers, and other projects such as the Tennessee Valley Authority provided both jobs and new sources of electricity to rural areas. The Social Security Act aimed to provide financial assistance and economic security, particularly for the elderly.

Not all people were able to enjoy the benefits of the New Deal, however. Farm laborers and domestic workers, many of them Black, were excluded from the 1935 Social Security Act, for example, and working conditions for millions remained less than ideal. Even so, many initiatives established by the New Deal still exist today.

OLE MAN RIVER

LOCATOR

KEY

1 By 1945 the Mississippi River had a large number of levees in place.

2 The Muskingum Basin reservoirs were built for the Ohio Valley Authority (OVA).

3 An extensive Missouri River basin reservoir system was proposed by 1945.

Triborough Bridge, LaGuardia Airport, the Lincoln Tunnel

Grand Coulee Dam

Bay Bridge

Hoover Dam

Arroyo Seco Parkway

UNITED STATES

Great Smoky Mountains National Park

San Antonio River Walk

Chickamauga Dam

New Orleans City Park

1933–1942 Over its lifetime, the CCC employed 3 million people, including at least 33,000 in California

Gulf of Mexico

Overseas Highway

PARKS, DAMS, BRIDGES, AND HIGHWAYS
The New Deal resulted in the construction of some major pieces of infrastructure, many of which can still be seen. Dams harnessed water power, while highways and bridges improved transportation, and new national parks helped preserve areas of natural beauty.

KEY

Major New Deal works

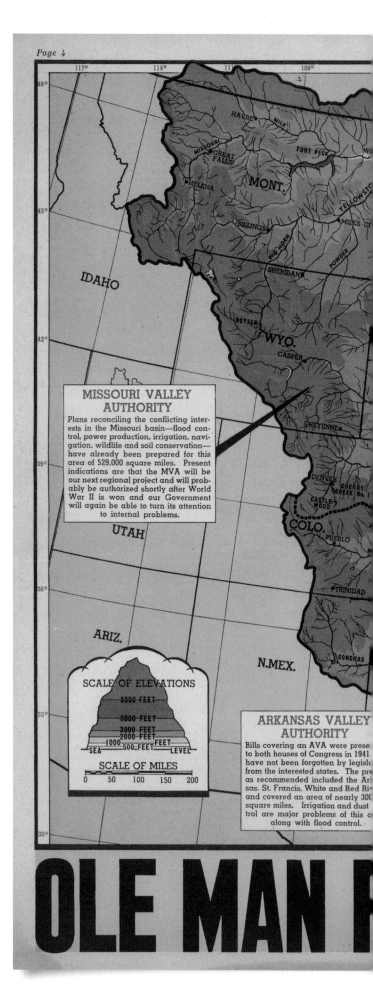

Page 4

IDAHO

MONT.

WYO.

UTAH

ARIZ.

N.MEX.

COLO.

MISSOURI VALLEY AUTHORITY
Plans reconciling the conflicting interests in the Missouri basin—flood control, power production, irrigation, navigation, wildlife and soil conservation—have already been prepared for this area of 529,000 square miles. Present indications are that the MVA will be our next regional project and will probably be authorized shortly after World War II is won and our Government will again be able to turn its attention to internal problems.

SCALE OF ELEVATIONS
8000 FEET
5000 FEET
3000 FEET
2000 FEET
1000 FEET
500 FEET
SEA LEVEL

SCALE OF MILES
0   50   100   150   200

ARKANSAS VALLEY AUTHORITY
Bills covering an AVA were prese to both houses of Congress in 1941 have not been forgotten by legisla from the interested states. The pr as recommended included the Ar sas, St. Francis, White and Red Ri and covered an area of nearly 300 square miles. Irrigation and dust trol are major problems of this o along with flood control.

OLE MAN

Sunday News, June 17, 1945

Page 5

UPPER MISSISSIPPI BASIN

Since only about 13% of the water in the lower river comes from the upper main stream, and the Upper Basin does not suffer from disastrous floods as frequently as the valleys of many of the tributaries, this area of over 175,000 square miles will probably have to wait a long time before a regional authority is created to meet its needs.

OHIO VALLEY AUTHORITY

This area of 164,000 square miles (including the Cumberland River valley, which may eventually become part of the TVA) is getting a great deal of attention as far as flood control is concerned, but not enough to prevent serious floods. The Ohio carries 36% of the water that goes into the main stream. The Tennessee and Cumberland Rivers account for 11%, leaving 25% to be controlled by an OVA when and if it is created. The Corps of Engineers of the Army has a flood control plan for the Ohio Valley and much of it is already realized. The social and economic problems to be met in this thickly populated area will make the OVA a tremendous undertaking, and an extremely important one. Up to the present, the OVA has figured in two bills offered in Congress but is not likely to reach the stage of decisive action until the war has been won.

LEGEND

COMPLETED OR UNDER CONSTRUCTION
LEVEES RESERVOIRS

AUTHORIZED BY CONGRESS
LEVEES RESERVOIRS

TENNESSEE VALLEY AUTHORITY

Created by act of Congress in 1933, the TVA can now boast of accomplishments that make it a model for similar projects all over the world. Flood control affecting an area of approximately 40,000 square miles has been achieved and demonstrated, with manifold social and economic advantages for the more than 4,000,000 inhabitants. Cheaper electricity, soil conservation, improved education, industrial growth and recreational facilities are only some of the objectives that have been attained in this great democratic experiment.

(NEWS map by Staff Artist–Sundberg)

MISSISSIPPI is a big name in American history. The great river and its tributaries have provided many millions of Americans with water, without which man cannot survive. However, the Mississippi brings tragedy as well as blessings to the humans whose lives depend on its whims. For more than 200 years, men have built barriers in an attempt to keep back the flood waters. Much of value has been accomplished, but the occurrence of disastrous floods in the last few months shows that much more remains to be done. This map pictures what has been done, what is already planned for the future, and great projects which are as yet only ideas in the minds of men.

Longitude West 93° of Greenwich

△ The New Deal's water authority projects
This newspaper illustration from 1945 shows how many of the New Deal's largest programs focused on harnessing the power of the Mississippi River and the waterways that drained into it by building dams, reservoirs, and hydroelectric plants. Time, money, and the scale of the projects proposed meant that not all of them would be realized.

Whimsical map of HOLLYWOOD showing STUDIOS, HOMES OF THE STARS AND POINTS OF INTEREST

COPYRIGHT · ALLIED ARTISTS · 1937

THE GOLDEN AGE OF HOLLYWOOD

From its first studio in 1911, Hollywood quickly became the entertainment capital of the world. By the 1930s, its monopoly over production and distribution enabled the release of hundreds of films annually.

During the "golden age" of Hollywood, roughly spanning the late 1920s to the 1960s, the film industry flourished with the emergence of iconic stars and legendary filmmakers. Notable figures such as Charlie Chaplin and Lillian Gish dominated the silent era (c. 1895–1930), while Mae West and Fred Astaire rose to fame with captivating performances in the early "talkies." Hollywood became famous as a place where anyone, from child actors such as Shirley Temple to distinguished stage veterans such as Sidney Poitier, could become an international celebrity. Directors Orson Welles, Cecil B. DeMille, and Alfred Hitchcock were in high demand, and each of the major Hollywood studios cultivated their own roster of directors, writers, and actors.

The movies of this era covered a range of genres, with Westerns, biographies, slapstick comedies, and musicals, and included enduring classics such as *Gone With the Wind* (1939), *Citizen Kane* (1941),

LOCATOR

KEY

1 Warner Bros., Paramount, RKO, and Universal could be found in the area around Sunset and Santa Monica Boulevards.

2 MGM and Twentieth Century-Fox were among the most successful of the "Big Five" studios, with MGM owning six lots.

3 Beverly Hills and Malibu in Los Angeles County, California, were home to many Hollywood stars.

and *Casablanca* (1942). New technologies—color film, audio-video synchronization, and animation—were used in films such as *The Jazz Singer* (1927) and *The Wizard of Oz* (1939). As Hollywood's influence grew, so did public concerns over depictions of sex and violence on screen. In response to this, in 1934 the Hays Code was drawn up, a self-enforced "moral code" for permissible content in Hollywood movies, which was upheld until the 1960s.

◁ **"Whimsical map of Hollywood," 1937**
This map shows the "Big Five"—Warner Bros., Paramount Pictures, RKO Radio Pictures, MGM, and Twentieth Century Fox—and other points of interest.

OSCAR MICHEAUX 1884–1951

Oscar Micheaux is recognized as the first Black US filmmaker. Initially a writer, he directed and produced 44 films throughout his career, beginning in the early 20th century. He ventured into filmmaking with the production of *The Homesteader* (1919)—a film based on his autobiographical novel *The Conquest: The Story of a Negro Pioneer* (1913). Micheaux's work countered negative portrayals of Black experiences through cinema, depicting the complexities and struggles faced by Black Americans. He addressed racial injustice, often using a multiracial or all-Black cast, while aiming to appeal to a wide range of audiences.

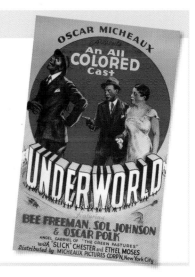

Movie poster for Micheaux's *Underworld* (1937)

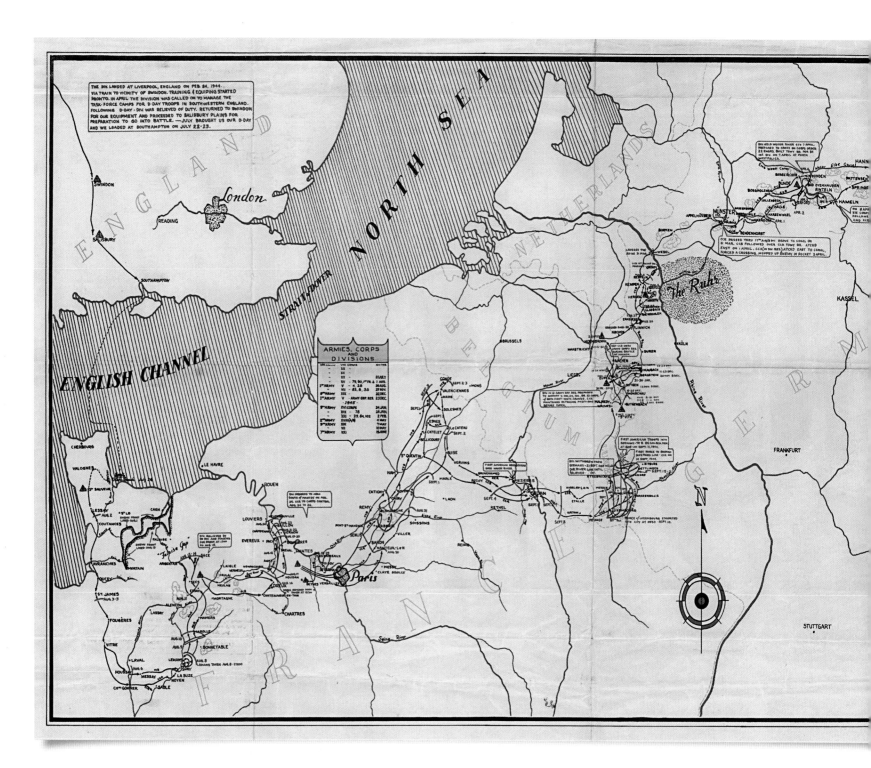

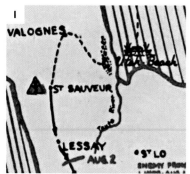

△ **Utah Beach, Normandy**
The 5th Armored Division landed in France at Utah Beach, and headed south to join the Allied advance across France.

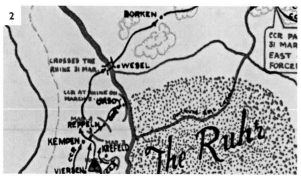

△ **The Battle of the Ruhr Pocket**
The 5th Armored Division crossed the Rhine River on March 30, 1945. Together with other Allied forces who had crossed the river earlier, they helped cut off Germany's principal industrial area of the Ruhr.

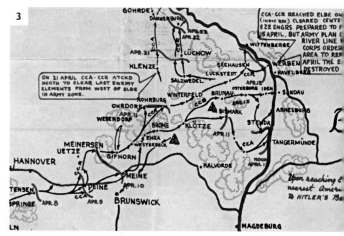

THE ATLANTIC THEATER

Beginning with its large-scale military operations in Europe, World War II transformed the relationship between the US and the rest of the world. The US not only gained the strength needed to help defeat Adolf Hitler's Germany, but also the confidence to use this new power on the world stage.

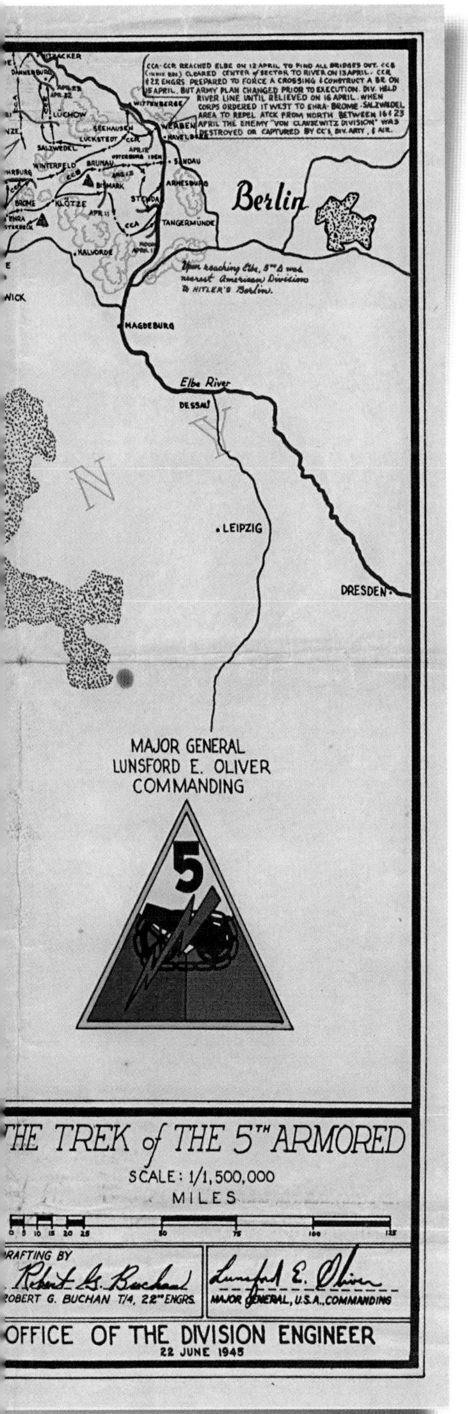

Europe's war began in September 1939 with the German and Soviet conquest of Poland. Poland's allies Britain and France declared war on Germany, as did Canada. Italy and Japan later allied with Germany as the main Axis powers. Despite its official neutrality, the US helped Britain by providing supplies, such as weapons and food, which increased after the Lend Lease Act passed in March 1941. This act sanctioned sharing war provisions with any nation deemed "vital to the defense of the United States." In the spring of 1941, US and Canadian navies began fighting German submarines in the Atlantic. The US declared war on Japan immediately after Pearl Harbor on December 7 (see pp.260–261), but formal hostilities with Germany began when Hitler declared war on the US on December 11. From then on, defeating Germany and Japan became the Allies' priority.

US president Franklin D. Roosevelt authorized the first peacetime military draft in October 1940, while the Two-Ocean Navy Act enacted earlier that year set

LOCATOR

in motion a huge expansion of its naval fleet. Other fighting services in the country followed suit, as did industrial production. The US Air Force became the world's strongest by late 1943, while truly substantial ground forces only saw combat after the D-Day invasion of Normandy, France, on June 6, 1944.

US and Canadian ground forces saw action in North Africa, Italy, and across northern Europe, while US air forces launched raids on German-controlled territory from England. More than 100,000 US troops died in the Atlantic theater.

Left margin map content:

Berlin

MAJOR GENERAL
LUNSFORD E. OLIVER
COMMANDING

5

THE TREK of THE 5TH ARMORED

SCALE: 1/1,500,000
MILES

DRAFTING BY

ROBERT G. BUCHAN T/4, 22ⁿᵈ ENGRS.   MAJOR GENERAL, U.S.A. COMMANDING

OFFICE OF THE DIVISION ENGINEER
22 JUNE 1945

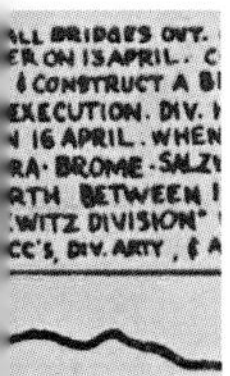

△ **Tactical trek**
The 5th Armored Division landed in Normandy, France, on July 24, 1944, about seven weeks after the main invasion force on D-Day. It finished the war closer to the German capital of Berlin than any other US formation. More than 800 of its soldiers died in action.

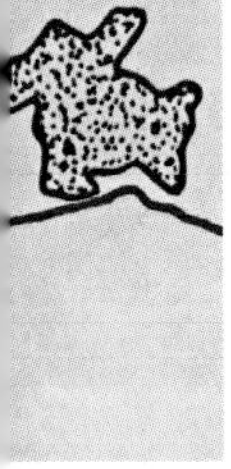

◁ **Strategic halt**
In mid-April, the 5th Armored reached the Elbe River near Berlin. In agreement with Soviet leaders, Allied Commander Dwight D. Eisenhower ordered his forces to halt their advance at this point, allowing Russian forces to take Berlin. Germany finally surrendered to the Western Allies on May 7.

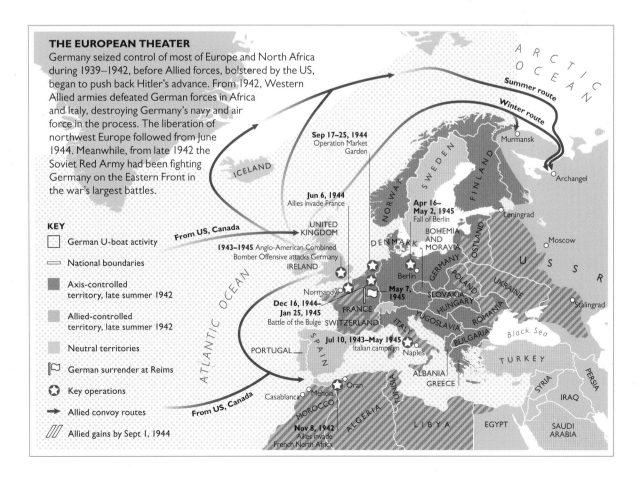

THE EUROPEAN THEATER
Germany seized control of most of Europe and North Africa during 1939–1942, before Allied forces, bolstered by the US, began to push back Hitler's advance. From 1942, Western Allied armies defeated German forces in Africa and Italy, destroying Germany's navy and air force in the process. The liberation of northwest Europe followed from June 1944. Meanwhile, from late 1942 the Soviet Red Army had been fighting Germany on the Eastern Front in the war's largest battles.

KEY
- German U-boat activity
- National boundaries
- Axis-controlled territory, late summer 1942
- Allied-controlled territory, late summer 1942
- Neutral territories
- German surrender at Reims
- Key operations
- Allied convoy routes
- Allied gains by Sept 1, 1944

Map labels:
Sep 17–25, 1944 Operation Market Garden
Jun 6, 1944 Allies invade France
Apr 16–May 2, 1945 Fall of Berlin
From US, Canada
1943–1945 Anglo-American Combined Bomber Offensive attacks Germany
Dec 16, 1944–Jan 25, 1945 Battle of the Bulge
May 7, 1945
Jul 10, 1943–May 1945 Italian campaign
Nov 8, 1942 Allies invade French North Africa
From US, Canada
Summer route
Winter route
Murmansk
Archangel
Leningrad
Moscow
Stalingrad

WORLD WAR II IN THE US

Mostly removed from the threat of bombing, the US was less directly affected by the war than other Allied powers. Although their forces lost tens of thousands, wartime production led to a booming economy.

△ **Pearl Harbor poster**
Direct US involvement in the war began with Japan's surprise attack on the US military base at Pearl Harbor in Hawaii on December 7, 1941. Roosevelt deemed it a "day that will live in infamy."

Compared to other countries, the US was slow to recover from the Great Depression of the 1930s, but by the end of World War II the country had been reinvigorated. Every statistic told a similar story. More than 17 percent of the workforce was unemployed in 1939, but by 1945 unemployment was below two percent, and average wages had risen more than 50 percent in real terms. The US armed forces were the most lavishly equipped in the world, and their supplies were vital to all of the other Allied nations.

Government contracts were issued at a markup, so industry prospered and agricultural prices soared. A mixture of social changes accompanied the economic boom. Many more women chose to work outside the home and support the war effort, although they still earned about a third less than men in comparable jobs. Wages of Black Americans rose faster than those of white Americans, largely due to the fact that their starting wages had been lower; the war also saw an increase in pay for war-related factory jobs. However, a large racial pay gap remained, and racism was as pernicious as ever. Personnel in the armed forces moved where the military sent them, and mixed with people from different backgrounds. So, too, did the millions of civilians who relocated to find war work. This led to changes in social attitudes in the direction of greater tolerance.

The US ended the war victorious, wealthier than it had ever been, and with goodwill from Allied and liberated nations. However, times were not easy for many people, and shortages of housing, schools and teachers, and health and childcare facilities were felt everywhere.

JAPANESE IMMIGRANTS IN THE US AND CANADA

During the war, the US and Canada detained around 150,000 people of Japanese descent—mostly American or Canadian citizens—and sent them to concentration camps. They were labeled as spies or saboteurs. Official inquiries in the 1980s found that racism motivated these events, and survivors received compensation.

Making parts for Douglas A-20 bombers, Long Beach, 1942
The Douglas Aircraft Company opened its Long Beach plant in late 1941. Its workforce grew dramatically during the war, with women making up around 40 percent of staff.

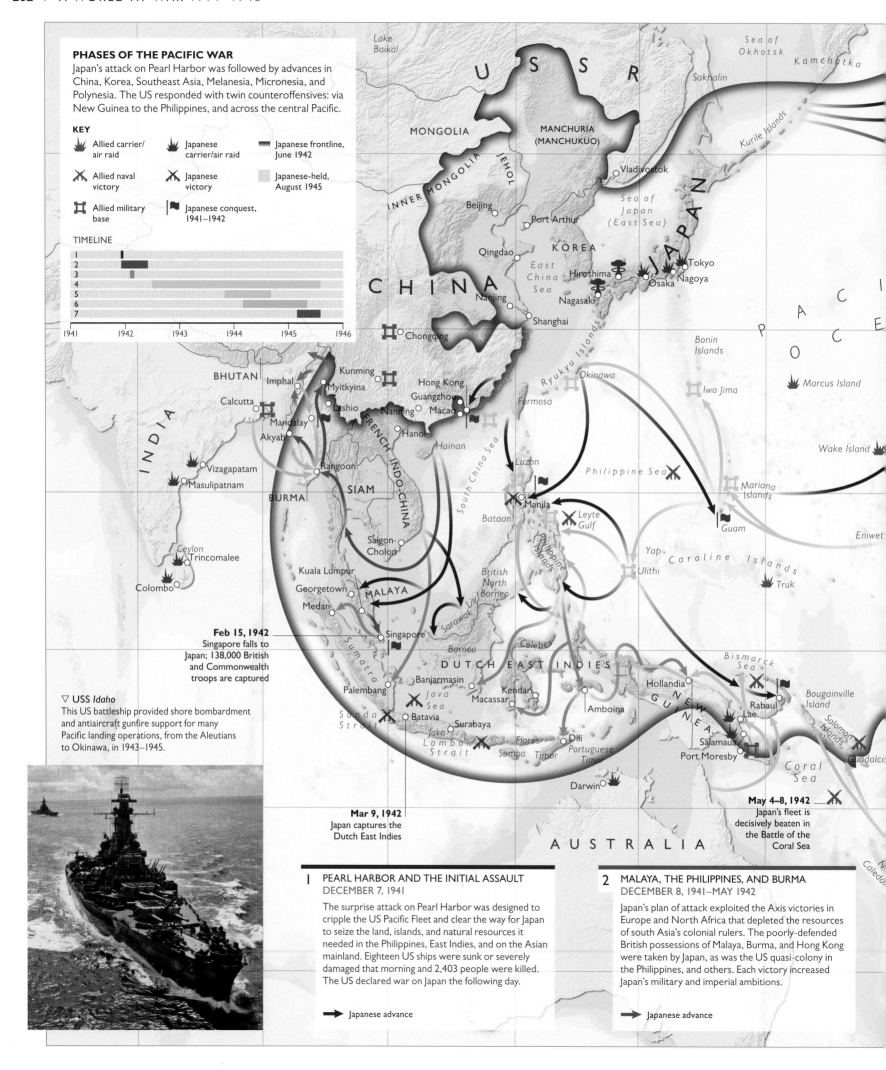

PHASES OF THE PACIFIC WAR

Japan's attack on Pearl Harbor was followed by advances in China, Korea, Southeast Asia, Melanesia, Micronesia, and Polynesia. The US responded with twin counteroffensives: via New Guinea to the Philippines, and across the central Pacific.

KEY

- Allied carrier/air raid
- Allied naval victory
- Allied military base
- Japanese carrier/air raid
- Japanese victory
- Japanese conquest, 1941–1942
- Japanese frontline, June 1942
- Japanese-held, August 1945

TIMELINE

1
2
3
4
5
6
7

1941 1942 1943 1944 1945 1946

Feb 15, 1942
Singapore falls to Japan; 138,000 British and Commonwealth troops are captured

▽ **USS Idaho**
This US battleship provided shore bombardment and antiaircraft gunfire support for many Pacific landing operations, from the Aleutians to Okinawa, in 1943–1945.

Mar 9, 1942
Japan captures the Dutch East Indies

May 4–8, 1942
Japan's fleet is decisively beaten in the Battle of the Coral Sea

1 PEARL HARBOR AND THE INITIAL ASSAULT
DECEMBER 7, 1941

The surprise attack on Pearl Harbor was designed to cripple the US Pacific Fleet and clear the way for Japan to seize the land, islands, and natural resources it needed in the Philippines, East Indies, and on the Asian mainland. Eighteen US ships were sunk or severely damaged that morning and 2,403 people were killed. The US declared war on Japan the following day.

→ Japanese advance

2 MALAYA, THE PHILIPPINES, AND BURMA
DECEMBER 8, 1941–MAY 1942

Japan's plan of attack exploited the Axis victories in Europe and North Africa that depleted the resources of south Asia's colonial rulers. The poorly-defended British possessions of Malaya, Burma, and Hong Kong were taken by Japan, as was the US quasi-colony in the Philippines, and others. Each victory increased Japan's military and imperial ambitions.

→ Japanese advance

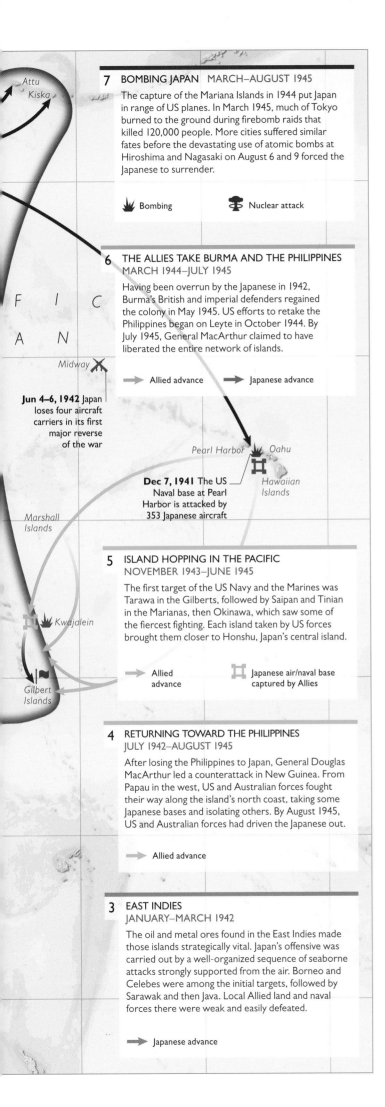

7 BOMBING JAPAN MARCH–AUGUST 1945

The capture of the Mariana Islands in 1944 put Japan in range of US planes. In March 1945, much of Tokyo burned to the ground during firebomb raids that killed 120,000 people. More cities suffered similar fates before the devastating use of atomic bombs at Hiroshima and Nagasaki on August 6 and 9 forced the Japanese to surrender.

- Bombing
- Nuclear attack

6 THE ALLIES TAKE BURMA AND THE PHILIPPINES MARCH 1944–JULY 1945

Having been overrun by the Japanese in 1942, Burma's British and imperial defenders regained the colony in May 1945. US efforts to retake the Philippines began on Leyte in October 1944. By July 1945, General MacArthur claimed to have liberated the entire network of islands.

- Allied advance
- Japanese advance

Jun 4–6, 1942 Japan loses four aircraft carriers in its first major reverse of the war

Pearl Harbor · Oahu

Dec 7, 1941 The US Naval base at Pearl Harbor is attacked by 353 Japanese aircraft

Hawaiian Islands

Marshall Islands

Kwajalein

5 ISLAND HOPPING IN THE PACIFIC NOVEMBER 1943–JUNE 1945

The first target of the US Navy and the Marines was Tarawa in the Gilberts, followed by Saipan and Tinian in the Marianas, then Okinawa, which saw some of the fiercest fighting. Each island taken by US forces brought them closer to Honshu, Japan's central island.

- Allied advance
- Japanese air/naval base captured by Allies

Gilbert Islands

4 RETURNING TOWARD THE PHILIPPINES JULY 1942–AUGUST 1945

After losing the Philippines to Japan, General Douglas MacArthur led a counterattack in New Guinea. From Papau in the west, US and Australian forces fought their way along the island's north coast, taking some Japanese bases and isolating others. By August 1945, US and Australian forces had driven the Japanese out.

- Allied advance

3 EAST INDIES JANUARY–MARCH 1942

The oil and metal ores found in the East Indies made those islands strategically vital. Japan's offensive was carried out by a well-organized sequence of seaborne attacks strongly supported from the air. Borneo and Celebes were among the initial targets, followed by Sarawak and then Java. Local Allied land and naval forces there were weak and easily defeated.

- Japanese advance

WORLD WAR II IN THE PACIFIC

Throughout the 1930s, the US viewed Japan's empire-building with suspicion. The US finally acted in late 1940, imposing a crippling trade embargo on Japan after it invaded French Indochina. As its economy worsened, Japan staked everything on an audacious attack that changed the course of the war.

On December 7, 1941, Japan attacked the US naval base at Pearl Harbor, propelling the US into the war. The Japanese admiral Isoroku Yamamoto had warned his superiors that the country's navy would only be able to win battles for six months before the US would recover and crush his fleet. His prediction proved correct.

By June 1942, Japanese advances had been halted after the battles of the Coral Sea and Midway; after this, the country was in retreat following reverses at Guadalcanal in the Solomon Islands in the second half of 1942. From this point, the empire that Japan's leaders called the "Greater East Asia Co-Prosperity Sphere" began to shrink as the US adopted a twin-track strategy against it. The army advanced by land along the north coast of New Guinea on its way to reconquering the Philippines, while a naval-led force drove across the Pacific, capturing island bases on the way.

From March 1945, Japan's cities were devastated by US air raids from airfields in the Marianas in preparation for an invasion of the Japanese Home Islands planned for later that year. This changed in August 1945, when the atomic bombing of Hiroshima and Nagasaki (see pp.264–265) and the simultaneous Soviet invasion of Manchuria forced Japan's surrender.

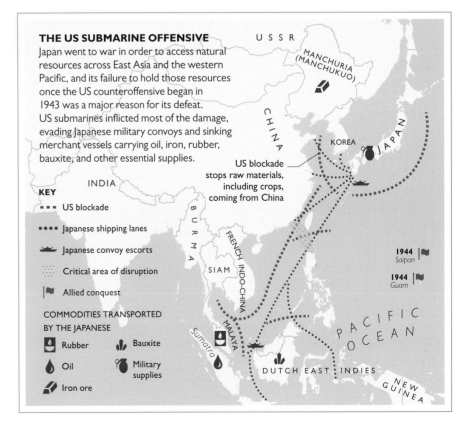

THE US SUBMARINE OFFENSIVE
Japan went to war in order to access natural resources across East Asia and the western Pacific, and its failure to hold those resources once the US counteroffensive began in 1943 was a major reason for its defeat. US submarines inflicted most of the damage, evading Japanese military convoys and sinking merchant vessels carrying oil, iron, rubber, bauxite, and other essential supplies.

US blockade stops raw materials, including crops, coming from China

KEY
- ---- US blockade
- •••• Japanese shipping lanes
- Japanese convoy escorts
- Critical area of disruption
- Allied conquest

COMMODITIES TRANSPORTED BY THE JAPANESE
- Rubber
- Oil
- Iron ore
- Bauxite
- Military supplies

1944 Saipan
1944 Guam

DEVELOPING NUCLEAR ARMS

In the 1930s, physicists theorized that collisions between atomic particles could develop into chain reactions giving off huge amounts of energy. World War II drove this research to the creation of atomic weapons.

The first major steps to turn prewar theories into reality were taken in Britain. During 1940–1941, government-backed researchers there concluded that an atom bomb was a practical possibility and worked out a plan to try to make one. Two types of bomb were considered—one based on uranium and the other on plutonium, a newly created element.

The British shared their conclusions with the US leadership, and this helped persuade President Roosevelt to set serious atom bomb research in motion in October 1941. By the fall of 1942, this work was known as the Manhattan Project and was commanded by a US Army engineer, General Leslie Groves. Its main research and development base was established at Los Alamos, New Mexico.

The researchers worked frantically, fearing that Germany might develop an atom bomb first, but the latter devoted few resources to the possibility and made no progress, as did Japan. The Soviets, in turn, did little themselves during the war but gained much information from spies targeting the Western research. They used this knowledge successfully in their postwar atomic developments.

After the successful test of the first device at Alamogordo, New Mexico in July 1945, the US used two atom bombs against Japan. A uranium-based weapon obliterated much of Hiroshima on August 6, and a plutonium weapon was dropped on Nagasaki on August 9. Around 80,000 people were killed in the first moments of the Hiroshima attack, a horrific toll that marked the start of a new era in warfare.

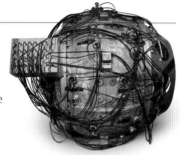

△ **The first atomic device**
"Gadget," seen here in replica, was a plutonium-fueled implosion weapon, c. 5 ft (1.5 m) across, with an explosive yield equivalent to 24,000 tons of TNT explosive.

J. ROBERT OPPENHEIMER 1904–1967

Known as the "father of the atomic bomb," Oppenheimer was an American theoretical physicist who, in 1943, became scientific director of the Los Alamos research establishment. He was a brilliant organizer and an inspirational leader, but his later reservations about the use and proliferation of nuclear weapons—and his prewar association with left-wing groups in the US—led to his security clearance being revoked in the 1950s sand ended his government career.

0.016 SEC.
N
100 METERS

0.090 SEC.
N
100 METERS

Testing the first bomb
A time-lapse showing the sequence of the explosion of "Gadget" at Alamogordo, New Mexico, on July 16, 1945. This device was similar in explosive power to the bomb, codenamed "Fat Man," dropped on Nagasaki.

4.0 SEC.
N
100 METERS

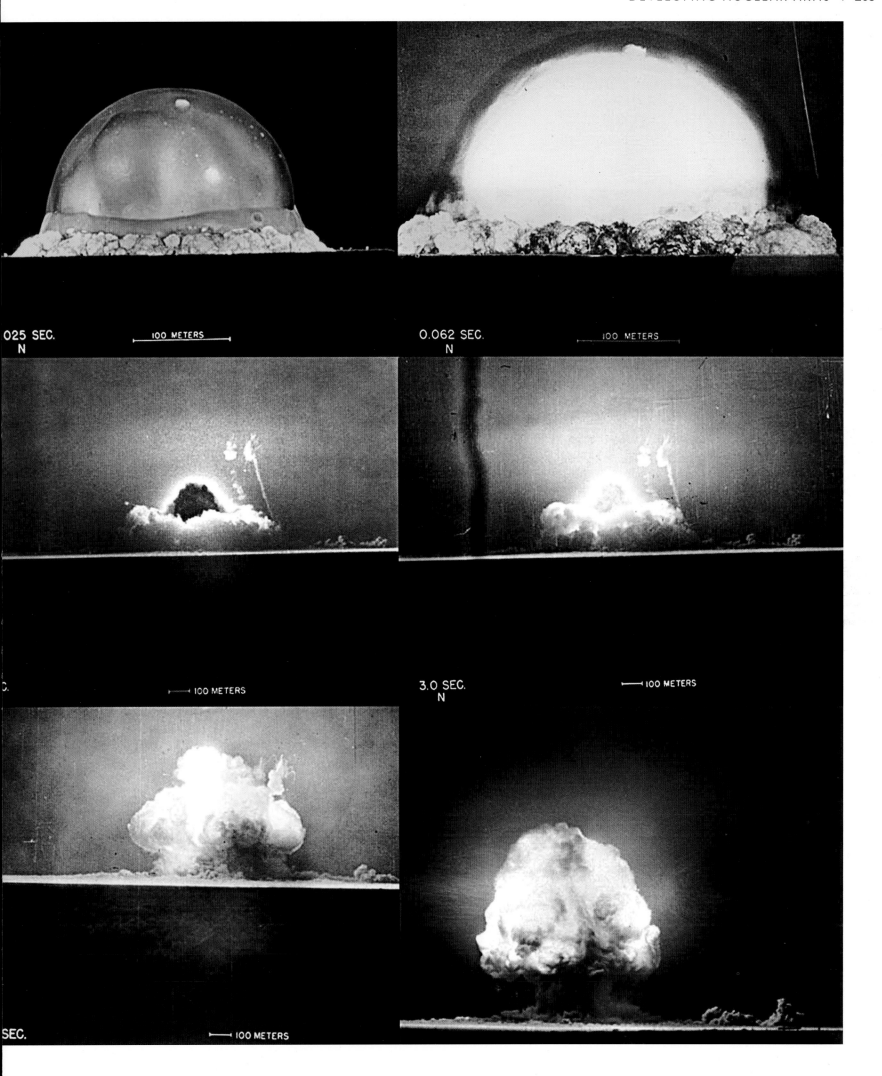

025 SEC.
N

100 METERS

0.062 SEC.
N

100 METERS

100 METERS

3.0 SEC.
N

100 METERS

SEC.

100 METERS

POSTWAR NORTH AMERICA

NORTH AMERICA ENTERED A TIME OF PROSPERITY AFTER WORLD WAR II, ALTHOUGH INEQUALITIES PERSISTED. ON THE WORLD STAGE, OLD ALLIANCES SWIFTLY TURNED TO THE MUTUAL ANTAGONISM OF THE COLD WAR, WITH THE EVER-PRESENT THREAT OF NUCLEAR WARFARE.

PEACE AND PROSPERITY

The end of World War II ushered in an era of extraordinary prosperity but also geopolitical tension for the nations of North America. While the postwar boom enriched and transformed the societies of the US, Canada, and Mexico, this new abundance was not shared by all.

△ **"European reconstruction"**
This poster from Italy commemorates the Marshall Plan for the rebuilding of western European countries after the destruction they suffered during World War II.

With the surrender of Germany and Japan in 1945, the most destructive war in human history came to an end. The world was forever changed, not merely by the defeat of fascism, but also by the political and economic transformations that would remake societies around the globe.

Postwar powers

Almost at once, the fragile wartime alliance between the world's two superpowers, the US and the Soviet Union, broke down into bitter rivalry, with each country pouring resources into Europe and Asia in a bid to impose their contrasting political and economic worldviews. While the US focused on the war-shattered countries of western Europe, the Soviet Union steadily increased its control over its neighbors in central and eastern Europe. By 1955, the world's major nations were divided into opposing military alliances: the US-backed North Atlantic Treaty Organization (NATO) and the pro-Soviet Warsaw Pact.

Across the Atlantic, the end of World War II left the countries of North America in an enviable

position. In contrast to a devastated Europe, North America itself had been virtually untouched by the war, with its cities and towns, industry, agriculture, and infrastructure all intact. This set the stage for an era of unprecedented peace and prosperity led by a triumphant US.

Economic boom

For the next 25 years, the US, Canada, and Mexico experienced a period of transformation in technology, society, and culture, powered by record economic growth. Living standards in the US and Canada were the highest in the world. The US government passed the G.I. Bill, which offered funding for higher education and loans to buy homes for servicemen returning to civilian life. This created a highly skilled workforce as the number of US citizens holding college degrees doubled from 1940 to 1950. Mexico, which also exited World War II in a strong economic position, embarked on a major expansion of its economy, industries, and cities that came to be called the "Mexican miracle."

Mass prosperity lifted millions into the middle class and brought about a revolution in the way people lived, worked, shopped, and traveled. New supermarkets and

> *"Our policy is directed … against hunger, poverty, desperation, and chaos."*
>
> GEORGE MARSHALL, JUNE 1947

◁ **Celebrating the Warsaw Pact**
This 1980 badge from East Germany celebrates the 25th anniversary of the foundation of the Warsaw Pact, the military alliance of the Soviet bloc.

A SUPERPOWER OF CONTRASTS

In the decades after World War II, the US occupied a position of economic, military and political dominance on the world stage. At home, its citizens enjoyed the fruits of mass prosperity, while abroad the country took on the leading role in an aggressive rivalry against the Communist bloc. While the US often portrayed itself as the champion of liberty, opportunity, and equality, the opulence of postwar US was unevenly distributed.

1944 The Bretton Woods Agreement establishes a system of financial exchange based on the US dollar

1944 The Servicemen's Readjustment Act, known as the G.I. Bill, allows returning servicemen to access education and loans

1946–1964 A "baby boom" begins, with more than 76 million births during this period

Mar 5, 1946 Winston Churchill gives a speech in Missouri using the metaphor of an "iron curtain" to describe Soviet influence over central and eastern Europe

1949 The Interstate Highway Act provides for the creation of a national road network

ECONOMIC PROSPERITY

ORIGINS OF THE COLD WAR

INDIGENOUS AND MIGRANT ISSUES

1940

1945

1950

1942–1964 The Bracero program allows Mexican workers to come to the US on temporary work permits

Jul–Aug 1945 The Potsdam Conference between the US, UK, and USSR meets to make a plan for the postwar world

Aug 1945 The US drops atomic bombs on the Japanese cities of Hiroshima and Nagasaki

1947 The Chinese Exclusion Act in Canada is repealed; significant barriers remain for Chinese migrants

◁ Oil in the Gulf of Mexico
Workers operate oil drilling equipment in the Gulf of Mexico in the 1960s. Improvements in technology throughout the 20th century have enabled US and Mexican oil companies to extend operations farther offshore in the Gulf of Mexico.

▽ Life behind the wheel, 1970s
Large automobiles and interstate highways became symbols of US affluence during the postwar era and beyond. Here a busy section of the Kennedy Expressway in the metropolitan area of Chicago, Illinois, runs alongside commuter rail tracks.

shopping malls competed with traditional shopping areas for the money of affluent North Americans. One of the main symbols of this new prosperity was the automobile, which became synonymous with the US way of life. The US automotive industry, which produced more than 80 percent of the world's cars, seemed to embody the success of the US free enterprise system in the postwar world. More than ever before, cars enabled people to live farther away from their workplaces, leading to the growth of suburbs as affluent North Americans sought refuge from chaotic and densely populated major cities. Automobiles also impacted the landscape of the US with the coming of the Interstate Highway System in 1956.

A new era of inequality

However, the prosperity of the postwar era was distributed unevenly. Indigenous peoples continued to struggle against persistent inequalities in legal recognition and status, economic opportunities, and access to education and health care. As they resisted policies of assimilation promoted by the US and Canadian governments in the decades following World War II, Indigenous communities continued to be among the most marginalized people in North American society. Migrant communities faced similar challenges. Despite the reliance of the US economy on immigrant labor, people of migrant backgrounds faced discrimination, exploitation, cultural exclusion, and the impact of restrictive immigration and citizenship laws.

1950–1970s Mexico undergoes a period of economic growth

1949 The North Atlantic Treaty Organization (NATO), an alliance of 10 western European countries with the US and Canada, is founded

1960 The US share of the global economy (Gross Domestic Product) peaks at 40 percent

1975 The Indian Self-Determination and Education Assistance Act delegates significant authority to tribal governments, a major reversal of the policy of termination

1960

1965

1970

1975

1954 Operation Wetback targets Mexican migrants in the largest mass deportation in US history

1956 The Indian Relocation Act is passed in the US to encourage Indigenous Americans to leave reservations and move to cities

1955 The Soviet Union establishes its own, anti-western military alliance, the Warsaw Pact

1965 The Immigration and Nationality Act abolishes the quota system of immigration in the US

1973 A major recession begins, marking the end of the postwar economic boom

Braceros in 1956
As part of the Bracero Program, Mexican laborers bound for the US await processing in Monterrey, Mexico. While the program included protections for laborers from unfair contracts, many still endured discrimination and exploitation in the US.

POSTWAR MIGRATIONS

The economic and social changes that occurred in the years after World War II meant that migration, both within the US and from nations abroad, continued to play an important role in the shaping of the country.

△ **A Cuban sports star**
Cuban-born Camilo Pascual played for a number of US baseball teams from the 1950s to the 1970s, including the Los Angeles Dodgers.

In contrast to the phases of relatively unrestricted immigration during the 19th and early 20th centuries, migration in the era of World War II and its aftermath was strictly controlled by federal policy that limited the numbers and national origins of prospective immigrants. While the Immigration and Nationality Act of 1952 repealed some racial exclusions (see pp.142–143) and allowed existing Asian immigrants in the US to become citizens, it reinforced a system of discriminatory quotas that effectively barred all but a few people outside of northern and western Europe from migrating to the US legally.

However, demographic shifts were underway from internal migrations, such as the Great Migration of Black Americans from the South (see pp.246–247). The Bracero Program had started in 1942 to bring temporary agricultural workers from Mexico, known as *braceros*, to the US. Originally meant to last until the end of World War II, it continued until 1964, with more than 4.5 million workers hired. Critics charged that immigration policy was unacceptably discriminatory, especially in the context of the growing Civil Rights Movement. A law abolishing the quota system and reforming immigration policy was signed by President Lyndon Johnson in 1965.

PUERTO RICAN LIFE IN THE US

Inhabitants of Puerto Rico, who had been granted full US citizenship since 1917, began moving to the US mainland during the 1950s in response to the collapse of the plantation economy on the island. Many settled in New York City, where a Puerto Rican neighborhood in northeast Manhattan became known as Spanish Harlem. The island's people, music, cuisine, and culture have been celebrated in the city since 1958 at the annual Puerto Rican Day Parade.

Puerto Rican folk singers in the US, 1939

THE POSTWAR WORLD

In the aftermath of World War II, the US and the Soviet Union emerged as superpowers, each seeking allies as they entered into a tense rivalry over conflicting ideologies. Nations also formed new regional and global alliances, such as the United Nations, to guard against future aggression.

After the Allies won World War II, they occupied different regions that had previously been under Axis control (see pp.260–261). The US and United Soviet Socialist Republic (USSR) started a "Cold War" of mutual antagonism without direct conflict (see pp.284–285). The two nations often involved wartime allies or areas they occupied in this conflict. Some areas, such as Korea (see pp.288–289), would permanently bear the marks of these postwar divisions. The US turned to many nations in Western Europe and the Western Hemisphere to form the North Atlantic Treaty Organization (NATO), while the USSR assembled the Warsaw Pact nations.

Much of the world needed help in recovering from World War II, and the US provided economic aid to many countries through the Marshall Plan (see below). The International Military Tribunal (IMT) was formed, and judges from Allied nations prosecuted former Axis leaders accused of war crimes and crimes against humanity. This marked a major shift in global relations, as countries came together to exert power over leaders and officials of other sovereign nations. Organizations such as IMT and the newly formed United Nations (UN) ushered in a new era of international cooperation and the willingness to intervene in, and on behalf of, other countries.

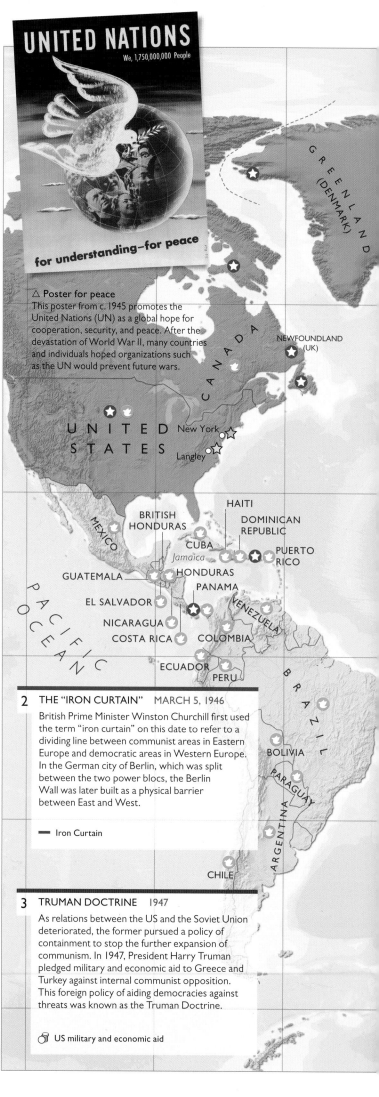

△ Poster for peace
This poster from c.1945 promotes the United Nations (UN) as a global hope for cooperation, security, and peace. After the devastation of World War II, many countries and individuals hoped organizations such as the UN would prevent future wars.

2 THE "IRON CURTAIN" MARCH 5, 1946
British Prime Minister Winston Churchill first used the term "iron curtain" on this date to refer to a dividing line between communist areas in Eastern Europe and democratic areas in Western Europe. In the German city of Berlin, which was split between the two power blocs, the Berlin Wall was later built as a physical barrier between East and West.

— Iron Curtain

3 TRUMAN DOCTRINE 1947
As relations between the US and the Soviet Union deteriorated, the former pursued a policy of containment to stop the further expansion of communism. In 1947, President Harry Truman pledged military and economic aid to Greece and Turkey against internal communist opposition. This foreign policy of aiding democracies against threats was known as the Truman Doctrine.

US military and economic aid

MARSHALL PLAN
George Marshall, the US Secretary of State, designed a program to provide economic relief to countries recovering from World War II, with the US sending more than $13 billion to Europe beginning in 1948. This aid helped provide stability in Europe and ensured the recipients became reliable trading partners for the US.

KEY

☐ Countries that received US aid

Aid received in million dollars (figures may vary as this was not the only aid received)

The USSR blocks Marshall Plan aid to countries in Eastern Europe

29 ICELAND
225 NORWAY
107 SWEDEN
273 DENMARK
1,083 NETHERLANDS
148 IRELAND
3,190 UNITED KINGDOM
FINLAND
559 BELGIUM
LUXEMBOURG
1,391 WEST GERMANY
EAST GERMANY
POLAND
CZECHOSLOVAKIA
U S S R
678 AUSTRIA
HUNGARY
SWITZERLAND
2,714 FRANCE
ROMANIA
YUGOSLAVIA
BULGARIA
1,509 ITALY
ALBANIA
51 PORTUGAL
707 GREECE
225 TURKEY

A long occupation leaves Belgium and Luxembourg in need of help

Switzerland is in a good economic position because it remained neutral during the war

Due to Franco's Axis sympathies, neutral Spain was deemed ineligible for aid

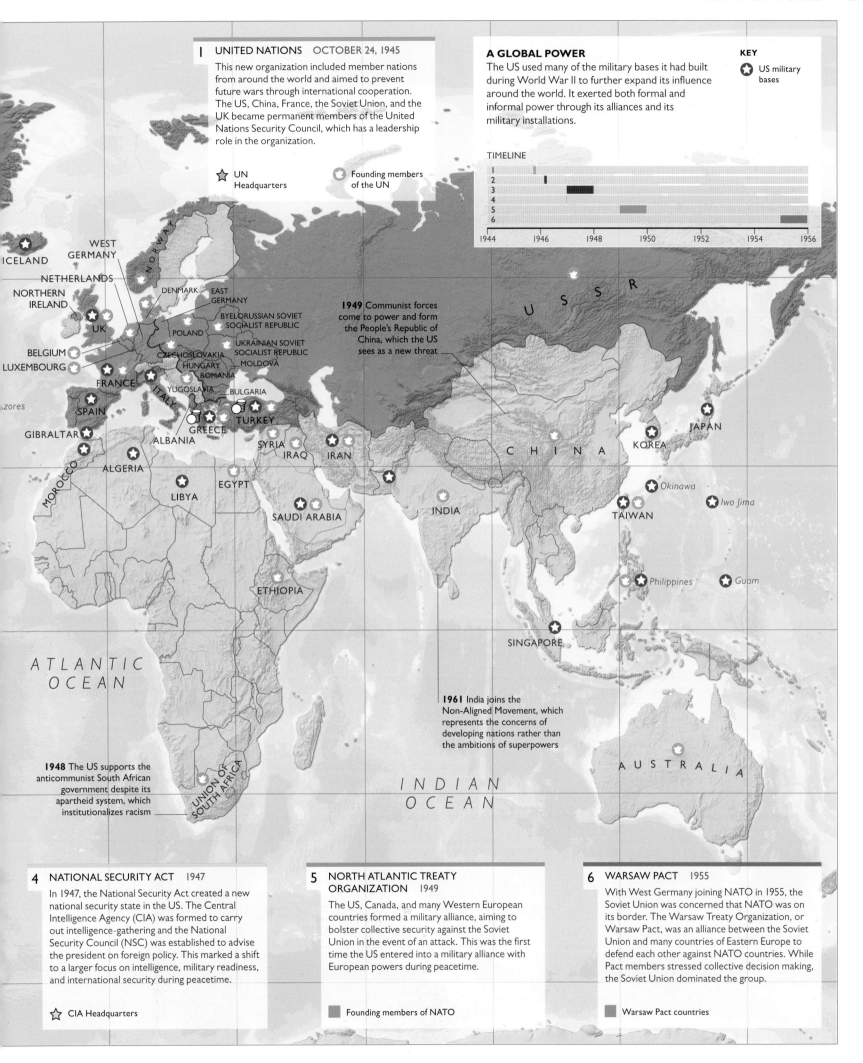

UNITED NATIONS OCTOBER 24, 1945

This new organization included member nations from around the world and aimed to prevent future wars through international cooperation. The US, China, France, the Soviet Union, and the UK became permanent members of the United Nations Security Council, which has a leadership role in the organization.

☆ UN Headquarters

◉ Founding members of the UN

A GLOBAL POWER

The US used many of the military bases it had built during World War II to further expand its influence around the world. It exerted both formal and informal power through its alliances and its military installations.

KEY

★ US military bases

TIMELINE

	1944	1946	1948	1950	1952	1954	1956
1							
2							
3							
4							
5							
6							

1949 Communist forces come to power and form the People's Republic of China, which the US sees as a new threat

1961 India joins the Non-Aligned Movement, which represents the concerns of developing nations rather than the ambitions of superpowers

1948 The US supports the anticommunist South African government despite its apartheid system, which institutionalizes racism

4 NATIONAL SECURITY ACT 1947

In 1947, the National Security Act created a new national security state in the US. The Central Intelligence Agency (CIA) was formed to carry out intelligence-gathering and the National Security Council (NSC) was established to advise the president on foreign policy. This marked a shift to a larger focus on intelligence, military readiness, and international security during peacetime.

☆ CIA Headquarters

5 NORTH ATLANTIC TREATY ORGANIZATION 1949

The US, Canada, and many Western European countries formed a military alliance, aiming to bolster collective security against the Soviet Union in the event of an attack. This was the first time the US entered into a military alliance with European powers during peacetime.

▪ Founding members of NATO

6 WARSAW PACT 1955

With West Germany joining NATO in 1955, the Soviet Union was concerned that NATO was on its border. The Warsaw Treaty Organization, or Warsaw Pact, was an alliance between the Soviet Union and many countries of Eastern Europe to defend each other against NATO countries. While Pact members stressed collective decision making, the Soviet Union dominated the group.

▪ Warsaw Pact countries

PROSPERITY IN MEXICO

Mexico experienced an economic boom in the decades after World War II. This period, called the "Mexican Miracle," saw Mexico became a more prosperous, urban, and industrial country.

△ **War poster**
Mexico provided the US with extensive material support during World War II, including sending combat troops to fight in the Pacific, and workers to help fill US labor shortages.

From the 1940s to the 1970s Mexico went through a period of sustained economic growth and rapid industrialization. As a member of the Allies during World War II, it provided labor and resources to the war effort, which boosted the Mexican economy and allowed the government to pursue ambitious policies after the war ended.

El milagro Mexicano (the Mexican Miracle) had a transformative effect on the country: GDP expanded by over six percent per year from 1952 to 1981. Economic growth was helped by the stable political situation throughout the period, in the form of virtual one-party rule by the Institutional Revolutionary Party (PRI). The government built up the country's industrial and manufacturing base, and prioritized commercial agriculture. More than ever, Mexico was becoming a capitalist, consumer society. This came at the cost of greater inequality, the erosion of workers' rights, an emphasis on urban rather than rural prosperity, and increased political corruption. The accumulation of vast foreign debt in the 1970s by the Mexican government led to a major economic crisis in 1982, and the end of the miracle (see pp.324–325).

THE MEXICAN OIL INDUSTRY

Mexico has long been an exporter of petroleum. The oil industry was nationalized in 1938 under the control of the state-owned company Petróleos Mexicanos, also known as Pemex. The discovery of enormous oil deposits in the late 1970s led initially to another economic boom, but the money the government borrowed to fund new oil extraction infrastructure ultimately paved the way for a crippling debt crisis.

Urban Mexico in the 1960s
This photograph of Chihuahua City in the 1960s portrays the modern, capitalist and urban society that Mexican governments sought to achieve during the period of economic boom.

INDIGENOUS PEOPLES' RIGHTS

Across the continent, the descendants of North America's first inhabitants continued to struggle for rights, recognition, and economic equality throughout the 20th century. A growing awareness of the injustices of the past led to significant, albeit uneven, progress.

The abolition in 1934 of the Dawes Act and its unpopular allotment system (see pp. 208-209) resulted in limited self-government and autonomy for Indigenous Americans. But this did not alleviate many of the significant economic challenges they faced, and in 1953 the federal government reverted to its earlier assimilationist approach. This was applied mainly through the policy known as termination, which undid the legal protections enjoyed by Indigenous Americans and removed their special legal status. It was only through activism and protest across the 1960s and 1970s that some of those protections and rights were restored by legislation.

In Canada, the government tried in the early 1970s to introduce termination-style policies to remove the rights extended to Indigenous peoples. They were forced to stop, however, in the face of popular unrest.

Mexico, with the largest Indigenous population in Central and South America, also encouraged assimilation. Common representations of Indigenous life and culture in Mexican art, such as in the murals of Diego Rivera, perhaps made the country appear more integrated than it was. Only in the 1990s, for example, would the plight of Mexico's rural Indigenous communities come to the fore (see pp.320–321).

> *"We ... tossed them the most nearly worthless scraps of a continent that had once been wholly theirs."*
>
> JOHN COLLIER, 1938

JOHN COLLIER AND THE "INDIAN NEW DEAL"

President Roosevelt appointed John Collier as Commissioner of Indian Affairs in 1933. Collier was far more sympathetic to the condition of Indigenous Americans than any of his predecessors and strongly opposed the policy of assimilation and allotment that had been in force since 1887. Under his leadership, the so-called "Indian New Deal" saw a partial restoration of land ownership to Indigenous peoples and a greater degree of self-government, alongside cultural and educational initiatives. Economic progress was limited, though, and incidences of poverty among Indigenous Americans remained high.

John Collier with a chief of the Crow people

---

3 TERMINATION 1945–1960s

The US government changed course once more during the Truman and Eisenhower administrations. Under the policy of termination, official attempts were made to end the special status of Indigenous Americans, renounce treaties with them, and dissolve their reservations. The Indian Relocation Act of 1956 forced large numbers of Indigenous people off their lands and into cities on the west coast, where many struggled to settle.

■ West coast area of resettlement

1953 The Klamath people and their Oregon reservation lose official recognition (are "terminated") by Congress

4 LEGAL RECOGNITION IN CANADA 1945–1969

A growing awareness of the need to address the inequalities experienced by First Nations communities led to important changes in the postwar period. Amendments to the Indian Act in 1951 allowed for a much greater degree of cultural and religious freedom. In 1960, legislation was passed giving Indigenous peoples an unrestricted right to vote in federal elections.

✎ Key legislation

1969–1971 Alcatraz Island in San Francisco Bay is occupied, or "reclaimed," by Indigenous "Indians of All Tribes" activists for 19 months from 1969 to 1971

5 A NEW APPROACH 1960s–1970s

Inspired by the African American Civil Rights Movement, Indigenous Americans pushed for greater freedoms, economic opportunities, and legal protections. Successful activism led to the end of the policy of termination with the signing of the Indian Self-Determination and Education Assistance Act in 1975. This heralded a return to the earlier spirit of the New Deal.

1940s–1960s The termination policy compels thousands of Indigenous Americans to leave their land and move to cities such as Chicago and Los Angeles

6 FIRST NATIONS RESIST ASSIMILATION 1969–1980s

In 1969, Canadian government plans to abolish the status of Indigenous people and convert reserves into private property were scrapped in the face of opposition. The Calder Case of 1973 established that Indigenous people could claim ownership of their ancestral homelands—a ruling that saw the Nisga'a of British Columbia attain self-government of part of the Nass River Valley.

■ British Columbia

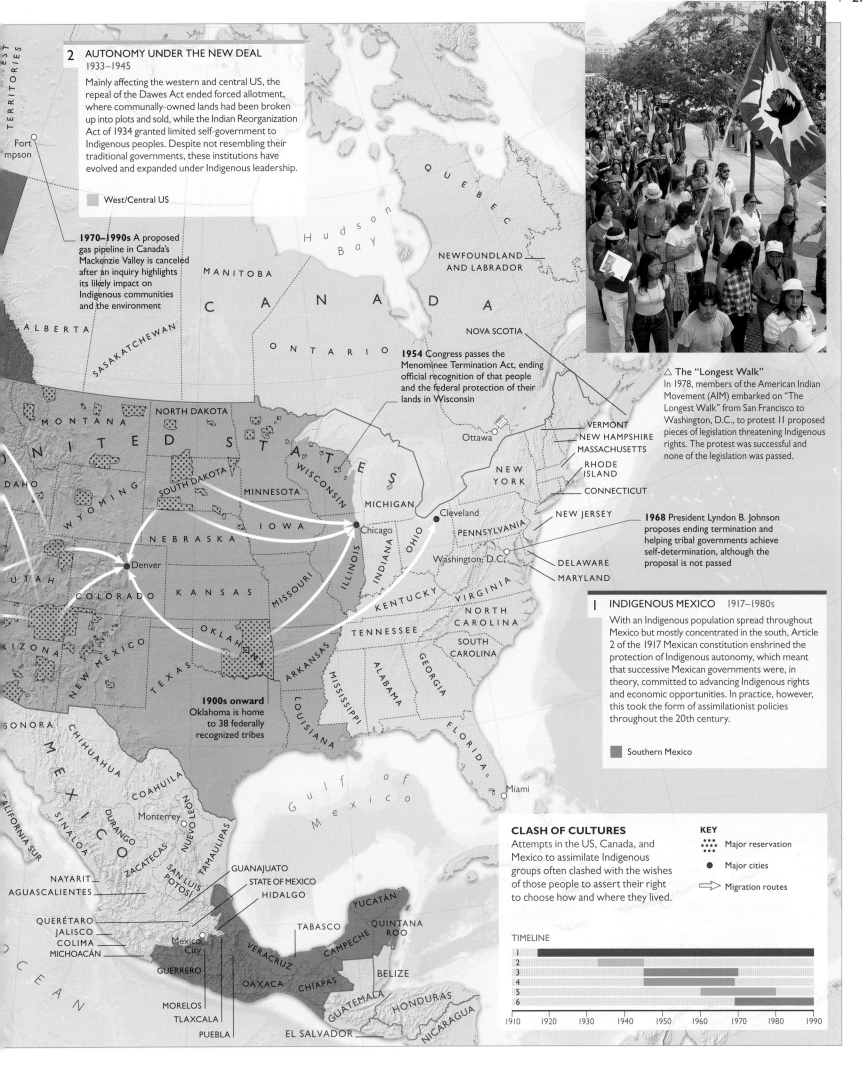

2 AUTONOMY UNDER THE NEW DEAL
1933–1945

Mainly affecting the western and central US, the repeal of the Dawes Act ended forced allotment, where communally-owned lands had been broken up into plots and sold, while the Indian Reorganization Act of 1934 granted limited self-government to Indigenous peoples. Despite not resembling their traditional governments, these institutions have evolved and expanded under Indigenous leadership.

■ West/Central US

1970–1990s A proposed gas pipeline in Canada's Mackenzie Valley is canceled after an inquiry highlights its likely impact on Indigenous communities and the environment

1954 Congress passes the Menominee Termination Act, ending official recognition of that people and the federal protection of their lands in Wisconsin

△ The "Longest Walk"
In 1978, members of the American Indian Movement (AIM) embarked on "The Longest Walk" from San Francisco to Washington, D.C., to protest 11 proposed pieces of legislation threatening Indigenous rights. The protest was successful and none of the legislation was passed.

1968 President Lyndon B. Johnson proposes ending termination and helping tribal governments achieve self-determination, although the proposal is not passed

1900s onward Oklahoma is home to 38 federally recognized tribes

1 INDIGENOUS MEXICO 1917–1980s

With an Indigenous population spread throughout Mexico but mostly concentrated in the south, Article 2 of the 1917 Mexican constitution enshrined the protection of Indigenous autonomy, which meant that successive Mexican governments were, in theory, committed to advancing Indigenous rights and economic opportunities. In practice, however, this took the form of assimilationist policies throughout the 20th century.

■ Southern Mexico

CLASH OF CULTURES

Attempts in the US, Canada, and Mexico to assimilate Indigenous groups often clashed with the wishes of those people to assert their right to choose how and where they lived.

KEY
⣿ Major reservation
● Major cities
⇨ Migration routes

TIMELINE
1910 1920 1930 1940 1950 1960 1970 1980 1990

Moving media
In the 1950s and 1960s, television sales greatly increased across the US. By 1963, most US households owned one, and more Americans got their news from televisions than from newspapers.

SUBURBIA AND CONSUMERISM

The US experienced an economic boom after World War II. Households were filled with the latest technologies, shopping centers opened around the country, and many people moved to newly built suburbs.

After World War II, unemployment in the US was at an all-time low. Workers earned higher wages, and new technologies—developed during the war—increased the speed of production and lowered the cost of goods. This, together with the removal of wartime rationing, encouraged a new focus on consumer culture.

Many Americans relocated to new, reasonably priced residential areas known as suburbs. Mass production methods, previously used in the construction of military housing, were utilized to build single-family homes quickly and affordably. Increased car ownership and newly built freeways allowed freestanding shopping centers to spread widely in the 1950s and 1960s. An expanding interstate system greatly improved the connectivity between suburbs and cities (see pp.280–281).

The Servicemen's Readjustment Act of 1944 (GI Bill) provided assistance with housing, unemployment insurance, and college education for war veterans. Around 8 million veterans had used the education benefits by 1951. However, not everyone benefited equally in the booming economy. Women were excluded from educational benefits and banks could refuse them home loans until 1974. Suburbs often had restrictive laws excluding Black homeowners, and many universities denied them educational benefits.

△ **Reaching consumers**
Companies such as Coca-Cola often published advertisements in popular magazines to attract customers and reach a wider consumer base.

REDLINING

Government appraisers used color coded maps to signal the level of "risk" for federally subsidized mortgages in different neighborhoods, as shown in this map of Detroit. Areas inhabited by Black communities were rated red, denoting risk, while all-white areas received green, the best rating. People in areas marked red could not secure loans, often preventing them from owning homes and leading to decades of economic inequality.

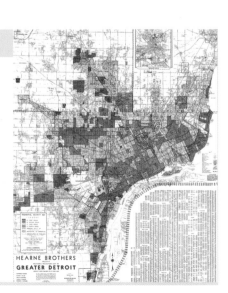

THE AUTOMOTIVE REVOLUTION

In the early 20th century, the growth of the automobile industry heralded one of the single most important shifts in US society. It brought about a complete transformation in the way people worked, lived, and traveled.

The automobile was seen more as a novelty than a useful device until industrialist Henry Ford's assembly line system facilitated manufacturing cars cheaply and on a large scale. The Ford Model T (1908) became an icon of the era. By 1920, the automotive revolution was in full swing, with more than 26 million registered cars by the end of the decade. People could now travel farther, faster, and with greater reliability than before.

The automobile industry became an integral part of the economy, employing thousands of workers, while also stimulating demand in other industries, such as steel and rubber production. Mass ownership of automobiles allowed people to live farther away from their jobs, driving societal shifts such as the growth of suburbs (see pp.278–279). Goods could now be shipped by road, in addition to rail. New businesses such as motels and roadside restaurants also sprang up to service the resultant boom in tourism and business travel.

This revolution culminated in the Federal-Aid Highway Act of 1956, signed into law by President Dwight

D. Eisenhower. This project to create an Interstate Highway System was unprecedented in its scale. Funding of $26 billion was approved for a 41,000-mile (65,983-km) network of wide, uniform highways, designed for high-speed driving.

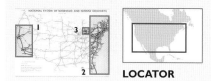

LOCATOR

KEY

1 Interstate 5 (built 1956–1979) links the western US to Mexico and Canada.

2 Interstate 95 (built 1956–2018) connects the eastern seaboard from Maine to Florida.

3 Detroit became an important center of automobile manufacturing.

▷ **Comprehensive connectivity**
This 1958 map depicts the planned Interstate Highway System. As well as increased mobility for the civilian population, reliable road infrastructure was required to support national defense during the Cold War.

THE RISE OF AIR TRAVEL

Commercial passenger airline services also grew rapidly throughout the first half of the 20th century. The introduction of jet liners in the 1950s, such as the iconic Boeing 707, ushered in a "golden age" of flying, featuring a much greater degree of luxury and comfort than early commercial flights. Unlike automobile travel, flying would remain a preserve of the wealthy until the 1970s.

Air travel in the 1950s was advertised as a luxury experience

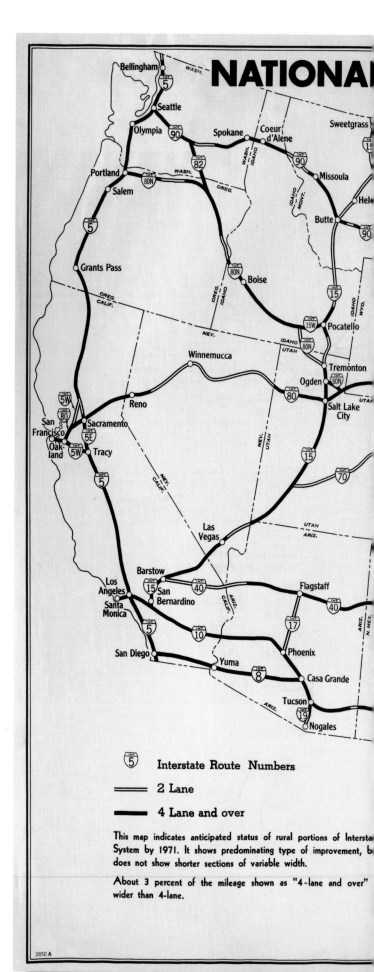

Interstate Route Numbers

═══ 2 Lane

━━━ 4 Lane and over

This map indicates anticipated status of rural portions of Interstate System by 1971. It shows predominating type of improvement, but does not show shorter sections of variable width.

About 3 percent of the mileage shown as "4-lane and over" wider than 4-lane.

STEM OF INTERSTATE AND DEFENSE HIGHWAYS

As of June, 1958

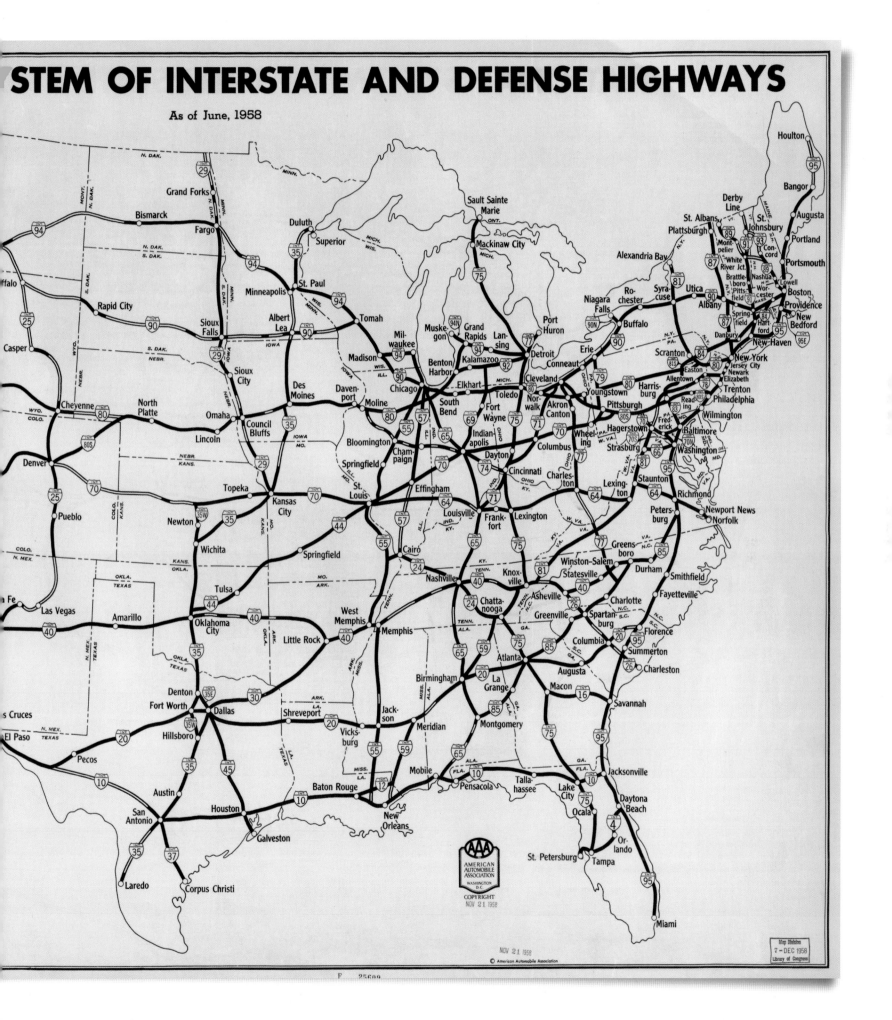

THE ATOMIC AGE

The creation of atomic weapons ushered in a new era of uncertainty as the US expanded its global power and engaged in a long Cold War with the USSR. At home, many people in North America fought for social justice and environmental protection, and society reflected the changing tastes of young people.

△ **Dwight D. Eisenhower**
After making his name as a World War II general, Dwight D. Eisenhower as president devoted much of his energy to containing the threat of his nation's former ally, the Soviet Union.

With the invention of the atomic bomb at the end of World War II, the US had exclusive access to the most powerful weapon ever created. When, in 1949, the Soviet Union created its own nuclear warheads, the two states became locked in a decades-long Cold War that drew other nations into their geopolitical conflict. While the US flexed its power internationally, its citizens called for more freedoms and protection at home, as witnessed by the Civil Rights campaigns of the 1950s and 1960s and the growing environmental movement across the continent. In an era of great social change, young people began to exert their power through music, culture, and protest.

Tension and turmoil

The Cold War saw the US, representing democracy and capitalism, pitted against the Soviet Union, standing for communism. The 1950s witnessed an economic boom in the US that made it a beacon for other nations struggling to rebuild their

economies after the war—a struggle the US did much to alleviate through trade and aid programs. The Cold War aided the economic success of the US, as it stimulated advances in weaponry and technology. By the late 1950s, the US and the Soviet Union were engaged in a "space race" where they relentlessly strove to outdo each other's achievements. When the Soviets successfully sent the first person into space in 1961, the US vowed to send a crewed mission to the moon before its great rival.

Although the US and the USSR never faced each other directly on the battlefield, they came close on several occasions—most notably during the Cuban Missile Crisis, but also in conflicts such as the Korean and Vietnam wars, where they and their proxies and allies engaged in long and bitter struggles. The first of these contests was deemed a success for the US, with South Korea able to hold off an invasion by communist North Korea. Vietnam, by contrast, became a bloody stalemate that cost the US dearly in terms of both money and casualties. After almost a decade of fighting, the US withdrew its forces from

◁ **Military vessels, November 1962**
A US military vessel (left) inspects the Soviet freighter *Ansov* as it leaves Cuba carrying what may be missiles. The Cuban Missile Crisis came to an end when the Soviet Union agreed to remove its nuclear weapons from Cuba.

> *"We knew the world would not be the same."*
>
> J. ROBERT OPPENHEIMER, ON THE CREATION OF THE ATOMIC BOMB

CHANGES AT HOME; CHANGES ABROAD

Although the US and the Soviets avoided direct confrontation, the atomic age was marked by many conflicts around the world involving the two nations or their allies. The US also increased its global reach through social, economic, and political means. The US-Soviet rivalry even extended into space. From the 1950s, North Americans campaigned for civil rights and social equality for marginalized groups.

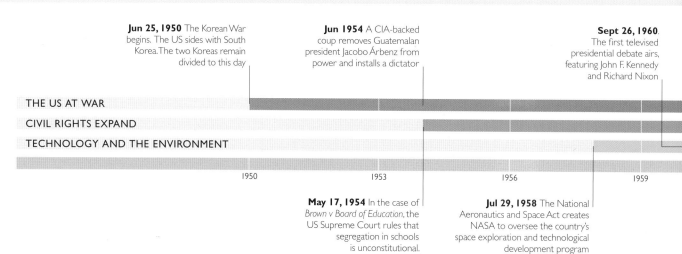

Jun 25, 1950 The Korean War begins. The US sides with South Korea. The two Koreas remain divided to this day

Jun 1954 A CIA-backed coup removes Guatemalan president Jacobo Árbenz from power and installs a dictator

Sept 26, 1960 The first televised presidential debate airs, featuring John F. Kennedy and Richard Nixon

THE US AT WAR

CIVIL RIGHTS EXPAND

TECHNOLOGY AND THE ENVIRONMENT

1950   1953   1956   1959

May 17, 1954 In the case of *Brown v Board of Education*, the US Supreme Court rules that segregation in schools is unconstitutional.

Jul 29, 1958 The National Aeronautics and Space Act creates NASA to oversee the country's space exploration and technological development program

◁ **Apollo 11 astronauts**
In 1961, President Kennedy promised that by the end of the decade the US would land men on the moon and bring them back safely. In July 1969, Neil Armstrong, Michael Collins, and Edwin "Buzz" Aldrin fulfilled that promise with the Apollo 11 mission.

▽ **The Vietnam War**
The US first sent combat troops to Vietnam in 1965. With each passing year the war became increasingly unpopular and the last US forces left the country in March 1973. South Vietnam fell to North Vietnam in 1975.

South Vietnam, which, within two years, fell to communist North Vietnam. The US faced much criticism for its actions in Vietnam, at home and from abroad. Nevertheless, it continued to intervene in the affairs of states where it was concerned about the growing influence of communism, especially in Central and South America. Several of the coups and regime changes that the US supported ended with the installation of dictators and repressive governments.

The people find their voice

In North America, change was on the horizon. Black civil rights campaigners pushed for racial equality, employing a mixed strategy of peaceful protest against the state and practical cooperation with it, resulting in groundbreaking legislation such as the Civil Rights Act of 1964. Other marginalized or discriminated-against groups such as women, the LGBTQ+ community, Indigenous peoples, and Latine peoples were also encouraged to fight for their rights. Alongside these campaigns for social and political equality, environmentalists demanded that the US government take better care of the planet, especially in the wake of ecological catastrophes such as the Three Mile Island nuclear power plant accident. This era also saw an expansion in culture and self-expression, particularly among the younger generation. Popular music became more experimental, rebellious, and questioning of authority, while young men going off to war exported US culture abroad and returned home with new, eastern-influenced beliefs and alternative approaches to living.

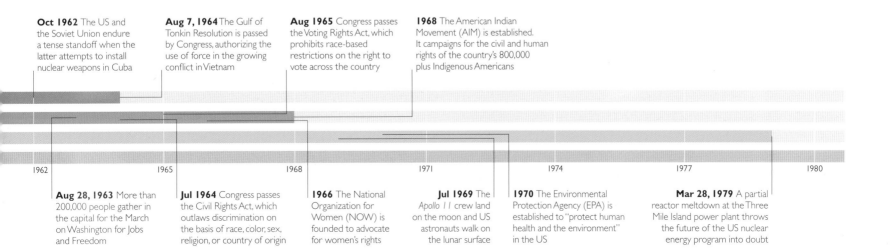

Oct 1962 The US and the Soviet Union endure a tense standoff when the latter attempts to install nuclear weapons in Cuba

Aug 7, 1964 The Gulf of Tonkin Resolution is passed by Congress, authorizing the use of force in the growing conflict in Vietnam

Aug 1965 Congress passes the Voting Rights Act, which prohibits race-based restrictions on the right to vote across the country

1968 The American Indian Movement (AIM) is established. It campaigns for the civil and human rights of the country's 800,000 plus Indigenous Americans

1962   1965   1968   1971   1974   1977   1980

Aug 28, 1963 More than 200,000 people gather in the capital for the March on Washington for Jobs and Freedom

Jul 1964 Congress passes the Civil Rights Act, which outlaws discrimination on the basis of race, color, sex, religion, or country of origin

1966 The National Organization for Women (NOW) is founded to advocate for women's rights

Jul 1969 The *Apollo 11* crew land on the moon and US astronauts walk on the lunar surface

1970 The Environmental Protection Agency (EPA) is established to "protect human health and the environment" in the US

Mar 28, 1979 A partial reactor meltdown at the Three Mile Island power plant throws the future of the US nuclear energy program into doubt

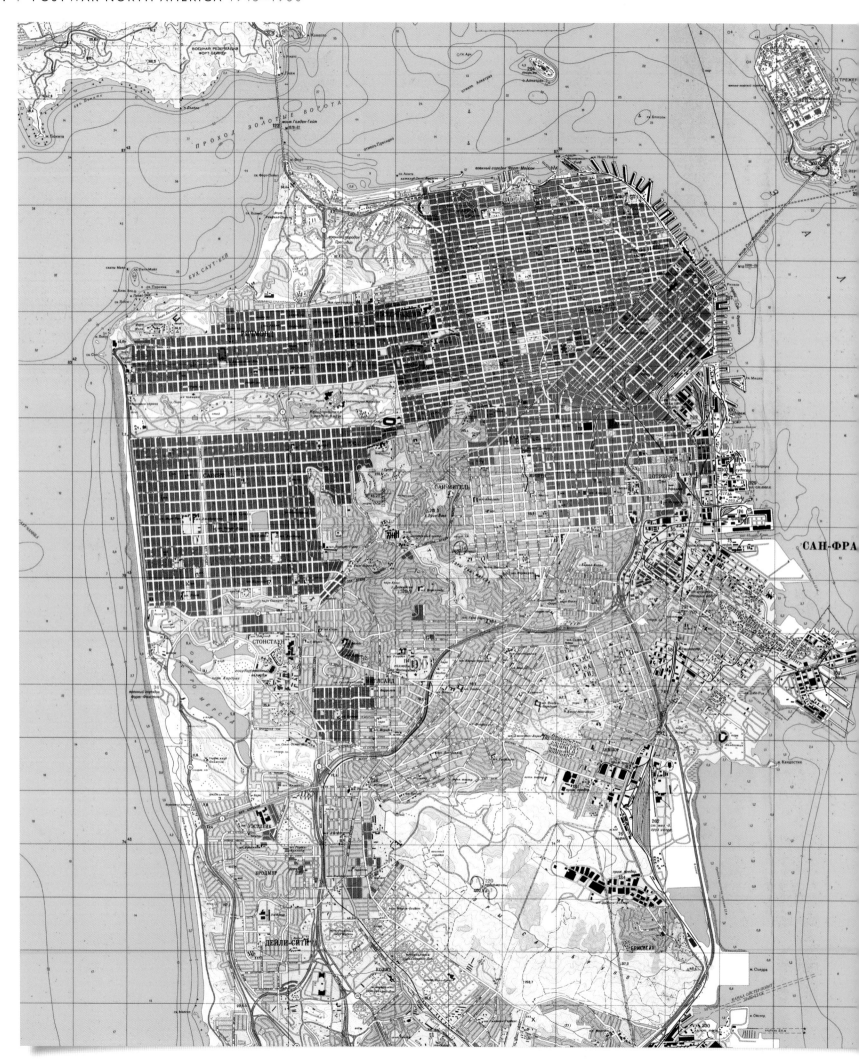

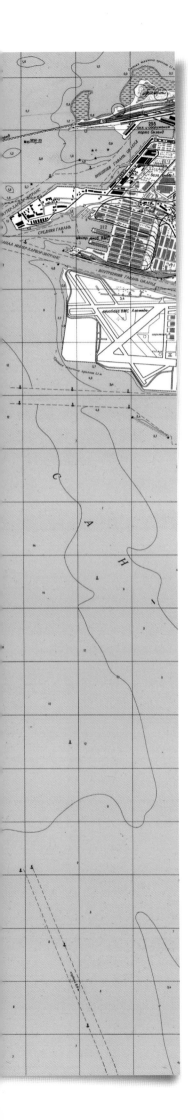

THE COLD WAR

After World War II, the US and Soviet Union clashed over their opposing government, economic, and social systems. They never fought directly, engaging in proxy wars instead. Each nation vied for the upper hand in military strength, economic success, and international alliances.

Allies during World War II, the US and the United Soviet Socialist Republic (USSR) fell out soon after over differing ideologies. The US championed democracy and capitalism; the USSR followed authoritarian communism. Both powers sought alliances, tried to influence other nations, developed new technology and weaponry, and engaged in proxy wars that devastated small countries in the Global South.

Berlin was at the center of one of the first major crises of the Cold War. In 1948, the US and its allies merged their occupation zones in Germany into a single economic and political unit in an effort to rebuild the country. The Soviets, who occupied the eastern part of the country surrounding Berlin, retaliated by blockading land and water routes into Western-occupied West Berlin, depriving the city of essential goods such as food and coal. This led the US and its allies to airlift these commodities into West Berlin until the USSR eventually ended the blockade in 1949.

Soon, Cuba became a site of tension between the two superpowers (see pp.304–305). After Fidel Castro came to power in 1959, he found a close ally in Soviet leader Nikita Khrushchev. Fearing Cuba would become a communist

KEY

1 The Soviet Union drew up Cyrillic maps of key cities worldwide. The detail and the inclusion of sensitive sites suggests spies were used to gather data.

2 US defenses against a possible attack included missiles sites, such as the Nike Missile Site SF-88 in Golden Gate National Recreation Area.

3 The financial district of San Francisco represented an important site for Soviet intelligence.

LOCATOR

◁ **Soviet map of San Francisco**
This 1980 Soviet map shows a detailed survey of San Francisco, including its commercial centers, military buildings, and transportation facilities. During the Cold War, both the US and the USSR used new surveillance technology and espionage to prepare maps of each other's territories.

threat right off the US coast, President Dwight D. Eisenhower developed and President John F. Kennedy approved a plan to train Cuban exiles to start an uprising against Castro. However, the operation, known as the Bay of Pigs invasion, failed. In 1962, US spy planes found evidence of the Soviet Union shipping supplies to build nuclear missile sites in Cuba. For a tense 13-day period, the US and USSR faced off, with the US creating a naval blockade around the island while Kennedy and Khrushchev negotiated peace. This was the closest the two nations came to going to war. They remained embroiled in a series of stand-offs until late 1991, when the Soviet superpower imploded, splitting into 15 independent nations.

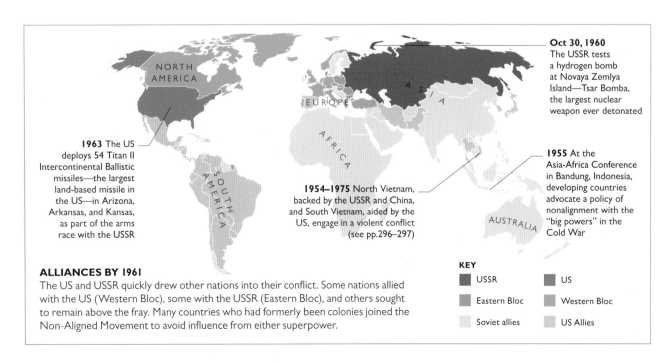

Oct 30, 1960 The USSR tests a hydrogen bomb at Novaya Zemlya Island—Tsar Bomba, the largest nuclear weapon ever detonated

1963 The US deploys 54 Titan II Intercontinental Ballistic missiles—the largest land-based missile in the US—in Arizona, Arkansas, and Kansas, as part of the arms race with the USSR

1954–1975 North Vietnam, backed by the USSR and China, and South Vietnam, aided by the US, engage in a violent conflict (see pp.296–297)

1955 At the Asia-Africa Conference in Bandung, Indonesia, developing countries advocate a policy of nonalignment with the "big powers" in the Cold War

ALLIANCES BY 1961
The US and USSR quickly drew other nations into their conflict. Some nations allied with the US (Western Bloc), some with the USSR (Eastern Bloc), and others sought to remain above the fray. Many countries who had formerly been colonies joined the Non-Aligned Movement to avoid influence from either superpower.

KEY
- USSR
- US
- Eastern Bloc
- Western Bloc
- Soviet allies
- US Allies

GLOBAL CAPITALISM

The US, with its vast economic power and influence, played a leading role in establishing a globalized capitalist system throughout the second half of the 20th century. US products, media, and manufacturing were increasingly exported around the world, and Mexico and Canada contributed to this economic expansion.

While international business was hardly a new phenomenon in the middle of the 20th century, the system of global capitalism reached unprecedented heights in the aftermath of World War II under an ascendant United States. The US emerged from the war with its industry and infrastructure almost singularly untouched among allied nations. This gave it a commanding advantage in setting the terms of international trade, and ultimately allowed it to remake the global economy in its own image. The Bretton Woods Agreement in 1944 led to a stable system of monetary exchange among 44 countries based on the US dollar. The Marshall Plan that rebuilt European countries in the aftermath of the conflict (see pp.272–273) also opened the markets of beneficiary nations to US products and businesses. Over the three decades of continuous economic expansion that followed the war, the US established itself as the world's richest country. Already the world's largest exporter (a position it held until overtaken by China in 2009), it came to dominate global commercial life. In the 1960s and 1970s, US corporations increasingly relocated manufacturing to Mexico, Japan, and South Korea, a trend that continued into the 1990s and early 2000s.

> "This free competitive economy has given us the highest standard of living in human history."
>
> REP. JOHN F. KENNEDY, 1952

ADVERTISING

Advertising became an important industry throughout the 20th century. The 1960s were a pivotal decade in what became known as the "creative revolution" in advertising. Firms based on New York City's Madison Avenue created memorable campaigns for a variety of products, including cars, fashion, appliances, and tobacco. This period also saw a shift toward television, in addition to print and radio, as a dominant medium for American advertising.

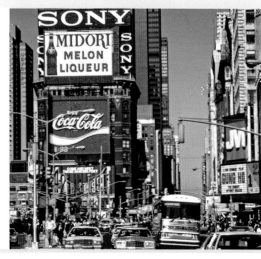

Times Square in 1986

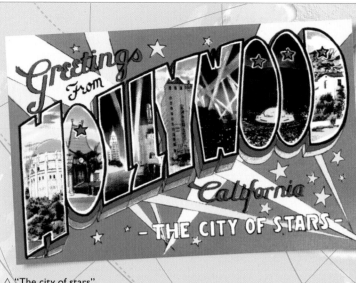

△ "The city of stars"
From the late 1920s to the 1940s, Hollywood, a district in the city of Los Angeles, emerged as the center of the US movie industry (see pp.256–257). It became home to the biggest movie studios and the most popular movie "stars." This tourism poster from the 1930s shows the city's iconic locations.

2 THE POSTWAR ECONOMIC BOOM
1945–1960

The US occupied a dominant economic position at the end of the World War II. The G.I. Bill, also known as the Servicemen's Readjustment Act of 1944, enabled millions of former soldiers to access education and reenter the workforce (see pp.278–279). An economic boom and mass prosperity unleashed pent-up demand for a wide range of new consumer goods.

3 AIR TRAVEL 1950s–1980s

By the mid-1950s, air travel was becoming increasingly common for both international and domestic journeys. 1958 was the first year more people crossed the Atlantic by plane than by ship. The introduction of large jetliners in the 1970s, such as the Boeing 747, put air travel within the reach of ordinary people.

 Major airports   - - - 1970s flight paths

4 THE CONTAINER REVOLUTION
1950s–1980s

The emergence of shipping containers and container ships to carry them revolutionized international shipping during the 1960s and 1970s. These containers can be easily stored on ships and offloaded onto freight trains. This transformed the speed and cost of international shipping and ports became specialized to process containers.

—— Container shipping routes   ⚓ Major ports

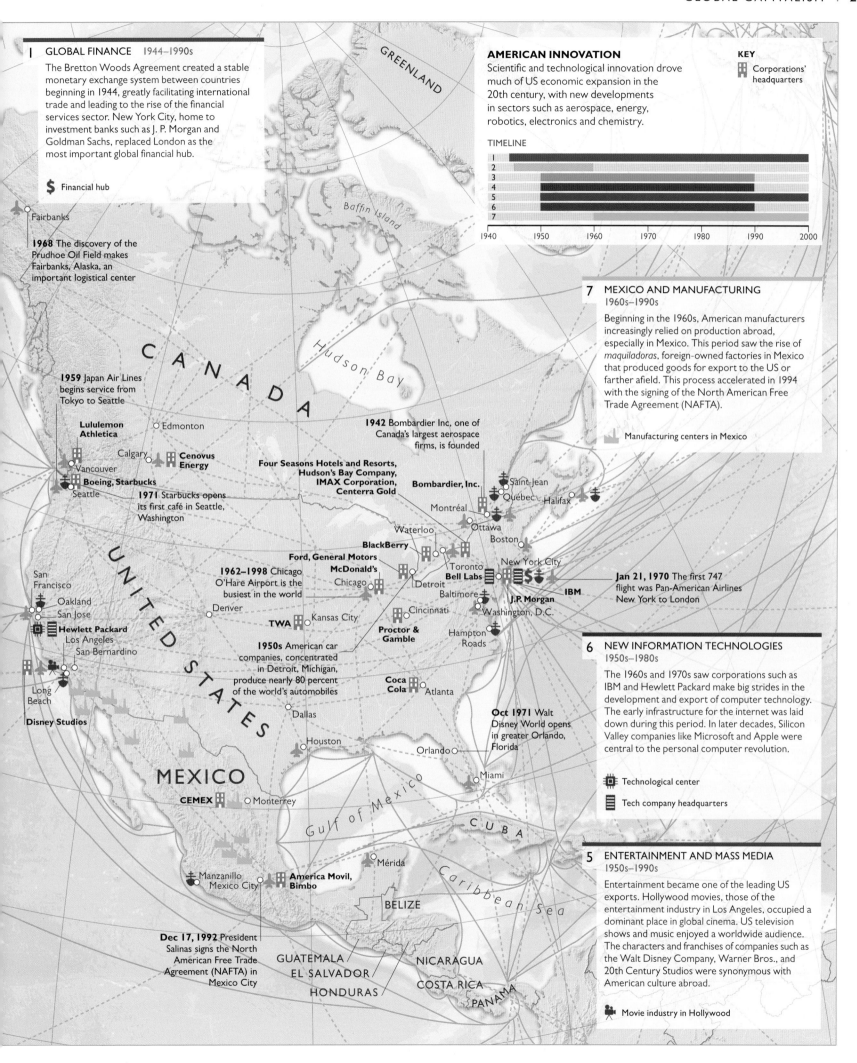

GLOBAL FINANCE 1944–1990s

The Bretton Woods Agreement created a stable monetary exchange system between countries beginning in 1944, greatly facilitating international trade and leading to the rise of the financial services sector. New York City, home to investment banks such as J. P. Morgan and Goldman Sachs, replaced London as the most important global financial hub.

$ Financial hub

GREENLAND

Baffin Island

Fairbanks

1968 The discovery of the Prudhoe Oil Field makes Fairbanks, Alaska, an important logistical center

AMERICAN INNOVATION

Scientific and technological innovation drove much of US economic expansion in the 20th century, with new developments in sectors such as aerospace, energy, robotics, electronics and chemistry.

KEY

Corporations' headquarters

TIMELINE

	1940	1950	1960	1970	1980	1990	2000
1							
2							
3							
4							
5							
6							
7							

7 MEXICO AND MANUFACTURING
1960s–1990s

Beginning in the 1960s, American manufacturers increasingly relied on production abroad, especially in Mexico. This period saw the rise of *maquiladoras*, foreign-owned factories in Mexico that produced goods for export to the US or farther afield. This process accelerated in 1994 with the signing of the North American Free Trade Agreement (NAFTA).

Manufacturing centers in Mexico

C A N A D A

Hudson Bay

1959 Japan Air Lines begins service from Tokyo to Seattle

Lululemon Athletica

Edmonton

Calgary   **Cenovus Energy**

Vancouver

Boeing, Starbucks

Seattle

1971 Starbucks opens its first café in Seattle, Washington

1942 Bombardier Inc, one of Canada's largest aerospace firms, is founded

Four Seasons Hotels and Resorts, Hudson's Bay Company, IMAX Corporation, Centerra Gold

Bombardier, Inc.

Saint-Jean

Québec

Halifax

Montréal

Ottawa

Waterloo

BlackBerry

Boston

Ford, General Motors

McDonald's

1962–1998 Chicago O'Hare Airport is the busiest in the world

Chicago

Detroit

Toronto

Bell Labs

New York City

J. P. Morgan

IBM

Baltimore

Jan 21, 1970 The first 747 flight was Pan-American Airlines New York to London

San Francisco

Oakland

San Jose

Denver

TWA

Kansas City

Cincinnati

Washington, D.C.

Hewlett Packard

Los Angeles

San Bernardino

1950s American car companies, concentrated in Detroit, Michigan, produce nearly 80 percent of the world's automobiles

Proctor & Gamble

Hampton Roads

6 NEW INFORMATION TECHNOLOGIES
1950s–1980s

The 1960s and 1970s saw corporations such as IBM and Hewlett Packard make big strides in the development and export of computer technology. The early infrastructure for the internet was laid down during this period. In later decades, Silicon Valley companies like Microsoft and Apple were central to the personal computer revolution.

Technological center

Tech company headquarters

Long Beach

Disney Studios

Dallas

Coca Cola

Atlanta

Houston

Oct 1971 Walt Disney World opens in greater Orlando, Florida

Orlando

U N I T E D   S T A T E S

Miami

M E X I C O

CEMEX   Monterrey

Gulf of Mexico

C U B A

5 ENTERTAINMENT AND MASS MEDIA
1950s–1990s

Entertainment became one of the leading US exports. Hollywood movies, those of the entertainment industry in Los Angeles, occupied a dominant place in global cinema. US television shows and music enjoyed a worldwide audience. The characters and franchises of companies such as the Walt Disney Company, Warner Bros., and 20th Century Studios were synonymous with American culture abroad.

Movie industry in Hollywood

Mérida

Caribbean Sea

Manzanillo

Mexico City

America Movil, Bimbo

BELIZE

Dec 17, 1992 President Salinas signs the North American Free Trade Agreement (NAFTA) in Mexico City

GUATEMALA

EL SALVADOR

HONDURAS

NICARAGUA

COSTA RICA

PANAMA

THE KOREAN WAR

In 1950, the US and other United Nations (UN) members went to war to support South Korea against North Korea. After a dynamic start to the conflict, the war dragged on in a stalemate, which eventually ended with the continued division of North and South Korea along the 38th parallel. This conflict was a landmark in the Cold War, and marked the start of US military involvement in East Asia in this era.

At the end of World War II, the US and the Soviet Union divided the Korean peninsula at the 38th parallel, with each occupying one region: North Korea, under the leadership of Kim Il-Sung, was a communist dictatorship and Soviet puppet state, and South Korea was formed as a constitutional republic aligned with the US.

In June 1950, following years of tension, North Korea invaded the South. The US asked the UN for support, and several UN countries committed troops to the conflict, though the majority of forces were American. The US wanted to prevent the spread of communism into South Korea, and it considered this war to be part of the larger Cold War fight between communism and the "free world." This conflict became one of the first major tests of the US in a Cold War proxy war. China joined the conflict, siding with North Korea.

The armistice that ended the fighting in July 1953 took two years to negotiate—longer than any other armistice in history. It ended hostilities, repatriated prisoners, and created a demilitarized zone (DMZ) that physically separated the two nations along a fortified border that stretched across the peninsula. This partition was intended to be temporary, and despite support for reunification on both sides of the DMZ, it continues to divide Korea into two heavily armed, antagonistic nations.

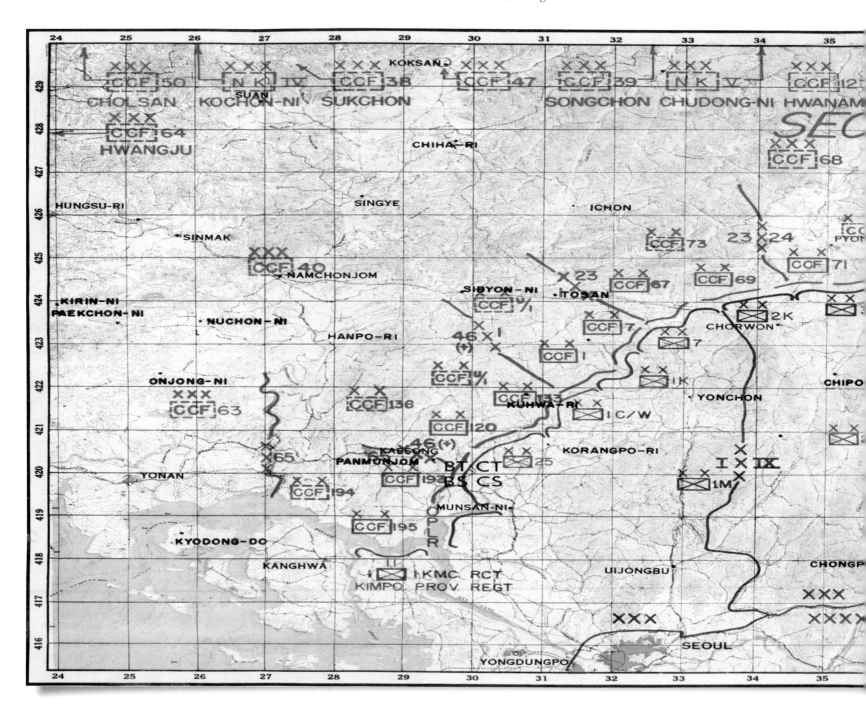

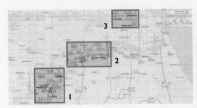

LOCATOR

KEY

1 Officials met in Panmunjom to negotiate and formalize the armistice. The entire process took two years to complete, between 1951 and 1953.

2 This 2½ mile- (4 km-) wide linear area became the permanent demilitarized zone between the Korean nations after the war ended.

3 Chinese and North Korean forces were allies during the war, and are shown in red on the map. China was promised Soviet supplies and arms.

▽ Situation map, May 30, 1953
In 1953, as officials worked on an armistice agreement, troops from North Korea, China, South Korea, the US, and the UN gathered along the area that would become a permanent division between North Korea and South Korea.

COURSE OF THE WAR
The early North Korean offensive pushed South Korean forces into the southeast corner of the country, near Pusan. UN forces countered the attack with an invasion at Pusan and a naval assault on the west coast, landing at Inchon. UN forces pushed even farther north, drawing Chinese forces into the war, which drove UN troops back to the region around the 38th parallel.

July 27, 1953
The border between the two nations is defined by the new armistice

KEY

→ North Korean attack, 1950

⏷ US fleet

⏺ UN landing at Inchon

→ UN counterattack

⇨ Chinese attack

▮ Koje-do prisoner of war camp

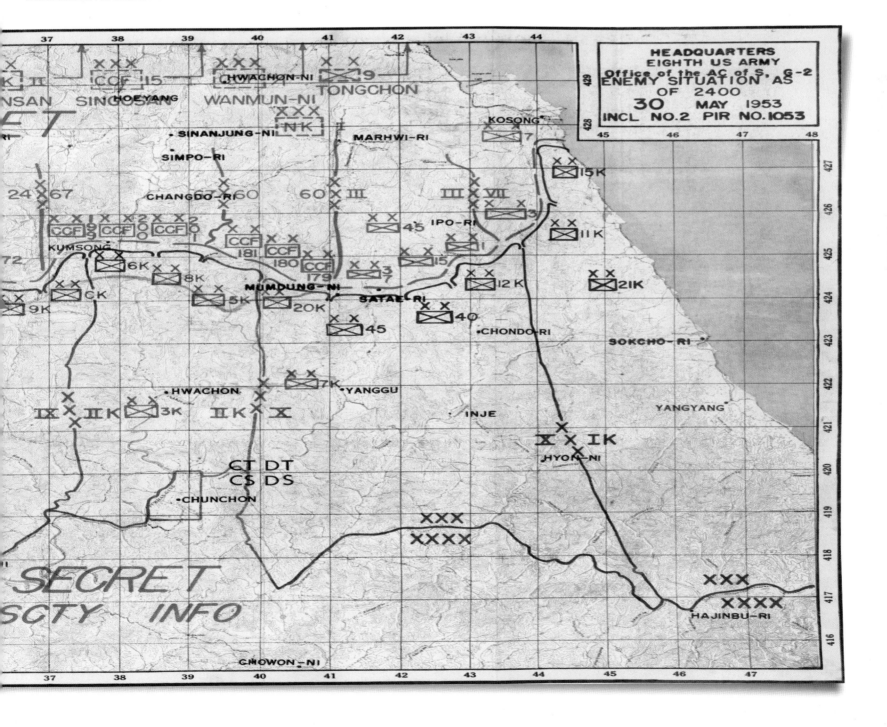

Addressing anticommunism
On June 26, 1963, President Kennedy delivered an anticommunism speech in Berlin. Germany, divided into the democratic West and the communist East, was often seen as a key battleground of the Cold War.

KENNEDY'S AMERICA

President John F. Kennedy represented a bold new international vision of the US. His policies often extended the country's presence in the wider context of the Cold War, including taking a stand against communist Cuba and participating in the race to the Moon.

The 1960 US presidential campaign pitted Democratic Party hopeful John F. Kennedy against the then vice president Richard M. Nixon. Kennedy won the election by a narrow margin and became the youngest man to be elected president of the US. A decorated World War II hero, he wanted the US to be a leader on the world stage, standing its ground against the Soviet Union in the ongoing Cold War (see pp.284–285).

△ **Kennedy's campaign**
This 1960 presidential election button features John F. Kennedy, who connected with voters through the first live televised presidential debates. The media played a major role in the campaign.

Combating communism

Kennedy sought to secure US borders through military, social, political, and economic influence. One of his many innovations, the Peace Corps, called on citizens to spread democracy and provide development assistance overseas. Cuba, with its communist agenda and proximity to the US, became a key front on which the Cold War played out. In 1961, US-funded Cuban exiles returned to Cuba to spark a revolution against Fidel Castro's rule, but failed to do so. A year later, the US nearly went to war with the Soviet Union over their plans to establish a nuclear weapons base in Cuba. After a tense two weeks, Kennedy successfully negotiated the removal of these weapons with Soviet Premier Nikita Khrushchev. Fearing the expansion of communism in east Asia (see pp.296–297), Kennedy sent military advisors to south Vietnam, which further entrenched US presence there. On November 22, 1963, Kennedy was assassinated, but his legacy continued.

THE SPACE RACE

President Kennedy called on the National Aeronautics and Space Administration (NASA) to land a "man on the Moon" by the end of the 1960s. The US feared losing the space race to the Soviet Union and poured billions of dollars into the space program over the 1960s.

Kennedy at Cape Canaveral Missile Test Annex in Florida, 1962

ENVIRONMENTAL PROTECTION

The second half of the 20th century was a transformative era for environmental protection in the US. The dangers posed by pollution, fossil fuels, and nuclear energy led to growing awareness of environmental issues.

The landscape of North America has long inspired discussions on the environment and humanity's role within it. In the 19th century, the conservation movement in the US sought to protect and preserve nature, a cause promoted by individuals such as Henry David Thoreau, John Muir, and President Theodore Roosevelt. It led to the creation of the country's first national parks, monuments, and, later, the National Park Service to oversee these federally protected lands. This campaign, however, came at a cost, as many Indigenous peoples were dispossessed of their ancestral lands in the process.

The 20th century, with its rapid technological progress, saw the emergence of many serious ecological threats. The advent of nuclear power provoked fears around radioactive contamination, and US biologist Rachel Carson's 1962 book *Silent Spring* brought awareness to the dangers of powerful pesticides, leading to a major shift in public attitudes toward environmental causes. Beginning in the 1970s, a combination of grassroots activism and government action led to the passage of significant legislation to protect the environment.

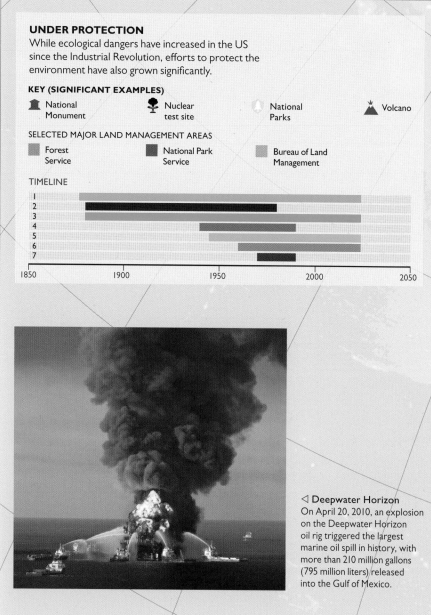

UNDER PROTECTION

While ecological dangers have increased in the US since the Industrial Revolution, efforts to protect the environment have also grown significantly.

KEY (SIGNIFICANT EXAMPLES)

National Monument
Nuclear test site
National Parks
Volcano

SELECTED MAJOR LAND MANAGEMENT AREAS

Forest Service
National Park Service
Bureau of Land Management

TIMELINE

◁ **Deepwater Horizon**
On April 20, 2010, an explosion on the Deepwater Horizon oil rig triggered the largest marine oil spill in history, with more than 210 million gallons (795 million liters) released into the Gulf of Mexico.

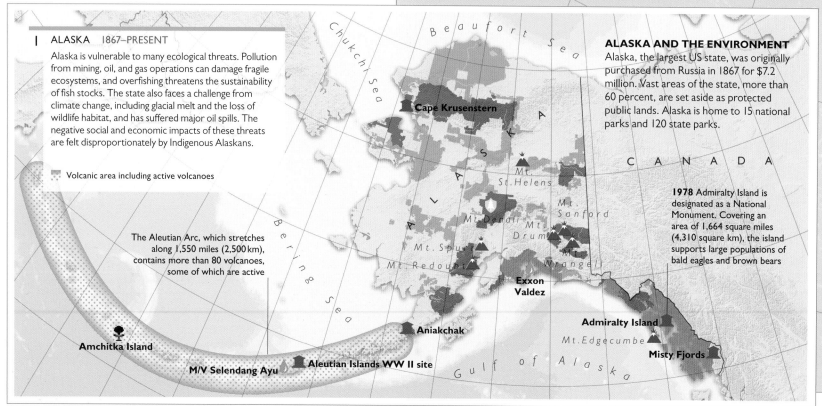

ALASKA 1867–PRESENT

Alaska is vulnerable to many ecological threats. Pollution from mining, oil, and gas operations can damage fragile ecosystems, and overfishing threatens the sustainability of fish stocks. The state also faces a challenge from climate change, including glacial melt and the loss of wildlife habitat, and has suffered major oil spills. The negative social and economic impacts of these threats are felt disproportionately by Indigenous Alaskans.

Volcanic area including active volcanoes

The Aleutian Arc, which stretches along 1,550 miles (2,500 km), contains more than 80 volcanoes, some of which are active

ALASKA AND THE ENVIRONMENT
Alaska, the largest US state, was originally purchased from Russia in 1867 for $7.2 million. Vast areas of the state, more than 60 percent, are set aside as protected public lands. Alaska is home to 15 national parks and 120 state parks.

1978 Admiralty Island is designated as a National Monument. Covering an area of 1,664 square miles (4,310 square km), the island supports large populations of bald eagles and brown bears

7 GOVERNMENT RESPONSE c.1970s–1980s

During the 1970s, realizing the need for extensive regulations for protecting the environment, the US government passed a series of landmark laws, including the Clean Water Act (1972), Endangered Species Act (1973), and the Toxic Substances Control Act (1976). The Environmental Protection Agency (EPA) and Occupational Health and Safety Administration (OSHA) were created in 1970 to allow for greater federal oversight and enforcement on environmental issues.

6 OIL SPILLS 1960s–PRESENT

Marine oil spills have had a devastating effect on sea life, wildlife habitat, and coastal communities. The 1989 *Exxon Valdez* accident spilled more than 10 million gallons (38 million liters) of crude oil into Prince William Sound, Alaska, and led to a massive loss of wildlife. It was the largest oil spill in US waters, until the 2010 Deepwater Horizon spill in the Gulf of Mexico. Following the *Exxon Valdez* accident, stricter laws now regulate the oil and gas industry.

Oil spill

5 NUCLEAR SCARE 1945–PRESENT

In 1979, a malfunction in the cooling system at the Three Mile Island nuclear power station caused the partial meltdown of a reactor, releasing radioactive material into the environment. While the damaged reactor was contained, and the workers and the nearby residents did not face any health issues, the accident raised serious concerns about the safety of nuclear power.

Nuclear accidents

1980 The eruption of Mount St. Helens kills 57 people and devastates a wide region around the volcano

1800s Over-logging results in the significant loss of old growth forests

1952–1969 Fires on the Cuyahoga River began a national conversation around water pollution

1989 The EPA and FBI raid the Rocky Flats nuclear weapons plant due to violations of environmental regulations

1951–1992 More than 900 nuclear weapons are tested at the Nevada Test Site

1908 Protected redwood groves in Marin County, California, are named for conservationist John Muir

1970s–1990s Once a thriving resort destination, the highly-saline Salton Sea has dramatically receded, creating toxic dust

FEDERAL LANDS

Around 30 percent of the land in the US is owned by the federal government. Various agencies have been established to manage these areas, such as the Forest Service (1905), National Park Service (1916), and Bureau of Land Management (1946).

2 THE PESTICIDE PROBLEM c.1870s–1970s

Dichlorodiphenyl trichloroethane (DDT) and other pesticides were widely used after World War II to combat malaria. While DDT was effective at eradicating agricultural pests and insect-borne diseases, its toxic effect on birds and fish became apparent only later; the bald eagle, the US national bird, was driven to the brink of extinction. In 1972, DDT was banned and laws were made to regulate the production and usage of pesticides.

3 NATIONAL PARKS c.1870s–PRESENT

The 19th century saw the emergence of national parks. These were areas of natural beauty safeguarded by the government for the enjoyment of the public. The efforts of Scottish-born naturalist John Muir, known as the "father of the national parks," were instrumental in creating a system of federally protected lands. Yellowstone was created as the first national park in 1872, followed by Sequoia and Yosemite in 1890.

4 TOXIC WASTE c.1940s–1980s

Numerous environmental disasters have brought the dangers of toxic waste disposal to the fore in the US. One of the worst cases was Love Canal, New York, a township built on top of Hooker Chemical Company's buried chemical waste dump. In the late 1970s, toxic waste leached out of containment drums, causing severe health problems to the residents.

Toxic contamination

Standing against segregation
Black protesters, as seen here in Birmingham, Alabama, in 1963, often faced violence from police and white locals. National media coverage of the brutal response to nonviolent protests helped publicize the message of the Civil Rights Movement.

THE FIGHT FOR CIVIL RIGHTS

Black Americans and Indigenous peoples spent decades fighting for equality, political representation, economic opportunity, and the enforcement of their civil rights. The height of the movement between the 1950s and 1970s witnessed dramatic clashes and great historical gains.

The struggle for Black American freedom focused on racial inequality in education, voting rights, and employment. The 1954 Supreme Court case *Brown v. Board of Education* ruled school segregation as unconstitutional, but some states were resistant to this change, provoking dramatic standoffs between students and pro-segregation groups. Black Americans from across the country participated in the movement, including student sit-ins and freedom rides that challenged transportation segregation, and groups such as the Student Nonviolent Coordinating Committee (SNCC) were formed to initiate nonviolent protest. However, despite legislature such as the 1964 Civil Rights Act and 1965 Voting Rights Act, political, social, and economic equality for Black Americans remained limited, inciting some activists toward violence under the slogan "Black Power." A key figure at this time was Malcolm X, who notably influenced later activists with his focus on Black nationalism.

△ **AIM poster**
The American Indian Movement fought for more rights and treaty recognition through protests such as the Trail of Broken Treaties march on Washington, D.C., in 1972.

Indigenous civil rights and tribal sovereignty

In 1953, Congress announced its termination of government support for Indigenous peoples, motivating groups such as the American Indian Movement (AIM), Chicanos, and Zapatistas to agitate for tribal land protection and Indigenous sovereignty (see pp.276–277).

MARTIN LUTHER KING JR. 1929–1968

King's leadership helped the Civil Rights Movement gain major achievements and attention. He united many groups through his 1963 March on Washington for Jobs and Freedom. King also fought for economic justice and international peace. In 1968, King was assassinated in Memphis while supporting a strike by Black sanitation workers. His death sparked anger and violence throughout the US.

THE VIETNAM WAR

In the 1960s and 1970s, the US engaged in offensive operations in conjunction with the forces of the Republic of Vietnam to defend South Vietnam against communist aggression. Back home, US involvement proved divisive, with many protesting the war.

Fearing the spread of communism, the US supported South Vietnam in its fight against the communist North. It sent military advisors to Vietnam as early as 1955. In 1964, US ships reported being fired on in the Gulf of Tonkin, and in 1965 the US sent in its first combat troops. Despite initial successes, its military faced several setbacks as they fought not only the North Vietnamese Army but also the National Liberation Front (NLF)—a political organization in South Vietnam that sided with the North. The NLF's military wing was called the Viet Cong.

In the US, people began questioning the moral and military necessity of this prolonged war. The anti–Vietnam War movement involved a range of people, from college students to Vietnam war veterans. Some protests targeted specific companies, such as Dow Chemical in Michigan, which made the incendiary gel napalm and the herbicide

LOCATOR

Agent Orange used to destroy forest cover and crops. Some demonstrations, such as the ones at Kent State University (Ohio) and Jackson State College (Mississippi) in 1970 turned violent, resulting in student deaths.

In 1969, US president Richard Nixon introduced "Vietnamization"—a policy to turn all fighting over to the South Vietnamese and equip them. It withdrew its troops from combat in 1973.

> *"North Vietnam cannot defeat or humiliate the United States. Only Americans can do that."*
>
> RICHARD NIXON, NOVEMBER 3, 1969

PUBLIC OUTRAGE

In 1971, secret government documents known as the Pentagon Papers were leaked to the press. These revealed that the US had a long history of supporting war in Vietnam, and highlighted problems with US strategy. Coinciding with a buildup of public antiwar sentiment that had been growing for several years, this leak fueled further protests (see pp.300–301).

Antiwar activists in Central Park, New York, in April 1967

▷ **Holding steady**
This map from the October 17, 1969, issue of the *Indianapolis News* shows 29 points where US and Allied troops were stationed in South Vietnam. By this point, US troops were gradually being withdrawn from Vietnam under the "Vietnamization" initiative.

◁ **Ho Chi Minh trail**
Named after North Vietnamese leader Ho Chi Minh, this trail was used by North Vietnam to send supplies, troops, and more through neighboring Cambodia and Laos into South Vietnam throughout the war.

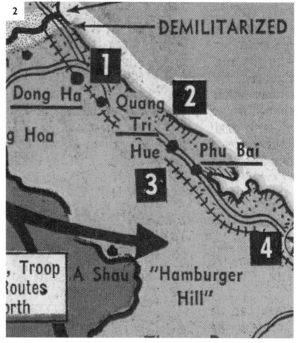

△ **The Tet Offensive**
During the 1968 lunar new year—or Tet—holiday, North Vietnamese forces launched a series of attacks throughout South Vietnam over three days. The longest battle of the offensive was fought in Hue city.

△ **Saigon**
In 1975, South Vietnam and its capital of Saigon fell to North Vietnam and many South Vietnamese fled in any way they could, escaping to nearby countries or the US.

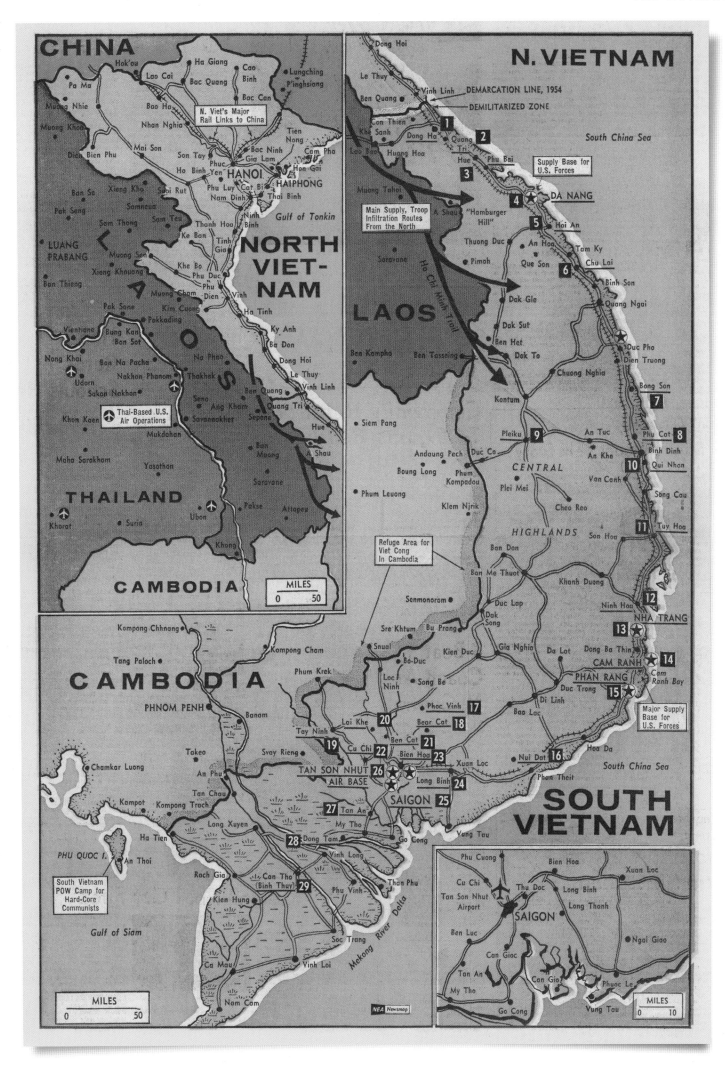

THE SPACE RACE

While scientists around the world focused on progress and collaborations, their governments and military were embroiled in political standoffs over technological superiority as the Cold War powers raced to achieve space flight and land on the moon.

As the Cold War intensified (see pp.284–285), the USSR gained the upper hand when it launched *Sputnik 1* in 1957, followed by Yuri Gagarin's historic mission in 1961. In response, the US set itself the ambitious goal of reaching the moon before the end of the decade. NASA's Mercury, Gemini, and early Apollo missions paved the way for successful crewed space and lunar exploration. Between 1969 and 1972, a total of 12 US astronauts walked on the moon, with another 12 orbiting Earth. In 1971, the Soviet Union launched *Salyut 1*, the first space station in Earth's orbit. The US countered by launching Skylab, the first crewed research laboratory in space, in 1973. The Apollo-Soyuz Test Project in 1975 allowed US and Soviet spacecrafts to dock together, marking the first successful collaboration in space between the two countries. By the late 1970s, the US shifted its focus to the outer planets and interstellar space, launching *Voyager 1* and *Voyager 2* in 1977. The two space probes offered humanity its first close-up views of other planets and moons in our solar system, and paved the way for future breakthroughs in space exploration.

> *"That's one small step for man, one giant leap for mankind."*
>
> NEIL ARMSTRONG, 1969

ART AND CULTURE IN THE SPACE AGE

For decades space travel was a mere fantasy, reserved for the cinema and science fiction. French director Georges Méliès' 1902 film *A Trip to the Moon*, widely believed to be the first sci-fi film, was just the beginning. It was followed by *Aelita, Queen of Mars* (Soviet Union) in 1924 and *2001: A Space Odyssey* in 1968, which was released at the height of the Cold War. As space exploration turned into tangible reality, a wave of cosmic-themed pop culture products emerged, influencing everything from cars and toys to literature and music.

Movie poster for Stanley Kubrick's groundbreaking *2001: A Space Odyssey*

An epic drama of adventure and exploration

2001: a space odyssey

LAUNCHING INTO SPACE

By the 1960s, the US and the USSR were locked in a contest to become the most advanced nation in space exploration. Each side used German engineers to bolster its rocket technology to enable travel to the moon and beyond.

KEY

▨ Nuclear superpower

TIMELINE

1	
2	
3	
4	
5	
6	
7	

1940 · 1950 · 1960 · 1970 · 1980

Oct 4–Dec 4, 1949 Two booster rockets called Little Joe are launched by NASA at Wallops Island, Virginia, to test the launch escape system and heat shield for Project Mercury crafts

1939 The Kirsten High-Speed Tunnel, used for aeronautical research tests, conducts first test at the University of Washington

Sept 1945 First seven German rocket scientists brought to Fort Strong, Long Island

1936 NASA's Jet Propulsion Laboratory is founded by researchers at Caltech for the construction and operation of spacecrafts; it later builds *Explorer I*

NORTH AMERICA

UNITED STATES

Seattle

McDonnell Aircraft Corporation

St. Louis

Boston

New York

Pasadena

Los Angeles

El Paso

Houston

Huntsville

Michoud Assembly Facility

New Orleans

Cape Canaveral Missile Test Center, Florida

North American Aviation

1945–1946 Wernher von Braun and his team are brought to Fort Bliss, Texas, to help develop an experimental cruise missile

Sept 12, 1962 US President John F. Kennedy gives historic "We Choose to Go to the Moon" speech at Rice University

Apr 11–17, 1970 The *Apollo 13* mission is aborted due to an explosion and the astronauts onboard splash down near Samoa

Samoa

Ordnance Rocket Center and Marshall Space Flight Center at Redstone Arsenal

SOUTH AMERICA

PACIFIC OCEAN

7 APOLLO 11 1969

Less than a year after *Apollo 7*, the first US crewed Apollo mission to orbit Earth, *Apollo 11* blasted off to the moon on July 16, 1969. On July 20, astronauts Neil Armstrong and Buzz Aldrin touched down and emerged for the first ever moonwalk. More than five hundred million people watched Armstrong take the first step on the moon.

▲ Key location

6 SATURN V ROCKET 1967–1973

Standing at 363 ft (111 m) tall, the enormous Saturn V made its first unmanned test flight, called *Apollo 4*, in 1967. A total of 13 Saturn V rockets were launched between 1967–1973, for the Apollo missions as well as to put Skylab into Earth's orbit.

▲ Key location

1 PROJECT PAPERCLIP 1945–1959

Project Paperclip was a government program to bring German and Austrian scientists (many with Nazi affiliations) to the US after World War II. Wernher von Braun and his team, who developed Germany's V-2 rocket, played a vital role in shaping US rocket and space programs, including the Redstone and Jupiter rockets.

▲ Key location

2 EARLY EFFORTS BY USSR 1957–1976

The Soviet Union launched *Sputnik 1* on October 4, 1957—the first artificial satellite to orbit Earth. Between 1959 and 1976, it also ran the Luna program, achieving many "firsts" in lunar exploration. On April 12, 1961, cosmonaut Yuri Gagarin became the first human to journey into space and to orbit Earth, aboard the *Vostok 1*.

△ Key location   ☐ Orenburg Oblast

3 EXPLORER 1 February 1, 1958

The first US satellite, *Explorer 1*, was successfully launched in 1958, marking the beginning of the US Space Age. This and subsequent Explorer missions were a result of the contributions made by scientists brought under Project Paperclip. However, it raised ethical questions about recruiting individuals with ties to the Nazi regime.

▲ Key location

The USSR Academy of Sciences oversees scientific leadership and supply of research instruments for *Sputnik 1*

1960s The USSR establishes Plesetsk Cosmodrome to launch military satellites

2006 The Yasny Cosmodrome is set up in Russia's Orenburg Oblast region and launches satellites into orbit using the Dnepr rocket for Kosmotras—a joint Russian, Ukrainian, and Kazakh project

Mar 1945 The Osenberg List, a catalog of scientists working for the Nazi regime, is found at Bonn University and used for Project Paperclip

1945 Scientists working on the V-2 rocket, developed at the Peenemünde Army Research Center, are captured by the US Army

1960s–1980s The Baikonur Cosmodrome functions as the principal operations center for the Soviet space program. Both *Sputnik 1* and *Vostok 1* are launched from here

4 MERCURY AND GEMINI 1958–1966

NASA's projects Mercury and Gemini aimed to develop the spacecraft that enabled astronauts to fly to and live in space. Weeks after Gagarin's launch, Alan Shepard became the first US astronaut to reach space on May 5 in a Mercury spacecraft called *Freedom 7*. A total of 16 crewed missions were launched under the two projects.

▲ Key location

5 THE APOLLO PROGRAM 1961–1972

When US President John F. Kennedy issued the challenge to be the first humans to land on the moon, it set the stage for NASA's Project Apollo. The program consisted of 10 successful crewed spaceflights—four tested equipment, while six others engaged in lunar exploration.

▲ Key location

2017–2020 NASA's James Webb Space Telescope undergoes environmental testing at Goddard to prepare it for launching

◁ *Apollo 11* Saturn V launch
This image shows NASA's Saturn V rocket minutes before liftoff. The rocket was launched from Pad A, Launch Complex 39 at the Kennedy Space Center in Cape Canaveral, Florida. It contained a lunar module called "Eagle" that was used by astronauts Neil Armstrong and Buzz Aldrin to land on the moon's surface.

NASA FACILITIES

In 1958, US President Dwight D. Eisenhower signed an order for the creation of a federal agency dedicated to research and development in the field of space exploration—the National Aeronautics and Space Administration (NASA). Headquartered in Washington, D.C., NASA has 20 centers and facilities across the country that carry out research, development, and testing for advance aeronautics and space technologies.

KEY
● Key facilities

PROTEST AND SOCIAL CHANGE

In the 1960s and 1970s, protests erupted across the US as people rallied against the Vietnam War and fought for the rights of oppressed people. Scandals rocked US politics, which led to a widespread mistrust of elected officials.

△ **Pride protest**
On June 28, 1970—in the first Stonewall anniversary march—gay and lesbian groups in New York protested for equal rights.

People in the US protested against the country's involvement in the Vietnam War (see pp.296–297), from college campuses to nationwide platforms. Groups such as the Students for a Democratic Society (SDS) advocated for expanded civil and economic rights for marginalized groups, particularly people of color. A larger counterculture revolution, associated with the hippie movement, opposed traditional social standards, such as consumerism and sexual conservatism. Patrons of the Stonewall Inn, a gay bar in New York, fought back during a police raid in 1969 when faced with threats of violence and arrest for their sexual orientation. This gave rise to the gay and lesbian rights movement, with organizations such as the Gay Liberation Front at the fore. Women pushed for an end to gender discrimination through organizations such as the National Organization for Women.

Politics and change

President Lyndon B. Johnson championed civil rights with his "Great Society" agenda of 1965. However, given the massive backlash to the Vietnam War, he decided not to run for reelection in 1968. Protesters headed to the Democratic National Convention in Chicago to support the candidacy of anti-war democrat Eugene McCarthy, but Johnson's vice president, Hubert Humphrey, was nominated instead. In clashes with the police, more than 600 protesters were arrested and many injured. Humphrey lost the election to Richard Nixon.

THE WATERGATE SCANDAL

On June 17, 1972, five men linked to Republican President Richard Nixon's reelection committee were arrested for breaking into the Democratic Party headquarters at the Watergate Hotel in Washington, D.C. Nixon's attempts to cover up his involvement were recorded on a taping system at the White House. When the tapes came to light, Nixon resigned rather than face impeachment.

Front cover of *Newsweek*'s coverage of the Watergate scandal

Arrests at "Days of Rage"
In October 1969, people headed to Chicago for four "Days of Rage"—a violent anti–Vietnam War protest that aimed to "Bring the War Home." Led by the Weathermen, a faction of the youth group SDS, protesters damaged public property and clashed with the police.

EARLY POPULAR MUSIC IN THE US

The 19th and 20th centuries saw the evolution of many new styles of popular music in the US. These new genres, including jazz, blues, and rock and roll, would inspire further musical creativity across the nation and around the world. Black artists and producers were instrumental in the growth of the US music industry.

The US has been fertile ground for musical creativity since the earliest days of the country, reflecting contributions from all over the world. The music of European immigrants, enslaved Africans, and their descendants formed an interwoven tapestry of influences and traditions leading to the emergence of a variety of popular styles throughout the 19th and 20th centuries.

The contribution of Black Americans has had an enormous impact on the US musical landscape. Beginning with the musical heritage of enslaved peoples, which included work songs, field hollers, church music, and West African traditions, Black artists and musical innovators produced the most iconic genres of US music—blues, ragtime, gospel, and jazz among others—in the decades after the Civil War. So great was the influence of Black music in global popular culture that the 1920s and 1930s became known as the "Jazz Age." These various styles were built upon during the 1940s and 1950s, creating further distinctive genres, most famously rock and roll. European musical heritage was also highly influential, ranging from the British and Irish roots of traditional folk, country, and bluegrass to the musical traditions of Jewish and Italian immigrants.

> *"Jazz...is the only unhampered, unhindered expression of complete freedom yet produced in this country"*
>
> DUKE ELLINGTON

SCOTT JOPLIN 1867/8–1917

Son of a formerly enslaved person, Scott Joplin was born in Texas in 1867 or 1868. He performed throughout the South and Midwest during the 1880s and 1890s, including at the 1893 World's Fair in Chicago. Known as the "King of Ragtime," his published compositions brought him great acclaim, especially his piano pieces *Maple Leaf Rag* (1899) and *The Entertainer* (1902). By the time of his death in 1917 at the age of 48, he had written more than 50 ragtime piano compositions, a ballet, and two operas.

Scott Joplin, His Complete Works, 1974

SPREADING MUSIC

Concerts, music festivals, and a vibrant recording industry all contributed to the proliferation of US popular music throughout the 20th century.

KEY

⊙ Major record label

♫ Key music festival

TIMELINE

	1700	1750	1800	1850	1900	1950	2000	2050
2								
3								
4								
5								
6								

MONTANA

OREGON

IDAHO

WYOMING

UNITED

UTAH

ARIZONA

CALIFORNIA

1967 Fantasy Fair and Magic Mountain Music Festival

1960s Founded by Black American entrepreneur Charles Sullivan in 1954, the Fillmore Auditorium in San Francisco becomes an iconic venue for psychedelic rock and the music of the counterculture

○ Filmore West

♫○ Marin County

♫○ San Jose **1968** Northern California Folk-Rock Festival

♫○ Monterey

1967 Monterey Pop Festival

Capitol Records ⊙ ○ Los Angeles

Fullerton

1954 Fender introduces the Stratocaster electric guitar. Still in production, the "Strat" is used in various genres, including rock and roll and R&B

6 ROCK AND ROLL 1940s–PRESENT

Rock and roll emerged during the 1940s and 1950s as a fusion of many genres and styles of popular music in the US, and quickly became associated with the electric guitar as its signature instrument. Early influential musicians included Elvis Presley, Jerry Lee Lewis, Little Richard, and Chuck Berry. Their enormous commercial success brought rock and roll into the mainstream.

■ Area of origin

5 COUNTRY AND BLUEGRASS 1920s–PRESENT

Country and bluegrass originated in the West and South—especially the Appalachian Mountains. These genres mostly evolved out of musical traditions from the British Isles, but were also influenced by slave spirituals, field songs, hymns, and blues that highlighted the rural and working-class life in the US, along with early country music . With characteristic instruments including the banjo (originally an African instrument), guitar, harmonica, and fiddle, they became popular genres in the 1920s, and remain so today.

⠿ Area of origin

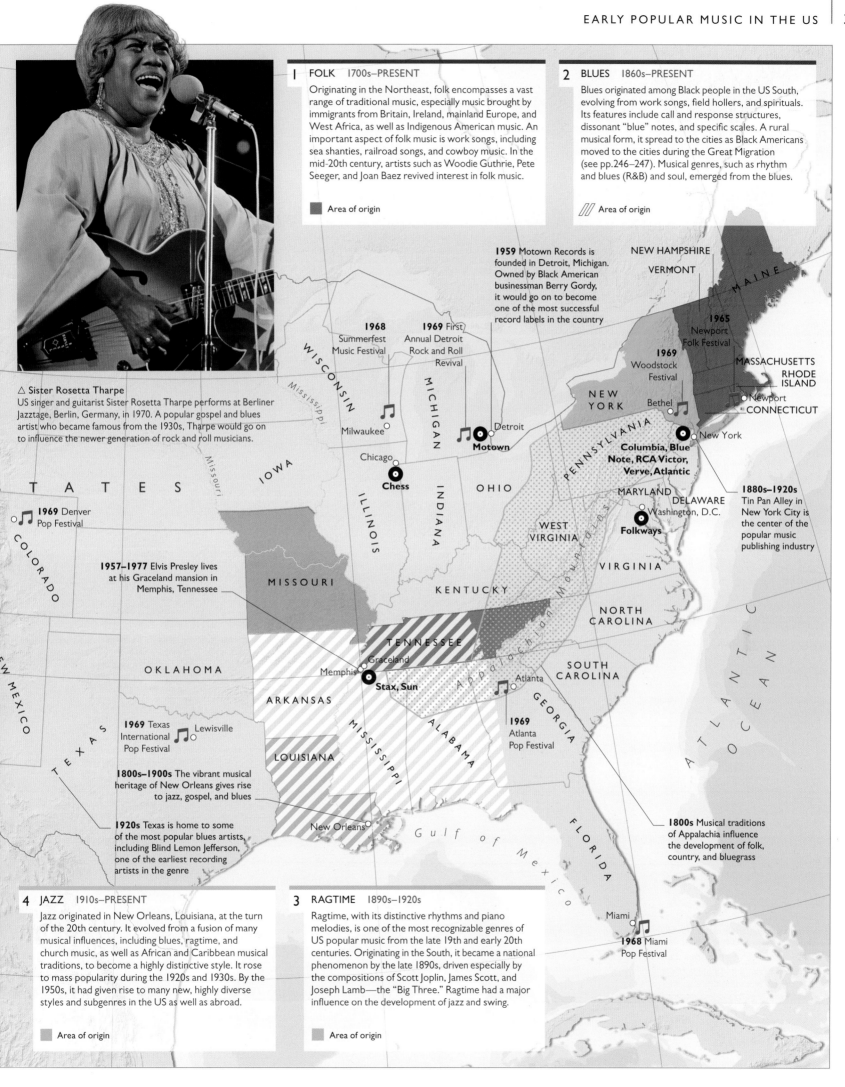

1 FOLK 1700s–PRESENT

Originating in the Northeast, folk encompasses a vast range of traditional music, especially music brought by immigrants from Britain, Ireland, mainland Europe, and West Africa, as well as Indigenous American music. An important aspect of folk music is work songs, including sea shanties, railroad songs, and cowboy music. In the mid-20th century, artists such as Woodie Guthrie, Pete Seeger, and Joan Baez revived interest in folk music.

■ Area of origin

2 BLUES 1860s–PRESENT

Blues originated among Black people in the US South, evolving from work songs, field hollers, and spirituals. Its features include call and response structures, dissonant "blue" notes, and specific scales. A rural musical form, it spread to the cities as Black Americans moved to the cities during the Great Migration (see pp.246–247). Musical genres, such as rhythm and blues (R&B) and soul, emerged from the blues.

/// Area of origin

△ **Sister Rosetta Tharpe**
US singer and guitarist Sister Rosetta Tharpe performs at Berliner Jazztage, Berlin, Germany, in 1970. A popular gospel and blues artist who became famous from the 1930s, Tharpe would go on to influence the newer generation of rock and roll musicians.

1959 Motown Records is founded in Detroit, Michigan. Owned by Black American businessman Berry Gordy, it would go on to become one of the most successful record labels in the country

1968 Summerfest Music Festival

1969 First Annual Detroit Rock and Roll Revival

1965 Newport Folk Festival

1969 Woodstock Festival

1880s–1920s Tin Pan Alley in New York City is the center of the popular music publishing industry

Columbia, Blue Note, RCA Victor, Verve, Atlantic

1969 Denver Pop Festival

1957–1977 Elvis Presley lives at his Graceland mansion in Memphis, Tennessee

1969 Texas International Pop Festival — Lewisville

1800s–1900s The vibrant musical heritage of New Orleans gives rise to jazz, gospel, and blues

1920s Texas is home to some of the most popular blues artists, including Blind Lemon Jefferson, one of the earliest recording artists in the genre

1800s Musical traditions of Appalachia influence the development of folk, country, and bluegrass

1969 Atlanta Pop Festival

1968 Miami Pop Festival

4 JAZZ 1910s–PRESENT

Jazz originated in New Orleans, Louisiana, at the turn of the 20th century. It evolved from a fusion of many musical influences, including blues, ragtime, and church music, as well as African and Caribbean musical traditions, to become a highly distinctive style. It rose to mass popularity during the 1920s and 1930s. By the 1950s, it had given rise to many new, highly diverse styles and subgenres in the US as well as abroad.

■ Area of origin

3 RAGTIME 1890s–1920s

Ragtime, with its distinctive rhythms and piano melodies, is one of the most recognizable genres of US popular music from the late 19th and early 20th centuries. Originating in the South, it became a national phenomenon by the late 1890s, driven especially by the compositions of Scott Joplin, James Scott, and Joseph Lamb—the "Big Three." Ragtime had a major influence on the development of jazz and swing.

■ Area of origin

EARLY US INTERVENTIONS

Since the declaration of the Monroe Doctrine in 1823, the US had considered South and Central America, as well as the Caribbean, to be within its sphere of influence. As the 20th century progressed, the US increasingly exercised its self-declared right to intervene across the hemisphere, especially in the post-1945 Cold War era.

The US had a long history, dating back to the 19th century, of intervention in the affairs of its neighbors beyond its southern border. While these earlier interventions had largely been to defend American business interests, the period after World War II saw a dramatic change in approach for the US. With the emergence of the Cold War (see pp.284–285), the foremost goal of the US was to prevent, by any means necessary, the formation of a

"I don't see why we need to stand by and watch a country go communist."

HENRY KISSINGER, US NATIONAL SECURITY ADVISOR

pro-Soviet government in the Western Hemisphere. To achieve this aim, the US supported a wide range of repressive regimes across the region, often offering the help of the CIA and the military.

The greatest disaster of this period for the US government was the 1959 Cuban Revolution. Cuba, located just 90 miles (145km) off the coast of Florida, had long been of vital strategic and economic importance to the United States. The revolution resulted in Cuba becoming a key ally of the Soviet Union. The attempt to station Soviet missiles in Cuba in 1962 brought the world to the brink of nuclear war. For the US government, Cuba's revolution was a catastrophe that could not be repeated anywhere else in the Americas. This result was even firmer resolve in Washington to use all the resources of the state to crush left-wing movements in Central America, South America, and the Caribbean.

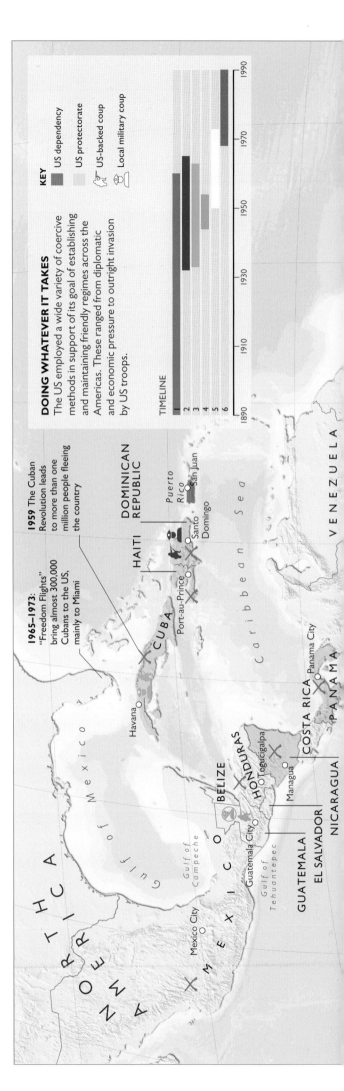

DOING WHATEVER IT TAKES

The US employed a wide variety of coercive methods in support of its goal of establishing and maintaining friendly regimes across the Americas. These ranged from diplomatic and economic pressure to outright invasion by US troops.

KEY

- US dependency
- US protectorate
- US-backed coup
- Local military coup

TIMELINE

1890 1910 1930 1950 1970 1990

1
2
3
4
5
6

1965–1973: "Freedom Flights" bring almost 300,000 Cubans to the US, mainly to Miami

1959 The Cuban Revolution leads to more than one million people fleeing the country

DOMINICAN REPUBLIC

Puerto Rico

San Juan

HAITI

Santo Domingo

Port-au-Prince

C U B A

Havana

Caribbean Sea

VENEZUELA

BELIZE

Guatemala City

Gulf of Tehuantepec

Gulf of Campeche

Mexico City

M E X I C O

G u l f   o f   M e x i c o

N O R T H   A M E R I C A

GUATEMALA

EL SALVADOR

HONDURAS

Tegucigalpa

Managua

NICARAGUA

COSTA RICA

PANAMA

Panama City

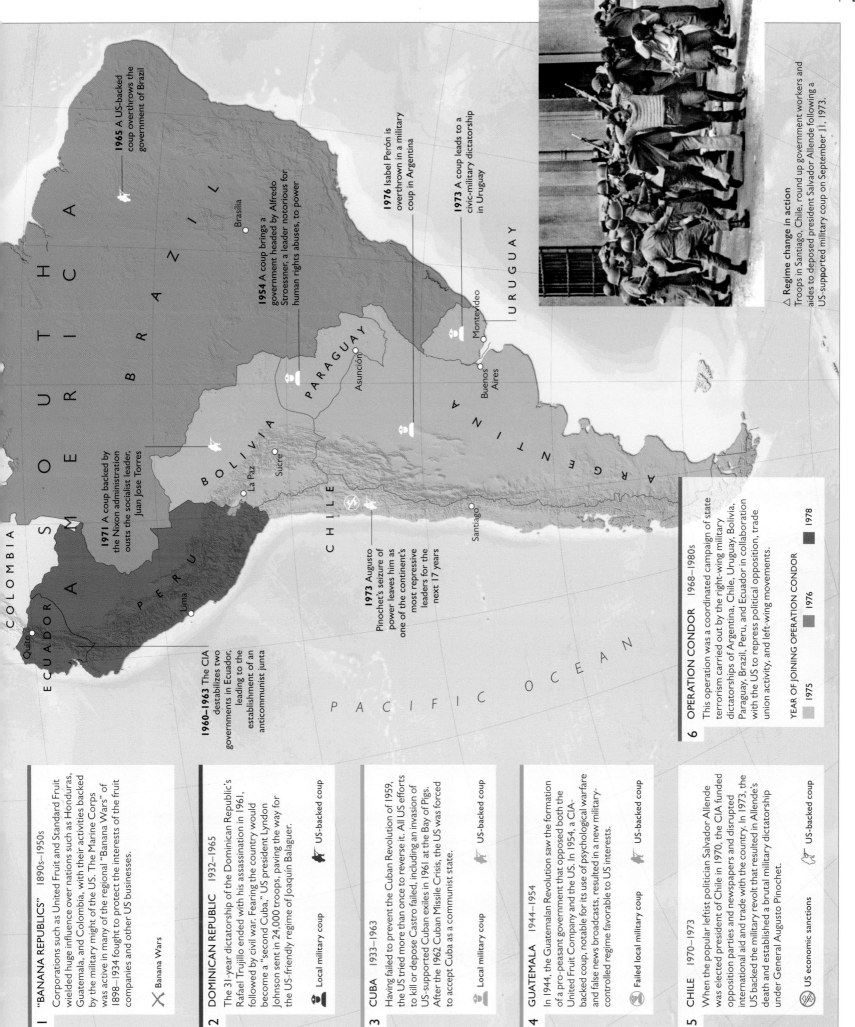

△ Regime change in action
Troops in Santiago, Chile, round up government workers and aides to deposed president Salvador Allende following a US-supported military coup on September 11, 1973.

1965 A US-backed coup overthrows the government of Brazil

Brasília

1954 A coup brings a government headed by Alfredo Stroessner, a leader notorious for human rights abuses, to power

1976 Isabel Perón is overthrown in a military coup in Argentina

1973 A coup leads to a civic-military dictatorship in Uruguay

Montevideo

1971 A coup backed by the Nixon administration ousts the socialist leader, Juan José Torres

1973 Augusto Pinochet's seizure of power leaves him as one of the continent's most repressive leaders for the next 17 years

1960–1963 The CIA destabilizes two governments in Ecuador, leading to the establishment of an anticommunist junta

URUGUAY
PARAGUAY
Asunción
Buenos Aires
BOLIVIA
La Paz
Sucre
CHILE
ARGENTINA
Santiago
PERU
Lima
COLOMBIA
ECUADOR
Quito
SOUTH AMERICA
BRAZIL

PACIFIC OCEAN

1 "BANANA REPUBLICS" 1890s–1950s

Corporations such as United Fruit and Standard Fruit wielded huge influence over nations such as Honduras, Guatemala, and Colombia, with their activities backed by the military might of the US. The Marine Corps was active in many of the regional "Banana Wars" of 1898–1934 fought to protect the interests of the fruit companies and other US businesses.

✕ Banana Wars

2 DOMINICAN REPUBLIC 1932–1965

The 31-year dictatorship of the Dominican Republic's Rafael Trujillo ended with his assassination in 1961, followed by civil war. Fearing the country would become a "second Cuba," US president Lyndon Johnson sent in 24,000 troops, paving the way for the US-friendly regime of Joaquín Balaguer.

Local military coup   US-backed coup

3 CUBA 1933–1963

Having failed to prevent the Cuban Revolution of 1959, the US tried more than once to reverse it. All US efforts to kill or depose Castro failed, including an invasion of US-supported Cuban exiles in 1961 at the Bay of Pigs. After the 1962 Cuban Missile Crisis, the US was forced to accept Cuba as a communist state.

Local military coup   US-backed coup

4 GUATEMALA 1944–1954

In 1944, the Guatemalan Revolution saw the formation of a pro-peasant government that opposed both the United Fruit Company and the US. In 1954, a CIA-backed coup, notable for its use of psychological warfare and false news broadcasts, resulted in a new military-controlled regime favorable to US interests.

Failed local military coup   US-backed coup

5 CHILE 1970–1973

When the popular leftist politician Salvador Allende was elected president of Chile in 1970, the CIA funded opposition parties and newspapers and disrupted international aid and trade with the country. In 1973, the US backed the military revolt that resulted in Allende's death and established a brutal military dictatorship under General Augusto Pinochet.

US economic sanctions   US-backed coup

6 OPERATION CONDOR 1968–1980s

This operation was a coordinated campaign of state terrorism carried out by the right-wing military dictatorships of Argentina, Chile, Uruguay, Bolivia, Paraguay, Brazil, Peru, and Ecuador in collaboration with the US to repress political opposition, trade union activity, and left-wing movements.

YEAR OF JOINING OPERATION CONDOR
1975   1976   1978

GLOBAL NORTH AMERICA

FROM THE 1980S, NORTH AMERICA ENTERED AN ERA OF BOLD ECONOMIC CHANGES. AS THE COLD WAR CAME TO AN END, THE US LAUNCHED NEW OVERSEAS MILITARY ACTIONS, AND THE UNSETTLED 21ST CENTURY SAW INCREASED POLITICAL DIVISIONS.

THE MODERN WORLD

As the 20th century drew to a close, the nations of North America seemed to enter an era of technological, economic, and social progress. However, this sense of optimism was challenged as the stability that followed the end of the Cold War proved to be short-lived.

The election of Ronald Reagan as president in 1980 marked an important turn for both domestic and foreign policy in the US (see pp.310–311). Reagan embarked on a series of controversial economic reforms at home, designed to revive the US economy still under strain from the stagflation of the 1970s. Internationally, he took a highly confrontational approach to the Cold War by increasing US military spending, expanding the country's nuclear arsenal, and intervening around the world to undermine socialist movements and regimes, especially throughout Latin America and the islands of the Caribbean.

▷ **Obama runs for president**
Barack Obama was born in Hawaii to an American mother and a Kenyan father. After serving as Senator of Illinois, he was elected the 44th president of the US in 2008.

International conflicts

The Cold War ended in 1991, but the US was soon drawn into conflicts elsewhere, leading a coalition of countries to liberate the Persian Gulf nation of Kuwait from its neighboring Iraq. In Operation Desert Storm, a war lasting two months, US forces expelled Iraqi forces from Kuwait, but stopped short of toppling the Iraqi regime.

On September 11, 2001, deadly terror attacks stunned the US and the world. Hijacked passenger planes flown into the World Trade Center in New York City and the Pentagon in Washington, D.C., claimed 2,977 lives. The US, led by President George W. Bush, responded by declaring a global "war on terror." Within weeks, it invaded Afghanistan, targeting the mastermind of the 9/11 attacks, Osama bin Laden, and the fundamentalist Taliban regime that sheltered him and his Al-Qaeda terrorist group. In 2003, this was followed by the invasion of Iraq to overthrow the rule of Saddam Hussein, a far more divisive move that saw an outpouring of antiwar protest around the world.

▽ **Fall of Baghdad**
The US hoped that the Iraqi people would greet the 2003 invasion force as liberators. Here, US soldiers tear down a statue of Saddam Hussein in Baghdad on April 9, 2003.

DAWN OF A NEW MILLENNIUM

While the end of the Cold War briefly left the US in a position of unchallenged geopolitical dominance, the societies of North America contended with a wide range of domestic and international crises in the 21st century. Terror attacks, economic crisis, political unrest and, most recently, the global COVID-19 pandemic—all presented significant challenges.

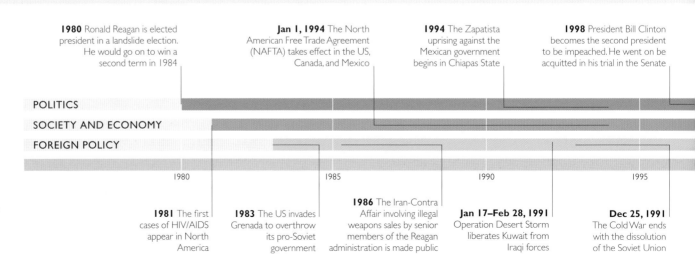

1980 Ronald Reagan is elected president in a landslide election. He would go on to win a second term in 1984

Jan 1, 1994 The North American Free Trade Agreement (NAFTA) takes effect in the US, Canada, and Mexico

1994 The Zapatista uprising against the Mexican government begins in Chiapas State

1998 President Bill Clinton becomes the second president to be impeached. He went on be acquitted in his trial in the Senate

POLITICS

SOCIETY AND ECONOMY

FOREIGN POLICY

1980   1985   1990   1995

1981 The first cases of HIV/AIDS appear in North America

1983 The US invades Grenada to overthrow its pro-Soviet government

1986 The Iran-Contra Affair involving illegal weapons sales by senior members of the Reagan administration is made public

Jan 17–Feb 28, 1991 Operation Desert Storm liberates Kuwait from Iraqi forces

Dec 25, 1991 The Cold War ends with the dissolution of the Soviet Union

◁ **US Capitol attack**
The 21st century has seen a sharp upsurge in political polarization across the US. On January 6, 2021, Donald Trump's supporters stormed the US Capitol building, prompted by his false accusations that fraud caused his loss in the 2020 election.

"… we are not as divided as our politics suggests … we are one people, we are one nation."

BARACK OBAMA, 2008

▽ **Pipeline protest**
In this image, an Indigenous American protests the Trump administration's decision to proceed with the Dakota Access Pipeline in 2017. A section of the proposed pipeline ran in proximity to the Standing Rock Sioux Reservation in North Dakota, potentially jeopardizing a key water source and desecrating cultural sites.

While the Iraqi army was quickly defeated, another armed Iraqi insurgency challenged US rule and evolved into a civil war that bogged down the US and its allies for years.

Society in flux

Mexico and Canada, too, were in a state of flux throughout this period. The emergence of a separatist movement in the French-speaking province of Quebec during the 1960s led to two referendums, in 1980 and in 1995, both of which rejected full political independence from Canada. In Mexico, the economic upheaval of the 1980s strained the decades-long rule of the Institutional Revolutionary Party (PRI). In 2000, Vicente Fox was elected the first non-PRI president of Mexico since 1929.

Across the continent, Indigenous and immigrant communities continued to struggle for rights and economic opportunities. In Canada and the US, this often took the form of legal disputes over rights to Indigenous land and the enforcement of immigration laws. In Mexico, the Zapatista uprising in 1994 became a global symbol of the Indigenous struggle against cultural and economic marginalization.

In the early 21st century, civil society in the US was split along racial, class, geographical, and religious lines. This situation was exacerbated by the global financial crisis of 2007–2008. There was a bitter partisan rivalry between the Democratic and Republican parties in the country. In 2008, Barack Obama was elected the first Black president of the US. The election of his successor, Donald Trump, became a rallying point for both the left and right, each offering radically different visions for the future. In 2020, with the onset of the COVID-19 pandemic (see pp.330–331), North America, and the world, grappled with the greatest public health emergency of modern times.

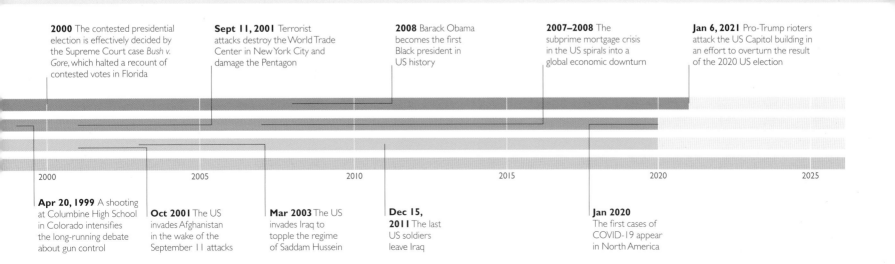

2000 The contested presidential election is effectively decided by the Supreme Court case *Bush v. Gore*, which halted a recount of contested votes in Florida

Sept 11, 2001 Terrorist attacks destroy the World Trade Center in New York City and damage the Pentagon

2008 Barack Obama becomes the first Black president in US history

2007–2008 The subprime mortgage crisis in the US spirals into a global economic downturn

Jan 6, 2021 Pro-Trump rioters attack the US Capitol building in an effort to overturn the result of the 2020 US election

2000   2005   2010   2015   2020   2025

Apr 20, 1999 A shooting at Columbine High School in Colorado intensifies the long-running debate about gun control

Oct 2001 The US invades Afghanistan in the wake of the September 11 attacks

Mar 2003 The US invades Iraq to topple the regime of Saddam Hussein

Dec 15, 2011 The last US soldiers leave Iraq

Jan 2020 The first cases of COVID-19 appear in North America

THE REAGAN ERA

The presidency of Ronald Reagan defined the style and substance of US politics during the 1980s. A vocal advocate of free-market economics, Reagan was a militant anticommunist and adopted a confrontational approach toward the Soviet Union.

△ **Campaign call**
This button from Reagan's 1980 campaign emphasizes fixing the perceived decline of the US. The slogan was reused in later elections, notably by Donald Trump in 2016.

Ronald Reagan was a Hollywood actor for almost 30 years before he went on to serve as governor of California from 1967 to 1975. During his presidential campaign, he created a powerful electoral coalition that included evangelical Christians, working-class voters, and traditional conservatives. This resulted in a landslide victory for him in 1980, in which he won 44 states, and an even larger landslide in the election of 1984, when he won 49 states.

The Reagan White House

As president, Reagan brought a conservative approach to economics, favoring limited government intervention, lower taxes, deregulation, and reigning in federal spending. As social policy, he advocated "traditional family values," prayer in public schools, and, together with First Lady Nancy Reagan, launched the "Just Say No" anti-drug campaign. He made numerous conservative appointments to the federal judiciary, including two Supreme Court Justices.

Reagan pursued an aggressive foreign policy, particularly with regard to the Cold War (see pp.284–285), and initiated a buildup of US military forces, both conventional and nuclear. He sought to develop missile defense technology in the Strategic Defense Initiative, or "Star Wars" program. The US supported anticommunist regimes and insurgencies, such as the Mujahideen in Afghanistan during the Soviet invasion, as well as the Contra rebels in Nicaragua.

REAGANOMICS

Reagan's approach to economics, dubbed Reaganomics, proved controversial even at the time. His supporters applauded higher employment, robust economic growth, and the end of the "stagflation" (simultaneous economic stagnation and inflation) that had plagued the US during the 1970s. On the other hand, his critics condemned a reduction in spending on social programs, widened income inequality, and tax cuts that benefited the wealthy.

Reagan wields the "Tax Ax," referring to tax cuts announced in the Tax Reform Act of 1986

Running for reelection
On August 23, 1984, Reagan accepted his nomination for reelection at the Republican National Convention in Dallas, Texas. He and his running mate, George H. W. Bush, won with 59 percent of the popular vote.

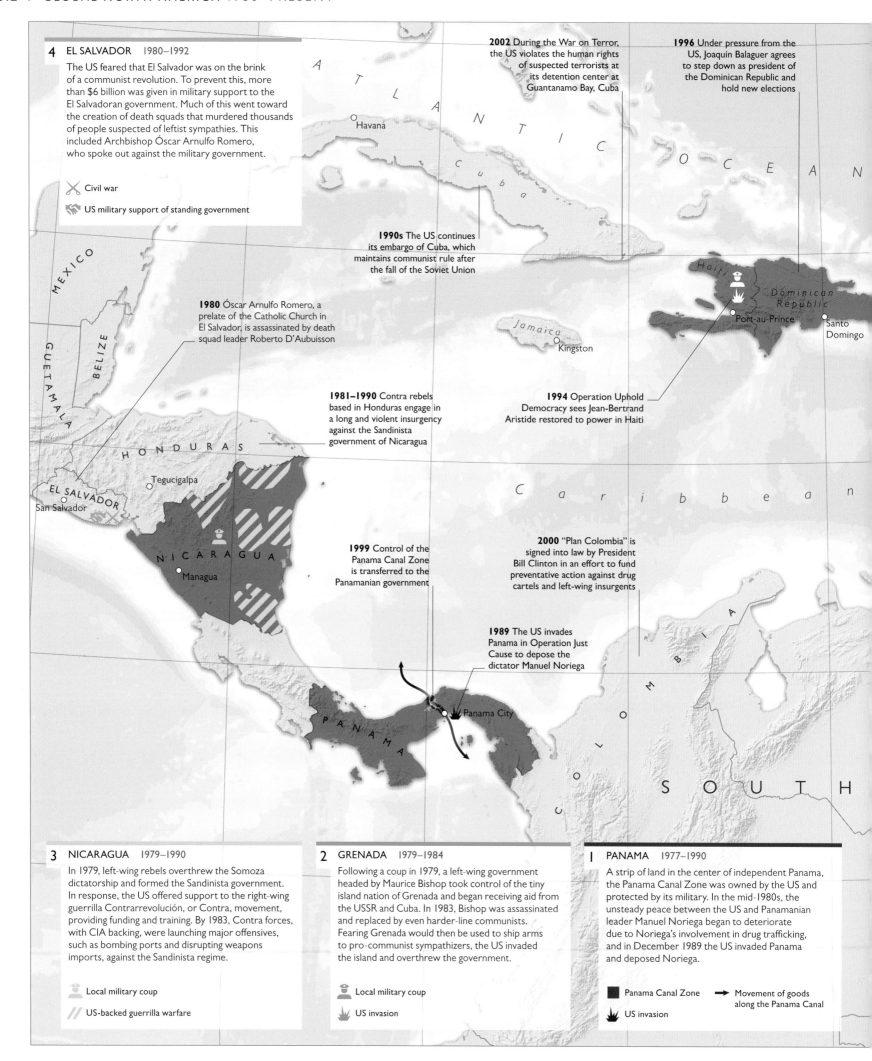

4 EL SALVADOR 1980–1992

The US feared that El Salvador was on the brink of a communist revolution. To prevent this, more than $6 billion was given in military support to the El Salvadoran government. Much of this went toward the creation of death squads that murdered thousands of people suspected of leftist sympathies. This included Archbishop Óscar Arnulfo Romero, who spoke out against the military government.

✂ Civil war

🤝 US military support of standing government

2002 During the War on Terror, the US violates the human rights of suspected terrorists at its detention center at Guantanamo Bay, Cuba

1996 Under pressure from the US, Joaquín Balaguer agrees to step down as president of the Dominican Republic and hold new elections

1990s The US continues its embargo of Cuba, which maintains communist rule after the fall of the Soviet Union

1980 Óscar Arnulfo Romero, a prelate of the Catholic Church in El Salvador, is assassinated by death squad leader Roberto D'Aubuisson

1981–1990 Contra rebels based in Honduras engage in a long and violent insurgency against the Sandinista government of Nicaragua

1994 Operation Uphold Democracy sees Jean-Bertrand Aristide restored to power in Haiti

1999 Control of the Panama Canal Zone is transferred to the Panamanian government

2000 "Plan Colombia" is signed into law by President Bill Clinton in an effort to fund preventative action against drug cartels and left-wing insurgents

1989 The US invades Panama in Operation Just Cause to depose the dictator Manuel Noriega

3 NICARAGUA 1979–1990

In 1979, left-wing rebels overthrew the Somoza dictatorship and formed the Sandinista government. In response, the US offered support to the right-wing guerrilla Contrarrevolución, or Contra, movement, providing funding and training. By 1983, Contra forces, with CIA backing, were launching major offensives, such as bombing ports and disrupting weapons imports, against the Sandinista regime.

👤 Local military coup

// US-backed guerrilla warfare

2 GRENADA 1979–1984

Following a coup in 1979, a left-wing government headed by Maurice Bishop took control of the tiny island nation of Grenada and began receiving aid from the USSR and Cuba. In 1983, Bishop was assassinated and replaced by even harder-line communists. Fearing Grenada would then be used to ship arms to pro-communist sympathizers, the US invaded the island and overthrew the government.

👤 Local military coup

🌱 US invasion

1 PANAMA 1977–1990

A strip of land in the center of independent Panama, the Panama Canal Zone was owned by the US and protected by its military. In the mid-1980s, the unsteady peace between the US and Panamanian leader Manuel Noriega began to deteriorate due to Noriega's involvement in drug trafficking, and in December 1989 the US invaded Panama and deposed Noriega.

■ Panama Canal Zone

🌱 US invasion

➡ Movement of goods along the Panama Canal

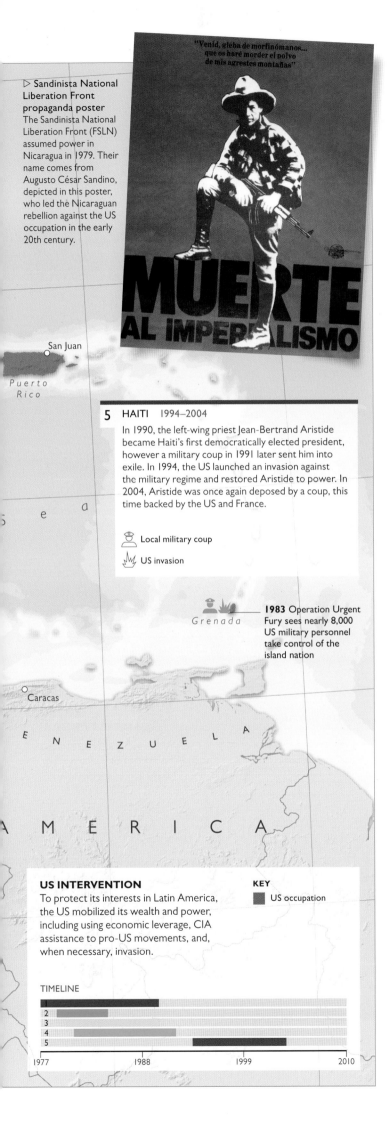

"Venid, gleba de morfinómanos... que os haré morder el polvo de mis agrestes montañas"

MUERTE AL IMPERIALISMO

▷ **Sandinista National Liberation Front propaganda poster**
The Sandinista National Liberation Front (FSLN) assumed power in Nicaragua in 1979. Their name comes from Augusto César Sandino, depicted in this poster, who led the Nicaraguan rebellion against the US occupation in the early 20th century.

San Juan

Puerto Rico

5   HAITI   1994–2004
In 1990, the left-wing priest Jean-Bertrand Aristide became Haiti's first democratically elected president, however a military coup in 1991 later sent him into exile. In 1994, the US launched an invasion against the military regime and restored Aristide to power. In 2004, Aristide was once again deposed by a coup, this time backed by the US and France.

🪖 Local military coup

🔥 US invasion

Grenada   **1983** Operation Urgent Fury sees nearly 8,000 US military personnel take control of the island nation

Caracas

V E N E Z U E L A

A M E R I C A

US INTERVENTION
To protect its interests in Latin America, the US mobilized its wealth and power, including using economic leverage, CIA assistance to pro-US movements, and, when necessary, invasion.

KEY
▮ US occupation

TIMELINE

1977   1988   1999   2010

LATER US INTERVENTIONS

As the Cold War continued into the 1980s, the US government remained committed to its policy of intervention in Latin American and Caribbean affairs. A series of invasions and occupations aimed to promote US interests and install anticommunist governments across the hemisphere.

In the late 20th century, US foreign policy continued to seek to prevent pro-Soviet governments taking power within the Western Hemisphere. The election of Ronald Reagan (see pp.310–311), who advocated a strongly confrontational approach to the Cold War, only intensified this attitude. Under his "Reagan Doctrine," the US provided aid to anticommunist resistance movements around the world. In Latin America, right-wing insurgencies and embattled pro-US governments received funding, equipment, and assistance from the CIA. A notorious example of this US interference was the Contra rebellion against the left-wing Nicaraguan

government, which eventually embroiled the Reagan administration in scandal when it resorted to covert and illegal arms sales to fund the rebels. In the case of Grenada in the Caribbean, a communist coup provoked fears in Washington that the island would become "another Cuba," and subsequently the US army invaded the nation and overthrew its socialist government in 1983.

At the close of the Cold War in 1991, anticommunism became less relevant as a policy objective, however the US continued to intervene in the region, with an increasing focus on fighting narcotics production and trafficking.

"And we must not break faith with those who are risking their lives … to defy Soviet-supported aggression …"

RONALD REAGAN, 1985

IRAN-CONTRA AFFAIR

The Iran-Contra Affair was the result of secret US sales of missiles to Iran to fund the ongoing right-wing Contra insurgency in Nicaragua, which the Reagan administration was committed to supporting. Both activities were against the law—Congress had cut off support to the Contras due to their involvement in cocaine trafficking, while Iran was under a weapons embargo. The exposure of the program in 1986 created a major political scandal that eventually resulted in criminal convictions for senior military officials plus high-ranking members of the CIA.

Lt. Col. Oliver North appearing before the congressional panel investigating the affair

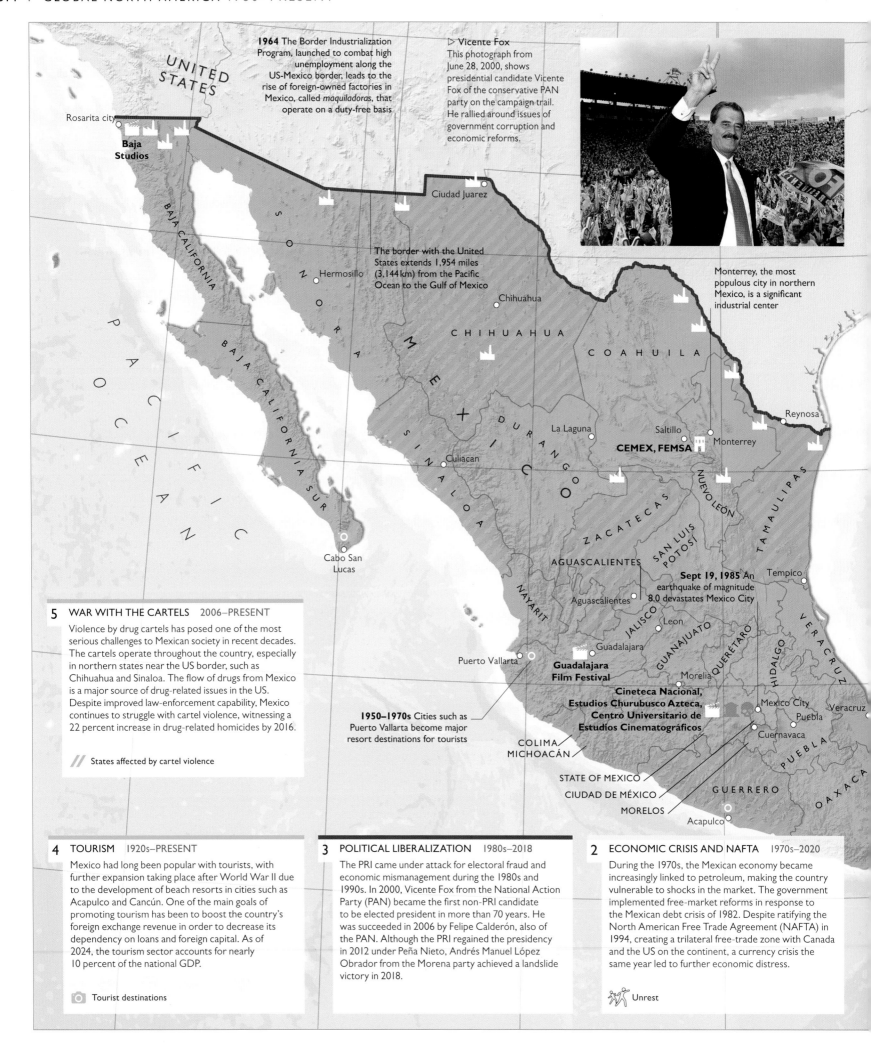

1964 The Border Industrialization Program, launched to combat high unemployment along the US-Mexico border, leads to the rise of foreign-owned factories in Mexico, called *maquiladoras*, that operate on a duty-free basis

▷ **Vicente Fox**
This photograph from June 28, 2000, shows presidential candidate Vicente Fox of the conservative PAN party on the campaign trail. He rallied around issues of government corruption and economic reforms.

The border with the United States extends 1,954 miles (3,144 km) from the Pacific Ocean to the Gulf of Mexico

Monterrey, the most populous city in northern Mexico, is a significant industrial center

CEMEX, FEMSA

Sept 19, 1985 An earthquake of magnitude 8.0 devastates Mexico City

Guadalajara Film Festival

1950–1970s Cities such as Puerto Vallarta become major resort destinations for tourists

Cineteca Nacional, Estudios Churubusco Azteca, Centro Universitario de Estudios Cinematográficos

5 WAR WITH THE CARTELS 2006–PRESENT
Violence by drug cartels has posed one of the most serious challenges to Mexican society in recent decades. The cartels operate throughout the country, especially in northern states near the US border, such as Chihuahua and Sinaloa. The flow of drugs from Mexico is a major source of drug-related issues in the US. Despite improved law-enforcement capability, Mexico continues to struggle with cartel violence, witnessing a 22 percent increase in drug-related homicides by 2016.

/// States affected by cartel violence

4 TOURISM 1920s–PRESENT
Mexico had long been popular with tourists, with further expansion taking place after World War II due to the development of beach resorts in cities such as Acapulco and Cancún. One of the main goals of promoting tourism has been to boost the country's foreign exchange revenue in order to decrease its dependency on loans and foreign capital. As of 2024, the tourism sector accounts for nearly 10 percent of the national GDP.

📷 Tourist destinations

3 POLITICAL LIBERALIZATION 1980s–2018
The PRI came under attack for electoral fraud and economic mismanagement during the 1980s and 1990s. In 2000, Vicente Fox from the National Action Party (PAN) became the first non-PRI candidate to be elected president in more than 70 years. He was succeeded in 2006 by Felipe Calderón, also of the PAN. Although the PRI regained the presidency in 2012 under Peña Nieto, Andrés Manuel López Obrador from the Morena party achieved a landslide victory in 2018.

2 ECONOMIC CRISIS AND NAFTA 1970s–2020
During the 1970s, the Mexican economy became increasingly linked to petroleum, making the country vulnerable to shocks in the market. The government implemented free-market reforms in response to the Mexican debt crisis of 1982. Despite ratifying the North American Free Trade Agreement (NAFTA) in 1994, creating a trilateral free-trade zone with Canada and the US on the continent, a currency crisis the same year led to further economic distress.

🏃 Unrest

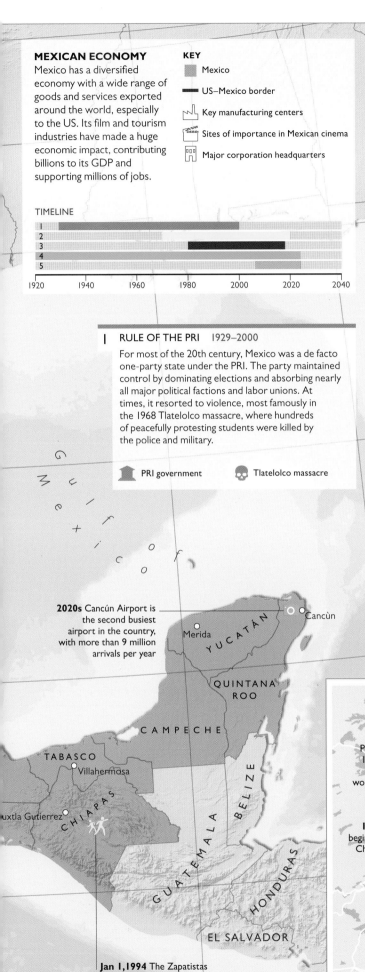

MEXICAN ECONOMY

Mexico has a diversified economy with a wide range of goods and services exported around the world, especially to the US. Its film and tourism industries have made a huge economic impact, contributing billions to its GDP and supporting millions of jobs.

KEY

- ▓ Mexico
- ▬ US–Mexico border
- ⚒ Key manufacturing centers
- 🎬 Sites of importance in Mexican cinema
- 🏛 Major corporation headquarters

TIMELINE

1
2
3
4
5

1920 1940 1960 1980 2000 2020 2040

I RULE OF THE PRI 1929–2000

For most of the 20th century, Mexico was a de facto one-party state under the PRI. The party maintained control by dominating elections and absorbing nearly all major political factions and labor unions. At times, it resorted to violence, most famously in the 1968 Tlatelolco massacre, where hundreds of peacefully protesting students were killed by the police and military.

- 🏛 PRI government
- 💀 Tlatelolco massacre

2020s Cancún Airport is the second busiest airport in the country, with more than 9 million arrivals per year

Jan 1,1994 The Zapatistas oppose NAFTA because they fear it will result in the exploitation of Indigenous peoples

MODERN MEXICO

In the second half of the 20th century, Mexico underwent political upheaval and economic turbulence as it navigated a complex relationship with the US. While the end of one-party rule brought a greater level of democracy, instability continued to persist, especially from cartel-related violence and economic issues.

Mexico had emerged from the revolution of 1910–1920 (see pp.238–239) with a new constitution and strong central government. The National Revolutionary Party, founded in 1929, consolidated the various victorious factions into a single national organization. Renamed the Institutional Revolutionary Party (PRI) in 1946, the party dominated Mexican politics and government without significant opposition for more than 70 years.

After World War II, Mexico witnessed three decades of continuous economic expansion and modernization. Called the "Mexican Miracle" (see pp.274–275), it was financed in large part by massive international loans. By the late 1970s, the economy began to falter, fueled by soaring public debt and an overreliance on oil exports. A sharp fall in oil prices led to a significant shortfall in revenue,

prompting the government to default on its debt payments. The outcome was the largest economic contraction in Mexican history since the Great Depression. Mexico's entry into the North American Free Trade Agreement (NAFTA) with Canada and the US led to further crises, including a devaluation of the peso and the emergence of the Zapatista insurgency in the state of Chiapas.

By the turn of the century, decades of instability and mismanagement had eroded support for the ruling PRI, culminating in a historic loss in the 2000 presidential elections and a transition to multiparty politics. Various governments since then have had to contend with an escalating war against drug cartels, continuing economic malaise, and the challenges posed by the COVID-19 pandemic.

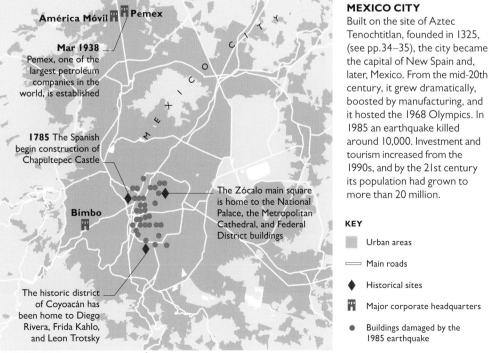

América Móvil 🏛🏛 **Pemex**

Mar 1938 Pemex, one of the largest petroleum companies in the world, is established

1785 The Spanish begin construction of Chapultepec Castle

Bimbo 🏛

The Zócalo main square is home to the National Palace, the Metropolitan Cathedral, and Federal District buildings

The historic district of Coyoacán has been home to Diego Rivera, Frida Kahlo, and Leon Trotsky

MEXICO CITY

Built on the site of Aztec Tenochtitlan, founded in 1325, (see pp.34–35), the city became the capital of New Spain and, later, Mexico. From the mid-20th century, it grew dramatically, boosted by manufacturing, and it hosted the 1968 Olympics. In 1985 an earthquake killed around 10,000. Investment and tourism increased from the 1990s, and by the 21st century its population had grown to more than 20 million.

KEY

- ▓ Urban areas
- ▭ Main roads
- ◆ Historical sites
- 🏛 Major corporate headquarters
- ● Buildings damaged by the 1985 earthquake

Flying the flag
During the 1980 referendum, impassioned crowds took to the streets of Quebec in a show of nationalistic fervor, many waving the province's fleur-de-lis flag. However, nearly 60 percent voted against separation.

QUÉBÉCOIS SEPARATISM

During the late 20th century, a strong sense of regional identity turned to nationalist ambitions in the predominately French-speaking Canadian province of Quebec, sparking political debate and crisis.

△ **Painting over differences**
Showing the Quebec flag being painted over, this banner conveys Québécois dissatisfaction at not being recognized as a "distinct society."

The Francophone province of Quebec had a long and sometimes tense history of linguistic and cultural distinctiveness from the rest of Canada, which is mostly Anglophone. These differences found expression in nationalist and separatist politics during the 1960s and 1970s, in what was called the Quiet Revolution.

The revolution started with the election of Jean Lesage as the Premier of Quebec in 1960. His Quebec Liberal Party undertook reforms emphasizing secularization, economic autonomy, and education. The nationalist and separatist Parti Québécois (PQ), founded in 1968, took this mandate a step further to campaign for the full independence of Quebec. In 1976, the PQ won a majority in provincial elections, prompting disquiet in the rest of Canada and leading to a national political conversation about the status of Quebec. In 1980, the PQ held a referendum in Quebec asking voters if they wanted to open negotiations with the national government for a path to sovereignty. This was rejected. In a second independence referendum held in 1995, the "No" campaign won out again, but by a much narrower margin.

THE OCTOBER CRISIS

In 1970, during what became known as the October Crisis, the militant separatist group Front de libération du Québec (FLQ) kidnapped British diplomat James Cross and provincial Labour Minister Pierre Laporte. In response, Prime Minister Pierre Trudeau invoked the War Measures Act, deploying troops and increasing police powers of arrest. The FLQ was banned and civil liberties suspended. While negotiations eventually secured the release of Cross, Laporte was murdered by his captors.

Army troops patrol the streets of Montreal in October 1970

PERSIAN GULF WAR

In 1991, the US and other coalition forces went to war with Iraq after its armed forces invaded Kuwait. The coalition's quick victory restored Kuwait's sovereignty, protected oil production in the region, and showcased new weapons technologies that changed the face of modern warfare.

In August 1990, Iraqi leader Saddam Hussein sent his army into Kuwait, aiming to take control of its oil fields and erase the large debt Iraq owed to the country. In response, the United Nations (UN) banned trade with Iraq, and the US organized a coalition opposed to Iraq whose 42 members included the Arab nations of Saudi Arabia, Syria, and Egypt. As tensions mounted, the UN authorized the use of force if the Iraqis did not leave Kuwait by January 15, 1991.

When that date passed with no withdrawal, the US-led coalition initiated an air campaign, called Operation Desert Storm, followed by a ground action, known as Operation Desert Sabre. President George H. W. Bush committed more than 400,000 US troops to the conflict, with the other coalition members sending 265,000 more. These soldiers fulfilled their objectives, but it was the use of sophisticated bombs and new military hardware that did the most damage. Global positioning systems (GPS) and geographic

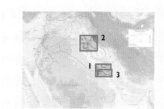

LOCATOR

information systems (GIS) allowed the coalition to navigate remote terrain and carry out precision strikes on power plants, oil refineries, military bases, and other strategic targets. Just five weeks after hostilities started, Iraq began to pull out of Kuwait.

Although the war was won, Saddam Hussein stayed in power and remained a threat to the region's peace and security. In 2003, emboldened by their success in the Gulf War, US forces took part in a second invasion of Iraq (see pp.324–325).

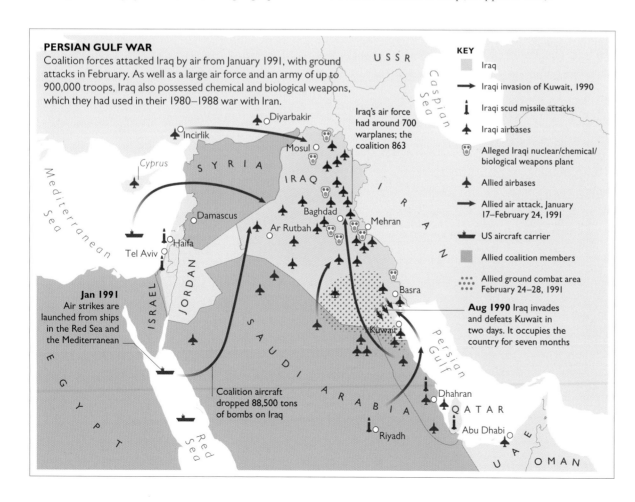

PERSIAN GULF WAR

Coalition forces attacked Iraq by air from January 1991, with ground attacks in February. As well as a large air force and an army of up to 900,000 troops, Iraq also possessed chemical and biological weapons, which they had used in their 1980–1988 war with Iran.

Iraq's air force had around 700 warplanes; the coalition 863

KEY

- Iraq
- → Iraqi invasion of Kuwait, 1990
- Iraqi scud missile attacks
- Iraqi airbases
- Alleged Iraqi nuclear/chemical/biological weapons plant
- Allied airbases
- → Allied air attack, January 17–February 24, 1991
- US aircraft carrier
- Allied coalition members
- Allied ground combat area February 24–28, 1991

Jan 1991 Air strikes are launched from ships in the Red Sea and the Mediterranean

Aug 1990 Iraq invades and defeats Kuwait in two days. It occupies the country for seven months

Coalition aircraft dropped 88,500 tons of bombs on Iraq

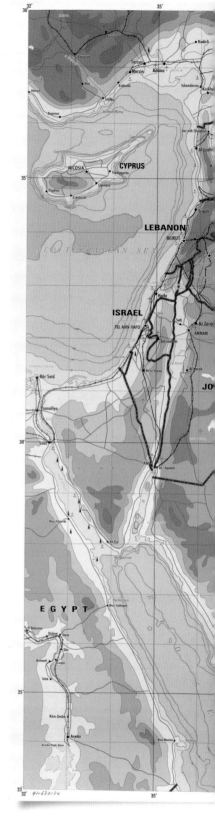

△ **Operation Desert Storm**
This US military briefing map shows the main transportation lines and airfields of the Persian Gulf region, including major targets in Iraq and Kuwait. The location of the many oil fields shows the strategic and geographic importance of petroleum in what was known as the Middle East.

▷ **Troops in Kuwait**
US and coalition ground forces entered Kuwait after 40 days of aerial bombing and quickly ended the war 100 hours later.

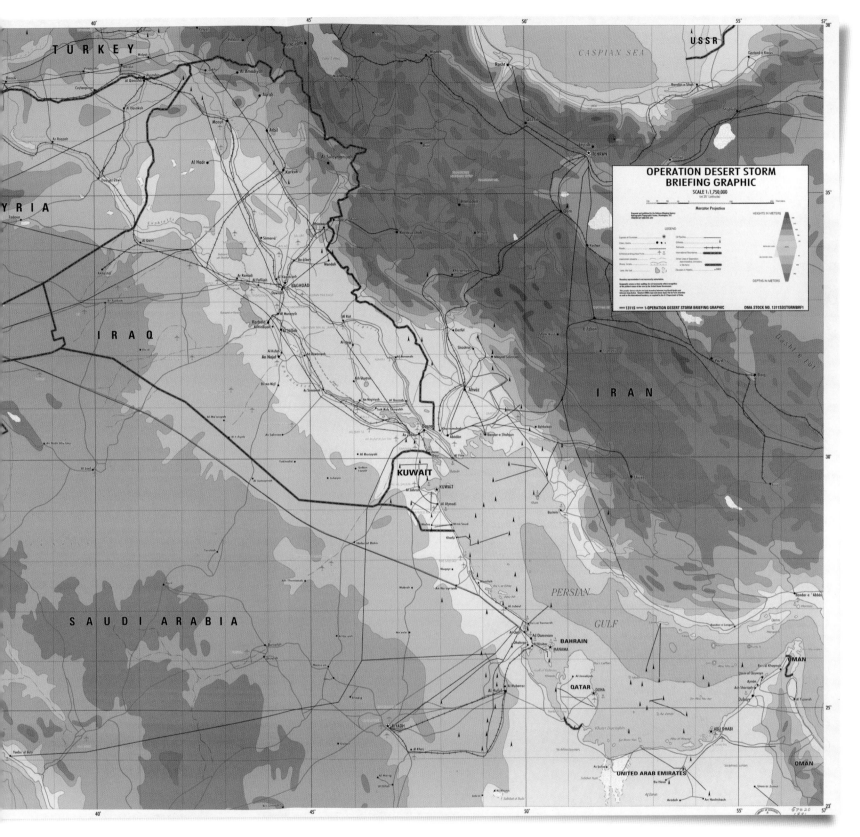

OPERATION DESERT STORM
BRIEFING GRAPHIC

SCALE 1:1,750,000
(at 25° Latitude)

Mercator Projection

LEGEND

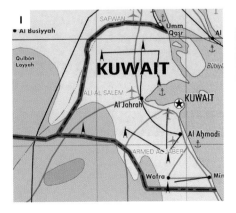

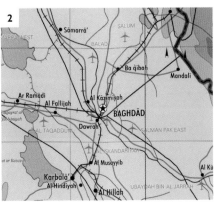

◁ Baghdad
Coalition bombs targeted the Iraq capital, an event broadcast worldwide in what has been described as the first war to be televised live.

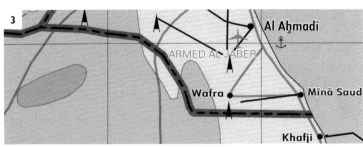

△ Kuwait–Saudi Arabia border
As a coalition member, Saudi Arabia provided supplies and served as a staging ground to launch attacks into Kuwait.

INDIGENOUS AND IMMIGRANT RIGHTS

Indigenous and immigrant communities in the US, Canada, and Mexico continued to challenge persistent discrimination and economic inequality in the later 20th and early 21st centuries.

Although some progress had been made to secure rights and recognition by the middle of the 20th century, Indigenous and immigrant communities remained severely marginalized in North America, especially in areas such as wealth inequality, access to education, and quality of health care. A significant figure in the early campaign for immigrant and Indigenous parity was Cesar Chavez, whose pioneering efforts to unionize agricultural workers boosted the emerging Chicano movement, which, in addition to calling for fair economic conditions for Mexican-Americans, and later Filipinos, further sought to promote cultural pride, solidarity, and visibility. To challenge what Chicano activists saw as a pervasive Anglocentrism in education, groups of teachers and students staged a walkout of public schools in East Los Angeles in 1968.

In recent decades, focus has shifted to the impact of global capitalism on Indigenous groups, particularly regarding their cultural and legal sovereignty. The Zapatista rebellion in Chiapas, Mexico, arose in response to the Mexican government's ratification of the North American Free Trade Agreement (NAFTA), which they argued opened Indigenous lands to exploitation by foreign corporations. Today, Indigenous groups in Canada and the US continue to oppose external development schemes on their land, most notably oil pipelines, which they view as a threat to their territory rights, environment, and cultural heritage.

> *"It's ironic that those who till the soil, cultivate and harvest the fruits, vegetables, and other foods that fill your tables with abundance have nothing left for themselves."*
>
> CESAR CHAVEZ, CIVIL RIGHTS ACTIVIST

SANCTUARY CITIES

In sanctuary cities, municipal governments refuse to cooperate with national immigration authorities in order to provide a safe haven for undocumented individuals, in some cases escaping economic or political disruption sanctioned by the US. This often brings these areas into conflict with the federal law. The movement began in the 1980s and gathered greater momentum in the early 2000s. It has now grown to include hundreds of municipalities throughout the US, including San Francisco, Los Angeles, and New York.

"Day Without Immigrants" protest, San Francisco, May 1, 2006

1 CHICANO MOVEMENT
1960s TO PRESENT

The Chicano movement of the 1960s and 1970s campaigned for the civil rights of Mexican-Americans and celebrated their cultural and linguistic identity. It called for greater political solidarity, access to education, and workers' rights. Prominent figures in the movement included labor leader and activist Cesar Chavez and the United Farm Workers union.

- Founding of advocacy group
- Founding of political party
- Chicano population

2 FIRST NATIONS ACTIVISM IN CANADA
1980s TO PRESENT

Conflict between Mohawk activists and land developers in Oka, Quebec lasted for 78 days in 1990 and resulted in a fatality. In response, the Canadian government launched the Inherent Right to Self-Government (IRSG) Policy in 1995 to enshrine First Nations self-determination as a constitutional principle. Further activism led to a class-action settlement against the legacy of Indigenous residential schools in 2007, demanding compensation for those affected.

- Indigenous activism

3 ZAPATISTAS
1994 TO PRESENT

The Zapatista movement launched a rebellion against the Mexican government in 1994, protesting the continued marginalization of predominately Indigenous communities in the Chiapas state and the impact of globalization on the rights of workers. Talks with the government in 1996 led to a cease-fire and partial deescalation of the conflict.

- Chiapas
- Sites of Indigenous activism

4 UNDOCUMENTED IN THE US
2000 TO PRESENT

In the 2000s, campaigns called for residency rights for individuals brought to the US from various other countries illegally as children. In 2012, President Obama issued a grant of temporary permits called Deferred Action for Childhood Arrivals (DACA). This was repealed in 2017 by President Trump, but was reinstated in 2021 by President Biden. Sanctuary cities offered support for undocumented migrants (see left).

- Mexico–US border
- Border fencing
- Sanctuary city

BRITISH COLUMBIA
WASHINGTON
OREGON
CALIFORNIA
NEVADA
San Francisco
Los Angeles
San Diego

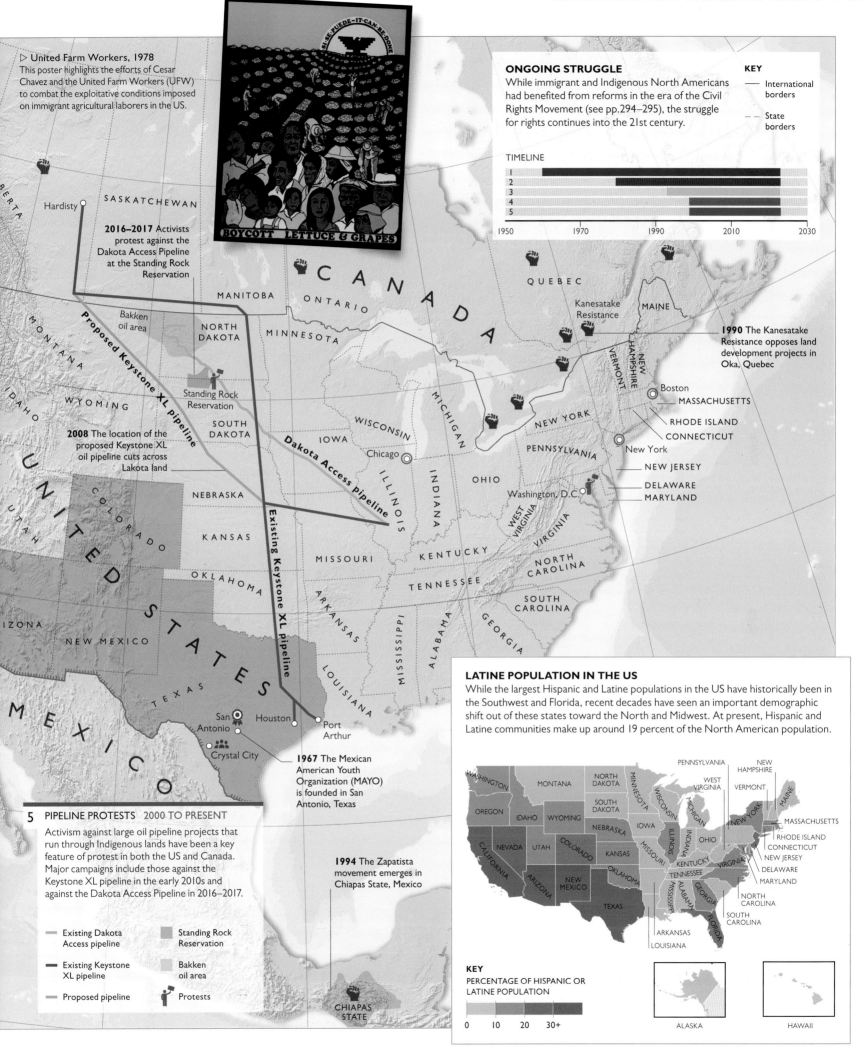

▷ United Farm Workers, 1978
This poster highlights the efforts of Cesar Chavez and the United Farm Workers (UFW) to combat the exploitative conditions imposed on immigrant agricultural laborers in the US.

ONGOING STRUGGLE
While immigrant and Indigenous North Americans had benefited from reforms in the era of the Civil Rights Movement (see pp.294–295), the struggle for rights continues into the 21st century.

KEY
— International borders
-- State borders

TIMELINE
1 2 3 4 5
1950   1970   1990   2010   2030

2016–2017 Activists protest against the Dakota Access Pipeline at the Standing Rock Reservation

1990 The Kanesatake Resistance opposes land development projects in Oka, Quebec

2008 The location of the proposed Keystone XL oil pipeline cuts across Lakota land

Hardisty
SASKATCHEWAN
ALBERTA
Bakken oil area
Proposed Keystone XL pipeline
MONTANA
IDAHO
WYOMING
Standing Rock Reservation
NORTH DAKOTA
MANITOBA
ONTARIO
CANADA
MINNESOTA
SOUTH DAKOTA
IOWA
WISCONSIN
MICHIGAN
Dakota Access pipeline
Chicago
ILLINOIS
INDIANA
OHIO
PENNSYLVANIA
NEW YORK
QUEBEC
MAINE
NEW HAMPSHIRE
VERMONT
Kanesatake Resistance
Boston
MASSACHUSETTS
RHODE ISLAND
CONNECTICUT
New York
NEW JERSEY
DELAWARE
MARYLAND
Washington, D.C.
WEST VIRGINIA
VIRGINIA
KENTUCKY
NORTH CAROLINA
TENNESSEE
SOUTH CAROLINA
GEORGIA
UNITED STATES
UTAH
COLORADO
NEBRASKA
KANSAS
MISSOURI
OKLAHOMA
ARKANSAS
MISSISSIPPI
ALABAMA
LOUISIANA
ARIZONA
NEW MEXICO
Existing Keystone XL pipeline
TEXAS
San Antonio
Houston
Port Arthur
Crystal City
MEXICO

1967 The Mexican American Youth Organization (MAYO) is founded in San Antonio, Texas

5 PIPELINE PROTESTS 2000 TO PRESENT
Activism against large oil pipeline projects that run through Indigenous lands have been a key feature of protest in both the US and Canada. Major campaigns include those against the Keystone XL pipeline in the early 2010s and against the Dakota Access Pipeline in 2016–2017.

1994 The Zapatista movement emerges in Chiapas State, Mexico

CHIAPAS STATE

— Existing Dakota Access pipeline
▨ Standing Rock Reservation
— Existing Keystone XL pipeline
▨ Bakken oil area
— Proposed pipeline
👤 Protests

LATINE POPULATION IN THE US
While the largest Hispanic and Latine populations in the US have historically been in the Southwest and Florida, recent decades have seen an important demographic shift out of these states toward the North and Midwest. At present, Hispanic and Latine communities make up around 19 percent of the North American population.

WASHINGTON
OREGON
IDAHO
MONTANA
WYOMING
NORTH DAKOTA
SOUTH DAKOTA
MINNESOTA
WISCONSIN
MICHIGAN
PENNSYLVANIA
NEW HAMPSHIRE
VERMONT
MAINE
WEST VIRGINIA
NEW YORK
MASSACHUSETTS
RHODE ISLAND
CONNECTICUT
NEW JERSEY
DELAWARE
MARYLAND
CALIFORNIA
NEVADA
UTAH
COLORADO
NEBRASKA
IOWA
ILLINOIS
INDIANA
OHIO
KENTUCKY
VIRGINIA
NORTH CAROLINA
ARIZONA
NEW MEXICO
KANSAS
MISSOURI
TENNESSEE
SOUTH CAROLINA
GEORGIA
OKLAHOMA
ARKANSAS
MISSISSIPPI
ALABAMA
TEXAS
LOUISIANA
FLORIDA

KEY
PERCENTAGE OF HISPANIC OR LATINE POPULATION
0   10   20   30+

ALASKA
HAWAII

THE WAR ON TERROR

After Al-Qaeda terrorists attacked several locations in the US in 2001, the US Government launched a "War on Terror" against the group's worldwide network. During this time, the US undertook prolonged war abroad and changes to security at home.

△ **Tracking terrorists**
Osama bin Laden, the leader of fundamentalist Islamic group Al-Qaeda, claimed responsibility for 9/11 becoming the "most wanted man in the world" and one of the US's main targets in the War on Terror.

On September 11, 2001, Al-Qaeda terrorists crashed two airplanes into the World Trade Center in New York City and another into the Pentagon outside Washington, D.C. Another plane was hijacked, but passengers intervened, and the plane crashed in a field in Pennsylvania. The second plane that hit the World Trade Center was caught on live television and many people watched it in real time. President George W. Bush quickly declared a "War on Terror" that targeted terrorists around the world. The US then went to war in Afghanistan in 2001 and then with Iraq in 2003 to end the dictatorship of Saddam Hussein and, supposedly, destroy any weapons of mass destruction.

Domestic security

The Department of Homeland Security began in 2003 to prevent terror attacks; secure borders; and handle immigration, customs, and disaster relief. Congress passed the PATRIOT Act, giving the government additional powers of surveillance to help counterterrorism efforts. Critics argue the act invades privacy because it allows the government to collect individual phone, email, bank, and internet activity.

US INVASION OF AFGHANISTAN

In 2001, the US launched Operation Enduring Freedom to capture terrorist leader Osama bin Laden and remove the Taliban government. The US military, with British allies, was quickly successful and the Taliban collapsed in 2001. After being tracked down in Abbottabad, Pakistan, Osama bin Laden, was killed by US troops in 2011 under the order of President Obama. However, the war continued until the US fully withdrew in 2021 and the Taliban returned to power.

Wreckage at Ground Zero
The Twin Towers—World Trade Center North and South Tower—collapsed as a result of the hijacked airliners crashing into them. A total of 2,753 people were killed in New York.

THE SECOND GULF WAR

In March 2003, the US under the leadership of President George W. Bush invaded Iraq with the aim of toppling Saddam Hussein. This decision would have profound consequences, leading to regional instability, economic damage, and the deaths of thousands.

The Persian Gulf War in 1991 (see pp.318–319) expelled Iraqi forces from Kuwait but allowed Saddam Hussein to remain in power. This led to tense relations between Iraq and the US. In 2003, against the backdrop of the expanding War on Terror (see pp.322–323), US forces supported by coalition allies invaded Iraq, this time with the explicit aim of regime change and imposing a new government friendly to US interests. The Iraqi army was swiftly defeated and all major cities were captured by coalition forces.

However, this victory was short-lived and the region soon saw the emergence of an Iraqi insurgency that launched attacks on occupying US troops and their allies for years. At the same time, sectarian tensions between Shi'a and Sunni Muslims, which had been kept at bay under Hussein's rule, spiraled into civil war. US forces withdrew in 2011, causing further instability that led to the formation of the radical Islamic State (later named ISIS), which drew coalition forces into another war until the end of 2018. More than 4,800 coalition soldiers were killed in combat operations, and hundreds of thousands of Iraqis, most of whom were civilians, were left dead and wounded.

> *"States like these, and their terrorist allies, constitute an axis of evil ..."*
>
> US PRESIDENT GEORGE W. BUSH, JANUARY 29, 2002

SADDAM HUSSEIN

Saddam Hussein (1937–2006), dictator of Iraq from 1979 until 2003, was a leading member of the Ba'ath Party, which promoted secularism and socialism within a framework of Arab nationalism. Hussein was initially an ally of the US, which supported Iraq in its 1980–1988 war against Iran, but relations later soured. This led to the Persian Gulf War of 1990–1991 (see pp.318–319), and the 2003 invasion of Iraq.

Saddam Hussein in Baghdad, Iraq, October 14, 1983

---

3 INVASION AND REGIME CHANGE
MARCH–MAY 2003

US forces commenced the attack with a "shock and awe" bombing campaign. The subsequent ground invasion led to the rapid defeat of the Iraqi army. Baghdad was captured on April 9, 2003, and Paul Bremer took control of the country as governor of an interim US authority. Among his first actions were the disbanding of the Iraqi military and the ruling Ba'ath Party.

⇨ US/UK troop movements   ⚑ City captured

2 PREPARING FOR WAR   2002–2003

The Bush administration justified its planned invasion with claims (later disproved) that Iraq had a stockpile of weapons of mass destruction. The US attempted to secure support from NATO allies but was only partially successful in assembling a "coalition of the willing." Despite international and domestic criticism of its plans, the US issued an ultimatum to Saddam Hussein on March 17, 2003.

°Damascus

1 THE ORIGINS OF THE CONFLICT
2001–2002

Relations between the US and Iraq had been hostile since the end of the Persian Gulf War in 1991. After the start of the War on Terror that began in the wake of the 9/11 attacks, Iraq seemed the next target for a US invasion, especially after George W. Bush declared Iraq to be a part of an "Axis of Evil."

°Ruwaished

TUR

SYRIA

✈ Ar Rutb

JORDAN   SAUD

COMBINED FORCES

The invasion force in 2003 comprised troops from the US, UK, Australia, and Poland. In some areas, Kurdish Peshmerga forces also conducted offensive operations against the Iraqi army. A further 37 countries provided troops to support the subsequent occupation.

KEY

▭ Kurdish territories since 1991	⫽ Disputed Kurdish territories since 1991	⫽ Sunni Triangle	✕ Major battle
⚑ City captured	⚒ Major oil field	✈ Major airfield	

MILITARY OCCUPATION ZONES

■ North   ■ North-Central   ■ South-Central   ■ South-East   ■ Western

TIMELINE

1
2
3
4
5
6

2000   2005   2010   2015   2020

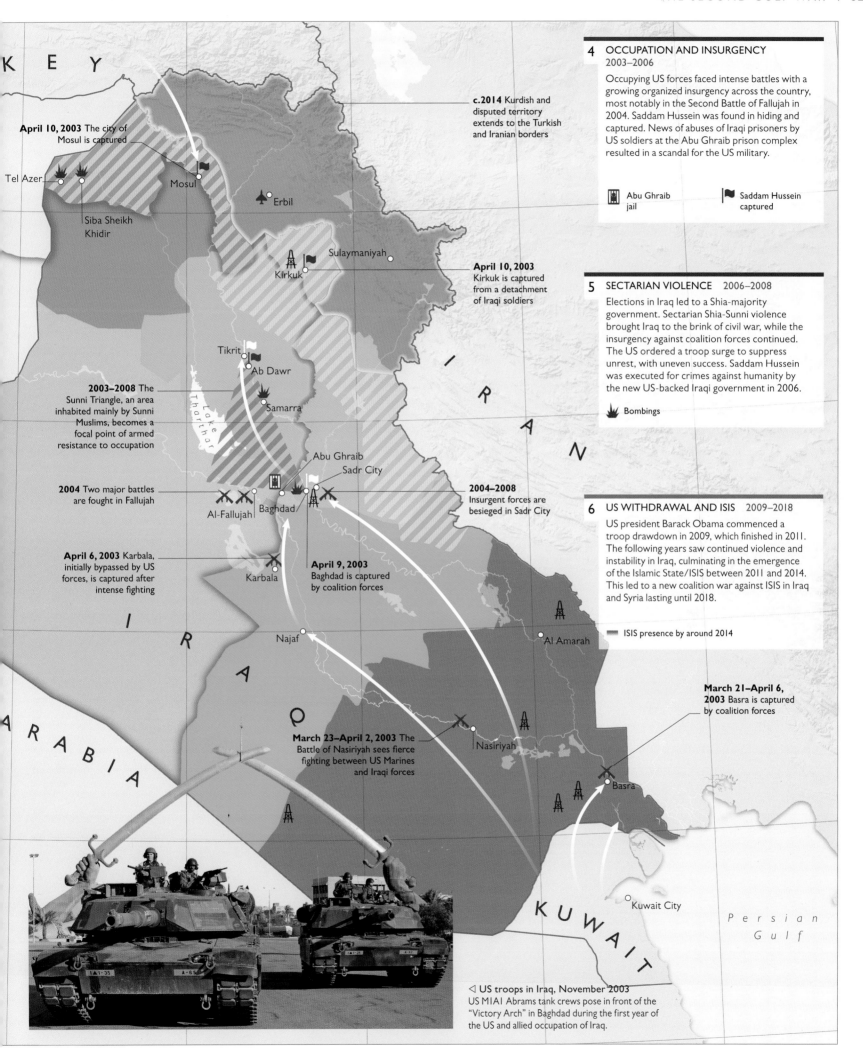

c.2014 Kurdish and disputed territory extends to the Turkish and Iranian borders

April 10, 2003 The city of Mosul is captured

April 10, 2003 Kirkuk is captured from a detachment of Iraqi soldiers

2003–2008 The Sunni Triangle, an area inhabited mainly by Sunni Muslims, becomes a focal point of armed resistance to occupation

2004 Two major battles are fought in Fallujah

April 6, 2003 Karbala, initially bypassed by US forces, is captured after intense fighting

April 9, 2003 Baghdad is captured by coalition forces

2004–2008 Insurgent forces are besieged in Sadr City

March 23–April 2, 2003 The Battle of Nasiriyah sees fierce fighting between US Marines and Iraqi forces

March 21–April 6, 2003 Basra is captured by coalition forces

4 OCCUPATION AND INSURGENCY 2003–2006

Occupying US forces faced intense battles with a growing organized insurgency across the country, most notably in the Second Battle of Fallujah in 2004. Saddam Hussein was found in hiding and captured. News of abuses of Iraqi prisoners by US soldiers at the Abu Ghraib prison complex resulted in a scandal for the US military.

Abu Ghraib jail   Saddam Hussein captured

5 SECTARIAN VIOLENCE 2006–2008

Elections in Iraq led to a Shia-majority government. Sectarian Shia-Sunni violence brought Iraq to the brink of civil war, while the insurgency against coalition forces continued. The US ordered a troop surge to suppress unrest, with uneven success. Saddam Hussein was executed for crimes against humanity by the new US-backed Iraqi government in 2006.

Bombings

6 US WITHDRAWAL AND ISIS 2009–2018

US president Barack Obama commenced a troop drawdown in 2009, which finished in 2011. The following years saw continued violence and instability in Iraq, culminating in the emergence of the Islamic State/ISIS between 2011 and 2014. This led to a new coalition war against ISIS in Iraq and Syria lasting until 2018.

ISIS presence by around 2014

◁ **US troops in Iraq, November 2003**
US M1A1 Abrams tank crews pose in front of the "Victory Arch" in Baghdad during the first year of the US and allied occupation of Iraq.

Financial woes
On September 16, 2008, traders at the Chicago Mercantile Exchange reacted with horror as billions of dollars were wiped off markets worldwide. This financial crisis spread beyond the financial industry, affecting many businesses.

GREAT RECESSION

The financial crash in 2008 was the worst economic crisis since the Great Depression. The collapse of banks and other financial institutions led to a lasting economic downturn that meant disruption, uncertainty, and unemployment for millions.

The early 21st century saw a boom in home ownership in the US. A large number of properties were financed by loans offered to customers with poor credit history, who would not usually qualify for a mortgage. These "subprime mortgages" were then turned into complex securities by global investment banks and traded for profit by banks and other investors. However, beginning in 2007, interest rates began to increase and house prices fell. Many subprime mortgages went into default, turning the banks' profits into catastrophic losses. This set off a financial chain reaction that damaged the global economy. Some banks and insurance companies, such as Lehman Brothers, went bankrupt (see box), while others, including Merrill Lynch and JP Morgan Chase were rescued by government bailout programs that paid hundreds of billions of dollars to prop up their balance sheets.

These actions prevented another Great Depression (see pp.250–251), but a severe and prolonged economic downturn followed that was nicknamed the "Great Recession." The US unemployment rate peaked at 10 percent in 2010, with more than 15 million people out of work. People protested what they saw as the unfairness of generous government support to the banks that had caused the crash while little was done for ordinary citizens.

> *"Our capital position at the moment is strong."*
>
> LEHMAN BROTHERS CFO IAN LOWITT, SEPTEMBER 10, 2008

LEHMAN BROTHERS

Lehman Brothers was the fourth-largest investment bank in the US with more than 25,000 employees. Heavily invested in mortgage-backed securities, it suddenly filed for bankruptcy on September 15, 2008, sending shock waves through the global economy. The financial crisis had come to a head and panic spread the world over. The majority of the company's employees immediately lost their jobs (right).

A DIVIDED AMERICA

The end of the 20th century saw a sharp increase in polarization, partisanship, and violence in the US. Not confined merely to politics, the fault lines in the nation's society reflect significant religious, cultural, racial, and economic divides.

While competition between rival political parties has long been a feature of the US system, the mid-20th century was characterized by a high level of bipartisan cooperation. This began to shift in the 1990s, especially during the later years of the Clinton presidency, the start of a trend that has resulted in the highest level of ideological polarization since the era of the Civil War. US citizens today are far less likely than a generation ago to vote "split ticket" (for candidates for multiple parties in the same election), marry a supporter of the opposing party, or even associate with people outside of their political alignment. This has contributed to significant personal animosity in US culture around partisan affiliation: a 2014 poll showed that around a third of respondents viewed members of the other party as a threat to the well-being of the country.

Elections in the US since 2000 have proved deeply divisive, and have exposed significant political and social splits between Democrats and Republicans on a wide range of issues: foreign policy, health care, environmental protection, gun control, immigration, racial justice, abortion, LGBTQ+ rights, and, more recently, the management of the Covid-19 pandemic. While it was once common for Democratic-leaning states to elect Republican officials and vice-versa, states now have a far more entrenched party identity. In two elections (2000 and 2016), the winner of the state-based electoral vote, which decides the presidency, went on to lose the national popular vote—a result that had last occurred in the 19th century.

US CAPITOL ATTACK

On January 6, 2021, thousands of supporters of President Trump stormed the US Capitol Building, many breaking through police cordons, to prevent Congress from certifying the electoral college for Joe Biden's election as president. Five died in the attack. The interior of the building was also heavily vandalized, causing more than $2.7 million in damages.

Protesters at the US Capitol

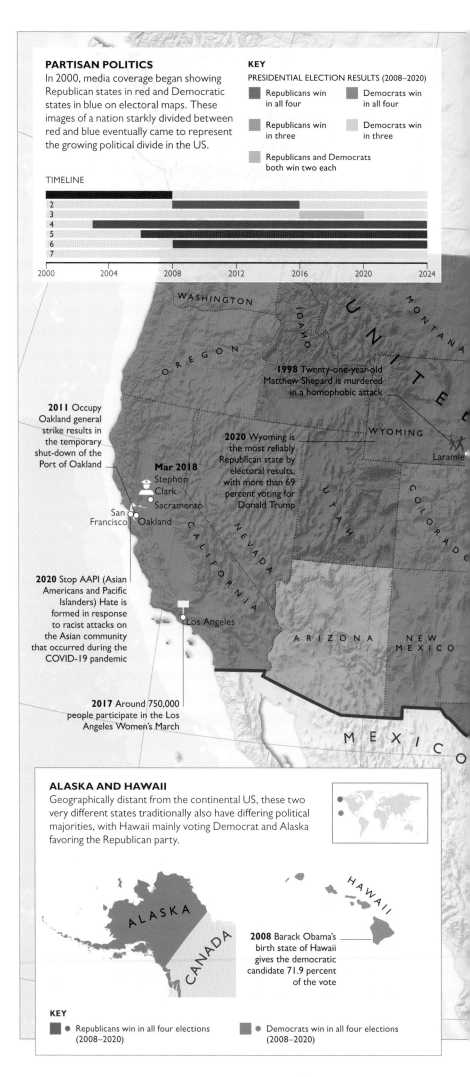

PARTISAN POLITICS

In 2000, media coverage began showing Republican states in red and Democratic states in blue on electoral maps. These images of a nation starkly divided between red and blue eventually came to represent the growing political divide in the US.

KEY
PRESIDENTIAL ELECTION RESULTS (2008–2020)

- Republicans win in all four
- Democrats win in all four
- Republicans win in three
- Democrats win in three
- Republicans and Democrats both win two each

TIMELINE

2000 · 2004 · 2008 · 2012 · 2016 · 2020 · 2024

1998 Twenty-one-year-old Matthew Shepard is murdered in a homophobic attack

2020 Wyoming is the most reliably Republican state by electoral results, with more than 69 percent voting for Donald Trump

2011 Occupy Oakland general strike results in the temporary shut-down of the Port of Oakland

Mar 2018 Stephon Clark, Sacramento

2020 Stop AAPI (Asian Americans and Pacific Islanders) Hate is formed in response to racist attacks on the Asian community that occurred during the COVID-19 pandemic

2017 Around 750,000 people participate in the Los Angeles Women's March

ALASKA AND HAWAII

Geographically distant from the continental US, these two very different states traditionally also have differing political majorities, with Hawaii mainly voting Democrat and Alaska favoring the Republican party.

2008 Barack Obama's birth state of Hawaii gives the democratic candidate 71.9 percent of the vote

KEY

- Republicans win in all four elections (2008–2020)
- Democrats win in all four elections (2008–2020)

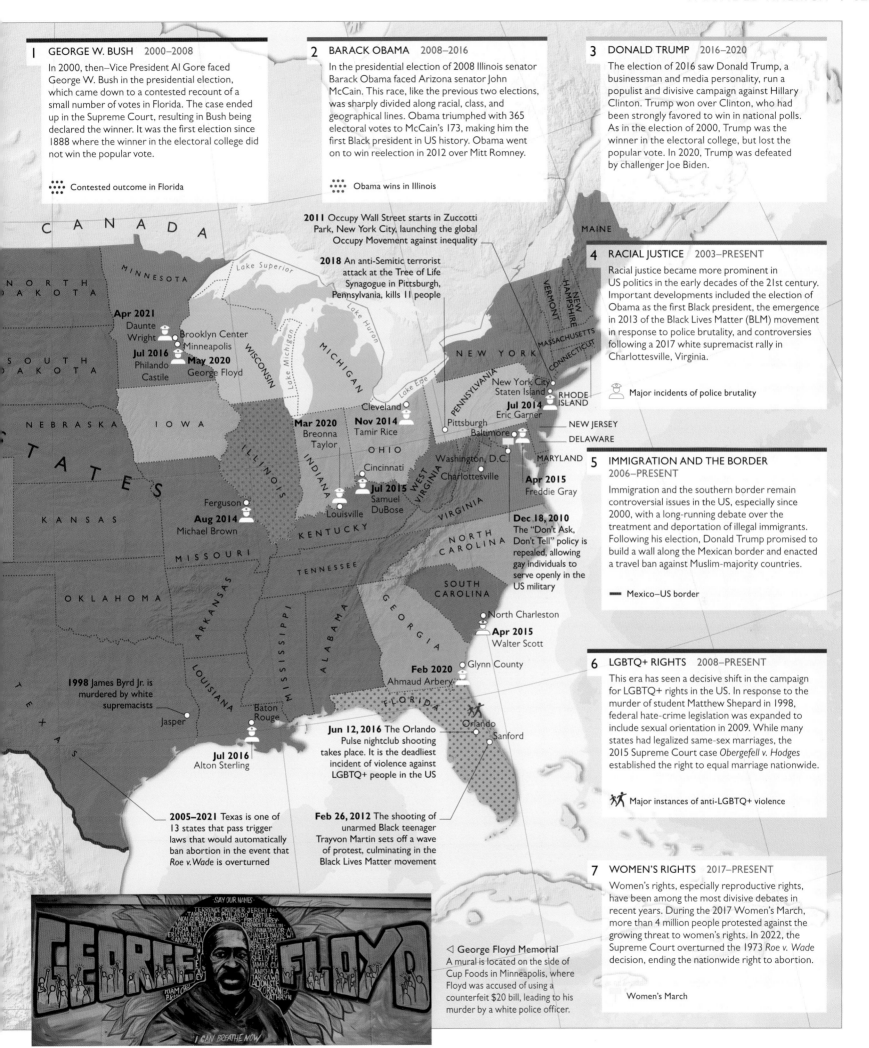

1 GEORGE W. BUSH 2000–2008

In 2000, then–Vice President Al Gore faced George W. Bush in the presidential election, which came down to a contested recount of a small number of votes in Florida. The case ended up in the Supreme Court, resulting in Bush being declared the winner. It was the first election since 1888 where the winner in the electoral college did not win the popular vote.

∷ Contested outcome in Florida

2 BARACK OBAMA 2008–2016

In the presidential election of 2008 Illinois senator Barack Obama faced Arizona senator John McCain. This race, like the previous two elections, was sharply divided along racial, class, and geographical lines. Obama triumphed with 365 electoral votes to McCain's 173, making him the first Black president in US history. Obama went on to win reelection in 2012 over Mitt Romney.

∷ Obama wins in Illinois

3 DONALD TRUMP 2016–2020

The election of 2016 saw Donald Trump, a businessman and media personality, run a populist and divisive campaign against Hillary Clinton. Trump won over Clinton, who had been strongly favored to win in national polls. As in the election of 2000, Trump was the winner in the electoral college, but lost the popular vote. In 2020, Trump was defeated by challenger Joe Biden.

4 RACIAL JUSTICE 2003–PRESENT

Racial justice became more prominent in US politics in the early decades of the 21st century. Important developments included the election of Obama as the first Black president, the emergence in 2013 of the Black Lives Matter (BLM) movement in response to police brutality, and controversies following a 2017 white supremacist rally in Charlottesville, Virginia.

👮 Major incidents of police brutality

5 IMMIGRATION AND THE BORDER 2006–PRESENT

Immigration and the southern border remain controversial issues in the US, especially since 2000, with a long-running debate over the treatment and deportation of illegal immigrants. Following his election, Donald Trump promised to build a wall along the Mexican border and enacted a travel ban against Muslim-majority countries.

— Mexico–US border

6 LGBTQ+ RIGHTS 2008–PRESENT

This era has seen a decisive shift in the campaign for LGBTQ+ rights in the US. In response to the murder of student Matthew Shepard in 1998, federal hate-crime legislation was expanded to include sexual orientation in 2009. While many states had legalized same-sex marriages, the 2015 Supreme Court case *Obergefell v. Hodges* established the right to equal marriage nationwide.

🏃 Major instances of anti-LGBTQ+ violence

7 WOMEN'S RIGHTS 2017–PRESENT

Women's rights, especially reproductive rights, have been among the most divisive debates in recent years. During the 2017 Women's March, more than 4 million people protested against the growing threat to women's rights. In 2022, the Supreme Court overturned the 1973 *Roe v. Wade* decision, ending the nationwide right to abortion.

Women's March

2011 Occupy Wall Street starts in Zuccotti Park, New York City, launching the global Occupy Movement against inequality

2018 An anti-Semitic terrorist attack at the Tree of Life Synagogue in Pittsburgh, Pennsylvania, kills 11 people

Apr 2021 Daunte Wright — Brooklyn Center Minneapolis

Jul 2016 Philando Castile

May 2020 George Floyd

Mar 2020 Breonna Taylor

Nov 2014 Tamir Rice — Cleveland

New York City — Staten Island

Jul 2014 Eric Garner

Pittsburgh — Baltimore

Cincinnati

Washington, D.C. — Charlottesville

Apr 2015 Freddie Gray

Jul 2015 Samuel DuBose — Louisville

Ferguson **Aug 2014** Michael Brown

Dec 18, 2010 The "Don't Ask, Don't Tell" policy is repealed, allowing gay individuals to serve openly in the US military

North Charleston **Apr 2015** Walter Scott

Feb 2020 Ahmaud Arbery — Glynn County

1998 James Byrd Jr. is murdered by white supremacists — Jasper

Baton Rouge

Jul 2016 Alton Sterling

Jun 12, 2016 The Orlando Pulse nightclub shooting takes place. It is the deadliest incident of violence against LGBTQ+ people in the US

Orlando — Sanford

2005–2021 Texas is one of 13 states that pass trigger laws that would automatically ban abortion in the event that *Roe v. Wade* is overturned

Feb 26, 2012 The shooting of unarmed Black teenager Trayvon Martin sets off a wave of protest, culminating in the Black Lives Matter movement

◁ **George Floyd Memorial**
A mural is located on the side of Cup Foods in Minneapolis, where Floyd was accused of using a counterfeit $20 bill, leading to his murder by a white police officer.

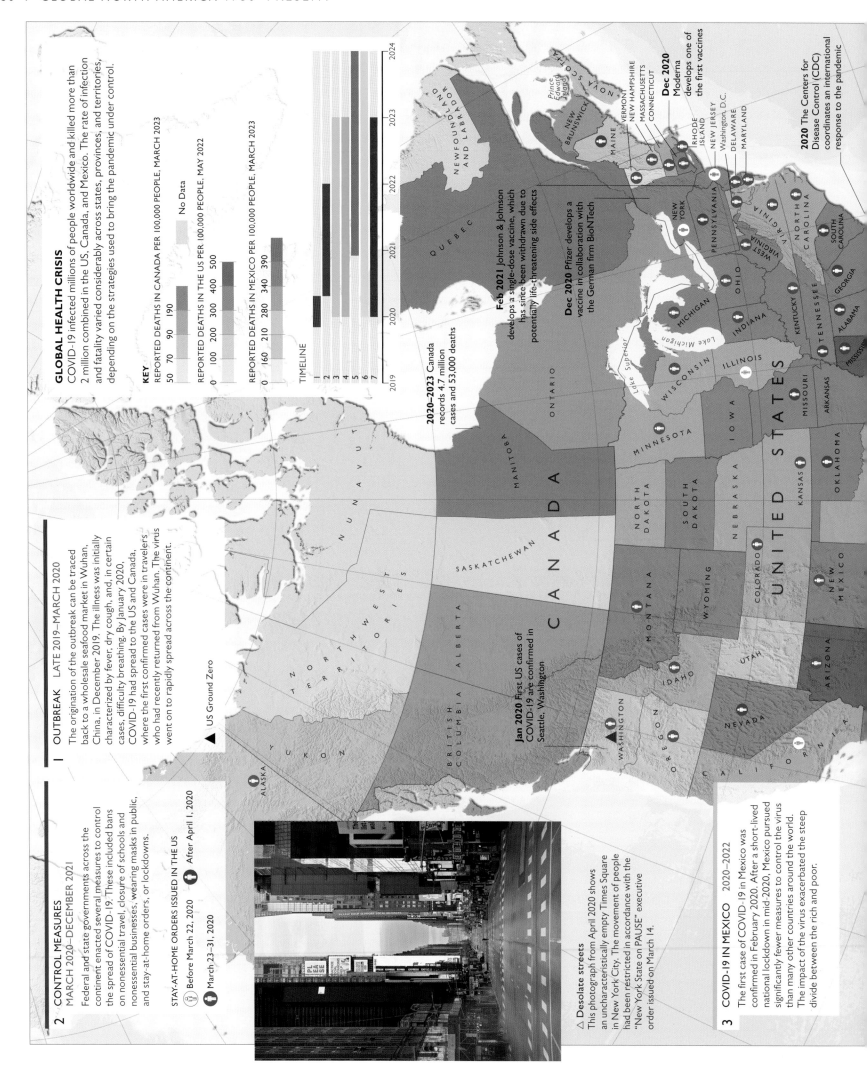

GLOBAL HEALTH CRISIS

COVID-19 infected millions of people worldwide and killed more than 2 million combined in the US, Canada, and Mexico. The rate of infection and fatality varied considerably across states, provinces, and territories, depending on the strategies used to bring the pandemic under control.

KEY

REPORTED DEATHS IN CANADA PER 100,000 PEOPLE, MARCH 2023

50 70 90 190

No Data

REPORTED DEATHS IN THE US PER 100,000 PEOPLE, MAY 2022

0 100 200 300 400 500

REPORTED DEATHS IN MEXICO PER 100,000 PEOPLE, MARCH 2023

0 160 210 280 340 390

TIMELINE

1
2
3
4
5
6
7

2019 2020 2021 2022 2023 2024

2020–2023 Canada records 4.7 million cases and 53,000 deaths

Feb 2021 Johnson & Johnson develops a single-dose vaccine, which has since been withdrawn due to potentially life-threatening side effects

Dec 2020 Pfizer develops a vaccine in collaboration with the German firm BioNTech

Dec 2020 Moderna develops one of the first vaccines

2020 The Centers for Disease Control (CDC) coordinates an international response to the pandemic

Jan 2020 First US cases of COVID-19 are confirmed in Seattle, Washington

▲ US Ground Zero

---

1 | OUTBREAK   LATE 2019–MARCH 2020

The origination of the outbreak can be traced back to a wholesale seafood market in Wuhan, China, in December 2019. The illness was initially characterized by fever, dry cough, and, in certain cases, difficulty breathing. By January 2020, COVID-19 had spread to the US and Canada, where the first confirmed cases were in travelers who had recently returned from Wuhan. The virus went on to rapidly spread across the continent.

---

2 | CONTROL MEASURES
MARCH 2020–DECEMBER 2021

Federal and state governments across the continent enacted several measures to control the spread of COVID-19. These included bans on nonessential travel, closure of schools and nonessential businesses, wearing masks in public, and stay-at-home orders, or lockdowns.

STAY-AT-HOME ORDERS ISSUED IN THE US

🏠 Before March 22, 2020   🏠 After April 1, 2020

🏠 March 23–31, 2020

△ Desolate streets

This photograph from April 2020 shows an uncharacteristically empty Times Square in New York City. The movement of people had been restricted in accordance with the "New York State on PAUSE" executive order issued on March 14.

---

3 | COVID-19 IN MEXICO   2020–2022

The first case of COVID-19 in Mexico was confirmed in February 2020. After a short-lived national lockdown in mid-2020, Mexico pursued significantly fewer measures to control the virus than many other countries around the world. The impact of the virus exacerbated the steep divide between the rich and poor.

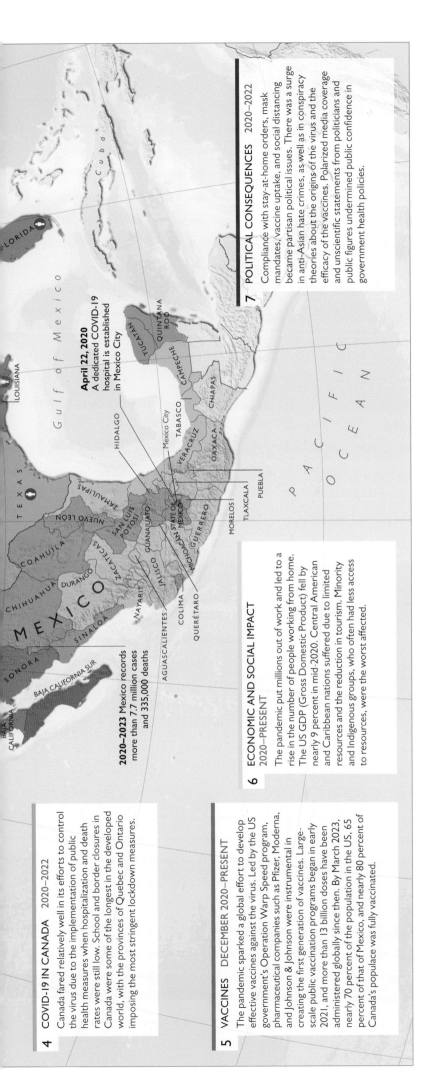

4 COVID-19 IN CANADA 2020–2022

Canada fared relatively well in its efforts to control the virus due to the implementation of public health measures when hospitalization and death rates were still low. School and border closures in Canada were some of the longest in the developed world, with the provinces of Quebec and Ontario imposing the most stringent lockdown measures.

5 VACCINES DECEMBER 2020–PRESENT

The pandemic sparked a global effort to develop effective vaccines against the virus. Led by the US government's Operation Warp Speed program, pharmaceutical companies such as Pfizer, Moderna, and Johnson & Johnson were instrumental in creating the first generation of vaccines. Large-scale public vaccination programs began in early 2021, and more than 13 billion doses have been administered globally since then. By March 2023, nearly 70 percent of the population in the US, 65 percent of that of Mexico, and nearly 80 percent of Canada's populace was fully vaccinated.

6 ECONOMIC AND SOCIAL IMPACT 2020–PRESENT

The pandemic put millions out of work and led to a rise in the number of people working from home. The US GDP (Gross Domestic Product) fell by nearly 9 percent in mid-2020. Central American and Caribbean nations suffered due to limited resources and the reduction in tourism. Minority and Indigenous groups, who often had less access to resources, were the worst affected.

7 POLITICAL CONSEQUENCES 2020–2022

Compliance with stay-at-home orders, mask mandates, vaccine uptake, and social distancing became partisan political issues. There was a surge in anti-Asian hate crimes, as well as in conspiracy theories about the origins of the virus and the efficacy of the vaccines. Polarized media coverage and unscientific statements from politicians and public figures undermined public confidence in government health policies.

April 22, 2020
A dedicated COVID-19 hospital is established in Mexico City

2020–2023 Mexico records more than 7.7 million cases and 335,000 deaths

IMPACT ON TRAVEL

From January 2020, the COVID-19 pandemic prompted countries to impose border closures and travel bans, leading to the abrupt curtailment of international travel, especially by air. The number of passengers on commercial flights dropped by more than 90 percent. Restrictive measures to control the spread of the virus included requirements for medical certificates, quarantine, or suspension of visa issuances. In the US, these measures were not lifted until November 2021, while Canada did so in October 2022.

Grounded aircraft at Pinal Airpark in Marana, Arizona, May 2020

THE COVID-19 PANDEMIC

In late 2019, a new and deadly virus began to spread around the world. The infectious disease strained the resources of health-care systems and led to catastrophic economic damage around the globe, including in the US, Canada, and Mexico. Vaccine production began in record time, but not before the pandemic had killed millions of people.

The first wave of the SARS-CoV-2 virus (severe acute respiratory syndrome coronavirus 2), now more commonly known as COVID-19, reached North America in early January 2020. The COVID-19 pandemic affected almost every facet of social, political, and economic life around the world. Governments scrambled to respond to the most significant global public health threat since the Great Influenza pandemic of 1918–1920.

By the middle of 2020, most North Americans were living under some form of lockdown intended to curb the spread of the virus. Economic crisis followed in the wake of these interventions, leading to the biggest downturn since the Great Depression (see pp.250–251) and restructuring working patterns for millions of people.

Hope emerged toward the end of 2020 as pharmaceutical companies, universities, and governments around the world worked together to develop effective vaccines against the virus. Mass vaccine rollouts allowed for an easing of restrictions and a gradual return to pre-pandemic normalcy. By the time the World Health Organization declared an end to the global health emergency in May 2023, the US was the hardest-hit country in the world, with more than 1.1 million deaths. The COVID-19 virus continues to evolve variant strains, leading to the development of new versions of the vaccines.

"This pandemic has magnified every existing inequality in our society …"

MELINDA GATES, INTERVIEW PUBLISHED IN
THE GUARDIAN, SEPTEMBER 2020

TIMELINE

INDIGENOUS NORTH AMERICA c. 30,000 YA–c. 1500

c. 30,000 YA

◁ **End of the mammoth**
Woolly mammoths were roughly the size of modern-day elephants and roamed the cold tundra of North America until about 10,000 years ago, when they became extinct.

c. 30,000 YA
Across the planet, Ice Age sea levels begin to fall, exposing a vast prehistoric land bridge—called Beringia, or the Bering land bridge—between Siberia and Alaska. At times, it is up to 620 miles (1,000 km) wide, and the size of British Columbia and Alberta combined.

c. 24,000–12,000 BCE
Asiatic peoples cross from Siberia into what is now western Alaska using the Bering land bridge. They disperse into the Arctic north, then down ice-free corridors along the Pacific coast and valleys of North America, where hunter-gatherer cultures develop.

c. 13,000 BCE
A hunter creates what becomes known as the Vero Beach bone. Incised with a carving of a mastodon or mammoth, it is now the oldest known example of Ice Age art in the Americas.

c. 11,500–10,800 BCE
The Clovis culture thrives in western North America. A hunter-gatherer culture, this community is named for its distinct stone and bone tools, which were first found with two mammoths near Clovis, in modern-day New Mexico. These tools are among the oldest confirmed stone tools found in North America.

9000–8000 BCE
Evidence points to hunting cultures in the Great Plains, southern California, and eastern North America. These include the Folsom complex—an archaeological pattern left by early inhabitants—in what is now the southwestern US; the San Dieguito complex, which occupies much of central North America; and the Eastern Fluted Point tradition, hunter-gatherer cultures in eastern North America.

c. 9000–5000 BCE
Agriculture begins in the Americas. Mesoamerican agriculturalists develop farming skills and domesticate wild plants, including maize (the first corn ever cultivated by humans), squash, and chile. The use of pottery becomes increasingly common.

8000–1000 BCE
Known as the Archaic stage in North American prehistory, this period is characterized by subsistence economies, supported through the exploitation of nuts, seeds, and shellfish. Archaic peoples develop skills in ceramic pottery, weaving, and early food cultivation.

8000 BCE
With the recession of the Laurentide ice cap, which covered most of North America, hunter-gatherers begin to migrate up the east side of the continent to occupy what is now New England, as well as the provinces of eastern Canada, and Newfoundland and Labrador. This is defined as the Maritime Archaic period. At the end of the Ice Age, floods mostly submerge the Bering land bridge. The Diomede Islands, the Pribilof Islands, and Saint Lawrence and King Islands are the last remnants of the land bridge seen above water today.

c. 5000 BCE
The Dorset culture emerges as groups adapt to the conditions of northern Canada (and later, Greenland). Dorset settlements are located on coasts and the people mainly hunt marine mammals. This culture begins to decline c. 4000 BCE as Pre-Dorset and Dorset Tradition groups move south, and they disappear c. 1500 BCE.

c. 5000 BCE
The Inuit and Aleut people cross the Bering Strait by boat from what is now Russia and settle in present-day Alaska. They gradually replace the Dorset culture and populate Arctic North America.

c. 3500 BCE
The Watson Brake, a pattern of 11 large mounds, is constructed in what is now Louisiana. Dated as about 5,400 years old, making it older than Stonehenge in the UK or the pyramids in Egypt, it is thought to be the oldest earthwork mound complex in North America. Mound Builder cultures cover areas around the Great Lakes, the Mississippi River, and the Ohio River Valley.

c. 2000–1500 BCE
Abandoning their previous hunter-gatherer lifestyle, Mesoamericans gradually establish villages in the areas now known as southern Mexico, Guatemala, and northern Belize.

28 tons
Weight of a stone head, San Lorenzo Tenochtitlán (25.4 metric tons).

▷ **Murals for the dead**
Colorful murals often lined the walls of the burial chambers the Zapotec built within their elaborate pyramid structures. The murals often depicted images of war.

◁ **Huge heads**
The Olmec people carved enormous heads from large basalt boulders. Some are nearly 12 ft (4 m) tall. It is thought that the monuments represent portraits of powerful individual rulers.

c. 800 BCE

c. 1500–1200 BCE
The Olmecs, the earliest complex society in the Americas, develop what we now call San Lorenzo Tenochtitlán, the site of the first known major Mesoamerican civilization. The excellent soil of the area allows for a more densely concentrated population than was ever seen in the Americas before. The Olmec people lay the foundation for later Mesoamerican civilizations, developing counting systems and building distinctive monuments in the form of colossal carved stone heads.

1350 BCE
The Zapotec people of what is today southern Mexico build a major urban settlement at the present-day site of San José Mogote in the Oaxaca Valley, which flourishes until c. 500 BCE. They develop a calendar and one of the first systems of written language that has been recorded in Mesoamerica.

1100 BCE
The people of the Olmec civilization build a second city at what is now known as La Venta in the modern-day state of Tabasco in Mexico. It was a civic and ceremonial center for the Olmec, and did not provide habitation for most people, who were relegated to outlier sites. The main complexes included the Great Pyramid, a large plaza, and an area used for religious practices.

c. 1000 BCE
The woolly mammoth dies out. While the reasons for its extinction are not known, both human over-hunting and the naturally warming climate after the Ice Age may have played a part. Archaic hunters migrate and adapt to these new climate conditions.

c. 1000 BCE –1100 CE
The Woodland period in North America is marked by advancement in agriculture, as well as the manufacture of pottery and the creation of burial mounds. This time period is divided into Early, Middle, and Late subperiods, which refer to intervals characterized by the first widespread use of pottery across the region, the rise and then decline of a vast exchange network across eastern North America, and finally, a period of increasing agricultural intensification and population growth.

c. 900 BCE
La Venta replaces San Lorenzo as the capital city and cultural center of the Olmecs. During this time, the cultural influence of the Olmecs begins to wane, but at its peak it is estimated that up to 18,000 people live in the city.

800–600 BCE
Settlers build the first villages in the Maya Lowlands, an area bordered by the Gulf of Mexico, the Caribbean Sea, and the Maya Highlands, which today encompasses Belize, parts of Mexico, and a part of Guatemala. The villages gradually develop into the powerful Maya civilization.

c. 800 BCE
A tablet-size writing stone, now known as the Cascajal Block, is created in what is now Mexico by the Olmec people. It is inscribed with glyphs that may represent

▷ **Creator deity**
This sculpture depicts the head of Quetzalcoatl from the Pyramid of the Feathered Serpent in Teotihuacán, Mexico, c. 200–300 CE. The Aztecs believed that he helped create mankind.

600 BCE

the earliest writing system in America. It lays undiscovered until it is unearthed by road builders in the 1990s (CE).

600–100 BCE
The Maya build urban centers including Tikal, Uaxactún, Dos Pilas, Calakmul, Palenque, and Río Bec. Many contain feats of engineering such as pyramids and inscribed stone monuments.

c. 500–400 BCE
The Zapotecs rise to control the Oaxaca Valley in modern-day Mexico and create

a city at what is now Monte Albán. It is the capital for more than 1,000 years.

500 BCE–1000 CE
The ancestors of Canada's First Nations peoples establish trade routes across northern North America. They create complex societies featuring urban settlement, monumental architecture, and widespread agriculture.

c. 500 BCE
In what is now the state of Ohio, the Adena people, small village communities

of hunter-gatherers who practice some horticulture, build impressive earthworks (the Adena are the ancestors of the later Hopewell culture). These are massive, log-lined tombs covered with conical earth mounds that scholars believe map the cosmos. The best-known remaining mound system is the Great Serpent Mound in Peebles, Ohio.

400 BCE
The people of the Olmec civilization abandon La Venta on the Gulf Coast.

Located in the Valley of Mexico, on the shore of Lake Texcoco, Cuicuilco becomes an important civic and religious center in the Mexican highlands. Originally settled by farmers, it grows until its population reaches more than 20,000 people, and a large temple pyramid is built there.

▽ Hohokam pottery
One of the distinctive features of the Hohokam culture was its pottery, often made of light brown clay with repeated, geometric markings in red. This Hohokam jar dates back to c. 850–950.

c. 400 BCE
The city of Teotihuacán is founded by an unknown people in the Valley of Mexico. By 400 CE it covers more than 8 square miles (20 square km) and becomes the most powerful city in the northern highlands of central America, with more than 125,000 inhabitants. It is an economic and religious center and its influence spreads through Mesoamerica.

100 BCE
A large volcanic eruption drives the inhabitants of Cuicuilco to the city of Teotihuacán, an event that rapidly increases the population there.

c. 50 BCE
The Maya develop the concept of place value, the value of each digit in a given number. They are the first people to do so in North America. They also introduce a calendar that has a cycle of 52 years, known as the Calendar Round, designed to reset once during every person's life. Additionally, they develop a more refined method of dating called the Long Count.

c. 100
People in Teotihuacán develop the cult of Quetzalcoatl, later a key figure in Aztec religion. Usually depicted as a feathered serpent, he is considered a creator deity who contributed to the birth of humankind. He is the patron god of priests, and is also linked to wind, the sun, the arts, and knowledge.

c. 100–500
The Hopewell Exchange, a network of Indigenous cultures, flourishes along rivers in the northeastern and midwestern Eastern Woodlands, a cultural area that occupies territory from the Atlantic coast to the Mississippi River, and from the Great Lakes to the Gulf of Mexico. The people are Mound Builders, burying their dead within the mounds. The Mound City Group, a restored complex of 25 mounds in modern Ohio, is one of the main remaining archaeological sites that gives insight into the Hopewell tradition.

c. 100
Ancestral Puebloan culture emerges in what is now the southwest US. The Ancestral Puebloans make pottery and practice agriculture, and are best known for building *kivas* (subterranean rooms used in religious and social rituals) and mining turquoise.

c. 150
The Pyramid of the Sun is built at Teotihuacán. At 738 ft (225 m) across and 246 ft (75 m) tall, it is the largest building in the city and one of the largest in Mesoamerica, forming part of the Avenue of the Dead. The name "Pyramid of the Sun" was bestowed later by the Aztecs.

c. 200
The Zapotec people reach the height of their artistic and political influence.

c. 200–1400
The Hohokam farming culture flourishes in the southern deserts of modern-day Arizona, creating extensive irrigation canals along the Salt and Gila rivers. By 1000, thousands of people live in Hohokam villages, well-maintained adobe structures that will remain inhabited for centuries. The Hohokam are ancestors of the Pima and Tohono O'odham people.

c. 250–900
The height of Maya civilization, also called the Classical period, is a time of building pyramids, temples, and ball courts in many Maya cities. More than 40 Maya cities thrive, mostly in the Maya lowlands, with populations of 5,000–50,000 people. Although the cities were often at war with each other, it was also a time of cultural prosperity.

c. 600–750
Teotihuacán is abandoned. This was possibly due to internal warfare, as archaeologists today have discovered signs of extensive burning on the buildings near the Avenue of the Dead.

800–1600
The Mississippian culture, a complex civilization in the midwestern, eastern, and southeastern present-day US, flourishes. They are known for building large, four-sided earthen mounds.

c. 800
Zapotec control of the great city of Monte Albán begins to decline and eventually collapses. The Mixtec people rise to power and assume control of the ancient city.

20,000

Number of pieces of turquoise excavated from the ruins at Chaco Canyon, New Mexico, an important Ancestral Puebloan center..

◁ **Window into Mayan life**
In the ancient Mayan city of Bonampak, colorful murals are still visible in a small house inside the acropolis. They depict peace and celebrations, war and sacrifice, music-making, and rituals.

◁ **Mayapán**
This Mayan incense burner represents the scribe of Mayapán, a city in Yucatan, Mexico (c. 1000–1542CE). The scribe's hand and feet are human, but the face is that of a monkey.

850–950
Many Maya centers in Guatemala and Mexico are abandoned, including the great city of Kaminaljuyu, which had been occupied for 2,000 years. The reasons for the abandonment are not clear, but may be due to overpopulation, disease, or extensive warfare. Maya cities continue in other regions.

900–1150
Chaco Canyon in northwestern New Mexico becomes a major center for the Ancestral Puebloan. There is evidence of agriculture and trade in the area, as well as turquoise jewelry-making.

900–950
The Toltecs rise to prominence in Oaxaca, establishing a capital called Tollan near today's Tula, Hidalgo, in Mexico. The Toltecs portray themselves as a conquering, warlike people in their mythology and stories.

987
The Toltecs capture the strategically important Maya city of Chichén Itzá, which has four sinkholes that provide year-round water.

c. 1000
Norse explorers arrive from Greenland. They call the Indigenous people Skraelings (a Norse term meaning something like "wretches") on Baffin Island, now Nunavut, and in Newfoundland and Labrador.

c. 1010
Icelandic explorer Thorfinn Karlsefni leads an expedition to North America, intending to create a colony in a northeastern coastal site called Vinland. His wife, Gudrid, gives birth to their son while they are in North America. The colony is abandoned due to internal dissent, but traces may survive today in the remains of a longhouse at L'Anse aux Meadows in Newfoundland, a Norse structure that is built in an Icelandic style.

1050
The largest pre-Columbian settlement north of the Aztec Empire is built at Cahokia, near present-day Collinsville, Illinois. It is a city of 120 mounds, built by the Mississippian culture. By 1300 it is a ghost town.

1142
The Haudenosaunee Confederacy is organized by Dekanahwideh (known as the Great Peacemaker) and his spokesperson, Hiawatha. They write the Great Law of Peace in beaded pictograms, which is later translated into many languages. The Confederacy aims to provide peaceful and equitable means of resolving disputes among its members.

c. 1150
The Aztec people begin to move south into the Valley of Mexico from their original home of Aztlan in northern Mexico.

100 ft (30 m)
The height of Monks Mound in Cahokia. It is the largest prehistoric earthen structure in the Western hemisphere.

1497

◁ **Solar deity**
This round Aztec sun stone is probably the most famous surviving work of Aztec art. The parent rock from which it was extracted comes from the Xitle volcano.

12 ft (3.6 m)

The width of the huge sun stone that was erected in Tenochtitlan by the Aztec people.

1150

The Chichimeca people (including the Aztec people) begin moving into the Valley of Mexico from the Bajío region of today's Mexico. The Toltec city of Tollan is destroyed and their power collapses.

1263

Mayapán is founded in the Yucatán Peninsula as the political and cultural capital of the Maya people during the Late Postclassic period (1220s–1440s). It has around 15,000 inhabitants, in more than 4,000 buildings. A tightly packed center contains religious structures including temples and altars.

c. 1300

The Aztec people settle at Chapultepec, in what is now Mexico City, but are attacked and forced to move to Culhua.

1300–1400

The Late Mississippian period is marked by warfare, turmoil, and population dispersal. Cultural and language traits from the Mississippian culture survive today in Indigenous groups such as the Osage and Seminole peoples.

c. 1325

The Aztec people move from Culhua in present-day Mexico City, to settle on an uninhabited island in Lake Mexico. They found the cities of Tenochtitlán and Tlatelolco. They build grand temples featuring images of fertility and warfare, and symbols representing their devotion to the sun. The Aztec people will soon dominate the region until their defeat by Spanish conquistadors in the 1500s.

1375

Acamapichtli, the first historical ruler of the Aztec people, is elected tlatoani ("speaker") in Tenochtitlan. He founds the first Tenochtitlan dynasty and strengthens ties with the nearby Tepanec state of Azcapotzalco (the capital of the Tepanec empire). They join forces to fight the Chichimeca and Toltec people.

1396

The Aztec people begin to build independent power.

c. 1428

The city states of Tenochtitlan, Texcoco, and Tlacopán form the Triple Alliance and begin to build the Aztec Empire.

1441

Mayapán, the capital of the Maya people, is abandoned, possibly due to drought.

1481

The Aztec people erect a huge sun stone in Tenochtitlan. It is 12 ft (3.6 m) across and weighs more than 54,000 lb (24,590 kg). Its purpose is not known but the sculpted motifs may represent Aztec cosmological beliefs, including a central image of their sun god.

1487

The Great Temple in Tenochtitlan is reopened after several spectacular expansions. The enlarged pyramid is dedicated to Huitzilopochtli, the Aztec god of sun and war, and the sacrifice of human victims to commemorate it is said to have lasted four days.

1492

Italian explorer Christopher Columbus reaches the West Indies. Pope Alexander VI issues the *Inter caetera* (or "Doctrine of Discovery"), a papal bull granting the monarchs of Spain the right to all lands to the west and south of a pole-to-pole line. The bull facilitates Europeans land claims in what they call the "New World."

1496

Diego Columbus, son of Christopher, establishes the first secure Spanish colony at Santo Domingo (on the island of Hispaniola, in what is now the Dominican Republic).

1497

As he searches for new territories for England, Italian explorer Giovanni Caboto reaches Newfoundland. Traveling with his sons, he is the first European to explore coastal North America since the Norse.

▷ **North American exploration**
Giovanni Caboto, or John Cabot, an Italian navigator, explored parts of North America for the English King Henry VII. This painting depicts Caboto and his son, Sebastian, leaving on their first voyage from Bristol, England in 1497.

COLONIZATION AND CONFLICT 1500–1750

1500

c.1500
The power and position of the last influential Mississippian culture center, Moundville, in present-day Alabama, declines. Permanent Spanish colonies are established in Cuba and Hispaniola. Diego Velázquez, then governor of Cuba, sends expeditions to explore the coasts of what are now Venezuela, Colombia, and other Caribbean islands.

1501
The Portuguese explorer Gaspar Corte-Real abducts two shiploads of Haudenosaunee and other peoples from Newfoundland and New England, selling them into slavery.

1502
Montezuma II becomes the ninth Aztec emperor or *tlatoani*, ruling over the empire and the city of Tenochtitlan. The first contact between the Indigenous civilizations of Mesoamerica and Europeans takes place during his reign.

1506–1518
The Huron-Wendat and Haudenosaunee begin exchanging goods with French traders pushing inland from the Atlantic coast.

The Haudenosaunee population declines when they come into contact with viruses, carried by the Europeans, to which they have no immunity.

1507
The continents are named by Europeans after the Italian explorer and navigator Amerigo Vespucci. Cartographer Martin Waldseemüller prints the name "America" on a map in recognition of Vespucci's claim that America was a new continent.

1511
The *encomienda* is introduced, a system that legally allowed Spanish people to enslave the populations they colonized. This continues Spain's mistreatment of Indigenous peoples in the Americas.

1513
Spanish colonizer Juan Ponce de León explores and names Florida. The Laws of Burgos are established, the first legal codes in what will become the US. They allow for the continued exploitation of Indigenous people, including the Calusa, who later rebel and kill León.

1517
King Charles V of Spain (r. 1516–1556) grants permission to forcibly transport 4,000 enslaved Africans to the Americas. Mayan warriors kill Francisco Hernández de Córdoba, the leader of the first Cuban expedition to Mesoamerica.

1519
A Spanish expedition under Hernán Cortés arrives in what is now Mexico. The Aztecs greet the Spanish as honored guests in the city of Tenochtitlan, but Cortés takes Montezuma II hostage.

1520
Montezuma II dies in captivity. His brother Cuitláhuac becomes *tlatoani*. Cortés and his soldiers loot Tenochtitlan, but the Aztecs retaliate. On what becomes known by the Spanish as *La Noche Triste* ("the Sad Night") they flee to Tlacopan, losing much of their looted treasure in flight.

1520–1700
"Virgin-soil" epidemics sweep through communities in North America, devastating populations whenever they encounter people without immunity. Many Indigenous peoples in Mesoamerica die from measles and other diseases, right up until the 1700s.

1521
Cortés recaptures Tenochtitlan with allies from Tlaxcala and Texcoco. He and his men defeat the Aztecs at Otumba, and Cuitláhuac surrenders, marking the end of the Aztec Empire.

◁ **Montezuma's headdress**
Tradition holds that this featherwork headgear was worn by Montezuma II, emperor of the Aztecs at the time of the Spanish conquest of their kingdom.

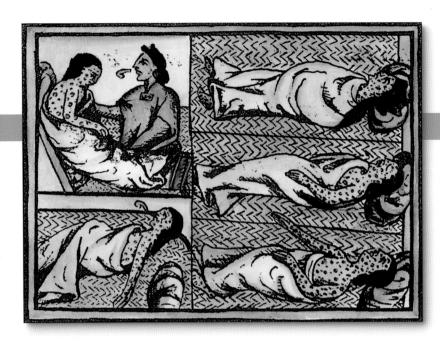

1586

◁ **The terrible impact of smallpox**
The Spanish brought smallpox to the Americas. In this 16th century illustration, an Aztec medicine man ministers to his stricken people.

90%

The percentage of Indigenous people killed by smallpox in the 1500s.

1523–1541
Spanish colonizer Pedro de Alvarado conquers the Maya people of Quiché and Kaqchikel in what is now Guatemala. The horses his men ride are new imports to the Americas.

1524
Italian explorer Giovanni da Verrazzano scouts the coast of North America on behalf of France, encountering Lenape (Delaware), Narragansett, and Wampanoag peoples. Mexico City is established on the ruins of Tenochtitlan while conquistadors begin colonizing the region. The Spanish king, Charles V, creates the Council of the Indies, a powerful body that governs in the area on the king's behalf.

1525
The Southern Athapaskan peoples migrate to the Southwest from West Central Canada; they will become the Ndé and the Navajo, among others.

1526
The first revolt of enslaved people in mainland North America, the San Miguel de Gualdape Slave Rebellion, occurs in modern-day Georgia and the Carolinas. After rebelling, the enslaved people escape to live with Indigenous peoples in the area.

1528
Spanish colonizer Francisco de Montejo leads an ultimately unsuccessful campaign against the Maya of Yucatán. His attempts to conquer the Yucatán continue until 1535.

1534
In the mistaken belief that he's reached Asia, Frenchman Jacques Cartier explores the Gulf of Saint Lawrence in present-day Canada. Welcomed by Huron-Wendat people to their island in the Montreal River, he names their island after himself.

1535
The Viceroyalty of New Spain is established, consisting of present-day Mexico, Central America, Florida, and parts of the southwest US. Ciudad de México becomes the capital of the Viceroyalty, and Antonio de Mendoza its first viceroy.

1537
Pope Paul III issues the *Sublimis Deus* decree, opposing the enslavement of Indigenous peoples in the Americas.

1540
Francisco Vásquez de Coronado searches for the treasure of the Seven Cities of Cibola, in what is now the southwestern US. The local Zuni people defend their territory, but are brutally overpowered. Coronado finds no treasure.

1541
After years plundering from present-day Florida to northern Arkansas and eastern Texas, Spanish colonizer Hernando de Soto reaches the Mississippi River; he dies before completing his journey.

1542
Spain's New Laws of the Indies for the Good Treatment and Preservation of the Indians abolish slavery and also end the *encomienda* system. The New Laws generate tremendous opposition from powerful colonists in the Viceroyalty.

1542
Silver deposits are discovered in northern Mexico. Towns founded near the mines include Zacatecas and San Luis Potosí. Along with Spanish silver mines in what is now Bolivia, these mines will produce more than 100,000 tons of silver by the early 1800s.

1545
King Charles V of Spain revokes the New Laws after a violent revolt in Peru the year before.

c.1550
French and British pirates entrench themselves on the island of Tortuga and others near Hispaniola. On the Central Mexican Plateau, the Chichimeca War breaks out between the Chichimeca people and the Spanish colonizers. Lasting until 1590, the 40-year campaign will be the longest and most expensive conflict between Spain and Indigenous peoples.

1565
The Spanish establish St. Augustine, Florida, now the oldest continuously occupied settlement of European origin in the US.

1571
The Mexican Inquisition is established to enforce Roman Catholic orthodoxy.

c.1575
Bernardino de Sahagún and Diego Durán are among the Catholic brothers who enlist Indigenous scribes and informants to help compile extensive information on Aztec culture.

1583
English explorer Humphrey Gilbert claims Newfoundland on behalf of England's Queen Elizabeth I, but doesn't establish a colony before leaving.

1585
English adventurer Sir Walter Raleigh establishes the Roanoke Colony in present-day North Carolina, after being welcomed by the Secotan people. Within five years, the colonists disappear under unknown circumstances. English colonists will try again to establish a colony there in 1587; it, too, is later found abandoned.

1586
An intense rivalry for control of the Americas emerges between Spain and England. English explorer Sir Francis Drake attacks and loots Santo Domingo, the Spanish capital of Hispaniola, leaving it in ruins.

▷ **Free by papal decree**
In 1537, Pope Paul III (1468–1549) issued the *Sublimis Deus*, which declared that Indigenous people in the Americas were "human beings ... not to be robbed of their freedom."

▷ **First Thanksgiving**
A romanticized depiction of the first Thanksgiving celebration. It was far more likely to have been a harvest feast prepared under the direction of the Indigenous people.

1598

1598

Spanish forces under Juan de Oñate march north from Mexico through the Rio Grande Valley. The Ndé and Pueblo push back, but the Spaniards establish a colony at Ohkay Owingeh. Oñate's campaign is brutal, enslaving and starving many Indigenous people.

1603

Along the Saint Lawrence River, French colonists form a defensive partnership with the Innu, Wolastoqiyik, and Mi'kmaq against the Algonquian and Huron-Wendat peoples. This develops into a military and political alliance between Mi'kmaq and French leaders, who share ties of religion and trade.

1607

The first permanent English colony in North America is founded at modern-day Jamestown, Virginia, marking the beginning of English colonization. The colonists occupy Tsenacomoco (Powhatan) territory, among 30 tribes and an estimated 20,000 Indigenous people.

144

The approximate number of original settlers in the colony at Jamestown.

1608

French explorer Samuel de Champlain establishes Quebec, the first permanent French colony in North America, and it quickly becomes a fur-trading center.

1609

Jesuit monks establish their first mission in North America at the French colony of Penobscot Bay, in what is now Maine. The First Anglo-Powhatan War begins, pitting the English colonists at Jamestown against an alliance of Indigenous peoples. Opechancanough, the premier Tsenacomoco chief, had been captured and taken to Europe as a youth, so he knew how to fight the English. However, England sent reinforcements and ultimately won in 1614.

1610

Searching for a northwest passage, English adventurer Henry Hudson explores the inland sea in what is now southeastern Canada. He and his men meet several Indigenous groups.

1610s

Membertou, Mi'kmaq chief and shaman in what is now Nova Scotia, becomes the first Indigenous leader baptized into Roman Catholicism by the French.

1613

During the First Anglo-Powhatan War, English soldiers in Virginia capture Chief Wahunsenacawh's (often called Powhatan) daughter, Mataoka (or Pocahontas). While captive, she learns English, converts to Christianity, and is given the name "Rebecca." She was later brought to England. It is believed that she was assaulted and eventually killed during her captivity.

1619

Approximately 30 people from the Kingdom of Ndongo in what is now Angola arrive in Jamestown; the first enslaved Africans in what will become the US. They arrive on the *White Lion*, an English ship, which had captured them from Portuguese enslavers.

1620

English Pilgrims aboard the *Mayflower* land in what they later name Plymouth, Massachusetts. Their contact with the Wampanoag people helps them survive during the struggle to build a colony.

1622

Led by Opechancanough, the Tsenacomoco attack the English colony at Jamestown, killing 300 and nearly wiping it out. This marks the start of the Second Anglo-Powhatan War. In revenge, the English murder Tsenacomoco at a supposed "peace conference" the next year.

1625

The French establish the colony of Saint Kitts, one of the earliest French colonies in the Caribbean. Control of the island will vary between the English, French, and Spanish.

1626

Walloon merchant Peter Minuit purchases Manhattan Island from the Lenape on behalf of the Dutch West India Company. Under his leadership, trade grows significantly in the area.

1628–1629

The Kirkes, brothers who raid on behalf of the English king, capture Quebec from the French during the Anglo-French War. It is returned to France in 1632 by the Treaty of Saint-Germain.

1630

The Great Puritan Migration of English people to the Massachusetts Bay colony begins. John Winthrop is appointed governor of the new colony, and a year later leaves England with 700 pilgrims. Thousands of English Puritans occupy

◁ **Mataoka**
Portrait of Mataoka (1595–1617), an Algonquian woman who helped the colonial settlement at Jamestown, Virginia. She was married to an Englishman and is depicted wearing English clothing.

modern-day Massachusetts, moving inland and displacing the Wampanoag and other Indigenous peoples.

1632–1636
The English king, Charles I, gives funding to found colonies in Maryland (1632) and in Rhode Island (1636). Both are based on principles of religious freedom: Maryland is a haven for persecuted Catholics, while Rhode Island welcomes all religious dissenters, including those fleeing the Puritans.

1636–1638
The first university on the North American continent, Harvard, is founded at Cambridge, Massachusetts. In its early years, Harvard primarily trains clergymen. From 1636 to 1638 the Pequot War sees the Pequot people

fighting an alliance of colonists from Massachusetts Bay, Plymouth, and Saybrook, plus warriors from the Narragansett and Mohegan nations. In 1637, the colonists massacre 500 Pequot people at their forts in what is now Mystic, Connecticut.

1638
The first reservation is established. Puritans near what is now New Haven, Connecticut, force the Quinnipiac people from their homelands, forbidding them to leave the reservation, and restricting their traditional practices. In what will become the western US, the Dakota peoples migrate from what is now northern Minnesota to the Great Plains. Their cultures come to rely on riding horses (reintroduced by Europeans) and hunting.

1640–1701
The Beaver Wars are fought, pitting the Haudenosaunee against the Huron-Wendat, other Algonquin-speaking peoples, and their French allies in the Great Lakes region. In 1649, the Haudenosaunee Confederacy destroys the Wendat Confederacy, a group of five Huron-Wendat bands who joined forces in

defense against the Haudenosaunee. Eventually, the wars push the Huron-Wendat people west to the Great Lakes.

1643
The New England Confederation is formed for mutual defense by the colonies of Massachusetts Bay, Plymouth, Saybrook, and New Haven.

▷ **Purchase of Manhattan**
Merchant Peter Minuit famously purchased Manhattan Island—where New York City would later be located—from the Lenape for 60 guilders, about $1,000 today.

FLOAT — PURCHASE OF MANHATTAN

1644–1646
The Third Anglo-Powhatan War is fought. Opechancanough is captured and killed. In 1646, England signs a peace treaty with the Tsenacomoco but breaks it a few years later. The Tsenacomoco are restricted to tribal reservations.

1647
Peter Stuyvesant becomes director general of the Dutch colony of New Netherland, along the northeast coast of what is now the US.

15

Number of Unangan women and children killed by Russian traders.

1661
In what will become New Mexico, the Spanish colonial governor and Catholic priests suppress the belief systems of the Pueblo people. Ceremonial dances are outlawed upon threat of death. Soldiers raid *kivas* (rooms used for religious rituals) and burn sacred objects such as *katsina* masks (masks for dancers, representing spirit beings).

1662
The Virginia Assembly tightens laws around slavery, decreeing that a child born to an enslaved woman would follow their mother into slavery, no matter who the father is. This secures the labor system upon which the colony relies, and ensures European-fathered children do not escape slavery.

1663
The English king, Charles II, grants the lands of what will become the Carolinas to eight of his supporters, called the Lords Proprietors. The French king, Louis XIV, makes New France—a large swath of North America stretching from Louisiana up to the Maritime Provinces in modern-day Canada—into a royal province, increasing the flow of French colonists to North America.

1664
The English seize the Dutch colony of New Netherland, hoping to bring most of the East Coast of North America under their rule; Peter Stuyvesant, the then-governor, capitulates.

1667
The Treaty of Breda ends the Anglo-Dutch war and confirms that New Netherland belongs to England. The Virginia Assembly closes a loophole that allows enslaved people to secure their children's freedom by baptizing them. This and other laws are codified in 1705.

1670
The Hudson's Bay Company is founded, establishing fur-trading posts and interactions with Indigenous groups in the Hudson's Bay region.

1675–1676
King Philip's War erupts between colonists and Indigenous nations in New England, led by the *sachem* (leader) of the Wampanoag, King Philip, who had taken his name when relations with the English were friendlier.

1676
In Bacon's Rebellion, the first uprising by colonists in North America, Virginians rebel against their governor, William Berkeley, after he refuses to expel the Indigenous peoples from the colony.

1680
Pueblo people in New Mexico rise up, killing missionaries and Spanish

△ **Massacre in the 17th century**
English colonists and their Indigenous allies set fire to the Pequot Fort near Stonington, Connecticut, in 1637, shooting anyone who fled and killing hundreds of Pequot people.

◁ *Kachina* doll
Carved *kachina* dolls were made by the Hopi people and used to instruct young women on the *katsinas*, or mystical beings of their religion, who were believed to control the natural world.

colonists, in what is now called the Pueblo Revolt. This, the only successful uprising against a colonizing power in North America, was led by the Pueblo religious leader Popé. The Pueblo successfully drive the Spanish out of New Mexico.

1682
William Penn founds Pennsylvania as a haven for Quakers and approves the Great Law, which allows for freedom of religious belief and practice there. He also negotiates peace with the Lenape peoples in the region. Robert de la Salle claims the entire area drained by the Mississippi River for France, naming it Louisiana after Louis XIV.

1685
The Code Noir is introduced in French colonies, regulating the treatment of enslaved and free people of color. It forbids the free movement of enslaved people and mandates their conversion to Catholicism.

1686
The Dominion of New England is created by the English king, James II, consolidating colonial governments. It stretches from modern-day Maine to New Jersey.

1688
Colonial governance is impacted by the Glorious Revolution in England, in which King James is dethroned and replaced by his daughter and her husband. Colonies are engulfed in King William's War, the first of six fought between New England and New France. Germantown Quakers petition for abolition in the first protest against slavery in North America. This petition becomes a human rights document.

1692
The Salem witch trials take place in what is now Massachusetts.

1697
The last pocket of Maya resistance is crushed at Tayasal in modern-day Guatemala.

1701
The Great Peace of Montreal ends the Beaver Wars and establishes a truce between the French and 39 Indigenous nations.

1702–1713
Queen Anne's War takes place in the Caribbean: a conflict between Spain, England, and France that reflects the tensions of the War of Spanish Succession in Europe. The Treaty of Utrecht ends the war, transferring territory between European powers.

1712
The New York Slave Revolt takes place: an uprising of 23 enslaved people in New York City.

1715–1717
In what is now South Carolina, the Yamasee War between British colonists and Indigenous peoples nearly wipes out the colony. Only the Cherokees' decision to aid the British against the Creek, a traditional Cherokee enemy, saves the colonists.

1722
The Haudenosaunee Confederacy becomes known as the Six Nations after the Tuscarora join.

1733
The last of the 13 colonies to be named, Georgia is established as a colony for debtors by James Oglethorpe, a member of parliament and social reformer.

1735
The Great Awakening, a revivalist movement led by Jonathan Edwards, sees an upswell of religious enthusiasm across the colonies.

1739
The Chickasaw War begins, with the Chickasaw people and their British allies fighting against the French and their Indigenous allies. It was sparked by the French colonial desire to eliminate the Chickasaw, having already wiped out the Natchez in 1730. The Stono Rebellion, a slave revolt, occurs in South Carolina. An alleged incident in which the Spanish coast guard lopped off a British captain's ear is used by the British to foment a conflict. Known as the War of Jenkins' Ear, it continues until 1748.

1744
King George's War, part of the War of Austrian Succession, is fought in North America. Lasting until 1748, it was the third of the four French and Indian Wars.

1745
Russian traders take Unangan (Aleut) women and children hostage to coerce Unangan men into trapping beaver and other animals for fur. On the island of Attu, 15 Unangan women and children are executed to set an example when the men do not return with furs.

△ Pueblo shield
An intimidating and meaningful symbol carried in ceremonial rituals, the shield pictured here hails from the Pueblo people of what is now the southwestern US.

FROM EMPIRES TO INDEPENDENCE 1750–1820

1750

1750s–1780s

In Mexico, the Bourbon Reforms, pushed by the Spanish crown, result in improvements in bureaucratic efficiency and economic development. At the same time, they increase the power of the Spanish in the region while decreasing that of the local elites.

1754

The Albany Congress, convened to negotiate a treaty with the Haudenosaunee people in the event of war with the French, approves the Pennsylvanian representative Benjamin Franklin's "Albany Plan." It provides for a president general named by Britain and a Grand Council of delegates from the colonies: the first attempt to unify them for mutual defense. It is rejected by both the colonies and the Crown.

1755

The first "Indian Department" is established in British North America. It aims to oversee the interactions between the colonizers and Indigenous peoples, and to secure the allegiance of the First Nations north of the Ohio River against North American and French colonies.

1755–1765

Indigenous people are brought into contact with colonizers who carry diseases from Europe and Eurasian origins through trading, exploration, warfare, and enslavement. Measles and smallpox epidemics kill thousands of Indigenous people in New York, Massachusetts, Connecticut, Rhode Island, and Pennsylvania, due to their lack of immunity to such diseases. Another illness, syphilis, likely developed in North America; it kills thousands.

1756–1763

Conflict between France, Britain, and their Indigenous allies begins in Pennsylvania in 1754. This sparks the larger Seven Years' War, with fighting among rival European empires around the globe. The North American theater of the war, sometimes known as the French and Indian War, draws in Indigenous American allies on either side. There are significant territorial changes as Britain gains control of Acadia (now Nova Scotia) and French Canada. The Proclamation of 1763 reserves lands west of the Appalachian Mountains for Indigenous peoples, restricting westward colonization.

1757

On August 10, one day after surrendering to the French general Louis-Joseph de Montcalm at Fort William Henry in northeastern New York, many British troops are killed in an ambush by

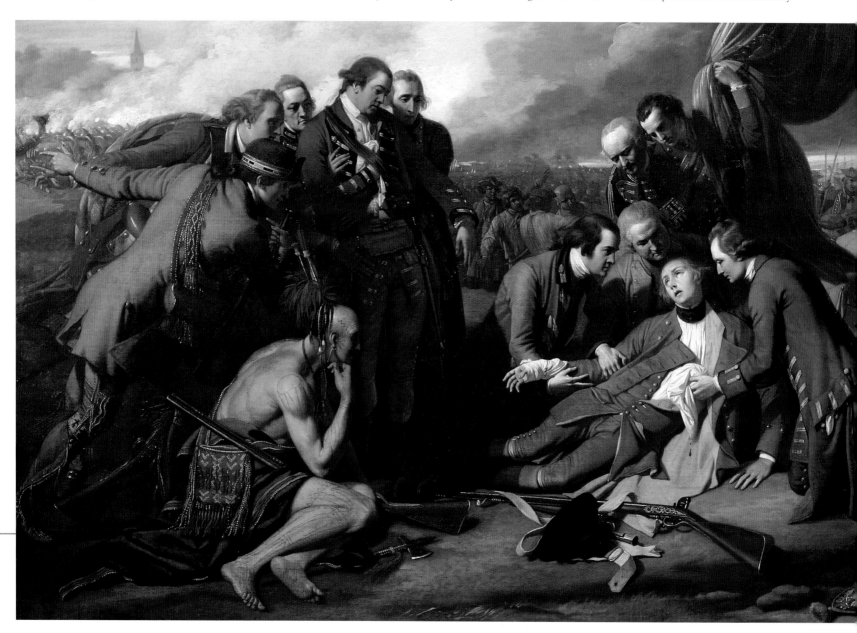

◁ **Anti-British sentiment runs high**
This teapot from the North American colonies shows colonial antagonism to the Stamp Act of 1765, regarded as unconstitutional. By displaying such messages, colonists showed their belief in the idea of "no taxation without representation."

1773

France's Indigenous allies. James Fenimore Cooper later uses this incident in his novel *The Last of the Mohicans*.

1759

A deciding event of the Seven Years' War occurs at the Battle of the Plains of Abraham, in Quebec. Both General de Montcalm and the British commander James Wolfe die in the fighting. The British capture Quebec. Although the fighting lasts only an hour, the war's final trajectory is made clear. In the Aleutian Islands, the Russian fur trade expands with the arrival of Stepan Glotov. He begins trading with the Unangan people, bringing scores of fox furs back to Russia.

1760

The Halifax Treaties, a series of peace agreements between Indigenous First Nations peoples and the British, are signed in Canada. They end more than 85 years of warfare and remain in effect to this day. In Boston, an enslaved man, Briton Hammon, publishes *A Narrative of the Uncommon Sufferings and Surprizing Deliverance of Briton Hammon, a Negro Man*. The book is believed to be the first autobiographical work written by an enslaved person of African descent living in British North America. In it, Hammon recounts his life, including a shipwreck, his service in the British Navy, and his subsequent re-enslavement.

1762

The Unangan people resist Russian occupation in the Aleutian Islands. A group of armed Unangan men attacks a party of Russian *promyshlenniki* (self-employed fur workers).

1763

The Treaty of Paris ends the Seven Years' War. Britain gains control of Canada, along with all French territory east of the Mississippi River, and formerly Spanish Florida. The Royal Proclamation of 1763 establishes British governance and recognizes Indigenous land rights, setting the stage for Indigenous land agreements in North America. It bans colonizers from occupying land west of the peaks of the Appalachian Mountains, but some ignore the rule. In protest over Britain's occupation of formerly French forts around the Great Lakes, Indigenous nations band together to fight a series of battles known as Pontiac's Rebellion. A group of colonial vigilantes, the Paxton Boys, kill 20 unarmed Conestoga people near Lancaster, Pennsylvania. Some of the victims are scalped. None of the vigilantes are prosecuted.

1765

The Stamp Act imposes a tax on all newspapers, legal documents, playing cards, dice, almanacs, and pamphlets in the British North American colonies. This raises the issue of taxation without representation, because the colonizers have no voice in the British Parliament. The purpose of the tax is to raise money for the British to occupy and defend North America, but colonizers fear the intrusions of an imperial government seeking to tighten control over the colonies.

1766

British Parliament repeals the Stamp Act, but passes the Declaratory Act, asserting its power to pass laws affecting the colonies. It declares that Parliament's authority is the same in the colonies as in Britain.

1767

The Townshend Acts are passed, outlining another series of taxes to be collected from the colonies in order to fund the British administration there, in hopes of keeping the local governors and judges loyal to the Crown. The acts increase the tension between the colonizers and the British government. In Mexico, the Jesuits, who are seen as having too much power in the Americas, are pushed out by order of King Carlos III of Spain as part of a wider expulsion from Spanish territories. In the British colonies, the Mason-Dixon Line survey is completed. It will later be widely agreed to be the demarcation between the US's North and South.

c. 1768–1771

The Cherokee War results from disputes over British colonization in Cherokee territory (what is now southwest North Carolina and southeast Tennessee).

1769

In Boston, tensions continue to increase between the British government and the colonizers. In June, customs officials seize John Hancock's sloop *Liberty* on the (likely false) charge that it was used for smuggling. In October, two regiments of British soldiers arrive in Boston. In California, the Spanish friar Father Junípero Serra establishes the first Franciscan mission there, in Baja. He will set up a further 8 of the 21 that are ultimately founded along the Californian coast between Baja and San Francisco.

1770

The Boston Massacre occurs when nine British soldiers fire into a crowd of colonizers, killing three and wounding eight, two of whom also later died. Propaganda, including a colored engraving by Paul Revere depicting the event, spreads through the region, provoking anti-Crown feeling.

1773

Objecting to the tax imposed on the sale of tea in North America, the radical Sons of Liberty throw boxes of it from British ships in Boston Harbor, in protest of the British Tea Act which allows the British East India Tea company a monopoly on selling Chinese tea in American colonies without paying taxes. This protest becomes known as the Boston Tea Party. When the British government

342

Number of tea chests thrown into Boston Harbor at the "Boston Tea Party."

◁ **The Death of General Wolfe**
US artist Benjamin West's famous painting shows the death of British general James Wolfe at the moment of victory in the 1759 Battle of the Plains of Abraham.

▷ **Newly minted**
The 1792 act of Congress established the US Mint and set the United States dollar as the country's standard currency.

1774

responds harshly, unrest in the colonies increases. In Silver Bluff, South Carolina, the Silver Bluff Baptist Church, now the oldest continuously operating Black church, is founded.

1774

In the Intolerable Acts, passed in reprisal for the Boston Tea Party, the British Parliament closes Boston Harbor to all shipping until payment is made for the destroyed tea, forbids public meetings, and forces colonizers to house and feed British soldiers in private homes. The Quebec Act, also passed by the British parliament, provides civil and religious liberties for French Canadians and expands the borders of Quebec to the Ohio River. It also guarantees the rights of Catholics and Indigenous peoples in the region. English religious leader Ann Lee arrives in New York. Later, she will found the colony of Shakers, a celibate, communal group that prizes simple design and personal expression of religious belief, while revering her as the female representation of God. In September, the First Continental Congress meets in Philadelphia; all 13 colonies except Georgia are represented.

After meeting in response to the British government's harsh retribution after the Boston Tea Party, the group approves the Suffolk Resolves, calling for organized opposition to the Intolerable Acts. They also draft a petition to King George asking for a repeal of the acts.

1775

On April 14, the Society for the Relief of Free Negroes Unlawfully Held in Bondage, the first antislavery society in the colonies, holds the first of four meetings in Philadelphia. Many of the men involved are Quakers and fervent abolitionists. On April 19, the American Revolution (also known as the American War of Independence) between the colonizers and the British begins with the Battles of Lexington and Concord, and will continue until 1783. The colonizers are warned that the British will attack their garrison of supplies at Concord by sea and are able to defend their holding, despite casualties. They harry the British forces as they retreat to Boston, blocking off their land access. The number of colonizers swells and in June, they establish the new Continental Army. George Washington is made

commander-in-chief because of his military experience in the French and Indian War. On June 17, after the Siege of Boston, the British fight their way out at the Battle of Bunker Hill, sustaining heavy losses. Despite their tactical loss, the revolutionaries surprise the British with their fierce resistance, and sustain far fewer casualties. On December 31, as they attempt to take Quebec, the Continental Army suffers its first major defeat, losing to the British in the Battle of Quebec. The Second Continental Congress begins convening in Philadelphia, with representatives from 12 of the 13 colonies attending.

1776

With war still raging, revolutionary Thomas Paine publishes *Common Sense*—a pamphlet outlining the advantages of American independence in clear and persuasive language. With more than half a million copies in print, the work helps to turn sentiment toward the revolutionaries. When compared proportionally to the population in the US, it is the best-selling American book of all time. On July 4, the Second Continental Congress adopts the Declaration of Independence. The document explains to the world why the 13 North American colonies no longer consider themselves to be under British rule. Representatives from all colonies sign. On September 9, the Continental Congress formally declares the name of the new nation to be the United States of America.

1777

In July, Vermont becomes the first political jurisdiction in the US to abolish slavery. In November, Congress adopts the Articles of Confederation; these acknowledge Indigenous American sovereignty and become the basis for the Constitution of the United States.

1778

The Continental Congress makes its first treaty with an Indigenous nation, the Lenape (Delaware), beginning a period of government-to-government agreements between 1778 and 1871, which use the treaty as the primary instrument of negotiation. In December, the British invade the deep South, capturing Savannah.

1780

Pennsylvania adopts the first gradual emancipation law, which holds that all children of enslaved people born after November 1, 1780, will be freed on their 28th birthday.

1780s

The peak of the transatlantic slave trade, with 78,000 enslaved people brought forcibly each year to the Americas. Between 1701 and 1810, more than three million arrive in the Caribbean.

1781

In Boston, Quock Walker, an enslaved man, successfully petitions for his freedom, basing his case on the Massachusetts constitution's declaration that "All men are born free and equal." His win sets Massachusetts on the path

12
The number (in millions) of people forcibly removed from their homelands during the transatlantic slave trade.

◁ **Drafting the Declaration of Independence**
The Committee of Five of the Second Continental Congress (from left, John Adams, Roger Sherman, Robert R. Livingston, Thomas Jefferson, and Benjamin Franklin), who drafted the Declaration of Independence, depicted in an 1817 oil painting by John Trumbull.

to abolishing slavery. The revolutionaries' victory at the Battle of Yorktown, achieved with the help of the French, leads to the surrender of British forces under General Cornwallis, effectively ending the American Revolution. Former loyalists flee the colonies, including 20,000 Black loyalists, who mostly end up in Nova Scotia.

1783
The Newburgh Conspiracy occurs in March, when Continental Army officers threaten to revolt. They consider taking violent action against Congress, but are dissuaded by General Washington. The Treaty of Paris officially ends the American Revolution, and establishes the border between the US and Canada. The Northwestern Confederacy, also called the United Indian Nation, forms in the Great Lakes to resist colonial

expansion after areas formerly part of Canada are ceded to the US in the Treaty of Paris.

1784
The Haldimand Proclamation goes into effect. It grants land on either side of the Grand River in Canada to the Six Nations in thanks for their support during the American Revolution. However, the grant is reduced over time and remains in dispute to this day. Russian fur traders, led by Grigorii Shelikhov, overwhelm the Sugpiaq people in a massacre at Refuge Rock on Kodiak Island, on Alaska's southern coast. Shelikhov founds the first permanent Russian colony in Alaska.

1785
The New York Society for the Promoting of the Manumission of

Slaves is founded by New Yorkers including John Jay and Alexander Hamilton. They seek to abolish slavery within New York State.

1786
New Brunswick is separated from Nova Scotia to become a separate British colony. In Massachusetts, Shays' Rebellion, an armed uprising over a debt crisis, highlights the need for a stronger central government.

1787
The US issues its first circulating coin, the Fugio cent, also known as the Franklin cent, a copper coin featuring an image of the sun. It is designed by Benjamin Franklin. In July, Congress enacts the Northwest Ordinance, which establishes formal procedures for transforming territories into new

states. It provides for the eventual establishment of Ohio, Indiana, Illinois, Michigan, Wisconsin, and Minnesota, and prohibits slavery in those states. It also provides for the eventual establishment of three to five states north of the Ohio River, and prohibits slavery there. The Free African Society, a mutual self-help group in Philadelphia, is created by Richard Allen and Absalom Jones. It is the first cultural organization established by Black people in North America. The Constitution of the United States is drafted in Philadelphia, creating the three distinct branches of government that exist today: the Judicial, the Executive, and the Legislative. Although it grants many rights to citizens, it excludes women, enslaved people, and Indigenous people. Slavery is enshrined for the next 20 years. Enslaved people are counted as only

△ **Slavery and plantation life**
In this engraving of a Southern plantation, enslaved people produce cotton, using Eli Whitney's cotton gin, while white men admire the cotton crop and reap the rewards of their labor.

◁ **Party for the Purchase**
In 1904, a World's Fair was held in St. Louis to celebrate the centennial of the Louisiana Purchase, when the US bought 828,000 square miles (more than 210,000 km²) of land from the French.

32:1
Ratio of men to women on the Lewis and Clark expedition. Sacagawea, the only woman, held an equal vote.

of their mothers' enslavers for life. US inventor Eli Whitney patents the cotton gin. He had learned how to separate seeds from raw cotton from an enslaved man known only as Sam. The development of the gin provides a huge boost to the slave-based cotton economy of the South. Industrialist Samuel Slater opens the first cotton mill, in Pawtucket, Rhode Island.

1794
In August, General Anthony Wayne defeats the Northwestern Confederacy at the Battle of Fallen Timbers, opening Ohio to colonization by white people. In Western Pennsylvania, President Washington demonstrates the power of the federal government to enforce its laws by using state militia to suppress the Whiskey Rebellion, a tax revolt by farmers. In Kodiak, Alaska, the first Russian Orthodox missionaries arrive and try to convert the Sugpiaq people.

1796
Jay's Treaty ushers in 10 years of peaceful trading and helps keep peace between the US and Britain by resolving several issues from the American Revolution. They are settled by arbitration, in its first modern usage.

1797
In the US, the Alien and Sedition Acts are passed to increase the requirements for those seeking citizenship. This triggers a migration of people from the US to Canada.

1799
The Russian czar, Paul I, grants the Russian-American Company a charter with exclusive rights to the fur trade in Russian-controlled Alaska, but the Russians find it hard to sustain a colony. The Seneca prophet Handsome Lake has his first religious revelation. He preaches that the Six Nations should live in peace with whites but maintain their Indigenous culture.

1800
Washington, in the District of Columbia, becomes the US capital. As a federal district, Washington, D.C., is neither a state nor in a state, and does not have voting representation in the US Congress. Congress rejects by a vote of 85 to 1 an antislavery petition offered by free Philadelphian African-Americans. On the island of Hispaniola, after eliminating his various rivals, Toussaint Louverture emerges as the leader of the former French colony of St. Domingue (now Haiti). In 1801 he invades the neighboring Spanish colony of Santo Domingo (now the Dominican Republic) and becomes the ruler of the whole of Hispaniola.

1801
The First Barbary War, fought by Sweden and the US against Tripolitania (roughly modern-day Libya) is the first US act of war on foreign soil. It arises when President Thomas Jefferson refuses to pay tribute to the Tripolitanian government. General

three-fifths of a man when counting the population for the House of Representatives.

1789
George Washington is inaugurated as the first President of the United States.

1790
The Indian Non-Intercourse Act is passed by the US Congress—the first law to regulate trade relations between colonizers and Indigenous Americans.

1791
In the French colony of St. Domingue, 100,000 enslaved people revolt in August, marking the start of the Haitian Revolution under the leadership of Jean-Jacques Dessalines and Toussaint Louverture. It will become the only uprising by enslaved people that ends in the founding of a state free of slavery. In the US, the Bill of Rights is ratified in December. This contains the first 10 amendments to the Constitution, which protect individual liberties from the power of central government. Vermont becomes the 14th state in the newly formed United States. The Constitutional Act is passed, dividing Canada into Upper Canada (Ontario) and Lower Canada (Quebec), each with its own government and legislative assembly.

1792
The US Mint is established in Philadelphia and the US dollar is designated the standard monetary unit.

1793
In February, the First Fugitive Slave Law is passed, which makes helping fugitive slaves a criminal offense. Legally, any enslaved person who is recaptured must be returned to their enslaver. It also makes the children of fugitive enslaved women the property

▷ **Jean-Jacques Dessalines**
A wooden bust of Jean-Jacques Dessalines, a leader of the Haitian Revolution who became the first emperor of Haiti.

▽ **Mapping uncharted territory**
In this painting from 1929, Lemhi Shoshone guide Sacagawea points the way to Lewis and Clark on their 8,000-mile journey to the Pacific coast.

William Eaton, US Consul General to Tunis, leading a small force of Marines and Arab mercenaries marches 500 miles (805 km) from Egypt to capture Tripoli's port of Derna. Tripolitania drops demands for the payments.

1803

The US federal government formally assigns the responsibility for providing medical care for Indigenous peoples to the US War Department. However, Congress does not allocate funding to pay for care. In April, the Louisiana Purchase is acquired by the US from France. The vast territory doubles the size of the country. Much of the purchased land remains under the control of Indigenous people, with the US essentially buying the right to subjugate them.

1804

In January, Jean-Jacques Dessalines proclaims Haiti's independence from France, becomes emperor there, and immediately abolishes slavery. In the US, the Ohio legislature passes the first "Black Laws," which are designed to restrict the legal rights of free Black people, part of the trend of imposing increasingly severe restrictions on all Black people in both the North and South before the Civil War. Ohio is the first non-slaveholding state to do so. Lewis and Clark are tasked by President Jefferson with exploring and mapping the newly acquired Louisiana Territory. Their expedition travels 8,000 miles as far as the Pacific, returning in 1806. Sacagawea, a Lemhi Shoshone woman who joins them in what is now North Dakota, serves as the expedition's guide as they travel toward the West Coast.

1805

In the Great Lakes region, Tecumseh—a Shawnee leader—and his brother, the prophet Lalawethika Tenskwatawa, begin to build a political and military confederacy (and religious movement) based on unity. Initially conceived as peaceful, they will eventually take up arms against the white population.

1807

New Jersey, where suffrage had been available to most women and Black people upon the formation of the state, begins to limit the right to vote to

1808

only "free, white males," part of a move toward the more general disenfranchisement of Black people. In September, US engineer Robert Fulton sails his new invention, the steamboat *Clermont*, on the Hudson River, inaugurating a new era of steam-powered transportation. The US Congress passes the Embargo Act, which prohibits US exports to Britain and France as a protest at their interference with US shipping.

1808

Napoleon's invasion of Spain and his capture of King Ferdinand VII disrupts Spanish rule, creating a power vacuum in Mexico. Calls for independence grow as the colonial government collapses. In

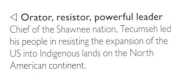

◁ **Orator, resistor, powerful leader**
Chief of the Shawnee nation, Tecumseh led his people in resisting the expansion of the US into Indigenous lands on the North American continent.

15

Number of stars and stripes on the original star-spangled banner.

March, the international slave trade is abolished in the US. The ban is widely ignored, however, and between 1808 and 1860, approximately 250,000 enslaved people are illegally brought into the country.

1809

The Treaty of Fort Wayne is negotiated by William Henry Harrison, governor of the Indiana Territory and superintendent of Indian Affairs. It takes three million acres (around 12,000 km²) from Indigenous peoples and gives them to the white population of Illinois and Indiana. Amish communities start colonizing eastern Ohio.

1810

In October, the US annexes the short-lived Republic of West Florida after American colonizers revolt against local Spanish control. The Mexican War of Independence begins, sparked by Father Miguel Hidalgo's famous call for independence from Spain, dubbed the "Cry from Delores."

1811

In January, the German Coast Uprising, led by Charles Deslondes, begins on the Louisiana plantation of Manual Andry. Fifteen enslaved men attack Andry, who survives to warn other plantation owners. In Mexico, the insurgent *caudillos* (warlords) including Miguel Hidalgo, Ignacio Allende, and Ignacio Aldama, are captured near the Wells of

Baján by Ignacio Elizondo, a royalist military officer who pretends to be a rebel in order to lure them into his trap. In Canada, the Hudson's Bay Company grants land to Scottish peer Thomas Douglas, who builds the Red River Colony there. The territory will eventually become part of Manitoba and the Missouri Territory.

1812

In June, the War of 1812 begins when the US government declares war on Britain over its interference with US shipping and impressments of US

seamen. In Canada, the Pemmican War, ignites as the Hudson's Bay Company and the North West Company skirmish, after the governor of Red River Colony bans export of pemmican (a type of dried meat) to forts owned by North West Company, in order to save it for the colony.

1813

As tensions rise in the Indiana Territory, the US launches a preemptive strike on the growing confederacy headed by Tecumseh in what will become known as Tecumseh's War. At the

◁ **Star-Spangled Banner**
Made in 1813 by flag maker Mary Pickersgill, the flag inspired the song written by Francis Scott Key, "The Star-Spangled Banner," after he saw the flag flying during the Battle of Baltimore.

1820

a combined British and Indigenous force meets the US Army, led by the Indiana Territory governor Harrison. Amid heavy fighting, the British troops flee, leaving Tecumseh's troops to fight alone. He is killed. The first Mexican constitution, the Constitution of Apatzingán, is enacted by the insurgent forces in the Congress of Anáhuac.

1814
In March, the Creek War ends at the Battle of Horseshoe Bend, when Chief Red Eagle surrenders to General Andrew Jackson. In August, the British set fire to the Presidential Mansion (now the White House) and the Capitol (which had been completed in 1800), avenging a US raid on York, Ontario. In September, the British bombard the US garrison at Fort McHenry in the Battle of Baltimore. The fort's battle flag has 15 stripes—the only official US flag to have more than 13—and inspires the composition of the song "The Star-Spangled Banner," which will become the US national anthem in 1931. In December, the Treaty of Ghent ends the War of 1812 and Britain agrees to relinquish claims to the Northwest Territory.

1815
At the Battle of New Orleans, unaware of the Treaty of Ghent, General Jackson defeats the British. Among his forces are Cherokee and Choctaw people, and 3,000 Black troops. In the ongoing Mexican War of Independence from Spain, José María Morelos, who had taken over command of the rebel militia from Hidalgo, is captured and executed. The American frigate, the USS *President*, is captured by the British. The second wave of Amish immigration from Europe to North America begins.

1816
Bishop Richard Allen officially creates the African Methodist Episcopal Church, the first wholly African-American church denomination in the US. Founded by Bushrod Washington (the nephew of George Washington), the American Colonization Society is established to encourage the migration of free Black people to Africa.

1817
Construction of the Erie Canal begins in July. It is designed to connect the Great Lakes to Albany, running from the Hudson River to Lake Erie. In December, General Jackson marches into Florida in order to stop raids by Indigenous people, fugitive enslaved people, and white outlaws on US territory, marking the beginning of the Seminole Wars—the bloodiest of all conflicts between US and Indigenous Americans. The US Congress drafts a bill to split the Mississippi Territory, creating the Alabama Territory.

1818
In the Treaty of 1818, the US and Britain set the boundary of the United States at the 49th parallel west of the Rockies, and address territorial issues in the Pacific Northwest. Oregon country is under joint US and British control.

1819
The US's first major economic depression produces political division, with calls for the democratization of state constitutions and an end to imprisonment for debt. In February, Spain cedes Florida to the United States through the Adams-Onís Treaty. This also delineates the boundary between the US and the Viceroyalty of Spain, in what is now Mexico.

1820
The Spanish Constitution of 1812 is reinstated in Spain in January, after King Ferdinand VII had abolished it in 1814. Its resurrection gives political rights of representation to Spanish Americans. In March, the Missouri Compromise is passed to address the issue of slavery in new territories. It is an attempt to balance the desires of northern states to prevent the expansion of slavery with those of southern states to expand it. Missouri is admitted as a slave state and Maine as a free state, while slavery is forbidden in the remaining Louisiana Purchase lands north of Oklahoma. The Compromise will remain in force for more than 30 years. The first plans for the removal of Indigenous people via resettlement are outlined in the Treaty of Doak's Stand. The Choctaw people cede nearly half their land for some in Indian Territory (now Oklahoma).

> *"We are to be ruined by paper, as we were by the old Continental paper."*
>
> THOMAS JEFFERSON, ON THE RISK OF A DEPRESSION, 1814

Battle of Tippecanoe, William Henry Harrison defeats Tenskwatawa and 500 Indigenous warriors. Tecumseh's warriors then join British forces in Canada, going to war against the US in the War of 1812. In June, Queenston housewife Laura Secord learns of a planned attack by US forces and walks 20 miles (32 km) to warn the British, who then defeat the US in the Battle of Beaver Dams. In July, the Creek War begins when conflict within the Muscogee tribes draws in the British and US. In October, at the Battle of the Thames (or Battle of Moraviantown),

▷ **Morelos money**
A 20-peso bill from Mexico featuring independence movement leader José María Morelos. He is featured more than anyone else on Mexico's paper money.

EXPANDING NATIONS 1820–1850

1821

1821

In March, the British North West Company and Hudson's Bay Company merge, covering territory from the Great Lakes to the Pacific Ocean. In September, reactionary forces secure Mexico's independence, led by Agustín de Iturbide, a former soldier in the royal Spanish army who switched sides to the insurgents. This ends more than a decade of revolutionary war. Iturbide and the Spanish viceroy, Juan de O'Donojú, sign the Treaty of Córdoba, ending Spanish control of Mexico and ratifying the Plan of Iguala. Under the Plan, Mexico will be ruled as a limited monarchy, with Catholicism as the official religion and equal rights for the minority Spanish and Mestizo populations, but not for the majority Indigenous, Black, or mixed-race population. In Alabama, a Cherokee man, Sequoyah, invents a system for writing down the Cherokee language. Now known as Sequoyah's Syllabary, this is the first written form of the Cherokee language. US frontier trader William Becknell establishes the Santa Fe Trail, a trade route between Missouri and New Mexico.

1822

Stephen Austin begins the colonization of what is now Texas. Austin is an American-born *empresario* (a contractor given the right to colonize land and recruit families to live there) whose father had gained a land grant from the Mexican government but died

before he could use it. Austin decides to continue the project. In May, Agustín de Iturbide declares himself Emperor of Mexico.

1823

In February, the first of three important US Supreme Court cases is held. Now known as the Marshall Trilogy, these court decisions have come to form the basis of Indigenous American law. In *Johnson v. McIntosh*, the court rules that since the federal government now controls the land, Indigenous populations have only a "right of occupancy" and hold no land titles. In March, Agustín de Iturbide is deposed (and later executed) by rebel soldier Antonio López de Santa Anna, who declares a Mexican republic. Guadalupe Victoria, a general who had fought for Mexican independence, becomes Mexico's first elected president. In December, US president James Monroe (elected in 1817) warns European nations against interfering in US affairs by issuing what is now called the Monroe Doctrine. The doctrine holds that any intervention can be seen as a hostile act, and is created out of concern about European and Russian territorial ambitions.

1824

The Bureau of Indian Affairs is set up within the US War Department, creating the bureaucracy that will later deliver the nation's "Manifest Destiny" objectives, which state that expansion to the Pacific is the nation's right. In what is now northern California, the Chumash revolt occurs when the people revolt against the Spanish and Mexican missionaries who have forced them into subjugation in their own lands. It begins in three of the Franciscan missions in Alta California, and spreads to the surrounding villages.

1825

The blockade by Mexican gunships of San Juan de Ulúa, an island in the Gulf of Mexico, ends with the surrender of Spanish forces in the town. It was the last Spanish stronghold in Mexico. In what is now Texas, Stephen Austin brings 300 families (known as the "Old 300") to his colony—the first group of colonizers from the US to Texas. The land area lies between the Brazos and the Colorado rivers, inland from the Gulf of Mexico. No previous Spanish or Mexican settlements exist there, but the area is occupied by Indigenous peoples, who attack the new colony. In Indiana, Welsh industrialist Robert Owen establishes the utopian community of New Harmony, an early socialist experiment. In Georgia, in the Treaty of Indian Springs, the Lower Creek Council led by Creek chief William McIntosh sells large amounts of Creek land to the US government for approximately $200,000. McIntosh is later assassinated by Upper Creek chief Menawa for making this concession. In the same year, the Kansa and Osage nations also cede land to the US. After the Treaties of St. Louis, a series of 14 agreements signed between the US and various Indigenous peoples, approximately 1,400 Missouri Shawnee people are forcibly relocated from Missouri to Kansas.

1826

Bytown is established in what is now Ontario, Canada. The town is named after Colonel John By, a supervising engineer for the construction of the Rideau Canal. Begun as a construction camp built on a bluff on the Ottawa River, the town is later renamed Ottawa and made capital of what will become

Canada. The area soon attracts merchants, contractors, and laborers. The US inventor Samuel Morey patents an internal combustion engine which uses the vapor of turpentine to power the machine. He is eventually able to employ it to power a carriage in an early prototype of an automobile. The Fredonian Rebellion at the end of the year is the first attempt by Texas to secede from Mexico. Colonists declare independence from Mexico and create the Republic of Fredonia in what is now Eastern Texas.

1827

Slavery is officially abolished in New York state, as a gradual abolition law passed in 1799 comes to full fruition. The last enslaved people are freed on July 4. Black Americans celebrate with a parade. The Cherokee people adopt a constitution modeled on that of the United States. It is developed largely in order to prevent the forced removal of the Cherokee people. The Democratic Party (now the US's oldest surviving political party) emerges after the Democratic-Republican Party (founded in 1790) divides. Martin Van Buren and Andrew Jackson are the founders.

1828

The first edition of The American Dictionary of the English Language is published. It is better known as

◁ **Military medal**
An award medal of the Military of Emperor Agustín de Iturbide of Mexico. Iturbide was emperor for less than a year.

▷ **The "Underground Railroad"**
Enslaved people escaping from the South to the North of the US were helped by an unofficial network of people, as depicted in this 1893 painting by Charles T. Webber.

◁ Reading and writing in Cherokee
Devised by a Cherokee man named Sequoyah, this syllabary shows the symbols used by the Cherokee people, making it possible to read and write in the Cherokee language.

1830

"The evil, sir, is enormous; the inevitable suffering incalculable."

EDWARD EVERETT, SECRETARY OF STATE, ON THE TRAIL OF TEARS

Webster's Dictionary, after its writer and publisher, Noah Webster. In March, Andrew Jackson is elected the seventh president of the United States. As a Tennessean, he is the first president from outside the states of Virginia or Massachusetts. His term inaugurates a mixture of reform and popular democracy, but also white supremacy, support for slavery, and subjugation and displacement of Indigenous peoples.

1829

In the Battle of Tampico, in what is now the Mexican state of Tamaulipas, the Spanish attempt to reclaim Mexico.

Mexico wins, under the leadership of Antonio López de Santa Anna, who becomes known as the Hero of Tampico. In August, in what are later known as the Cincinnati riots, more than half of the city's Black residents are driven out by white mob violence. This marks the beginning of more than 100 years of sustained white violence against Northern Black urban communities. The British scientist James Smithson bequeaths £100,000 to the US to found the Smithsonian Institution in Washington D.C. The money, which was paid in gold sovereigns, is sent from England in 11 crates.

1830

Peaking around 1830, the "Underground Railroad"—a network of abolitionists, secret routes, and safe houses—helps enslaved people escape from Southern states to freedom in the North. It is so named because railroad terms are used to reference the workings of the system: routes are known as "lines" and the people who help along the way are known as "conductors." Assisting the escape of enslaved people are free Black people (including formerly enslaved people) and Northern abolitionists, philanthropists, and church leaders. During the subsequent decade, the US government signs numerous treaties with Indigenous peoples to provide agricultural assistance, education, health care, payments, cattle, and merchandise in return for millions of acres of land. In total, Congress ratifies 389 treaties with Indigenous peoples between

1778 and 1886. In May, President Jackson passes the Indian Removal Act. It authorizes the US Army to force Cherokee, Chickasaw, Choctaw, Creek, and Seminole peoples—including some of Jackson's former allies in the War of 1812—out of Georgia and other states. In September, Black delegates meet in Philadelphia at the first National Negro Convention to devise ways to challenge slavery in the South and racial discrimination in the North. Joseph Smith, a church leader in New York state, publishes the *Book of Mormon*, a religious text of the Latter-Day Saint movement. The work gains him thousands of followers, and Smith goes on to found Church of Jesus Christ of Latter-Day Saints, also known as Mormonism. The religious movement grows into a worldwide organization by the end of the 20th century. The first section of the

▽ **Nat Turner's rebellion**
In 1831, Nat Turner led a violent revolt that struck fear into the white population of Virginia. The Southampton Insurrection, as it became known, was the deadliest revolt by enslaved people in US history.

1831

Baltimore and Ohio Railroad opens. It is the first common carrier railroad, carrying people, goods, or services for the general public.

1831

In the second of the Marshall Trilogy hearings, *Cherokee Nation v. State of Georgia*, the US Supreme Court rules that Indigenous nations are not subject to state law. An effective enslaved people's revolt in US history takes place in August, when Nat Turner leads a rebellion in Virginia. Approximately 60 white people are killed. In its aftermath, white mobs murder more than 120 Black people, many of whom were not involved in the revolt. As part of a general trend of laws restricting literacy in the Southern states, North Carolina enacts a statute that bans the teaching of enslaved people to read and write. Alabama also makes it illegal for enslaved or free Black people to preach. As part of the ongoing effect of the 1830 Indian Removal Act, the next two decades see the US government force thousands of

Indigenous people—including nearly one-third of the Choctaw Nation— to walk 500 miles (more than 800 km) on relocation marches along what becomes known as the "Trail of Tears." It is estimated that up to 15,000 people die of starvation, exposure, and disease on the journey to Indian Territory. This land, encompassing all land west of the Mississippi River, has been set aside for the relocation of Indigenous peoples, but will gradually be reduced over the coming years. Eventually it will become the state of Oklahoma. The Nimiipuu (Nez Percé) people send a delegation 2,000 miles (more than 3,200 km) from what is now Idaho to St. Louis, Missouri, to look for explorer William Clark, whom they had met when he lived with them for a month in 1806. They are also keen to meet Bible teachers, sparking an influx of missionaries into the Pacific Northwest.

1832

Sauk and Fox people unsuccessfully seek to recover territory in Illinois that had been surrendered to the

US in the Black Hawk War. In March, in the last of the Marshall Trilogy cases, *Worcester v. State of Georgia*, the Supreme Court rules that the federal government, not the states, has jurisdiction over Indigenous territories. In Salem, Massachusetts, a group of free Black women found the Salem Female Anti-Slavery Society, the first Black women's abolitionist society. In addition to promoting abolitionism, the society helps people who are newly freed or have recently escaped from slavery, provides educational and job training opportunities for free Black youth, fights segregationist laws and practices, and lobbies against plans to deport all free Black people in the US to Africa. The Rideau Canal is completed, one of several canals built in the Canadas. It links the Ottawa River, at what is now Ottawa, with Lake Ontario at what is now Kingston, Ontario. It is 125 miles (200 km) long and has 24 locks. The cholera epidemic reaches North America from England, where the disease is rampant. Quarantine stations are set up in Quebec to deal with the tens of thousands of immigrants arriving from England but the disease continues to spread, reaching New York City and then the midwestern US states. In Mexico, Santa Anna is elected president, for the first of five terms. His strong centralist policies anger residents of Texas, which is still under Mexican rule. In Charleston, South Carolina, freed Black man Denmark Vesey is hanged along with 35 others for allegedly plotting a rebellion. The discovery of this plot stokes fears among white people in the US South. In Ontario, the Ojibwe people hand over huge tracts of land to the Canadian government in

exchange for reserves, payments, and hunting and fishing rights. Mexico is recognized as an independent nation by the US at the end of the year, when President James Monroe welcomes José Manuel Zozaya as the first Mexican diplomat to represent his country in the US.

1833

The American Anti-Slavery Society is founded in Philadelphia under the leadership of William Lloyd Garrison, with the intention of advocating for the immediate abolition of slavery in the US. The society will go on to sponsor lecture tours by formerly enslaved people, including Frederick Douglass. These prove to be its most effective technique for recruiting others to the abolitionist cause.

1834

The US Department of War forcibly removes the remaining 20,000 Muscogee Creek people from Alabama, relocating them to Indian Territory. South Carolina bans the teaching of Black people, enslaved or free, within its borders. In the British-governed colony of Lower Canada, politicians Louis-Joseph Papineau and Augustin-Norbert Morin publish the Ninety-Two Resolutions, a long series of demands for political reforms. The document is a critique of the entire colonial political system. None of the resolutions are enacted. Mexico seizes control of the Californian missions. It frees the

▷ **Memories on buffalo hide**
Lone Dog's Winter Count, a record of the Yanktonai people's history painted on animal hides. This entry shows disease epidemics, starting from the center and spiraling outward.

▷ **Tribute to *Amistad***
Sculptor Ed Hamilton's 1992 memorial pays tribute to the men of the *Amistad*, who mutinied and eventually secured their freedom after a long court battle.

Chumash people, who had been enslaved by the Spanish in California for 65 years. Ignoring promises of reparation to Indigenous people, Mexico gives land grants to families of Spanish descent. The British parliament's Slavery Abolition Act outlaws slavery in all British-controlled lands, which include the Canadas and islands in the Caribbean.

1835

The first known assassination attempt on a US president occurs when an unemployed house painter named Richard Lawrence hides on the porch of the US Capitol building and attempts to shoot President Andrew Jackson in the heart. The gun misfires, saving Jackson. In January, the US national debt is declared to be $0 for the first and, thus far, only time in history. The Second Seminole War begins when the US forces the Seminole people to move from a reservation in what is now central Florida to the Creek reservation west of the Mississippi River. It will become the longest of the wars of Indian removal, lasting seven years. The Texas Revolution begins, with Texas colonists revolting against the Mexican government. It lasts until 1836. The Battle of the Alamo is a pivotal event in the war, when Mexican soldiers retake Fort Alamo after a siege in which they kill most of the soldiers who had held it. In Georgia, the Treaty of New Echota cedes all Cherokee lands east of Mississippi to the US government, and forces the Cherokee people to move to Indian Territory in the West, as part of what becomes known as the Trail of Tears.

1836

The Texas Revolution ends with the Battle of San Jacinto, when rebel leader General Sam Houston defeats a Mexican army in a battle lasting only 18 minutes. This completes the seizure of Texas from Mexico, and Texas declares its independence. The Champlain and Saint Lawrence Railroad opens, the first public railroad in the Canadas. It connects La Prairie (near Montréal) to Saint-Jean-sur-Richelieu. In North America, a new wave of epidemics begins, decimating Indigenous populations. A smallpox epidemic in the American West kills 10,000 people in the Northern Plains alone. Peoples affected include the Siksika (Blackfoot), Kainai (Blood), Chaticks Si Chaticks (Pawnee), Nakoda (Assiniboine), Numakiki (Mandan), Sahnish (Arikara), and Dakota, among many others.

1837

In both Upper and Lower Canada, British colonial rule and the privileges of the elite lead to widespread discontent and rebellions break out. These are crushed by colonial militia and British troops, but the rebels plant the seeds of responsible government and lay the foundations for the creation of modern Canada. The US Department of War forcibly removes the Chickasaw people from Mississippi, Kentucky, Alabama, and Tennessee to Indian Territory. The Chickasaw people negotiate compensation for lost lands from the US government, receiving more than $500,000. Missouri is the latest state to continue the anti-literacy crackdown by banning the education of free Black people.

1838

The Great Western Steamship Company begins operating the first regular transatlantic steamer service, from the British port of Bristol to New York City. The US government begins the forced removal of about 860 members of the Potawatomi nation from Indiana to reservation lands in what is now Kansas. More than 40 people will die during the journey, most of them children. It is now known as the Potawatomi Trail of Death. In Maryland,

10

Number of thousands of Indigenous people killed in the Northern Plains by the smallpox epidemic of 1836.

enslaved Black man Frederick Douglass makes his third attempt to escape to freedom. He boards a train heading north disguised as a sailor and carrying identification papers from a free Black seaman. He travels to Philadelphia, and continues to New York City where he becomes a free man after a journey lasting fewer than 24 hours.

1839
In Upper Canada, the Crown Lands Act is passed. It disenfranchises First Nations peoples by affirming that Indigenous lands belong to the British Crown unless specifically titled to an individual. Near the coast of Cuba, there is a mutiny by enslaved men on the Spanish ship *Amistad*. Led by Joseph Cinqué, the mutineers kill the captain and the cook but spare the life of the navigator, so he can sail them back to Sierra Leone. Instead the navigator sails the *Amistad* north and the US Navy seizes the ship off Long Island, New York. The case ends up in the US Supreme Court and the mutineers are declared free men, illegally kidnapped, in a decision that bolsters the abolitionist movement. Thirty-five of the survivors are repatriated to their homelands in Sierra Leone.

1840
The British Parliament passes the Act of Union, which abolishes the legislatures of Upper and Lower Canada, and

instead establishes a new political entity: the Province of Canada. Representation between the two areas becomes more equal. Explorer Captain Charles Wilkes circumvents Antarctica and claims Wilkes Land for the United States. He and his men prove that Antarctica is a land continent by exploring more than 1,500 miles (2,400 km) of its coast.

1841
On May 1, the first wagon train leaves from Independence, Missouri, to what will become California, led by colonizer John Bidwell. Part of what is known as the Western Emigration Society, nearly 70 adults, almost all of them men, travel in the train. Their journey takes until November 4.

1842
The Webster–Ashburton Treaty is signed in Washington D.C. It resolves various US–Canadian boundary disputes, establishing that the two parties would share use of the Great Lakes.

1843
In a mass exodus, nearly a thousand people follow John Gantt, a former US Army captain and fur trader, into the American Northwest, using what becomes known as the Oregon Trail, a 2,100-mile (3,380-km) route from

Missouri to present-day Oregon. Formerly enslaved people Sojourner Truth and William Wells Brown become involved in the growing antislavery movement and begin campaigning.

1844
US inventors Samuel Morse and Alfred Vail complete the first electromagnetic telegraph line between Washington, D.C., and Baltimore and send the first telegraphic message. In Illinois, the founder of the Church of Jesus Christ of Latter-Day Saints, Joseph Smith, and his brother are shot and killed by an angry mob as they await trial. The two had been charged with inciting a riot after Smith had ordered the destruction of the printing press of the *Nauvoo Expositor*. The newspaper had been critical of Smith and accused him of practicing polygamy, as well as treason against the State of Illinois. The US and China sign the Treaty of Wangxia, which forces the Chinese to grant the US territories and trading powers—the same intrusive terms granted to Britain. The Oregon Exclusion Law comes into effect, prohibiting Black citizens from entering or remaining in the territory, while also prohibiting slavery there.

1845
Having escaped slavery, Frederick Douglass publishes the first of three volumes of his autobiography, *Narrative of the Life of Frederick Douglass, an American Slave, Written by Himself*. He becomes an international leader in the abolitionist movement, famed for his oratory and writing. Political journalist John L. O'Sullivan coins the slogan "Manifest Destiny" to promote the US's territorial ambitions to extend west to the Pacific. The Irish potato famine begins, lasting until 1952. It sparks mass emigration to Canada and the US. Up to two million people will emigrate

during the famine years. Because transportation costs to British North American ports are cheaper than fares to other destinations, most Irish refugees head to North America, especially to Quebec, Montreal, and New York City. In March, the US Congress approves the annexation of Texas, authorized by President John Tyler. Texas becomes the 28th state in the Union in December. This will trigger the Mexican–American War the following year.

1846
The Oregon Treaty formalizes the border between Canada and the US along the 49th parallel, ending joint occupancy of Pacific Northwest. The Mexican–American War begins, after the US Army is sent into Texas following skirmishes between US and Mexican residents of the region. The US invades Mexico, and also hopes to acquire land in New Mexico and California, so sends troops there, too. In search of a place to practice the tenets of his unorthodox new religion freely, the second leader of the Church of Jesus Christ of Latter-Day Saints, Brigham Young, leads the Mormons up the Missouri River from Illinois to Utah and eventually Salt Lake City. The US whaling industry reaches its peak. After US whalers venture north and kill a previously unknown species, the bowhead whale, near Big Diomede Island, commercial whalers begin hunting in the waters of the Bering Strait in earnest. In time, the intensity of this commercial whaling erodes the whale and walrus populations on which Yup'ik and Inuit people rely for food and materials and destroys those traditions.

△ **Dot dot dash**
Samuel Morse's telegraph key, which sent the first US telegraph message in 1844. His first message was a Bible verse: "What hath God wrought!" which was suggested by a friend.

1848

Swiss colonist John Sutter finds gold on his property in California, sparking the Gold Rush. Thousands of people hoping to make their fortunes travel to California in search of gold. The flow of hopeful gold prospectors intensifies in 1849, giving rise to the term "forty-niners." The Gold Rush expands the population of California, further displacing the local Indigenous people. In the Treaty of Guadalupe Hidalgo that marks the end of the Mexican-American War, Mexico cedes California, Arizona, New Mexico, Nevada, and Utah to the US and gives up its claim to Texas in exchange for $20 million. The Rio Grande River becomes the southern boundary of Texas. The Seneca Falls Convention, the first women's rights conference in the US, takes place in New York, organized by abolitionists and women's rights activists Elizabeth Cady Stanton and Lucretia Mott.

1849

In January, Elizabeth Blackwell earns her medical degree, becoming the first female doctor in the US. She will continue to advocate for women's medical education for the rest of her life. Reverend and abolitionist William King establishes the Buxton Settlement in Southern Ontario as a refuge for freedom seeking enslaved people and free Black people. Vancouver Island becomes a British Crown colony and is leased to the Hudson's Bay Company. In Montreal, a mob of the pro-British Tory elite burns down the Parliament Building in protest over the local government's decision to compensate French Canadians for their losses in earlier rebellions. The capital subsequently moves to Toronto. In September, Harriet Tubman escapes from the plantation in Maryland on which she had been enslaved. With the help of the Underground Railroad, she travels across the border into Pennsylvania, where slavery is illegal.

1850

In the Compromise of 1850, the US Congress admits California to the Union as a free state, where slavery is illegal, but allows white voters in New Mexico and Utah to decide for themselves whether slavery will be legal there. Congress also establishes a boundary between Texas and the US; calls for the abolition of the slave trade in Washington, D.C.; and passes the Fugitive Slave Act, which requires authorities in free states to return escaped people to their enslavers. Harriet Tubman makes the first of many journeys through the Underground Railroad network to Maryland to bring others to freedom.

△ **Unsustainable practice**
This 19th-century painting depicts men harpooning a sperm whale. Commercial whaling reached its peak in the US in the 1840s, depleting resources for Indigenous people.

DISRUPTION AND EXPANSION 1850–1880

1851

1851

The US government passes the first of several Indian Appropriations acts. These acts set aside funds to force Indigenous people to move to and live on reservations. Indigenous people living on reservations are restricted in their capacity to fish, hunt, and forage for traditional foods. For some Indigenous people, the government organizes food rations, which introduces wheat flour, grease, and sugar into their diet. Railroads are built farther into the West, encouraging colonization and encroaching yet more on Indian lands.

1852

On March 20, US author Harriet Beecher Stowe's *Uncle Tom's Cabin* is published for the first time in book form. An abolitionist and member of the religiously prominent Beecher family, Stowe and her husband use their home as a stop on the Underground Railroad, and she says the idea for the novel came to her in a vision during a church service. On July 5, Frederick Douglass gives his famous "Hypocrisy of American Slavery" speech in an address to the Rochester Ladies' Anti-Slavery Society in New York. In it he eloquently attacks the idea that a nation can celebrate its independence and freedom when millions of enslaved people are still in bondage.

22

Number of Roman Catholic people killed in Louisville, KY, on Bloody Monday by Protestant aggressors.

1853

California begins to confine its Indigenous population to reservations, beginning with the Tejon Reservation in the San Joaquin Valley. The Tejon people, who traditionally forage for food, are expected to farm the land, but a drought destroys the crops, so they return to their traditional ways. In May, a yellow fever epidemic kills thousands of people in the southern US and Mexico, many of them recent immigrants to the continent. In July, Commodore Matthew Perry arrives in Edo Bay, Japan, tasked by President Millard Fillmore with a diplomatic mission for the US. He is assigned to negotiate a trade treaty with Japan, despite the latter's policy of self-isolation, which it has maintained for around 200 years.

1854

In this year alone, more than 215,000 Germans arrive in the US; this decade sees German immigration peak, with more than one million arriving into the country. The Sioux Wars begin, a series of conflicts between the US and the Sioux people that will last for more than three decades. Tensions run high due to drought, the continued encroachment onto Sioux lands, and the poor treatment of the Sioux people by colonists and US soldiers. In March, the Republican Party is formed in Michigan in opposition of the extension of slavery into the Western territories. In Virginia, Anthony Burns, an enslaved man, escapes bondage and flees to Boston. His capture, trial, and eventual return to his enslaver after rioters seek to free him outrage many people and

increase support for abolition. The US Congress passes the Kansas–Nebraska Act, creating two new areas, the Kansas Territory and Nebraska Territory, and repealing the Missouri Compromise of 1820. As a result, the populations of the new territories are allowed to determine for themselves whether to be free or slave territories. This leads to the so-called Bleeding Kansas civil disruptions, which continue until 1859, as both pro- and antislavery factions head into the new territories to colonize them. The US buys what is now southern Arizona from Mexico in the Gadsden Purchase. Cherokee author John Rollin Ridge publishes *The Life and Adventures of Joaquin Murieta*, the first novel by an Indigenous American published in the US. Ridge writes under the name "Yellow Bird." Although it receives much attention, it is later widely plagiarized and brings Ridge little fortune. La Reforma begins in Mexico, a liberal political and social revolution under the leadership of Benito Juarez, a highly educated Zapotec man. Many Mexicans believe that their country's future depends on widespread reform.

1855

The Liberty Party of New York nominates Frederick Douglass for the office of secretary of state, the first Black candidate to be nominated for a state-wide office in the US. In California, the Klamath and Salmon River War (Red Cap War) erupts for three months. The colonizers in the region want the local Indigenous people to disarm, which some refuse to do. The US Army is eventually drawn into the war to defend the colonists, and there are

fatalities on both sides before the Indigenous peoples are forced to relocate by the army. In Louisville, Kentucky, on what becomes known as Bloody Monday, Protestants attack Irish and German Catholic neighborhoods, killing 22 people. In late October, the first official US expedition to Fiji is initiated; the US Navy sends a warship to demand compensation from the Indigenous peoples after they allegedly commit arson on the US commercial agent in Fiji during the civil war there.

1856

In Kansas Territory, the Bleeding Kansas tensions continue with what becomes known as the Pottawatomie Massacre. Abolitionist John Brown and other antislavery colonists preside over the killing of five pro-slavery men.

PRICE, TWENTY-FIVE CENTS.

THE BOSTON SLAVE RIOT,
AND
TRIAL
OF
Anthony Burns,

BOSTON:
FETRIDGE AND COMPANY
1854.

◁ **Fugitive returned**
The cover of a pamphlet announcing the trial of Anthony Burns, who was tried in Boston and returned to slavery in Virginia under the Fugitive Slave Law.

▷ **Minstrel puppets**
Puppets were used in Civil War–era minstrel shows, which often featured racist songs and skits. The rise of the minstrel show coincided with the growth of the abolitionist movement.

1857

In the US, Dred Scott, an enslaved man, petitions for freedom for himself and his wife, citing the fact that his enslavers had taken him from a slaveholding state to free territories, and therefore he had been freed by default. The case goes all the way to the US Supreme Court, which not only rules that the couple remain in bondage, but also declares that Black people are not citizens of the United States. This decision in March adds to the tension between pro- and antislavery campaigners. In August, what is now known as the Panic of 1857 erupts in the US. It is a financial crisis caused by the declining international economy and the overexpansion of the domestic economy. News of the panic spreads rapidly, enabled by the recent invention of the telegraph. In New York City, the last residents are evicted from Seneca

Village, a settlement of mostly Black landowners. The land where Seneca Village stood will become the location of New York's Central Park. In May, when forces of the US government arrive in Utah Territory to enforce government administration in the area, they meet armed resistance from Mormon colonists. Known as the Utah War, the fighting lasts for more than a year.

1858

The Reform War begins in Mexico, following on from La Reforma of 1854. Conservative clergy, military, and landowners fight the liberal government for the next two years over the reforms they are trying to implement. These include the redistribution of land owned by the Roman Catholic Church and others to increase the number of Indigenous land owners. The policies fail,

and in fact much of the land is bought up by rich speculators, further exacerbating inequality in the country. John O'Mahony, an Irish immigrant to the US, founds the Fenian Brotherhood, a secret organization supporting Irish republicans, who seek Ireland's independence from Britain. In May, a group of pro-slavery men ride through Trading Post, in Kansas Territory. They capture 11 local pro-abolitionists, force them into a ravine, and proceed to shoot at them, killing five, in what becomes known as the Marais des Cygnes Massacre. The massacre becomes one of the foremost examples of the violence that shakes the area during the Bleeding Kansas years, centered around the debate about whether the territory should be a slave or free state upon entering the Union. In June, senate candidate Abraham Lincoln delivers his famous "House Divided" speech in

Illinois, in which he declares that a house divided against itself cannot stand, referring to the nation's rupture over slavery. In July, the first significant discovery of gold in the Rocky Mountains sees the beginning of the Pike's Peak Gold Rush in the Kansas and Nebraska territories (now Denver). More than 100,000 people will make their way to the area to try to make their fortunes.

1859

The Arkansas Act 151 bans the manumission and residence of free Black or mixed-race people in the state, declaring that any remaining after the year's end will be enslaved or fined. The remains of the crew of HMS *Erebus*, a British ship that was part of Sir John Franklin's 1845 Arctic expedition to find the Northwest Passage, are located after years of fruitless searches. The location confirm that Franklin had failed in his mission. US businessman Edwin Drake, hired by the Seneca Oil Company, strikes oil in Titusville, Pennsylvania, and builds the first oil well in the US. In Harpers Ferry in what will become West Virginia, John Brown and other abolitionists attempt to seize arms from the US Armory with the aim of arming enslaved people in a rebellion. Brown and others are arrested.

1860

The US population reaches 31.4 million, with a Black population of 4.4 million, including 487,970 free men, women, and

◁ **Fateful voyage**
In this c.1850 painting by François Musin, Franklin's ship HMS *Erebus* is depicted trapped in the Arctic ice during the explorer's third expedition to find a Northwest Passage.

children. In California, after the gold rush brings thousands of colonists, the Indigenous population has declined from 310,000 in 1769 to 30,000 by 1860. Using relay teams of horse-mounted riders, the Pony Express begins delivering mail between Missouri and California. The service covers nearly 2,000 miles (3,220 km) and has more than 190 stations, requiring 10 days to complete the circuit. In November, Abraham Lincoln, the Republican candidate, is elected president. His success further exposes the ideological differences between those who want to abolish slavery and those who hope to keep the practice going. In response to Lincoln's election, South Carolina secedes from the Union in December.

1861

Liberals recover control of Mexico City after the Reform War, strengthening

Benito Juarez's position as president. However, the war has left Mexico penniless and bankrupt, so Juarez suspends interest payments on the foreign debt that Mexico owes to Britain, France, and Spain. In February, at the Montgomery Convention in Alabama, the seceded states South Carolina, Mississippi, Florida, Alabama, Georgia, and Louisiana form their own government. Texas secedes in February and joins the Confederacy in March, and Virginia, Arkansas, Tennessee, and North Carolina join later in the year. The Confederacy elects Jefferson Davis as its president. In the Battle of Fort Sumter in April, the South Carolina militia besieges the fort, the last Union post in the state. After a siege, the US Army surrenders the fort; the battle marks the start of the American Civil War. The First Louisiana Native Guard of the Confederate Army launches in New Orleans, the first

military unit of Black officers fighting for Southern independence. In July, Confederates win the Battle of Bull Run, in Prince William County, Virginia. It is the first major conflict of the Civil War. The Union begins to blockade southern ports, preventing supplies from entering or leaving by water. The US Congress passes the First Confiscation Act, which restricts the rights of Confederate enslavers. Spanish, British, and French forces form the Tripartite Expedition, a coalition that seeks to force loan repayments on the government of Benito Juárez, following his suspension of repayments on Mexican government bonds.

1862

The Port Royal Experiment begins in South Carolina. After the Union Army occupies Sea Islands, white plantation owners flee, along with the Confederate

Army. The Union Army gives formerly enslaved people land abandoned by planters to work, and they are paid wages for their labor. A new era in naval warfare begins with the Battle of the *Monitor* and *Merrimack*, off the Virginia coast. This sees the first battle between ironclad ships, the Confederates' CSS *Virginia* (formerly Merrimack) and the Union's USS Monitor. At the Battle of Shiloh, the first major Civil War conflict in Tennessee, both sides suffer huge casualties, but the Union is eventually victorious, reinforcing the reputation of General Ulysses S. Grant. On April 25, the Union naval fleet arrives at New Orleans, where they demand the surrender of the city. Within two days the forts fall and the mouth of the Mississippi River is under the Union's control. In Charleston, South Carolina, Robert Smalls and other enslaved crewmates take control of the CSS

1865

I0 Number of days it took to complete the Pony Express circuit, which used more than 400 horses and 80 riders.

Mississippi River. In November, four months after the Battle of Gettysburg, President Lincoln delivers the Gettysburg Address at the battlefield, honoring the Union dead and reinforcing the ideals of equality and freedom set out in the Declaration of Independence.

1864
In April, the French install Austrian archduke Maximilian as emperor of Mexico, beginning the Second Mexican Empire. US Congress passes a bill authorizing equal pay, equipment, arms, and health care for Black troops in the Union Army. Grant moves his troops south to pin down Lee's Confederate forces at Petersburg, near Richmond, Virginia. General William T. Sherman captures Atlanta for the Union, the first important southern city to fall into Union hands. In August, the US Army brings to an end 20 years of Navajo resistance by forcing them off their homelands in what is now Arizona and New Mexico. On what becomes known as the Navajo Long Walk, Navajos are marched 300 miles (483 km) at gunpoint to Fort Sumner, at Bosque Redondo in today's New Mexico. Hundreds die during the 18-day ordeal. On November 29, under the leadership of Colonel John Chivington, a citizen-army in Colorado attacks an Indigenous camp at Sand Creek, killing and mutilating more than 150 Cheyenne and Arapaho people, many of them women, children, and the

edlerly. In December, General Sherman finishes his "March to the Sea," reaching the coast after a 37-day scorched-earth campaign through Confederate lands, and captures Savannah.

1865
Building on the Emancipation Proclamation, the Thirteenth Amendment to US Constitution passes in February, outlawing slavery throughout the United States. In April, General Lee surrenders to Grant at Appomattox Court House, effectively ending the Civil War. On April 14, Confederate sympathizer John Wilkes Booth shoots President Lincoln in the head at a theater in Washington, D.C.; Lincoln dies the next day. Lincoln is the first US president to be assassinated. Over the next two years, some southern states pass new "Black codes," designed to limit the freedom granted to Black people by the North and to reinstate the control they once had over them through slavery. In June, Cherokee chief, Stand Watie, is the last Confederate general in the field to surrender in the Civil War. The Little Arkansas Treaty is signed in October, between the US government and the Kiowa, Comanche, Na'isha (Plains Apache), Southern Cheyenne, and Southern Arapaho people, but it does not hold, leading to the Plains War. The flash point comes along the Bozeman Trail, which runs from Fort Laramie, in today's Wyoming, to Virginia City, Montana Territory. Red Cloud, a charismatic Sioux chief, gathers a coalition of Indigenous people to keep

Planter, a Confederate steamship. Smalls steers his family and other enslaved people on board to freedom in the North. After the Battle of Seven Pines in late May, Robert E. Lee replaces the wounded Confederate general Joseph Johnston, renaming his command the Army of Northern Virginia. Lee's army attacks the Union Army under General George McClellan in the Seven Days' Battles, beginning at Mechanicsville, near Richmond, Virginia, on June 26 and ending at Malvern Hill on July 1. In July, Congress permits the enlistment of Black soldiers in the US Army. At the Second Battle of Bull Run in August, General Stonewall Jackson and General Lee defeat the Union Army. In September, the Battle of Antietam, in Maryland, is the bloodiest single day of the Civil War. It brings to an end General Lee's plan for a Confederate invasion of Maryland and halts the Confederate advance into the North. In December, the Confederate Army wins a victory at Fredericksburg after Union forces conduct a risky river crossing in an attempt to win a victory on Confederate soil before the release of the Emancipation Proclamation in January of the next year. The Homestead Act grants 160 acres in the western US

to any family who agrees to farm them for five years, accelerating the colonization of the West.

1863
The Emancipation Proclamation frees all enslaved people in any state opposing the Union government, thus converting the Civil War into a quest for liberty. It also means that the Union can now recruit Black soldiers. Nearly 180,000 Black men enlist during the remaining years of the war. In May, in Battle Creek, Michigan, the Seventh-Day Adventist Church is formally recognized as an organization. In June, the French capture Mexico City as part of their campaign to force the collection of Mexican debts, and President Juarez flees north to San Luis Potosi. In July, General Lee attempts to invade the North via Pennsylvania. After three days of brutal fighting at the Battle of Gettysburg, Union forces prevail and Lee withdraws. This intense battle is often considered the turning point in the Civil War. Also in July, the Siege of Vicksburg ends when the city surrenders to General Grant (who will later become US president), bringing the Mississippi under Union control. The city of Vicksburg was the last key remaining point of Confederate defense on the

◁ **Turning point**
The Battle of Gettysburg, depicted in this c.1887 print, raged in Pennsylvania from July 1–3, 1863, and marked the turning point of the Civil War.

▷ **Hood of horror**
This Ku Klux Klan (KKK) hood was designed to hide the wearer's identity and cause terror. The KKK developed shortly after the Civil War as a virulently racist and violent hate group.

1866

white people from appropriating the lands. In Tennessee, the Ku Klux Klan (KKK) is founded in an attempt to impose white supremacy through the use of violence and intimidation.

1866

Emperor Napoleon III of France withdraws his troops from Mexico, leaving Emperor Maximilian in a dangerous position, with little support. In the US, the Civil Rights Act confers citizenship upon Black Americans for the first time and guarantees equal rights with white citizens, protected by law. In May, during the Memphis Massacre, white civilians and police in Memphis, Tennessee, kill 46 Black Americans and injure many more, burning 90 houses, 12 schools, and four churches. In July, the Fourteenth Amendment passes, assuring equal rights as citizens to all those born or naturalized in the US. Tennessee ratifies this amendment and so becomes the first rebel state to be readmitted to the Union. Cowboys move 260,000 head of cattle from Texas to railheads in Kansas,

Missouri, and Iowa in the first large-scale cattle drive, in order to transport them for sale elsewhere.

1867

US Secretary of State William Seward guides the purchase of Alaska from Russia for $7.2 million. The few Russian colonists that remain leave soon after the purchase. The Reconstruction Acts outline the terms for readmission to the US for the rebel states. The acts divide the former Confederate states into five military districts, each with an appointed military governor. Tennessee is exempt from this because it has already been readmitted to the Union. The Acts mark the beginning of Radical Reconstruction, when the vehemently antislavery Radical Republicans push for more rights and protection for free Black people. Emperor Maximilian of Mexico is captured, sentenced to death, and executed by firing squad at Querétaro. Mexico is restored as a republic. The British North America Act unites the three separate territories of Canada, Nova Scotia, and New

Brunswick into a single entity, named the Dominion of Canada. The British government gives the new dominion a parliamentary structure similar to its own. Provision is also made within the act for other colonies and territories of British North America to negotiate their entry into the dominion. William "Buffalo Bill" Cody earns his nickname hunting buffalo for construction workers on the Kansas Pacific Railroad.

1868

The Radical Republicans impeach President Andrew Johnson for his lack of cooperation in the Reconstruction plans. He is the first US president to be impeached, but is not removed from office. The Rupert's Land Act passes control of Rupert's Land—an area stretching from what is now Montana to Quebec—from the Hudson's Bay Company to the Dominion of Canada. The Treaty of Bosque Redondo allows Navajo people to leave the reservation in New Mexico, where conditions are appalling, and return to a portion of their former lands. With this, Navajo

internment ends, but 2,000 people have died while imprisoned. In the Opelousas Massacre in Louisiana, white supremacists opposed to Reconstruction and suffrage for Black Americans murder an estimated 200 to 300 Black Americans. An armed uprising against Spanish rule in Puerto Rico, the Grito de Lares, is unsuccessful and quickly quelled by the Spanish militia. In October, the Ten Years' War begins in Cuba when a group of planters and patriots call for freedom from Spain. It is the first of three wars of liberation that will be fought in Cuba over the next 30 years. In the Washita Massacre in Oklahoma, Colonel George Armstrong Custer's US Army cavalry attacks a Cheyenne village on the Washita River, killing more than 100 people. As part of the Fort Laramie treaty with Sioux, the US government recognizes the Black Hills of Dakota as the Great Sioux Reservation, the exclusive territory of the Sioux and Arapaho people. But when miners and colonizers discover gold in the Black Hills, they begin moving onto the land en masse. Representative John Willis Menard is the first Black American elected to Congress (specifically, the House of Representatives); he is denied his seat. The Fifteenth Amendment to the US constitution makes it illegal to deny the right to vote on racial grounds.

1869

In January, Elizabeth Cady Stanton becomes the first woman to testify before the US Congress, advocating for women's inalienable rights, including the right to vote. Later that year, she and Susan B. Anthony form the National Woman Suffrage Association (NWSA), which argues

△ **Cattle drive**
Cowboys are depicted herding cattle between Texas and Kansas in this woodcut print from the 1870s.

against the proposed Fifteenth Amendment to the US Constitution (proposing to give Black men the right to vote), and instead calling for voting rights to be extended to all woman and all Black Americans at the same time. In March, Ulysses S. Grant is elected as the 18th US president. A war hero and a

supporter of the Radical Republican's policies of Reconstruction, he wins the election easily. Outlaw Jesse James commits his first confirmed bank robbery in Gallatin, Missouri, along with his brother, Frank, and other members of their gang. The first transcontinental railroad in North America is completed when the Union Pacific and Central Pacific railroads meet at Promontory Summit, Utah. The Red River Rebellion in Winnipeg, an uprising of the Red River Colony against the Canadian government, prompts the creation of Manitoba as a province of Canada.

1870

US industrialist John D. Rockefeller establishes the Standard Oil Company in Ohio. Its success will make Rockefeller one of world's first billionaires. The First Ghost Dance Movement begins, an Indigenous spiritual movement of hope and renewal that originates with Wodziwob, a Paiute man in Nevada. It seeks to bring about the departure of white people and the return of lands and natural resources to the Indigenous people. Hiram R. Revels, elected to the Senate from Mississippi, becomes the first Black American to serve in the Senate. As in all US states at this time, it is the legislature rather than the citizens that elects the state's senators.

1871

The Indian Appropriations Act is passed, part of President Grant's Peace Policy of 1868. An attempt to protect the rights of Indigenous people, it stipulates that the US government will stop treating Indigenous people of the Great Plains and Canadian Prairies as "an independent nation, tribe, or power," instead they are to be treated as wards of the state. In Mexico, in the Plan de la Noria, rebel General Porfirio Diaz issues a manifesto and call to arms, intending to oust Mexican President Juarez and reconstitute the nation. He fails. US Civil War veterans establish the National Rifle Association to promote marksmanship. With the Ku Klux Klan Act, President Grant attempts to suppress the Klan in southern US states. British Columbia joins the Canadian dominion.

1872

White "Boomers" begin to colonize territory reserved for Indigenous Americans in what is now Oklahoma. The Dominion Lands Act in Canada aims to encourage colonization of the prairies and prevent the US from claiming the area. In the US, the General Mining Act allows individuals and corporations to stake claims to land in the West without consulting Indigenous peoples. In Pittsburgh, industrialist Andrew Carnegie establishes the first Bessemer mills in the country for mass-producing steel, which is key in the construction of the railroads and other industries. Beginning in 1872 and lasting into the next year, the Modoc War is fought between the Modoc people and the US Army in what is now California and Oregon. After the conflict subsides, the remaining Modoc people are sent to live on a reservation in what is now Oklahoma as prisoners of war. P. B. S. Pinchback, one of the most prominent Black American officeholders during the Reconstruction, becomes the first Black governor of a US state (Louisiana). His tenure lasts only 35

> "May God continue the unity of our Country, as this Railroad unites the two great Oceans …"
>
> INSCRIPTION, GOLDEN RAILROAD SPIKE, 1869

◁ **Great leader**
This bas-relief depicts In-mut-too-yah-lat-lat (Joseph), chief of the Nimiipuu (Nez Percé), who led his people during their forced relocation from their ancestral lands in Oregon to reservations.

1873

days, but he manages to pass 10 acts of legislature.

1873

In April, the Colfax Massacre occurs in Louisiana when a mob of former Confederate soldiers joined by Ku Klux Klan members kill as many as 150 Black militia men who are trying to surrender after occupying the courthouse in Colfax. In June, a group of US hunters cross into Canadian territory seeking bison and wolf. In the Cypress Hills Massacre, they murder more than 20 Nakoda Assiniboine people, triggering the formation of the North-West Mounted Police by the Canadian government to keep peace between traders and Indigenous people. Prince Edward Island joins the Dominion of Canada in July. Attending an Illinois country fair, Joseph Glidden catches his first sight of barbed wire, and later invents a machine to mass-produce it. In September, the Financial Panic of 1873 sees an end to the expansion in the world's economy, which had been building since the 1840s. In the US alone, 5,183 businesses fail, and the depression in the US and Europe will last until 1879. Canadian prime minister John Macdonald resigns in November after the Pacific Scandal, which revealed that private interests had paid for the election-related expenses of the Conservative Party in order to influence politicians in the bid for a national rail contract. MacDonald will later return to the post and continue to pursue the construction of the Canadian Pacific Railway. US President Grant sets aside a portion of the Wallowa Valley in what will become Oregon for the Nimiipuu (Nez Percé), but it is rescinded two years later, leading to the Nez Percé war.

1874

In the US South, a white-supremacist paramilitary terrorist group is formed called the White League. It aims to intimidate Black men from voting and prevent the Republican Party from organizing by targeting Republican officeholders. Unlike the KKK and other secretive groups, they operate openly in communities. The Greenback Party is formed by those affected by the Panic of 1873; they hold an anti-monopoly ideology and will field candidates in the next three presidential elections.

1875

Hawaii signs a trade treaty with the US, granting the US exclusive trading rights. In Tennessee, the state legislature approves the first of what will be known as Jim Crow Laws, introducing legalized racial segregation in public spaces ("Jim Crow" is a derogatory term for a Black American person). Other southern states follow. In response, the US Civil Rights Act outlaws segregation on public transportation, in hotels, and in restaurants. Religious leader Mary Baker Eddy publishes the key text of what will become the Christian Science religion: *Science and Health with Key to the Scriptures*. Also in March, the US government passes the Page Act, the first restrictive federal immigration law in the US. It effectively prohibits the entry of Chinese women, marking the end of open borders for the country.

1876

The Great Sioux War begins, a series of battles and negotiations between the US government and an alliance of Lakota Sioux and Northern Cheyenne people, led by chiefs Ta-sunko-witko (Crazy Horse) and Tatanka Iyotake (Sitting Bull). The Indigenous people try to protect their land in the Black Hills, Dakota Territory, against white prospectors who are looking for gold. The Canadian government passes the Indian Act, which governs the state's interactions with registered Indigenous people, their bands (governing units), and the reserves. The act grants the Canadian government control over many aspects of Indigenous peoples' lives, including the management of housing, health services, the environment, and other resources. In Mexico, a revolutionary army under General Fidencio Hernandez marches on Oaxaca and proclaims General Diaz its leader. The incumbent president, Lerdo de Tejada, is deposed. Later in the year, José María Iglesias, president of Mexico's supreme court, condemns the prior election of Lerdo as fraudulent, and proclaims himself president. He later concedes to Diaz. At the Battle of Little Bighorn, commonly called "Custer's Last Stand," combined forces of Lakota Sioux, Northern Cheyenne, and Arapaho peoples defeat the US Army 7th Cavalry Regiment led by General Custer, wiping out 5 of the 12 companies in his division. More than half of the US forces die. In September, members of the James-Younger gang of outlaws are killed in Minnesota; the legendary Jesse James and his brother Frank escape.

1877

The Nez Percé War begins when the Indigenous people refuse to move from their homeland in Oregon's Wallowa Valley. Federal troops pursue and capture them and their leader, In-mut-too-yah-lat-lat (Chief Joseph), forcing them to live on a reservation in what is now Oklahoma and Kansas. Dodge City, Kansas, is the largest cattle-shipping town in the US. The Compromise of 1877, an informal agreement between southern Democrats and Republican allies, ends Reconstruction in southern states. Porfirio Diaz enters Mexico City and assumes the Mexican presidency, which becomes a *de facto* dictatorship that embeds poverty and inequality. In New Mexico, William H. Bonney, cattle rustler and outlaw, makes his name as Billy the Kid. The US Army pursues Tatanka Iyotake (Sitting Bull) and his people after they refuse to surrender; they are exiled to Canada.

1878

In February, US inventor Thomas Edison patents the phonograph. The Posse Comitatus Act is signed by President Rutherford B. Hayes in June, limiting the ability of the US federal government to deploy federal military forces to manage domestic policies. The law is a response to a rollback of Reconstruction in the South. Opera singer Marie Selika Williams is the first Black American to perform at the White House. A bill in favor of women's suffrage is introduced in the US Senate for the first time, but such a bill will not pass for decades.

1879

The first off-reservation boarding school is established in the US; Lakota children are forced to attend the Carlisle Indian Training and Industrial School. It is designed to forcibly assimilate Indigenous children into white society.

▷ **Forced assimilation**
At Carlisle Indian Industrial School in Pennsylvania, Indigenous children were taken from their families and forced to give up their own culture.

15,000

Number of Chinese workers who built the Trans-Canada Railway.

Members of the Blackfoot Confederacy remember this year as *Itsistsitsis/awenimiopi*, meaning "when first/no more buffalo," indicating the decline of buffalo on the prairie. In the National Policy, an economic program, Canadian prime minister John Macdonald renews his commitment to the construction of the Canadian Pacific Railway. In what becomes known as the "Exodus," around 6,000 Black Americans leave Louisiana and Mississippi for Kansas to escape persecution. Decades of Indian policy are reversed in the US when Judge Elmer Scipio Dundy declares in federal court that Indigenous Americans are legally defined as people under federal law.

1880

Sergeant George Jordan of the 9th Cavalry, commanding a detachment of Buffalo Soldiers (the nickname for Black American troops), leads a successful defense of Tularosa, New Mexico Territory, against Apache people. Tatanka Iyotake (Sitting Bull) returns from exile in Canada. He later joins Bill Cody's Wild West Show. At Silver Bow Basin (now known as Juneau, Alaska), Tlingit chief Kowee shows gold to white prospectors. This draws other prospectors to the area and leads to clashes with Tlingit and other Indigenous Alaskan people, although mining continues. By this year, more than 100,000 Chinese men and 3,000 Chinese women are living in the western US, mostly employed as service workers.

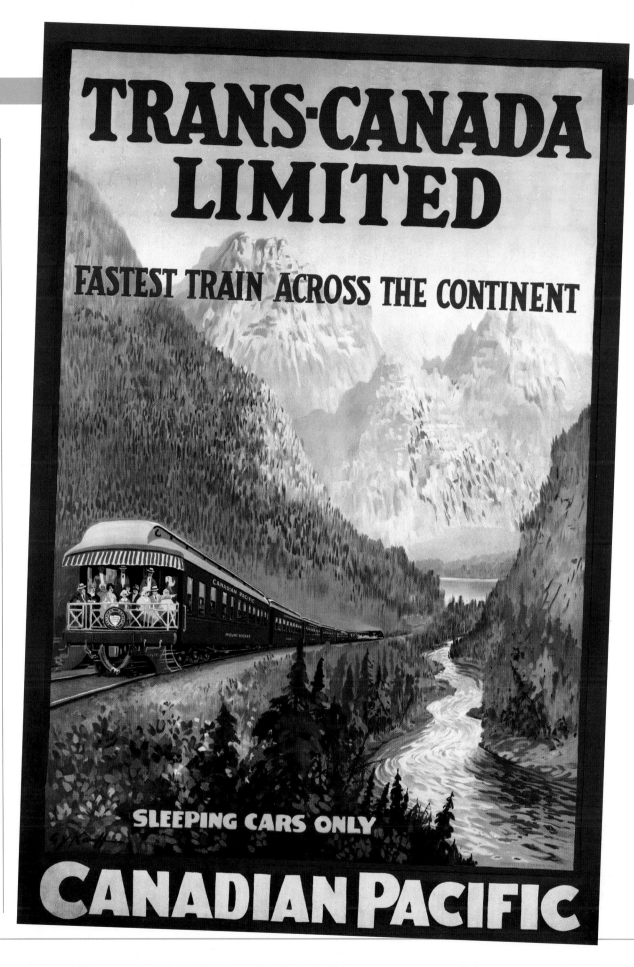

△ **Spanning the continent**
This 1924 poster depicts the Canadian Pacific Railway. The project survived a bribery scandal and the resignation of its mastermind, Prime Minister John Macdonald.

ACROSS NORTH AMERICA 1880–1914

1880

1880s

Known as the Gilded Age, this decade sees rapid economic growth in the US, especially in the railroad, factory, mining, and ranching industries.

1881

In Atlanta, Spelman College is founded, the first college for Black women in the US. It awards its first degree in 1901. In April, after a hearing about the murder of two Mexican *vaqueros* (cowboys), tensions run high outside a courthouse in El Paso, Texas. In the ensuing confrontation, four men die—three of them killed by Marshall Dallas Stoudenmire, an expert marksman—in what becomes known as the Four Dead in Five Seconds Gunfight. Nurse Clara Barton opens the US branch of the Red Cross in May and becomes its president. In July, the Sioux chief Tatanka Iyotanka (Sitting Bull) leads the last of his fugitive peoples to surrender to US troops at Fort Buford in the Dakota Territory. In September, Charles Guiteau assassinates US president James A. Garfield less than four months into his presidency. Mistakenly believing that Garfield owes him a political post in return for his help during the election, Guiteau shoots Garfield at a Baltimore train station in July. Garfield dies 79 days later. Guiteau's trial begins in November and he is later executed.

1882

The outlaw Jesse James is killed by Robert Ford, a new recruit to his gang who had hoped to collect reward money for his death, and to receive amnesty for any prior crimes. James and his brother Frank had terrorized the West for years, robbing stagecoaches, trains, and banks, often violently. Ford is initially charged with murder but is later given a full pardon. In Alaska, after a shaman is accidentally killed while working on a whaling ship, Tlingit villagers seize the Killisnoo Whaling Station and take two hostages. Despite the subsequent release of the hostages, the US Navy shells the Tlingit villages of Angoon, Kake, and Wrangel in response. The US government passes the Chinese Exclusion Act, beginning a 10-year ban on Chinese laborers immigrating to the US. The act is made permanent in 1902.

1883

Five landmark civil rights cases heard in the US Supreme Court lead to the decision that the Thirteenth and Fourteenth Amendments do not empower Congress to outlaw racial discrimination by private individuals or corporations. This reverses the Civil Rights Act of 1875. The Courts of Indian Offenses are established to prosecute those involved in traditional ceremonies, an attempt to repress Indigenous culture and impose Christianity. The Brooklyn Bridge, the longest suspension bridge in the world, is opened between Brooklyn and lower Manhattan. It is designed by John A. Roebling, who oversees the construction until his death, when his son, Washington Roebling, carries on the work. After the younger Roebling's health declines due to caisson disease (also known as the bends), his wife, Emily, takes over supervision of the project. In Nebraska, Buffalo Bill Cody forms his Wild West Show. With sharpshooting and historical reenactments, the first outdoor Western show goes on to tour the globe, even performing for European royalty. The Friends of the Indians group pushes for assimilation of Indigenous culture into US culture. They claim to speak on behalf of Indigenous people, but in fact they represent the interests of the US Office of Indian Affairs.

1884

Military rule comes to an end in Alaska. It had been in place since Alaska was originally purchased 17 years beforehand, but is now replaced by civil government as part of a US district. The district government's concerns about the

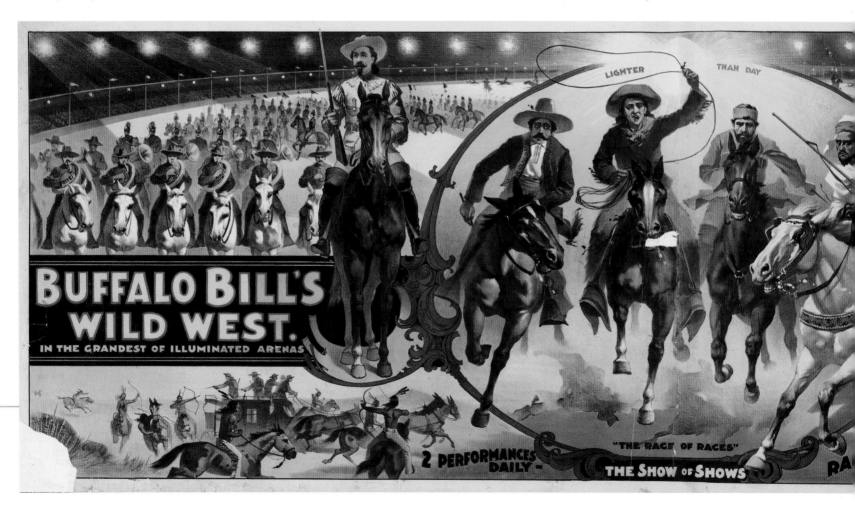

▽ **The creature within**
Masks such as this one from around 1910 were used by the Kwakwaka'wakw peoples in the Pacific Northwest during ceremonial dances. The mask opens to show the transformation between animal and human.

▷ **Symbol of freedom**
Created by French sculptor Frédéric Auguste Bartholdi and erected in New York Harbor, the Statue of Liberty shows an allegorical figure breaking free from the chains that bind her.

1887

deteriorating health of the Indigenous population, due to tuberculosis and alcohol consumption, spark calls for the provision of health care for Indigenous Alaskan people, but little is accomplished. The Washington Monument is completed in Washington, D.C. An obelisk on the National Mall, it is built to honor George Washington, the first president of the United States. *The Adventures of Huckleberry Finn* by Mark Twain (the pen name of Samuel Clemens) is published in Canada and the UK. Now considered a classic, the book was one of the first US novels to be written in vernacular English. It is released in the US the following year.

1885
In the Frog Lake Massacre, Kapapamahchakwew (Wandering Spirit) and other Cree people in the band of Mistahi-maskwa (Big Bear) kill nine white men at Frog Lake, Saskatchewan, during the North-West Rebellion in Canada. The Canadian government sends troops to put the rebellion down. At Batoche, the decisive battle of the rebellion, the Canadian authorities capture Indigenous leader Louis Riel. Riel is tried for treason, and hanged on November 16. As a result, Canada becomes deeply polarized along ethno-religious lines. The federal government outlaws the potlatch ceremony (a gift-giving ceremony used to affirm social status) and the Tamanawas winter dances, both practiced by the Indigenous peoples of the Pacific Northwest. The Electoral Franchise Act restricts the vote in Canada to propertied men over 21. It excludes women, Indigenous people west of Ontario, and those designated "Chinese" or "Mongolian." The Canadian federal government also introduces the pass system in the aftermath of the North-West Rebellion. Under it, Indigenous people must present a travel document authorized by an Indigenous agent in order to leave and return to their reserves. The measure is designed to prevent large gatherings. The Canadian Pacific Railway is completed, with a symbolic last spike driven in at Craigellachie, British Columbia. The railroad stretches 12,500 miles (more than 20,000 km) from Montreal to Vancouver. It also serves several cities in the northern US.

1886
The Yup'ik people in Alaska mark this year as the "great die out" of seals, bowhead whales, and caribou. The resulting famine prompts Captain Michael Healy of the US Revenue Cutter Service to introduce reindeer to the area, to replace caribou and alleviate some of the suffering of the Indigenous people. He transports reindeer in batches of 20 or more from Siberia, on his ship the *Bear*. In Atlanta, Coca-Cola is created by John S. Pemberton. Made from cocaine, kola nuts, and citrus juices, it is originally marketed as a temperance (nonalcoholic) drink and patent medicine. In what becomes known as the Haymarket Affair, a peaceful demonstration in Chicago against police brutality is shattered when someone in the crowd throws a bomb at the police as they attempt to disperse the meeting. In the resulting gunfire, around 11 people are killed and dozens injured. The Apache leader Goyathlay (Geronimo) surrenders after a decade of resistance. Goyathlay and around 30 of his followers are forced onto railroad cars and sent to Fort Marion in St. Augustine, Florida, where they are imprisoned. The American Federation of Labor is created to protect workers' rights by coordinating the work of multiple unions. In April, Vancouver is incorporated as a city. The Statue of Liberty, carried by ship from France, is erected on Bedloe's Island (now Liberty Island) in the approach to New York Harbor. A gift from France to the US to commemorate the two nations' friendship, it is dedicated on October 28 and stands 151 ft (46 m) tall.

1,200
Number of performers appearing in a Wild West Show at any one time.

1887
An early attempt to constrain corporate power, the US Interstate Commerce Act

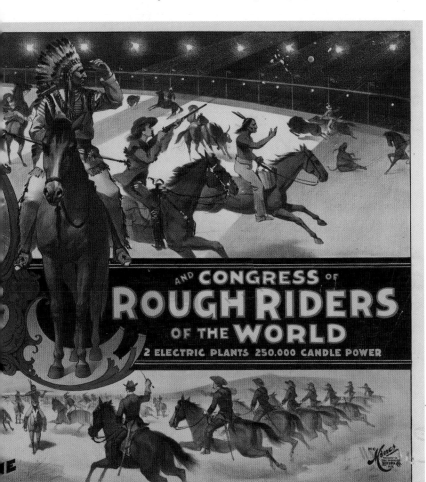

◁ **Western spectacle**
Buffalo Bill's Wild West Show included performers such as sharpshooter Annie Oakley, and prominent Indigenous Americans such as Tatanka Iyotanka (Sitting Bull) and Goyathlay (Geronimo).

◁ **Sobriety in the 19th century**
Engraved with images of General Clinton B. Fisk and John A. Brooks of the Temperance Party, prohibition medals showed support for banning the sale of alcoholic beverages in the US.

2,000

Approximate number killed in the Johnstown Flood, Pennsylvania, 1889.

is passed to regulate the railroad industry and curb monopolistic practices. US president Grover Cleveland signs the Dawes Severalty Act, which deprives Indigenous Americans of their tribal lands, giving each an allotment of up to 320 acres instead. The remaining tribal lands are sold. By 1934, Indigenous landholdings have been reduced from 138 million acres (560,000 sq km) to 48 million acres (194,000 sq km).

1888

The National Geographic Society is founded in Washington, D.C., and grows to become one of the largest nonprofit scientific and educational organizations in the world, focusing on the studies of geology, archeology, environmental conservation, and world cultures. The International Council of Women is formed and holds its first convention in Washington, D.C., in the spring. Women's suffrage is avoided as a discussion point at the conference, as the attendees remain split over whether to pursue it. In April, the company Eastman Kodak is founded, releasing a film roll camera invented by entrepreneur George Eastman and photography businessman Henry A. Strong. In August, a 23-year-old Black man, Amos Miller, is lynched after being dragged out of a courthouse in Franklin, Tennessee, where he is awaiting trial.

1889

The Johnstown Flood kills more than 2,000 people in Western Pennsylvania, after a dam collapses. Clara Barton brings her newly formed Red Cross to provide disaster relief. The Peasant Farm Policy is implemented in Canada. It limits Indigenous agriculture and the tools people can use on the prairies, impeding the growth of First Nations farms. The first International Conference of American States creates the International Union of American Republics, a forerunner of the Pan-American Union. In the first Land Run into Oklahoma, the federal government opens up nearly two million acres (8,100 km²) in Indian Territory to white colonization. A further six more land runs are organized before the government decides to end this inefficient way of distributing land.

1890

The Manitoba Schools Question, a debate over whether Catholics and Protestants should be educated separately, marks the first major clash in independent Canada between French and British interests. The Afro-American League is founded in Chicago, under the leadership of journalist and civil rights leader Timothy Thomas Fortune, to fight for full citizenship and equality for Black Americans. The Mississippi Plan, developed by white conservatives, attempts to disenfranchise Black voters with the aim of overthrowing Republican control of the state. The plan uses threats of violence and white supremacist intimidation. In September, in response to mounting pressure from the US Congress, the president of the Church of Jesus Christ of Latter-Day Saints (the Mormons) issues a manifesto stating that he would submit to the anti-polygamy laws. The church formally accepts the manifesto a month later. In December, Tatanka Iyotanka (Sitting Bull) is murdered during a confrontation with Tribal police officers, sent by the local US federal agent. A Hunkpapa Lakota leader, he had led his people in resistance against the federal government for many years. Later that month, nearly 300 Sioux people, led by Si Tanka (Big Foot), are shot and killed by US troops, in what will become known as the Wounded Knee Massacre. It is the deadliest mass shooting in US history. In 1990, the US Congress will pass a resolution of "deep regret" for the killings.

1891

Canadian–American professor and athlete James Naismith invents basketball at a Young Men's Christian Association (YMCA) college in Springfield, Massachusetts. He was trying to devise a means of keeping his class active indoors on a rainy day.

1892

Ellis Island in New York Harbor opens as the point of reception for immigrants arriving in the US. By the time it closes in 1954, 12 million people will have made their way through the processing station there. The closing of the Homestead Steel Works near Pittsburgh in a dispute with unions leads to confrontation and violence. The Homestead Strike becomes a major industrial action in US history, and sets back efforts to unionize steelworkers.

1893

The Panic of 1893 is triggered by a decline in the US federal gold reserves. It causes a severe economic depression nationwide, impacting farmers, workers, and businessmen, who see prices, wages, and profits fall. The Anti-Saloon League is founded in Ohio, and the temperance movement, which has grown in the late 19th century, begins pressing for the prohibition of alcohol. The 1893 Chicago World's Fair marks the 400th anniversary of Christopher Columbus's arrival in the New World, and showcases US exceptionalism. The Hawaiian Kingdom of Queen Lili'uokalani is overthrown in a *coup d'état* by seven US businessmen and six Hawaiian Kingdom subjects, with assistance from the US Marines. The US Congress will apologize for the nation's role in the rebellion in 1993. In Colorado, women are granted suffrage after a voter referendum. It is the first suffrage law to pass by popular legislation.

1894

In September, President Cleveland pardons polygamous members of the Church of Jesus Christ of Latter-Day Saints. This restores

▷ **Four-wheeled first**
The Ford Quadricycle consisted of a simple metal frame with four bicycle wheels, powered by a gas engine. The hand-built vehicle was very expensive to produce.

▽ **Fortune seekers**
This colorized photo shows Dawson City, in Canada's Yukon territory, the center of the Klondike Gold Rush. The population fluctuated at times between a few dozen and more than 15,000 people.

their property and civil rights, which had been rescinded during efforts to eliminate polygamy in Utah Territory.

1895

In February, uprisings across the island mark the start of the Cuban War of Independence. The country's fight for independence from Spain lasts until 1898. In what is later known as the Atlanta Compromise, Black reformer and educator Booker T. Washington gives a speech in which he promotes a policy of gradualism and accommodation to solve the social ills affecting Black Americans. William Randolph Hearst begins building his press empire by buying the *New York Journal*.

1896

Utah is admitted to the Union as the 45th state. Polygamy is outlawed in the new state's constitution. In May's *Plessy v. Ferguson* ruling, the US Supreme Court rules that it is legal for a state to provide "separate but equal" facilities for Black people, declaring that the South's Jim Crow laws do not conflict with the Thirteenth and Fourteenth Amendments. This decision legitimizes many of the Jim Crow laws in the South that oppress Black people. Inventor and industrialist Henry Ford test-drives his first four-wheeled internal combustion vehicle, the Quadricycle. Canada's first French-speaking and Roman Catholic premier, Wilfrid Laurier, wins the first of four

10,000

New members of the United Mine Workers Union in 1897.

consecutive elections as prime minster. He will serve for 15 years, the longest tenure of a Canadian prime minister. In August, reports of gold emerge from what becomes known as Bonanza Creek, a tributary of the Klondike, in northwestern Canada, triggering the Klondike Gold Rush.

1897

In January, Martha Hughes Cannon of Utah takes office as the first female state senator in the US. To win, she defeats her own husband, who is also on the ballot. In March, the White Rose Mission opens for the first time on East 97th Street in New York. It's aim is to help young Black women who have arrived from the southern states or the West Indies. In the same month, the American Negro

Academy opens in Washington, D.C., the first organization to promote classical learning for Black American students. The use of strikes as a negotiation tactic gathers momentum when coal miners in Western Pennsylvania and West Virginia walk out on strike. Their action brings about an eight-hour working day in the mines. In the Lattimer Massacre, at least 19 striking anthracite coal miners in Western Pennsylvania are killed in a confrontation with a sheriff's posse. Many more are wounded. The massacre prompts 10,000 new members to join the United Mine Workers Union.

1898

The *USS Maine* sinks in Havana harbor after an explosion, killing hundreds onboard. Newspapers blame Spain for

the incident, and whip up anti-Spanish feeling. The Spanish–American War erupts when the US intervenes in the Cuban struggle for independence in an attempt to protect its investments, which are threatened by the conflict. In the Treaty of Paris, ending the war, Spain cedes Puerto Rico and Guam to the US, which makes the US the dominant foreign influence in the Caribbean. In Canada, the completion of the narrow-gauge Newfoundland Railway brings sport hunters to hunt the caribou populations. This has a disastrous impact on the culture of Mi'kmaq people, who depend on caribou. The Curtis Act expands US federal authority over Indigenous populations within the Indian Territory. It results in the breakup of tribal governments and communal

▷ **W. E. B. Du Bois**
Du Bois was a civil rights activist and intellectual who helped found the National Association for the Advancement of Colored People (NAACP), with the aim of improving the lives of Black Americans.

1899

lands. In Canada, the Yukon Territory is separated from the Northwest Territories to become Canada's second northern territory. The Louisiana Legislature introduces a "grandfather clause" into the state's constitution. The clause decrees that only those with ancestors registered to vote before 1867 have suffrage, effectively disfranchising virtually all Black voters in the state.

1899
In Treaty 8, the Beaver and Chipewyan First Nations people surrender just less than 325,000 square miles (840,000 sq km) of lands in present-day British Columbia, Alberta, and Saskatchewan to the Canadian Crown. They are promised land and hunting rights as well as financial and medical support. In East Asia, the US creates its "Open Door policy." This is a key tenet of US foreign policy and aims to keep China open for trade. Canadian troops are sent to South Africa to fight for the British in the Second Boer War. The Philippine–American War begins after the US takes control of the Philippines from the Spanish at the end of the Spanish–American War, despite the Philippines declaring their independence.

1900
A Category 4 hurricane demolishes the seaside resort of Galveston in Texas. Around 8,000 people die and more than 3,600 buildings in the city are destroyed. Every home there suffers at least some damage. It remains among the deadliest Atlantic hurricanes on record.

1901
The Texas oil boom begins, with the discovery of the 75,000-barrel-a-day Lucas Gusher near Beaumont, Texas in January. By late June, there are 13 oil wells on the field. US Congress confers citizenship on all Indigenous Americans in Oklahoma Territory.

In September, President McKinley is shot by anarchist Leon Czolgosz while visiting the Pan-American Exhibition in Buffalo. He dies a week later due to gangrene, and his vice-president, Theodore Roosevelt, takes over. In the first transatlantic radio transmission, Italian inventor Guglielmo Marconi sends a message in Morse code 2,100 miles (3,380 km), from Cornwall to Newfoundland.

1902
On May 20, with US control of the country at an end, Cuba achieves formal independence and declares itself the Republic of Cuba. The Philippine–American War ends and the Philippines finally gain their independence. In the Rolling Mill Mine disaster in Johnstown, Pennsylvania, 112 miners—mostly Eastern European immigrants—are killed in an explosion and the subsequent afterdamp (an asphyxiating gas that often follows mine disasters). In September, 115 people are crushed to death in the Shiloh Baptist Church Stampede, when a crowd who had gathered to hear Booker T. Washington panic and run.

1903
The Hay Herrán treaty is signed by the US and Colombia, although it is not ratified by the Senate of Colombia, who are unhappy with terms offered. It would have allowed the US a renewable lease of 100 years on a 6-mile-wide (9.5-km) strip across the planned canal zone of Panama. Panama separates from Columbia to declare an independent republic. Later, the Hay-Bunau-Varilla Treaty grants

rights to the US to build and indefinitely administer the Panama Canal Zone and its defenses. Cuba and the US sign the Agreement for the Lease to the United States of Lands in Cuba for Coaling and Naval Stations. It requires Cuba to accept a permanent US military presence in Guantanamo Bay. The first baseball World Series is played between nine leading US teams from the National League and the American League. In the first powered flight, Orville Wright travels 40 yd (37 m) at Kitty Hawk in North Carolina in a Wright Flyer, a biplane. The UK and US settle the Alaska boundary dispute, which had been ongoing since the purchase of Alaska by the US. Canadians are disappointed that the settlement does not give them a sea-water port to connect to the Yukon.

1904
The Roosevelt Corollary, an addition to the Monroe Doctrine, asserts the right of the US to intervene in order to "stabilize" the economic affairs of small states in the Caribbean and Central America if they are unable to pay their international debts. In February, in what becomes known as the Santo Domingo Affair, the US launches a punitive military expedition against the Dominican Republic after the death of a seaman from the *USS Yankee*.

1905
Alberta and Saskatchewan join the dominion as the eighth and ninth provinces of Canada. Protesting the racial segregation introduced on streetcars in Nashville, Tennessee, Black community

leaders organize the Nashville Streetcar Boycott and set up their own transportation network. In the US, the Niagara Movement is founded by Black American intellectuals and activists, led by W. E. B. Du Bois and William Monroe Trotter. They reject Booker T. Washington's gradualist approach and favor a more aggressive stance.

1906
On August 13 in Brownsville, Texas, approximately a dozen Black troops riot against segregation and in the process kill a local citizen. When the identity of the killer cannot be determined, President Roosevelt dishonorably discharges three companies of Black soldiers. Mobs of armed white men attack random Black Americans in what becomes known as the Atlanta Race Riot in September, resulting in the deaths of 10 Black and 2 white people. It is triggered when local newspapers publish lurid and unsubstantiated accounts of supposed rapes of white women by Black men. Fire destroys much of San Francisco following the most violent earthquake in the city's history, which kills up to 3,000 people. It remains the most deadly earthquake in US history. The US Congress passes the Naturalization Act, which provides definitive requirements for naturalization as a US citizen, and

16 Number of baseball teams forming part of the sport's first governing body, the National Association of Base Ball Players.

▷ **Home run**
The first officially recorded game of baseball in North America took place in Ontario in 1838, and the first in US history in 1846 in New Jersey. Mitts were introduced in the 1870s.

14,000

Number of US sailors in the 16 battleships of the Great White Fleet.

limits racial eligibility for citizenship. It also requires citizens to learn English in order to become naturalized. The Northwest Passage is finally navigated by Norwegian explorer Roald Amundsen and his crew on a 70-ft (21-m) fishing boat, in a journey taking three years.

1907

As part of the "banana wars," President Roosevelt sends US Marines to Honduras, when political unrest there threatens the commercial interests of US-owned fruit companies, which dominate the banana export sector. Charles Curtis becomes the first Indigenous American US Senator. Representing Kansas, he will go on to be senate majority leader before becoming vice-president. President Roosevelt sends the "Great White Fleet" of US Navy battleships on a tour of the world, demonstrating US power. Oklahoma Territory is merged with Indian Territory and becomes the state of Oklahoma.

1908

The Federal Bureau of Investigation (FBI) is set up in Washington, D.C., as the investigative force of the Department of Justice. In the Springfield Race Riot, the first major riot in a Northern city in nearly half a century, two Black people and four white people are killed when a mob of white people wage a two-day assault on the Black community. The first Model T Ford rolls off the production line at the Piquette Avenue Plant in Detroit,

Michigan. It becomes the first mass-market automobile, affordable to most middle-class homes in the US.

1909

In response to the Springfield Riot, the National Association for the Advancement of Colored People (NAACP) is founded in New York City. Canadian explorer Joseph-Elzéar Bernier claims islands in the Arctic Archipelago and a section of the Arctic up to the North Pole for Canada. After the Nicaraguan government executes two US citizens, President William Howard Taft sends in US Marines, who help oust President Zelaya.

1910

The Royal Canadian Navy is created by the Naval Service Act, following the creation of the Royal Canadian Regiment in 1883. US film director D. W. Griffith directs *In Old California*, the first film shot in the California village of Hollywood. The Mexican Revolution begins when revolutionary Francisco I. Madero González declares war on the Díaz regime and issues the Plan of San Luis Potosí, promising democracy, federalism, agrarian reform, and workers' rights.

1911

Madero becomes president in Mexico but the revolution continues. Emiliano Zapata, a leading revolutionary figure, issues the Plan of Ayala under the slogan "Land and Liberty." He denounces Madero, and calls for radical redistribution of land. The Nestor Film Company opens the first film studio in Hollywood, California, on Sunset Boulevard. John D. Rockefeller's Standard Oil Company is broken up by US antitrust legislation.

1912

The *Titanic* sinks on its maiden voyage from the British port of Southampton to

New York after colliding with an iceberg. Approximately 1,500 people on board die. A series of protests and uprisings in Cuba, the War of 1912—also known as the Little Race War, the Negro Rebellion, or The Twelve—sees conflict between Afro-Cuban rebels and the armed forces of Cuba, supported by US forces.

1913

In February, Grand Central Terminal in New York City reopens after being rebuilt. It is the largest train station in the world at the time. Following riots in Mexico City, Madero is overthrown by his own military chief, General Victoriano Huerta, who declares himself dictator. In March, the Woman Suffrage Procession take place in Washington,

D.C., the day before Woodrow Wilson's presidential inauguration, in protest at women's exclusion from the democratic process. The Great Dayton Flood in Ohio kills 428 people. The Canadian Arctic Expedition, led by Vilhjalmur Stefansson, sets off to the north in July. It includes Iñupiat, Inuvialuit, and Inuinnait people and asserts Canada's sovereignty in the Arctic Archipelago. The Lincoln Highway, the first road across the US, is dedicated in October. Beginning on October 31, the Indianapolis Streetcar Strike involves thousands of protesters and shuts down the city's transportation network. The Ford Motor Company creates the world's first moving assembly line, enabling rapid production of cars.

▷ *Soldaderas* **join the revolution**
A large number of women joined or were forced to join the Mexican Revolution and served in the military. They were *soldaderas*: armed combatants, camp followers, or medical personnel.

A WORLD AT WAR 1914–1945

1914

1914

A year after President Madero is killed in a coup led by General Victoriano Huerta, nine US soldiers are arrested and detained by Huerta's army for allegedly entering a prohibited zone in Tampico, Mexico, in what becomes known as the Tampico Affair. US President Woodrow Wilson sends Marines to occupy the port of Veracruz. This invasion, which leads to the deaths of 19 Americans and hundreds of Mexicans, inflames anti-American sentiment in Mexico, and Huerta flees the capital soon after. In May, the worst peacetime disaster in Canadian maritime history occurs when the RMS *Empress of Ireland* sinks after colliding with another ship near the mouth of the Saint Lawrence River. More than 1,000 people die. In June, the assassination of Austrian archduke Franz Ferdinand triggers World War I in Europe. The conflict originates between the Allies (led by France and Britain at first) and the Central Powers (led by Germany). President Wilson proclaims US neutrality, although, as a British dominion, Canada is drawn into the conflict. Marcus Garvey, a Black nationalist and Pan-Africanist (someone who promotes the idea of unity for people of African descent), founds the Universal Negro

Improvement Association in July. It aims to inspire racial pride and unity. At its height, the organization claims nearly two million members. In August, Canada opens the first permanent internment camp at Fort Henry, Ontario, for enemy aliens (people who reside in Canada but come from states at war with it). Many of those held at Fort Henry are of Ukrainian descent. The First Canadian Contingent sails from Québec City for England. The largest convoy ever to cross the Atlantic, it comprises more than 31,000 volunteer troops aboard 31 ocean liners, escorted by Royal Navy warships. Many English-speaking Canadians have links to Britain and are keen to support the British Empire at war. Also sailing in this convoy is a contingent from the British Dominion of Newfoundland, which at this time still remains separate from Canada.

1915

The US occupies Haiti to prevent an anti-American government forming after President Vilbrun Sam is assassinated. US forces help install a pro-American president, Philippe Sudré Dartiguenave. The US will occupy Haiti for the next 19 years.

1916

In what will become known as the Great Migration, Black Americans leave the Southern states for Northern cities, where there are greater economic opportunities and no Jim Crow laws. By the 1970s, six million people will have made the move. The Jazz Age begins, originating in New Orleans and moving north with the Great Migration as musicians leave the South. Black musicians such as Louis Armstrong would go on to bring jazz to Chicago and New York. In March, the Mexican revolutionary "Pancho" Villa attacks a military garrison in the New Mexican town of Columbus, possibly to steal

6 million

The number of people who moved from the South in the Great Migration.

supplies. The assault, the first military incursion into US territory since 1812, kills around 17 Americans and destroys much of the town center. President Wilson responds by sending 10,000 troops into Mexico in pursuit of Villa. They will withdraw a year later, having failed to capture the guerrilla leader.

1917

The constitution of Mexico is approved by a constituent assembly in Santiago de Querétaro. It's the first such document in the world to grant social rights, such as the right to education and the right to housing, and is still in use today. The Zimmermann Telegram, a coded message sent by German foreign secretary Arthur Zimmerman to the German ambassador to Mexico, Heinrich von Eckardt, is intercepted by the British and given to the US. In the telegram, Germany secretly offers to restore territories that Mexico lost in the Mexican–American War in exchange for a Mexican attack on the US. This offer accelerates the entry of the US into the war against Germany. Soon after, the US recognizes the government of General Venustiano Carranza, leader of one of the factions in the Mexican Revolution, in exchange for Mexico's continued neutrality. In the US, President Wilson signs the Jones-Shafroth Act into law, granting US citizenship to Puerto Ricans. Although it remains a US territory, Puerto Rico will have its own House of Representatives

and Senate, elected by democratic vote. In France, four divisions of the Canadian Expeditionary Force fight together for the first time at the Battle of Vimy Ridge, against the German 6th Army. The conflict becomes celebrated as a national symbol of achievement and sacrifice, and as a formative milestone in the creation of Canada's national identity. The US declares war on Germany in April, and on the Austro-Hungarian Empire in December. On July 28, in what is now known as the Silent Parade, nearly 10,000 Black Americans and their supporters march down Fifth Avenue in Manhattan as part of an NAACP-organized protest against lynchings, race riots, and the denial of rights. It is the first major civil rights demonstration in the US. In Canada, a massive explosion devastates Halifax, after the French cargo ship the SS *Mont-Blanc* collides with a Norwegian ship, the SS *Imo*. The French ship was loaded with munitions that caught fire before exploding, causing severe damage and killing nearly 1,800 people.

△ **From folk hero to revolutionary soldier**
Francisco Villa (also known as "Pancho") was a Mexican bandit who began his career robbing wealthy miners, making him a local folk hero. He later became a general in the Mexican Revolution.

▷ **Blinded by gas**
Gassed, a painting by John Singer Sargent from 1919, depicts the effects of a mustard gas attack on US troops on the Western Front in World War I. Many men are temporarily blinded.

◁ **Cotton Club clapper**
This wooden clapper promoting singer
and actor Ethel Waters is from the
Cotton Club, a nightclub and mainstay
of the Harlem Renaissance.

1919

1918

In January, in a speech called the Fourteen Points, President Wilson lays out to the US Congress detailed proposals aimed at world peace once World War I has ended. The US experiences its first "Red Scare," a period of public fear of far-left and communist movements. Hysteria foments around Bolshevism and anarchism following a series of violent communist revolutions in Europe. Leftist radicals worldwide are emboldened by the Bolshevik Revolution in Russia and are eager to respond to Lenin's call for world revolution. This triggers bouts of mass paranoia in the US. The Harlem Renaissance begins, a Black cultural movement centered in the Upper Manhattan district of Harlem. Many cultural figures are involved, including writers such as Langston Hughes and Zora Neale Hurston, and musicians Jelly Roll Morton, Ethel Waters, and Louis Armstrong.

Prohibition of alcohol in Canada is enacted federally by an Order in Council, as part of the war effort. It will end in 1919. Women in Canada win the right to vote in federal elections but Indigenous and Asian women are excluded. US troops arrive in Europe at the rate of 10,000 a day. By September, there are 1.2 million US troops in France. They help turn the tide of World War I because Germany cannot replace its devastating losses in manpower. A loosely connected series of strikes, riots, and labor conflicts begin across Canada, largely organized by the One Big Union (OBU). They are sparked by the Vancouver general strike, which takes place after prominent labor activist Albert "Ginger" Goodwin is shot by police. The conflicts will last until 1925. A group of Choctaw people from Oklahoma pioneer the use of Indigenous American languages as military code in World War I, since the German troops cannot understand the language. They become known as the Choctaw code talkers. Indigenous code talkers speaking

many different languages will go on to be used in both world wars. On November 11, Germany signs an armistice, signaling the first step toward ending World War I. More than 116,000 Americans and 66,000 Canadians have been killed in the conflict.

1919

Canada's Immigration Act excludes communists, Mennonites, Doukhobors, and other religious groups from entering the country. It also excludes Austrian, Hungarian, and Turkish people, and others whose home countries had fought against Canada during World War I. The May Day riots occur in Cleveland, Ohio, protesting the imprisonment of the Socialist Party leader, Eugene Debs, as well as the US intervention against the Bolsheviks in the Russian Civil War, which had erupted after the Bolshevik seizure of power. Also in May, the Winnipeg General Strike begins, the largest in Canada's history. Almost the entire

working population of Winnipeg takes part in the strike, fighting for better treatment at work. More than 30,000 workers walk off their jobs alongside soldiers returning from World War I, shutting down the majority of the city's privately owned factories, shops, and trains. During what will become known as the "Red Summer," white supremacist terrorism and racial riots occur in at least 26 cities across the US. British aviators John Alcock and Arthur Whitten Brown fly from St. John's in Newfoundland to Clifden in Ireland on the first nonstop transatlantic flight. The journey is nearly 2,000 miles (3,200 km) and takes around 16 hours. The duo fly in a modified World War I Vickers Vimy bomber. In the Great Steel Strike, steelworkers across the US walk off the job in an attempt to create a major confrontation with industrial management. They want to negotiate for better working conditions, but the strike collapses after four months with nothing achieved. In an attempt to

▽ Recognition for code talkers
This American congressional gold medal was awarded in 2013 to the Choctaw code talkers who pioneered the use of Indigenous American languages as military code during World War I.

▷ Carnage on Wall Street
This photo depicts the chaos on the street and the crowd of people who gathered just after the 1920 bombing on Wall Street in Manhattan. A wagon full of dynamite exploded at lunchtime.

1920

disentangle themselves from the increasingly powerful Hollywood movie studios and produce and distribute their own films, the actors Mary Pickford, Douglas Fairbanks, and Charlie Chaplin, along with the director D. W. Griffith, form the United Artists Corporation. Anarchists in the US send a series of coordinated mail bombs to politicians, anti-anarchist officials, anti-immigration officials, businessmen, and a journalist. The majority of the bombs do not detonate but at least one person is injured. Anarchists also set off eight large bombs in different US cities in June. These bombings contribute to the ongoing hysteria of the Red Scare. The Treaty of Versailles is drawn up at the Paris Peace Conference in order to officially end World War I. US President Wilson advocates for the treaty to include a plan for the League of Nations, the first organization for international cooperation and peacekeeping. His idea has public support, yet on his return to the US he is disappointed to find that Congress votes to opt out of the league and fails to ratify the treaty. Although this undermines the effectiveness of the league, the Treaty of Versailles is still signed in Germany, and the US will go on to sign its own peace agreement with Germany in 1921.

1920

The Roaring Twenties begin in the US and other Western countries, a period characterized by economic prosperity fueled by technological progress, new opportunities, and optimism. It is a time of social change, with women especially experiencing a period of progressive freedom. Jazz music flourishes, and art and literature also experience radical shifts. In January, the Xalapa Earthquake hits Mexico, with its epicenter in Puebla and Veracruz. Killing around 700 people, it is one of the deadliest Mexican earthquakes to date. The Battle of Port-au-Prince ends the Second Caco War in Haiti, a rebellion that had erupted in 1918 against US occupation. In the US, the Palmer Raids, a series of raids and arrests by the Department of Justice, target non-citizen socialists, anarchists, radical unionists, and immigrants, all charged with planning to overthrow the government. By 1920, more than 10,000 arrests are made, and the immigrants caught up in these raids are deported back to Europe, including the anarchist Emma Goldman, who previously had attempted to assassinate the industrialist Henry Clay Frick. The passing of the Eighteenth Amendment brings Prohibition into effect in the US, three months after the Volstead Act has provided guidelines for enforcement. Bootlegging and the illegal sale of alcohol becomes widespread. Prohibition lasts until 1933, when the Twenty-First Amendment repeals the Eighteenth. Canada is admitted to the League of Nations independently of Britain. The Indian Act is amended in Canada, reducing First Nations rights. Among other stipulations, the act makes it mandatory for Indigenous parents to send their children to a residential school and allows the Department of Indian Affairs to ban the hereditary rule of bands. The act is repealed two years later, but reintroduced in a modified form in 1933. The Nineteenth Amendment to the US Constitution is ratified, guaranteeing women the right to vote, but it fails to fully enfranchise Black American, Asian American, Hispanic American, and Indigenous American women. In the Wall Street bombing, a terrorist attack kills 30 people in Lower Manhattan when an unknown man drives a horse-drawn wagon full of dynamite up to the J.P. Morgan building. He gets out and the wagon explodes. The case remains unsolved. Ten years of violent revolution in Mexico are brought to an end in a successful coup by General Álvaro Obregón, who becomes president.

24.9%

The unemployment rate in the US at the peak of the Great Depression.

1921

The Emergency Quota Act in the US restricts the flow of people from southern and eastern Europe into the country; Mexican people are excluded from quota requirements. Between May 31 and June 1, violence against Black Americans peaks in what becomes known as the Tulsa Race Massacre, after a white woman accuses a Black man of rape in Tulsa, Oklahoma. Between 36 and 300 people are killed in white supremacy riots that last two days, and 35 blocks of Greenwood, a Black neighborhood, are burned down. In Canada, the Slave, Dogrib, Hare, Loucheux, and other Indigenous peoples cede the Mackenzie River region of the Northwest Territories to the federal government. William Lyon Mackenzie King begins the first of his three non-consecutive terms as Canadian prime minister. He establishes Canada's reputation as a middle-tier world power, and will become the longest-serving prime minister in Canadian history. The Washington Conference, an international

naval disarmament gathering, commences. It initiates the process of limiting the navies of major nations. *The Sheik,* a film starring Rudolph Valentino, is released in the US in November. While toned down from its source material—a novel of the same name, which included scenes of sexual violence and racial tension—it creates a moral outcry due to his "European style," which is seen as unmasculine.

1922

The Teapot Dome Scandal rocks President Warren G. Harding's government. In the greatest US corruption scandal until Watergate in 1972, several prominent government officials are revealed to be involved in a bribery scheme centered around leasing federal oil reserves. Harding's government never recovers.

1923

The Levi Chief Deskaheh sails to Geneva to ask the League of Nations to recognize the Six Nations of Grand River as a sovereign nation. He is not allowed to address the organization, but gives speeches across the country. In the Bucareli Treaty, Mexico agrees to respect the rights of US oil companies, and repay losses suffered by US companies during the Mexican Revolution, in exchange for US recognition of the Mexican government.

1924

The Immigration Act of 1924 extends US immigration restrictions to East and South Asian people and sets quotas for immigrants arriving from Eastern and Central Europe. The act creates the US Border Control force and establishes stations to formally admit Mexican workers and to collect visa fees and taxes from those entering. The US again takes a leadership role on the world stage when lawyer Charles Dawes, who later becomes US vice-president, develops the Dawes Plan, which temporarily resolves the issue of unpaid German reparations to the Allied nations for World War I. The Indian Citizenship Act declares all Indigenous Americans to be US citizens. Previously, citizenship had only been granted to Indigenous people based on factors such as whether a person had accepted a deal for land rights, had a certain percentage of Indigenous ancestry, was a veteran, or had married a US citizen.

1925

While still only 26 years old, Al Capone takes over Johnny Torrio's gangster organization in Chicago, called the Chicago Outfit. His leadership ushers in extreme violence. If a business refused to buy beer from his organization, Capone would often order the building to be blown up. At the Scopes trial, biology teacher John Scopes is prosecuted for breaking state law by teaching the concept of evolution as established science to his class in Dayton, Tennessee. While the trial is staged mainly for publicity, it does underline the growing controversy between modernists, who are eager to include new and scientific knowledge into their beliefs, and Christian fundamentalists, who reject this. The Ku Klux Klan (KKK), a violent white supremacist organization, marches on Washington, D.C., to demand an all-white, protestant US. The KKK had been revived in 1915 by William Joseph Simmons, a suspended Methodist preacher, at Stone Mountain, Georgia. Lynchings of Black Americans continue during this time, among them a number of returning soldiers still in uniform.

1926

In Canada, Governor General Lord Byng of Vimy refuses Prime Minister Mackenzie King's request to dissolve parliament and call an election, triggering a constitutional crisis that will become known as the King-Byng Affair. Byng instead asks opposition leader Arthur Meighen to form a government, which in turn is quickly defeated. The affair plays a role in the Balfour Report later in the year, in which each dominion of the British Empire is declared to be of equal status with Britain.

1927

By 1927, US media mogul William Randolph Hearst owns a nationwide string of daily newspapers, the largest in the country. His sensationalist style will influence US journalism to the present day. Actor Mae West is

◁ **Freedom for filmmaking**
The movie studio and distribution company United Artists Corporation was formed by actor and director Charlie Chaplin, actors Mary Pickford and Douglas Fairbanks, and director D. W. Griffith.

1928

▽ **First flight**
Charles A. Lindbergh piloted the *Spirit of St. Louis* on the first solo, nonstop flight across the Atlantic. The flight took 33 hours and 30 minutes.

sentenced to eight days in jail when the play *Sex*, which she wrote, produced, and starred in, is judged to be obscene. In the first solo nonstop transatlantic flight, US aviator Charles Lindbergh flies solo across the Atlantic, from New York to Paris, in his single-engine plane, *Spirit of St. Louis*. It is a journey of 3,600 miles (5,800 km), takes 33.5 hours, and makes Lindbergh an international celebrity. In the US, sculptor Gutzon Borglum begins the massive task of carving the portraits of four US presidents (Washington, Jefferson, Roosevelt, and Lincoln) into the granite rock face of Mount Rushmore. Work will not be completed until 1941.

1928
Álvaro Obregón, the leading figure in Mexico's anticlerical revolution, is shot by a Roman Catholic assassin. The US Secretary of State Frank B. Kellogg and his French counterpart, Aristide Briand, write the Kellogg-Briand Pact. Another international peacekeeping effort, it is created separately from the League of Nations. The US, France, and Germany are the first to sign it, and signatory states promise not to use war to resolve disputes. It remains in effect today.

1929
Canada's government begins to impose Christian names on Inuit citizens, partly to enforce authority. In Chicago, seven members of the Bugs Moran gang are lined up against a wall and machine-gunned by rival gangsters in what becomes known as the Saint Valentine's

Day Massacre. The shooting is part of a battle for control of the city by various gangs. Herbert Hoover becomes president of the US, with Charles Curtis becoming the first Indigenous American vice-president. Hoover is an engineer and proponent of progressivism, seeking to implement efficiency in business and public service. His administration at first promotes standardization, elimination of waste, and international trade. In Mexico, Plutarco Calles establishes the National Revolutionary Party. It will hold power, under different names, for the rest of the century. On Thursday, October 24, panic selling causes a Wall Street stock market crash that leads to the Great Depression. The worst global economic downturn in history, it lasts for the next 10 years. In the US, high unemployment and poverty, low profits, and deflation are just some of the consequences of the Great Depression. Americans begin to view Mexican workers as competitors for jobs, prompting the creation of a repatriation program for Mexicans and Mexican-Americans. From 1929 to 1939, the US forcibly relocates more than 400,000 people from Arizona, California, and Texas to Mexico.

1930
The Hays Code is created to set exacting standards of public decency in US movies. The film studios agree to abide by the Hays Code in part to avoid governmental restrictions and appease pressure groups. In May, the Chrysler Building opens in New York as the

world's tallest building. The Manhattan skyline continues to change as more skyscrapers—including the Empire State Building in 1931—are built in response to an increasing population and the need for office space. The Smoot-Hawley Tariff Act implements protectionist policies in the US by placing tariffs on more than 20,000 imported goods. Wallace D. Fard founds the Nation of Islam as a Black separatist movement in the US. While it uses Muslim terms and elements of the Islamic faith, it differs considerably from the traditional teachings of the religion and incorporates Black nationalist ideas. Military commander Rafael Trujillo becomes the dictator of the Dominican Republic. He will rule the country for more than 30 years.

1931
In a trial in Alabama, nine Black teenagers, known as the Scottsboro Boys, are wrongly convicted of gang rape by an all-white jury. The publicity

around the case increases public awareness of the problems of all-white juries who do not reflect the racial makeup of the area they are representing in court. Violence erupts during a confrontation between the Royal Canadian Mounted Police and striking coal miners, in what is now called the Estevan Riot. It is eventually resolved when both the mine operators and employees agree on a contract for better conditions for the miners. In October, gangster Al Capone is jailed for tax evasion. He is never convicted of murder, despite his alleged involvement in brutal gang violence, including the Saint Valentine's Day Massacre. The George Washington Bridge opens over the Hudson River that links New York City with New Jersey. At the time, it is the world's longest suspension bridge, with a main span of 3,500 ft (1,067 m). The British Parliament passes the Statute of Westminster, which defines and formalizes the concept of the British Commonwealth. It formally recognizes Canada's *de facto* independence following World War I, as well as the sovereign right of each dominion to control its own domestic and foreign affairs, to establish its own diplomatic

120 mph
The top speed of the *Spirit of St. Louis* (193 kph). Its construction was completed in 60 days.

▽ **Skyscraper boom**
This photo shows the Art Deco Chrysler Building among other skyscrapers in Manhattan. It was the tallest building in the world for 11 months after it was built in 1930, before others superseded it.

corps, and (except for Newfoundland) to be separately represented in the League of Nations.

1932
US aviator Amelia Earhart lands her airplane in Ireland 15 hours after leaving Newfoundland, becoming the first woman to fly solo across the Atlantic. In the US, in what becomes known as the Bonus Army Conflict, 43,000 war veterans and their families descend on Washington, D.C., to demand early cash redemption of their service bonus certificates in the hope of alleviating economic hardship. General Douglas MacArthur leads a military response, using tanks and cavalry to disperse the protesters. In Europe, a refugee crisis begins as Jewish people flee increasing anti-Semitic violence. More than 110,000 refugees reach the US by 1941, but hundreds of thousands more applicants are rejected; Canada accepts fewer than 5,000 refugees in the years that follow.

1933
Franklin Delano Roosevelt, often referred to as "FDR," becomes president of the US for the first of four terms. He offers "a new deal for the American people," in a series of programs, public works projects, financial reforms, and governmental regulations that seek to alleviate the ongoing impact of the Great Depression. Under Roosevelt's leadership, the US focuses on using cooperation and trade with Latin America rather than military force in order to maintain stability, in what is termed the Good Neighbor Policy.

1934
In March, the Tydings-McDuffie Act comes into effect in the Philippines, which establishes a process for the islands, still a US territory, to gain independence over the course of a 10-year period. It also limits Filipino immigration into the US. *Tender Is the Night*, F. Scott Fitzgerald's last novel, is published, initially serialized in *Scribner* magazine. As part of the Good Neighbor Policy, the US ends its occupation of Haiti, but still maintains economic connections there. On the prairies of the US and Canada, in what becomes known as the Dust Bowl, droughts and dust storms drive farmers off their land and deepen the Great Depression. The Indian Reorganization Act (also known as the Wheeler–Howard Act) restores tribal ownership of land in the US national reservations and encourages the preservation and recovery of Indigenous Americans' cultural traditions. In December, Japan

renounces the Washington Naval Treaty and London Naval Treaty, which had historically limited its construction of naval ships. The National Archives of the United States is established in Washington, D.C., dedicated to preserving governmental and historic records.

1935
In Canada, under the leadership of Arthur "Slim" Evans, more than 1,000 workers join the Relief Camp Workers' Union and begin what is known as the On-to-Ottawa Trek in protest of the conditions and wages in government relief work camps. In the US, President Roosevelt launches the second part of his stabilizing program, called the Second New Deal. Along with other measures, it passes the Social Security Act to help US citizens facing old age, unemployment, and illness. It also creates the Works Progress Administration, a national work relief program, the efforts of which are still widely visible in the US today. In Mexico, President Lázaro Cárdenas, who had been elected in 1934, redistributes land to the rural poor, creating *ejidos* (cultivated communal land used for agriculture) and destroying the *hacienda*

system (a form of indentured servitude linked to Spanish colonialism). During his administration, Cárdenas will redistribute huge quantities of land, around a tenth of which is expropriated from US nationals. The US Congress passes the first of three neutrality acts, an attempt to keep the US neutral as Europe moves again toward war.

1936
The Boulder Dam (which will be renamed the Hoover Dam in 1947) is completed on the Colorado River, on the border between Arizona and Nevada. It is a huge arch-gravity dam, blocking Lake Mead and creating hydroelectric power. The dam causes massive ecological changes to the Colorado River itself, and the ecosystems within the Grand Canyon, since it eliminates the natural flooding process.

1937
The Golden Gate Bridge, linking San Francisco and Marin County in California, opens as the world's newest, longest, and tallest suspension bridge, with a main span of 4,200 ft (1,280 m). In what becomes known as the Parsley Massacre, dictator Rafael Trujillo orders the slaughter of 20,000 Haitian people living in the Dominican Republic. Nearly all Haitian people in the country are either murdered or flee to Haiti. Amelia Earhart disappears four weeks into her attempt to fly around the world, along with her navigator Fred Noonan. To this day their disappearance remains a mystery.

1938
In Canada, as part of the Métis Population Betterment Act, 12 temporary settlements in the province of Alberta are created for the Métis people. When it is eventually revealed that the Métis people cannot survive

◁ **Hoover for president**
This 1928 Republican note card shows endorsements for Herbert Hoover for president and Charles Curtis for vice-president. They were successful in 1929.

▽ **Great Golden Gate**
In this 1937 view, San Francisco's Golden Gate Bridge is having its roadbed installed. It was completed the same year and the opening celebration lasted for a week.

1939

on some of this land because it is unsuitable for agriculture, hunting, or fishing, several of the settlements are rescinded and the land is given back to the government. The House Un-American Activities Committee is formed in the US House of Representatives to investigate politically subversive groups. Citizens suspected of having ties to the Communist Party are interrogated in court and asked to inform on others. Mexico nationalizes its oil industry, including the holdings of foreign oil companies. In Vancouver, Canada, the Relief Project Workers' Union (an extension of the Relief Camp Workers' Union) stages a month long sit-down strike, refusing to work and occupying the post office unlawfully. This culminates in "Bloody Sunday," a violent confrontation between the strikers and police on June 19.

1939

In what becomes known as the "Voyage of the Damned," the MS *St. Louis,* a German passenger ship attempting to rescue Jewish refugees from Nazi Germany, is turned away from Cuba, the US, and Canada and forced to return to Europe. It is estimated that nearly 30 percent of the people on the ship are later murdered during the Holocaust. Germany invades

Poland, provoking Britain and France to declare war on Germany, beginning World War II. The Allies are soon joined by British Commonwealth countries, with Canada declaring war on Germany in September. During the war, the Canadian government mobilizes money, supplies, and volunteers to support the British war effort while boosting its own domestic economy and morale on the home front. Canada will also play a military role protecting Allied convoys against German submarines and fighting the German Army in Western Europe.

1940

In the Destroyers for Bases deal, the US government provides 50 navy destroyers to the Allies in return for a 99-year lease on British naval and air bases in the Caribbean. Educator and Black activist Booker T. Washington becomes the first Black American to be depicted on a US postage stamp. In May, the first McDonald's restaurant opens in San Bernardino, California. In September, Japan enters World War II with the invasion of French Indochina and officially forms the Axis alliance with Germany and Italy, who had entered the war in June. In November, Franklin D. Roosevelt wins the US presidential election to

become the first and only president to complete three terms (he will be elected to a fourth but will die before its completion).

1941

President Roosevelt delivers his famous Four Freedoms speech, which articulates his vision of the rights of all humankind. The four freedoms he seeks to protect are freedom of speech and of worship, and freedom from want or from fear. His vision serves as an argument for the US to enter World War II and is used to encourage public support for this involvement. The US Army creates the all-Black Tuskegee Air Squadron. Roosevelt desegregates war production plants and creates the Fair Employment Practices Committee (FEPC), which bans discriminatory practices in all federal and war-supporting facilities. The desperate need for factory labor to build the war machine needed for World War II leads to a migration of Black Americans from the South to the North and West. This migration will transform US politics, as Black people, who were still often restricted from voting in the South, start to vote in large numbers. The Lend-Lease Act enables Roosevelt to provide help to the Allies in the form of material aid (for example food and ammunition) without violating the US's official neutrality. Roosevelt and the British prime minister, Winston Churchill, publish a joint declaration, called the Atlantic Charter, which paves the way for the eventual creation of the United Nations. The US builds the first of the mass-produced Liberty ships—the SS

Patrick Henry—to help supply the Allies in Europe with food and war material. On December 7, Japanese planes attack the US naval fleet at Pearl Harbor in a surprise strike that kills more than 2,400 people. They sink 180 aircraft and damage 19 ships, sinking three. Roosevelt calls it a "day which will live on in infamy." The next day, the US enters World War II on the side of the Allies. This marks the start of the Pacific War, which will be fought in eastern Asia, the Pacific Ocean, the Indian Ocean, and Oceania.

1942

US physicist J. Robert Oppenheimer is appointed director of the Manhattan Project, a top-secret research project to develop a nuclear weapon. US forces defending the Philippines surrender to the Japanese after the Battle of Bataan. It is the largest surrender in both US and Philippine history. More than 75,000 troops from both countries are forcibly transferred from the Bataan Peninsula to Camp O'Donnell on Luzon Island on a death march, and many prisoners of war are killed or die en route. In late spring and early summer, Allied victories against the Japanese navy in the battles of the Coral Sea and Midway mark a turning point in the Pacific War. In August, US military forces land on Guadalcanal in the Solomon Islands, driving north across the islands toward Japan itself. In December, the Battle of the Atlantic reaches a peak, with 1.5 million tons (more than 1.36 million metric tons) of shipping sunk in the last quarter of the year.

75

The length of time, in minutes, of the attack on Pearl Harbor. The US declared war on Japan and its allies the next day.

◁ **Tuskegee airmen**
This military honors and rank medal grouping belonged to the Tuskegee Airmen, a group of Black pilots and airmen who flew in World War II. They trained at Tuskegee Army Air Field in Alabama.

1943

In Los Angeles, violence erupts between US servicemen and young Mexican-Americans who wear zoot suits. Popular in California, zoot suits are baggy, boldly colored, often striped suits, most famously worn by the bandleader Cab Calloway. The servicemen see such suits as too flamboyant and wasteful due to the cloth rationing at the time. Racism also plays a part in the conflicts, which become known as the Zoot Suit Riots. The Los Alamos Laboratory, a centralized facility designed to coordinate the research of the Manhattan Project, begins operations at the University of California, with the mission to design and build the world's first atomic bombs. In Beaumont, Harlem, and Detroit, race riots break out due to resentments over the inequalities between Black and white people. On July 10, Allied forces invade the Italian island of Sicily, and in September, US General Dwight D. Eisenhower announces to the Allied forces that Italy has surrendered. At the Tehran Conference, the Allied leaders Franklin D. Roosevelt, Joseph Stalin of Russia, and Winston Churchill of Britain decide to open a second front against the German forces, forcing them to fight on their eastern flank as well as on the Western Front. The closing of the Works Progress Administration by Roosevelt marks the official end of the Great Depression.

1944

In Canada, registered Indigenous veterans who have served in World War II are permitted to vote in federal elections (along with their spouses) without losing their tribal status, with some conditions. The Aztec Eagles, a Mexican flying squadron, begin training in the US. They later serve as part of the US Air Force in the Philippines. At the Bretton Woods Conference, delegates from 44 nations agree on new rules for the postwar global monetary system, creating both the World Bank and the International Monetary Fund. On June 6, now known as D-Day, US and Canadian troops are among Allied forces that land in Normandy, in the north of France, to drive German occupiers from western Europe. It is the largest amphibious invasion in history. In September, the first of thousands of war brides arrive in Canada, mainly from Britain. They had met and married Canadian servicemen serving overseas. At the Dumbarton Oaks Conference, delegates from 39 nations meet near Washington, D.C., to plan the future United Nations. In April, President Roosevelt dies and is replaced by his vice-president, Harry S. Truman.

1945

In February, the Soviet Union hosts the Yalta Conference, which gathers the leaders of the US, Britain, and the Soviet Union to discuss the progress of the war and their vision of the postwar period. The Alaska Equal Rights Act of 1945 is passed by Alaska's territorial Senate, the first antidiscrimination law passed in a US state or territory in the 20th century. It prohibits discrimination due to race. Also in February, US naval forces begin their attempt to wrest control of the island of Iwo Jima (just south of Japan) from Japanese forces in the Battle of Iwo Jima. By March, the US has control of the island. In April, US troops reach Ohrdruf, the first Nazi concentration camp to be liberated by an Allied army. The discovery of the camp shocks the soldiers; it is the first time they have seen the horror inflicted by the Nazis during the Holocaust. General Eisenhower visits the site on April 12 and is also shaken when faced with the full evidence of Nazi brutality. Delegates from 50 nations meet in San Francisco for the United Nations Conference on International Organization (also known as the San Francisco Conference). The aim is to build on political objectives set out in the Dumbarton Oaks and Yalta conferences. The United Nations is founded in San Francisco after the delegates sign the United Nations Charter, but it is not ratified until October. The war ends in Europe after the Allies force the German troops back to Berlin, where the Soviet Union closes in on Nazi headquarters and Germany officially surrenders. May 8 is declared Victory in Europe Day (or VE Day) and is met with widespread celebration. In August, US military planes drop atomic bombs on the Japanese cities of Hiroshima and Nagasaki. The bombs have been developed as part of the Manhattan Project. This action forces the end of the war as the final Axis power, the Japanese, surrender.

▷ **Prelude to war**
Thick smoke rolls out of a burning ship during the surprise attack by Japan on Pearl Harbor, the US naval base in Hawaii, in 1941. The attack destroyed or damaged 19 US Navy ships.

POSTWAR NORTH AMERICA 1945–1980

1946

1946
In Canada, businesswoman Viola Desmond challenges segregation. She is dragged out of a movie theater in Nova Scotia and booked by police after she refuses to move from the main floor of the theater to the balcony, where Black patrons are segregated. Her decision to contest her charges raises awareness of the racism experienced by Black Canadians. In December, Miguel Alemán becomes the first civilian president of Mexico since Francisco Madero in 1911. The ruling party (Partido de la Revolución Mexicana) is renamed the Partido Revolucionario Institucional (PRI), and will continue its dominance for the next 50 years.

1947
In what becomes known as the Truman Doctrine, US president Harry S. Truman defines postwar US foreign policy by pledging support for any nation that defends itself against communism. This pledge will lead to an increase in US foreign intervention. Under the threat of denying them any financial aid, the US pressures France and Italy into purging communists from their governments. The US Congress passes the National Security Act, which provides for the creation of the Central Intelligence Agency (the CIA), a nonmilitary force for gathering foreign intelligence.

1948
In March, Soviet representatives walk out of a meeting of the Allied Control Council, effectively ending the wartime alliance. This added to the brewing postwar rivalries between the US, the USSR, and their respective allies that would become known as the Cold War. The council had been set up to govern the Allied occupation zones in Germany and Austria after the end of World War II. In April, George Marshall, the US Secretary of State, launches an initiative to distribute aid to 16 European countries. This becomes known as the Marshall Plan. The first country to benefit is Greece, whose government is fighting communist rebels. The US will ultimately transfer more than $13 billion in aid to Europe. The Berlin Blockade

1949
Newfoundland joins Canada as its 10th province, completing the Confederation. The North Atlantic Treaty Organization (NATO) is set up by the US and Canada, together with Britain and other European countries, for the purposes of collective security.

1950
The Korean War begins when North Korea, with the backing of the USSR, invades South Korea. It will last until 1953. Canadians and Americans fight

government employees, Hollywood stars, academics, left-wing politicians, and labor union activists are blacklisted. In May, the Royal Canadian Mounted Police schooner RCMPV *St. Roch* becomes the first ship to circumnavigate North America, traveling through both the Panama Canal and the Northwest Passage. In September, the US evangelist Billy Graham forms the Billy Graham Evangelistic Association to preach his Christian message globally. Graham becomes one of the most influential evangelists in the world.

1951
In February, the Twenty-Second Amendment to the US Constitution is ratified. It limits anyone from serving more than two consecutive presidential terms. In March, Julius and Ethel Rosenberg are convicted for spying for the USSR. They will be executed in 1953, becoming the first US civilians to be executed for such charges and the first to be executed during peacetime.

1952
Vincent Massey is sworn in as the first Canadian-born governor general of Canada. In Cuba, Fulgencio Batista takes power through a coup. He will rule as dictator until 1959, and his secret police use violence, torture, and public executions to keep him in power.

1953
Former US army general Dwight D. Eisenhower becomes president of the US. His tenure is marked by his belief in

> "I feel that the majority of people should decide for themselves what government they want."
>
> CONVICTED SPY JULIUS ROSENBERG, LATER EXECUTED

is of the first international crises of the Cold War. It begins in June, when the USSR blocks the Western Allies' access to railroads, roads, and other routes into Allied-controlled areas of Berlin. The Allies organized the Berlin Airlift to bring supplies to those in need in West Berlin. The blockade ends in 1949 when the Soviets reopen access to West Berlin. Relations between the US and the USSR break down further with the publication of documents detailing collaboration between the Soviets and the Germans, and the subsequent publication of a book entitled *The Falsifiers of History*, partly written by Joseph Stalin, which attacks the Allies.

in the war under United Nations' command against communist North Korea. In response to Soviet atom bomb tests, and perceived threats from the Cold War and the Korean War, the US develops a hydrogen bomb, and begins stockpiling nuclear weapons. Canada also begins storing nuclear missiles and warheads for the US. Senator Joseph McCarthy claims in a speech to know the names of 205 communists in the US State Department, leading to a period of political paranoia and persecution of left-wing individuals known as the era of McCarthyism. McCarthyism also targets homosexuals and stirs up a moral panic known as the Lavender Scare. McCarthyism wanes in the late 1950s, but only after many

◁ **European recovery**
A poster announcing the arrival of aid in Europe from the Marshall Plan. The slogan says: "Make Way for the Marshall Plan." Launched in 1948, the plan sent aid to postwar western Europe.

▷ **Courageous stand**
One of the Little Rock Nine, Elizabeth Eckford, ignored the hostile screams and stares of fellow students on her first day of school in 1957.

◁ **Keeping life going**
A plane used in the Berlin Airlift. In total the airlift delivered more than 2.3 million tons (2.1 million metric tons) of food, fuel, machinery, and other supplies and cost $224 million.

1958

the Domino Theory, which holds that communism will spread from one country to the next. It is used to justify US intervention around the world. He also builds up the nation's stockpile of nuclear weapons. In Cuba, Fidel Castro and rebels attack the Moncada Barracks. They form the 26th of July Movement and in subsequent years fight to oust Batista. In August, President Eisenhower implements Operation Ajax, a covert coup operation to overthrow the democratically elected Iranian prime minister, Mohammad Mosaddegh, and strengthen the Shah of Iran.

1954

In July, France and the Viet Minh sign the Geneva Peace Accord, dividing Vietnam into a northern section, under the control of the communists, led by Ho Chi Minh, and a southern section, led by the Catholic anticommunist Ngô Đình Diêm.

Escalating tensions between north and south soon lead to the Vietnam War, with the US providing military aid to the south. In the landmark *Brown v. Board of Education* case, the US Supreme Court rules that segregation in public schools is illegal. In Guatemala, a *coup d'état* ousts the left-wing President Jacobo Árbenz. This is carried out with CIA support and the US installs a military dictator. The Nova Scotia Association for the Advancement of Colored People pressures the province's government to pass the Fair Employment Act of 1955 and the Fair Accommodations Act of 1959 to end segregation in Nova Scotia.

1955

Disneyland opens in California, an event watched on television by 90 million Americans. In August, Emmett Till, a Black 14-year-old boy, is abducted and lynched in Drew, Mississippi, by a white

mob after being accused of offending a white woman. His mother, Mamie Till-Mobley, shows his brutalized body in an open casket at his funeral. In court, his killers are acquitted. The case draws continued national attention to the persecution of Black Americans. In December, Baptist pastor and civil rights campaigner Martin Luther King Jr. leads the Montgomery Bus Boycott after Rosa Parks is arrested for refusing to give up her seat to a white man.

1957

A group of nine Black American students (later known as the Little Rock Nine) enroll at Little Rock Central High School in an effort to integrate the school. On the orders of the governor of Arkansas, they are kept from entering by the Arkansas National Guard. President Eisenhower sends military troops to enforce desegregation. In October,

Francois Duvalier, known as Papa Doc, is elected president of Haiti. His regime, supported by an undercover death squad, the Tonton Macoute, rapidly becomes despotic.

1958

In June, the *Loving v. Virginia* case is decided. In this landmark civil rights ruling, the US Supreme Court unanimously determines that laws banning interracial marriage violate the Equal Protection and Due Process Clauses of the Fourteenth Amendment to the US Constitution. In July, the National Aeronautics and Space Administration (NASA) is founded following the success of the USSR in launching its Sputnik satellite. Canada and the US then cofound the North American Aerospace Defense Command (NORAD) to jointly protect the security of North American airspace.

1959

1959

In Cuba, Fidel Castro defeats the Cuban army and ousts Batista, installing a communist regime. Alaska becomes the 49th state in the US. It is the largest state by area. Hawaii becomes the 50th state, the only one outside North America. It comprises more than 135 islands. In 1893, the US had overthrown Hawaii's Indigenous government (in 1993, they will apologize for this action). The Saint Lawrence Seaway, a system of locks and canals in Canada and the US, is built as a joint project linking the Great Lakes and the Atlantic Ocean.

1960

The Guatemalan Civil War begins, fought between the US-backed government and left-wing guerrilla groups inspired by Castro's victory in Cuba. Up to 200,000 people will be "disappeared" during the war, including many Mayan people. The war lasts until 1996. In Greensboro, North Carolina Black student activists hold a sit-in in a segregated Woolworth's dining area. This sparks nonviolent civil rights protests and begins a series of sit-ins in the South. John Lesage is elected as prime minister of Quebec, heralding the beginning of Quebec's "quiet revolution" of secularization and modernization in French Canada. In May, Soviet forces shoot down a US U-2 spy plane and capture the pilot, Gary Powers, taking him hostage, before exchanging him for a Russian spy in 1962. In July, Canadian First Nations peoples gain the vote in federal elections while retaining their status and treaty rights. However, Indigenous people are still excluded from voting in some provinces. The Congo Crisis begins in what is now the Democratic Republic of the Congo. The CIA-backed president, Joseph Kasa-Vubu, ousts democratically elected Prime Minister Patrice Lumumba from office. Later, the CIA-backed Colonel Mobutu Sese Seko quickly mobilizes his forces to seize power through a military coup d'état and Lumumba is assassinated.

1961

In January, John F. Kennedy becomes president of the US. In his inaugural address, he famously tells Americans to "ask not what your country can do for you—ask what you can do for your country." The Peace Corps is established in March by President Kennedy, enabling US volunteers to provide international development

◁ **The assassination of Malcolm X**
Civil rights activist Malcolm X was assassinated in 1965 in New York City. He was one of the most significant figures within the US Black nationalist movement.

21

The total duration, in years, of the Vietnam War (1954–1975).

assistance. In April, 1,500 Cuban exiles, backed by the US, invade Cuba's Bay of Pigs in an attempt to topple the Castro regime. The invasion fails; Rafael Trujillo is assassinated. In May, US astronaut Alan Shepard becomes the first American in space, with a suborbital flight in *Freedom 7*. President Kennedy commits the US to placing a man on the Moon and bringing him back safely by 1970. From 1961 to 1964, the Cold War continues as weapons are built on a massive scale and in huge numbers. The arsenal of nuclear weapons in the US increases by 50 percent, as does the number of B-52 bombers used to deliver them. President Kennedy authorizes 23 new Polaris submarines, each of which carries 16 nuclear missiles. Kennedy also calls on cities to construct fallout shelters. The Berlin Crisis begins in June, with President Kennedy refusing to withdraw armed forces from West Berlin. East German leaders order the building of a wall around West Berlin, which will become known as the Berlin Wall.

1962
The Canadian Minister of Citizenship and Immigration, Ellen Fairclough, dismantles the "White Canada" immigration policy during her term, mostly eliminating racial discrimination

in immigration policy that had been in place since 1910. The Trans-Canada Highway is completed in July, stretching some 5,000 miles (8,050 km) across the continent. In October, US intelligence reveals nuclear missile bases under construction in Cuba, causing an international confrontation now known as the Cuban Missile Crisis. President Kennedy sends the US Navy to prevent the delivery of Soviet missiles to Cuba. A deal between President Kennedy and Soviet premier Nikita Khrushchev defuses the crisis and averts a potential nuclear war.

1963
The KKK bombs the 16th Street Baptist church in Birmingham, Alabama, a center of the civil rights movement. Four young Black girls are killed in the blast. The tragedy marks a turning point in the US civil rights movement. At the March on Washington for Jobs and Freedom, a massive peaceful civil rights protest, Martin Luther King Jr. delivers his most famous address, the "I Have a Dream" speech. US environmentalist Rachel Carson publishes *Silent Spring*, an impassioned warning of impending ecological disaster. She kick-starts the environmental movement in the US, which over the next decades involves campaigns against nuclear weapons and power, acid rain, ozone depletion, deforestation, and climate change. It remains vital today. The Partial Test Ban Treaty, signed by the US, USSR, and UK, is the first of many international attempts to limit the threat of nuclear war. On November 22,

President Kennedy is shot and killed while riding in a motorcade through downtown Dallas, Texas. Vice-President Lyndon B. Johnson becomes president.

1964
In June, Papa Doc Duvalier declares himself Haiti's president for life. In the US, a volunteer voter registration campaign called Freedom Summer kicks off in June, bringing dozens of young adults to the South to help register Black voters. In Mississippi, three volunteers are arrested under false pretenses, then murdered by the KKK upon their release, shocking the nation. US President Lyndon B. Johnson pushes through the Civil Rights Act in July despite strong Senate opposition. The act gives the federal government more power to protect citizens against discrimination on the basis of race, religion, sex, or national origin. In August, false reports of an attack by North Vietnam on US forces lead to the Gulf of Tonkin incident. This triggers increased US intervention against North Vietnam in the ongoing Vietnam War.

1965
Operation Rolling Thunder sees an escalation of US involvement in the Vietnam War. The US begins a regular bombing campaign against North Vietnam, and ground troops are sent to Vietnam. By 1969, more than 500,000 US military personnel are stationed there. In March, civil rights protesters attempt three nonviolent marches in Alabama, from Selma to Montgomery. Alabama state police

viciously attack the marchers, including future US Representative John Lewis. Martin Luther King Jr. and many other prominent civil rights leaders join the third and final march. US Marines intervene in the civil war in the Dominican Republic to prevent a communist takeover. Tensions had been running high since supporters of the overthrown president, Juan Bosch, ousted the militarily installed president Donald Reid Cabral from office two years earlier. In the US, Black activist and advocate for Black empowerment, Malcolm X, is assassinated when giving a speech in the Audubon Ballroom in New York. In August, the Voting Rights Act passes, a major step in the civil rights fight. It aims to overcome legal barriers at the state and local levels that prevent Black Americans from exercising their right to vote. President Johnson issues Executive Order 11246, which establishes requirements for nondiscriminatory practices in hiring and employment on the part of US government contractors. In Los Angeles, six days of civil unrest follow a police brutality incident against a Black man. The Watts riots, as they become known, are eventually quelled by the National Guard but are the worst violence seen in Los Angeles until 1992. President Johnson increases the military draft numbers from 17,000 to 35,000 men per month and makes burning a draft card a crime. The antiwar protest movement grows, spurred on by the unfolding military disaster in Vietnam.

◁ **Castro seizes power**
Fidel Castro celebrating with his soldiers in 1959 in Havana, Cuba, after overthrowing Batista's government. Castro began a program of nationalization, centralization, and consolidation.

▷ **Anti-Vietnam War feeling runs high**
By 1970, there was huge opposition to the Vietnam War, especially during periods of intense drafting. Many protesters wore pins such as this one decorated with flowers and peace symbols.

▽ Peace, love, and mud
Despite poor organization, half a million people attended Woodstock music festival in 1968 in Bethel, New York. Performers included Jimi Hendrix, Joe Cocker, and Santana.

1966

1966

After the civil war, Joaquín Balaguer, a close associate of former dictator Rafael Trujillo, is elected president of the Dominican Republic for a second time. His presidency will be marked by violence and terror, with 11,000 people tortured or forcibly "disappeared." However, he also liberalizes the government. As part of the emerging Black Power movement, the Black Panther Party is founded in Oakland, California, to launch a more aggressive campaign for civil rights.

1967

The Equal Rights for Indian Women Association (ERIW) is established in Québec. A provincial organization, ERIW is founded by Mohawk women's rights activist Mary Two-Axe Earley, who is fighting the loss of Indian status suffered by Indigenous women married to non-status Indians. ERIW faces strong resistance from male leaders in First Nations communities. Canada mounts the Expo 67 world's fair as the centerpiece of its centennial celebrations. Sixty-two nations participate in the fair, which sees daily attendance of half a million at times. In October, appointed by President Johnson, Thurgood Marshall becomes the first Black justice of the US Supreme Court. The summer of 1967 becomes known as the Summer of Love. As many as 100,000 people, mostly hippies, converge in San Francisco's Haight-Ashbury neighborhood, which becomes the epicenter of the "free love" movement across the US.

1968

On April 4, Martin Luther King Jr. is assassinated in Memphis, Tennessee, by escaped convict James Earl Ray. The evening before, King preaches that the civil rights movement should go on without him. In Canada, Pierre Trudeau begins 16 almost unbroken years as Liberal leader and prime minister. Former US Attorney General Robert Kennedy—John F. Kennedy's brother and a presidential hopeful—is assassinated by Sirhan Sirhan in the Ambassador Hotel in Los Angeles. In response to police brutality and racial profiling, the American Indian Movement is founded. An urban-focused movement, it grows rapidly in the coming years to become the driving force behind the Indigenous civil rights movement. In October's Tlatelolco Massacre, Mexican security forces and military open fire on people who are protesting the lack of social justice and democracy in Mexico under the ruling PRI party. The massacre takes place in the Tlatelolco Plaza, killing at least 100 people, just 10 days before the Olympic Games open in Mexico. In December, NASA's *Apollo 8* mission becomes the first to orbit the moon.

1969

Republican Richard Nixon becomes the 37th president of the US on his second attempt, having lost to John F. Kennedy in 1960. In a first step toward the internet, the ARPANET goes live, linking computers in four US cities. In June, the Stonewall riots, a series of violent confrontations between police and gay rights activists take place outside the Stonewall Inn, a gay bar in Greenwich Village, New York City. The events of that night become a catalyst for an organized US campaign for gay and lesbian rights. Neil Armstrong, commander of the NASA space mission *Apollo 11*, sets foot on the moon in July and says, "That's one small step for man, one giant leap for mankind." In August, nearly half a million people show up for the Woodstock Music and Art Fair at a dairy farm in Bethel, New York. The three-day festival features many of the era's most popular music acts. In Canada, September's Official Languages Act gives French and English equal status. In November, the Indians of All Tribes, a group of Indigenous American protesters, occupy Alcatraz Island off San Francisco, declaring their intention to use the island for an Indigenous

◁ Unbought and unbossed
A political poster for Shirley Chisholm from 1972 featuring her campaign slogan. She was the first Black woman to be elected to US Congress and became the first woman to run for US president.

school, cultural center, and museum. Armed federal marshals remove the last protesters on June 11, 1971.

1970

In Vietnam, the Viet Minh opposition are hiding out in Cambodia, so US President Nixon sends troops into Cambodia to destroy Viet Minh bases. Back in the US, in May national guards kill four students during an anti–Vietnam War demonstration at Kent State University in Ohio. Later that month, police also kill two students at the all-Black Jackson State College in Mississippi when they fire into a dormitory during a riot. As many as 100,000 demonstrators converge on Washington, D.C., to protest the student killings and Nixon's incursion into Cambodia. A group of Indigenous Americans, led by the San Francisco–based group the United Native Americans, set up camp atop Mount Rushmore to protest the broken Treaty of Fort Laramie. In Canada, the assassination of vice-premier Pierre Laporte by the Front de Libération du Québec triggers what becomes known as the October Crisis, when Prime Minister Trudeau evokes the martial law powers of the War Measures Act to crack down on separatist terrorists in Quebec.

1971

Greenpeace is founded in Canada to campaign against US nuclear testing. In Haiti, Jean-Claude Duvalier, the 19-year-old son of Papa Doc, nicknamed "Baby Doc," succeeds his father as president. He will remain in power until overthrown by a popular uprising in 1986. The Pentagon Papers are published in *The New York Times*, revealing evidence of official deception concerning the US's involvement in Vietnam.

1972

Shirley Chisholm runs for US president. She is the first female candidate for president of the US and, by running to be the Democratic Party's nominee, the first Black American candidate from a major party. In May, the first Strategic Arms Limitation Talks (SALT 1) negotiations are concluded and signed by the US and USSR, including the first treaty to place limits and restraints on ballistic missiles. The Watergate Scandal erupts, causing a constitutional crisis for President Nixon. The scandal stems from the Nixon administration's attempt to cover up its involvement in a break-in at the Democratic National Committee headquarters in the Watergate Building. Nixon helped orchestrate the cover-up and ends up resigning in 1974 before he can be impeached. In another major scandal for the US government, a whistleblower reveals details of the Tuskegee syphilis experiment. This was a program that had run since 1932 in Alabama to study the effects of untreated syphilis among African American men. In October, as part of the Trail of Broken Treaties movement, hundreds of Indigenous Americans drive to Washington, D.C., to demand the recognition of Indigenous tribes, the abolition of the Bureau of Indian Affairs, and federal protections for Indigenous cultures and religions. They occupy the Bureau of Indian Affairs office for a week. In Canada, the Supreme Court rules that the Canadian Bill of Rights does not apply to the Indian Act section which determined Indigenous women married to non-status Indians lose their Indian status.

1973

The Paris Peace Accords ends the US combat role in Vietnam, which did not achieve its objectives and left millions dead. In January, the Calder Case is the first time that Canadian law acknowledges that the Indigenous title to land existed prior to the colonization of the continent and was not merely derived from statutory law. In the US, through *Roe v. Wade*, the Supreme Court establishes that prohibiting abortion violates a woman's right to privacy. In the Wounded Knee Occupation, some 200 Oglala Lakota (Oglala Sioux) and American Indian Movement members seize and occupy the town of Wounded Knee, South Dakota, for 71 days. In October, Arab oil-exporting countries cause an economic crisis by denying oil to western countries supporting Israel, including the US and Canada. The average retail price of a gallon of gasoline rises by 43 percent.

1974

The Canadian province of Quebec introduces Bill 22, which makes French the province's sole official language.

1975

Microsoft is founded in the US by school friends Bill Gates and Paul Allen. By 2022, it will be the world's largest software maker. The Indian Self-Determination and Education Assistance Act is passed in the US. It provides recognition and funds to Indigenous nations who have been disbanded, their people relocated, and land sold.

1976

Huge oil reserves are discovered in the southern Gulf of Mexico. The Cantarell oil field becomes one of the largest in the world, producing more than one million barrels per day by 1981. Jose López Portillo, elected Mexican president in 1976, borrows huge sums of foreign money against this oil to fund a campaign of industrial expansion, social welfare, and high-yield agriculture. But the oil turns out to be low grade, leaving Mexico with the world's largest foreign debt. In the US, Steve Wozniak and Steve Jobs design and market a personal computer, calling it the Apple, and found the technology company of the same name.

1977

The Torrijos–Carter treaties are signed by the US and Panama to provide for the gradual transfer of the Canal Zone from US to Panamanian control.

1978

Starting from Alcatraz Island, California, hundreds of protesters begin the Longest Walk, a transcontinental trek for Indigenous American justice. By the time marchers reach Washington, D.C., five months later, they number 30,000. The American Indian Religious Freedom Act gives Indigenous Americans the right to use certain lands and controlled substances for religious ceremonies.

1979

The partial meltdown of a US nuclear power station at Three Mile Island, near Harrisburg, Pennsylvania, spreads radioactive steam over a large surrounding area.

▷ The rise of technology
In 1976, Steve Jobs, Steve Wozniak, and Ronald Wayne launched Apple Computer, Inc., with the Apple I desktop computer.

GLOBAL NORTH AMERICA 1980–PRESENT

1980

1980

The Mariel boatlift transports 125,000 Cubans (including a large number of Afro-Cubans) to Florida. In the Quebec independence referendum, 60 percent vote against the proposal to request greater independence from Canada; 40 percent vote in favor. In Florida, riots break out in Liberty City, Miami, after police officers are acquitted of the killing of Arthur McDuffie, an unarmed Black man. Fifteen people die in what become known as the Miami riots, the worst the nation had seen since those in Detroit in 1967. The Maine Indian Claims Settlement Act grants Indigenous peoples $81.5 million for land taken from them more than 150 years earlier.

1981

Ronald Reagan is elected US president and prioritizes the "War on Drugs" with the "Just Say No" campaign led by his wife, Nancy. After 444 days, the Iran hostage crisis ends with the release of 52 US diplomats, staff, and citizens who had been taken hostage in the US embassy in Tehran in 1979. A military operation to rescue the hostages the previous year had failed,

8

Number of US servicemen killed during the Iranian hostage crisis.

leaving eight US servicemen dead. The US space agency, NASA, returns to space with the launch of its first shuttle mission. Doctors discover clusters of patients with rare cancers and pneumonia among gay men in San Francisco, New York, and Los Angeles. The new disease is named acquired immune deficiency syndrome (AIDS). Due to its initial prominence in the gay community, homophobia prevents it from being properly acknowledged, studied, and treated for many years.

1982

The Constitution Act of 1982 amends the Canadian Constitution to recognize and affirm Indigenous land and treaty rights. Section 37 of the constitution is also subsequently amended, obligating the federal and provincial governments to consult with Indigenous peoples on outstanding issues. Leaders from Canada's Indigenous groups form the Assembly of First Nations (AFN) from the National Indian Brotherhood. The AFN aims to promote the interests of First Nations. In the US, Sun Myung Moon, founder of the Unification Church (whose members are also called "Moonies"), is convicted of tax fraud and imprisoned. Mexican president José López Portillo nationalizes the banking industry. Mexico renegotiates its external debt with the International Monetary Fund. The agreement requires all public industry to be privatized, removes subsidies, shrinks and eliminates import taxes, and increases foreign investment.

1983

President Reagan proposes a Strategic Defense Initiative (SDI) against nuclear attack, which is given the nickname "Star Wars" after the movie. The US invades Grenada when President Reagan sends marines to depose the nation's communist rulers after the execution of the prime minister, Maurice Bishop.

1984

Because of the South Florida Drug Task Force's successful crackdown on drugs, traffickers turn to Mexican marijuana smugglers to move cocaine across the US-Mexican border. By the mid-1980s, this has become the major transit route for cocaine into the US. The Inuvialuit people and the Canadian federal government sign the Inuvialuit Final Agreement, a massive Western Arctic land claim. An earthquake in Mexico City causes 10,000 deaths and $3 billion–$4 billion in damage.

1986

President Reagan launches an air strike against Libya, accusing Libyan leader Muammar Gaddafi of involvement in international terrorism. The space shuttle *Challenger* breaks apart shortly after take-off, killing all seven crew members aboard, including Christa McAuliffe, an American schoolteacher who joined the group as part of NASA's "Teacher in Space" program. Many schoolchildren watch the disaster unfold on live TV. The Iran-Contra affair is uncovered, revealing that between 1981 and 1986, the Reagan administration had been covertly allowing the illegal sale of arms to Iran, which was subject to an arms embargo at the time. The administration had hoped to divert the proceeds to fund the Contras, anticommunist insurgents fighting the Marxist provisional government in Nicaragua. However, this contravened the Boland Amendment, which US Congress had passed in 1984, banning US military aid to the Contras.

1987

The US Congress begins an investigation into the Iran-Contra affair, eventually clearing President Reagan of direct involvement. In October, the US stock market collapses, with the Dow Jones index losing 22 percent of its value in one day—later dubbed Black Monday.

1988

In July, Mexico holds its first presidential election since the Institutional Revolutionary Party (PRI) took power in 1929. Carlos Salinas de Gortari of the PRI is elected president in what is widely seen as a rigged election. The true results are never made public.

1989

In response to the 1988 election in Mexico, the Party of the Democratic Revolution (PRD) is established. The supertanker *Exxon Valdez* spills 11 million tons (more than 12 million metric tons) of oil in Prince William Sound, Alaska. More than 1,300 miles

◁ **Spaceflight disasters**
After the loss of *Challenger* in 1986, *Columbia* (pictured) carried out repeated missions but broke up upon reentry in 2003, killing all seven crew members on board.

(nearly 3,000 km) of coastline are affected, and the ecology of the region is devastated.

1990
Drug companies begin pushing the use of highly addictive opioids for the treatment of chronic pain, marking the start of the "opioid crisis." The number of deaths from opioid overdoses will increase every decade. US troops capture Panama's dictator, Manuel Noriega, and take him to Miami on drug trafficking charges. He will be convicted in 1992. The Meech Lake Accord collapses after Indigenous leaders refuse to ratify it due to its failure to provide for Indigenous people. A siege begins at Oka, Québec, when police attempt to storm a barricade erected by the Mohawk people to block the expansion of a golf course. In the wake of this,

the Royal Commission on Aboriginal Peoples is set up to study the relationship between Indigenous peoples, the government, and Canadian society. In August, the Gulf War begins after Iraq invades Kuwait. The US launches Operation Desert Shield, a buildup of US and Allied forces from a coalition of 25 other NATO countries.

1991
Operation Desert Storm, an aerial bombing campaign against Iraq, results

in the liberation of Kuwait by February. The splitting of the USSR signals the end of the Cold War. Relations thaw between the US, under President Reagan, and the USSR, led by Mikhail Gorbachev.

1992
Riots in Los Angeles follow the acquittal of policemen who were recorded beating Rodney King in 1991. Mexico, Canada, and the US sign the North American Free Trade Agreement (NAFTA), which results in an enormous increase in legitimate trade across the US-Mexico border. The agreement is controversial in Mexico, and opposed by the leftist party, the PRD, which begins to win increasing support.

1993
In the Waco Siege, 82 Branch Davidians—members of a religious cult

led by David Koresh—burn to death in their Waco, Texas, headquarters to avoid surrendering to law enforcement officials, four of whom are also killed. In the Canadian parliament, the separatist Bloc Québécois becomes the official opposition party. Mayans in rural Chiapas stage an armed uprising against the Mexican government.

1994
Two leading members of Mexico's ruling party, the PRI, Luis Donaldo Colosio Murrieta and José Francisco Ruiz Massieu, are assassinated. A remaining PRI candidate, Ernesto Zedillo Ponce de Leon, is elected president and immediately faces a banking crisis when the value of the Mexican peso plunges in international markets. The US loans Mexico $20 billion, which helps stabilize its currency.

▷ Panic in the stock market
The front page of the *New York Daily News* from October 20, 1987, which broke the news of the stock market's dramatic plummet the day before, on so-called Black Monday.

△ Earthquake devastation
People had to flee for their lives during an earthquake in Mexico in September 1985. The earthquake caused 10,000 deaths and catastrophic damage to buildings in Mexico City.

1995

A massive bomb destroys federal buildings in Oklahoma City, killing 168 people on the second anniversary of the Waco Siege. Terry Nichols and Timothy McVeigh, who hold anti-government views and want to avenge those killed in Waco, are later convicted and McVeigh is executed. Louis Farrakhan's Nation of Islam organizes a Million Man March into Washington, D.C. More than 500,000 Black men gather to promote racial unity and family values and to combat negative racial stereotypes. In Canada, two incidents of First Nations activism in British Columbia garner national attention. Indigenous Upper Nicola people block roads leading into Douglas Lake Ranch, while a stand-off occurs between Ts'peten Defenders and their allies and the Royal Canadian Mounted Police at Gustafsen Lake. Both end peacefully. In the Second Quebec referendum, 51 percent vote no on independence.

1996

The final report from the Royal Commission on Aboriginal Peoples states that many of the 1876 Indian Act's measures were oppressive. It notes that "Recognition as 'Indian' in Canadian law often had nothing to do with whether a person was actually of Indian ancestry."

1998

US cruise missiles attack al-Qaeda bases in Afghanistan and a suspected chemical factory in Khartoum. US president Bill Clinton denies having an inappropriate relationship with a White House intern, Monica Lewinsky, saying, "I did not have sexual relations with that woman, Ms. Lewinsky." He later admits that he did.

1999

The US Senate begins an impeachment trial of President Clinton for perjury and obstruction. President Clinton escapes impeachment. Two teenage boys open fire in Columbine High School in Littleton, Colorado, murdering 13 people, including one teacher. Bombs that they planned to use to destroy survivors fleeing the building fail to detonate. The massacre sparks a national debate about gun control and ownership in the US. Despite later copycat massacres, the issue is still unresolved. A Nunavut semiautonomous territory is created for the Inuit from central and eastern portions of the Northwest Territories. The Supreme Court of Canada rules that treaties from the 1760s guaranteed Mi'kmaq people the rights to fish, hunt, and log year-round. The ruling sparks controversy, as the Mi'kmaq begin to fish lobster out of season. Angry non-Indigenous fishermen destroy lobster traps and other equipment, sink a boat, and carry out an armed blockade of Yarmouth Harbor, Nova Scotia. The conflict ends when an agreement is reached that allows the Mi'kmaq to fish for subsistence only. The Canadian House of Commons votes 217–48 in favor of a bill that would give the Nisga'a of northwest British Columbia the right to self-government. The band receive 800 square miles (2,000 km^2) of land and C$190 million. In return they agree to pay taxes and relinquish future claims.

2000

Vicente Fox, of the opposition Partido de Acción Nacional (PAN), is elected as Mexican president, ending more than 70 years of PRI rule. Fox focuses on improving trade relations with the US, calming civil unrest, and reducing corruption, crime, and drug trafficking. Later, with reforms slowing and his opponents gaining ground, Fox will also

 Territorial flag
Adopted in 1999, the official flag of Nunavut features a sacred stone monument. The colors represent the land, sea, and sky and the North star is also represented.

2008

face large-scale protests by farmers frustrated with the inequalities of the NAFTA trade agreement.

2001

Osama bin Laden, leader of the Islamic extremist group al-Qaeda, masterminds massive terror attacks in the US on September 11. Islamic militants hijack four planes, two of which are flown into the World Trade Center towers in Manhattan. Another is flown into the Pentagon building in Washington, D.C., and the fourth crashes into farmland in rural Western Pennsylvania when passengers rebel and try to overpower the hijackers, who had intended to fly it into the Capitol Building. Almost 3,000 people die in the attacks. President George W. Bush declares a war on terrorism that draws the US into multiple conflicts. In British Columbia, the tribal council of the Nuu-chah-nulth, the largest Indigenous group in the province, agree to a treaty with the provincial and federal governments, giving the group more autonomy over its territories and a large one-time payment. The giant Texas energy company Enron files for bankruptcy after disclosure of major accountancy fraud. In October, the US invades Afghanistan and topples the Taliban, ending their protection of al-Qaeda. The war in Afghanistan will continue for two decades. Richard Reid, a British terrorist linked to al-Qaeda, tries to bring down a Paris-Miami flight but fails to light the explosive in his shoe. Screening of passengers' shoes becomes standard on commercial flights.

2002

The US begins to detain suspected al-Qaeda terrorists in Guantanamo Bay, a US military base in Cuba, indefinitely and often without legal rights.

2003

Marking the beginning of the eight-year Second Gulf War, the US and several coalition allies invade Iraq and oust President Saddam Hussein, triggering widespread protests. Bush's administration justifies the invasion as necessary to prevent Hussein from developing weapons of mass destruction, but these claims are later revealed to be false.

2004

A social networking site, Facebook, is formed by Harvard college friends Mark Zuckerberg, Andrew McCollum, Dustin Moskovitz, Eduardo Saverin, and Chris Hughes. In Iraq, the US suffers 95 casualties in the Second Battle of Fallujah, the deadliest battle for US troops since Vietnam. The al-Qaeda fighters are largely defeated but small-scale attacks later multiply across Iraq. Massachusetts becomes the first US state to legalize same-sex marriage.

2005

Hurricane Katrina brings flooding and chaos to New Orleans and other coastal areas, and kills more than 1,500. The Bush administration is widely criticized for its ineffective handling of the disaster.

445

Cost to the US taxpayer in millions of dollars to keep the remaining 40 detainees held in Guantanamo Bay.

2006

Felipe Calderón of PAN wins the Mexican presidency with 36 percent of the vote (less than one percentage point over the PRD's Andrés Manuel López Obrador). In his first months in office, Calderón moves away from the pro-business, free-trade promises of his campaign, expressing his desire to address some of the issues of poverty and social injustice championed by the PRD. Twitter, a social media site, is launched and soon develops a role as an important source for breaking news and political stories, allowing citizen journalists to report almost instantaneously from the site of incidents. The Mexican drug war begins, when the government launches Operation Michoacán against the Familia Michoacana, a cartel and organized crime syndicate. It aims to reduce violence and dismantle the drug cartels, and is a joint effort involving the Secretariats of Defense, Navy, and Public Security and the Attorney General's Office. Years of fighting follow. The US Supreme Court rules that the military courts set up to try detainees in Guantanamo Bay are illegal. Nancy Pelosi becomes the first female Speaker of the US House of Representatives in the country's history. She leads the Democratic majority in the House.

2007

The US and Mexico jointly announce the Mérida Initiative, a multi-year security cooperation agreement through which the US government will provide financial assistance, equipment, training, and intelligence to Mexico and other Central American countries to help them fight drug trafficking, transnational organized crime, and money laundering. The Great Recession begins, lasting into 2008. It is triggered in part by the subprime mortgage crisis, which saw US homes abruptly decline in price after the collapse of a housing bubble (in which home values were artificially inflated). At Virginia Tech, an undergraduate student kills 32 and wounds 17 others in a shooting with semiautomatic pistols. It is the deadliest killing on a college campus.

2008

The Dow Jones index suffers its largest ever one-day fall, of 777 points, when the US House of Representatives rejects an emergency package proposed by President Bush. In Canada, the Truth and Reconciliation Commission releases a damning report into the country's residential school system for Indigenous children, which had been administered by the Catholic Church. With testimony from survivors, families, and

KEEP HOPE ALIVE ★ OBAMA · PRESIDENT · 2008 ★

◁ **Two-time winner**
Campaign buttons were produced for the Democratic presidential candidate Barack Obama, who was elected in 2008 and again in 2012, with Joe Biden as his vice-president.

communities, the report reveals shocking systemic abuse that amounts to cultural genocide. It concludes that at least 4,100 students died at the schools. In November, Barack Obama is elected on the Democratic ticket to become the first Black president of the United States. Joe Biden is elected vice-president.

2009
The World Health Organization declares that "swine flu" (strain H1N1) spreading from Mexico has reached the status of a pandemic. US president Obama signs an order that the Guantanamo Bay detention camp is to be closed within a year; it remains open.

2010
In Haiti, a 7.0 magnitude earthquake kills 230,000 and causes huge damage to buildings. In the Gulf of Mexico, an explosion destroys British Petroleum's Deepwater Horizon oil rig, killing 11 and starting the largest oil spill in US history. Federal estimates are that more than 210 million gallons (795 million l) of oil have spilled into the sea from the disaster. A massive restructuring plan for health care in the US, the Affordable Care Act (also known as Obamacare), is passed by Congress and signed into law by President Obama.

2011
The architect of the 9/11 terrorist attacks, Osama bin Laden, is shot and killed by elite US naval forces in Pakistan. Having gradually reduced its military presence in Iraq over the past four years, the US formally withdraws its troops, ending the Iraq War.

2012
In Florida, Trayvon Martin, an unarmed 17-year-old Black American high school student walking home after buying candy, is killed by a vigilante, George Zimmerman. When Zimmerman is acquitted under Florida's Stand Your Ground law, protests occur across the country. At Sandy Hook Elementary School, in Newtown, Connecticut, a gunman shoots 26 people, including 20 young children, again sparking a national conversation about gun control and mental illness. Hurricane Sandy, a Category 3 Atlantic storm, causes $70 billion in damage and kills 233 people. Four Canadian women start Idle No More as a national (and online) movement of marches and teach-ins, raising awareness of Indigenous rights and advocating for self-determination.

2013
US National Security Agency employee Edward Snowden releases classified documents to journalists concerning mass surveillance by the agency. His actions prompt a national discussion about spying and privacy. In Canada, severe floods in Alberta displace more than 100,000 people. Thirty-two states of local emergency are declared in the region.

2014
The terrorist group ISIS begins its offensive in northern Iraq, leading to intervention in Iraq and Syria by a US-led coalition. In Canada, the National Operational

"Justice has been done."

PRESIDENT BARACK OBAMA IN MAY 2011, AFTER US TROOPS KILL OSAMA BIN LADEN

Review on Missing and Murdered Aboriginal Women is established and identifies 1,181 missing and murdered Indigenous women and girls in police databases. The final report, released in 2019, will reveal that persistent and deliberate human rights violations are the source of Canada's staggering rates of violence against Indigenous women, girls, and LGBTQ+ people.

2015
In Charleston, South Carolina, a white supremacist shoots and kills nine Black people during a Bible study at Emanuel African Methodist Episcopal Church.

KEEP IT IN THE GROUND

2016
US troops withdraw from Afghanistan after 15 years. One of the most powerful drug traffickers in the world, El Chapo, is captured in Mexico. The Supreme Court of Canada rules unanimously that the legal definition of "Indian"—as laid out in the Constitution—includes Métis and non-status Indigenous people. While this ruling does not grant Indian status to those people, it helps to facilitate possible negotiations over traditional land rights and access to education and health programs. Indigenous people gather in North Dakota to protest the Dakota Access Pipeline, which runs through Indigenous lands in the Dakotas, Iowa, and Illinois. Although the US courts will eventually rule against the pipeline, it remains in operation while decisions are appealed. In Orlando, Florida, a man murders 49 people in a homophobic attack on the Pulse Nightclub. The event is classified as a hate crime. Real estate developer and reality television star Donald Trump is elected president.

2017
The US outlines demands for a renegotiated North American Free Trade Agreement. While the Mexican government fights to save NAFTA during talks in Washington, thousands of Mexican farmers and workers protest, demanding the deal be scrapped. The Puebla earthquake damages the Mexican states of Puebla and Morelos and the Greater Mexico City area. More than 6,000 are injured. Allegations emerge of hundreds of incidents of sexual abuse against film producer Harvey Weinstein.

▷ **Placard plea**
Protests led by Indigenous people against the Dakota Access Pipeline began in 2016 amid concerns about its environmental impact, including its potential to cause an oil spill, and threats to sacred lands and artifacts.

This leads to a wave of similar accusations from within Hollywood and other areas of primarily the English-speaking world in what becomes known as the "#Me Too" movement. It raises awareness worldwide of sexual harassment and abuse. The Supreme Court of Canada rules that Indigenous peoples do not have the power to veto resource development projects such as pipelines. The Chippewas of the Thames First Nation had appealed the approval of a modification to a pipeline which runs through Chippewa territory near London, Ontario. Later the Energy East Pipeline Project is canceled in a victory for Indigenous communities. At Marjory Stoneman Douglas High School in Florida, 17 people are murdered by a student in the February 14 Parkland shooting. This triggers the March for Our Lives in 900 locations worldwide.

2018

Populist candidate Andrés Manuel López Obrador is elected president of Mexico. He wants to challenge "elites," boost the military, and concentrate power in the executive while undermining checks and balances. US President Trump meets North Korean dictator Kim Jong Un and becomes the first sitting US president to set foot in North Korea. The Camp Fire rages through California, killing 85 people and destroying 240 square miles (621 km²). It is the deadliest and most expensive wildfire in California's history.

2019

US president Trump is impeached over allegations of abuse of power and obstruction of Congress related to his dealings with Ukraine. He is acquitted by the US Senate.

2020

The COVID-19 pandemic reaches North America. It will kill more than 7 million people worldwide. The US government launches Operation Warp Speed to produce effective vaccines by the end of the year, scaling up to wide availability in 2021. The murder of George Floyd, an unarmed Black man, by Minneapolis police sparks protests in the US and worldwide in the "Black Lives Matter" movement. Joe Biden wins the US presidency, but Donald Trump leads a fraudulent effort to prevent official recognition of his defeat, culminating in domestic terrorists using violence to block the certification of the election results.

2021

In the January 6 insurrection, supporters of President Trump violently attack the US Capitol Building, leading to five deaths. Many elected officials, including Vice-President Mike Pence, have to barricade themselves or flee from the invaders for safety. Hundreds of people involved will be arrested in the coming years. On January 13, Trump is impeached a second time, although he is acquitted again after his trial. President Biden is sworn in, along with Kamala Harris, who is the first Black, first Asian-American, and first female vice-president. In Canada, hundreds of unmarked graves are found in the grounds of two former residential schools. British Columbia will commit millions of dollars to help First Nations communities search for more residential school graves. The annual Canada Day celebrations on Parliament Hill are replaced this year by a "Cancel Canada Day" rally, organized by Idle No More and the Anishinaabe nation and attended by thousands. Inuk leader Mary Simon becomes Canada's first Indigenous governor general. Haitian President Jovenel Moïse is assassinated in a midnight attack by unknown mercenaries. An earthquake in Haiti kills more than 2,000 people. The US, UK, and Australia sign a trilateral security partnership for the Indo-Pacific region.

2022

The US Supreme Court overturns the constitutional protection for abortion confirmed in *Roe v. Wade* (1973). Abortion is made illegal in many states.

△ **Solidarity for survivors**
Several hundred survivors of sexual abuse, harassment, and assault marched with their supporters in Hollywood in 2017 as part of the #Me Too movement.

INDEX

The main information is shown in **bold** page numbers. Cities and place names in the United States and Canada can be found under the entry for the State or Province.

ACKNOWLEDGMENTS

Dorling Kindersley would like to thank the following people for their help in the preparation of this book: Ekta Chadha and Janet Mohun for editorial assistance; Vaibhav Rastogi for design assistance; Aditya Katyal for picture research assistance; Mrinmoy Mazumdar for technical assistance; Patricia McCormack for additional consulting; Priyanka Lamichhane and Michaela Weglinksi for fact checking; Joy Evatt for proofreading; and Elizabeth Wise for indexing.

The publisher would like to thank the following for their kind permission to reproduce their photographs:

(Key: a-above; b-below/bottom; c-center; f-far; l-left; r-right; t-top)

2 Dorling Kindersley: Lynton Gardiner / American Museum of Natural History (c). **10-11 Alamy Stock Photo:** Gary Whitton. **12 Alamy Stock Photo:** Granger—Historical Picture Archive (cl); Dan Leeth (tl). **13 Dreamstime.com:** Sean Pavone (cr). **Los Angeles County Museum of Art:** Gift of the 2003 Collectors Committee (M.2003.44) (tl). **14 Getty Images / iStock:** MasterLu (cr). **16 Getty Images / iStock:** Calvin Jennings (bl). **18 Copyright Kenneth Garrett** (bc). **19 Shutterstock.com:** Josemar Franco (bl). **20-21 Alamy Stock Photo:** Gary Whitton (t). **20 Dreamstime.com:** W.scott Mcgill (br). **21 Blackwater Draw Museum Photo Archives at Eastern. New Mexico University.** (br). **22 Dorling Kindersley:** Gary Ombler / University of Pennsylvania Museum of Archaeology and Anthropology (tr). **24-25 Alamy Stock Photo:** Science History Images / Photo Researchers (l). **25 Alamy Stock Photo:** Granger—Historical Picture Archive (cra); Tom Till (br). **26 Getty Images:** De Agostini / Dea / G. Cappelli (tc). **27 Dorling Kindersley:** Gary Ombler / University of Pennsylvania Museum of Archaeology and Anthropology (cr). **28 Alamy Stock Photo:** Retro AdArchives (clb). **The Cleveland Museum Of Art:** Gift of James C. Gruener in memory of his wife, Florence Crowell Gruener / 1983.190 (ca). **29 Alamy Stock Photo:** The Granger Collection (cr). **National Museum of the American Indian, Smithsonian Institution:** 10 / 3534 (tr). **30 Alamy Stock Photo:** The Picture Art Collection (bc). **31 Alamy Stock Photo:** Photo12 / Ann Ronan Picture Library (tr). **32 Alamy Stock Photo:** Peter Horree (tl). **34-35 Library of Congress, Washington, D.C.:** Codex Azcatitlan. [Place of Publication Not Identified: Publisher Not Identified, 1530] Pdf. https://www.loc.gov/item/2021668122/. (t). **34 Alamy Stock Photo:** World History Archive (br). **35 Alamy Stock Photo:** Granger—Historical Picture Archive (br). **36 Getty Images:** Universal Images Group / Werner Forman (tl). **37 Alamy Stock Photo:** Classic Image (br). **38 Library of Congress, Washington, D.C.:** L. Prang & Co. Columbus Taking Possession of the New Country. Bahamas San Salvador Island, 1893. Boston, U.S.A.: Published by the Prang Educational Co. Photograph. https://www.loc.gov/item/91481671/. (br). **39 Bridgeman Images:** NPL—DeA Picture Library (br). **40 Alamy Stock Photo:** Jimlop collection (bl). **40-41 Getty Images:** De Agostini / Dea Picture Library. **42-43 Alamy Stock Photo:** North Wind Picture Archives. **44 Alamy Stock Photo:** Heritage Image Partnership Ltd / Fine Art Images (cla); history_docu_photo (cr). **45 Alamy Stock Photo:** The Print Collector / Heritage Images (cra). **Getty Images:** Hulton Archive / Heritage Images (tl). **46 Alamy Stock Photo:** Granger—Historical Picture Archive (bl). **47 Alamy Stock Photo:** Chico Sanchez (br). **48-49 Library of Congress, Washington, D.C.:** Homann, Johann Baptist, and Homann Erben. Regni Mexicani seu Novæ Hispaniæ, Floridæ, Novæ Angliæ, Carolinæ, Virginiæ, et Pennsylvaniæ, nec non insvlarvm archipelagi Mexicani in America septentrionali. [Noribergæ Homann Erben, 1759] Map. https://www.loc.gov/item/74690812/.. **50 Alamy Stock Photo:** The Picture Art Collection (cla). **51 Getty Images:** Hulton Archive / Print Collector / Ann Ronan Pictures (cr). **52-53 Getty Images:** De Agostini / Dea Picture Library. **54-55 Alamy Stock Photo:** The Picture Art Collection. **56 Alamy Stock Photo:** Lebrecht Music & Arts (bc). **57 Alamy Stock Photo:** Granger—Historical Picture Archive (br). **58 Alamy Stock Photo:** The Granger Collection (cr). **59 Alamy Stock Photo:** Glasshouse Images / JT Vintage (cla); incamerastock / ICP (cb). **National Museum of the American Indian, Smithsonian Institution:** 5 / 3150 (t). **60-61 Alamy Stock Photo:** Granger—Historical Picture Archive. **62-63 Alamy Stock Photo:** Granger—Historical Picture Archive. **64-65 Alamy Stock Photo:** Science History Images. **66-67 Library of Congress, Washington, D.C.:** Highsmith, Carol M, photographer. First floor WPA mural at elevator at the U.S. Courthouse, Albuquerque, New Mexico. United States Albuquerque New Mexico, 2013. April. Photograph. https://www.loc.gov/item/2013634301/. (t). **66 Alamy Stock Photo:** CMA / BOT (br). **67 Alamy Stock Photo:** Carver Mostardi (br). **69 Alamy Stock Photo:** The Granger Collection (tr). **70-71 Library of Congress, Washington, D.C.:** Fer, Nicolas De. La Californie ou Nouvelle Caroline: teatro de los trabajos, Apostolicos de la Compa. e Jesus en la America Septe. [Paris: N. de Fer, 1720] Map. https://www.loc.gov/item/98687119/. (l). **72 Alamy Stock Photo:** World History Archive (cl). **73 Alamy Stock Photo:** Science History Images (br). **74-75 Alamy Stock Photo:** North Wind Picture Archives (r). **74 Alamy Stock Photo:** VTR (bc). **National Museum of the American Indian, Smithsonian Institution:** 11 / 1317 (cla). **76 Yale Center for British Art, Paul Mellon Collection:** B1981.25.74 (tr). **77 Alamy Stock Photo:** World History Archive (br). **78-79 Library of Congress, Washington, D.C.:** A new map of North America, shewing the advantages obtain'd therein to England by the peace. [London: Royal Magazine, May, 1763] Map. https://www.loc.gov/item/2015591095/.. **80-81 Alamy Stock Photo:** Everett Collection Inc / Ron Harvey. **82 Getty Images:** Hulton Fine Art Collection / Culture Club (tl). **The Metropolitan Museum of Art:** Gift of John Stewart Kennedy, 1897 (cl). **83 Alamy Stock Photo:** The Granger Collection (crb). **Getty Images:** Hulton Archive / Print Collector / Ann Ronan Pictures (t). **84-85 Alamy Stock Photo:** Everett Collection Inc / Ron Harvey. **86-87 Alamy Stock Photo:** The Granger Collection (r). **86 Alamy Stock Photo:** North Wind Picture Archives (cla). **Bridgeman Images:** New-York Historical Society (bc). **88-89 Library of Congress, Washington, D.C.:** Bowles, Carington. North America, and the West Indies; a new map, wherein the British Empire and its limits, according to the definitive treaty of peace, in , are accurately described, and the dominions possessed by the Spaniards, the French, & other European States. The whole compiled from all the new surveys, and authentic memoirs that have hitherto appeared. [London, 1774] Map. https://www.loc.gov/item/74694268/.. **90 National Museum of American History / Smithsonian Institution:** Harry T. Peters "America on Stone" Lithography Collection (bc). **91 Alamy Stock Photo:** IanDagnall Computing (cr). **92 Dreamstime.com:** Rosemarie Mosteller (br). **94-95 The New York Public Library:** Lionel Pincus and Princess Firyal Map Division, The New York Public Library. "An accurate map of the United States of America : according to the Treaty of Peace of 1783." The New York Public Library Digital Collections. 1794-10. https://digitalcollections.nypl.org/items/510d47da-f0ce-a3d9-e040-e00a18064a99. **97 Alamy Stock Photo:** Darling Archive (br); Granger—Historical Picture Archive (tl). **98-99 123RF.com:** sergeyussr. **100 Alamy Stock Photo:** ARTGEN (br). **101 Alamy Stock Photo:** LM / BT (tr). **102 Alamy Stock Photo:** Penta Springs Limited / Artokoloro (cra). **Bridgeman Images:** Peter Newark Pictures (clb). **103 Alamy Stock Photo:** Greg Vaughn (tl). **National Museum of American History / Smithsonian Institution:** (cr). **104 Alamy Stock Photo:** Penta Springs Limited / Artokoloro (tl). **105 Alamy Stock Photo:** Granger—Historical Picture Archive (br). **106-107 Alamy Stock Photo:** piemags / DCM. **108 Alamy Stock Photo:** YA / BOT (bc). **108-109 Alamy Stock Photo:** Everett Collection Inc / Ron Harvey (r). **110-111 Bibliothèque nationale de France, Paris:** ark: / 12148 / btv1b53006821k. **112-113 Library of Congress, Washington, D.C.:** Sebree, William. Plan of Fort Meigs' and its environs: compricing sic the operations of the American forces, under Genl. W.H. Harrison, and the British Army and their allies, under Genl. Proctor and Tecumseh. [1813] Map. https://www.loc.gov/item/2004625488/.. **114-115 Alamy Stock Photo:** Granger—Historical Picture Archive (l). **115 Alamy Stock Photo:** Art Collection 3 (br); Granger—Historical Picture Archive (ca). **116-117 Library of Congress, Washington, D.C.:** Genthe, Arnold, photographer. In front of the Joss House, Chinatown, San Francisco. , None. Between 1896 and 1906. Photograph. https://www.loc.gov/item/2018704928/.. **118 Alamy Stock Photo:** Sutters Mill (cr). **The US National Archives and Records Administration:** 306420 (tl). **119 Alamy Stock Photo:** The Picture Art Collection (cr). **© The Trustees of the British Museum. All rights reserved:** (tl). **120 National Museum of the American Indian, Smithsonian Institution:** 27 / 40 (bl). **121 Alamy Stock Photo:** Science History Images / Photo Researchers (br). **122-123 David Rumsey Map Collection, David Rumsey Map Center, Stanford Libraries:** 0373049. **123 Alamy Stock Photo:** North Wind Picture Archives (tr). **124-125 Library of Congress, Washington, D.C.:** Pughe, J. S. , Artist. His foresight/J.S. Pughe. Europe, 1901. N.Y.: J. Ottmann Lith. Co., Puck Bldg., October 9. Photograph. https://www.loc.gov/item/2010651471/.. **125 Alamy Stock Photo:** The Granger Collection (br); Pictures Now (cra). **126 Library of Congress, Washington, D.C.:** Crofutt, George A. American Progress. , ca. 1873. Photograph. https://www.loc.gov/item/97507547/. (bc). **126-127 David Rumsey Map Collection, David Rumsey Map Center, Stanford Libraries:** 2439000. **128 Bridgeman Images:** The Stapleton Collection (bl). **129 Library of Congress, Washington, D.C.:** Mitchell, Edward H., Publisher. Chief Washakie. United States, None. [San francisco: edward h. mitchell, publisher, between 1900 and 1920] Photograph. https://www.loc.gov/item/2016653228/. (br). **130-131 Bridgeman Images:** Philadelphia History Museum at the Atwater Kent / Courtesy of Historical Society of Pennsylvania Collection. **132-133 David Rumsey Map Collection, David Rumsey Map Center, Stanford Libraries:** 5024001. **134-135 Alamy Stock Photo:** Everett Collection Historical (l). **135 Alamy Stock Photo:** Granger—Historical Picture Archive (br). **National Museum of American History / Smithsonian Institution:** Adriana Scalamandre Bitter and Edwin Ward Bitter for the Bitter Family Collection (cra). **136-137 Library of Congress, Washington, D.C.:** Norris, William, and Daniel K Minor. Map of the railroads and canals, finished, unfinished, and in contemplation, in the United States. New York: Railroad Journal, 1834. Map. https://www.loc.gov/item/96688053/.. **136 Alamy Stock Photo:** YA / BOT (bc). **138-139 Library of Congress, Washington, D.C.:** Zamora, Rafael, and Vincente Quiroga. Croquis del terro, camino, bosques, barrancas, cerro y beredas de Cerro-gordo con las posiciones de las topas Mejicanas y Americanas con sus respectivos Generales Cuerpos y Baterias el dis 18 de Abril de. [1847] Map. https://www.loc.gov/item/gm72002050/.. **140 Courtesy of the California History Room, California State Library, Sacramento, California.** (tr). **141 Alamy Stock Photo:** Science History Images / Photo Researchers (br). **142-143 Library of Congress, Washington, D.C.:** Genthe, Arnold, photographer. In front of the Joss House, Chinatown, San Francisco. , None. Between 1896 and 1906. Photograph. https://www.loc.gov/item/2018704928/. (l). **143 Alamy Stock Photo:** World Archive (br). **144 Getty Images:** Bettmann (bl). **145 Getty Images:** Nextrecord Archives (br). **146 Alamy Stock Photo:** Science History Images (bc). **146-147 Alamy Stock Photo:** Archive World (r). **148-149 Alamy Stock Photo:** Chronicle (t). **149 Alamy Stock Photo:** Historic Images (br). **150-151 Library of Congress, Washington, D.C.:** Currier & Ives, Publisher, and Parsons & Atwater.

The City of Chicago/sketched & drawn on stone by Parsons & Atwater. United States Chicago Illinois, ca. 1874. New York: Published by Currier & Ives. Photograph. https://www.loc.gov/item/90715977/.. **152 Alamy Stock Photo:** North Wind Picture Archives (cl); YA / BOT (cra). **153 Alamy Stock Photo:** Niday Picture Library (tl, crb). **154 Alamy Stock Photo:** UPI (tl). **155 Alamy Stock Photo:** North Wind Picture Archives (br). **156-157 David Rumsey Map Collection, David Rumsey Map Center, Stanford Libraries:** 3236001. **159 Getty Images:** Moment / mikroman6 (tr). **160 Alamy Stock Photo:** Archive Images (tl). **161 Alamy Stock Photo:** Granger—Historical Picture Archive (br). **162-163 Alamy Stock Photo:** Wetdryvac. **164 Alamy Stock Photo:** piemags / CMB (bc). **165 Alamy Stock Photo:** History and Art Collection (tr). **166-167 Library of Congress, Washington, D.C.:** Bermuda Hundred, Va. African-American teamsters near the signal tower. United States Virginia Bermuda Hundred, 1864. Photograph. https://www.loc.gov/item/2018666610/. (r). **166 Bridgeman Images:** (cl). **Library of Congress, Washington, D.C.:** Moore, Henry P, photographer. Sweet potato planting, Hopkinson's Plantation. South Carolina Edisto Island, 1862. [April 8] Photograph. https://www.loc.gov/item/2010651644/. (bc). **168-169 The New York Public Library:** Schomburg Center for Research in Black Culture, Jean Blackwell Hutson Research and Reference Division, The New York Public Library. "Status of slavery in the United States, 1775-1865" The New York Public Library Digital Collections. 1893. https://digitalcollections.nypl.org/items/510d47df-fd18-a3d9-e040-e00a18064a99. **170 The New York Public Library:** The Miriam and Ira D. Wallach Division of Art, Prints and Photographs: Photography Collection, The New York Public Library. "15th Amendment, or the Darkey's millenium: 40 acres of land and a mule." The New York Public Library Digital Collections. 1850—1930. https://digitalcollections.nypl.org/items/510d47e0-121c-a3d9-e040-e00a18064a99 (bc). **171 Library of Congress, Washington, D.C.:** Waud, Alfred R. , Artist. "The first vote"/AW monogram ; drawn by A.R. Waud. , 1867. Photograph. https://www.loc.gov/item/00651117/. (tr). **172 Alamy Stock Photo:** Niday Picture Library (cra). **The Metropolitan Museum of Art:** Gift of Charles and Valerie Diker, 1999 (cla). **173 Alamy Stock Photo:** 914 collection (crb); Jonathan Holstein (tr). **174-175 Library of Congress, Washington, D.C.:** Detroit Publishing Co., Copyright Claimant, and Publisher Detroit Publishing Co. Sorting Cotton. United States Pensacola Florida, None. [Between 1900 and 1910] Photograph. https://www.loc.gov/item/2016794737/. (r). **174 Alamy Stock Photo:** Historic Collection (bl). **177 Alamy Stock Photo:** Granger—Historical Picture Archive (bl). **178 Alamy Stock Photo:** Independent Picture Service (br). **179 Alamy Stock Photo:** UtCon Collection (br). **180-181 Library of Congress, Washington, D.C.:** Detroit Publishing Co., Publisher. Jewish market on the East Side, New York, N.Y. United States New York New York State, None. [Between 1890 and 1901] Photograph. https://www.loc.gov/item/2016801830/. (r). **180 Getty Images:** Corbis Historical / Stefano Bianchetti (bc). **Library of Congress, Washington, D.C.:** Tefilah mi-kol ha-shanah: Minah eanah: le-holkhe derekh ule-ovre yamim leha-noim li-medinat Ameria ...: eyne minyaur oyzgabe oyf fayner perl shrif. Fyorda: Zrndorffer & Sommer, 1842. Pdf. https://www.loc.gov/item/98826664/. (cla). **182 Imperial War Museum:** FLA 5361 (bl). **182-183 David Rumsey Map Collection, David Rumsey Map Center, Stanford Libraries:** 2094008. **184-185 Library of Congress, Washington, D.C.:** Currier & Ives, Publisher, and Parsons & Atwater. The City of Chicago/sketched & drawn on stone by Parsons & Atwater. United States Chicago Illinois, ca. 1874. New York: Published by Currier & Ives. Photograph. https://www.loc.gov/item/90715977/.. **186 Image PDP02923 courtesy of the BC Archives:** John Clayton White (bc). **186-187 Library of Congress, Washington, D.C.:** Millroy, J. J. Millroy's map of Alaska and the Klondyke gold fields. [S.l, 1897] Map. https://www.loc.gov/item/99446191/.. **188-189 Library of Congress, Washington, D.C.:** Detroit Publishing Co., Publisher. Mulberry Street, New York City. United States New York Mulberry Street New York State, ca. 1900. Photograph. https://www.loc.gov/item/2016794146/.. **190 Alamy Stock Photo:** KGPA Ltd / The Keasbury-Gordon Photograph Archive (cr). **Getty Images:** Hulton Archive / Oxford Science Archive / Print Collector (cla). **191 Getty Images:** Archive Photos / MPI / Stringer (cr). **Library of Congress, Washington, D.C.:** Bain News Service, Publisher. Strike Pickets. , 1910. Feb. date created or published later by Bain. Photograph. https://www.loc.gov/item/2014684501/. (tl). **192-193 Library of Congress, Washington, D.C.:** Geo. H. Walker & Co. Road map of the Boston district showing the metropolitan park system. [Boston: The Company, 1905, 1905] Map. https://www.loc.gov/item/88693304/.. **194-195 Alamy Stock Photo:** PictureLux / The Hollywood Archive (l). **195 Alamy Stock Photo:** Granger—Historical Picture Archive (cra, bc). **197 Alamy Stock Photo:** Chronicle (tl). **Library of Congress, Washington, D.C.:** Keppler, Udo J., Artist. His 128th birthday--"Gee, but this is an awful stretch!"/Keppler. , 1904. Photograph. https://www.loc.gov/item/98511150/. (br). **198-199 Alamy Stock Photo:** Phil Cardamone. **200-201 Library of Congress, Washington, D.C.:** Detroit Publishing Co., Publisher. Mulberry Street, New York City. United States New York Mulberry Street New York State, ca. 1900. Photograph. https://www.loc.gov/item/2016794146/. (l). **201 Alamy Stock Photo:** Granger—Historical Picture Archive (br). **Bridgeman Images:** Luisa Ricciarini (cr). **202-203 David Rumsey Map Collection, David Rumsey Map Center, Stanford Libraries:** 0019009. **204-205 Library of Congress, Washington, D.C.:** Rand Mcnally And Company. Rand, McNally & Co.'s map of the United States showing, in six degrees the density of population. [S.l, 1892] Map. https://www.loc.gov/item/99446196/.. **206-207 Library of Congress, Washington, D.C.:** Bain News Service, Publisher. Strikers storming horse-drawn car, Philadelphia. [No Date Recorded on Caption Card] Photograph. https://www.loc.gov/item/2014684532/. (r). **206 Alamy Stock Photo:** The Granger Collection (cl, bl). **208-209 Library of Congress, Washington, D.C.:** United States Office Of Indian Affairs, and T. J Morgan. Map showing Indian reservations within the limits of the United States. Washington, D.C.: Office of Indian Affairs, 1892. Map. https://www.loc.gov/item/2009579467/.. **210 Library of Congress, Washington, D.C.:** Smoking rubber, Brazil. Brazil, ca. 1890. [Between and 1923] Photograph. https://www.loc.gov/item/91483207/. (bc). **211 Alamy Stock Photo:** Science History Images / Photo Researchers (tr). **212-213 Image owned by True North Publishing, sold and distributed through texasmapstore.com. 212 Alamy Stock Photo:** Granger—Historical Picture Archive (bc). **214 Getty Images:** Corbis Historical / Ipsumpix (cla). **The Metropolitan Museum of Art:** The Charles and Valerie Diker Collection of Native American Art, Gift of Charles and Valerie Diker, 2021 (cb). **215 Alamy Stock Photo:** The Picture Art Collection (tl). **Getty Images:** Bettmann (cra). **216-217 Library of Congress, Washington, D.C.:** Goff, Eugenia A. Wheeler, Henry Slade Goff, and Fort Dearborn Publishing Co. Goff's historical map of the Spanish-American War in the West Indies. [S.l, 1898] Map. https://www.loc.gov/item/98687149/.. **218 Library of Congress, Washington, D.C.:** Lee, Russell, photographer. Negro drinking at "Colored" water cooler in streetcar terminal, Oklahoma City, Oklahoma. United States Oklahoma City Oklahoma, 1939. July. Photograph. https://www.loc.gov/item/2017740552/. (bc). **219 Alamy Stock Photo:** Granger—Historical Picture Archive (br). **220-221 Alamy Stock Photo:** Granger—Historical Picture Archive. **222-223 Image courtesy of Manitoba Historical Maps:** https://www.flickr.com/photos/manitobamaps/4147912216. **224 Alamy Stock Photo:** Vintage_Space (bl). **225 Alamy Stock Photo:** The Print Collector / Heritage Images (bc). **226-227 Library of Congress, Washington, D.C.:** Niox, G, Mexican National Construction Company, and United States War Department. Office Of The Chief Of Engineers. Map of the Mexican National Railway showing the lines granted by the Mexican government to the Mexican National Construction Company Palmer-Sullivan concession. [Washington: Published in the office of the Chief of Engineers, U.S.A, 1881] Map. https://www.loc.gov/item/2006635259/.. **227 Alamy Stock Photo:** Historic Collection (br/Reference For Natural Resources Map). **228-229 David Rumsey Map Collection, David Rumsey Map Center, Stanford Libraries:** 0724027. **230-231 Alamy Stock Photo:** MPVHistory. **232 Library of Congress, Washington, D.C.:** Stwer, Willy, Artist. Deutsches U-Boot, einen bewaffneten englischen fischdampfer vernichtend/Willy Stwer. , 1916. [Berlin: Galerie-Verlag, G.m.b.H., Potsdamerstr. 97] Photograph. https://www.loc.gov/item/2002697970/. (tl). **Shutterstock.com:** Yaroslaff (cb). **233 Alamy Stock Photo:** Glasshouse Images / Circa Images (tl); Hi-Story (cr). **234 Library of Congress, Washington, D.C.:** Hine, Lewis Wickes, photographer. Row of tenements, 260 to 268 Elizabeth St., N.Y., in which a great deal of finishing of clothes is carried on. See photo of , which shows condition of halls. See also photo 2828, one of the families at work. Location: New York, New York State. United States New York New York State, 1912. March. Photograph. https://www.loc.gov/item/2018677059/. (bc). **235 Getty Images / iStock:** Retrofile RF / George Marks (br). **236-237 Alamy Stock Photo:** Granger—Historical Picture Archive (r). **236 Alamy Stock Photo:** Shawshots (bc). **Library of Congress, Washington, D.C.:** Spear, Fred, Artist, and Willard Dickerman Straight. Enlist/Fred Spear. United States, 1915. [New York: Sackett & Wilhelms Corporation, or 1916] Photograph. https://www.loc.gov/item/00651156/. (cl). **238-239 Library of Congress, Washington, D.C.:** Rand Mcnally And Company. Atlas of the Mexican conflict: containing detailed maps showing the territory involved, pertinent statistics of Mexico and the United States, summary of recent events in Mexico. Chicago ; New York: Rand McNally & Co, 1913. Map. https://www.loc.gov/item/2012589700/. (l). **239 Library of Congress, Washington, D.C.:** Bain News Service, Publisher. Emelio Zapata. , 1911. Photograph. https://www.loc.gov/item/2014694879/. (br). **240 Alamy Stock Photo:** Alpha Historica (tc). **241 Bridgeman Images:** Look and Learn (crb). **242 Alamy Stock Photo:** Vintage_Space (cla). **Dreamstime.com:** Meunierd (bc). **242-243 Alamy Stock Photo:** SuperStock / ACME / Sydney Morning Herald (r). **244 Depositphotos Inc:** everett225 (bc). **245 Bridgeman Images:** Prismatic Pictures (cr). **246-247 Library of Congress, Washington, D.C.:** Fitzsimmons, Samuel. Distribution of Negro population by county: showing each county with 500 or more Negro population. [Washington, D.C.: Samuel Fitzsimmons, Copyright, 1956] Map. https://www.loc.gov/item/2013593062/.. **246 Getty Images:** Bettmann (bc). **248 Alamy Stock Photo:** IanDagnall Computing (tl). **Smithsonian American Art Museum:** Transfer from the General Services Administration (cr). **249 Alamy Stock Photo:** Everett Collection Inc (cr). **Getty Images:** Corbis Historical / Museum of Flight Foundation (tl). **251 Getty Images:** Bettmann (br); Hulton Archive / Hulton Archive (tr). **252-253 Library of Congress, Washington, D.C.:** Lange, Dorothea, photographer. Untitled photo, possibly related to: Family between Dallas and Austin, Texas. The people have left their home and connections in South Texas, and hope to reach the Arkansas Delta for work in the cotton fields. Penniless people. No food and three gallons of gas in the tank. The father is trying to repair a tire. Three children. Father says, "It's tough but life's tough anyway you take it". United States Texas, 1936. Aug. Photograph. https://www.loc.gov/item/2017768097/.. **252 Alamy Stock Photo:** Granger—Historical Picture Archive (cla). **Library of Congress, Washington, D.C.:** Kernodle, D. L, photographer. Dust storm. Baca County, Colorado. Baca County United States Colorado, 1936. Photograph. https://www.loc.gov/item/2017759525/. (bl). **254-255 David Rumsey Map Collection, David Rumsey Map Center, Stanford Libraries:** 13663000. **256-257 David Rumsey Map**

Collection, David Rumsey Map Center, Stanford Libraries: 9672000. 257 Alamy Stock Photo: Everett Collection, Inc. (br). 258-259 Curtis Wright Maps. 260 Alamy Stock Photo: Everett Collection Historical (bc). Library of Congress, Washington, D.C.: Perlin, Bernard, Artist, and Funder/Sponsor United States Office Of War Information. Avenge December 7/ Bernard Perlin. United States, 1942. Washington, D.C.: Office of War Information, U.S. Government Printing Office. Photograph. https://www.loc.gov/item/90712763/. (cla). 260-261 Alamy Stock Photo: MPVHistory (r). 262 Alamy Stock Photo: mccool (bl). 264-265 Alamy Stock Photo: Everett Collection Historical (r). 264 Alamy Stock Photo: Granger—Historical Picture Archive (bc); Sipa US / Sam Wasson (ca). 266-267 Alamy Stock Photo: M&N. 268 Alamy Stock Photo: ARCHIVIO GBB (tl); INTERFOTO / History (cb). 269 Alamy Stock Photo: Classicstock / H. Armstrong Roberts (tl). Getty Images: Archive Photos / ClassicStock / R. Krubner (cr). 270-271 National Museum of American History / Smithsonian Institution: (l). 271 Library of Congress, Washington, D.C.: Cowell, Sidney Robertson, Collector. Aurora Calderon, Elinor Rodriguez, and Cruz Losada, group portrait, photograph. Oakland California, 1939. Photograph. https://www.loc.gov/item/2017701220/. (br). National Museum of American History / Smithsonian Institution: (cra). 272 The US National Archives and Records Administration: 515906 (tr). 274 Getty Images: Bettmann (bl). The US National Archives and Records Administration: 513803 (cla). 274-275 Alamy Stock Photo: M&N (r). 276 Alamy Stock Photo: Associated Press (bc). 277 Getty Images: Corbis Historical / Wally McNamee (tr). 278-279 Getty Images: Archive Photos / H. Armstrong Roberts / ClassicStock (l). 279 Getty Images: Picture Post / Stringer (cra). Digital Scholarship Lab, University of Richmond: Home Owners' Loan Corporation (br). 280-281 Library of Congress, Washington, D.C.: American Automobile Association. National system of interstate and defense highways: as of June. Washington, D.C.: The Association, 1958. Map. https://www.loc.gov/item/2011593044//.. 280 Alamy Stock Photo: Pictorial Press Ltd (bc). 282 Bridgeman Images: Peter Newark American Pictures (cla). Getty Images: Bettmann (cb). 283 Alamy Stock Photo: Associated Press / Horst Faas (cr). NASA: (tl). 284-285 1:25,000 scale Soviet City Plan of San Fransisco copyright 2024 East View Geospatial (geospatial.com). 286 Alamy Stock Photo: Patti McConville (bc); Retro AdArchives (tr). 288-289 Image courtesy of the National Army Museum, London: NAM. 2002-02-918-2. 290-291 Getty Images: Archive Photos / PhotoQuest (l). 291 Alamy Stock Photo: Granger—Historical Picture Archive (cra). NASA: KSC-62C-1443 (br). 292 Alamy Stock Photo: Geopix (cr). 294-295 Getty Images: Bettmann (b). 295 Alamy Stock Photo: PA Images (bc). Library of Congress, Washington, D.C.: American Indian Movement, Sponsor/Advertiser. Support the American Indian Movement. , None. [Between 1968 and 1980] Photograph. https://www.loc.gov/item/2016648080/. (cr). 296-297 Curtis Wright Maps. 296 Getty Images: New York Daily News Archive / Leonard Detrick (bc). 298 Alamy Stock Photo: Shawshots (bc). 299 NASA: (bl). 300-301 Getty Images: Archive Photos / David Fenton (l). 300 Alamy Stock Photo: Retro AdArchives (bc). Getty Images: Premium Archive / Fred W. McDarrah (cla). 302 Alamy Stock Photo: Records (bc). 303 Getty Images: Premium Archive / Jan Persson (tl). 304 Alamy Stock Photo: IanDagnall Computing (tc). 305 Reuters: STRINGER (tr). 306-307 123RF.com: rabbit75123. 308 Getty Images: Wathiq Khuzaie / Stringer (cl); Scott Olson (cra). 309 Alamy Stock Photo: Sipa US / Annabelle Marcovici (cr); Carrie Schreck (tl). 310-311 The US National Archives and Records Administration: 75853575 (r). 310 Alamy Stock Photo: Archive PL (cl). Getty Images: The Chronicle Collection / Diana Walker (bc). 313 Getty Images: Bettmann (br); Universal Images Group / Universal History Archive (tl). 314 Getty Images: AFP / Ramon Cavallo / Stringer (tr). 316-317 Getty Images: Toronto Star / Boris Spremo (l). 317 Alamy Stock Photo: Associated Press / The Canadian Press (br). Getty Images: The Chronicle Collection / Steve Liss (ca). 318-319 Library of Congress, Washington, D.C.: United States Defense Mapping Agency. Hydrographic/Topographic Center. Operation Desert Storm briefing graphic. [Washington, D.C.: The Center, 1991] Map. https://www.loc.gov/item/91682184//.. 320 Alamy Stock Photo: Shelly Rivoli (bc). 321 National Museum of American History / Smithsonian Institution: (tc). US Census Bureau: Map of Latino population based on data from-"HISPANIC OR LATINO, AND NOT HISPANIC OR LATINO BY RACE." Decennial Census, DEC Redistricting Data (PL 94-171), Table P2, 2020, https://data.census.gov/table/DECENNIALPL2020.P2?q=P2: HISPANIC OR LATINO, AND NOT HISPANIC OR LATINO BY RACE&g=010XX00US$0500000. Accessed on March 8, 2024 (br). 322-323 Magnum Photos: Steve McCurry (r). 322 Alamy Stock Photo: Everett Collection Inc (bc). Getty Images: Corbis Historical / Viviane Moos (cl). 324 Getty Images: Gamma-Rapho / Chip HIRES (bc). 325 Alamy Stock Photo: Everett Collection Historical (bl). 326-327 Alamy Stock Photo: Associated Press / M. Spencer Green (l). 327 Reuters: Joshua Lott (br). 328 Getty Images: Samuel Corum / Stringer (bl). 329 Getty Images: MediaNews Group / St. Paul Pioneer Press / John Autey / Creator and artist Cadex Herrera and principal artist, Xena Goldman and Greta McLain. / (bl). 330 Getty Images: Photodisc / Matt Henry Gunther (br). 331 Getty Images: Christian Petersen (tr). 332-333 Getty Images: Archive Farms / Burton Holmes. 334-335 Alamy Stock Photo: Album (b). 335 Dreamstime.com: (tl). 336 Alamy Stock Photo: Evgeny Haritonov (tr). 336-337 Alamy Stock Photo: ART Collection (bl). 337 Alamy Stock Photo: Zuri Swimmer (cra). 338 Alamy Stock Photo: Adriana Rosas (l). 339 Alamy Stock Photo: The Print Collector / Heritage Images (br). Dorling Kindersley: Andy Crawford / University Museum of Archaeology and Anthropology, Cambridge (tl). 340 Shutterstock.com: Gianni Dagli Orti (b). 341 Alamy

Stock Photo: The Granger Collection (tl); Heritage Image Partnership Ltd (br). 342 Alamy Stock Photo: Science History Images / Photo Researchers (bl). 342-343 Shutterstock.com: Everett Collection (tr). 343 Bridgeman Images: Look and Learn (br). 344 Alamy Stock Photo: The Granger Collection (t). 345 Dorling Kindersley: Alan Keohane / Hopi Learning Centre, Arizona (tl); Lynton Gardiner / American Museum of Natural History (br). 346-347 Alamy Stock Photo: GL Archive (bl). 347 Bridgeman Images: Don Troiani. All Rights Reserved 2024 (tc). 348 Alamy Stock Photo: Universal Art Archive (bl). National Museum of American History / Smithsonian Institution: United States Mint (tr). 349 Alamy Stock Photo: North Wind Picture Archives (t). 350 Alamy Stock Photo: Archivart (tl). 351 Alamy Stock Photo: Granger—Historical Picture Archive (b). Bridgeman Images: Michael Graham-Stewart (br). 352-353 National Museum of American History / Smithsonian Institution: Gift of Eben Appleton (tc). 352 Getty Images: Hulton Archive / Stringer (bl). 353 Alamy Stock Photo: Falkenstein / Bildagentur-online Historical Collect. (c). 354 Alamy Stock Photo: YA / BOT (bl). Getty Images / iStock: DigitalVision Vectors / Nastasic (tr). 355 Alamy Stock Photo: Granger—Historical Picture Archive (b). 356 Alamy Stock Photo: Everett Collection Inc / Ron Harvey (cla). 356-57 National Museum of the American Indian, Smithsonian Institution: 1 / 617 (bc). 357 Alamy Stock Photo: Stillman Rogers / "Amistad Memorial" by Ed Hamilton, © Ed Hamilton 1992 (tr). 358 Alamy Stock Photo: Gado Images / Ken Florey Suffrage Collection (tr); Science History Images / Photo Researchers (bl). 359 Alamy Stock Photo: Classic Image (t). 360-361 Alamy Stock Photo: Pictorial Press Ltd (bc). 360 Alamy Stock Photo: The Granger Collection (bl). 361 National Museum of American History / Smithsonian Institution: Gift of Hazelle H. and J. Woodson Rollins (tr/male, tr/female). 362 Alamy Stock Photo: Archive Images (b). 363 Alamy Stock Photo: World History Archive (tl). Collection of the Smithsonian National Museum of African American History and Culture: Gift of Therbia Parker (br). 364 Alamy Stock Photo: North Wind Picture Archives (clb). 365 Getty Images: Archive Photos / Kean Collection (tr). 366 Alamy Stock Photo: Heritage Image Partnership Ltd (br). Smithsonian American Art Museum: Gift of Mrs. Carlyle Jones (tl). 367 Alamy Stock Photo: Vintage Travel and Advertising Archive (r). 368-369 Library of Congress, Washington, D.C.: Buffalo Bill's Wild West and Congress of Rough Riders of the World In the grandest of illuminated arenas, 2 electric plants, 250,000 candle power. , 1895. [N.Y.: The Springer Litho. Co] Photograph. https://www.loc.gov/item/2002719218/. (bl). 369 Alamy Stock Photo: ARCHIVIO GBB (tr). © The Trustees of the British Museum. All rights reserved: (cla). 370 Alamy Stock Photo: Shawshots (tc); Transcol (br). 371 Getty Images: Archive Farms / Burton Holmes (cra). 372 Alamy Stock Photo: Science History Images (tr). 373 Bridgeman Images: Peter Newark American Pictures (br). 374-375 Alamy Stock Photo: De Luan (br). 374 Getty Images: Hulton Archive / Topical Press Agency / Stringer (cla). 375 Collection of the Smithsonian National Museum of African American History and Culture: Gift of Dwandalyn R. Reece in memory of Pauline Watkins Reece (tl). 376 Alamy Stock Photo: Zip Lexing (cla). Getty Images: Moviepix / Topical Press Agency / Stringer (br). 377 Library of Congress, Washington, D.C.: Crowd gathered following the explosion on Wall St., car overturned in foreground, ambulance behind it. Wall Street New York, 1920. [, printed later] Photograph. https://www.loc.gov/item/2003663321/. (t). 378 National Air and Space Museum, Smithsonian Institution: Gift of the Spirit of St. Louis Corporation (t). 379 Getty Images: Universal Images Group / Independent Picture Service (bl). Library of Congress, Washington, D.C.: Underhill, Irving, -1960, photographer. Chrysler Bldg. & other skyscrapers. New York, 1930. [New York] Photograph. https://www.loc.gov/item/2015647627/. (cra). 380 Getty Images: Archive Photos / Underwood Archives (cla). 381 Alamy Stock Photo: The Color Archives (br); The Protected Art Archive (tl). 382 Alamy Stock Photo: Album (bl); PF-(aircraft) (tr). 383 Getty Images: Bettmann (b). 384 Alamy Stock Photo: World History Archive (b). 385 Alamy Stock Photo: Gado Images / Stuart Lutz (br). Getty Images: The Chronicle Collection / Bob Parent (tl). 386 Shutterstock.com: Warner Bros / Kobal (cla). 387 Library of Congress, Washington, D.C.: Bring U.S. together. Vote Chisholm , unbought and unbossed. , 1972. [United States: N.G. Slater Corporation] Photograph. https://www.loc.gov/item/2014646807/. (tl). Science Museum Group: (br). 388 NASA: (bl). 389 Getty Images: New York Daily News Archive (bl); Sygma / Sergio Dorantes (t). 390 Alamy Stock Photo: Geopix (t). Dorling Kindersley: Simon Mumford / The Flag Institute (br). 391 Alamy Stock Photo: Trinity Mirror / Mirrorpix (cra). 392 Alamy Stock Photo: Granger—Historical Picture Archive (tl). Getty Images: Alex Wong (bc). 393 Getty Images: AFP / Mark Ralston (t)

All other images © Dorling Kindersley Limited